CIPM® PROGRAM LEVEL II VOLUME 1

2024

© 2023 CFA Institute. All rights reserved.

No part of this publication may be reproduced or transmitted in any form or by any means, electronic or mechanical, including photocopy, recording, or any information storage and retrieval system, without permission of the copyright holder. Requests for permission to make copies of any part of the work should be mailed to: CFA Institute, Permissions Department, 915 East High Street, Charlottesville, VA 22902.

CFA®, Chartered Financial Analysts®, AIMR-PPS®, and GIPS® are just a few of the trademarks owned by CFA Institute. To view a list of CFA Institute trademarks and the Guide for the Use of CFA Institute Marks, please visit our website at www.cfainstitute.org.

ISBN 978-1-953337-88-7

September 2023

CONTENTS

How to Use the CIPM Program Curriculum   iii
    Exam Scheduling   iii
    CIPM Learning Ecosystem   iii
    Features Overview   iv
    Curriculum Development   vi
    Organization of the Curriculum   vi
    Candidate Resources   vi
    Feedback   vii

Ethical and Professional Standards

Study Session 1   **Ethical and Professional Standards**   3

Reading 1   **CFA Institute Code of Ethics and Standards of Professional Conduct**   5
    Preamble   5
    The Code of Ethics   6
    Standards of Professional Conduct   6

Reading 2   ***Standards of Practice Handbook*, Eleventh Edition**   11
    Standard I: Professionalism   11
    Standard II: Integrity of Capital Markets   45
    Standard III: Duties to Clients   62
    Standard IV: Duties to Employers   94
    Standard V: Investment Analysis, Recommendations, and Actions   115
    Standard VI: Conflicts of Interest   137
    Standard VII: Responsibilities as a CFA Institute Member or CFA Candidate   153
    Practice Problems   163
    Solutions   181

Performance Evaluation: Measurement, Attribution, and Appraisal

Study Session 2   **Performance Measurement**   193

Reading 3   **Topics in Return Measurement**   195
    Introduction   195
    Long–Short Performance Measurement   196
    Derivatives Performance Measurement   205
    Multicurrency Performance Measurement   224
    Conclusion and Summary   240
    ◘ *A Primer on Derivatives*   242
    Practice Problems   269
    Solutions   280

Reading 4   **Topics in Data Integrity**   289
    Introduction   289
    Performance Discrepancies: Investment Manager vs. Custodian   290

◘ indicates an optional segment

	Performance Discrepancies: NAV-Based vs. End-of-Day Time-Weighted Performance	296
	Maintenance of Composite Data	301
	Summary	308
	Practice Problems	310
	Solutions	313
Study Session 3	**Performance Attribution**	**317**
Reading 5	**Strategy Benchmarks: From the Investment Manager's Perspective**	**319**
	Normal (Or Neutral) Weights	320
	Two Types of Investment Disciplines	321
	General Framework of an Institutional Process	322
	Performance Comparisons, Tracking Error, and Information Ratio	328
	Conclusion	333
	Practice Problems	335
	Solutions	339
Reading 6	**Topics in Return Attribution**	**341**
	Introduction	341
	Attribution Analysis for Portfolios Containing Short Positions	342
	Attribution Analysis for a Portfolio Containing Derivatives	347
	Multi-currency Attribution	358
	Multi-period Attribution	374
	Multi-asset and Balanced Attribution Analysis	376
	Summary	379
	Practice Problems	382
	Solutions	387
Reading 7	**Introduction to Fixed-Income Attribution**	**391**
	Introduction	391
	Fixed-Income Attribution: Classification of Approaches	392
	Scenario for the Worked Examples	394
	Exposure Decomposition—Duration Based	400
	Yield Curve Decomposition—Duration Based	411
	Yield Curve Decomposition—Full Repricing	429
	Comparison of Attribution Results	446
	Summary	449
	◉ *Fixed Income Fundamentals*	451
	Practice Problems	473
	Solutions	481
	Glossary	**G-1**

◉ indicates an optional segment

How to Use the CIPM Program Curriculum

Welcome to the Level II of the Certificate in Investment Performance Measurement (CIPM®) Program. This exciting and rewarding program of study reflects your desire to become a serious portfolio evaluation professional. You are pursuing a program noted for its high ethical standards and the depth of knowledge, skills, and abilities it develops. Your commitment to the CIPM Program should be educationally and professionally rewarding. CIPM certificants are dedicated to life-long learning and maintaining currency with the ever-changing dynamics of a challenging profession. The CIPM Program represents the first step towards a career-long commitment to professional education.

To begin your study:

1. Schedule your examination.
2. Access the CIPM Learning Ecosystem and access your study materials.

EXAM SCHEDULING

Examinations are provided online by our testing partner, Pearson VUE. We suggest you schedule your exam appointment with them as soon as possible, because appointments are first-come, first-served. With 24 hours notice, Pearson VUE allows you to reschedule your exam to another available time and place within the same exam window. Rescheduling your exam appointment must be completed within the exam scheduling window. When you schedule or reschedule your exam appointment with Pearson VUE, you will receive an e-mail confirmation. Contact Pearson VUE www.pearsonvue.com/contact/ if you do not receive a confirmation of your appointment.

CIPM LEARNING ECOSYSTEM

The Learning Ecosystem is a customized learning program that makes studying for the CIPM Exam enjoyable, efficient, and effective. The Learning Ecosystem is an online portal that adapts to your needs, strengths, and weaknesses, serving you the right material at the right time and focusing on the areas you need to focus on the most. It helps you stay focused, engaged, and on track while you study.

> **TIP**
>
> Everything you need is in one place. We provide an eBook version of the curriculum for your convenience should that be your preferred method of study. The Learning Ecosystem contains the exact same content. There is no need to do both. If you elect to use the eBook, you may still log into the Learning Ecosystem to take advantage of study tools, such as flashcards, practice tests, and the mock exam.

© 2020 CFA Institute. All rights reserved.

FEATURES OVERVIEW

The Learning Ecosystem is web-based and accessible through all common browsers.

- The Learning Ecosystem is designed to work well on whatever device is convenient at the moment, whether your desktop, tablet, or smartphone.
- Your progress through the course is automatically recorded so you can seamlessly switch between devices.

> **TIP**
>
> If you are accessing the Learning Ecosystem on a mobile device, it is possible to preload some content for times when you will not have continuous internet access. While you still have Internet access, log in to the Learning Ecosystem and launch your next study activity. This content will remain available when internet access is cut off, for example if you are on mass transit.

Home: Dashboard

Here you will find a summary of your progress through the material and a summary of your strengths and weaknesses with the content.

Study Plans

There are two kinds of study plans from which to choose: structured and adaptive.

- The structured plan will help you keep track of the time remaining before your exam and will suggest the number of activities to complete each day to stay on track. The structured plan will take you through the content in the same order as it appears in the eBook.
- The adaptive plan will begin with a short pre-test to establish a baseline for your existing knowledge. From that point forward, the system will track and adapt to your strengths and weaknesses with the content each time you interact with it. For example, it may adjust your pace through the material to spend less time on content where you are strong and more time on content where you comparatively weaker.

> **TIP**
>
> You are not stuck with your choice of study plan. You can switch back and forth between the structured and adaptive plans. When you switch from one study plan to the other your progress is not lost, and you do not need to start again at the beginning.

> **TIP**
>
> Whichever study plan you choose, studying consistently is the key to success.

Study Tasks

Whichever study plan you are using, the Learning Ecosystem will always let you know which study task is next. Study tasks can include reading a lesson, completing practice questions, completing chapter review questions, reviewing flashcards, or taking a mock exam.

- Lessons are composed of the same content found in the eBook.
- Practiced questions help you review and make sure you understood what you have learned.
- Flashcards test your understanding and recall of important terms and definitions.
- The mock exam is of similar length and weight as the live examination and can help gauge your overall readiness for the live exam.

> **TIP**
>
> As you work through lessons, practice problems, and flashcards, the Learning Ecosystem will frequently ask you to assess your confidence in knowing the material being covered. This information is tracked and presented to you in your Learning History. In the case of the adaptive plan, this information may supplement the system's understanding of your relative strengths and weaknesses.

> **TIP**
>
> If you are studying primarily from the eBook, you can still access the study tools in the Learning Ecosystem without working through a study plan. All of the study tools are accessible directly through the tabs within the menu bar on the left side of the Learning Ecosystem screen.

Other Study Resources

The Learning Ecosystem provides resources that supplement your study tasks.

- The Game Center makes reviewing your flashcards more enjoyable by presenting them within the context of a game in which you may compete with fellow candidates.
- Discussion boards are a place where you can confer with fellow candidates when you need a little extra help or a motivational nudge.

> **TIP**
>
> Discussion boards are **not** actively monitored or moderated by CFA Institute; please use them with that caution in mind. Our vendor monitors the boards for vulgarity and inflammatory language; to speak with a CFA Institute representative please contact us at info@cfainstitute.org.

> **TIP**
> For technical support assistance or to give us feedback on the Learning Ecosystem or course of study, you may also use the messaging feature.

- The Learning History tab reports trends in your performance over time with tracking on how you have done on practice tests and the mock exam. Additionally, the learning history summarizes your confidence in the topics within the program.

CURRICULUM DEVELOPMENT

The CIPM Program curriculum is grounded in the practice of the portfolio evaluation profession. CFA Institute performs a continuous practice analysis with investment professionals around the world to determine the knowledge, skills, and abilities that are relevant to the profession. Regional expert panels and targeted surveys are conducted to verify and reinforce the insights from practice analysis. The practice analysis process ultimately defines the CIPM Candidate Body of Knowledge (CBOK™).

The examinations are written by practicing certificants and are designed to allow you to demonstrate your mastery of the CBOK as set forth in the CIPM Program curriculum. As you structure your personal study program, you should emphasize mastery of the CBOK and the practical application of that knowledge. For more information on the practice analysis, CBOK, and development of the CIPM Program curriculum, please visit www.cfainstitute.org/programs/cipm/courseofstudy/Pages/index.aspx.

ORGANIZATION OF THE CURRICULUM

The reading assignments are the basis for all examination questions, and are selected or developed specifically to teach the CBOK. These readings are drawn from CIPM Program-commissioned content, textbook chapters, and professional journal articles. Learning outcome statements are listed with each lesson. These LOS indicate what you should be able to accomplish after studying the lesson. We encourage you to review how to properly use LOS, and the descriptions of commonly used LOS "command words," at http://www.cfainstitute.org/programs/cipm/courseofstudy/Pages/cipm_learning_outcome_statements.aspx. The command words signal the depth of learning you are expected to achieve from the reading. You should use the LOS to guide and focus your study, as each examination question is based on an assigned lesson and one or more LOS. However, the lessons provide context for the LOS and enable you to apply a principle or concept in a variety of scenarios. *Candidates are responsible for the entirety of all required material in the curriculum.*

CANDIDATE RESOURCES

CFA Institute provides a web page that contains numerous resources to help in your successful completion of the CIPM Program. On this page you will find links to testing policies (calculator policy, ID policy, and others); exam details and logistics; testing accommodations; curriculum errata; and a detailed glossary of terms. You should visit this site often to obtain current information: www.cfainstitute.org/programs/cipm/Pages/index.aspx.

FEEDBACK

At CFA Institute, we are committed to delivering a comprehensive and rigorous curriculum for the development of competent, ethically grounded investment professionals. We rely on candidate and member feedback as we work to incorporate content, design, and packaging improvements. You can be assured that we will continue to listen to your suggestions. Please send any comments or feedback—or perceived errors—to info@cfainstitute.org. Ongoing improvements in the curriculum will help you prepare for success on the upcoming examinations, and for a lifetime of learning as a serious investment professional.

Ethical and Professional Standards

STUDY SESSION

Study Session 1 Ethical and Professional Standards

TOPIC LEVEL LEARNING OUTCOME

The candidate should be able to evaluate situations and apply the provisions of the CFA Institute Code of Ethics and Standards of Professional Conduct in specific situations.

© 2020 CFA Institute. All rights reserved.

ETHICAL AND PROFESSIONAL STANDARDS
STUDY SESSION

1

Ethical and Professional Standards

The CIPM Level I curriculum introduced ethical reasoning and presented the provisions of the CFA Institute Code of Ethics and Standards of Professional Conduct. At Level II, you are expected to demonstrate your ability to recognize ethical issues that you may encounter and to apply the ethical principles and standards governing your professional conduct.

Note: This study session makes use of the 11th edition of the CFA Institute *Standards of Practice Handbook* (SOPH) to focus on applications of the Code and Standards and recommended procedures for complying with them.[1] The guidance, recommendations, and applications provided in SOPH supplement the CFA Institute Code and Standards. Recognizing that the following list is not exhaustive, the following exchanges may help with your understanding the reading:

SOPH Terminology		
CFA Institute	→	CIPM Association
CFA	→	CIPM
Members and Membership	→	Pertains to the CIPM Association and CFA Institute
Program, Candidates and Candidacy	→	Pertains to the CIPM Program and the CFA Program
Designation	→	Pertains to the Certificate in Investment Performance Measurement (CIPM) designation and the CFA designation

(continued)

---

[1] Until October 1, 2019, existing CIPM certificants may be members of either the CIP Association or CFA Institute. While the Code and Standards for each organization are substantially similar, each certificant will be held to the Code and Standards of the organization of which they are a member. New CIPM certificants will join CFA Institute, thus this material is focused on the CFA Institute Code of Ethics and Standards of Professional Conduct.

© 2020 CFA Institute. All rights reserved.

SOPH Terminology		
Exams	→	CIPM and CFA exams
CFA marks	→	CIPM marks ("Certificate in Investment Performance Measurement" or "CIPM")
Charter/Charterholders	→	Certificate/Certificants or Certificate Holders

READING ASSIGNMENTS

1 CFA Institute Code of Ethics and Standards of Professional Conduct
2 *Standards of Practice Handbook*, Eleventh Edition

READING
1

CFA Institute Code of Ethics and Standards of Professional Conduct

LEARNING OUTCOME STATEMENTS	
Mastery	The candidate should be able to:
☐	a. evaluate procedures for complying with the CFA Institute Standards of Professional Conduct;
☐	b. explain the individual's responsibilities as a candidate or member, including references to membership in CFA Institute, the CIPM designation, and candidacy in the CIPM program;
☐	c. evaluate circumstances, identify violations, and formulate appropriate corrective actions based on the CFA Institute Code of Ethics and Standards of Professional Conduct.

PREAMBLE

The CFA Institute Code of Ethics and Standards of Professional Conduct are fundamental to the values of CFA Institute and essential to achieving its mission to lead the investment profession globally by promoting the highest standards of ethics, education, and professional excellence for the ultimate benefit of society. High ethical standards are critical to maintaining the public's trust in financial markets and in the investment profession. Since their creation in the 1960s, the Code and Standards have promoted the integrity of CFA Institute members and served as a model for measuring the ethics of investment professionals globally, regardless of job function, cultural differences, or local laws and regulations. All CFA Institute members (including holders of the Chartered Financial Analyst [CFA] and Certificate in Investment Performance Measurement [CIPM] designations) and CFA and CIPM Program candidates have the personal responsibility to embrace and uphold the provisions of the Code and Standards and are encouraged to notify their employer of this responsibility. Violations may result in disciplinary sanctions by CFA Institute. Sanctions can include revocation of membership, revocation of candidacy in the CFA or CIPM Program, and revocation of the right to use the CFA or CIPM designation.

© 2015 CFA Institute. All rights reserved.

THE CODE OF ETHICS

Members of CFA Institute (including CFA charterholders and CIPM certificants) and candidates for the CFA and CIPM designations ("Members and Candidates") must:

- Act with integrity, competence, diligence, and respect and in an ethical manner with the public, clients, prospective clients, employers, employees, colleagues in the investment profession, and other participants in the global capital markets.
- Place the integrity of the investment profession and the interests of clients above their own personal interests.
- Use reasonable care and exercise independent professional judgment when conducting investment analysis, making investment recommendations, taking investment actions, and engaging in other professional activities.
- Practice and encourage others to practice in a professional and ethical manner that will reflect credit on themselves and the profession.
- Promote the integrity and viability of the global capital markets for the ultimate benefit of society.
- Maintain and improve their professional competence and strive to maintain and improve the competence of other investment professionals.

STANDARDS OF PROFESSIONAL CONDUCT

I. PROFESSIONALISM

   A Knowledge of the Law

   Members and Candidates must understand and comply with all applicable laws, rules, and regulations (including the CFA Institute Code of Ethics and Standards of Professional Conduct) of any government, regulatory organization, licensing agency, or professional association governing their professional activities. In the event of conflict, Members and Candidates must comply with the more strict law, rule, or regulation. Members and Candidates must not knowingly participate or assist in and must dissociate from any violation of such laws, rules, or regulations.

   B Independence and Objectivity

   Members and Candidates must use reasonable care and judgment to achieve and maintain independence and objectivity in their professional activities. Members and Candidates must not offer, solicit, or accept any gift, benefit, compensation, or consideration that reasonably could be expected to compromise their own or another's independence and objectivity.

   C Misrepresentation

   Members and Candidates must not knowingly make any misrepresentations relating to investment analysis, recommendations, actions, or other professional activities.

   D Misconduct

   Members and Candidates must not engage in any professional conduct involving dishonesty, fraud, or deceit or commit any act that reflects adversely on their professional reputation, integrity, or competence.

II. INTEGRITY OF CAPITAL MARKETS

   A Material Nonpublic Information

Standards of Professional Conduct

Members and Candidates who possess material nonpublic information that could affect the value of an investment must not act or cause others to act on the information.

B Market Manipulation

Members and Candidates must not engage in practices that distort prices or artificially inflate trading volume with the intent to mislead market participants.

III. DUTIES TO CLIENTS

A Loyalty, Prudence, and Care

Members and Candidates have a duty of loyalty to their clients and must act with reasonable care and exercise prudent judgment. Members and Candidates must act for the benefit of their clients and place their clients' interests before their employer's or their own interests.

B Fair Dealing

Members and Candidates must deal fairly and objectively with all clients when providing investment analysis, making investment recommendations, taking investment action, or engaging in other professional activities.

C Suitability

1 When Members and Candidates are in an advisory relationship with a client, they must:

   a Make a reasonable inquiry into a client's or prospective client's investment experience, risk and return objectives, and financial constraints prior to making any investment recommendation or taking investment action and must reassess and update this information regularly.

   b Determine that an investment is suitable to the client's financial situation and consistent with the client's written objectives, mandates, and constraints before making an investment recommendation or taking investment action.

   c Judge the suitability of investments in the context of the client's total portfolio.

2 When Members and Candidates are responsible for managing a portfolio to a specific mandate, strategy, or style, they must make only investment recommendations or take only investment actions that are consistent with the stated objectives and constraints of the portfolio.

D Performance Presentation

When communicating investment performance information, Members and Candidates must make reasonable efforts to ensure that it is fair, accurate, and complete.

E Preservation of Confidentiality

Members and Candidates must keep information about current, former, and prospective clients confidential unless:

1 The information concerns illegal activities on the part of the client or prospective client,

2 Disclosure is required by law, or

3 The client or prospective client permits disclosure of the information.

IV. DUTIES TO EMPLOYERS

A Loyalty

In matters related to their employment, Members and Candidates must act for the benefit of their employer and not deprive their employer of the advantage of their skills and abilities, divulge confidential information, or otherwise cause harm to their employer.

B Additional Compensation Arrangements

Members and Candidates must not accept gifts, benefits, compensation, or consideration that competes with or might reasonably be expected to create a conflict of interest with their employer's interest unless they obtain written consent from all parties involved.

C Responsibilities of Supervisors

Members and Candidates must make reasonable efforts to ensure that anyone subject to their supervision or authority complies with applicable laws, rules, regulations, and the Code and Standards.

V. INVESTMENT ANALYSIS, RECOMMENDATIONS, AND ACTIONS

A Diligence and Reasonable Basis

Members and Candidates must:

1 Exercise diligence, independence, and thoroughness in analyzing investments, making investment recommendations, and taking investment actions.

2 Have a reasonable and adequate basis, supported by appropriate research and investigation, for any investment analysis, recommendation, or action.

B Communication with Clients and Prospective Clients

Members and Candidates must:

1 Disclose to clients and prospective clients the basic format and general principles of the investment processes they use to analyze investments, select securities, and construct portfolios and must promptly disclose any changes that might materially affect those processes.

2 Disclose to clients and prospective clients significant limitations and risks associated with the investment process.

3 Use reasonable judgment in identifying which factors are important to their investment analyses, recommendations, or actions and include those factors in communications with clients and prospective clients.

4 Distinguish between fact and opinion in the presentation of investment analysis and recommendations.

C Record Retention

Members and Candidates must develop and maintain appropriate records to support their investment analyses, recommendations, actions, and other investment-related communications with clients and prospective clients.

VI. CONFLICTS OF INTEREST

A Disclosure of Conflicts

Members and Candidates must make full and fair disclosure of all matters that could reasonably be expected to impair their independence and objectivity or interfere with respective duties to their clients, prospective clients, and employer. Members and Candidates must ensure that such disclosures are prominent, are delivered in plain language, and communicate the relevant information effectively.

B Priority of Transactions

Standards of Professional Conduct

Investment transactions for clients and employers must have priority over investment transactions in which a Member or Candidate is the beneficial owner.

C Referral Fees

Members and Candidates must disclose to their employer, clients, and prospective clients, as appropriate, any compensation, consideration, or benefit received from or paid to others for the recommendation of products or services.

VII. RESPONSIBILITIES AS A CFA INSTITUTE MEMBER OR CFA CANDIDATE

A Conduct as Participants in CFA Institute Programs

Members and Candidates must not engage in any conduct that compromises the reputation or integrity of CFA Institute or the CFA designation or the integrity, validity, or security of CFA Institute programs.

B Reference to CFA Institute, the CFA Designation, and the CFA Program

When referring to CFA Institute, CFA Institute membership, the CFA designation, or candidacy in the CFA Program, Members and Candidates must not misrepresent or exaggerate the meaning or implications of membership in CFA Institute, holding the CFA designation, or candidacy in the CFA Program.

READING
2

Standards of Practice Handbook, Eleventh Edition

STANDARD I: PROFESSIONALISM

Standard I(A) Knowledge of the Law

> Members and Candidates must understand and comply with all applicable laws, rules, and regulations (including the CFA Institute Code of Ethics and Standards of Professional Conduct) of any government, regulatory organization, licensing agency, or professional association governing their professional activities. In the event of conflict, Members and Candidates must comply with the more strict law, rule, or regulation. Members and Candidates must not knowingly participate or assist in and must dissociate from any violation of such laws, rules, or regulations.

Guidance

Highlights:

- *Relationship between the Code and Standards and Applicable Law*
- *Participation in or Association with Violations by Others*
- *Investment Products and Applicable Laws*

Members and candidates must understand the applicable laws and regulations of the countries and jurisdictions where they engage in professional activities. These activities may include, but are not limited to, trading of securities or other financial instruments, providing investment advice, conducting research, or performing other investment services. On the basis of their reasonable and good faith understanding, members and candidates must comply with the laws and regulations that directly govern their professional activities and resulting outcomes and that protect the interests of the clients.

When questions arise, members and candidates should know their firm's policies and procedures for accessing compliance guidance. This standard does not require members and candidates to become experts, however, in compliance. Additionally, members and candidates are not required to have detailed knowledge of or be experts on all the laws that could potentially govern their activities.

© 2014 CFA Institute. All rights reserved.

During times of changing regulations, members and candidates must remain vigilant in maintaining their knowledge of the requirements for their professional activities. New financial products and processes, along with uncovered ethical missteps, create an environment for recurring and potentially wide-ranging regulatory changes. Members and candidates are also continually provided improved and enhanced methods of communicating with both clients and potential clients, such as mobile applications and web-based social networking platforms. As new local, regional, and global requirements are updated to address these and other changes, members, candidates, and their firms must adjust their procedures and practices to remain in compliance.

Relationship between the Code and Standards and Applicable Law

Some members or candidates may live, work, or provide investment services to clients living in a country that has no law or regulation governing a particular action or that has laws or regulations that differ from the requirements of the Code and Standards. When applicable law and the Code and Standards require different conduct, members and candidates must follow the more strict of the applicable law or the Code and Standards.

"Applicable law" is the law that governs the member's or candidate's conduct. Which law applies will depend on the particular facts and circumstances of each case. The "more strict" law or regulation is the law or regulation that imposes greater restrictions on the action of the member or candidate or calls for the member or candidate to exert a greater degree of action that protects the interests of investors. For example, applicable law or regulation may not require members and candidates to disclose referral fees received from or paid to others for the recommendation of investment products or services. Because the Code and Standards impose this obligation, however, members and candidates must disclose the existence of such fees.

Members and candidates must adhere to the following principles:

- Members and candidates must comply with applicable laws or regulations related to their professional activities.

- Members and candidates must not engage in conduct that constitutes a violation of the Code and Standards, even though it may otherwise be legal.

- In the absence of any applicable law or regulation or when the Code and Standards impose a higher degree of responsibility than applicable laws and regulations, members and candidates must adhere to the Code and Standards. Applications of these principles are outlined in Exhibit 1.

The applicable laws governing the responsibilities of a member or candidate should be viewed as the minimal threshold of acceptable actions. When members and candidates take actions that exceed the minimal requirements, they further support the conduct required of Standard I(A).

CFA Institute members are obligated to abide by the CFA Institute Articles of Incorporation, Bylaws, Code of Ethics, Standards of Professional Conduct, Rules of Procedure, Membership Agreement, and other applicable rules promulgated by CFA Institute, all as amended periodically. CFA candidates who are not members must also abide by these documents (except for the Membership Agreement) as well as rules and regulations related to the administration of the CFA examination, the Candidate Responsibility Statement, and the Candidate Pledge.

Participation in or Association with Violations by Others

Members and candidates are responsible for violations in which they *knowingly* participate or assist. Although members and candidates are presumed to have knowledge of all applicable laws, rules, and regulations, CFA Institute acknowledges that members may not recognize violations if they are not aware of all the facts giving rise to

Standard I: Professionalism

the violations. Standard I(A) applies when members and candidates know or should know that their conduct may contribute to a violation of applicable laws, rules, or regulations or the Code and Standards.

If a member or candidate has reasonable grounds to believe that imminent or ongoing client or employer activities are illegal or unethical, the member or candidate must dissociate, or separate, from the activity. In extreme cases, dissociation may require a member or candidate to leave his or her employment. Members and candidates may take the following intermediate steps to dissociate from ethical violations of others when direct discussions with the person or persons committing the violation are unsuccessful. The first step should be to attempt to stop the behavior by bringing it to the attention of the employer through a supervisor or the firm's compliance department. If this attempt is unsuccessful, then members and candidates have a responsibility to step away and dissociate from the activity. Dissociation practices will differ on the basis of the member's or candidate's role in the investment industry. It may include removing one's name from written reports or recommendations, asking for a different assignment, or refusing to accept a new client or continue to advise a current client. Inaction combined with continuing association with those involved in illegal or unethical conduct may be construed as participation or assistance in the illegal or unethical conduct.

CFA Institute strongly encourages members and candidates to report potential violations of the Code and Standards committed by fellow members and candidates. Although a failure to report is less likely to be construed as a violation than a failure to dissociate from unethical conduct, the impact of inactivity on the integrity of capital markets can be significant. Although the Code and Standards do not compel members and candidates to report violations to their governmental or regulatory organizations unless such disclosure is mandatory under applicable law (voluntary reporting is often referred to as whistleblowing), such disclosure may be prudent under certain circumstances. Members and candidates should consult their legal and compliance advisers for guidance.

Additionally, CFA Institute encourages members, nonmembers, clients, and the investing public to report violations of the Code and Standards by CFA Institute members or CFA candidates by submitting a complaint in writing to the CFA Institute Professional Conduct Program via e-mail (pcprogram@cfainstitute.org) or the CFA Institute website (www.cfainstitute.org).

Investment Products and Applicable Laws

Members and candidates involved in creating or maintaining investment services or investment products or packages of securities and/or derivatives should be mindful of where these products or packages will be sold as well as their places of origination. The applicable laws and regulations of the countries or regions of origination and expected sale should be understood by those responsible for the supervision of the services or creation and maintenance of the products or packages. Members or candidates should make reasonable efforts to review whether associated firms that are distributing products or services developed by their employing firm also abide by the laws and regulations of the countries and regions of distribution. Members and candidates should undertake the necessary due diligence when transacting cross-border business to understand the multiple applicable laws and regulations in order to protect the reputation of their firm and themselves.

Given the complexity that can arise with business transactions in today's market, there may be some uncertainty surrounding which laws or regulations are considered applicable when activities are being conducted in multiple jurisdictions. Members and candidates should seek the appropriate guidance, potentially including the firm's compliance or legal departments and legal counsel outside the organization, to gain a reasonable understanding of their responsibilities and how to implement them appropriately.

> **Exhibit 1 Global Application of the Code and Standards**
>
> Members and candidates who practice in multiple jurisdictions may be subject to varied securities laws and regulations. If applicable law is stricter than the requirements of the Code and Standards, members and candidates must adhere to applicable law; otherwise, they must adhere to the Code and Standards. The following chart provides illustrations involving a member who may be subject to the securities laws and regulations of three different types of countries:
>
> NS: country with no securities laws or regulations
>
> LS: country with *less* strict securities laws and regulations than the Code and Standards
>
> MS: country with *more* strict securities laws and regulations than the Code and Standards
>
> | Applicable Law | Duties | Explanation |
> |---|---|---|
> | Member resides in NS country, does business in LS country; LS law applies. | Member must adhere to the Code and Standards. | Because applicable law is less strict than the Code and Standards, the member must adhere to the Code and Standards. |
> | Member resides in NS country, does business in MS country; MS law applies. | Member must adhere to the law of MS country. | Because applicable law is stricter than the Code and Standards, member must adhere to the more strict applicable law. |
> | Member resides in LS country, does business in NS country; LS law applies. | Member must adhere to the Code and Standards. | Because applicable law is less strict than the Code and Standards, member must adhere to the Code and Standards. |
> | Member resides in LS country, does business in MS country; MS law applies. | Member must adhere to the law of MS country. | Because applicable law is stricter than the Code and Standards, member must adhere to the more strict applicable law. |
> | Member resides in LS country, does business in NS country; LS law applies, but it states that law of locality where business is conducted governs. | Member must adhere to the Code and Standards. | Because applicable law states that the law of the locality where the business is conducted governs and there is no local law, the member must adhere to the Code and Standards. |
> | Member resides in LS country, does business in MS country; LS law applies, but it states that law of locality where business is conducted governs. | Member must adhere to the law of MS country. | Because applicable law of the locality where the business is conducted governs and local law is stricter than the Code and Standards, member must adhere to the more strict applicable law. |

Standard I: Professionalism

Exhibit 1 (Continued)

Applicable Law	Duties	Explanation
Member resides in MS country, does business in LS country; MS law applies.	Member must adhere to the law of MS country.	Because applicable law is stricter than the Code and Standards, member must adhere to the more strict applicable law.
Member resides in MS country, does business in LS country; MS law applies, but it states that law of locality where business is conducted governs.	Member must adhere to the Code and Standards.	Because applicable law states that the law of the locality where the business is conducted governs and local law is less strict than the Code and Standards, member must adhere to the Code and Standards.
Member resides in MS country, does business in LS country with a client who is a citizen of LS country; MS law applies, but it states that the law of the client's home country governs.	Member must adhere to the Code and Standards.	Because applicable law states that the law of the client's home country governs (which is less strict than the Code and Standards), member must adhere to the Code and Standards.
Member resides in MS country, does business in LS country with a client who is a citizen of MS country; MS law applies, but it states that the law of the client's home country governs.	Member must adhere to the law of MS country.	Because applicable law states that the law of the client's home country governs and the law of the client's home country is stricter than the Code and Standards, the member must adhere to the more strict applicable law.

Recommended Procedures for Compliance

Members and Candidates

Suggested methods by which members and candidates can acquire and maintain understanding of applicable laws, rules, and regulations include the following:

- *Stay informed*: Members and candidates should establish or encourage their employers to establish a procedure by which employees are regularly informed about changes in applicable laws, rules, regulations, and case law. In many instances, the employer's compliance department or legal counsel can provide such information in the form of memorandums distributed to employees in the organization. Also, participation in an internal or external continuing education program is a practical method of staying current.

- *Review procedures*: Members and candidates should review, or encourage their employers to review, the firm's written compliance procedures on a regular basis to ensure that the procedures reflect current law and provide adequate guidance to employees about what is permissible conduct under the law and/

or the Code and Standards. Recommended compliance procedures for specific items of the Code and Standards are discussed in this *Handbook* in the "Guidance" sections associated with each standard.

- *Maintain current files*: Members and candidates should maintain or encourage their employers to maintain readily accessible current reference copies of applicable statutes, rules, regulations, and important cases.

Distribution Area Laws

Members and candidates should make reasonable efforts to understand the applicable laws—both country and regional—for the countries and regions where their investment products are developed and are most likely to be distributed to clients.

Legal Counsel

When in doubt about the appropriate action to undertake, it is recommended that a member or candidate seek the advice of compliance personnel or legal counsel concerning legal requirements. If a potential violation is being committed by a fellow employee, it may also be prudent for the member or candidate to seek the advice of the firm's compliance department or legal counsel.

Dissociation

When dissociating from an activity that violates the Code and Standards, members and candidates should document the violation and urge their firms to attempt to persuade the perpetrator(s) to cease such conduct. To dissociate from the conduct, a member or candidate may have to resign his or her employment.

Firms

The formality and complexity of compliance procedures for firms depend on the nature and size of the organization and the nature of its investment operations. Members and candidates should encourage their firms to consider the following policies and procedures to support the principles of Standard I(A):

- *Develop and/or adopt a code of ethics*: The ethical culture of an organization starts at the top. Members and candidates should encourage their supervisors or managers to adopt a code of ethics. Adhering to a code of ethics facilitates solutions when people face ethical dilemmas and can prevent the need for employees to resort to a "whistleblowing" solution publicly alleging concealed misconduct. CFA Institute has published the *Asset Manager Code of Professional Conduct*, which firms may adopt or use as the basis for their codes (visit www.cfainstitute.org).

- *Provide information on applicable laws*: Pertinent information that highlights applicable laws and regulations might be distributed to employees or made available in a central location. Information sources might include primary information developed by the relevant government, governmental agencies, regulatory organizations, licensing agencies, and professional associations (e.g., from their websites); law firm memorandums or newsletters; and association memorandums or publications (e.g., *CFA Institute Magazine*).

- *Establish procedures for reporting violations*: Firms might provide written protocols for reporting suspected violations of laws, regulations, or company policies.

Standard I: Professionalism

Application of the Standard

Example 1 (Notification of Known Violations):

Michael Allen works for a brokerage firm and is responsible for an underwriting of securities. A company official gives Allen information indicating that the financial statements Allen filed with the regulator overstate the issuer's earnings. Allen seeks the advice of the brokerage firm's general counsel, who states that it would be difficult for the regulator to prove that Allen has been involved in any wrongdoing.

> *Comment*: Although it is recommended that members and candidates seek the advice of legal counsel, the reliance on such advice does not absolve a member or candidate from the requirement to comply with the law or regulation. Allen should report this situation to his supervisor, seek an independent legal opinion, and determine whether the regulator should be notified of the error.

Example 2 (Dissociating from a Violation):

Lawrence Brown's employer, an investment banking firm, is the principal underwriter for an issue of convertible debentures by the Courtney Company. Brown discovers that the Courtney Company has concealed severe third-quarter losses in its foreign operations. The preliminary prospectus has already been distributed.

> *Comment*: Knowing that the preliminary prospectus is misleading, Brown should report his findings to the appropriate supervisory persons in his firm. If the matter is not remedied and Brown's employer does not dissociate from the underwriting, Brown should sever all his connections with the underwriting. Brown should also seek legal advice to determine whether additional reporting or other action should be taken.

Example 3 (Dissociating from a Violation):

Kamisha Washington's firm advertises its past performance record by showing the 10-year return of a composite of its client accounts. Washington discovers, however, that the composite omits the performance of accounts that have left the firm during the 10-year period, whereas the description of the composite indicates the inclusion of all firm accounts. This omission has led to an inflated performance figure. Washington is asked to use promotional material that includes the erroneous performance number when soliciting business for the firm.

> *Comment*: Misrepresenting performance is a violation of the Code and Standards. Although she did not calculate the performance herself, Washington would be assisting in violating Standard I(A) if she were to use the inflated performance number when soliciting clients. She must dissociate herself from the activity. If discussing the misleading number with the person responsible is not an option for correcting the problem, she can bring the situation to the attention of her supervisor or the compliance department at her firm. If her firm is unwilling to recalculate performance, she must refrain from using the misleading promotional material and should notify the firm of her reasons. If the firm insists that she use the material, she should consider whether her obligation to dissociate from the activity requires her to seek other employment.

Example 4 (Following the Highest Requirements):

James Collins is an investment analyst for a major Wall Street brokerage firm. He works in a developing country with a rapidly modernizing economy and a growing capital market. Local securities laws are minimal—in form and content—and include no punitive prohibitions against insider trading.

> *Comment*: Collins must abide by the requirements of the Code and Standards, which might be more strict than the rules of the developing country. He should be aware of the risks that a small market and the absence of a fairly regulated flow of information to the market represent to his ability to obtain information and make timely judgments. He should include this factor in formulating his advice to clients. In handling material nonpublic information that accidentally comes into his possession, he must follow Standard II(A)–Material Nonpublic Information.

Example 5 (Following the Highest Requirements):

Laura Jameson works for a multinational investment adviser based in the United States. Jameson lives and works as a registered investment adviser in the tiny, but wealthy, island nation of Karramba. Karramba's securities laws state that no investment adviser registered and working in that country can participate in initial public offerings (IPOs) for the adviser's personal account. Jameson, believing that, as a US citizen working for a US-based company, she should comply only with US law, has ignored this Karrambian law. In addition, Jameson believes that as a charterholder, as long as she adheres to the Code and Standards requirement that she disclose her participation in any IPO to her employer and clients when such ownership creates a conflict of interest, she is meeting the highest ethical requirements.

> *Comment*: Jameson is in violation of Standard I(A). As a registered investment adviser in Karramba, Jameson is prevented by Karrambian securities law from participating in IPOs regardless of the law of her home country. In addition, because the law of the country where she is working is stricter than the Code and Standards, she must follow the stricter requirements of the local law rather than the requirements of the Code and Standards.

Example 6 (Laws and Regulations Based on Religious Tenets):

Amanda Janney is employed as a fixed-income portfolio manager for a large international firm. She is on a team within her firm that is responsible for creating and managing a fixed-income hedge fund to be sold throughout the firm's distribution centers to high-net-worth clients. Her firm receives expressions of interest from potential clients from the Middle East who are seeking investments that comply with Islamic law. The marketing and promotional materials for the fixed-income hedge fund do not specify whether or not the fund is a suitable investment for an investor seeking compliance with Islamic law. Because the fund is being distributed globally, Janney is concerned about the reputation of the fund and the firm and believes disclosure of whether or not the fund complies with Islamic law could help minimize potential mistakes with placing this investment.

> *Comment*: As the financial market continues to become globalized, members and candidates will need to be aware of the differences between cultural and religious laws and requirements as well as the different governmental laws and regulations. Janney and the firm could be proactive in their efforts to acknowledge areas where the new fund may not be suitable for clients.

Example 7 (Reporting Potential Unethical Actions):

Krista Blume is a junior portfolio manager for high-net-worth portfolios at a large global investment manager. She observes a number of new portfolios and relationships coming from a country in Europe where the firm did not have previous business and is told that a broker in that country is responsible for this new business. At a meeting on allocation of research resources to third-party research firms, Blume notes that this broker has been added to the list and is allocated payments for research. However, she knows the portfolios do not invest in securities in the broker's country, and she has not seen any research come from this broker. Blume asks her supervisor about the name being on the list and is told that someone in marketing is receiving the research and that the name being on the list is OK. She believes that what may be going on is that the broker is being paid for new business through the inappropriate research payments, and she wishes to dissociate from the misconduct.

> *Comment*: Blume should follow the firm's policies and procedures for reporting potential unethical activity, which may include discussions with her supervisor or someone in a designated compliance department. She should communicate her concerns appropriately while advocating for disclosure between the new broker relationship and the research payments.

Example 8 (Failure to Maintain Knowledge of the Law):

Colleen White is excited to use new technology to communicate with clients and potential clients. She recently began posting investment information, including performance reports and investment opinions and recommendations, to her Facebook page. In addition, she sends out brief announcements, opinions, and thoughts via her Twitter account (for example, "Prospects for future growth of XYZ company look good! #makingmoney4U"). Prior to White's use of these social media platforms, the local regulator had issued new requirements and guidance governing online electronic communication. White's communications appear to conflict with the recent regulatory announcements.

> *Comment*: White is in violation of Standard I(A) because her communications do not comply with the existing guidance and regulation governing use of social media. White must be aware of the evolving legal requirements pertaining to new and dynamic areas of the financial services industry that are applicable to her. She should seek guidance from appropriate, knowledgeable, and reliable sources, such as her firm's compliance department, external service providers, or outside counsel, unless she diligently follows legal and regulatory trends affecting her professional responsibilities.

Standard I(B) Independence and Objectivity

> Members and Candidates must use reasonable care and judgment to achieve and maintain independence and objectivity in their professional activities. Members and Candidates must not offer, solicit, or accept any gift, benefit, compensation, or consideration that reasonably could be expected to compromise their own or another's independence and objectivity.

Guidance

Highlights:

- *Buy-Side Clients*
- *Fund Manager and Custodial Relationships*
- *Investment Banking Relationships*
- *Performance Measurement and Attribution*
- *Public Companies*
- *Credit Rating Agency Opinions*
- *Influence during the Manager Selection/Procurement Process*
- *Issuer-Paid Research*
- *Travel Funding*

Standard I(B) states the responsibility of CFA Institute members and candidates in the CFA Program to maintain independence and objectivity so that their clients will have the benefit of their work and opinions unaffected by any potential conflict of interest or other circumstance adversely affecting their judgment. Every member and candidate should endeavor to avoid situations that could cause or be perceived to cause a loss of independence or objectivity in recommending investments or taking investment action.

External sources may try to influence the investment process by offering analysts and portfolio managers a variety of benefits. Corporations may seek expanded research coverage, issuers and underwriters may wish to promote new securities offerings, brokers may want to increase commission business, and independent rating agencies may be influenced by the company requesting the rating. Benefits may include gifts, invitations to lavish functions, tickets, favors, or job referrals. One type of benefit is the allocation of shares in oversubscribed IPOs to investment managers for their personal accounts. This practice affords managers the opportunity to make quick profits that may not be available to their clients. Such a practice is prohibited under Standard I(B). Modest gifts and entertainment are acceptable, but special care must be taken by members and candidates to resist subtle and not-so-subtle pressures to act in conflict with the interests of their clients. Best practice dictates that members and candidates reject any offer of gift or entertainment that could be expected to threaten their independence and objectivity.

Receiving a gift, benefit, or consideration from a *client* can be distinguished from gifts given by entities seeking to influence a member or candidate to the detriment of other clients. In a client relationship, the client has already entered some type of compensation arrangement with the member, candidate, or his or her firm. A gift from a client could be considered supplementary compensation. The potential for obtaining influence to the detriment of other clients, although present, is not as great as in situations where no compensation arrangement exists. When possible, prior to accepting "bonuses" or gifts from clients, members and candidates should disclose to their employers such benefits offered by clients. If notification is not possible prior to acceptance, members and candidates must disclose to their employer benefits previously accepted from clients. Disclosure allows the employer of a member or candidate to make an independent determination about the extent to which the gift may affect the member's or candidate's independence and objectivity.

Members and candidates may also come under pressure from their own firms to, for example, issue favorable research reports or recommendations for certain companies with potential or continuing business relationships with the firm. The situation may be aggravated if an executive of the company sits on the bank or investment firm's board

Standard I: Professionalism

and attempts to interfere in investment decision making. Members and candidates acting in a sales or marketing capacity must be especially mindful of their objectivity in promoting appropriate investments for their clients.

Left unmanaged, pressures that threaten independence place research analysts in a difficult position and may jeopardize their ability to act independently and objectively. One of the ways that research analysts have coped with these pressures in the past is to use subtle and ambiguous language in their recommendations or to temper the tone of their research reports. Such subtleties are lost on some investors, however, who reasonably expect research reports and recommendations to be straightforward and transparent and to communicate clearly an analyst's views based on unbiased analysis and independent judgment.

Members and candidates are personally responsible for maintaining independence and objectivity when preparing research reports, making investment recommendations, and taking investment action on behalf of clients. Recommendations must convey the member's or candidate's true opinions, free of bias from internal or external pressures, and be stated in clear and unambiguous language.

Members and candidates also should be aware that some of their professional or social activities within CFA Institute or its member societies may subtly threaten their independence or objectivity. When seeking corporate financial support for conventions, seminars, or even weekly society luncheons, the members or candidates responsible for the activities should evaluate both the actual effect of such solicitations on their independence and whether their objectivity might be perceived to be compromised in the eyes of their clients.

Buy-Side Clients

One source of pressure on sell-side analysts is buy-side clients. Institutional clients are traditionally the primary users of sell-side research, either directly or with soft dollar brokerage. Portfolio managers may have significant positions in the security of a company under review. A rating downgrade may adversely affect the portfolio's performance, particularly in the short term, because the sensitivity of stock prices to ratings changes has increased in recent years. A downgrade may also affect the manager's compensation, which is usually tied to portfolio performance. Moreover, portfolio performance is subject to media and public scrutiny, which may affect the manager's professional reputation. Consequently, some portfolio managers implicitly or explicitly support sell-side ratings inflation.

Portfolio managers have a responsibility to respect and foster the intellectual honesty of sell-side research. Therefore, it is improper for portfolio managers to threaten or engage in retaliatory practices, such as reporting sell-side analysts to the covered company in order to instigate negative corporate reactions. Although most portfolio managers do not engage in such practices, the perception by the research analyst that a reprisal is possible may cause concern and make it difficult for the analyst to maintain independence and objectivity.

Fund Manager and Custodial Relationships

Research analysts are not the only people who must be concerned with maintaining their independence. Members and candidates who are responsible for hiring and retaining outside managers and third-party custodians should not accepts gifts, entertainment, or travel funding that may be perceived as impairing their decisions. The use of secondary fund managers has evolved into a common practice to manage specific asset allocations. The use of third-party custodians is common practice for independent investment advisory firms and helps them with trading capabilities and reporting requirements. Primary and secondary fund managers, as well as third-party custodians, often arrange educational and marketing events to inform others about their business strategies, investment process, or custodial services. Members and candidates must review the merits of each offer individually in determining whether they may attend yet maintain their independence.

Investment Banking Relationships

Some sell-side firms may exert pressure on their analysts to issue favorable research reports on current or prospective investment banking clients. For many of these firms, income from investment banking has become increasingly important to overall firm profitability because brokerage income has declined as a result of price competition. Consequently, firms offering investment banking services work hard to develop and maintain relationships with investment banking clients and prospects. These companies are often covered by the firm's research analysts because companies often select their investment banks on the basis of the reputation of their research analysts, the quality of their work, and their standing in the industry.

In some countries, research analysts frequently work closely with their investment banking colleagues to help evaluate prospective investment banking clients. In other countries, because of past abuses in managing the obvious conflicts of interest, regulators have established clear rules prohibiting the interaction of these groups. Although collaboration between research analysts and investment banking colleagues may benefit the firm and enhance market efficiency (e.g., by allowing firms to assess risks more accurately and make better pricing assumptions), it requires firms to carefully balance the conflicts of interest inherent in the collaboration. Having analysts work with investment bankers is appropriate only when the conflicts are adequately and effectively managed and disclosed. Firm managers have a responsibility to provide an environment in which analysts are neither coerced nor enticed into issuing research that does not reflect their true opinions. Firms should require public disclosure of actual conflicts of interest to investors.

Members, candidates, and their firms must adopt and follow perceived best practices in maintaining independence and objectivity in the corporate culture and protecting analysts from undue pressure by their investment banking colleagues. The "firewalls" traditionally built between these two functions must be managed to minimize conflicts of interest; indeed, enhanced firewall policies may go as far as prohibiting all communications between these groups. A key element of an enhanced firewall is separate reporting structures for personnel on the research side and personnel on the investment banking side. For example, investment banking personnel should not have any authority to approve, disapprove, or make changes to research reports or recommendations. Another element should be a compensation arrangement that minimizes the pressures on research analysts and rewards objectivity and accuracy. Compensation arrangements should not link analyst remuneration directly to investment banking assignments in which the analyst may participate as a team member. Firms should also regularly review their policies and procedures to determine whether analysts are adequately safeguarded and to improve the transparency of disclosures relating to conflicts of interest. The highest level of transparency is achieved when disclosures are prominent and specific rather than marginalized and generic.

Performance Measurement and Attribution

Members and candidates working within a firm's investment performance measurement department may also be presented with situations that challenge their independence and objectivity. As performance analysts, their analyses may reveal instances where managers may appear to have strayed from their mandate. Additionally, the performance analyst may receive requests to alter the construction of composite indexes owing to negative results for a selected account or fund. The member or candidate must not allow internal or external influences to affect their independence and objectivity as they faithfully complete their performance calculation and analysis-related responsibilities.

Public Companies

Analysts may be pressured to issue favorable reports and recommendations by the companies they follow. Not every stock is a "buy," and not every research report is favorable—for many reasons, including the cyclical nature of many business activities and market fluctuations. For instance, a "good company" does not always translate into a "good stock" rating if the current stock price is fully valued. In making an investment recommendation, the analyst is responsible for anticipating, interpreting, and assessing a company's prospects and stock price performance in a factual manner. Many company managers, however, believe that their company's stock is undervalued, and these managers may find it difficult to accept critical research reports or ratings downgrades. Company managers' compensation may also be dependent on stock performance.

Due diligence in financial research and analysis involves gathering information from a wide variety of sources, including public disclosure documents (such as proxy statements, annual reports, and other regulatory filings) and also company management and investor-relations personnel, suppliers, customers, competitors, and other relevant sources. Research analysts may justifiably fear that companies will limit their ability to conduct thorough research by denying analysts who have "negative" views direct access to company managers and/or barring them from conference calls and other communication venues. Retaliatory practices include companies bringing legal action against analysts personally and/or their firms to seek monetary damages for the economic effects of negative reports and recommendations. Although few companies engage in such behavior, the perception that a reprisal is possible is a reasonable concern for analysts. This concern may make it difficult for them to conduct the comprehensive research needed to make objective recommendations. For further information and guidance, members and candidates should refer to the CFA Institute publication *Best Practice Guidelines Governing Analyst/Corporate Issuer Relations* (www.cfainstitute.org).

Credit Rating Agency Opinions

Credit rating agencies provide a service by grading the fixed-income products offered by companies. Analysts face challenges related to incentives and compensation schemes that may be tied to the final rating and successful placement of the product. Members and candidates employed at rating agencies should ensure that procedures and processes at the agencies prevent undue influences from a sponsoring company during the analysis. Members and candidates should abide by their agencies' and the industry's standards of conduct regarding the analytical process and the distribution of their reports.

The work of credit rating agencies also raises concerns similar to those inherent in investment banking relationships. Analysts may face pressure to issue ratings at a specific level because of other services the agency offers companies—namely, advising on the development of structured products. The rating agencies need to develop the necessary firewalls and protections to allow the independent operations of their different business lines.

When using information provided by credit rating agencies, members and candidates should be mindful of the potential conflicts of interest. And because of the potential conflicts, members and candidates may need to independently validate the rating granted.

Influence during the Manager Selection/Procurement Process

Members and candidates may find themselves on either side of the manager selection process. An individual may be on the hiring side as a representative of a pension organization or an investment committee member of an endowment or a charitable organization. Additionally, other members may be representing their organizations in attempts to earn new investment allocation mandates. The responsibility of members and candidates to maintain their independence and objectivity extends to the hiring or firing of those who provide business services beyond investment management.

When serving in a hiring capacity, members and candidates should not solicit gifts, contributions, or other compensation that may affect their independence and objectivity. Solicitations do not have to benefit members and candidates personally to conflict with Standard I(B). Requesting contributions to a favorite charity or political organization may also be perceived as an attempt to influence the decision-making process. Additionally, members and candidates serving in a hiring capacity should refuse gifts, donations, and other offered compensation that may be perceived to influence their decision-making process.

When working to earn a new investment allocation, members and candidates should not offer gifts, contributions, or other compensation to influence the decision of the hiring representative. The offering of these items with the intent to impair the independence and objectivity of another person would not comply with Standard I(B). Such prohibited actions may include offering donations to a charitable organization or political candidate referred by the hiring representative.

A clear example of improperly influencing hiring representatives was displayed in the "pay-to-play" scandal involving government-sponsored pension funds in the United States. Managers looking to gain lucrative allocations from the large funds made requested donations to the political campaigns of individuals directly responsible for the hiring decisions. This scandal and other similar events have led to new laws requiring additional reporting concerning political contributions and bans on hiring—or hiring delays for—managers that made campaign contributions to representatives associated with the decision-making process.

Issuer-Paid Research

In light of the recent reduction of sell-side research coverage, many companies, seeking to increase visibility both in the financial markets and with potential investors, have hired analysts to produce research reports analyzing their companies. These reports bridge the gap created by the lack of coverage and can be an effective method of communicating with investors.

Issuer-paid research conducted by independent analysts, however, is fraught with potential conflicts. Depending on how the research is written and distributed, investors may be misled into believing that the research is from an independent source when, in reality, it has been paid for by the subject company.

Members and candidates must adhere to strict standards of conduct that govern how the research is to be conducted and what disclosures must be made in the report. Analysts must engage in thorough, independent, and unbiased analysis and must fully disclose potential conflicts of interest, including the nature of their compensation. Otherwise, analysts risk misleading investors.

Investors need clear, credible, and thorough information about companies, and they need research based on independent thought. At a minimum, issuer-paid research should include a thorough analysis of the company's financial statements based on publicly disclosed information, benchmarking within a peer group, and industry analysis. Analysts must exercise diligence, independence, and thoroughness in conducting their research in an objective manner. Analysts must distinguish between fact and opinion in their reports. Conclusions must have a reasonable and adequate basis and must be supported by appropriate research.

Standard I: Professionalism

Independent analysts must also strictly limit the type of compensation that they accept for conducting issuer-paid research. Otherwise, the content and conclusions of the reports could reasonably be expected to be determined or affected by compensation from the sponsoring companies. Compensation that might influence the research report could be direct, such as payment based on the conclusions of the report, or indirect, such as stock warrants or other equity instruments that could increase in value on the basis of positive coverage in the report. In such instances, the independent analyst has an incentive to avoid including negative information or making negative conclusions. Best practice is for independent analysts, prior to writing their reports, to negotiate only a flat fee for their work that is not linked to their conclusions or recommendations.

Travel Funding

The benefits related to accepting paid travel extend beyond the cost savings to the member or candidate and his firm, such as the chance to talk exclusively with the executives of a company or learning more about the investment options provided by an investment organization. Acceptance also comes with potential concerns; for example, members and candidates may be influenced by these discussions when flying on a corporate or chartered jet or attending sponsored conferences where many expenses, including airfare and lodging, are covered. To avoid the appearance of compromising their independence and objectivity, best practice dictates that members and candidates always use commercial transportation at their expense or at the expense of their firm rather than accept paid travel arrangements from an outside company. Should commercial transportation be unavailable, members and candidates may accept modestly arranged travel to participate in appropriate information-gathering events, such as a property tour.

Recommended Procedures for Compliance

Members and candidates should adhere to the following practices and should encourage their firms to establish procedures to avoid violations of Standard I(B):

- *Protect the integrity of opinions*: Members, candidates, and their firms should establish policies stating that every research report concerning the securities of a corporate client should reflect the unbiased opinion of the analyst. Firms should also design compensation systems that protect the integrity of the investment decision process by maintaining the independence and objectivity of analysts.
- *Create a restricted list*: If the firm is unwilling to permit dissemination of adverse opinions about a corporate client, members and candidates should encourage the firm to remove the controversial company from the research universe and put it on a restricted list so that the firm disseminates only factual information about the company.
- *Restrict special cost arrangements*: When attending meetings at an issuer's headquarters, members and candidates should pay for commercial transportation and hotel charges. No corporate issuer should reimburse members or candidates for air transportation. Members and candidates should encourage issuers to limit the use of corporate aircraft to situations in which commercial transportation is not available or in which efficient movement could not otherwise be arranged. Members and candidates should take particular care that when frequent meetings are held between an individual issuer and an individual member or candidate, the issuer should not always host the member or candidate.

- *Limit gifts*: Members and candidates must limit the acceptance of gratuities and/or gifts to token items. Standard I(B) does not preclude customary, ordinary business-related entertainment as long as its purpose is not to influence or reward members or candidates. Firms should consider a strict value limit for acceptable gifts that is based on the local or regional customs and should address whether the limit is per gift or an aggregate annual value.
- *Restrict investments*: Members and candidates should encourage their investment firms to develop formal policies related to employee purchases of equity or equity-related IPOs. Firms should require prior approval for employee participation in IPOs, with prompt disclosure of investment actions taken following the offering. Strict limits should be imposed on investment personnel acquiring securities in private placements.
- *Review procedures*: Members and candidates should encourage their firms to implement effective supervisory and review procedures to ensure that analysts and portfolio managers comply with policies relating to their personal investment activities.
- *Independence policy*: Members, candidates, and their firms should establish a formal written policy on the independence and objectivity of research and implement reporting structures and review procedures to ensure that research analysts do not report to and are not supervised or controlled by any department of the firm that could compromise the independence of the analyst. More detailed recommendations related to a firm's policies regarding research objectivity are set forth in the CFA Institute statement *Research Objectivity Standards* (www.cfainstitute.org).
- *Appointed officer*: Firms should appoint a senior officer with oversight responsibilities for compliance with the firm's code of ethics and all regulations concerning its business. Firms should provide every employee with the procedures and policies for reporting potentially unethical behavior, violations of regulations, or other activities that may harm the firm's reputation.

Application of the Standard

Example 1 (Travel Expenses):

Steven Taylor, a mining analyst with Bronson Brokers, is invited by Precision Metals to join a group of his peers in a tour of mining facilities in several western US states. The company arranges for chartered group flights from site to site and for accommodations in Spartan Motels, the only chain with accommodations near the mines, for three nights. Taylor allows Precision Metals to pick up his tab, as do the other analysts, with one exception—John Adams, an employee of a large trust company who insists on following his company's policy and paying for his hotel room himself.

> *Comment*: The policy of the company where Adams works complies closely with Standard I(B) by avoiding even the appearance of a conflict of interest, but Taylor and the other analysts were not necessarily violating Standard I(B). In general, when allowing companies to pay for travel and/or accommodations in these circumstances, members and candidates must use their judgment. They must be on guard that such arrangements not impinge on a member's or candidate's independence and objectivity. In this example, the trip was strictly for business and Taylor was not accepting irrelevant or lavish hospitality. The itinerary required chartered flights, for which analysts were not expected to pay. The accommodations were modest. These arrangements are not unusual and did not violate Standard I(B) as long as Taylor's independence and objectivity were not compromised. In

Standard I: Professionalism

the final analysis, members and candidates should consider both whether they can remain objective and whether their integrity might be perceived by their clients to have been compromised.

Example 2 (Research Independence):

Susan Dillon, an analyst in the corporate finance department of an investment services firm, is making a presentation to a potential new business client that includes the promise that her firm will provide full research coverage of the potential client.

> *Comment*: Dillon may agree to provide research coverage, but she must not commit her firm's research department to providing a favorable recommendation. The firm's recommendation (favorable, neutral, or unfavorable) must be based on an independent and objective investigation and analysis of the company and its securities.

Example 3 (Research Independence and Intrafirm Pressure):

Walter Fritz is an equity analyst with Hilton Brokerage who covers the mining industry. He has concluded that the stock of Metals & Mining is overpriced at its current level, but he is concerned that a negative research report will hurt the good relationship between Metals & Mining and the investment banking division of his firm. In fact, a senior manager of Hilton Brokerage has just sent him a copy of a proposal his firm has made to Metals & Mining to underwrite a debt offering. Fritz needs to produce a report right away and is concerned about issuing a less-than-favorable rating.

> *Comment*: Fritz's analysis of Metals & Mining must be objective and based solely on consideration of company fundamentals. Any pressure from other divisions of his firm is inappropriate. This conflict could have been eliminated if, in anticipation of the offering, Hilton Brokerage had placed Metals & Mining on a restricted list for its sales force.

Example 4 (Research Independence and Issuer Relationship Pressure):

As in Example 3, Walter Fritz has concluded that Metals & Mining stock is overvalued at its current level, but he is concerned that a negative research report might jeopardize a close rapport that he has nurtured over the years with Metals & Mining's CEO, chief finance officer, and investment relations officer. Fritz is concerned that a negative report might result also in management retaliation—for instance, cutting him off from participating in conference calls when a quarterly earnings release is made, denying him the ability to ask questions on such calls, and/or denying him access to top management for arranging group meetings between Hilton Brokerage clients and top Metals & Mining managers.

> *Comment*: As in Example 3, Fritz's analysis must be objective and based solely on consideration of company fundamentals. Any pressure from Metals & Mining is inappropriate. Fritz should reinforce the integrity of his conclusions by stressing that his investment recommendation is based on relative valuation, which may include qualitative issues with respect to Metals & Mining's management.

Example 5 (Research Independence and Sales Pressure):

As support for the sales effort of her corporate bond department, Lindsey Warner offers credit guidance to purchasers of fixed-income securities. Her compensation is closely linked to the performance of the corporate bond department. Near the quarter's end, Warner's firm has a large inventory position in the bonds of Milton, Ltd., and has been unable to sell the bonds because of Milton's recent announcement of an operating problem. Salespeople have asked her to contact large clients to push the bonds.

> *Comment*: Unethical sales practices create significant potential violations of the Code and Standards. Warner's opinion of the Milton bonds must not be affected by internal pressure or compensation. In this case, Warner must refuse to push the Milton bonds unless she is able to justify that the market price has already adjusted for the operating problem.

Example 6 (Research Independence and Prior Coverage):

Jill Jorund is a securities analyst following airline stocks and a rising star at her firm. Her boss has been carrying a "buy" recommendation on International Airlines and asks Jorund to take over coverage of that airline. He tells Jorund that under no circumstances should the prevailing buy recommendation be changed.

> *Comment*: Jorund must be independent and objective in her analysis of International Airlines. If she believes that her boss's instructions have compromised her, she has two options: She can tell her boss that she cannot cover the company under these constraints, or she can take over coverage of the company, reach her own independent conclusions, and if they conflict with her boss's opinion, share the conclusions with her boss or other supervisors in the firm so that they can make appropriate recommendations. Jorund must issue only recommendations that reflect her independent and objective opinion.

Example 7 (Gifts and Entertainment from Related Party):

Edward Grant directs a large amount of his commission business to a New York–based brokerage house. In appreciation for all the business, the brokerage house gives Grant two tickets to the World Cup in South Africa, two nights at a nearby resort, several meals, and transportation via limousine to the game. Grant fails to disclose receiving this package to his supervisor.

> *Comment*: Grant has violated Standard I(B) because accepting these substantial gifts may impede his independence and objectivity. Every member and candidate should endeavor to avoid situations that might cause or be perceived to cause a loss of independence or objectivity in recommending investments or taking investment action. By accepting the trip, Grant has opened himself up to the accusation that he may give the broker favored treatment in return.

Example 8 (Gifts and Entertainment from Client):

Theresa Green manages the portfolio of Ian Knowlden, a client of Tisbury Investments. Green achieves an annual return for Knowlden that is consistently better than that of the benchmark she and the client previously agreed to. As a reward, Knowlden offers Green two tickets to Wimbledon and the use of Knowlden's flat in London for a week. Green discloses this gift to her supervisor at Tisbury.

> *Comment*: Green is in compliance with Standard I(B) because she disclosed the gift from one of her clients in accordance with the firm's policies. Members and candidates may accept bonuses or gifts from clients as long as they disclose them to their employer because gifts in a client relationship are deemed less likely to affect a member's or candidate's objectivity and independence than gifts in other situations. Disclosure is required, however, so that supervisors can monitor such situations to guard against

employees favoring a gift-giving client to the detriment of other fee-paying clients (such as by allocating a greater proportion of IPO stock to the gift-giving client's portfolio).

Best practices for monitoring include comparing the transaction costs of the Knowlden account with the costs of other accounts managed by Green and other similar accounts within Tisbury. The supervisor could also compare the performance returns with the returns of other clients with the same mandate. This comparison will assist in determining whether a pattern of favoritism by Green is disadvantaging other Tisbury clients or the possibility that this favoritism could affect her future behavior.

Example 9 (Travel Expenses from External Manager):

Tom Wayne is the investment manager of the Franklin City Employees Pension Plan. He recently completed a successful search for a firm to manage the foreign equity allocation of the plan's diversified portfolio. He followed the plan's standard procedure of seeking presentations from a number of qualified firms and recommended that his board select Penguin Advisors because of its experience, well-defined investment strategy, and performance record. The firm claims compliance with the Global Investment Performance Standards (GIPS) and has been verified. Following the selection of Penguin, a reporter from the *Franklin City Record* calls to ask if there was any connection between this action and the fact that Penguin was one of the sponsors of an "investment fact-finding trip to Asia" that Wayne made earlier in the year. The trip was one of several conducted by the Pension Investment Academy, which had arranged the itinerary of meetings with economic, government, and corporate officials in major cities in several Asian countries. The Pension Investment Academy obtains support for the cost of these trips from a number of investment managers, including Penguin Advisors; the Academy then pays the travel expenses of the various pension plan managers on the trip and provides all meals and accommodations. The president of Penguin Advisors was also one of the travelers on the trip.

> *Comment*: Although Wayne can probably put to good use the knowledge he gained from the trip in selecting portfolio managers and in other areas of managing the pension plan, his recommendation of Penguin Advisors may be tainted by the possible conflict incurred when he participated in a trip partly paid for by Penguin Advisors and when he was in the daily company of the president of Penguin Advisors. To avoid violating Standard I(B), Wayne's basic expenses for travel and accommodations should have been paid by his employer or the pension plan; contact with the president of Penguin Advisors should have been limited to informational or educational events only; and the trip, the organizer, and the sponsor should have been made a matter of public record. Even if his actions were not in violation of Standard I(B), Wayne should have been sensitive to the public perception of the trip when reported in the newspaper and the extent to which the subjective elements of his decision might have been affected by the familiarity that the daily contact of such a trip would encourage. This advantage would probably not be shared by firms competing with Penguin Advisors.

Example 10 (Research Independence and Compensation Arrangements):

Javier Herrero recently left his job as a research analyst for a large investment adviser. While looking for a new position, he was hired by an investor-relations firm to write a research report on one of its clients, a small educational software company. The investor-relations firm hopes to generate investor interest in the technology company. The firm will pay Herrero a flat fee plus a bonus if any new investors buy stock in the company as a result of Herrero's report.

Comment: If Herrero accepts this payment arrangement, he will be in violation of Standard I(B) because the compensation arrangement can reasonably be expected to compromise his independence and objectivity. Herrero will receive a bonus for attracting investors, which provides an incentive to draft a positive report regardless of the facts and to ignore or play down any negative information about the company. Herrero should accept only a flat fee that is not tied to the conclusions or recommendations of the report. Issuer-paid research that is objective and unbiased can be done under the right circumstances as long as the analyst takes steps to maintain his or her objectivity and includes in the report proper disclosures regarding potential conflicts of interest.

Example 11 (Recommendation Objectivity and Service Fees):

Two years ago, Bob Wade, trust manager for Central Midas Bank, was approached by Western Funds about promoting its family of funds, with special interest in the service-fee class of funds. To entice Central to promote this class, Western Funds offered to pay the bank a service fee of 0.25%. Without disclosing the fee being offered to the bank, Wade asked one of the investment managers to review Western's funds to determine whether they were suitable for clients of Central Midas Bank. The manager completed the normal due diligence review and determined that the new funds were fairly valued in the market with fee structures on a par with competitors. Wade decided to accept Western's offer and instructed the team of portfolio managers to exclusively promote these funds and the service-fee class to clients seeking to invest new funds or transfer from their current investments.

Now, two years later, the funds managed by Western begin to underperform their peers. Wade is counting on the fees to reach his profitability targets and continues to push these funds as acceptable investments for Central's clients.

Comment: Wade is violating Standard I(B) because the fee arrangement has affected the objectivity of his recommendations. Wade is relying on the fee as a component of the department's profitability and is unwilling to offer other products that may affect the fees received.
See also Standard VI(A)–Disclosure of Conflicts.

Example 12 (Recommendation Objectivity):

Bob Thompson has been doing research for the portfolio manager of the fixed-income department. His assignment is to do sensitivity analysis on securitized subprime mortgages. He has discussed with the manager possible scenarios to use to calculate expected returns. A key assumption in such calculations is housing price appreciation (HPA) because it drives "prepays" (prepayments of mortgages) and losses. Thompson is concerned with the significant appreciation experienced over the previous five years as a result of the increased availability of funds from subprime mortgages. Thompson insists that the analysis should include a scenario run with –10% for Year 1, –5% for Year 2, and then (to project a worst-case scenario) 0% for Years 3 through 5. The manager replies that these assumptions are too dire because there has never been a time in their available database when HPA was negative.

Thompson conducts his research to better understand the risks inherent in these securities and evaluates these securities in the worst-case scenario, an unlikely but possible environment. Based on the results of the enhanced scenarios, Thompson does not recommend the purchase of the securitization. Against the general market trends, the manager follows Thompson's recommendation and does not invest. The following year, the housing market collapses. In avoiding the subprime investments, the manager's portfolio outperforms its peer group that year.

Standard I: Professionalism

Comment: Thompson's actions in running the worst-case scenario against the protests of the portfolio manager are in alignment with the principles of Standard I(B). Thompson did not allow his research to be pressured by the general trends of the market or the manager's desire to limit the research to historical norms.

See also Standard V(A)–Diligence and Reasonable Basis.

Example 13 (Influencing Manager Selection Decisions):

Adrian Mandel, CFA, is a senior portfolio manager for ZZYY Capital Management who oversees a team of investment professionals who manage labor union pension funds. A few years ago, ZZYY sought to win a competitive asset manager search to manage a significant allocation of the pension fund of the United Doughnut and Pretzel Bakers Union (UDPBU). UDPBU's investment board is chaired by a recognized key decision maker and long-time leader of the union, Ernesto Gomez. To improve ZZYY's chances of winning the competition, Mandel made significant monetary contributions to Gomez's union reelection campaign fund. Even after ZZYY was hired as a primary manager of the pension, Mandel believed that his firm's position was not secure. Mandel continued to contribute to Gomez's reelection campaign chest as well as to entertain lavishly the union leader and his family at top restaurants on a regular basis. All of Mandel's outlays were routinely handled as marketing expenses reimbursed by ZZYY's expense accounts and were disclosed to his senior management as being instrumental in maintaining a strong close relationship with an important client.

Comment: Mandel not only offered but actually gave monetary gifts, benefits, and other considerations that reasonably could be expected to compromise Gomez's objectivity. Therefore, Mandel was in violation of Standard I(B).

Example 14 (Influencing Manager Selection Decisions):

Adrian Mandel, CFA, had heard about the manager search competition for the UDPBU Pension Fund through a broker/dealer contact. The contact told him that a well-known retired professional golfer, Bobby "The Bear" Finlay, who had become a licensed broker/dealer serving as a pension consultant, was orchestrating the UDPBU manager search. Finlay had gained celebrity status with several labor union pension fund boards by entertaining their respective board members and regaling them with colorful stories of fellow pro golfers' antics in clubhouses around the world. Mandel decided to improve ZZYY's chances of being invited to participate in the search competition by befriending Finlay to curry his favor. Knowing Finlay's love of entertainment, Mandel wined and dined Finlay at high-profile bistros where Finlay could glow in the fan recognition lavished on him by all the other patrons. Mandel's endeavors paid off handsomely when Finlay recommended to the UDPBU board that ZZYY be entered as one of three finalist asset management firms in its search.

Comment: Similar to Example 13, Mandel lavished gifts, benefits, and other considerations in the form of expensive entertainment that could reasonably be expected to influence the consultant to recommend the hiring of his firm. Therefore, Mandel was in violation of Standard I(B).

Example 15 (Fund Manager Relationships):

Amie Scott is a performance analyst within her firm with responsibilities for analyzing the performance of external managers. While completing her quarterly analysis, Scott notices a change in one manager's reported composite construction. The change concealed the bad performance of a particularly large account by placing that account into a new residual composite. This change allowed the manager to remain at the top of the list of manager performance. Scott knows her firm has a large allocation to this manager, and the fund's manager is a close personal friend of the CEO. She needs to deliver her final report but is concerned with pointing out the composite change.

> *Comment*: Scott would be in violation of Standard I(B) if she did not disclose the change in her final report. The analysis of managers' performance should not be influenced by personal relationships or the size of the allocation to the outside managers. By not including the change, Scott would not be providing an independent analysis of the performance metrics for her firm.

Example 16 (Intrafirm Pressure):

Jill Stein is head of performance measurement for her firm. During the last quarter, many members of the organization's research department were removed because of the poor quality of their recommendations. The subpar research caused one larger account holder to experience significant underperformance, which resulted in the client withdrawing his money after the end of the quarter. The head of sales requests that Stein remove this account from the firm's performance composite because the performance decline can be attributed to the departed research team and not the client's adviser.

> *Comment*: Pressure from other internal departments can create situations that cause a member or candidate to violate the Code and Standards. Stein must maintain her independence and objectivity and refuse to exclude specific accounts from the firm's performance composites to which they belong. As long as the client invested under a strategy similar to that of the defined composite, it cannot be excluded because of the poor stock selections that led to the underperformance and asset withdrawal.

Standard I(C) Misrepresentation

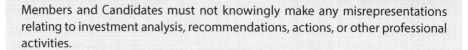

Members and Candidates must not knowingly make any misrepresentations relating to investment analysis, recommendations, actions, or other professional activities.

Guidance

Highlights:

- *Impact on Investment Practice*
- *Performance Reporting*
- *Social Media*
- *Omissions*
- *Plagiarism*
- *Work Completed for Employer*

Trust is the foundation of the investment profession. Investors must be able to rely on the statements and information provided to them by those with whom the investors have trusted their financial well-being. Investment professionals who make false or

Standard I: Professionalism

misleading statements not only harm investors but also reduce the level of investor confidence in the investment profession and threaten the integrity of capital markets as a whole.

A misrepresentation is any untrue statement or omission of a fact or any statement that is otherwise false or misleading. A member or candidate must not knowingly omit or misrepresent information or give a false impression of a firm, organization, or security in the member's or candidate's oral representations, advertising (whether in the press or through brochures), electronic communications, or written materials (whether publicly disseminated or not). In this context, "knowingly" means that the member or candidate either knows or should have known that the misrepresentation was being made or that omitted information could alter the investment decision-making process.

Written materials include, but are not limited to, research reports, underwriting documents, company financial reports, market letters, newspaper columns, and books. Electronic communications include, but are not limited to, internet communications, webpages, mobile applications, and e-mails. Members and candidates who use webpages should regularly monitor materials posted on these sites to ensure that they contain current information. Members and candidates should also ensure that all reasonable precautions have been taken to protect the site's integrity and security and that the site does not misrepresent any information and does provide full disclosure.

Standard I(C) prohibits members and candidates from guaranteeing clients any specific return on volatile investments. Most investments contain some element of risk that makes their return inherently unpredictable. For such investments, guaranteeing either a particular rate of return or a guaranteed preservation of investment capital (e.g., "I can guarantee that you will earn 8% on equities this year" or "I can guarantee that you will not lose money on this investment") is misleading to investors. Standard I(C) does not prohibit members and candidates from providing clients with information on investment products that have guarantees built into the structure of the products themselves or for which an institution has agreed to cover any losses.

Impact on Investment Practice

Members and candidates must not misrepresent any aspect of their practice, including (but not limited to) their qualifications or credentials, the qualifications or services provided by their firm, their performance record and the record of their firm, and the characteristics of an investment. Any misrepresentation made by a member or candidate relating to the member's or candidate's professional activities is a breach of this standard.

Members and candidates should exercise care and diligence when incorporating third-party information. Misrepresentations resulting from the use of the credit ratings, research, testimonials, or marketing materials of outside parties become the responsibility of the investment professional when it affects that professional's business practices.

Investing through outside managers continues to expand as an acceptable method of investing in areas outside a firm's core competencies. Members and candidates must disclose their intended use of external managers and must not represent those managers' investment practices as their own. Although the level of involvement of outside managers may change over time, appropriate disclosures by members and candidates are important in avoiding misrepresentations, especially if the primary activity is to invest directly with a single external manager. Standard V(B)–Communication with Clients and Prospective Clients discusses in further detail communicating the firm's investment practices.

Performance Reporting

The performance benchmark selection process is another area where misrepresentations may occur. Members and candidates may misrepresent the success of their performance record through presenting benchmarks that are not comparable to their strategies. Further, clients can be misled if the benchmark's results are not reported on a basis comparable to that of the fund's or client's results. Best practice is selecting the most appropriate available benchmark from a universe of available options. The transparent presentation of appropriate performance benchmarks is an important aspect in providing clients with information that is useful in making investment decisions.

However, Standard I(C) does not require that a benchmark always be provided in order to comply. Some investment strategies may not lend themselves to displaying an appropriate benchmark because of the complexity or diversity of the investments included. Furthermore, some investment strategies may use reference indexes that do not reflect the opportunity set of the invested assets—for example, a hedge fund comparing its performance with a "cash plus" basis. When such a benchmark is used, members and candidates should make reasonable efforts to ensure that they disclose the reasons behind the use of this reference index to avoid misrepresentations of their performance. Members and candidates should discuss with clients on a continuous basis the appropriate benchmark to be used for performance evaluations and related fee calculations.

Reporting misrepresentations may also occur when valuations for illiquid or non-traded securities are available from more than one source. When different options are available, members and candidates may be tempted to switch providers to obtain higher security valuations. The process of shopping for values may misrepresent a security's worth, lead to misinformed decisions to sell or hold an investment, and result in overcharging clients advisory fees.

Members and candidates should take reasonable steps to provide accurate and reliable security pricing information to clients on a consistent basis. Changing pricing providers should not be based solely on the justification that the new provider reports a higher current value of a security. Consistency in the reported information will improve the perception of the valuation process for illiquid securities. Clients will likely have additional confidence that they were able to make an informed decision about continuing to hold these securities in their portfolios.

Social Media

The advancement of online discussion forums and communication platforms, commonly referred to as "social media," is placing additional responsibilities on members and candidates. When communicating through social media channels, members and candidates should provide only the same information they are allowed to distribute to clients and potential clients through other traditional forms of communication. The online or interactive aspects of social media do not remove the need to be open and honest about the information being distributed.

Along with understanding and following existing and newly developing rules and regulations regarding the allowed use of social media, members and candidates should also ensure that all communications in this format adhere to the requirements of the Code and Standards. The perceived anonymity granted through these platforms may entice individuals to misrepresent their qualifications or abilities or those of their employer. Actions undertaken through social media that knowingly misrepresent investment recommendations or professional activities are considered a violation of Standard I(C).

Standard I: Professionalism

Omissions

The omission of a fact or outcome can be misleading, especially given the growing use of models and technical analysis processes. Many members and candidates rely on such models and processes to scan for new investment opportunities, to develop investment vehicles, and to produce investment recommendations and ratings. When inputs are knowingly omitted, the resulting outcomes may provide misleading information to those who rely on it for making investment decisions. Additionally, the outcomes from models shall not be presented as fact because they represent the expected results based on the inputs and analysis process incorporated.

Omissions in the performance measurement and attribution process can also misrepresent a manager's performance and skill. Members and candidates should encourage their firms to develop strict policies for composite development to prevent cherry picking—situations in which selected accounts are presented as representative of the firm's abilities. The omission of any accounts appropriate for the defined composite may misrepresent to clients the success of the manager's implementation of its strategy.

Plagiarism

Standard I(C) also prohibits plagiarism in the preparation of material for distribution to employers, associates, clients, prospects, or the general public. Plagiarism is defined as copying or using in substantially the same form materials prepared by others without acknowledging the source of the material or identifying the author and publisher of such material. Members and candidates must not copy (or represent as their own) original ideas or material without permission and must acknowledge and identify the source of ideas or material that is not their own.

The investment profession uses a myriad of financial, economic, and statistical data in the investment decision-making process. Through various publications and presentations, the investment professional is constantly exposed to the work of others and to the temptation to use that work without proper acknowledgment.

Misrepresentation through plagiarism in investment management can take various forms. The simplest and most flagrant example is to take a research report or study done by another firm or person, change the names, and release the material as one's own original analysis. This action is a clear violation of Standard I(C). Other practices include (1) using excerpts from articles or reports prepared by others either verbatim or with only slight changes in wording without acknowledgment, (2) citing specific quotations as attributable to "leading analysts" and "investment experts" without naming the specific references, (3) presenting statistical estimates of forecasts prepared by others and identifying the sources but without including the qualifying statements or caveats that may have been used, (4) using charts and graphs without stating their sources, and (5) copying proprietary computerized spreadsheets or algorithms without seeking the cooperation or authorization of their creators.

In the case of distributing third-party, outsourced research, members and candidates may use and distribute such reports as long as they do not represent themselves as the report's authors. Indeed, the member or candidate may add value for the client by sifting through research and repackaging it for clients. In such cases, clients should be fully informed that they are paying for the ability of the member or candidate to find the best research from a wide variety of sources. Members and candidates must not misrepresent their abilities, the extent of their expertise, or the extent of their work in a way that would mislead their clients or prospective clients. Members and candidates should disclose whether the research being presented to clients comes from another source—from either within or outside the member's or candidate's firm. This allows clients to understand who has the expertise behind the report or whether the work is being done by the analyst, other members of the firm, or an outside party.

Standard I(C) also applies to plagiarism in oral communications, such as through group meetings; visits with associates, clients, and customers; use of audio/video media (which is rapidly increasing); and telecommunications, including electronic data transfer and the outright copying of electronic media.

One of the most egregious practices in violation of this standard is the preparation of research reports based on multiple sources of information without acknowledging the sources. Examples of information from such sources include ideas, statistical compilations, and forecasts combined to give the appearance of original work. Although there is no monopoly on ideas, members and candidates must give credit where it is clearly due. Analysts should not use undocumented forecasts, earnings projections, asset values, and so on. Sources must be revealed to bring the responsibility directly back to the author of the report or the firm involved.

Work Completed for Employer

The preceding paragraphs address actions that would constitute a violation of Standard I(C). In some situations, however, members or candidates may use research conducted or models developed by others within the same firm without committing a violation. The most common example relates to the situation in which one (or more) of the original analysts is no longer with the firm. Research and models developed while employed by a firm are the property of the firm. The firm retains the right to continue using the work completed after a member or candidate has left the organization. The firm may issue future reports without providing attribution to the prior analysts. A member or candidate cannot, however, reissue a previously released report solely under his or her name.

Recommended Procedures for Compliance

Factual Presentations

Members and candidates can prevent unintentional misrepresentations of their qualifications or the services they or their firms provide if each member and candidate understands the limit of the firm's or individual's capabilities and the need to be accurate and complete in presentations. Firms can provide guidance for employees who make written or oral presentations to clients or potential clients by providing a written list of the firm's available services and a description of the firm's qualifications. This list should suggest ways of describing the firm's services, qualifications, and compensation that are both accurate and suitable for client or customer presentations. Firms can also help prevent misrepresentation by specifically designating which employees are authorized to speak on behalf of the firm. Regardless of whether the firm provides guidance, members and candidates should make certain that they understand the services the firm can perform and its qualifications.

Qualification Summary

In addition, to ensure accurate presentations to clients, each member and candidate should prepare a summary of his or her own qualifications and experience and a list of the services the member or candidate is capable of performing. Firms can assist member and candidate compliance by periodically reviewing employee correspondence and documents that contain representations of individual or firm qualifications.

Verify Outside Information

When providing information to clients from a third party, members and candidates share a responsibility for the accuracy of the marketing and distribution materials that pertain to the third party's capabilities, services, and products. Misrepresentation by third parties can damage the member's or candidate's reputation, the reputation of the firm, and the integrity of the capital markets. Members and candidates should encourage their employers to develop procedures for verifying information of third-party firms.

Maintain Webpages

Members and candidates who publish a webpage should regularly monitor materials posted on the site to ensure that the site contains current information. Members and candidates should also ensure that all reasonable precautions have been taken to protect the site's integrity, confidentiality, and security and that the site does not misrepresent any information and provides full disclosure.

Plagiarism Policy

To avoid plagiarism in preparing research reports or conclusions of analysis, members and candidates should take the following steps:

- *Maintain copies*: Keep copies of all research reports, articles containing research ideas, material with new statistical methodologies, and other materials that were relied on in preparing the research report.
- *Attribute quotations*: Attribute to their sources any direct quotations, including projections, tables, statistics, model/product ideas, and new methodologies prepared by persons other than recognized financial and statistical reporting services or similar sources.
- *Attribute summaries*: Attribute to their sources any paraphrases or summaries of material prepared by others. For example, to support his analysis of Brown Company's competitive position, the author of a research report on Brown might summarize another analyst's report on Brown's chief competitor, but the author of the Brown report must acknowledge in his own report the reliance on the other analyst's report.

Application of the Standard

Example 1 (Disclosure of Issuer-Paid Research):

Anthony McGuire is an issuer-paid analyst hired by publicly traded companies to electronically promote their stocks. McGuire creates a website that promotes his research efforts as a seemingly independent analyst. McGuire posts a profile and a strong buy recommendation for each company on the website indicating that the stock is expected to increase in value. He does not disclose the contractual relationships with the companies he covers on his website, in the research reports he issues, or in the statements he makes about the companies in internet chat rooms.

> *Comment*: McGuire has violated Standard I(C) because the website is misleading to potential investors. Even if the recommendations are valid and supported with thorough research, his omissions regarding the true relationship between himself and the companies he covers constitute a misrepresentation. McGuire has also violated Standard VI(A)–Disclosure of Conflicts by not disclosing the existence of an arrangement with the companies through which he receives compensation in exchange for his services.

Example 2 (Correction of Unintentional Errors):

Hijan Yao is responsible for the creation and distribution of the marketing materials for his firm, which claims compliance with the GIPS standards. Yao creates and distributes a presentation of performance by the firm's Asian equity composite that states the composite has ¥350 billion in assets. In fact, the composite has only ¥35 billion in assets, and the higher figure on the presentation is a result of a typographical error. Nevertheless, the erroneous material is distributed to a number of clients before Yao catches the mistake.

> *Comment*: Once the error is discovered, Yao must take steps to cease distribution of the incorrect material and correct the error by informing those who have received the erroneous information. Because Yao did not knowingly make the misrepresentation, however, he did not violate Standard I(C). Because his firm claims compliance with the GIPS standards, it must also comply with the GIPS Guidance Statement on Error Correction in relation to the error.

Example 3 (Noncorrection of Known Errors):

Syed Muhammad is the president of an investment management firm. The promotional material for the firm, created by the firm's marketing department, incorrectly claims that Muhammad has an advanced degree in finance from a prestigious business school in addition to the CFA designation. Although Muhammad attended the school for a short period of time, he did not receive a degree. Over the years, Muhammad and others in the firm have distributed this material to numerous prospective clients and consultants.

> *Comment*: Even though Muhammad may not have been directly responsible for the misrepresentation of his credentials in the firm's promotional material, he used this material numerous times over an extended period and should have known of the misrepresentation. Thus, Muhammad has violated Standard I(C).

Example 4 (Plagiarism):

Cindy Grant, a research analyst for a Canadian brokerage firm, has specialized in the Canadian mining industry for the past 10 years. She recently read an extensive research report on Jefferson Mining, Ltd., by Jeremy Barton, another analyst. Barton provided extensive statistics on the mineral reserves, production capacity, selling rates, and marketing factors affecting Jefferson's operations. He also noted that initial drilling results on a new ore body, which had not been made public, might show the existence of mineral zones that could increase the life of Jefferson's main mines, but Barton cited no specific data as to the initial drilling results. Grant called an officer of Jefferson, who gave her the initial drilling results over the telephone. The data indicated that the expected life of the main mines would be tripled. Grant added these statistics to Barton's report and circulated it within her firm as her own report.

> *Comment*: Grant plagiarized Barton's report by reproducing large parts of it in her own report without acknowledgment.

Example 5 (Misrepresentation of Information):

When Ricki Marks sells mortgage-backed derivatives called "interest-only strips" (IOs) to public pension plan clients, she describes them as "guaranteed by the US government." Purchasers of the IOs are entitled only to the interest stream generated by the mortgages, however, not the notional principal itself. One particular municipality's investment policies and local law require that securities purchased by its public pension plans be guaranteed by the US government. Although the underlying mortgages are guaranteed, neither the investor's investment nor the interest stream on the IOs

Standard I: Professionalism

is guaranteed. When interest rates decline, causing an increase in prepayment of mortgages, interest payments to the IOs' investors decline, and these investors lose a portion of their investment.

> *Comment*: Marks violated Standard I(C) by misrepresenting the terms and character of the investment.

Example 6 (Potential Information Misrepresentation):

Khalouck Abdrabbo manages the investments of several high-net-worth individuals in the United States who are approaching retirement. Abdrabbo advises these individuals that a portion of their investments be moved from equity to bank-sponsored certificates of deposit and money market accounts so that the principal will be "guaranteed" up to a certain amount. The interest is not guaranteed.

> *Comment*: Although there is risk that the institution offering the certificates of deposits and money market accounts could go bankrupt, in the United States, these accounts are insured by the US government through the Federal Deposit Insurance Corporation. Therefore, using the term "guaranteed" in this context is not inappropriate as long as the amount is within the government-insured limit. Abdrabbo should explain these facts to the clients.

Example 7 (Plagiarism):

Steve Swanson is a senior analyst in the investment research department of Ballard and Company. Apex Corporation has asked Ballard to assist in acquiring the majority ownership of stock in the Campbell Company, a financial consulting firm, and to prepare a report recommending that stockholders of Campbell agree to the acquisition. Another investment firm, Davis and Company, had already prepared a report for Apex analyzing both Apex and Campbell and recommending an exchange ratio. Apex has given the Davis report to Ballard officers, who have passed it on to Swanson. Swanson reviews the Davis report and other available material on Apex and Campbell. From his analysis, he concludes that the common stocks of Campbell and Apex represent good value at their current prices; he believes, however, that the Davis report does not consider all the factors a Campbell stockholder would need to know to make a decision. Swanson reports his conclusions to the partner in charge, who tells him to "use the Davis report, change a few words, sign your name, and get it out."

> *Comment*: If Swanson does as requested, he will violate Standard I(C). He could refer to those portions of the Davis report that he agrees with if he identifies Davis as the source; he could then add his own analysis and conclusions to the report before signing and distributing it.

Example 8 (Plagiarism):

Claude Browning, a quantitative analyst for Double Alpha, Inc., returns from a seminar in great excitement. At that seminar, Jack Jorrely, a well-known quantitative analyst at a national brokerage firm, discussed one of his new models in great detail, and Browning is intrigued by the new concepts. He proceeds to test the model, making some minor mechanical changes but retaining the concepts, until he produces some very positive results. Browning quickly announces to his supervisors at Double Alpha that he has discovered a new model and that clients and prospective clients should be informed of this positive finding as ongoing proof of Double Alpha's continuing innovation and ability to add value.

Comment: Although Browning tested Jorrely's model on his own and even slightly modified it, he must still acknowledge the original source of the idea. Browning can certainly take credit for the final, practical results; he can also support his conclusions with his own test. The credit for the innovative thinking, however, must be awarded to Jorrely.

Example 9 (Plagiarism):

Fernando Zubia would like to include in his firm's marketing materials some "plain-language" descriptions of various concepts, such as the price-to-earnings (P/E) multiple and why standard deviation is used as a measure of risk. The descriptions come from other sources, but Zubia wishes to use them without reference to the original authors. Would this use of material be a violation of Standard I(C)?

Comment: Copying verbatim any material without acknowledgement, including plain-language descriptions of the P/E multiple and standard deviation, violates Standard I(C). Even though these concepts are general, best practice would be for Zubia to describe them in his own words or cite the sources from which the descriptions are quoted. Members and candidates would be violating Standard I(C) if they either were responsible for creating marketing materials without attribution or knowingly use plagiarized materials.

Example 10 (Plagiarism):

Through a mainstream media outlet, Erika Schneider learns about a study that she would like to cite in her research. Should she cite both the mainstream intermediary source as well as the author of the study itself when using that information?

Comment: In all instances, a member or candidate must cite the actual source of the information. Best practice for Schneider would be to obtain the information directly from the author and review it before citing it in a report. In that case, Schneider would not need to report how she found out about the information. For example, suppose Schneider read in the *Financial Times* about a study issued by CFA Institute; best practice for Schneider would be to obtain a copy of the study from CFA Institute, review it, and then cite it in her report. If she does not use any interpretation of the report from the *Financial Times* and the newspaper does not add value to the report itself, the newspaper is merely a conduit of the original information and does not need to be cited. If she does not obtain the report and review the information, Schneider runs the risk of relying on second-hand information that may misstate facts. If, for example, the *Financial Times* erroneously reported some information from the original CFA Institute study and Schneider copied that erroneous information without acknowledging CFA Institute, she could be the object of complaints. Best practice would be either to obtain the complete study from its original author and cite only that author or to use the information provided by the intermediary and cite both sources.

Example 11 (Misrepresentation of Information):

Paul Ostrowski runs a two-person investment management firm. Ostrowski's firm subscribes to a service from a large investment research firm that provides research reports that can be repackaged by smaller firms for those firms' clients. Ostrowski's firm distributes these reports to clients as its own work.

Standard I: Professionalism

> *Comment*: Ostrowski can rely on third-party research that has a reasonable and adequate basis, but he cannot imply that he is the author of such research. If he does, Ostrowski is misrepresenting the extent of his work in a way that misleads the firm's clients or prospective clients.

Example 12 (Misrepresentation of Information):

Tom Stafford is part of a team within Appleton Investment Management responsible for managing a pool of assets for Open Air Bank, which distributes structured securities to offshore clients. He becomes aware that Open Air is promoting the structured securities as a much less risky investment than the investment management policy followed by him and the team to manage the original pool of assets. Also, Open Air has procured an independent rating for the pool that significantly overstates the quality of the investments. Stafford communicates his concerns to his supervisor, who responds that Open Air owns the product and is responsible for all marketing and distribution. Stafford's supervisor goes on to say that the product is outside of the US regulatory regime that Appleton follows and that all risks of the product are disclosed at the bottom of page 184 of the prospectus.

> *Comment*: As a member of the investment team, Stafford is qualified to recognize the degree of accuracy of the materials that characterize the portfolio, and he is correct to be worried about Appleton's responsibility for a misrepresentation of the risks. Thus, he should continue to pursue the issue of Open Air's inaccurate promotion of the portfolio according to the firm's policies and procedures.
>
> The Code and Standards stress protecting the reputation of the firm and the sustainability and integrity of the capital markets. Misrepresenting the quality and risks associated with the investment pool may lead to negative consequences for others well beyond the direct investors.

Example 13 (Avoiding a Misrepresentation):

Trina Smith is a fixed-income portfolio manager at a pension fund. She has observed that the market for highly structured mortgages is the focus of salespeople she meets and that these products represent a significant number of trading opportunities. In discussions about this topic with her team, Smith learns that calculating yields on changing cash flows within the deal structure requires very specialized vendor software. After more research, they find out that each deal is unique and that deals can have more than a dozen layers and changing cash flow priorities. Smith comes to the conclusion that, because of the complexity of these securities, the team cannot effectively distinguish between potentially good and bad investment options. To avoid misrepresenting their understanding, the team decides that the highly structured mortgage segment of the securitized market should not become part of the core of the fund's portfolio; they will allow some of the less complex securities to be part of the core.

> *Comment*: Smith is in compliance with Standard I(C) by not investing in securities that she and her team cannot effectively understand. Because she is not able to describe the risk and return profile of the securities to the pension fund beneficiaries and trustees, she appropriately limits the fund's exposure to this sector.

Example 14 (Misrepresenting Composite Construction):

Robert Palmer is head of performance for a fund manager. When asked to provide performance numbers to fund rating agencies, he avoids mentioning that the fund manager is quite liberal in composite construction. The reason accounts are included/

excluded is not fully explained. The performance values reported to the rating agencies for the composites, although accurate for the accounts shown each period, may not present a true representation of the fund manager's ability.

> Comment: "Cherry picking" accounts to include in either published reports or information provided to rating agencies conflicts with Standard I(C). Moving accounts into or out of a composite to influence the overall performance results materially misrepresents the reported values over time. Palmer should work with his firm to strengthen its reporting practices concerning composite construction to avoid misrepresenting the firm's track record or the quality of the information being provided.

Example 15 (Presenting Out-of-Date Information):

David Finch is a sales director at a commercial bank, where he directs the bank's client advisers in the sale of third-party mutual funds. Each quarter, he holds a division-wide training session where he provides fact sheets on investment funds the bank is allowed to offer to clients. These fact sheets, which can be redistributed to potential clients, are created by the fund firms and contain information about the funds, including investment strategy and target distribution rates.

Finch knows that some of the fact sheets are out of date; for example, one long-only fund approved the use of significant leverage last quarter as a method to enhance returns. He continues to provide the sheets to the sales team without updates because the bank has no control over the marketing material released by the mutual fund firms.

> Comment: Finch is violating Standard I(C) by providing information that misrepresents aspects of the funds. By not providing the sales team and, ultimately, the clients with the updated information, he is misrepresenting the potential risks associated with the funds with outdated fact sheets. Finch can instruct the sales team to clarify the deficiencies in the fact sheets with clients and ensure they have the most recent fund prospectus document before accepting orders for investing in any fund.

Example 16 (Overemphasis of Firm Results):

Bob Anderson is chief compliance officer for Optima Asset Management Company, a firm currently offering eight funds to clients. Seven of the eight had 10-year returns below the median for their respective sectors. Anderson approves a recent advertisement, which includes this statement: "Optima Asset Management is achieving excellent returns for its investors. The Optima Emerging Markets Equity fund, for example, has 10-year returns that exceed the sector median by more than 10%."

> Comment: From the information provided it is difficult to determine whether a violation has occurred as long as the sector outperformance is correct. Anderson may be attempting to mislead potential clients by citing the performance of the sole fund that achieved such results. Past performance is often used to demonstrate a firm's skill and abilities in comparison to funds in the same sectors.
>
> However, if all the funds outperformed their respective benchmarks, then Anderson's assertion that the company "is achieving excellent returns" may be factual. Funds may exhibit positive returns for investors, exceed benchmarks, and yet have returns below the median in their sectors.
>
> Members and candidates need to ensure that their marketing efforts do not include statements that misrepresent their skills and abilities to remain compliant with Standard I(C). Unless the returns of a single fund reflect the performance of a firm as a whole, the use of a singular fund for performance comparisons should be avoided.

Standard I(D) Misconduct

Members and Candidates must not engage in any professional conduct involving dishonesty, fraud, or deceit or commit any act that reflects adversely on their professional reputation, integrity, or competence.

Guidance

Whereas Standard I(A) addresses the obligation of members and candidates to comply with applicable law that governs their professional activities, Standard I(D) addresses *all* conduct that reflects poorly on the professional integrity, good reputation, or competence of members and candidates. Any act that involves lying, cheating, stealing, or other dishonest conduct is a violation of this standard if the offense reflects adversely on a member's or candidate's professional activities. Although CFA Institute discourages any sort of unethical behavior by members and candidates, the Code and Standards are primarily aimed at conduct and actions related to a member's or candidate's professional life.

Conduct that damages trustworthiness or competence may include behavior that, although not illegal, nevertheless negatively affects a member's or candidate's ability to perform his or her responsibilities. For example, abusing alcohol during business hours might constitute a violation of this standard because it could have a detrimental effect on the member's or candidate's ability to fulfill his or her professional responsibilities. Personal bankruptcy may not reflect on the integrity or trustworthiness of the person declaring bankruptcy, but if the circumstances of the bankruptcy involve fraudulent or deceitful business conduct, the bankruptcy may be a violation of this standard.

In some cases, the absence of appropriate conduct or the lack of sufficient effort may be a violation of Standard I(D). The integrity of the investment profession is built on trust. A member or candidate—whether an investment banker, rating or research analyst, or portfolio manager—is expected to conduct the necessary due diligence to properly understand the nature and risks of an investment before making an investment recommendation. By not taking these steps and, instead, relying on someone else in the process to perform them, members or candidates may violate the trust their clients have placed in them. This loss of trust may have a significant impact on the reputation of the member or candidate and the operations of the financial market as a whole.

Individuals may attempt to abuse the CFA Institute Professional Conduct Program by actively seeking CFA Institute enforcement of the Code and Standards, and Standard I(D) in particular, as a method of settling personal, political, or other disputes unrelated to professional ethics. CFA Institute is aware of this issue, and appropriate disciplinary policies, procedures, and enforcement mechanisms are in place to address misuse of the Code and Standards and the Professional Conduct Program in this way.

Recommended Procedures for Compliance

In addition to ensuring that their own behavior is consistent with Standard I(D), to prevent general misconduct, members and candidates should encourage their firms to adopt the following policies and procedures to support the principles of Standard I(D):

- *Code of ethics*: Develop and/or adopt a code of ethics to which every employee must subscribe, and make clear that any personal behavior that reflects poorly on the individual involved, the institution as a whole, or the investment industry will not be tolerated.

- *List of violations*: Disseminate to all employees a list of potential violations and associated disciplinary sanctions, up to and including dismissal from the firm.
- *Employee references*: Check references of potential employees to ensure that they are of good character and not ineligible to work in the investment industry because of past infractions of the law.

Application of the Standard

Example 1 (Professionalism and Competence):

Simon Sasserman is a trust investment officer at a bank in a small affluent town. He enjoys lunching every day with friends at the country club, where his clients have observed him having numerous drinks. Back at work after lunch, he clearly is intoxicated while making investment decisions. His colleagues make a point of handling any business with Sasserman in the morning because they distrust his judgment after lunch.

> *Comment*: Sasserman's excessive drinking at lunch and subsequent intoxication at work constitute a violation of Standard I(D) because this conduct has raised questions about his professionalism and competence. His behavior reflects poorly on him, his employer, and the investment industry.

Example 2 (Fraud and Deceit):

Howard Hoffman, a security analyst at ATZ Brothers, Inc., a large brokerage house, submits reimbursement forms over a two-year period to ATZ's self-funded health insurance program for more than two dozen bills, most of which have been altered to increase the amount due. An investigation by the firm's director of employee benefits uncovers the inappropriate conduct. ATZ subsequently terminates Hoffman's employment and notifies CFA Institute.

> *Comment*: Hoffman violated Standard I(D) because he engaged in intentional conduct involving fraud and deceit in the workplace that adversely reflected on his integrity.

Example 3 (Fraud and Deceit):

Jody Brink, an analyst covering the automotive industry, volunteers much of her spare time to local charities. The board of one of the charitable institutions decides to buy five new vans to deliver hot lunches to low-income elderly people. Brink offers to donate her time to handle purchasing agreements. To pay a long-standing debt to a friend who operates an automobile dealership—and to compensate herself for her trouble—she agrees to a price 20% higher than normal and splits the surcharge with her friend. The director of the charity ultimately discovers the scheme and tells Brink that her services, donated or otherwise, are no longer required.

> *Comment*: Brink engaged in conduct involving dishonesty, fraud, and misrepresentation and has violated Standard I(D).

Example 4 (Personal Actions and Integrity):

Carmen Garcia manages a mutual fund dedicated to socially responsible investing. She is also an environmental activist. As the result of her participation in nonviolent protests, Garcia has been arrested on numerous occasions for trespassing on the property of a large petrochemical plant that is accused of damaging the environment.

Standard II: Integrity of Capital Markets

Comment: Generally, Standard I(D) is not meant to cover legal transgressions resulting from acts of civil disobedience in support of personal beliefs because such conduct does not reflect poorly on the member's or candidate's professional reputation, integrity, or competence.

Example 5 (Professional Misconduct):

Meredith Rasmussen works on a buy-side trading desk of an investment management firm and concentrates on in-house trades for a hedge fund subsidiary managed by a team at the investment management firm. The hedge fund has been very successful and is marketed globally by the firm. From her experience as the trader for much of the activity of the fund, Rasmussen has become quite knowledgeable about the hedge fund's strategy, tactics, and performance. When a distinct break in the market occurs and many of the securities involved in the hedge fund's strategy decline markedly in value, Rasmussen observes that the reported performance of the hedge fund does not reflect this decline. In her experience, the lack of effect is a very unlikely occurrence. She approaches the head of trading about her concern and is told that she should not ask any questions and that the fund is big and successful and is not her concern. She is fairly sure something is not right, so she contacts the compliance officer, who also tells her to stay away from the issue of the hedge fund's reporting.

Comment: Rasmussen has clearly come across an error in policies, procedures, and compliance practices within the firm's operations. According to the firm's procedures for reporting potentially unethical activity, she should pursue the issue by gathering some proof of her reason for doubt. Should all internal communications within the firm not satisfy her concerns, Rasmussen should consider reporting the potential unethical activity to the appropriate regulator.

See also Standard IV(A) for guidance on whistleblowing and Standard IV(C) for the duties of a supervisor.

STANDARD II: INTEGRITY OF CAPITAL MARKETS

Standard II(A) Material Nonpublic Information

Members and Candidates who possess material nonpublic information that could affect the value of an investment must not act or cause others to act on the information.

Guidance

Highlights:

- *What Is "Material" Information?*
- *What Constitutes "Nonpublic" Information?*
- *Mosaic Theory*
- *Social Media*

- *Using Industry Experts*
- *Investment Research Reports*

Trading or inducing others to trade on material nonpublic information erodes confidence in capital markets, institutions, and investment professionals by supporting the idea that those with inside information and special access can take unfair advantage of the general investing public. Although trading on inside information may lead to short-term profits, in the long run, individuals and the profession as a whole suffer from such trading. These actions have caused and will continue to cause investors to avoid capital markets because the markets are perceived to be "rigged" in favor of the knowledgeable insider. When the investing public avoids capital markets, the markets and capital allocation become less efficient and less supportive of strong and vibrant economies. Standard II(A) promotes and maintains a high level of confidence in market integrity, which is one of the foundations of the investment profession.

The prohibition on using this information goes beyond the direct buying and selling of individual securities or bonds. Members and candidates must not use material nonpublic information to influence their investment actions related to derivatives (e.g., swaps or option contracts), mutual funds, or other alternative investments. *Any* trading based on material nonpublic information constitutes a violation of Standard II(A). The expansion of financial products and the increasing interconnectivity of financial markets globally have resulted in new potential opportunities for trading on material nonpublic information.

What Is "Material" Information?

Information is "material" if its disclosure would probably have an impact on the price of a security or if reasonable investors would want to know the information before making an investment decision. In other words, information is material if it would significantly alter the total mix of information currently available about a security in such a way that the price of the security would be affected.

The specificity of the information, the extent of its difference from public information, its nature, and its reliability are key factors in determining whether a particular piece of information fits the definition of material. For example, material information may include, but is not limited to, information on the following:

- earnings;
- mergers, acquisitions, tender offers, or joint ventures;
- changes in assets or asset quality;
- innovative products, processes, or discoveries (e.g., new product trials or research efforts);
- new licenses, patents, registered trademarks, or regulatory approval/rejection of a product;
- developments regarding customers or suppliers (e.g., the acquisition or loss of a contract);
- changes in management;
- change in auditor notification or the fact that the issuer may no longer rely on an auditor's report or qualified opinion;
- events regarding the issuer's securities (e.g., defaults on senior securities, calls of securities for redemption, repurchase plans, stock splits, changes in dividends, changes to the rights of security holders, and public or private sales of additional securities);
- bankruptcies;
- significant legal disputes;

Standard II: Integrity of Capital Markets

- government reports of economic trends (employment, housing starts, currency information, etc.);
- orders for large trades before they are executed; and
- new or changing equity or debt ratings issued by a third party (e.g., sell-side recommendations and credit ratings).

In addition to the substance and specificity of the information, the source or relative reliability of the information also determines materiality. The less reliable a source, the less likely the information provided would be considered material. For example, factual information from a corporate insider regarding a significant new contract for a company is likely to be material, whereas an assumption based on speculation by a competitor about the same contract is likely to be less reliable and, therefore, not material. Additionally, information about trials of a new drug, product, or service under development from qualified personnel involved in the trials is likely to be material, whereas educated conjecture by subject experts not connected to the trials is unlikely to be material.

Also, the more ambiguous the effect of the information on price, the less material that information is considered. If it is unclear whether and to what extent the information will affect the price of a security, the information may not be considered material. The passage of time may also render information that was once important immaterial.

What Constitutes "Nonpublic" Information?

Information is "nonpublic" until it has been disseminated or is available to the marketplace in general (as opposed to a select group of investors). "Disseminated" can be defined as "made known." For example, a company report of profits that is posted on the internet and distributed widely through a press release or accompanied by a filing has been effectively disseminated to the marketplace. Members and candidates must have a reasonable expectation that people have received the information before it can be considered public. It is not necessary, however, to wait for the slowest method of delivery. Once the information is disseminated to the market, it is public information that is no longer covered by this standard.

Members and candidates must be particularly aware of information that is selectively disclosed by corporations to a small group of investors, analysts, or other market participants. Information that is made available to analysts remains nonpublic until it is made available to investors in general. Corporations that disclose information on a limited basis create the potential for insider-trading violations.

Issues of selective disclosure often arise when a corporate insider provides material information to analysts in a briefing or conference call before that information is released to the public. Analysts must be aware that a disclosure made to a room full of analysts does not necessarily make the disclosed information "public." Analysts should also be alert to the possibility that they are selectively receiving material nonpublic information when a company provides them with guidance or interpretation of such publicly available information as financial statements or regulatory filings.

A member or candidate may use insider information provided legitimately by the source company for the specific purpose of conducting due diligence according to the business agreement between the parties for such activities as mergers, loan underwriting, credit ratings, and offering engagements. In such instances, the investment professional would not be considered in violation of Standard II(A) by using the material information. However, the use of insider information provided by the source company for other purposes, especially to trade or entice others to trade the securities of the firm, conflicts with this standard.

Mosaic Theory

A financial analyst gathers and interprets large quantities of information from many sources. The analyst may use significant conclusions derived from the analysis of public and nonmaterial nonpublic information as the basis for investment recommendations and decisions even if those conclusions would have been material inside information had they been communicated directly to the analyst by a company. Under the "mosaic theory," financial analysts are free to act on this collection, or mosaic, of information without risking violation.

The practice of financial analysis depends on the free flow of information. For the fair and efficient operation of the capital markets, analysts and investors must have the greatest amount of information possible to facilitate making well-informed investment decisions about how and where to invest capital. Accurate, timely, and intelligible communication is essential if analysts and investors are to obtain the data needed to make informed decisions about how and where to invest capital. These disclosures must go beyond the information mandated by the reporting requirements of the securities laws and should include specific business information about items used to guide a company's future growth, such as new products, capital projects, and the competitive environment. Analysts seek and use such information to compare and contrast investment alternatives.

Much of the information used by analysts comes directly from companies. Analysts often receive such information through contacts with corporate insiders, especially investor-relations staff and financial officers. Information may be disseminated in the form of press releases, through oral presentations by company executives in analysts' meetings or conference calls, or during analysts' visits to company premises. In seeking to develop the most accurate and complete picture of a company, analysts should also reach beyond contacts with companies themselves and collect information from other sources, such as customers, contractors, suppliers, and the companies' competitors.

Analysts are in the business of formulating opinions and insights that are not obvious to the general investing public about the attractiveness of particular securities. In the course of their work, analysts actively seek out corporate information not generally known to the market for the express purpose of analyzing that information, forming an opinion on its significance, and informing their clients, who can be expected to trade on the basis of the recommendation. Analysts' initiatives to discover and analyze information and communicate their findings to their clients significantly enhance market efficiency, thus benefiting all investors (see *Dirks v. Securities and Exchange Commission*). Accordingly, violations of Standard II(A) will *not* result when a perceptive analyst reaches a conclusion about a corporate action or event through an analysis of public information and items of nonmaterial nonpublic information.

Investment professionals should note, however, that although analysts are free to use mosaic information in their research reports, they should save and document all their research [see Standard V(C)–Record Retention]. Evidence of the analyst's knowledge of public and nonmaterial nonpublic information about a corporation strengthens the assertion that the analyst reached his or her conclusions solely through appropriate methods rather than through the use of material nonpublic information.

Social Media

The continuing advancement in technology allows members, candidates, and the industry at large to exchange information at rates not previously available. It is important for investment professionals to understand the implications of using information from the internet and social media platforms because all such information may not actually be considered public.

Standard II: Integrity of Capital Markets

Some social media platforms require membership in specific groups in order to access the published content. Members and candidates participating in groups with membership limitations should verify that material information obtained from these sources can also be accessed from a source that would be considered available to the public (e.g., company filings, webpages, and press releases).

Members and candidates may use social media platforms to communicate with clients or investors without conflicting with this standard. As long as the information reaches all clients or is open to the investing public, the use of these platforms would be comparable with other traditional forms of communications, such as e-mails and press releases. Members and candidates, as required by Standard I(A), should also complete all appropriate regulatory filings related to information distributed through social media platforms.

Using Industry Experts

The increased demand for insights for understanding the complexities of some industries has led to an expansion of engagement with outside experts. As the level of engagement increased, new businesses formed to connect analysts and investors with individuals who have specialized knowledge of their industry (e.g., technology or pharmaceuticals). These networks offer investors the opportunity to reach beyond their usual business circles to speak with experts regarding economic conditions, industry trends, and technical issues relating to specific products and services.

Members and candidates may provide compensation to individuals for their insights without violating this standard. However, members and candidates are ultimately responsible for ensuring that they are not requesting or acting on confidential information received from external experts, which is in violation of security regulations and laws or duties to others. As the recent string of insider-trading cases displayed, some experts are willing to provide confidential and protected information for the right incentive.

Firms connecting experts with members or candidates often require both parties to sign agreements concerning the disclosure of material nonpublic information. Even with the protections from such compliance practices, if an expert provides material nonpublic information, members and candidates would be prohibited from taking investment actions on the associated firm until the information became publicly known to the market.

Investment Research Reports

When a particularly well-known or respected analyst issues a report or makes changes to his or her recommendation, that information alone may have an effect on the market and thus may be considered material. Theoretically, under Standard II(A), such a report would have to be made public at the time it was distributed to clients. The analyst is not a company insider, however, and does not have access to inside information. Presumably, the analyst created the report from information available to the public (mosaic theory) and by using his or her expertise to interpret the information. The analyst's hard work, paid for by the client, generated the conclusions.

Simply because the public in general would find the conclusions material does not require that the analyst make his or her work public. Investors who are not clients of the analyst can either do the work themselves or become clients of the analyst to gain access to the analyst's expertise.

Recommended Procedures for Compliance

Achieve Public Dissemination

If a member or candidate determines that information is material, the member or candidate should make reasonable efforts to achieve public dissemination of the information. These efforts usually entail encouraging the issuing company to make the information public. If public dissemination is not possible, the member or candidate must communicate the information only to the designated supervisory and compliance personnel within the member's or candidate's firm and must not take investment action or alter current investment recommendations on the basis of the information. Moreover, members and candidates must not knowingly engage in any conduct that may induce company insiders to privately disclose material nonpublic information.

Adopt Compliance Procedures

Members and candidates should encourage their firms to adopt compliance procedures to prevent the misuse of material nonpublic information. Particularly important is improving compliance in such areas as the review of employee and proprietary trading, the review of investment recommendations, documentation of firm procedures, and the supervision of interdepartmental communications in multiservice firms. Compliance procedures should suit the particular characteristics of a firm, including its size and the nature of its business.

Members and candidates are encouraged to inform their supervisor and compliance personnel of suspected inappropriate use of material nonpublic information as the basis for security trading activities or recommendations being made within their firm.

Adopt Disclosure Procedures

Members and candidates should encourage their firms to develop and follow disclosure policies designed to ensure that information is disseminated to the marketplace in an equitable manner. For example, analysts from small firms should receive the same information and attention from a company as analysts from large firms receive. Similarly, companies should not provide certain information to buy-side analysts but not to sell-side analysts, or vice versa. Furthermore, a company should not discriminate among analysts in the provision of information or "blackball" particular analysts who have given negative reports on the company in the past.

Within investment and research firms, members and candidates should encourage the development of and compliance with procedures for distributing new and updated investment opinions to clients. Recommendations of this nature may represent material market-moving information that needs to be communicated to all clients fairly.

Issue Press Releases

Companies should consider issuing press releases prior to analyst meetings and conference calls and scripting those meetings and calls to decrease the chance that further information will be disclosed. If material nonpublic information is disclosed for the first time in an analyst meeting or call, the company should promptly issue a press release or otherwise make the information publicly available.

Standard II: Integrity of Capital Markets

Firewall Elements

An information barrier commonly referred to as a "firewall" is the most widely used approach for preventing the communication of material nonpublic information within firms. It restricts the flow of confidential information to those who need to know the information to perform their jobs effectively. The minimum elements of such a system include, but are not limited to, the following:

- substantial control of relevant interdepartmental communications, preferably through a clearance area within the firm in either the compliance or legal department;
- review of employee trading through the maintenance of "watch," "restricted," and "rumor" lists;
- documentation of the procedures designed to limit the flow of information between departments and of the actions taken to enforce those procedures; and
- heightened review or restriction of proprietary trading while a firm is in possession of material nonpublic information.

Appropriate Interdepartmental Communications

Although documentation requirements must, for practical reasons, take into account the differences between the activities of small firms and those of large, multiservice firms, firms of all sizes and types benefit by improving the documentation of their internal enforcement of firewall procedures. Therefore, even at small firms, procedures concerning interdepartmental communication, the review of trading activity, and the investigation of possible violations should be compiled and formalized.

Physical Separation of Departments

As a practical matter, to the greatest extent possible, firms should consider the physical separation of departments and files to prevent the communication of sensitive information that should not be shared. For example, the investment banking and corporate finance areas of a brokerage firm should be separated from the sales and research departments, and a bank's commercial lending department should be segregated from its trust and research departments.

Prevention of Personnel Overlap

There should be no overlap of personnel between the investment banking and corporate finance areas of a brokerage firm and the sales and research departments or between a bank's commercial lending department and its trust and research departments. For a firewall to be effective in a multiservice firm, an employee should be on only one side of the firewall at any time. Inside knowledge may not be limited to information about a specific offering or the current financial condition of a company. Analysts may be exposed to much information about the company, including new product developments or future budget projections that clearly constitute inside knowledge and thus preclude the analyst from returning to his or her research function. For example, an analyst who follows a particular company may provide limited assistance to the investment bankers under carefully controlled circumstances when the firm's investment banking department is involved in a deal with the company. That analyst must then be treated as though he or she were an investment banker; the analyst must remain on the investment banking side of the wall until any information he or she learns is publicly disclosed. In short, the analyst cannot use any information learned in the course of the project for research purposes and cannot share that information with colleagues in the research department.

A Reporting System

A primary objective of an effective firewall procedure is to establish a reporting system in which authorized people review and approve communications between departments. If an employee behind a firewall believes that he or she needs to share confidential information with someone on the other side of the wall, the employee should consult a designated compliance officer to determine whether sharing the information is necessary and how much information should be shared. If the sharing is necessary, the compliance officer should coordinate the process of "looking over the wall" so that the necessary information will be shared and the integrity of the procedure will be maintained.

A single supervisor or compliance officer should have the specific authority and responsibility of deciding whether information is material and whether it is sufficiently public to be used as the basis for investment decisions. Ideally, the supervisor or compliance officer responsible for communicating information to a firm's research or brokerage area would not be a member of that area.

Personal Trading Limitations

Firms should consider restrictions or prohibitions on personal trading by employees and should carefully monitor both proprietary trading and personal trading by employees. Firms should require employees to make periodic reports (to the extent that such reporting is not already required by securities laws) of their own transactions and transactions made for the benefit of family members. Securities should be placed on a restricted list when a firm has or may have material nonpublic information. The broad distribution of a restricted list often triggers the sort of trading the list was developed to avoid. Therefore, a watch list shown to only the few people responsible for compliance should be used to monitor transactions in specified securities. The use of a watch list in combination with a restricted list is an increasingly common means of ensuring effective control of personal trading.

Record Maintenance

Multiservice firms should maintain written records of the communications between various departments. Firms should place a high priority on training and should consider instituting comprehensive training programs, particularly for employees in sensitive areas.

Proprietary Trading Procedures

Procedures concerning the restriction or review of a firm's proprietary trading while the firm possesses material nonpublic information will necessarily depend on the types of proprietary trading in which the firm may engage. A prohibition on all types of proprietary activity when a firm comes into possession of material nonpublic information is *not* appropriate. For example, when a firm acts as a market maker, a prohibition on proprietary trading may be counterproductive to the goals of maintaining the confidentiality of information and market liquidity. This concern is particularly important in the relationships between small, regional broker/dealers and small issuers. In many situations, a firm will take a small issuer public with the understanding that the firm will continue to be a market maker in the stock. In such instances, a withdrawal by the firm from market-making activities would be a clear tip to outsiders. Firms that continue market-making activity while in the possession of material nonpublic information should, however, instruct their market makers to remain passive with respect to the market—that is, to take only the contra side of unsolicited customer trades.

In risk-arbitrage trading, the case for a trading prohibition is more compelling than it is in the case of market making. The impetus for arbitrage trading is neither passive nor reactive, and the potential for illegal profits is greater than in market making. The most prudent course for firms is to suspend arbitrage activity when a security is placed on the watch list. Those firms that continue arbitrage activity face a high hurdle in proving the adequacy of their internal procedures for preventing trading on material nonpublic information and must demonstrate a stringent review and documentation of firm trades.

Communication to All Employees

Members and candidates should encourage their employers to circulate written compliance policies and guidelines to all employees. Policies and guidelines should be used in conjunction with training programs aimed at enabling employees to recognize material nonpublic information. Such information is not always clearly identifiable.

Employees must be given sufficient training to either make an informed decision or to realize they need to consult a supervisor or compliance officer before engaging in questionable transactions. Appropriate policies reinforce that using material nonpublic information is illegal in many countries. Such trading activities based on material nonpublic information undermine the integrity of the individual, the firm, and the capital markets.

Application of the Standard

Example 1 (Acting on Nonpublic Information):

Frank Barnes, the president and controlling shareholder of the SmartTown clothing chain, decides to accept a tender offer and sell the family business at a price almost double the market price of its shares. He describes this decision to his sister (SmartTown's treasurer), who conveys it to her daughter (who owns no stock in the family company at present), who tells her husband, Staple. Staple, however, tells his stockbroker, Alex Halsey, who immediately buys SmartTown stock for himself.

> *Comment*: The information regarding the pending sale is both material and nonpublic. Staple has violated Standard II(A) by communicating the inside information to his broker. Halsey also has violated the standard by buying the shares on the basis of material nonpublic information.

Example 2 (Controlling Nonpublic Information):

Samuel Peter, an analyst with Scotland and Pierce Incorporated, is assisting his firm with a secondary offering for Bright Ideas Lamp Company. Peter participates, via telephone conference call, in a meeting with Scotland and Pierce investment banking employees and Bright Ideas' CEO. Peter is advised that the company's earnings projections for the next year have significantly dropped. Throughout the telephone conference call, several Scotland and Pierce salespeople and portfolio managers walk in and out of Peter's office, where the telephone call is taking place. As a result, they are aware of the drop in projected earnings for Bright Ideas. Before the conference call is concluded, the salespeople trade the stock of the company on behalf of the firm's clients and other firm personnel trade the stock in a firm proprietary account and in employees' personal accounts.

> *Comment*: Peter has violated Standard II(A) because he failed to prevent the transfer and misuse of material nonpublic information to others in his firm. Peter's firm should have adopted information barriers to prevent the communication of nonpublic information between departments of the firm. The salespeople and portfolio managers who traded on the information have also violated Standard II(A) by trading on inside information.

Example 3 (Selective Disclosure of Material Information):

Elizabeth Levenson is based in Taipei and covers the Taiwanese market for her firm, which is based in Singapore. She is invited, together with the other 10 largest shareholders of a manufacturing company, to meet the finance director of that company. During the meeting, the finance director states that the company expects its workforce to strike next Friday, which will cripple productivity and distribution. Can Levenson use this information as a basis to change her rating on the company from "buy" to "sell"?

> *Comment*: Levenson must first determine whether the material information is public. According to Standard II(A), if the company has not made this information public (a small group forum does not qualify as a method of public dissemination), she cannot use the information.

Example 4 (Determining Materiality):

Leah Fechtman is trying to decide whether to hold or sell shares of an oil-and-gas exploration company that she owns in several of the funds she manages. Although the company has underperformed the index for some time already, the trends in the industry sector signal that companies of this type might become takeover targets. While she is considering her decision, her doctor, who casually follows the markets, mentions that she thinks that the company in question will soon be bought out by a large multinational conglomerate and that it would be a good idea to buy the stock right now. After talking to various investment professionals and checking their opinions on the company as well as checking industry trends, Fechtman decides the next day to accumulate more stock in the oil-and-gas exploration company.

> *Comment*: Although information on an expected takeover bid may be of the type that is generally material and nonpublic, in this case, the source of information is unreliable, so the information cannot be considered material. Therefore, Fechtman is not prohibited from trading the stock on the basis of this information.

Example 5 (Applying the Mosaic Theory):

Jagdish Teja is a buy-side analyst covering the furniture industry. Looking for an attractive company to recommend as a buy, he analyzes several furniture makers by studying their financial reports and visiting their operations. He also talks to some designers and retailers to find out which furniture styles are trendy and popular. Although none of the companies that he analyzes are a clear buy, he discovers that one of them, Swan Furniture Company (SFC), may be in financial trouble. SFC's extravagant new designs have been introduced at substantial cost. Even though these designs initially attracted attention, the public is now buying more conservative furniture from other makers. Based on this information and on a profit-and-loss analysis, Teja believes that SFC's next quarter earnings will drop substantially. He issues a sell recommendation for SFC. Immediately after receiving that recommendation, investment managers start reducing the SFC stock in their portfolios.

> *Comment*: Information on quarterly earnings data is material and nonpublic. Teja arrived at his conclusion about the earnings drop on the basis of public information and on pieces of nonmaterial nonpublic information (such as opinions of designers and retailers). Therefore, trading based on Teja's correct conclusion is not prohibited by Standard II(A).

Example 6 (Applying the Mosaic Theory):

Roger Clement is a senior financial analyst who specializes in the European automobile sector at Rivoli Capital. Because he has been repeatedly nominated by many leading industry magazines and newsletters as a "best analyst" for the automobile industry, he is widely regarded as an authority on the sector. After speaking with representatives of Turgot Chariots—a European auto manufacturer with sales primarily in South Korea—and after conducting interviews with salespeople, labor leaders, his firm's Korean currency analysts, and banking officials, Clement analyzed Turgot Chariots and concluded that (1) its newly introduced model will probably not meet sales expectations, (2) its corporate restructuring strategy may well face serious opposition from unions, (3) the depreciation of the Korean won should lead to pressure on margins for the industry in general and Turgot's market segment in particular, and (4) banks could take a tougher-than-expected stance in the upcoming round of credit renegotiations with the company. For these reasons, he changes his conclusion about the company from "market outperform" to "market underperform." Clement retains the support material used to reach his conclusion in case questions later arise.

> *Comment*: To reach a conclusion about the value of the company, Clement has pieced together a number of nonmaterial or public bits of information that affect Turgot Chariots. Therefore, under the mosaic theory, Clement has not violated Standard II(A) in drafting the report.

Example 7 (Analyst Recommendations as Material Nonpublic Information):

The next day, Clement is preparing to be interviewed on a global financial news television program where he will discuss his changed recommendation on Turgot Chariots for the first time in public. While preparing for the program, he mentions to the show's producers and Mary Zito, the journalist who will be interviewing him, the information he will be discussing. Just prior to going on the air, Zito sells her holdings in Turgot Chariots. She also phones her father with the information because she knows that he and other family members have investments in Turgot Chariots.

> *Comment*: When Zito receives advance notice of Clement's change of opinion, she knows it will have a material impact on the stock price, even if she is not totally aware of Clement's underlying reasoning. She is not a client of Clement but obtains early access to the material nonpublic information prior to publication. Her trades are thus based on material nonpublic information and violate Standard II(A).
>
> Zito further violates the Standard by relaying the information to her father. It would not matter if he or any other family member traded; the act of providing the information violates Standard II(A). The fact that the information is provided to a family member does not absolve someone of the prohibition of using or communicating material nonpublic information.

Example 8 (Acting on Nonpublic Information):

Ashton Kellogg is a retired investment professional who manages his own portfolio. He owns shares in National Savings, a large local bank. A close friend and golfing buddy, John Mayfield, is a senior executive at National. National has seen its stock price drop considerably, and the news and outlook are not good. In a conversation about the economy and the banking industry on the golf course, Mayfield relays the information that National will surprise the investment community in a few days when it announces excellent earnings for the quarter. Kellogg is pleasantly surprised by this information, and thinking that Mayfield, as a senior executive, knows the law and would not disclose inside information, he doubles his position in the bank. Subsequently,

National announces that it had good operating earnings but had to set aside reserves for anticipated significant losses on its loan portfolio. The combined news causes the stock to go down 60%.

> *Comment*: Even though Kellogg believes that Mayfield would not break the law by disclosing inside information and money was lost on the purchase, Kellogg should not have purchased additional shares of National. It is the member's or candidate's responsibility to make sure, before executing investment actions, that comments about earnings are not material nonpublic information. Kellogg has violated Standard II(A).

Example 9 (Mosaic Theory):

John Doll is a research analyst for a hedge fund that also sells its research to a select group of paying client investment firms. Doll's focus is medical technology companies and products, and he has been in the business long enough and has been successful enough to build up a very credible network of friends and experts in the business. Doll has been working on a major research report recommending Boyce Health, a medical device manufacturer. He recently ran into an old acquaintance at a wedding who is a senior executive at Boyce, and Doll asked about the business. Doll was drawn to a statement that the executive, who has responsibilities in the new products area, made about a product: "I would not get too excited about the medium-term prospects; we have a lot of work to do first." Doll incorporated this and other information about the new Boyce product in his long-term recommendation of Boyce.

> *Comment*: Doll's conversation with the senior executive is part of the mosaic of information used in recommending Boyce. When holding discussions with a firm executive, Doll would need to guard against soliciting or obtaining material nonpublic information. Before issuing the report, the executive's statement about the continuing development of the product would need to be weighed against the other known public facts to determine whether it would be considered material.

Example 10 (Materiality Determination):

Larry Nadler, a trader for a mutual fund, gets a text message from another firm's trader, whom he has known for years. The message indicates a software company is going to report strong earnings when the firm publicly announces in two days. Nadler has a buy order from a portfolio manager within his firm to purchase several hundred thousand shares of the stock. Nadler is aggressive in placing the portfolio manager's order and completes the purchases by the following morning, a day ahead of the firm's planned earnings announcement.

> *Comment*: There are often rumors and whisper numbers before a release of any kind. The text message from the other trader would most likely be considered market noise. Unless Nadler knew that the trader had an ongoing business relationship with the public firm, he had no reason to suspect he was receiving material nonpublic information that would prevent him from completing the trading request of the portfolio manager.

Example 11 (Using an Expert Network):

Mary McCoy is the senior drug analyst at a mutual fund. Her firm hires a service that connects her to experts in the treatment of cancer. Through various phone conversations, McCoy enhances her understanding of the latest therapies for successful treatment. This information is critical to Mary making informed recommendations of the companies producing these drugs.

Comment: McCoy is appropriately using the expert networks to enhance her evaluation process. She has neither asked for nor received information that may be considered material and nonpublic, such as preliminary trial results. McCoy is allowed to seek advice from professionals within the industry that she follows.

Example 12 (Using an Expert Network):

Tom Watson is a research analyst working for a hedge fund. To stay informed, Watson relies on outside experts for information on such industries as technology and pharmaceuticals, where new advancements occur frequently. The meetings with the industry experts often are arranged through networks or placement agents that have specific policies and procedures in place to deter the exchange of material nonpublic information.

Watson arranges a call to discuss future prospects for one of the fund's existing technology company holdings, a company that was testing a new semiconductor product. The scientist leading the tests indicates his disappointment with the performance of the new semiconductor. Following the call, Watson relays the insights he received to others at the fund. The fund sells its current position in the company and buys many put options because the market is anticipating the success of the new semiconductor and the share price reflects the market's optimism.

Comment: Watson has violated Standard II(A) by passing along material nonpublic information concerning the ongoing product tests, which the fund used to trade in the securities and options of the related company. Watson cannot simply rely on the agreements signed by individuals who participate in expert networks that state that he has not received information that would prohibit his trading activity. He must make his own determination whether information he received through these arrangements reaches a materiality threshold that would affect his trading abilities.

Standard II(B) Market Manipulation

Members and Candidates must not engage in practices that distort prices or artificially inflate trading volume with the intent to mislead market participants.

Guidance

Highlights:

- *Information-Based Manipulation*
- *Transaction-Based Manipulation*

Standard II(B) requires that members and candidates uphold market integrity by prohibiting market manipulation. Market manipulation includes practices that distort security prices or trading volume with the intent to deceive people or entities that rely on information in the market. Market manipulation damages the interests of all investors by disrupting the smooth functioning of financial markets and lowering investor confidence.

Market manipulation may lead to a lack of trust in the fairness of the capital markets, resulting in higher risk premiums and reduced investor participation. A reduction in the efficiency of a local capital market may negatively affect the growth and economic health of the country and may also influence the operations of the globally interconnected capital markets. Although market manipulation may be less likely to occur in mature financial markets than in emerging markets, cross-border investing increasingly exposes all global investors to the potential for such practices.

Market manipulation includes (1) the dissemination of false or misleading information and (2) transactions that deceive or would be likely to mislead market participants by distorting the price-setting mechanism of financial instruments. The development of new products and technologies increases the incentives, means, and opportunities for market manipulation. Additionally, the increasing complexity and sophistication of the technologies used for communicating with market participants have created new avenues for manipulation.

Information-Based Manipulation

Information-based manipulation includes, but is not limited to, spreading false rumors to induce trading by others. For example, members and candidates must refrain from "pumping up" the price of an investment by issuing misleading positive information or overly optimistic projections of a security's worth only to later "dump" the investment (i.e., sell it) once the price, fueled by the misleading information's effect on other market participants, reaches an artificially high level.

Transaction-Based Manipulation

Transaction-based manipulation involves instances where a member or candidate knew or should have known that his or her actions could affect the pricing of a security. This type of manipulation includes, but is not limited to, the following:

- transactions that artificially affect prices or volume to give the impression of activity or price movement in a financial instrument, which represent a diversion from the expectations of a fair and efficient market, and
- securing a controlling, dominant position in a financial instrument to exploit and manipulate the price of a related derivative and/or the underlying asset.

Standard II(B) is not intended to preclude transactions undertaken on legitimate trading strategies based on perceived market inefficiencies. The intent of the action is critical to determining whether it is a violation of this standard.

Application of the Standard

Example 1 (Independent Analysis and Company Promotion):

The principal owner of Financial Information Services (FIS) entered into an agreement with two microcap companies to promote the companies' stock in exchange for stock and cash compensation. The principal owner caused FIS to disseminate e-mails, design and maintain several websites, and distribute an online investment newsletter—all of which recommended investment in the two companies. The systematic publication of purportedly independent analyses and recommendations containing inaccurate and highly promotional and speculative statements increased public investment in the companies and led to dramatically higher stock prices.

> *Comment*: The principal owner of FIS violated Standard II(B) by using inaccurate reporting and misleading information under the guise of independent analysis to artificially increase the stock price of the companies. Furthermore, the principal owner violated Standard V(A)–Diligence and Reasonable Basis by not having a reasonable and adequate basis for recommending the two

companies and violated Standard VI(A)–Disclosure of Conflicts by not disclosing to investors the compensation agreements (which constituted a conflict of interest).

Example 2 (Personal Trading Practices and Price):

John Gray is a private investor in Belgium who bought a large position several years ago in Fame Pharmaceuticals, a German small-cap security with limited average trading volume. He has now decided to significantly reduce his holdings owing to the poor price performance. Gray is worried that the low trading volume for the stock may cause the price to decline further as he attempts to sell his large position.

Gray devises a plan to divide his holdings into multiple accounts in different brokerage firms and private banks in the names of family members, friends, and even a private religious institution. He then creates a rumor campaign on various blogs and social media outlets promoting the company.

Gray begins to buy and sell the stock using the accounts in hopes of raising the trading volume and the price. He conducts the trades through multiple brokers, selling slightly larger positions than he bought on a tactical schedule, and over time, he is able to reduce his holding as desired without negatively affecting the sale price.

> *Comment*: John violated Standard II(B) by fraudulently creating the appearance that there was a greater investor interest in the stock through the online rumors. Additionally, through his trading strategy, he created the appearance that there was greater liquidity in the stock than actually existed. He was able to manipulate the price through both misinformation and trading practices.

Example 3 (Creating Artificial Price Volatility):

Matthew Murphy is an analyst at Divisadero Securities & Co., which has a significant number of hedge funds among its most important brokerage clients. Some of the hedge funds hold short positions on Wirewolf Semiconductor. Two trading days before the publication of a quarter-end report, Murphy alerts his sales force that he is about to issue a research report on Wirewolf that will include the following opinions:

- quarterly revenues are likely to fall short of management's guidance,
- earnings will be as much as 5 cents per share (or more than 10%) below consensus, and
- Wirewolf's highly respected chief financial officer may be about to join another company.

Knowing that Wirewolf has already entered its declared quarter-end "quiet period" before reporting earnings (and thus would be reluctant to respond to rumors), Murphy times the release of his research report specifically to sensationalize the negative aspects of the message in order to create significant downward pressure on Wirewolf's stock—to the distinct advantage of Divisadero's hedge fund clients. The report's conclusions are based on speculation, not on fact. The next day, the research report is broadcast to all of Divisadero's clients and to the usual newswire services.

Before Wirewolf's investor-relations department can assess the damage on the final trading day of the quarter and refute Murphy's report, its stock opens trading sharply lower, allowing Divisadero's clients to cover their short positions at substantial gains.

> *Comment*: Murphy violated Standard II(B) by aiming to create artificial price volatility designed to have a material impact on the price of an issuer's stock. Moreover, by lacking an adequate basis for the recommendation, Murphy also violated Standard V(A)–Diligence and Reasonable Basis.

Example 4 (Personal Trading and Volume):

Rajesh Sekar manages two funds—an equity fund and a balanced fund—whose equity components are supposed to be managed in accordance with the same model. According to that model, the funds' holdings in stock of Digital Design Inc. (DD) are excessive. Reduction of the DD holdings would not be easy, however, because the stock has low liquidity in the stock market. Sekar decides to start trading larger portions of DD stock back and forth between his two funds to slowly increase the price; he believes market participants will see growing volume and increasing price and become interested in the stock. If other investors are willing to buy the DD stock because of such interest, then Sekar will be able to get rid of at least some of his overweight position without inducing price decreases. In this way, the whole transaction will be for the benefit of fund participants, even if additional brokers' commissions are incurred.

> *Comment*: Sekar's plan would be beneficial for his funds' participants but is based on artificial distortion of both trading volume and the price of the DD stock and thus constitutes a violation of Standard II(B).

Example 5 ("Pump-Priming" Strategy):

ACME Futures Exchange is launching a new bond futures contract. To convince investors, traders, arbitrageurs, hedgers, and so on, to use its contract, the exchange attempts to demonstrate that it has the best liquidity. To do so, it enters into agreements with members in which they commit to a substantial minimum trading volume on the new contract over a specific period in exchange for substantial reductions of their regular commissions.

> *Comment*: The formal liquidity of a market is determined by the obligations set on market makers, but the actual liquidity of a market is better estimated by the actual trading volume and bid–ask spreads. Attempts to mislead participants about the actual liquidity of the market constitute a violation of Standard II(B). In this example, investors have been intentionally misled to believe they chose the most liquid instrument for some specific purpose, but they could eventually see the actual liquidity of the contract significantly reduced after the term of the agreement expires. If the ACME Futures Exchange fully discloses its agreement with members to boost transactions over some initial launch period, it will not violate Standard II(B). ACME's intent is not to harm investors but, on the contrary, to give them a better service. For that purpose, it may engage in a liquidity-pumping strategy, but the strategy must be disclosed.

Example 6 (Creating Artificial Price Volatility):

Emily Gordon, an analyst of household products companies, is employed by a research boutique, Picador & Co. Based on information that she has gathered during a trip through Latin America, she believes that Hygene, Inc., a major marketer of personal care products, has generated better-than-expected sales from its new product initiatives in South America. After modestly boosting her projections for revenue and for gross profit margin in her worksheet models for Hygene, Gordon estimates that her earnings projection of US$2.00 per diluted share for the current year may be as much as 5% too low. She contacts the chief financial officer (CFO) of Hygene to try to gain confirmation of her findings from her trip and to get some feedback regarding her revised models. The CFO declines to comment and reiterates management's most recent guidance of US$1.95–US$2.05 for the year.

Gordon decides to try to force a comment from the company by telling Picador & Co. clients who follow a momentum investment style that consensus earnings projections for Hygene are much too low; she explains that she is considering raising her published estimate by an ambitious US$0.15 to US$2.15 per share. She believes that when word of an unrealistically high earnings projection filters back to Hygene's investor-relations department, the company will feel compelled to update its earnings guidance. Meanwhile, Gordon hopes that she is at least correct with respect to the earnings direction and that she will help clients who act on her insights to profit from a quick gain by trading on her advice.

Comment: By exaggerating her earnings projections in order to try to fuel a quick gain in Hygene's stock price, Gordon is in violation of Standard II(B). Furthermore, by virtue of previewing her intentions of revising upward her earnings projections to only a select group of clients, she is in violation of Standard III(B)–Fair Dealing. However, it would have been acceptable for Gordon to write a report that

- framed her earnings projection in a range of possible outcomes,
- outlined clearly the assumptions used in her Hygene models that took into consideration the findings from her trip through Latin America, and
- was distributed to all Picador & Co. clients in an equitable manner.

Example 7 (Pump and Dump Strategy):

In an effort to pump up the price of his holdings in Moosehead & Belfast Railroad Company, Steve Weinberg logs on to several investor chat rooms on the internet to start rumors that the company is about to expand its rail network in anticipation of receiving a large contract for shipping lumber.

Comment: Weinberg has violated Standard II(B) by disseminating false information about Moosehead & Belfast with the intent to mislead market participants.

Example 8 (Manipulating Model Inputs):

Bill Mandeville supervises a structured financing team for Superior Investment Bank. His responsibilities include packaging new structured investment products and managing Superior's relationship with relevant rating agencies. To achieve the best rating possible, Mandeville uses mostly positive scenarios as model inputs—scenarios that reflect minimal downside risk in the assets underlying the structured products. The resulting output statistics in the rating request and underwriting prospectus support the idea that the new structured products have minimal potential downside risk. Additionally, Mandeville's compensation from Superior is partially based on both the level of the rating assigned and the successful sale of new structured investment products but does not have a link to the long-term performance of the instruments.

Mandeville is extremely successful and leads Superior as the top originator of structured investment products for the next two years. In the third year, the economy experiences difficulties and the values of the assets underlying structured products significantly decline. The subsequent defaults lead to major turmoil in the capital markets, the demise of Superior Investment Bank, and the loss of Mandeville's employment.

Comment: Mandeville manipulates the inputs of a model to minimize associated risk to achieve higher ratings. His understanding of structured products allows him to skillfully decide which inputs to include in support of the desired rating and price. This information manipulation for short-term gain, which is in violation of Standard II(B), ultimately causes significant damage to many parties and the capital markets as a whole. Mandeville should have realized that promoting a rating and price with inaccurate information could cause not only a loss of price confidence in the particular structured product but also a loss of investor trust in the system. Such loss of confidence affects the ability of the capital markets to operate efficiently.

Example 9 (Information Manipulation):

Allen King is a performance analyst for Torrey Investment Funds. King believes that the portfolio manager for the firm's small- and microcap equity fund dislikes him because the manager never offers him tickets to the local baseball team's games but does offer tickets to other employees. To incite a potential regulatory review of the manager, King creates user profiles on several online forums under the portfolio manager's name and starts rumors about potential mergers for several of the smaller companies in the portfolio. As the prices of these companies' stocks increase, the portfolio manager sells the position, which leads to an investigation by the regulator as King desired.

> *Comment*: King has violated Standard II(B) even though he did not personally profit from the market's reaction to the rumor. In posting the false information, King misleads others into believing the companies were likely to be acquired. Although his intent was to create trouble for the portfolio manager, his actions clearly manipulated the factual information that was available to the market.

STANDARD III: DUTIES TO CLIENTS

Standard III(A) Loyalty, Prudence, and Care

> Members and Candidates have a duty of loyalty to their clients and must act with reasonable care and exercise prudent judgment. Members and Candidates must act for the benefit of their clients and place their clients' interests before their employer's or their own interests.

Guidance

Highlights:

- *Understanding the Application of Loyalty, Prudence, and Care*
- *Identifying the Actual Investment Client*
- *Developing the Client's Portfolio*
- *Soft Commission Policies*
- *Proxy Voting Policies*

Standard III(A) clarifies that client interests are paramount. A member's or candidate's responsibility to a client includes a duty of loyalty and a duty to exercise reasonable care. Investment actions must be carried out for the sole benefit of the client and in a manner the member or candidate believes, given the known facts and circumstances,

Standard III: Duties to Clients

to be in the best interest of the client. Members and candidates must exercise the same level of prudence, judgment, and care that they would apply in the management and disposition of their own interests in similar circumstances.

Prudence requires caution and discretion. The exercise of prudence by investment professionals requires that they act with the care, skill, and diligence that a reasonable person acting in a like capacity and familiar with such matters would use. In the context of managing a client's portfolio, prudence requires following the investment parameters set forth by the client and balancing risk and return. Acting with care requires members and candidates to act in a prudent and judicious manner in avoiding harm to clients.

Standard III(A) sets minimum expectations for members and candidates when fulfilling their responsibilities to their clients. Regulatory and legal requirements for such duties can vary across the investment industry depending on a variety of factors, including job function of the investment professional, the existence of an adviser/client relationship, and the nature of the recommendations being offered. From the perspective of the end user of financial services, these different standards can be arcane and confusing, leaving investors unsure of what level of service to expect from investment professionals they employ. The single standard of conduct described in Standard III(A) benefits investors by establishing a benchmark for the duties of loyalty, prudence, and care and clarifies that all CFA Institute members and candidates, regardless of job title, local laws, or cultural differences, are required to comply with these fundamental responsibilities. Investors hiring members or candidates who must adhere to the duty of loyalty, prudence, and care set forth in this standard can be confident that these responsibilities are a requirement regardless of any legally imposed fiduciary duties.

Standard III(A), however, is not a substitute for a member's or candidate's legal or regulatory obligations. As stated in Standard I(A), members and candidates must abide by the most strict requirements imposed on them by regulators or the Code and Standards, including any legally imposed fiduciary duty. Members and candidates must also be aware of whether they have "custody" or effective control of client assets. If so, a heightened level of responsibility arises. Members and candidates are considered to have custody if they have any direct or indirect access to client funds. Members and candidates must manage any pool of assets in their control in accordance with the terms of the governing documents (such as trust documents and investment management agreements), which are the primary determinant of the manager's powers and duties. Whenever their actions are contrary to provisions of those instruments or applicable law, members and candidates are at risk of violating Standard III(A).

Understanding the Application of Loyalty, Prudence, and Care

Standard III(A) establishes a minimum benchmark for the duties of loyalty, prudence, and care that are required of all members and candidates regardless of whether a legal fiduciary duty applies. Although fiduciary duty often encompasses the principles of loyalty, prudence, and care, Standard III(A) does not render all members and candidates fiduciaries. The responsibilities of members and candidates for fulfilling their obligations under this standard depend greatly on the nature of their professional responsibilities and the relationships they have with clients. The conduct of members and candidates may or may not rise to the level of being a fiduciary, depending on the type of client, whether the member or candidate is giving investment advice, and the many facts and circumstances surrounding a particular transaction or client relationship.

Fiduciary duties are often imposed by law or regulation when an individual or institution is charged with the duty of acting for the benefit of another party, such as managing investment assets. The duty required in fiduciary relationships exceeds what is acceptable in many other business relationships because a fiduciary is in an enhanced position of trust. Although members and candidates must comply with any legally imposed fiduciary duty, the Code and Standards neither impose such a legal responsibility nor require all members or candidates to act as fiduciaries. However, Standard III(A) requires members and candidates to work in the client's best interest no matter what the job function.

A member or candidate who does not provide advisory services to a client but who acts only as a trade execution professional must prudently work in the client's interest when completing requested trades. Acting in the client's best interest requires these professionals to use their skills and diligence to execute trades in the most favorable terms that can be achieved. Members and candidates operating in such positions must use care to operate within the parameters set by the client's trading instructions.

Members and candidates may also operate in a blended environment where they execute client trades and offer advice on a limited set of investment options. The extent of the advisory arrangement and limitations should be outlined in the agreement with the client at the outset of the relationship. For instance, members and candidates should inform clients that the advice provided will be limited to the propriety products of the firm and not include other products available on the market. Clients who want access to a wider range of investment products would have the information necessary to decide not to engage with members or candidates working under these restrictions.

Members and candidates operating in this blended context would comply with their obligations by recommending the allowable products that are consistent with the client's objectives and risk tolerance. They would exercise care through diligently aligning the client's needs with the attributes of the products being recommended. Members and candidates should place the client's interests first by disregarding any firm or personal interest in motivating a recommended transaction.

There is a large variety of professional relationships that members and candidates have with their clients. Standard III(A) requires them to fulfill the obligations outlined explicitly or implicitly in the client agreements to the best of their abilities and with loyalty, prudence, and care. Whether a member or candidate is structuring a new securitization transaction, completing a credit rating analysis, or leading a public company, he or she must work with prudence and care in delivering the agreed-on services.

Identifying the Actual Investment Client

The first step for members and candidates in fulfilling their duty of loyalty to clients is to determine the identity of the "client" to whom the duty of loyalty is owed. In the context of an investment manager managing the personal assets of an individual, the client is easily identified. When the manager is responsible for the portfolios of pension plans or trusts, however, the client is not the person or entity who hires the manager but, rather, the beneficiaries of the plan or trust. The duty of loyalty is owed to the ultimate beneficiaries.

In some situations, an actual client or group of beneficiaries may not exist. Members and candidates managing a fund to an index or an expected mandate owe the duty of loyalty, prudence, and care to invest in a manner consistent with the stated mandate. The decisions of a fund's manager, although benefiting all fund investors, do not have to be based on an individual investor's requirements and risk profile. Client loyalty and care for those investing in the fund are the responsibility of members and candidates who have an advisory relationship with those individuals.

Situations involving potential conflicts of interest with respect to responsibilities to clients may be extremely complex because they may involve a number of competing interests. The duty of loyalty, prudence, and care applies to a large number of persons in varying capacities, but the exact duties may differ in many respects in accord with the relationship with each client or each type of account in which the assets are managed. Members and candidates must not only put their obligations to clients first in all dealings but also endeavor to avoid all real or potential conflicts of interest.

Standard III: Duties to Clients

Members and candidates with positions whose responsibilities do not include direct investment management also have "clients" that must be considered. Just as there are various types of advisory relationships, members and candidates must look at their roles and responsibilities when making a determination of who their clients are. Sometimes the client is easily identifiable; such is the case in the relationship between a company executive and the firm's public shareholders. At other times, the client may be the investing public as a whole, in which case the goals of independence and objectivity of research surpass the goal of loyalty to a single organization.

Developing the Client's Portfolio

The duty of loyalty, prudence, and care owed to the individual client is especially important because the professional investment manager typically possesses greater knowledge in the investment arena than the client does. This disparity places the individual client in a vulnerable position; the client must trust the manager. The manager in these situations should ensure that the client's objectives and expectations for the performance of the account are realistic and suitable to the client's circumstances and that the risks involved are appropriate. In most circumstances, recommended investment strategies should relate to the long-term objectives and circumstances of the client.

Particular care must be taken to detect whether the goals of the investment manager or the firm in conducting business, selling products, and executing security transactions potentially conflict with the best interests and objectives of the client. When members and candidates cannot avoid potential conflicts between their firm and clients' interests, they must provide clear and factual disclosures of the circumstances to the clients.

Members and candidates must follow any guidelines set by their clients for the management of their assets. Some clients, such as charitable organizations and pension plans, have strict investment policies that limit investment options to certain types or classes of investment or prohibit investment in certain securities. Other organizations have aggressive policies that do not prohibit investments by type but, instead, set criteria on the basis of the portfolio's total risk and return.

Investment decisions must be judged in the context of the total portfolio rather than by individual investment within the portfolio. The member's or candidate's duty is satisfied with respect to a particular investment if the individual has thoroughly considered the investment's place in the overall portfolio, the risk of loss and opportunity for gains, tax implications, and the diversification, liquidity, cash flow, and overall return requirements of the assets or the portion of the assets for which the manager is responsible.

Soft Commission Policies

An investment manager often has discretion over the selection of brokers executing transactions. Conflicts may arise when an investment manager uses client brokerage to purchase research services, a practice commonly called "soft dollars" or "soft commissions." A member or candidate who pays a higher brokerage commission than he or she would normally pay to allow for the purchase of goods or services, without corresponding benefit to the client, violates the duty of loyalty to the client.

From time to time, a client will direct a manager to use the client's brokerage to purchase goods or services for the client, a practice that is commonly called "directed brokerage." Because brokerage commission is an asset of the client and is used to benefit that client, not the manager, such a practice does not violate any duty of loyalty. However, a member or candidate is obligated to seek "best price" and "best execution" and be assured by the client that the goods or services purchased from the brokerage will benefit the account beneficiaries. "Best execution" refers to a trading process that seeks to maximize the value of the client's portfolio within the client's stated investment objectives and constraints. In addition, the member or candidate should disclose to the client that the client may not be getting best execution from the directed brokerage.

Proxy Voting Policies

The duty of loyalty, prudence, and care may apply in a number of situations facing the investment professional besides those related directly to investing assets.

Part of a member's or candidate's duty of loyalty includes voting proxies in an informed and responsible manner. Proxies have economic value to a client, and members and candidates must ensure that they properly safeguard and maximize this value. An investment manager who fails to vote, casts a vote without considering the impact of the question, or votes blindly with management on nonroutine governance issues (e.g., a change in company capitalization) may violate this standard. Voting of proxies is an integral part of the management of investments.

A cost–benefit analysis may show that voting all proxies may not benefit the client, so voting proxies may not be necessary in all instances. Members and candidates should disclose to clients their proxy voting policies.

Recommended Procedures for Compliance

Regular Account Information

Members and candidates with control of client assets (1) should submit to each client, at least quarterly, an itemized statement showing the funds and securities in the custody or possession of the member or candidate plus all debits, credits, and transactions that occurred during the period, (2) should disclose to the client where the assets are to be maintained, as well as where or when they are moved, and (3) should separate the client's assets from any other party's assets, including the member's or candidate's own assets.

Client Approval

If a member or candidate is uncertain about the appropriate course of action with respect to a client, the member or candidate should consider what he or she would expect or demand if the member or candidate were the client. If in doubt, a member or candidate should disclose the questionable matter in writing to the client and obtain client approval.

Firm Policies

Members and candidates should address and encourage their firms to address the following topics when drafting the statements or manuals containing their policies and procedures regarding responsibilities to clients:

- *Follow all applicable rules and laws*: Members and candidates must follow all legal requirements and applicable provisions of the Code and Standards.
- *Establish the investment objectives of the client*: Make a reasonable inquiry into a client's investment experience, risk and return objectives, and financial constraints prior to making investment recommendations or taking investment actions.
- *Consider all the information when taking actions*: When taking investment actions, members and candidates must consider the appropriateness and suitability of the investment relative to (1) the client's needs and circumstances, (2) the investment's basic characteristics, and (3) the basic characteristics of the total portfolio.

Standard III: Duties to Clients

- *Diversify*: Members and candidates should diversify investments to reduce the risk of loss, unless diversification is not consistent with plan guidelines or is contrary to the account objectives.
- *Carry out regular reviews*: Members and candidates should establish regular review schedules to ensure that the investments held in the account adhere to the terms of the governing documents.
- *Deal fairly with all clients with respect to investment actions*: Members and candidates must not favor some clients over others and should establish policies for allocating trades and disseminating investment recommendations.
- *Disclose conflicts of interest*: Members and candidates must disclose all actual and potential conflicts of interest so that clients can evaluate those conflicts.
- *Disclose compensation arrangements*: Members and candidates should make their clients aware of all forms of manager compensation.
- *Vote proxies*: In most cases, members and candidates should determine who is authorized to vote shares and vote proxies in the best interests of the clients and ultimate beneficiaries.
- *Maintain confidentiality*: Members and candidates must preserve the confidentiality of client information.
- *Seek best execution*: Unless directed by the client as ultimate beneficiary, members and candidates must seek best execution for their clients. (Best execution is defined in the preceding text.)
- *Place client interests first*: Members and candidates must serve the best interests of clients.

Application of the Standard

Example 1 (Identifying the Client—Plan Participants):

First Country Bank serves as trustee for the Miller Company's pension plan. Miller is the target of a hostile takeover attempt by Newton, Inc. In attempting to ward off Newton, Miller's managers persuade Julian Wiley, an investment manager at First Country Bank, to purchase Miller common stock in the open market for the employee pension plan. Miller's officials indicate that such action would be favorably received and would probably result in other accounts being placed with the bank. Although Wiley believes the stock is overvalued and would not ordinarily buy it, he purchases the stock to support Miller's managers, to maintain Miller's good favor toward the bank, and to realize additional new business. The heavy stock purchases cause Miller's market price to rise to such a level that Newton retracts its takeover bid.

> *Comment*: Standard III(A) requires that a member or candidate, in evaluating a takeover bid, act prudently and solely in the interests of plan participants and beneficiaries. To meet this requirement, a member or candidate must carefully evaluate the long-term prospects of the company against the short-term prospects presented by the takeover offer and by the ability to invest elsewhere. In this instance, Wiley, acting on behalf of his employer, which was the trustee for a pension plan, clearly violated Standard III(A). He used the pension plan to perpetuate existing management, perhaps to the detriment of plan participants and the company's shareholders, and to benefit himself. Wiley's responsibilities to the plan participants and beneficiaries should have taken precedence over any ties of his bank to corporate managers and over his self-interest. Wiley had a duty to examine the takeover offer on its own merits and to make an independent decision.

The guiding principle is the appropriateness of the investment decision to the pension plan, not whether the decision benefited Wiley or the company that hired him.

Example 2 (Client Commission Practices):

JNI, a successful investment counseling firm, serves as investment manager for the pension plans of several large regionally based companies. Its trading activities generate a significant amount of commission-related business. JNI uses the brokerage and research services of many firms, but most of its trading activity is handled through a large brokerage company, Thompson, Inc., because the executives of the two firms have a close friendship. Thompson's commission structure is high in comparison with charges for similar brokerage services from other firms. JNI considers Thompson's research services and execution capabilities average. In exchange for JNI directing its brokerage to Thompson, Thompson absorbs a number of JNI overhead expenses, including those for rent.

> *Comment*: JNI executives are breaching their responsibilities by using client brokerage for services that do not benefit JNI clients and by not obtaining best price and best execution for their clients. Because JNI executives are not upholding their duty of loyalty, they are violating Standard III(A).

Example 3 (Brokerage Arrangements):

Charlotte Everett, a struggling independent investment adviser, serves as investment manager for the pension plans of several companies. One of her brokers, Scott Company, is close to consummating management agreements with prospective new clients whereby Everett would manage the new client accounts and trade the accounts exclusively through Scott. One of Everett's existing clients, Crayton Corporation, has directed Everett to place securities transactions for Crayton's account exclusively through Scott. But to induce Scott to exert efforts to send more new accounts to her, Everett also directs transactions to Scott from other clients without their knowledge.

> *Comment*: Everett has an obligation at all times to seek best price and best execution on all trades. Everett may direct new client trades exclusively through Scott Company as long as Everett receives best price and execution on the trades or receives a written statement from new clients that she is *not* to seek best price and execution and that they are aware of the consequence for their accounts. Everett may trade other accounts through Scott as a reward for directing clients to Everett only if the accounts receive best price and execution and the practice is disclosed to the accounts. Because Everett does not disclose the directed trading, Everett has violated Standard III(A).

Example 4 (Brokerage Arrangements):

Emilie Rome is a trust officer for Paget Trust Company. Rome's supervisor is responsible for reviewing Rome's trust account transactions and her monthly reports of personal stock transactions. Rome has been using Nathan Gray, a broker, almost exclusively for trust account brokerage transactions. When Gray makes a market in stocks, he has been giving Rome a lower price for personal purchases and a higher price for sales than he gives to Rome's trust accounts and other investors.

> *Comment*: Rome is violating her duty of loyalty to the bank's trust accounts by using Gray for brokerage transactions simply because Gray trades Rome's personal account on favorable terms. Rome is placing her own interests before those of her clients.

Standard III: Duties to Clients

Example 5 (Client Commission Practices):

Lauren Parker, an analyst with Provo Advisors, covers South American equities for her firm. She likes to travel to the markets for which she is responsible and decides to go on a trip to Chile, Argentina, and Brazil. The trip is sponsored by SouthAM, Inc., a research firm with a small broker/dealer affiliate that uses the clearing facilities of a larger New York brokerage house. SouthAM specializes in arranging South American trips for analysts during which they can meet with central bank officials, government ministers, local economists, and senior executives of corporations. SouthAM accepts commission dollars at a ratio of 2 to 1 against the hard-dollar costs of the research fee for the trip. Parker is not sure that SouthAM's execution is competitive, but without informing her supervisor, she directs the trading desk at Provo to start giving commission business to SouthAM so she can take the trip. SouthAM has conveniently timed the briefing trip to coincide with the beginning of Carnival season, so Parker also decides to spend five days of vacation in Rio de Janeiro at the end of the trip. Parker uses commission dollars to pay for the five days of hotel expenses.

> *Comment*: Parker is violating Standard III(A) by not exercising her duty of loyalty to her clients. She should have determined whether the commissions charged by SouthAM are reasonable in relation to the benefit of the research provided by the trip. She also should have determined whether best execution and prices could be received from SouthAM. In addition, the five extra days are not part of the research effort because they do not assist in the investment decision making. Thus, the hotel expenses for the five days should not be paid for with client assets.

Example 6 (Excessive Trading):

Vida Knauss manages the portfolios of a number of high-net-worth individuals. A major part of her investment management fee is based on trading commissions. Knauss engages in extensive trading for each of her clients to ensure that she attains the minimum commission level set by her firm. Although the securities purchased and sold for the clients are appropriate and fall within the acceptable asset classes for the clients, the amount of trading for each account exceeds what is necessary to accomplish the client's investment objectives.

> *Comment*: Knauss has violated Standard III(A) because she is using the assets of her clients to benefit her firm and herself.

Example 7 (Managing Family Accounts):

Adam Dill recently joined New Investments Asset Managers. To assist Dill in building a book of clients, both his father and brother opened new fee-paying accounts. Dill followed all the firm's procedures in noting his relationships with these clients and in developing their investment policy statements.

After several years, the number of Dill's clients has grown, but he still manages the original accounts of his family members. An IPO is coming to market that is a suitable investment for many of his clients, including his brother. Dill does not receive the amount of stock he requested, so to avoid any appearance of a conflict of interest, he does not allocate any shares to his brother's account.

> *Comment*: Dill has violated Standard III(A) because he is not acting for the benefit of his brother's account as well as his other accounts. The brother's account is a regular fee-paying account comparable to the accounts of his other clients. By not allocating the shares proportionately across *all* accounts for which he thought the IPO was suitable, Dill is disadvantaging specific clients.

Dill would have been correct in not allocating shares to his brother's account if that account was being managed outside the normal fee structure of the firm.

Example 8 (Identifying the Client):

Donna Hensley has been hired by a law firm to testify as an expert witness. Although the testimony is intended to represent impartial advice, she is concerned that her work may have negative consequences for the law firm. If the law firm is Hensley's client, how does she ensure that her testimony will not violate the required duty of loyalty, prudence, and care to one's client?

Comment: In this situation, the law firm represents Hensley's employer and the aspect of "who is the client" is not well defined. When acting as an expert witness, Hensley is bound by the standard of independence and objectivity in the same manner as an independent research analyst would be bound. Hensley must not let the law firm influence the testimony she provides in the legal proceedings.

Example 9 (Identifying the Client):

Jon Miller is a mutual fund portfolio manager. The fund is focused on the global financial services sector. Wanda Spears is a private wealth manager in the same city as Miller and is a friend of Miller. At a local CFA Institute society meeting, Spears mentions to Miller that her new client is an investor in Miller's fund. She states that the two of them now share a responsibility to this client.

Comment: Spears' statement is not totally correct. Because she provides the advisory services to her new client, she alone is bound by the duty of loyalty to this client. Miller's responsibility is to manage the fund according to the investment policy statement of the fund. His actions should not be influenced by the needs of any particular fund investor.

Example 10 (Client Loyalty):

After providing client account investment performance to the external-facing departments but prior to it being finalized for release to clients, Teresa Nguyen, an investment performance analyst, notices the reporting system missed a trade. Correcting the omission resulted in a large loss for a client that had previously placed the firm on "watch" for potential termination owing to underperformance in prior periods. Nguyen knows this news is unpleasant but informs the appropriate individuals that the report needs to be updated before releasing it to the client.

Comment: Nguyen's actions align with the requirements of Standard III(A). Even though the correction may lead to the firm's termination by the client, withholding information on errors would not be in the best interest of the client.

Example 11 (Execution-Only Responsibilities):

Baftija Sulejman recently became a candidate in the CFA Program. He is a broker who executes client-directed trades for several high-net-worth individuals. Sulejman does not provide any investment advice and only executes the trading decisions made by clients. He is concerned that the Code and Standards impose a fiduciary duty on him in his dealing with clients and sends an e-mail to the CFA Ethics Helpdesk (ethics@cfainstitute.org) to seek guidance on this issue.

Comment: In this instance, Sulejman serves in an execution-only capacity and his duty of loyalty, prudence, and care is centered on the skill and diligence used when executing trades—namely, by seeking best execution and making trades within the parameters set by the clients (instructions on quantity, price, timing, etc.). Acting in the best interests of the client dictates that trades are executed on the most favorable terms that can be achieved for the client. Given this job function, the requirements of the Code and Standards for loyalty, prudence, and care clearly do not impose a fiduciary duty.

Standard III(B) Fair Dealing

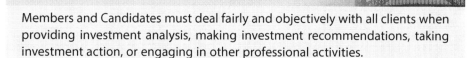

Members and Candidates must deal fairly and objectively with all clients when providing investment analysis, making investment recommendations, taking investment action, or engaging in other professional activities.

Guidance

Highlights:

- *Investment Recommendations*
- *Investment Action*

Standard III(B) requires members and candidates to treat all clients fairly when disseminating investment recommendations or making material changes to prior investment recommendations or when taking investment action with regard to general purchases, new issues, or secondary offerings. Only through the fair treatment of all parties can the investment management profession maintain the confidence of the investing public.

When an investment adviser has multiple clients, the potential exists for the adviser to favor one client over another. This favoritism may take various forms—from the quality and timing of services provided to the allocation of investment opportunities.

The term "fairly" implies that the member or candidate must take care not to discriminate against any clients when disseminating investment recommendations or taking investment action. Standard III(B) does not state "equally" because members and candidates could not possibly reach all clients at exactly the same time—whether by printed mail, telephone (including text messaging), computer (including internet updates and e-mail distribution), facsimile (fax), or wire. Each client has unique needs, investment criteria, and investment objectives, so not all investment opportunities are suitable for all clients. In addition, members and candidates may provide more personal, specialized, or in-depth service to clients who are willing to pay for premium services through higher management fees or higher levels of brokerage. Members and candidates may differentiate their services to clients, but different levels of service must not disadvantage or negatively affect clients. In addition, the different service levels should be disclosed to clients and prospective clients and should be available to everyone (i.e., different service levels should not be offered selectively).

Standard III(B) covers conduct in two broadly defined categories—investment recommendations and investment action.

Investment Recommendations

The first category of conduct involves members and candidates whose primary function is the preparation of investment recommendations to be disseminated either to the public or within a firm for the use of others in making investment decisions. This group includes members and candidates employed by investment counseling, advisory, or consulting firms as well as banks, brokerage firms, and insurance companies. The criterion is that the member's or candidate's primary responsibility is the preparation of recommendations to be acted on by others, including those in the member's or candidate's organization.

An investment recommendation is any opinion expressed by a member or candidate in regard to purchasing, selling, or holding a given security or other investment. The opinion may be disseminated to customers or clients through an initial detailed research report, through a brief update report, by addition to or deletion from a list of recommended securities, or simply by oral communication. A recommendation that is distributed to anyone outside the organization is considered a communication for general distribution under Standard III(B).

Standard III(B) addresses the manner in which investment recommendations or changes in prior recommendations are disseminated to clients. Each member or candidate is obligated to ensure that information is disseminated in such a manner that all clients have a fair opportunity to act on every recommendation. Communicating with all clients on a uniform basis presents practical problems for members and candidates because of differences in timing and methods of communication with various types of customers and clients. Members and candidates should encourage their firms to design an equitable system to prevent selective or discriminatory disclosure and should inform clients about what kind of communications they will receive.

The duty to clients imposed by Standard III(B) may be more critical when members or candidates change their recommendations than when they make initial recommendations. Material changes in a member's or candidate's prior investment recommendations because of subsequent research should be communicated to all current clients; particular care should be taken that the information reaches those clients who the member or candidate knows have acted on or been affected by the earlier advice. Clients who do not know that the member or candidate has changed a recommendation and who, therefore, place orders contrary to a current recommendation should be advised of the changed recommendation before the order is accepted.

Investment Action

The second category of conduct includes those members and candidates whose primary function is taking investment action (portfolio management) on the basis of recommendations prepared internally or received from external sources. Investment action, like investment recommendations, can affect market value. Consequently, Standard III(B) requires that members or candidates treat all clients fairly in light of their investment objectives and circumstances. For example, when making investments in new offerings or in secondary financings, members and candidates should distribute the issues to all customers for whom the investments are appropriate in a manner consistent with the policies of the firm for allocating blocks of stock. If the issue is oversubscribed, then the issue should be prorated to all subscribers. This action should be taken on a round-lot basis to avoid odd-lot distributions. In addition, if the issue is oversubscribed, members and candidates should forgo any sales to themselves or their immediate families in order to free up additional shares for clients. If the investment professional's family-member accounts are managed similarly to the accounts of other clients of the firm, however, the family-member accounts should not be excluded from buying such shares.

Standard III: Duties to Clients

Members and candidates must make every effort to treat all individual and institutional clients in a fair and impartial manner. A member or candidate may have multiple relationships with an institution; for example, the member or candidate may be a corporate trustee, pension fund manager, manager of funds for individuals employed by the customer, loan originator, or creditor. A member or candidate must exercise care to treat all clients fairly.

Members and candidates should disclose to clients and prospective clients the documented allocation procedures they or their firms have in place and how the procedures would affect the client or prospect. The disclosure should be clear and complete so that the client can make an informed investment decision. Even when complete disclosure is made, however, members and candidates must put client interests ahead of their own. A member's or candidate's duty of fairness and loyalty to clients can never be overridden by client consent to patently unfair allocation procedures.

Treating clients fairly also means that members and candidates should not take advantage of their position in the industry to the detriment of clients. For instance, in the context of IPOs, members and candidates must make bona fide public distributions of "hot issue" securities (defined as securities of a public offering that are trading at a premium in the secondary market whenever such trading commences because of the great demand for the securities). Members and candidates are prohibited from withholding such securities for their own benefit and must not use such securities as a reward or incentive to gain benefit.

Recommended Procedures for Compliance

Develop Firm Policies

Although Standard III(B) refers to a member's or candidate's responsibility to deal fairly and objectively with clients, members and candidates should also encourage their firms to establish compliance procedures requiring all employees who disseminate investment recommendations or take investment actions to treat customers and clients fairly. At the very least, a member or candidate should recommend appropriate procedures to management if none are in place. And the member or candidate should make management aware of possible violations of fair-dealing practices within the firm when they come to the attention of the member or candidate.

The extent of the formality and complexity of such compliance procedures depends on the nature and size of the organization and the type of securities involved. An investment adviser who is a sole proprietor and handles only discretionary accounts might not disseminate recommendations to the public, but that adviser should have formal written procedures to ensure that all clients receive fair investment action.

Good business practice dictates that initial recommendations be made available to all customers who indicate an interest. Although a member or candidate need not communicate a recommendation to all customers, the selection process by which customers receive information should be based on suitability and known interest, not on any preferred or favored status. A common practice to assure fair dealing is to communicate recommendations simultaneously within the firm and to customers.

Members and candidates should consider the following points when establishing fair-dealing compliance procedures:

- *Limit the number of people involved*: Members and candidates should make reasonable efforts to limit the number of people who are privy to the fact that a recommendation is going to be disseminated.
- *Shorten the time frame between decision and dissemination*: Members and candidates should make reasonable efforts to limit the amount of time that elapses between the decision to make an investment recommendation and the time the actual recommendation is disseminated. If a detailed institutional

recommendation that might take two or three weeks to publish is in preparation, a short summary report including the conclusion might be published in advance. In an organization where both a research committee and an investment policy committee must approve a recommendation, the meetings should be held on the same day if possible. The process of reviewing reports and printing and mailing them, faxing them, or distributing them by e-mail necessarily involves the passage of time, sometimes long periods of time. In large firms with extensive review processes, the time factor is usually not within the control of the analyst who prepares the report. Thus, many firms and their analysts communicate to customers and firm personnel the new or changed recommendations by an update or "flash" report. The communication technique might be fax, e-mail, wire, or short written report.

- *Publish guidelines for pre-dissemination behavior*: Members and candidates should encourage firms to develop guidelines that prohibit personnel who have prior knowledge of an investment recommendation from discussing or taking any action on the pending recommendation.

- *Simultaneous dissemination*: Members and candidates should establish procedures for the timing of dissemination of investment recommendations so that all clients are treated fairly—that is, are informed at approximately the same time. For example, if a firm is going to announce a new recommendation, supervisory personnel should time the announcement to avoid placing any client or group of clients at an unfair advantage relative to other clients. A communication to all branch offices should be sent at the time of the general announcement. (When appropriate, the firm should accompany the announcement of a new recommendation with a statement that trading restrictions for the firm's employees are now in effect. The trading restrictions should stay in effect until the recommendation is widely distributed to all relevant clients.) Once this distribution has occurred, the member or candidate may follow up separately with individual clients, but members and candidates should not give favored clients advance information when such advance notification may disadvantage other clients.

- *Maintain a list of clients and their holdings*: Members and candidates should maintain a list of all clients and the securities or other investments each client holds in order to facilitate notification of customers or clients of a change in an investment recommendation. If a particular security or other investment is to be sold, such a list can be used to ensure that all holders are treated fairly in the liquidation of that particular investment.

- *Develop and document trade allocation procedures*: When formulating procedures for allocating trades, members and candidates should develop a set of guiding principles that ensure

    - fairness to advisory clients, both in priority of execution of orders and in the allocation of the price obtained in execution of block orders or trades,
    - timeliness and efficiency in the execution of orders, and
    - accuracy of the member's or candidate's records as to trade orders and client account positions.

With these principles in mind, members and candidates should develop or encourage their firm to develop written allocation procedures, with particular attention to procedures for block trades and new issues. Procedures to consider are as follows:

- requiring orders and modifications or cancellations of orders to be documented and time stamped;

Standard III: Duties to Clients

- processing and executing orders on a first-in, first-out basis with consideration of bundling orders for efficiency as appropriate for the asset class or the security;
- developing a policy to address such issues as calculating execution prices and "partial fills" when trades are grouped, or in a block, for efficiency;
- giving all client accounts participating in a block trade the same execution price and charging the same commission;
- when the full amount of the block order is not executed, allocating partially executed orders among the participating client accounts pro rata on the basis of order size while not going below an established minimum lot size for some securities (e.g., bonds); and
- when allocating trades for new issues, obtaining advance indications of interest, allocating securities by client (rather than portfolio manager), and providing a method for calculating allocations.

Disclose Trade Allocation Procedures

Members and candidates should disclose to clients and prospective clients how they select accounts to participate in an order and how they determine the amount of securities each account will buy or sell. Trade allocation procedures must be fair and equitable, and disclosure of inequitable allocation methods does not relieve the member or candidate of this obligation.

Establish Systematic Account Review

Member and candidate supervisors should review each account on a regular basis to ensure that no client or customer is being given preferential treatment and that the investment actions taken for each account are suitable for each account's objectives. Because investments should be based on individual needs and circumstances, an investment manager may have good reasons for placing a given security or other investment in one account while selling it from another account and should fully document the reasons behind both sides of the transaction. Members and candidates should encourage firms to establish review procedures, however, to detect whether trading in one account is being used to benefit a favored client.

Disclose Levels of Service

Members and candidates should disclose to all clients whether the organization offers different levels of service to clients for the same fee or different fees. Different levels of service should not be offered to clients selectively.

Application of the Standard

Example 1 (Selective Disclosure):

Bradley Ames, a well-known and respected analyst, follows the computer industry. In the course of his research, he finds that a small, relatively unknown company whose shares are traded over the counter has just signed significant contracts with some of the companies he follows. After a considerable amount of investigation, Ames decides to write a research report on the small company and recommend purchase of its shares. While the report is being reviewed by the company for factual accuracy, Ames schedules a luncheon with several of his best clients to discuss the company. At the luncheon, he mentions the purchase recommendation scheduled to be sent early the following week to all the firm's clients.

Comment: Ames has violated Standard III(B) by disseminating the purchase recommendation to the clients with whom he has lunch a week before the recommendation is sent to all clients.

Example 2 (Fair Dealing between Funds):

Spencer Rivers, president of XYZ Corporation, moves his company's growth-oriented pension fund to a particular bank primarily because of the excellent investment performance achieved by the bank's commingled fund for the prior five-year period. Later, Rivers compares the results of his pension fund with those of the bank's commingled fund. He is startled to learn that, even though the two accounts have the same investment objectives and similar portfolios, his company's pension fund has significantly underperformed the bank's commingled fund. Questioning this result at his next meeting with the pension fund's manager, Rivers is told that, as a matter of policy, when a new security is placed on the recommended list, Morgan Jackson, the pension fund manager, first purchases the security for the commingled account and then purchases it on a pro rata basis for all other pension fund accounts. Similarly, when a sale is recommended, the security is sold first from the commingled account and then sold on a pro rata basis from all other accounts. Rivers also learns that if the bank cannot get enough shares (especially of hot issues) to be meaningful to all the accounts, its policy is to place the new issues only in the commingled account.

Seeing that Rivers is neither satisfied nor pleased by the explanation, Jackson quickly adds that nondiscretionary pension accounts and personal trust accounts have a lower priority on purchase and sale recommendations than discretionary pension fund accounts. Furthermore, Jackson states, the company's pension fund had the opportunity to invest up to 5% in the commingled fund.

Comment: The bank's policy does not treat all customers fairly, and Jackson has violated her duty to her clients by giving priority to the growth-oriented commingled fund over all other funds and to discretionary accounts over nondiscretionary accounts. Jackson must execute orders on a systematic basis that is fair to all clients. In addition, trade allocation procedures should be disclosed to all clients when they become clients. Of course, in this case, disclosure of the bank's policy would not change the fact that the policy is unfair.

Example 3 (Fair Dealing and IPO Distribution):

Dominic Morris works for a small regional securities firm. His work consists of corporate finance activities and investing for institutional clients. Arena, Ltd., is planning to go public. The partners have secured rights to buy an arena football league franchise and are planning to use the funds from the issue to complete the purchase. Because arena football is the current rage, Morris believes he has a hot issue on his hands. He has quietly negotiated some options for himself for helping convince Arena to do the financing through his securities firm. When he seeks expressions of interest, the institutional buyers oversubscribe the issue. Morris, assuming that the institutions have the financial clout to drive the stock up, then fills all orders (including his own) and decreases the institutional blocks.

Comment: Morris has violated Standard III(B) by not treating all customers fairly. He should not have taken any shares himself and should have prorated the shares offered among all clients. In addition, he should have disclosed to his firm and to his clients that he received options as part of the deal [see Standard VI(A)–Disclosure of Conflicts].

Standard III: Duties to Clients

Example 4 (Fair Dealing and Transaction Allocation):

Eleanor Preston, the chief investment officer of Porter Williams Investments (PWI), a medium-size money management firm, has been trying to retain a client, Colby Company. Management at Colby, which accounts for almost half of PWI's revenues, recently told Preston that if the performance of its account did not improve, it would find a new money manager. Shortly after this threat, Preston purchases mortgage-backed securities (MBSs) for several accounts, including Colby's. Preston is busy with a number of transactions that day, so she fails to allocate the trades immediately or write up the trade tickets. A few days later, when Preston is allocating trades, she notes that some of the MBSs have significantly increased in price and some have dropped. Preston decides to allocate the profitable trades to Colby and spread the losing trades among several other PWI accounts.

> *Comment*: Preston has violated Standard III(B) by failing to deal fairly with her clients in taking these investment actions. Preston should have allocated the trades prior to executing the orders, or she should have had a systematic approach to allocating the trades, such as pro rata, as soon as practical after they were executed. Among other things, Preston must disclose to the client that the adviser may act as broker for, receive commissions from, and have a potential conflict of interest regarding both parties in agency cross-transactions. After the disclosure, she should obtain from the client consent authorizing such transactions in advance.

Example 5 (Selective Disclosure):

Saunders Industrial Waste Management (SIWM) publicly indicates to analysts that it is comfortable with the somewhat disappointing earnings-per-share projection of US$1.16 for the quarter. Bernard Roberts, an analyst at Coffey Investments, is confident that SIWM management has understated the forecasted earnings so that the real announcement will cause an "upside surprise" and boost the price of SIWM stock. The "whisper number" (rumored) estimate based on extensive research and discussed among knowledgeable analysts is higher than US$1.16. Roberts repeats the US$1.16 figure in his research report to all Coffey clients but informally tells his large clients that he expects the earnings per share to be higher, making SIWM a good buy.

> *Comment*: By not sharing his opinion regarding the potential for a significant upside earnings surprise with all clients, Roberts is not treating all clients fairly and has violated Standard III(B).

Example 6 (Additional Services for Select Clients):

Jenpin Weng uses e-mail to issue a new recommendation to all his clients. He then calls his three largest institutional clients to discuss the recommendation in detail.

> *Comment*: Weng has not violated Standard III(B) because he widely disseminated the recommendation and provided the information to all his clients prior to discussing it with a select few. Weng's largest clients received additional personal service because they presumably pay higher fees or because they have a large amount of assets under Weng's management. If Weng had discussed the report with a select group of clients prior to distributing it to all his clients, he would have violated Standard III(B).

Example 7 (Minimum Lot Allocations):

Lynn Hampton is a well-respected private wealth manager in her community with a diversified client base. She determines that a new 10-year bond being offered by Healthy Pharmaceuticals is appropriate for five of her clients. Three clients request to purchase US$10,000 each, and the other two request US$50,000 each. The minimum lot size is established at US$5,000, and the issue is oversubscribed at the time of placement. Her firm's policy is that odd-lot allocations, especially those below the minimum, should be avoided because they may affect the liquidity of the security at the time of sale.

Hampton is informed she will receive only US$55,000 of the offering for all accounts. Hampton distributes the bond investments as follows: The three accounts that requested US$10,000 are allocated US$5,000 each, and the two accounts that requested US$50,000 are allocated US$20,000 each.

> *Comment*: Hampton has not violated Standard III(B), even though the distribution is not on a completely pro rata basis because of the required minimum lot size. With the total allocation being significantly below the amount requested, Hampton ensured that each client received at least the minimum lot size of the issue. This approach allowed the clients to efficiently sell the bond later if necessary.

Example 8 (Excessive Trading):

Ling Chan manages the accounts for many pension plans, including the plan of his father's employer. Chan developed similar but not identical investment policies for each client, so the investment portfolios are rarely the same. To minimize the cost to his father's pension plan, he intentionally trades more frequently in the accounts of other clients to ensure the required brokerage is incurred to continue receiving free research for use by all the pensions.

> *Comment*: Chan is violating Standard III(B) because his trading actions are disadvantaging his clients to enhance a relationship with a preferred client. All clients are benefiting from the research being provided and should incur their fair portion of the costs. This does not mean that additional trading should occur if a client has not paid an equal portion of the commission; trading should occur only as required by the strategy.

Example 9 (Limited Social Media Disclosures):

Mary Burdette was recently hired by Fundamental Investment Management (FIM) as a junior auto industry analyst. Burdette is expected to expand the social media presence of the firm because she is active with various networks, including Facebook, LinkedIn, and Twitter. Although Burdette's supervisor, Joe Graf, has never used social media, he encourages Burdette to explore opportunities to increase FIM's online presence and ability to share content, communicate, and broadcast information to clients. In response to Graf's encouragement, Burdette is working on a proposal detailing the advantages of getting FIM onto Twitter in addition to launching a company Facebook page.

As part of her auto industry research for FIM, Burdette is completing a report on the financial impact of Sun Drive Auto Ltd.'s new solar technology for compact automobiles. This research report will be her first for FIM, and she believes Sun Drive's technology could revolutionize the auto industry. In her excitement, Burdette sends a quick tweet to FIM Twitter followers summarizing her "buy" recommendation for Sun Drive Auto stock.

> *Comment*: Burdette has violated Standard III(B) by sending an investment recommendation to a select group of contacts prior to distributing it to all clients. Burdette must make sure she has received the appropriate training about FIM's policies and procedures, including the appropriate business use of personal social media networks before engaging in such activities.
>
> See Standard IV(C) for guidance related to the duties of the supervisor.

Example 10 (Fair Dealing between Clients):

Paul Rove, performance analyst for Alpha-Beta Investment Management, is describing to the firm's chief investment officer (CIO) two new reports he would like to develop to assist the firm in meeting its obligations to treat clients fairly. Because many of the firm's clients have similar investment objectives and portfolios, Rove suggests a report detailing securities owned across several clients and the percentage of the portfolio the security represents. The second report would compare the monthly performance of portfolios with similar strategies. The outliers within each report would be submitted to the CIO for review.

> *Comment*: As a performance analyst, Rove likely has little direct contact with clients and thus has limited opportunity to treat clients differently. The recommended reports comply with Standard III(B) while helping the firm conduct after-the-fact reviews of how effectively the firm's advisers are dealing with their clients' portfolios. Reports that monitor the fair treatment of clients are an important oversight tool to ensure that clients are treated fairly.

Standard III(C) Suitability

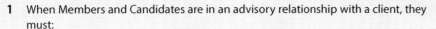

1. When Members and Candidates are in an advisory relationship with a client, they must:

   a. Make a reasonable inquiry into a client's or prospective client's investment experience, risk and return objectives, and financial constraints prior to making any investment recommendation or taking investment action and must reassess and update this information regularly.

   b. Determine that an investment is suitable to the client's financial situation and consistent with the client's written objectives, mandates, and constraints before making an investment recommendation or taking investment action.

   c. Judge the suitability of investments in the context of the client's total portfolio.

2. When Members and Candidates are responsible for managing a portfolio to a specific mandate, strategy, or style, they must make only investment recommendations or take only investment actions that are consistent with the stated objectives and constraints of the portfolio.

Guidance

Highlights:

- *Developing an Investment Policy*
- *Understanding the Client's Risk Profile*
- *Updating an Investment Policy*
- *The Need for Diversification*
- *Addressing Unsolicited Trading Requests*
- *Managing to an Index or Mandate*

Standard III(C) requires that members and candidates who are in an investment advisory relationship with clients consider carefully the needs, circumstances, and objectives of the clients when determining the appropriateness and suitability of a given investment or course of investment action. An appropriate suitability determination will not, however, prevent some investments or investment actions from losing value.

In judging the suitability of a potential investment, the member or candidate should review many aspects of the client's knowledge, experience related to investing, and financial situation. These aspects include, but are not limited to, the risk profile of the investment as compared with the constraints of the client, the impact of the investment on the diversity of the portfolio, and whether the client has the means or net worth to assume the associated risk. The investment professional's determination of suitability should reflect only the investment recommendations or actions that a prudent person would be willing to undertake. Not every investment opportunity will be suitable for every portfolio, regardless of the potential return being offered.

The responsibilities of members and candidates to gather information and make a suitability analysis prior to making a recommendation or taking investment action fall on those members and candidates who provide investment advice in the course of an advisory relationship with a client. Other members and candidates may be simply executing specific instructions for retail clients when buying or selling securities, such as shares in mutual funds. These members and candidates and some others, such as sell-side analysts, may not have the opportunity to judge the suitability of a particular investment for the ultimate client.

Developing an Investment Policy

When an advisory relationship exists, members and candidates must gather client information at the inception of the relationship. Such information includes the client's financial circumstances, personal data (such as age and occupation) that are relevant to investment decisions, attitudes toward risk, and objectives in investing. This information should be incorporated into a written investment policy statement (IPS) that addresses the client's risk tolerance, return requirements, and all investment constraints (including time horizon, liquidity needs, tax concerns, legal and regulatory factors, and unique circumstances). Without identifying such client factors, members and candidates cannot judge whether a particular investment or strategy is suitable for a particular client. The IPS also should identify and describe the roles and responsibilities of the parties to the advisory relationship and investment process, as well as schedules for review and evaluation of the IPS. After formulating long-term capital market expectations, members and candidates can assist in developing an appropriate strategic asset allocation and investment program for the client, whether these are presented in separate documents or incorporated in the IPS or in appendices to the IPS.

Understanding the Client's Risk Profile

One of the most important factors to be considered in matching appropriateness and suitability of an investment with a client's needs and circumstances is measuring that client's tolerance for risk. The investment professional must consider the possibilities of rapidly changing investment environments and their likely impact on a client's holdings, both individual securities and the collective portfolio. The risk of many investment strategies can and should be analyzed and quantified in advance.

The use of synthetic investment vehicles and derivative investment products has introduced particular issues of risk. Members and candidates should pay careful attention to the leverage inherent in many of these vehicles or products when considering them for use in a client's investment program. Such leverage and limited liquidity, depending on the degree to which they are hedged, bear directly on the issue of suitability for the client.

Standard III: Duties to Clients

Updating an Investment Policy

Updating the IPS should be repeated at least annually and also prior to material changes to any specific investment recommendations or decisions on behalf of the client. The effort to determine the needs and circumstances of each client is not a one-time occurrence. Investment recommendations or decisions are usually part of an ongoing process that takes into account the diversity and changing nature of portfolio and client characteristics. The passage of time is bound to produce changes that are important with respect to investment objectives.

For an individual client, important changes might include the number of dependents, personal tax status, health, liquidity needs, risk tolerance, amount of wealth beyond that represented in the portfolio, and extent to which compensation and other income provide for current income needs. With respect to an institutional client, such changes might relate to the magnitude of unfunded liabilities in a pension fund, the withdrawal privileges in an employee savings plan, or the distribution requirements of a charitable foundation. Without efforts to update information concerning client factors, one or more factors could change without the investment manager's knowledge.

Suitability review can be done most effectively when the client fully discloses his or her complete financial portfolio, including those portions not managed by the member or candidate. If clients withhold information about their financial portfolios, the suitability analysis conducted by members and candidates cannot be expected to be complete; it must be based on the information provided.

The Need for Diversification

The investment profession has long recognized that combining several different investments is likely to provide a more acceptable level of risk exposure than having all assets in a single investment. The unique characteristics (or risks) of an individual investment may become partially or entirely neutralized when it is combined with other individual investments within a portfolio. Some reasonable amount of diversification is thus the norm for many portfolios, especially those managed by individuals or institutions that have some degree of legal fiduciary responsibility.

An investment with high relative risk on its own may be a suitable investment in the context of the entire portfolio or when the client's stated objectives contemplate speculative or risky investments. The manager may be responsible for only a portion of the client's total portfolio, or the client may not have provided a full financial picture. Members and candidates can be responsible for assessing the suitability of an investment only on the basis of the information and criteria actually provided by the client.

Addressing Unsolicited Trading Requests

Members and candidates may receive requests from a client for trades that do not properly align with the risk and return objectives outlined in the client's investment policy statement. These transaction requests may be based on the client's individual biases or professional experience. Members and candidates will need to make reasonable efforts to balance their clients' trading requests with their responsibilities to follow the agreed-on investment policy statement.

In cases of unsolicited trade requests that a member or candidate knows are unsuitable for a client, the member or candidate should refrain from making the trade until he or she discusses the concerns with the client. The discussions and resulting actions may encompass a variety of scenarios depending on how the requested unsuitable investment relates to the client's full portfolio.

Many times, an unsolicited request may be expected to have only a minimum impact on the entire portfolio because the size of the requested trade is small or the trade would result in a limited change to the portfolio's risk profile. In discussing the trade, the member or candidate should focus on educating the investor on how the request deviates from the current policy statement. Following the discussion, the member or candidate may follow his or her firm's policies regarding the necessary client approval for executing unsuitable trades. At a minimum, the client should acknowledge the discussion and accept the conditions that make the recommendation unsuitable.

Should the unsolicited request be expected to have a material impact on the portfolio, the member or candidate should use this opportunity to update the investment policy statement. Doing so would allow the client to fully understand the potential effect of the requested trade on his or her current goals or risk levels.

Members and candidates may have some clients who decline to modify their policy statements while insisting an unsolicited trade be made. In such instances, members or candidates will need to evaluate the effectiveness of their services to the client. The options available to the members or candidates will depend on the services provided by their employer. Some firms may allow for the trade to be executed in a new unmanaged account. If alternative options are not available, members and candidates ultimately will need to determine whether they should continue the advisory arrangement with the client.

Managing to an Index or Mandate

Some members and candidates do not manage money for individuals but are responsible for managing a fund to an index or an expected mandate. The responsibility of these members and candidates is to invest in a manner consistent with the stated mandate. For example, a member or candidate who serves as the fund manager for a large-cap income fund would not be following the fund mandate by investing heavily in small-cap or start-up companies whose stock is speculative in nature. Members and candidates who manage pooled assets to a specific mandate are not responsible for determining the suitability of the *fund* as an investment for investors who may be purchasing shares in the fund. The responsibility for determining the suitability of an investment for clients can be conferred only on members and candidates who have an advisory relationship with clients.

Recommended Procedures for Compliance

Investment Policy Statement

To fulfill the basic provisions of Standard III(C), a member or candidate should put the needs and circumstances of each client and the client's investment objectives into a written investment policy statement. In formulating an investment policy for the client, the member or candidate should take the following into consideration:

- client identification—(1) type and nature of client, (2) the existence of separate beneficiaries, and (3) approximate portion of total client assets that the member or candidate is managing;
- investor objectives—(1) return objectives (income, growth in principal, maintenance of purchasing power) and (2) risk tolerance (suitability, stability of values);
- investor constraints—(1) liquidity needs, (2) expected cash flows (patterns of additions and/or withdrawals), (3) investable funds (assets and liabilities or other commitments), (4) time horizon, (5) tax considerations, (6) regulatory and legal circumstances, (7) investor preferences, prohibitions, circumstances, and unique needs, and (8) proxy voting responsibilities and guidance; and
- performance measurement benchmarks.

Regular Updates

The investor's objectives and constraints should be maintained and reviewed periodically to reflect any changes in the client's circumstances. Members and candidates should regularly compare client constraints with capital market expectations to arrive at an appropriate asset allocation. Changes in either factor may result in a fundamental change in asset allocation. Annual review is reasonable unless business or other reasons, such as a major change in market conditions, dictate more frequent review. Members and candidates should document attempts to carry out such a review if circumstances prevent it.

Suitability Test Policies

With the increase in regulatory required suitability tests, members and candidates should encourage their firms to develop related policies and procedures. The procedures will differ according to the size of the firm and the scope of the services offered to its clients.

The test procedures should require the investment professional to look beyond the potential return of the investment and include the following:

- an analysis of the impact on the portfolio's diversification,
- a comparison of the investment risks with the client's assessed risk tolerance, and
- the fit of the investment with the required investment strategy.

Application of the Standard

Example 1 (Investment Suitability—Risk Profile):

Caleb Smith, an investment adviser, has two clients: Larry Robertson, 60 years old, and Gabriel Lanai, 40 years old. Both clients earn roughly the same salary, but Robertson has a much higher risk tolerance because he has a large asset base. Robertson is willing to invest part of his assets very aggressively; Lanai wants only to achieve a steady rate of return with low volatility to pay for his children's education. Smith recommends investing 20% of both portfolios in zero-yield, small-cap, high-technology equity issues.

> *Comment*: In Robertson's case, the investment may be appropriate because of his financial circumstances and aggressive investment position, but this investment is not suitable for Lanai. Smith is violating Standard III(C) by applying Robertson's investment strategy to Lanai because the two clients' financial circumstances and objectives differ.

Example 2 (Investment Suitability—Entire Portfolio):

Jessica McDowell, an investment adviser, suggests to Brian Crosby, a risk-averse client, that covered call options be used in his equity portfolio. The purpose would be to enhance Crosby's income and partially offset any untimely depreciation in the portfolio's value should the stock market or other circumstances affect his holdings unfavorably. McDowell educates Crosby about all possible outcomes, including the risk of incurring an added tax liability if a stock rises in price and is called away and, conversely, the risk of his holdings losing protection on the downside if prices drop sharply.

> *Comment*: When determining suitability of an investment, the primary focus should be the characteristics of the client's entire portfolio, not the characteristics of single securities on an issue-by-issue basis. The basic characteristics of the entire portfolio will largely determine whether investment recommendations are taking client factors into account. Therefore,

the most important aspects of a particular investment are those that will affect the characteristics of the total portfolio. In this case, McDowell properly considers the investment in the context of the entire portfolio and thoroughly explains the investment to the client.

Example 3 (IPS Updating):

In a regular meeting with client Seth Jones, the portfolio managers at Blue Chip Investment Advisors are careful to allow some time to review his current needs and circumstances. In doing so, they learn that some significant changes have recently taken place in his life. A wealthy uncle left Jones an inheritance that increased his net worth fourfold, to US$1 million.

> *Comment*: The inheritance has significantly increased Jones's ability (and possibly his willingness) to assume risk and has diminished the average yield required to meet his current income needs. Jones's financial circumstances have definitely changed, so Blue Chip managers must update Jones's investment policy statement to reflect how his investment objectives have changed. Accordingly, the Blue Chip portfolio managers should consider a somewhat higher equity ratio for his portfolio than was called for by the previous circumstances, and the managers' specific common stock recommendations might be heavily tilted toward low-yield, growth-oriented issues.

Example 4 (Following an Investment Mandate):

Louis Perkowski manages a high-income mutual fund. He purchases zero-dividend stock in a financial services company because he believes the stock is undervalued and is in a potential growth industry, which makes it an attractive investment.

> *Comment*: A zero-dividend stock does not seem to fit the mandate of the fund that Perkowski is managing. Unless Perkowski's investment fits within the mandate or is within the realm of allowable investments the fund has made clear in its disclosures, Perkowski has violated Standard III(C).

Example 5 (IPS Requirements and Limitations):

Max Gubler, chief investment officer of a property/casualty insurance subsidiary of a large financial conglomerate, wants to improve the diversification of the subsidiary's investment portfolio and increase its returns. The subsidiary's investment policy statement provides for highly liquid investments, such as large-cap equities and government, supranational, and corporate bonds with a minimum credit rating of AA and maturity of no more than five years. In a recent presentation, a venture capital group offered very attractive prospective returns on some of its private equity funds that provide seed capital to ventures. An exit strategy was already contemplated, but investors would have to observe a minimum three-year lockup period and a subsequent laddered exit option for a maximum of one-third of their shares per year. Gubler does not want to miss this opportunity. After extensive analysis, with the intent to optimize the return on the equity assets within the subsidiary's current portfolio, he invests 4% in this seed fund, leaving the portfolio's total equity exposure still well below its upper limit.

> *Comment*: Gubler is violating Standard III(A)–Loyalty, Prudence, and Care as well as Standard III(C). His new investment locks up part of the subsidiary's assets for at least three years and up to as many as five years and possibly beyond. The IPS requires investments in highly liquid investments and describes accepted asset classes; private equity investments with a lockup period certainly do not qualify. Even without a lockup period, an asset class with only an occasional, and thus implicitly illiquid, market

Standard III: Duties to Clients

may not be suitable for the portfolio. Although an IPS typically describes objectives and constraints in great detail, the manager must also make every effort to understand the client's business and circumstances. Doing so should enable the manager to recognize, understand, and discuss with the client other factors that may be or may become material in the investment management process.

Example 6 (Submanager and IPS Reviews):

Paul Ostrowski's investment management business has grown significantly over the past couple of years, and some clients want to diversify internationally. Ostrowski decides to find a submanager to handle the expected international investments. Because this will be his first subadviser, Ostrowski uses the CFA Institute model "request for proposal" to design a questionnaire for his search. By his deadline, he receives seven completed questionnaires from a variety of domestic and international firms trying to gain his business. Ostrowski reviews all the applications in detail and decides to select the firm that charges the lowest fees because doing so will have the least impact on his firm's bottom line.

> *Comment*: When selecting an external manager or subadviser, Ostrowski needs to ensure that the new manager's services are appropriate for his clients. This due diligence includes comparing the risk profile of the clients with the investment strategy of the manager. In basing the decision on the fee structure alone, Ostrowski may be violating Standard III(C).
>
> When clients ask to diversify into international products, it is an appropriate time to review and update the clients' IPSs. Ostrowski's review may determine that the risk of international investments modifies the risk profiles of the clients or does not represent an appropriate investment.
>
> See also Standard V(A)–Diligence and Reasonable Basis for further discussion of the review process needed in selecting appropriate submanagers.

Example 7 (Investment Suitability—Risk Profile):

Samantha Snead, a portfolio manager for Thomas Investment Counsel, Inc., specializes in managing public retirement funds and defined benefit pension plan accounts, all of which have long-term investment objectives. A year ago, Snead's employer, in an attempt to motivate and retain key investment professionals, introduced a bonus compensation system that rewards portfolio managers on the basis of quarterly performance relative to their peers and to certain benchmark indexes. In an attempt to improve the short-term performance of her accounts, Snead changes her investment strategy and purchases several high-beta stocks for client portfolios. These purchases are seemingly contrary to the clients' investment policy statements. Following their purchase, an officer of Griffin Corporation, one of Snead's pension fund clients, asks why Griffin Corporation's portfolio seems to be dominated by high-beta stocks of companies that often appear among the most actively traded issues. No change in objective or strategy has been recommended by Snead during the year.

> *Comment*: Snead violated Standard III(C) by investing the clients' assets in high-beta stocks. These high-risk investments are contrary to the long-term risk profile established in the clients' IPSs. Snead has changed the investment strategy of the clients in an attempt to reap short-term rewards offered by her firm's new compensation arrangement, not in response to changes in clients' investment policy statements.
>
> See also Standard VI(A)–Disclosure of Conflicts.

Example 8 (Investment Suitability):

Andre Shrub owns and operates Conduit, an investment advisory firm. Prior to opening Conduit, Shrub was an account manager with Elite Investment, a hedge fund managed by his good friend Adam Reed. To attract clients to a new Conduit fund, Shrub offers lower-than-normal management fees. He can do so because the fund consists of two top-performing funds managed by Reed. Given his personal friendship with Reed and the prior performance record of these two funds, Shrub believes this new fund is a winning combination for all parties. Clients quickly invest with Conduit to gain access to the Elite funds. No one is turned away because Conduit is seeking to expand its assets under management.

> *Comment*: Shrub has violated Standard III(C) because the risk profile of the new fund may not be suitable for every client. As an investment adviser, Shrub needs to establish an investment policy statement for each client and recommend only investments that match each client's risk and return profile in the IPS. Shrub is required to act as more than a simple sales agent for Elite.
>
> Although Shrub cannot disobey the direct request of a client to purchase a specific security, he should fully discuss the risks of a planned purchase and provide reasons why it might not be suitable for a client. This requirement may lead members and candidates to decline new customers if those customers' requested investment decisions are significantly out of line with their stated requirements.
>
> See also Standard V(A)–Diligence and Reasonable Basis.

Standard III(D) Performance Presentation

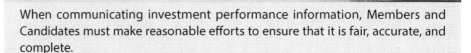

When communicating investment performance information, Members and Candidates must make reasonable efforts to ensure that it is fair, accurate, and complete.

Guidance

Standard III(D) requires members and candidates to provide credible performance information to clients and prospective clients and to avoid misstating performance or misleading clients and prospective clients about the investment performance of members or candidates or their firms. This standard encourages full disclosure of investment performance data to clients and prospective clients.

Standard III(D) covers any practice that would lead to misrepresentation of a member's or candidate's performance record, whether the practice involves performance presentation or performance measurement. This standard prohibits misrepresentations of past performance or reasonably expected performance. A member or candidate must give a fair and complete presentation of performance information whenever communicating data with respect to the performance history of individual accounts, composites or groups of accounts, or composites of an analyst's or firm's performance results. Furthermore, members and candidates should not state or imply that clients will obtain or benefit from a rate of return that was generated in the past.

Standard III: Duties to Clients

The requirements of this standard are not limited to members and candidates managing separate accounts. Whenever a member or candidate provides performance information for which the manager is claiming responsibility, such as for pooled funds, the history must be accurate. Research analysts promoting the success or accuracy of their recommendations must ensure that their claims are fair, accurate, and complete.

If the presentation is brief, the member or candidate must make available to clients and prospects, on request, the detailed information supporting that communication. Best practice dictates that brief presentations include a reference to the limited nature of the information provided.

Recommended Procedures for Compliance

Apply the GIPS Standards

For members and candidates who are showing the performance history of the assets they manage, compliance with the GIPS standards is the best method to meet their obligations under Standard III(D). Members and candidates should encourage their firms to comply with the GIPS standards.

Compliance without Applying GIPS Standards

Members and candidates can also meet their obligations under Standard III(D) by

- considering the knowledge and sophistication of the audience to whom a performance presentation is addressed,
- presenting the performance of the weighted composite of similar portfolios rather than using a single representative account,
- including terminated accounts as part of performance history with a clear indication of when the accounts were terminated,
- including disclosures that fully explain the performance results being reported (for example, stating, when appropriate, that results are simulated when model results are used, clearly indicating when the performance record is that of a prior entity, or disclosing whether the performance is gross of fees, net of fees, or after tax), and
- maintaining the data and records used to calculate the performance being presented.

Application of the Standard

Example 1 (Performance Calculation and Length of Time):

Kyle Taylor of Taylor Trust Company, noting the performance of Taylor's common trust fund for the past two years, states in a brochure sent to his potential clients, "You can expect steady 25% annual compound growth of the value of your investments over the year." Taylor Trust's common trust fund did increase at the rate of 25% per year for the past year, which mirrored the increase of the entire market. The fund has never averaged that growth for more than one year, however, and the average rate of growth of all of its trust accounts for five years is 5% per year.

> *Comment*: Taylor's brochure is in violation of Standard III(D). Taylor should have disclosed that the 25% growth occurred only in one year. Additionally, Taylor did not include client accounts other than those in the firm's common trust fund. A general claim of firm performance should take into account the performance of all categories of accounts. Finally, by

stating that clients can expect a steady 25% annual compound growth rate, Taylor is also violating Standard I(C)–Misrepresentation, which prohibits assurances or guarantees regarding an investment.

Example 2 (Performance Calculation and Asset Weighting):

Anna Judd, a senior partner of Alexander Capital Management, circulates a performance report for the capital appreciation accounts for the years 1988 through 2004. The firm claims compliance with the GIPS standards. Returns are not calculated in accordance with the requirements of the GIPS standards, however, because the composites are not asset weighted.

> *Comment*: Judd is in violation of Standard III(D). When claiming compliance with the GIPS standards, firms must meet *all* of the requirements, make mandatory disclosures, and meet any other requirements that apply to that firm's specific situation. Judd's violation is not from any misuse of the data but from a false claim of GIPS compliance.

Example 3 (Performance Presentation and Prior Fund/Employer):

Aaron McCoy is vice president and managing partner of the equity investment group of Mastermind Financial Advisors, a new business. Mastermind recruited McCoy because he had a proven six-year track record with G&P Financial. In developing Mastermind's advertising and marketing campaign, McCoy prepares an advertisement that includes the equity investment performance he achieved at G&P Financial. The advertisement for Mastermind does not identify the equity performance as being earned while at G&P. The advertisement is distributed to existing clients and prospective clients of Mastermind.

> *Comment*: McCoy has violated Standard III(D) by distributing an advertisement that contains material misrepresentations about the historical performance of Mastermind. Standard III(D) requires that members and candidates make every reasonable effort to ensure that performance information is a fair, accurate, and complete representation of an individual's or firm's performance. As a general matter, this standard does not prohibit showing past performance of funds managed at a prior firm as part of a performance track record as long as showing that record is accompanied by appropriate disclosures about where the performance took place and the person's specific role in achieving that performance. If McCoy chooses to use his past performance from G&P in Mastermind's advertising, he should make full disclosure of the source of the historical performance.

Example 4 (Performance Presentation and Simulated Results):

Jed Davis has developed a mutual fund selection product based on historical information from the 1990–95 period. Davis tested his methodology by applying it retroactively to data from the 1996–2003 period, thus producing simulated performance results for those years. In January 2004, Davis's employer decided to offer the product and Davis began promoting it through trade journal advertisements and direct dissemination to clients. The advertisements included the performance results for the 1996–2003 period but did not indicate that the results were simulated.

> *Comment*: Davis violated Standard III(D) by failing to clearly identify simulated performance results. Standard III(D) prohibits members and candidates from making any statements that misrepresent the performance achieved by them or their firms and requires members and candidates to make every reasonable effort to ensure that performance information

presented to clients is fair, accurate, and complete. Use of simulated results should be accompanied by full disclosure as to the source of the performance data, including the fact that the results from 1995 through 2003 were the result of applying the model retroactively to that time period.

Example 5 (Performance Calculation and Selected Accounts Only):

In a presentation prepared for prospective clients, William Kilmer shows the rates of return realized over a five-year period by a "composite" of his firm's discretionary accounts that have a "balanced" objective. This composite, however, consisted of only a few of the accounts that met the balanced criterion set by the firm, excluded accounts under a certain asset level without disclosing the fact of their exclusion, and included accounts that did not have the balanced mandate because those accounts would boost the investment results. In addition, to achieve better results, Kilmer manipulated the narrow range of accounts included in the composite by changing the accounts that made up the composite over time.

> *Comment*: Kilmer violated Standard III(D) by misrepresenting the facts in the promotional material sent to prospective clients, distorting his firm's performance record, and failing to include disclosures that would have clarified the presentation.

Example 6 (Performance Attribution Changes):

Art Purell is reviewing the quarterly performance attribution reports for distribution to clients. Purell works for an investment management firm with a bottom-up, fundamentals-driven investment process that seeks to add value through stock selection. The attribution methodology currently compares each stock with its sector. The attribution report indicates that the value added this quarter came from asset allocation and that stock selection contributed negatively to the calculated return.

Through running several different scenarios, Purell discovers that calculating attribution by comparing each stock with its industry and then rolling the effect to the sector level improves the appearance of the manager's stock selection activities. Because the firm defines the attribution terms and the results better reflect the stated strategy, Purell recommends that the client reports should use the revised methodology.

> *Comment*: Modifying the attribution methodology without proper notifications to clients would fail to meet the requirements of Standard III(D). Purell's recommendation is being done solely for the interest of the firm to improve its perceived ability to meet the stated investment strategy. Such changes are unfair to clients and obscure the facts regarding the firm's abilities.
>
> Had Purell believed the new methodology offered improvements to the original model, then he would have needed to report the results of both calculations to the client. The report should also include the reasons why the new methodology is preferred, which would allow the client to make a meaningful comparison to prior results and provide a basis for comparing future attributions.

Example 7 (Performance Calculation Methodology Disclosure):

While developing a new reporting package for existing clients, Alisha Singh, a performance analyst, discovers that her company's new system automatically calculates both time-weighted and money-weighted returns. She asks the head of client services and retention which value would be preferred given that the firm has various investment strategies that include bonds, equities, securities without leverage, and alternatives. Singh is told not to label the return value so that the firm may show whichever value is greatest for the period.

> *Comment*: Following these instructions would lead to Singh violating Standard III(D). In reporting inconsistent return values, Singh would not be providing complete information to the firm's clients. Full information is provided when clients have sufficient information to judge the performance generated by the firm.

Example 8 (Performance Calculation Methodology Disclosure):

Richmond Equity Investors manages a long–short equity fund in which clients can trade once a week (on Fridays). For transparency reasons, a daily net asset value of the fund is calculated by Richmond. The monthly fact sheets of the fund report month-to-date and year-to-date performance. Richmond publishes the performance based on the higher of the last trading day of the month (typically, not the last business day) or the last business day of the month as determined by Richmond. The fact sheet mentions only that the data are as of the end of the month, without giving the exact date. Maggie Clark, the investment performance analyst in charge of the calculations, is concerned about the frequent changes and asks her supervisor whether they are appropriate.

> *Comment*: Clark's actions in questioning the changing performance metric comply with Standard III(D). She has shown concern that these changes are not presenting an accurate and complete picture of the performance generated.

Standard III(E) Preservation of Confidentiality

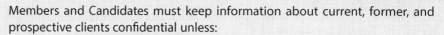

Members and Candidates must keep information about current, former, and prospective clients confidential unless:

1. The information concerns illegal activities on the part of the client;
2. Disclosure is required by law; or
3. The client or prospective client permits disclosure of the information.

Guidance

Highlights:

- *Status of Client*
- *Compliance with Laws*
- *Electronic Information and Security*
- *Professional Conduct Investigations by CFA Institute*

Standard III(E) requires that members and candidates preserve the confidentiality of information communicated to them by their clients, prospective clients, and former clients. This standard is applicable when (1) the member or candidate receives information because of his or her special ability to conduct a portion of the client's business or personal affairs and (2) the member or candidate receives information that arises

Standard III: Duties to Clients

from or is relevant to that portion of the client's business that is the subject of the special or confidential relationship. If disclosure of the information is required by law or the information concerns illegal activities by the client, however, the member or candidate may have an obligation to report the activities to the appropriate authorities.

Status of Client

This standard protects the confidentiality of client information even if the person or entity is no longer a client of the member or candidate. Therefore, members and candidates must continue to maintain the confidentiality of client records even after the client relationship has ended. If a client or former client expressly authorizes the member or candidate to disclose information, however, the member or candidate may follow the terms of the authorization and provide the information.

Compliance with Laws

As a general matter, members and candidates must comply with applicable law. If applicable law requires disclosure of client information in certain circumstances, members and candidates must comply with the law. Similarly, if applicable law requires members and candidates to maintain confidentiality, even if the information concerns illegal activities on the part of the client, members and candidates should not disclose such information. Additionally, applicable laws, such as inter-departmental communication restrictions within financial institutions, can impose limitations on information flow about a client within an entity that may lead to a violation of confidentiality. When in doubt, members and candidates should consult with their employer's compliance personnel or legal counsel before disclosing confidential information about clients.

Electronic Information and Security

Because of the ever-increasing volume of electronically stored information, members and candidates need to be particularly aware of possible accidental disclosures. Many employers have strict policies about how to electronically communicate sensitive client information and store client information on personal laptops, mobile devices, or portable disk/flash drives. In recent years, regulatory authorities have imposed stricter data security laws applying to the use of mobile remote digital communication, including the use of social media, that must be considered. Standard III(E) does not require members or candidates to become experts in information security technology, but they should have a thorough understanding of the policies of their employer. The size and operations of the firm will lead to differing policies for ensuring the security of confidential information maintained within the firm. Members and candidates should encourage their firm to conduct regular periodic training on confidentiality procedures for all firm personnel, including portfolio associates, receptionists, and other non-investment staff who have routine direct contact with clients and their records.

Professional Conduct Investigations by CFA Institute

The requirements of Standard III(E) are not intended to prevent members and candidates from cooperating with an investigation by the CFA Institute Professional Conduct Program (PCP). When permissible under applicable law, members and candidates shall consider the PCP an extension of themselves when requested to provide information about a client in support of a PCP investigation into their own conduct. Members and candidates are encouraged to cooperate with investigations into the conduct of others. Any information turned over to the PCP is kept in the strictest confidence. Members and candidates will not be considered in violation of this standard by forwarding confidential information to the PCP.

Recommended Procedures for Compliance

The simplest, most conservative, and most effective way to comply with Standard III(E) is to avoid disclosing any information received from a client except to authorized fellow employees who are also working for the client. In some instances, however, a member or candidate may want to disclose information received from clients that is outside the scope of the confidential relationship and does not involve illegal activities. Before making such a disclosure, a member or candidate should ask the following:

- In what context was the information disclosed? If disclosed in a discussion of work being performed for the client, is the information relevant to the work?
- Is the information background material that, if disclosed, will enable the member or candidate to improve service to the client?

Members and candidates need to understand and follow their firm's electronic information communication and storage procedures. If the firm does not have procedures in place, members and candidates should encourage the development of procedures that appropriately reflect the firm's size and business operations.

Communicating with Clients

Technological changes are constantly enhancing the methods that are used to communicate with clients and prospective clients. Members and candidates should make reasonable efforts to ensure that firm-supported communication methods and compliance procedures follow practices designed for preventing accidental distribution of confidential information. Given the rate at which technology changes, a regular review of privacy protection measures is encouraged.

Members and candidates should be diligent in discussing with clients the appropriate methods for providing confidential information. It is important to convey to clients that not all firm-sponsored resources may be appropriate for such communications.

Application of the Standard

Example 1 (Possessing Confidential Information):

Sarah Connor, a financial analyst employed by Johnson Investment Counselors, Inc., provides investment advice to the trustees of City Medical Center. The trustees have given her a number of internal reports concerning City Medical's needs for physical plant renovation and expansion. They have asked Connor to recommend investments that would generate capital appreciation in endowment funds to meet projected capital expenditures. Connor is approached by a local businessman, Thomas Kasey, who is considering a substantial contribution either to City Medical Center or to another local hospital. Kasey wants to find out the building plans of both institutions before making a decision, but he does not want to speak to the trustees.

> *Comment*: The trustees gave Connor the internal reports so she could advise them on how to manage their endowment funds. Because the information in the reports is clearly both confidential and within the scope of the confidential relationship, Standard III(E) requires that Connor refuse to divulge information to Kasey.

Example 2 (Disclosing Confidential Information):

Lynn Moody is an investment officer at the Lester Trust Company. She has an advisory customer who has talked to her about giving approximately US$50,000 to charity to reduce her income taxes. Moody is also treasurer of the Home for Indigent Widows (HIW), which is planning its annual giving campaign. HIW hopes to expand its list

Standard III: Duties to Clients

of prospects, particularly those capable of substantial gifts. Moody recommends that HIW's vice president for corporate gifts call on her customer and ask for a donation in the US$50,000 range.

> *Comment*: Even though the attempt to help the Home for Indigent Widows was well intended, Moody violated Standard III(E) by revealing confidential information about her client.

Example 3 (Disclosing Possible Illegal Activity):

Government officials approach Casey Samuel, the portfolio manager for Garcia Company's pension plan, to examine pension fund records. They tell her that Garcia's corporate tax returns are being audited and the pension fund is being reviewed. Two days earlier, Samuel had learned in a regular investment review with Garcia officers that potentially excessive and improper charges were being made to the pension plan by Garcia. Samuel consults her employer's general counsel and is advised that Garcia has probably violated tax and fiduciary regulations and laws.

> *Comment*: Samuel should inform her supervisor of these activities, and her employer should take steps, with Garcia, to remedy the violations. If that approach is not successful, Samuel and her employer should seek advice of legal counsel to determine the appropriate steps to be taken. Samuel may well have a duty to disclose the evidence she has of the continuing legal violations and to resign as asset manager for Garcia.

Example 4 (Disclosing Possible Illegal Activity):

David Bradford manages money for a family-owned real estate development corporation. He also manages the individual portfolios of several of the family members and officers of the corporation, including the chief financial officer (CFO). Based on the financial records of the corporation and some questionable practices of the CFO that Bradford has observed, Bradford believes that the CFO is embezzling money from the corporation and putting it into his personal investment account.

> *Comment*: Bradford should check with his firm's compliance department or appropriate legal counsel to determine whether applicable securities regulations require reporting the CFO's financial records.

Example 5 (Accidental Disclosure of Confidential Information):

Lynn Moody is an investment officer at the Lester Trust Company (LTC). She has stewardship of a significant number of individually managed taxable accounts. In addition to receiving quarterly written reports, about a dozen high-net-worth individuals have indicated to Moody a willingness to receive communications about overall economic and financial market outlooks directly from her by way of a social media platform. Under the direction of her firm's technology and compliance departments, she established a new group page on an existing social media platform specifically for her clients. In the instructions provided to clients, Moody asked them to "join" the group so they may be granted access to the posted content. The instructions also advised clients that all comments posted would be available to the public and thus the platform was not an appropriate method for communicating personal or confidential information.

Six months later, in early January, Moody posted LTC's year-end "Market Outlook." The report outlined a new asset allocation strategy that the firm is adding to its recommendations in the new year. Moody introduced the publication with a note informing her clients that she would be discussing the changes with them individually in their upcoming meetings.

One of Moody's clients responded directly on the group page that his family recently experienced a major change in their financial profile. The client described highly personal and confidential details of the event. Unfortunately, all clients that were part of the group were also able to read the detailed posting until Moody was able to have the comment removed.

Comment: Moody has taken reasonable steps for protecting the confidentiality of client information while using the social media platform. She provided instructions clarifying that all information posted to the site would be publically viewable to all group members and warned against using this method for communicating confidential information. The accidental disclosure of confidential information by a client is not under Moody's control. Her actions to remove the information promptly once she became aware further align with Standard III(E).

In understanding the potential sensitivity clients express surrounding the confidentiality of personal information, this event highlights a need for further training. Moody might advocate for additional warnings or controls for clients when they consider using social media platforms for two-way communications.

STANDARD IV: DUTIES TO EMPLOYERS

Standard IV(A) Loyalty

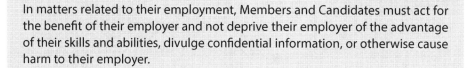

In matters related to their employment, Members and Candidates must act for the benefit of their employer and not deprive their employer of the advantage of their skills and abilities, divulge confidential information, or otherwise cause harm to their employer.

Guidance

Highlights:

- *Employer Responsibilities*
- *Independent Practice*
- *Leaving an Employer*
- *Use of Social Media*
- *Whistleblowing*
- *Nature of Employment*

Standard IV(A) requires members and candidates to protect the interests of their firm by refraining from any conduct that would injure the firm, deprive it of profit, or deprive it of the member's or candidate's skills and ability. Members and candidates must always place the interests of clients above the interests of their employer but should also consider the effects of their conduct on the sustainability and integrity of the employer firm. In matters related to their employment, members and candidates must not engage in conduct that harms the interests of their employer. Implicit in

Standard IV: Duties to Employers

this standard is the obligation of members and candidates to comply with the policies and procedures established by their employers that govern the employer–employee relationship—to the extent that such policies and procedures do not conflict with applicable laws, rules, or regulations or the Code and Standards.

This standard is not meant to be a blanket requirement to place employer interests ahead of personal interests in all matters. The standard does not require members and candidates to subordinate important personal and family obligations to their work. Members and candidates should enter into a dialogue with their employer about balancing personal and employment obligations when personal matters may interfere with their work on a regular or significant basis.

Employer Responsibilities

The employer–employee relationship imposes duties and responsibilities on both parties. Employers must recognize the duties and responsibilities that they owe to their employees if they expect to have content and productive employees.

Members and candidates are encouraged to provide their employer with a copy of the Code and Standards. These materials will inform the employer of the responsibilities of a CFA Institute member or a candidate in the CFA Program. The Code and Standards also serve as a basis for questioning employer policies and practices that conflict with these responsibilities.

Employers are not obligated to adhere to the Code and Standards. In expecting to retain competent employees who are members and candidates, however, they should not develop conflicting policies and procedures. The employer is responsible for a positive working environment, which includes an ethical workplace. Senior management has the additional responsibility to devise compensation structures and incentive arrangements that do not encourage unethical behavior.

Independent Practice

Included in Standard IV(A) is the requirement that members and candidates abstain from independent competitive activity that could conflict with the interests of their employer. Although Standard IV(A) does not preclude members or candidates from entering into an independent business while still employed, members and candidates who plan to engage in independent practice for compensation must notify their employer and describe the types of services they will render to prospective independent clients, the expected duration of the services, and the compensation for the services. Members and candidates should not render services until they receive consent from their employer to all of the terms of the arrangement. "Practice" means any service that the employer currently makes available for remuneration. "Undertaking independent practice" means engaging in competitive business, as opposed to making preparations to begin such practice.

Leaving an Employer

When members and candidates are planning to leave their current employer, they must continue to act in the employer's best interest. They must not engage in any activities that would conflict with this duty until their resignation becomes effective. It is difficult to define specific guidelines for those members and candidates who are planning to compete with their employer as part of a new venture. The circumstances of each situation must be reviewed to distinguish permissible preparations from violations of duty. Activities that might constitute a violation, especially in combination, include the following:

- misappropriation of trade secrets,
- misuse of confidential information,
- solicitation of the employer's clients prior to cessation of employment,

- self-dealing (appropriating for one's own property a business opportunity or information belonging to one's employer), and
- misappropriation of clients or client lists.

A departing employee is generally free to make arrangements or preparations to go into a competitive business before terminating the relationship with his or her employer as long as such preparations do not breach the employee's duty of loyalty. A member or candidate who is contemplating seeking other employment must not contact existing clients or potential clients prior to leaving his or her employer for purposes of soliciting their business for the new employer. Once notice is provided to the employer of the intent to resign, the member or candidate must follow the employer's policies and procedures related to notifying clients of his or her planned departure. In addition, the member or candidate must not take records or files to a new employer without the written permission of the previous employer.

Once an employee has left the firm, the skills and experience that an employee obtained while employed are not "confidential" or "privileged" information. Similarly, simple knowledge of the names and existence of former clients is generally not confidential information unless deemed such by an agreement or by law. Standard IV(A) does not prohibit experience or knowledge gained at one employer from being used at another employer. Firm records or work performed on behalf of the firm that is stored in paper copy or electronically for the member's or candidate's convenience while employed, however, should be erased or returned to the employer unless the firm gives permission to keep those records after employment ends.

The standard does not prohibit former employees from contacting clients of their previous firm as long as the contact information does not come from the records of the former employer or violate an applicable "noncompete agreement." Members and candidates are free to use public information after departing to contact former clients without violating Standard IV(A) as long as there is no specific agreement not to do so.

Employers often require employees to sign noncompete agreements that preclude a departing employee from engaging in certain conduct. Members and candidates should take care to review the terms of any such agreement when leaving their employer to determine what, if any, conduct those agreements may prohibit.

In some markets, there are agreements between employers within an industry that outline information that departing employees are permitted to take upon resignation, such as the "Protocol for Broker Recruiting" in the United States. These agreements ease individuals' transition between firms that have agreed to follow the outlined procedures. Members and candidates who move between firms that sign such agreements may rely on the protections provided as long as they faithfully adhere to all the procedures outlined.

For example, under the agreement between many US brokers, individuals are allowed to take some general client contact information when departing. To be protected, a copy of the information the individual is taking must be provided to the local management team for review. Additionally, the specific client information may only be used by the departing employee and not others employed by the new firm.

Use of Social Media

The growth in various online networking platforms, such as LinkedIn, Twitter, and Facebook (commonly referred to as social media platforms), is providing new opportunities and challenges for businesses. Members and candidates should understand and abide by all applicable firm policies and regulations as to the acceptable use of social media platforms to interact with clients and prospective clients. This is especially important when a member or candidate is planning to leave an employer.

Social media use makes determining how and when departure notification is delivered to clients more complex. Members and candidates may have developed profiles on these platforms that include connections with individuals who are clients of the firm, as well as individuals unrelated to their employer. Communications through social media platforms that potentially reach current clients should adhere to the employer's policies and procedures regarding notification of departing employees.

Social media connections with clients are also raising questions concerning the differences between public information and firm property. Specific accounts and user profiles of members and candidates may be created for solely professional reasons, including firm-approved accounts for client engagements. Such firm-approved business-related accounts would be considered part of the firm's assets, thus requiring members and candidates to transfer or delete the accounts as directed by their firm's policies and procedures. Best practice for members and candidates is to maintain separate accounts for their personal and professional social media activities. Members and candidates should discuss with their employers how profiles should be treated when a single account includes personal connections and also is used to conduct aspects of their professional activities.

Whistleblowing

A member's or candidate's personal interests, as well as the interests of his or her employer, are secondary to protecting the integrity of capital markets and the interests of clients. Therefore, circumstances may arise (e.g., when an employer is engaged in illegal or unethical activity) in which members and candidates must act contrary to their employer's interests in order to comply with their duties to the market and clients. In such instances, activities that would normally violate a member's or candidate's duty to his or her employer (such as contradicting employer instructions, violating certain policies and procedures, or preserving a record by copying employer records) may be justified. Such action would be permitted only if the intent is clearly aimed at protecting clients or the integrity of the market, not for personal gain.

Nature of Employment

A wide variety of business relationships exists within the investment industry. For instance, a member or candidate may be an employee or an independent contractor. Members and candidates must determine whether they are employees or independent contractors in order to determine the applicability of Standard IV(A). This issue will be decided largely by the degree of control exercised by the employing entity over the member or candidate. Factors determining control include whether the member's or candidate's hours, work location, and other parameters of the job are set; whether facilities are provided to the member or candidate; whether the member's or candidate's expenses are reimbursed; whether the member or candidate seeks work from other employers; and the number of clients or employers the member or candidate works for.

A member's or candidate's duties within an independent contractor relationship are governed by the oral or written agreement between the member and the client. Members and candidates should take care to define clearly the scope of their responsibilities and the expectations of each client within the context of each relationship. Once a member or candidate establishes a relationship with a client, the member or candidate has a duty to abide by the terms of the agreement.

Recommended Procedures for Compliance

Employers may establish codes of conduct and operating procedures for their employees to follow. Members and candidates should fully understand the policies to ensure that they are not in conflict with the Code and Standards. The following topics identify policies that members and candidates should encourage their firms to adopt if the policies are not currently in place.

Competition Policy

A member or candidate must understand any restrictions placed by the employer on offering similar services outside the firm while employed by the firm. The policy may outline the procedures for requesting approval to undertake the outside service or may be a strict prohibition of such service. If a member's or candidate's employer elects to have its employees sign a noncompete agreement as part of the employment agreement, the member or candidate should ensure that the details are clear and fully explained prior to signing the agreement.

Termination Policy

Members and candidates should clearly understand the termination policies of their employer. Termination policies should establish clear procedures regarding the resignation process, including addressing how the termination will be disclosed to clients and staff and whether updates posted through social media platforms will be allowed. The firm's policy may also outline the procedures for transferring ongoing research and account management responsibilities. Finally, the procedures should address agreements that allow departing employees to remove specific client-related information upon resignation.

Incident-Reporting Procedures

Members and candidates should be aware of their firm's policies related to whistleblowing and encourage their firm to adopt industry best practices in this area. Many firms are required by regulatory mandates to establish confidential and anonymous reporting procedures that allow employees to report potentially unethical and illegal activities in the firm.

Employee Classification

Members and candidates should understand their status within their employer firm. Firms are encouraged to adopt a standardized classification structure (e.g., part time, full time, outside contractor) for their employees and indicate how each of the firm's policies applies to each employee class.

Application of the Standard

Example 1 (Soliciting Former Clients):

Samuel Magee manages pension accounts for Trust Assets, Inc., but has become frustrated with the working environment and has been offered a position with Fiduciary Management. Before resigning from Trust Assets, Magee asks four big accounts to leave that firm and open accounts with Fiduciary. Magee also persuades several prospective clients to sign agreements with Fiduciary Management. Magee had previously made presentations to these prospects on behalf of Trust Assets.

> *Comment*: Magee violated the employee–employer principle requiring him to act solely for his employer's benefit. Magee's duty is to Trust Assets as long as he is employed there. The solicitation of Trust Assets' current clients and prospective clients is unethical and violates Standard IV(A).

Example 2 (Former Employer's Documents and Files):

James Hightower has been employed by Jason Investment Management Corporation for 15 years. He began as an analyst but assumed increasing responsibilities and is now a senior portfolio manager and a member of the firm's investment policy committee. Hightower has decided to leave Jason Investment and start his own investment management business. He has been careful not to tell any of Jason's clients that he is leaving; he does not want to be accused of breaching his duty to Jason by soliciting Jason's clients before his departure. Hightower is planning to copy and take with him the following documents and information he developed or worked on while at Jason: (1) the client list, with addresses, telephone numbers, and other pertinent client information; (2) client account statements; (3) sample marketing presentations to prospective clients containing Jason's performance record; (4) Jason's recommended list of securities; (5) computer models to determine asset allocations for accounts with various objectives; (6) computer models for stock selection; and (7) personal computer spreadsheets for Hightower's major corporate recommendations, which he developed when he was an analyst.

> *Comment*: Except with the consent of their employer, departing members and candidates may not take employer property, which includes books, records, reports, and other materials, because taking such materials may interfere with their employer's business opportunities. Taking any employer records, even those the member or candidate prepared, violates Standard IV(A). Employer records include items stored in hard copy or any other medium (e.g., home computers, portable storage devices, cell phones).

Example 3 (Addressing Rumors):

Reuben Winston manages all-equity portfolios at Target Asset Management (TAM), a large, established investment counselor. Ten years previously, Philpott & Company, which manages a family of global bond mutual funds, acquired TAM in a diversification move. After the merger, the combined operations prospered in the fixed-income business but the equity management business at TAM languished. Lately, a few of the equity pension accounts that had been with TAM before the merger have terminated their relationships with TAM. One day, Winston finds on his voice mail the following message from a concerned client: "Hey! I just heard that Philpott is close to announcing the sale of your firm's equity management business to Rugged Life. What is going on?" Not being aware of any such deal, Winston and his associates are stunned. Their internal inquiries are met with denials from Philpott management, but the rumors persist. Feeling left in the dark, Winston contemplates leading an employee buyout of TAM's equity management business.

> *Comment*: An employee-led buyout of TAM's equity asset management business would be consistent with Standard IV(A) because it would rest on the permission of the employer and, ultimately, the clients. In this case, however, in which employees suspect the senior managers or principals are not truthful or forthcoming, Winston should consult legal counsel to determine appropriate action.

Example 4 (Ownership of Completed Prior Work):

Laura Clay, who is unemployed, wants part-time consulting work while seeking a full-time analyst position. During an interview at Bradley Associates, a large institutional asset manager, Clay is told that the firm has no immediate research openings but would be willing to pay her a flat fee to complete a study of the wireless communications industry within a given period of time. Clay would be allowed unlimited access to Bradley's research files and would be welcome to come to the offices and use whatever support facilities are available during normal working hours. Bradley's research director does not seek any exclusivity for Clay's output, and the two agree to the arrangement on a handshake. As Clay nears completion of the study, she is offered an analyst job in the research department of Winston & Company, a brokerage firm, and she is pondering submitting the draft of her wireless study for publication by Winston.

Comment: Although she is under no written contractual obligation to Bradley, Clay has an obligation to let Bradley act on the output of her study before Winston & Company or Clay uses the information to their advantage. That is, unless Bradley gives permission to Clay and waives its rights to her wireless report, Clay would be in violation of Standard IV(A) if she were to immediately recommend to Winston the same transactions recommended in the report to Bradley. Furthermore, Clay must not take from Bradley any research file material or other property that she may have used.

Example 5 (Ownership of Completed Prior Work):

Emma Madeline, a recent college graduate and a candidate in the CFA Program, spends her summer as an unpaid intern at Murdoch and Lowell. The senior managers at Murdoch are attempting to bring the firm into compliance with the GIPS standards, and Madeline is assigned to assist in its efforts. Two months into her internship, Madeline applies for a job at McMillan & Company, which has plans to become GIPS compliant. Madeline accepts the job with McMillan. Before leaving Murdoch, she copies the firm's software that she helped develop because she believes this software will assist her in her new position.

Comment: Even though Madeline does not receive monetary compensation for her services at Murdoch, she has used firm resources in creating the software and is considered an employee because she receives compensation and benefits in the form of work experience and knowledge. By copying the software, Madeline violated Standard IV(A) because she misappropriated Murdoch's property without permission.

Example 6 (Soliciting Former Clients):

Dennis Elliot has hired Sam Chisolm, who previously worked for a competing firm. Chisolm left his former firm after 18 years of employment. When Chisolm begins working for Elliot, he wants to contact his former clients because he knows them well and is certain that many will follow him to his new employer. Is Chisolm in violation of Standard IV(A) if he contacts his former clients?

Comment: Because client records are the property of the firm, contacting former clients for any reason through the use of client lists or other information taken from a former employer without permission would be a violation of Standard IV(A). In addition, the nature and extent of the contact with former clients may be governed by the terms of any noncompete agreement signed by the employee and the former employer that covers contact with former clients after employment.

Simple knowledge of the names and existence of former clients is not confidential information, just as skills or experience that an employee obtains while employed are not "confidential" or "privileged" information. The Code and Standards do not impose a prohibition on the use of experience or knowledge gained at one employer from being used at another employer. The Code and Standards also do not prohibit former employees from contacting clients of their previous firm, in the absence of a noncompete agreement. Members and candidates are free to use public information about their former firm after departing to contact former clients without violating Standard IV(A).

Standard IV: Duties to Employers

> In the absence of a noncompete agreement, as long as Chisolm maintains his duty of loyalty to his employer before joining Elliot's firm, does not take steps to solicit clients until he has left his former firm, and does not use material from his former employer without its permission after he has left, he is not in violation of the Code and Standards.

Example 7 (Starting a New Firm):

Geraldine Allen currently works at a registered investment company as an equity analyst. Without notice to her employer, she registers with government authorities to start an investment company that will compete with her employer, but she does not actively seek clients. Does registration of this competing company with the appropriate regulatory authorities constitute a violation of Standard IV(A)?

> *Comment*: Allen's preparation for the new business by registering with the regulatory authorities does not conflict with the work for her employer if the preparations have been done on Allen's own time outside the office and if Allen will not be soliciting clients for the business or otherwise operating the new company until she has left her current employer.

Example 8 (Competing with Current Employer):

Several employees are planning to depart their current employer within a few weeks and have been careful to not engage in any activities that would conflict with their duty to their current employer. They have just learned that one of their employer's clients has undertaken a request for proposal (RFP) to review and possibly hire a new investment consultant. The RFP has been sent to the employer and all of its competitors. The group believes that the new entity to be formed would be qualified to respond to the RFP and be eligible for the business. The RFP submission period is likely to conclude before the employees' resignations are effective. Is it permissible for the group of departing employees to respond to the RFP for their anticipated new firm?

> *Comment*: A group of employees responding to an RFP that their employer is also responding to would lead to direct competition between the employees and the employer. Such conduct violates Standard IV(A) unless the group of employees receives permission from their employer as well as the entity sending out the RFP.

Example 9 (Externally Compensated Assignments):

Alfonso Mota is a research analyst with Tyson Investments. He works part time as a mayor for his hometown, a position for which he receives compensation. Must Mota seek permission from Tyson to serve as mayor?

> *Comment*: If Mota's mayoral duties are so extensive and time-consuming that they might detract from his ability to fulfill his responsibilities at Tyson, he should discuss his outside activities with his employer and come to a mutual agreement regarding how to manage his personal commitments with his responsibilities to his employer.

Example 10 (Soliciting Former Clients):

After leaving her employer, Shawna McQuillen establishes her own money management business. While with her former employer, she did not sign a noncompete agreement that would have prevented her from soliciting former clients. Upon her departure, she does not take any of her client lists or contact information and she clears her personal computer of any employer records, including client contact information. She obtains the phone numbers of her former clients through public records and contacts them to solicit their business.

> *Comment*: McQuillen is not in violation of Standard IV(A) because she has not used information or records from her former employer and is not prevented by an agreement with her former employer from soliciting her former clients.

Example 11 (Whistleblowing Actions):

Meredith Rasmussen works on a buy-side trading desk and concentrates on in-house trades for a hedge fund subsidiary managed by a team at the investment management firm. The hedge fund has been very successful and is marketed globally by the firm. From her experience as the trader for much of the activity of the fund, Rasmussen has become quite knowledgeable about the hedge fund's strategy, tactics, and performance. When a distinct break in the market occurs, however, and many of the securities involved in the hedge fund's strategy decline markedly in value, Rasmussen observes that the reported performance of the hedge fund does not reflect this decline. In her experience, the lack of any effect is a very unlikely occurrence. She approaches the head of trading about her concern and is told that she should not ask any questions and that the fund is big and successful and is not her concern. She is fairly sure something is not right, so she contacts the compliance officer, who also tells her to stay away from the issue of this hedge fund's reporting.

> *Comment*: Rasmussen has clearly come upon an error in policies, procedures, and compliance practices in the firm's operations. Having been unsuccessful in finding a resolution with her supervisor and the compliance officer, Rasmussen should consult the firm's whistleblowing policy to determine the appropriate next step toward informing management of her concerns. The potentially unethical actions of the investment management division are appropriate grounds for further disclosure, so Rasmussen's whistleblowing would not represent a violation of Standard IV(A).
>
> See also Standard I(D)–Misconduct and Standard IV(C)–Responsibilities of Supervisors.

Example 12 (Soliciting Former Clients):

Angel Crome has been a private banker for YBSafe Bank for the past eight years. She has been very successful and built a considerable client portfolio during that time but is extremely frustrated by the recent loss of reputation by her current employer and subsequent client insecurity. A locally renowned headhunter contacted Crome a few days ago and offered her an interesting job with a competing private bank. This bank offers a substantial signing bonus for advisers with their own client portfolios. Crome figures that she can solicit at least 70% of her clients to follow her and gladly enters into the new employment contract.

> *Comment*: Crome may contact former clients upon termination of her employment with YBSafe Bank, but she is prohibited from using client records built by and kept with her in her capacity as an employee of YBSafe Bank. Client lists are proprietary information of her former employer and must not be used for her or her new employer's benefit. The use of written, electronic, or any other form of records other than publicly available information to contact her former clients at YBSafe Bank will be a violation of Standard IV(A).

Standard IV: Duties to Employers

Example 13 (Notification of Code and Standards):

Krista Smith is a relatively new assistant trader for the fixed-income desk of a major investment bank. She is on a team responsible for structuring collateralized debt obligations (CDOs) made up of securities in the inventory of the trading desk. At a meeting of the team, senior executives explain the opportunity to eventually separate the CDO into various risk-rated tranches to be sold to the clients of the firm. After the senior executives leave the meeting, the head trader announces various responsibilities of each member of the team and then says, "This is a good time to unload some of the junk we have been stuck with for a while and disguise it with ratings and a thick, unreadable prospectus, so don't be shy in putting this CDO together. Just kidding." Smith is worried by this remark and asks some of her colleagues what the head trader meant. They all respond that he was just kidding but that there is some truth in the remark because the CDO is seen by management as an opportunity to improve the quality of the securities in the firm's inventory.

Concerned about the ethical environment of the workplace, Smith decides to talk to her supervisor about her concerns and provides the head trader with a copy of the Code and Standards. Smith discusses the principle of placing the client above the interest of the firm and the possibility that the development of the new CDO will not adhere to this responsibility. The head trader assures Smith that the appropriate analysis will be conducted when determining the appropriate securities for collateral. Furthermore, the ratings are assigned by an independent firm and the prospectus will include full and factual disclosures. Smith is reassured by the meeting, but she also reviews the company's procedures and requirements for reporting potential violations of company policy and securities laws.

> *Comment*: Smith's review of the company policies and procedures for reporting violations allows her to be prepared to report through the appropriate whistleblower process if she decides that the CDO development process involves unethical actions by others. Smith's actions comply with the Code and Standards principles of placing the client's interests first and being loyal to her employer. In providing her supervisor with a copy of the Code and Standards, Smith is highlighting the high level of ethical conduct she is required to adhere to in her professional activities.

Example 14 (Leaving an Employer):

Laura Webb just left her position as portfolio analyst at Research Systems, Inc. (RSI). Her employment contract included a non-solicitation agreement that requires her to wait two years before soliciting RSI clients for any investment-related services. Upon leaving, Webb was informed that RSI would contact clients immediately about her departure and introduce her replacement.

While working at RSI, Webb connected with clients, other industry associates, and friends through her LinkedIn network. Her business and personal relationships were intermingled because she considered many of her clients to be personal friends. Realizing that her LinkedIn network would be a valuable resource for new employment opportunities, she updated her profile several days following her departure from RSI. LinkedIn automatically sent a notification to Webb's entire network that her employment status had been changed in her profile.

> *Comment*: Prior to her departure, Webb should have discussed any client information contained in her social media networks. By updating her LinkedIn profile after RSI notified clients and after her employment ended, she has appropriately placed her employer's interests ahead of her own personal interests. In addition, she has not violated the non-solicitation agreement with RSI, unless it prohibited any contact with clients during the two-year period.

Example 15 (Confidential Firm Information):

Sanjay Gupta is a research analyst at Naram Investment Management (NIM). NIM uses a team-based research process to develop recommendations on investment opportunities covered by the team members. Gupta, like others, provides commentary for NIM's clients through the company blog, which is posted weekly on the NIM password-protected website. According to NIM's policy, every contribution to the website must be approved by the company's compliance department before posting. Any opinions expressed on the website are disclosed as representing the perspective of NIM.

Gupta also writes a personal blog to share his experiences with friends and family. As with most blogs, Gupta's personal blog is widely available to interested readers through various internet search engines. Occasionally, when he disagrees with the team-based research opinions of NIM, Gupta uses his personal blog to express his own opinions as a counterpoint to the commentary posted on the NIM website. Gupta believes this provides his readers with a more complete perspective on these investment opportunities.

> *Comment*: Gupta is in violation of Standard IV(A) for disclosing confidential firm information through his personal blog. The recommendations on the firm's blog to clients are not freely available across the internet, but his personal blog post indirectly provides the firm's recommendations.
>
> Additionally, by posting research commentary on his personal blog, Gupta is using firm resources for his personal advantage. To comply with Standard IV(A), members and candidates must receive consent from their employer prior to using company resources.

Standard IV(B) Additional Compensation Arrangements

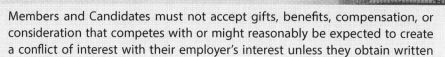

Members and Candidates must not accept gifts, benefits, compensation, or consideration that competes with or might reasonably be expected to create a conflict of interest with their employer's interest unless they obtain written consent from all parties involved.

Guidance

Standard IV(B) requires members and candidates to obtain permission from their employer before accepting compensation or other benefits from third parties for the services rendered to the employer or for any services that might create a conflict with their employer's interest. Compensation and benefits include direct compensation by the client and any indirect compensation or other benefits received from third parties. "Written consent" includes any form of communication that can be documented (for example, communication via e-mail that can be retrieved and documented).

Members and candidates must obtain permission for additional compensation/benefits because such arrangements may affect loyalties and objectivity and create potential conflicts of interest. Disclosure allows an employer to consider the outside arrangements when evaluating the actions and motivations of members and candidates. Moreover, the employer is entitled to have full knowledge of all compensation/benefit arrangements so as to be able to assess the true cost of the services members or candidates are providing.

Standard IV: Duties to Employers

There may be instances in which a member or candidate is hired by an employer on a "part-time" basis. "Part-time" status applies to employees who do not commit the full number of hours required for a normal work week. Members and candidates should discuss possible limitations to their abilities to provide services that may be competitive with their employer during the negotiation and hiring process. The requirements of Standard IV(B) would be applicable to limitations identified at that time.

Recommended Procedures for Compliance

Members and candidates should make an immediate written report to their supervisor and compliance officer specifying any compensation they propose to receive for services in addition to the compensation or benefits received from their employer. The details of the report should be confirmed by the party offering the additional compensation, including performance incentives offered by clients. This written report should state the terms of any agreement under which a member or candidate will receive additional compensation; "terms" include the nature of the compensation, the approximate amount of compensation, and the duration of the agreement.

Application of the Standard

Example 1 (Notification of Client Bonus Compensation):

Geoff Whitman, a portfolio analyst for Adams Trust Company, manages the account of Carol Cochran, a client. Whitman is paid a salary by his employer, and Cochran pays the trust company a standard fee based on the market value of assets in her portfolio. Cochran proposes to Whitman that "any year that my portfolio achieves at least a 15% return before taxes, you and your wife can fly to Monaco at my expense and use my condominium during the third week of January." Whitman does not inform his employer of the arrangement and vacations in Monaco the following January as Cochran's guest.

> *Comment*: Whitman violated Standard IV(B) by failing to inform his employer in writing of this supplemental, contingent compensation arrangement. The nature of the arrangement could have resulted in partiality to Cochran's account, which could have detracted from Whitman's performance with respect to other accounts he handles for Adams Trust. Whitman must obtain the consent of his employer to accept such a supplemental benefit.

Example 2 (Notification of Outside Compensation):

Terry Jones sits on the board of directors of Exercise Unlimited, Inc. In return for his services on the board, Jones receives unlimited membership privileges for his family at all Exercise Unlimited facilities. Jones purchases Exercise Unlimited stock for the client accounts for which it is appropriate. Jones does not disclose this arrangement to his employer because he does not receive monetary compensation for his services to the board.

> *Comment*: Jones has violated Standard IV(B) by failing to disclose to his employer benefits received in exchange for his services on the board of directors. The nonmonetary compensation may create a conflict of interest in the same manner as being paid to serve as a director.

Example 3 (Prior Approval for Outside Compensation):

Jonathan Hollis is an analyst of oil-and-gas companies for Specialty Investment Management. He is currently recommending the purchase of ABC Oil Company shares and has published a long, well-thought-out research report to substantiate his recommendation. Several weeks after publishing the report, Hollis receives a call from the investor-relations office of ABC Oil saying that Thomas Andrews, CEO of the company, saw the report and really liked the analyst's grasp of the business and his company. The investor-relations officer invites Hollis to visit ABC Oil to discuss the industry further. ABC Oil offers to send a company plane to pick Hollis up and arrange for his accommodations while visiting. Hollis, after gaining the appropriate approvals, accepts the meeting with the CEO but declines the offered travel arrangements.

Several weeks later, Andrews and Hollis meet to discuss the oil business and Hollis's report. Following the meeting, Hollis joins Andrews and the investment relations officer for dinner at an upscale restaurant near ABC Oil's headquarters.

Upon returning to Specialty Investment Management, Hollis provides a full review of the meeting to the director of research, including a disclosure of the dinner attended.

> *Comment*: Hollis's actions did not violate Standard IV(B). Through gaining approval before accepting the meeting and declining the offered travel arrangements, Hollis sought to avoid any potential conflicts of interest between his company and ABC Oil. Because the location of the dinner was not available prior to arrival and Hollis notified his company of the dinner upon his return, accepting the dinner should not impair his objectivity. By disclosing the dinner, Hollis has enabled Specialty Investment Management to assess whether it has any impact on future reports and recommendations by Hollis related to ABC Oil.

Standard IV(C) Responsibilities of Supervisors

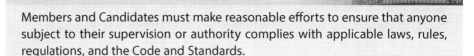

Members and Candidates must make reasonable efforts to ensure that anyone subject to their supervision or authority complies with applicable laws, rules, regulations, and the Code and Standards.

Guidance

Highlights:

- *System for Supervision*
- *Supervision Includes Detection*

Standard IV(C) states that members and candidates must promote actions by all employees under their supervision and authority to comply with applicable laws, rules, regulations, and firm policies and the Code and Standards.

Any investment professional who has employees subject to her or his control or influence—whether or not the employees are CFA Institute members, CFA charterholders, or candidates in the CFA Program—exercises supervisory responsibility. Members and candidates acting as supervisors must also have in-depth knowledge of the Code and Standards so that they can apply this knowledge in discharging their supervisory responsibilities.

Standard IV: Duties to Employers

The conduct that constitutes reasonable supervision in a particular case depends on the number of employees supervised and the work performed by those employees. Members and candidates with oversight responsibilities for large numbers of employees may not be able to personally evaluate the conduct of these employees on a continuing basis. These members and candidates may delegate supervisory duties to subordinates who directly oversee the other employees. A member's or candidate's responsibilities under Standard IV(C) include instructing those subordinates to whom supervision is delegated about methods to promote compliance, including preventing and detecting violations of laws, rules, regulations, firm policies, and the Code and Standards.

At a minimum, Standard IV(C) requires that members and candidates with supervisory responsibility make reasonable efforts to prevent and detect violations by ensuring the establishment of effective compliance systems. However, an effective compliance system goes beyond enacting a code of ethics, establishing policies and procedures to achieve compliance with the code and applicable law, and reviewing employee actions to determine whether they are following the rules.

To be effective supervisors, members and candidates should implement education and training programs on a recurring or regular basis for employees under their supervision. Such programs will assist the employees with meeting their professional obligations to practice in an ethical manner within the applicable legal system. Further, establishing incentives—monetary or otherwise—for employees not only to meet business goals but also to reward ethical behavior offers supervisors another way to assist employees in complying with their legal and ethical obligations.

Often, especially in large organizations, members and candidates may have supervisory responsibility but not the authority to establish or modify firm-wide compliance policies and procedures or incentive structures. Such limitations should not prevent a member or candidate from working with his or her own superiors and within the firm structure to develop and implement effective compliance tools, including but not limited to:

- a code of ethics,
- compliance policies and procedures,
- education and training programs,
- an incentive structure that rewards ethical conduct, and
- adoption of firm-wide best practice standards (e.g., the GIPS standards, the CFA Institute Asset Manager Code of Professional Conduct).

A member or candidate with supervisory responsibility should bring an inadequate compliance system to the attention of the firm's senior managers and recommend corrective action. If the member or candidate clearly cannot discharge supervisory responsibilities because of the absence of a compliance system or because of an inadequate compliance system, the member or candidate should decline in writing to accept supervisory responsibility until the firm adopts reasonable procedures to allow adequate exercise of supervisory responsibility.

System for Supervision

Members and candidates with supervisory responsibility must understand what constitutes an adequate compliance system for their firms and make reasonable efforts to see that appropriate compliance procedures are established, documented, communicated to covered personnel, and followed. "Adequate" procedures are those designed to meet industry standards, regulatory requirements, the requirements of the Code and Standards, and the circumstances of the firm. Once compliance procedures are established, the supervisor must also make reasonable efforts to ensure that the procedures are monitored and enforced.

To be effective, compliance procedures must be in place prior to the occurrence of a violation of the law or the Code and Standards. Although compliance procedures cannot be designed to anticipate every potential violation, they should be designed to anticipate the activities most likely to result in misconduct. Compliance programs must be appropriate for the size and nature of the organization. The member or candidate should review model compliance procedures or other industry programs to ensure that the firm's procedures meet the minimum industry standards.

Once a supervisor learns that an employee has violated or may have violated the law or the Code and Standards, the supervisor must promptly initiate an assessment to determine the extent of the wrongdoing. Relying on an employee's statements about the extent of the violation or assurances that the wrongdoing will not reoccur is not enough. Reporting the misconduct up the chain of command and warning the employee to cease the activity are also not enough. Pending the outcome of the investigation, a supervisor should take steps to ensure that the violation will not be repeated, such as placing limits on the employee's activities or increasing the monitoring of the employee's activities.

Supervision Includes Detection

Members and candidates with supervisory responsibility must also make reasonable efforts to detect violations of laws, rules, regulations, firm policies, and the Code and Standards. The supervisors exercise reasonable supervision by establishing and implementing written compliance procedures and ensuring that those procedures are followed through periodic review. If a member or candidate has adopted reasonable procedures and taken steps to institute an effective compliance program, then the member or candidate may not be in violation of Standard IV(C) if he or she does not detect violations that occur despite these efforts. The fact that violations do occur may indicate, however, that the compliance procedures are inadequate. In addition, in some cases, merely enacting such procedures may not be sufficient to fulfill the duty required by Standard IV(C). A member or candidate may be in violation of Standard IV(C) if he or she knows or should know that the procedures designed to promote compliance, including detecting and preventing violations, are not being followed.

Recommended Procedures for Compliance

Codes of Ethics or Compliance Procedures

Members and candidates are encouraged to recommend that their employers adopt a code of ethics. Adoption of a code of ethics is critical to establishing a strong ethical foundation for investment advisory firms and their employees. Codes of ethics formally emphasize and reinforce the client loyalty responsibilities of investment firm personnel, protect investing clients by deterring misconduct, and protect the firm's reputation for integrity.

There is a distinction, however, between codes of ethics and the specific policies and procedures needed to ensure compliance with the codes and with securities laws and regulations. Although both are important, codes of ethics should consist of fundamental, principle-based ethical and fiduciary concepts that are applicable to all of the firm's employees. In this way, firms can best convey to employees and clients the ethical ideals that investment advisers strive to achieve. These concepts need to be implemented, however, by detailed, firm-wide compliance policies and procedures. Compliance procedures assist the firm's personnel in fulfilling the responsibilities enumerated in the code of ethics and make probable that the ideals expressed in the code of ethics will be adhered to in the day-to-day operation of the firm.

Stand-alone codes of ethics should be written in plain language and should address general fiduciary concepts. They should be unencumbered by numerous detailed procedures. Codes presented in this way are the most effective in stressing to employees

Standard IV: Duties to Employers

that they are in positions of trust and must act with integrity at all times. Mingling compliance procedures in the firm's code of ethics goes against the goal of reinforcing the ethical obligations of employees.

Separating the code of ethics from compliance procedures will also reduce, if not eliminate, the legal terminology and "boilerplate" language that can make the underlying ethical principles incomprehensible to the average person. Above all, to ensure the creation of a culture of ethics and integrity rather than one that merely focuses on following the rules, the principles in the code of ethics must be stated in a way that is accessible and understandable to everyone in the firm.

Members and candidates should encourage their employers to provide their codes of ethics to clients. In this case also, a simple, straightforward code of ethics will be best understood by clients. Unencumbered by the compliance procedures, the code of ethics will be effective in conveying that the firm is committed to conducting business in an ethical manner and in the best interests of the clients.

Adequate Compliance Procedures

A supervisor complies with Standard IV(C) by identifying situations in which legal violations or violations of the Code and Standards are likely to occur and by establishing and enforcing compliance procedures to prevent such violations. Adequate compliance procedures should

- be contained in a clearly written and accessible manual that is tailored to the firm's operations,
- be drafted so that the procedures are easy to understand,
- designate a compliance officer whose authority and responsibility are clearly defined and who has the necessary resources and authority to implement the firm's compliance procedures,
- describe the hierarchy of supervision and assign duties among supervisors,
- implement a system of checks and balances,
- outline the scope of the procedures,
- outline procedures to document the monitoring and testing of compliance procedures,
- outline permissible conduct, and
- delineate procedures for reporting violations and sanctions.

Once a compliance program is in place, a supervisor should

- disseminate the contents of the program to appropriate personnel,
- periodically update procedures to ensure that the measures are adequate under the law,
- continually educate personnel regarding the compliance procedures,
- issue periodic reminders of the procedures to appropriate personnel,
- incorporate a professional conduct evaluation as part of an employee's performance review,
- review the actions of employees to ensure compliance and identify violators, and
- take the necessary steps to enforce the procedures once a violation has occurred.

Once a violation is discovered, a supervisor should

- respond promptly,

- conduct a thorough investigation of the activities to determine the scope of the wrongdoing,
- increase supervision or place appropriate limitations on the wrongdoer pending the outcome of the investigation, and
- review procedures for potential changes necessary to prevent future violations from occurring.

Implementation of Compliance Education and Training

No amount of ethics education and awareness will deter someone determined to commit fraud for personal enrichment. But the vast majority of investment professionals strive to achieve personal success with dedicated service to their clients and employers.

Regular ethics and compliance training, in conjunction with adoption of a code of ethics, is critical to investment firms seeking to establish a strong culture of integrity and to provide an environment in which employees routinely engage in ethical conduct in compliance with the law. Training and education assist individuals in both recognizing areas that are prone to ethical and legal pitfalls and identifying those circumstances and influences that can impair ethical judgment.

By implementing educational programs, supervisors can train their subordinates to put into practice what the firm's code of ethics requires. Education helps employees make the link between legal and ethical conduct and the long-term success of the business; a strong culture of compliance signals to clients and potential clients that the firm has truly embraced ethical conduct as fundamental to the firm's mission to serve its clients.

Establish an Appropriate Incentive Structure

Even if individuals want to make the right choices and follow an ethical course of conduct and are aware of the obstacles that may trip them up, they can still be influenced to act improperly by a corporate culture that embraces a "succeed at all costs" mentality, stresses results regardless of the methods used to achieve those results, and does not reward ethical behavior. Supervisors can reinforce an individual's natural desire to "do the right thing" by building a culture of integrity in the workplace.

Supervisors and firms must look closely at their incentive structure to determine whether the structure encourages profits and returns at the expense of ethically appropriate conduct. Reward structures may turn a blind eye to how desired outcomes are achieved and encourage dysfunctional or counterproductive behavior. Only when compensation and incentives are firmly tied to client interests and *how* outcomes are achieved, rather than *how much* is generated for the firm, will employees work to achieve a culture of integrity.

Application of the Standard

Example 1 (Supervising Research Activities):

Jane Mattock, senior vice president and head of the research department of H&V, Inc., a regional brokerage firm, has decided to change her recommendation for Timber Products from buy to sell. In line with H&V's procedures, she orally advises certain other H&V executives of her proposed actions before the report is prepared for publication. As a result of Mattock's conversation with Dieter Frampton, one of the H&V executives accountable to Mattock, Frampton immediately sells Timber's stock from his own account and from certain discretionary client accounts. In addition, other personnel inform certain institutional customers of the changed recommendation before it is printed and disseminated to all H&V customers who have received previous Timber reports.

Standard IV: Duties to Employers

> *Comment*: Mattock has violated Standard IV(C) by failing to reasonably and adequately supervise the actions of those accountable to her. She did not prevent or establish reasonable procedures designed to prevent dissemination of or trading on the information by those who knew of her changed recommendation. She must ensure that her firm has procedures for reviewing or recording any trading in the stock of a corporation that has been the subject of an unpublished change in recommendation. Adequate procedures would have informed the subordinates of their duties and detected sales by Frampton and selected customers.

Example 2 (Supervising Research Activities):

Deion Miller is the research director for Jamestown Investment Programs. The portfolio managers have become critical of Miller and his staff because the Jamestown portfolios do not include any stock that has been the subject of a merger or tender offer. Georgia Ginn, a member of Miller's staff, tells Miller that she has been studying a local company, Excelsior, Inc., and recommends its purchase. Ginn adds that the company has been widely rumored to be the subject of a merger study by a well-known conglomerate and discussions between them are under way. At Miller's request, Ginn prepares a memo recommending the stock. Miller passes along Ginn's memo to the portfolio managers prior to leaving for vacation, and he notes that he has not reviewed the memo. As a result of the memo, the portfolio managers buy Excelsior stock immediately. The day Miller returns to the office, he learns that Ginn's only sources for the report were her brother, who is an acquisitions analyst with Acme Industries, the "well-known conglomerate," and that the merger discussions were planned but not held.

> *Comment*: Miller violated Standard IV(C) by not exercising reasonable supervision when he disseminated the memo without checking to ensure that Ginn had a reasonable and adequate basis for her recommendations and that Ginn was not relying on material nonpublic information.

Example 3 (Supervising Trading Activities):

David Edwards, a trainee trader at Wheeler & Company, a major national brokerage firm, assists a customer in paying for the securities of Highland, Inc., by using anticipated profits from the immediate sale of the same securities. Despite the fact that Highland is not on Wheeler's recommended list, a large volume of its stock is traded through Wheeler in this manner. Roberta Ann Mason is a Wheeler vice president responsible for supervising compliance with the securities laws in the trading department. Part of her compensation from Wheeler is based on commission revenues from the trading department. Although she notices the increased trading activity, she does nothing to investigate or halt it.

> *Comment*: Mason's failure to adequately review and investigate purchase orders in Highland stock executed by Edwards and her failure to supervise the trainee's activities violate Standard IV(C). Supervisors should be especially sensitive to actual or potential conflicts between their own self-interests and their supervisory responsibilities.

Example 4 (Supervising Trading Activities and Record Keeping):

Samantha Tabbing is senior vice president and portfolio manager for Crozet, Inc., a registered investment advisory and registered broker/dealer firm. She reports to Charles Henry, the president of Crozet. Crozet serves as the investment adviser and principal underwriter for ABC and XYZ public mutual funds. The two funds' prospectuses allow Crozet to trade financial futures for the funds for the limited purpose of hedging against market risks. Henry, extremely impressed by Tabbing's performance in the past two years, directs Tabbing to act as portfolio manager for the funds. For the benefit of its employees, Crozet has also organized the Crozet Employee Profit-Sharing Plan (CEPSP), a defined contribution retirement plan. Henry assigns Tabbing to manage 20% of the assets of CEPSP. Tabbing's investment objective for her portion of CEPSP's assets is aggressive growth. Unbeknownst to Henry, Tabbing frequently places S&P 500 Index purchase and sale orders for the funds and the CEPSP without providing the futures commission merchants (FCMs) who take the orders with any prior or simultaneous designation of the account for which the trade has been placed. Frequently, neither Tabbing nor anyone else at Crozet completes an internal trade ticket to record the time an order was placed or the specific account for which the order was intended. FCMs often designate a specific account only after the trade, when Tabbing provides such designation. Crozet has no written operating procedures or compliance manual concerning its futures trading, and its compliance department does not review such trading. After observing the market's movement, Tabbing assigns to CEPSP the S&P 500 positions with more favorable execution prices and assigns positions with less favorable execution prices to the funds.

> *Comment*: Henry violated Standard IV(C) by failing to adequately supervise Tabbing with respect to her S&P 500 trading. Henry further violated Standard IV(C) by failing to establish record-keeping and reporting procedures to prevent or detect Tabbing's violations. Henry must make a reasonable effort to determine that adequate compliance procedures covering all employee trading activity are established, documented, communicated, and followed.

Example 5 (Accepting Responsibility):

Meredith Rasmussen works on a buy-side trading desk and concentrates on in-house trades for a hedge fund subsidiary managed by a team at the investment management firm. The hedge fund has been very successful and is marketed globally by the firm. From her experience as the trader for much of the activity of the fund, Rasmussen has become quite knowledgeable about the hedge fund's strategy, tactics, and performance. When a distinct break in the market occurs and many of the securities involved in the hedge fund's strategy decline markedly in value, however, Rasmussen observes that the reported performance of the hedge fund does not at all reflect this decline. From her experience, this lack of an effect is a very unlikely occurrence. She approaches the head of trading about her concern and is told that she should not ask any questions and that the fund is too big and successful and is not her concern. She is fairly sure something is not right, so she contacts the compliance officer and is again told to stay away from the hedge fund reporting issue.

> *Comment*: Rasmussen has clearly come upon an error in policies, procedures, and compliance practices within the firm's operations. According to Standard IV(C), the supervisor and the compliance officer have the responsibility to review the concerns brought forth by Rasmussen. Supervisors have the responsibility of establishing and encouraging an ethical culture in the firm. The dismissal of Rasmussen's question violates Standard IV(C) and undermines the firm's ethical operations.
>
> See also Standard I(D)–Misconduct and, for guidance on whistleblowing, Standard IV(A)–Loyalty.

Example 6 (Inadequate Procedures):

Brendan Witt, a former junior sell-side technology analyst, decided to return to school to earn an MBA. To keep his research skills and industry knowledge sharp, Witt accepted a position with On-line and Informed, an independent internet-based

Standard IV: Duties to Employers

research company. The position requires the publication of a recommendation and report on a different company every month. Initially, Witt is a regular contributor of new research and a participant in the associated discussion boards that generally have positive comments on the technology sector. Over time, his ability to manage his educational requirements and his work requirements begin to conflict with one another. Knowing a recommendation is due the next day for On-line, Witt creates a report based on a few news articles and what the conventional wisdom of the markets has deemed the "hot" security of the day.

>   *Comment*: Allowing the report submitted by Witt to be posted highlights a lack of compliance procedures by the research firm. Witt's supervisor needs to work with the management of On-line to develop an appropriate review process to ensure that all contracted analysts comply with the requirements.
>
>   See also Standard V(A)–Diligence and Reasonable Basis because it relates to Witt's responsibility for substantiating a recommendation.

Example 7 (Inadequate Supervision):

Michael Papis is the chief investment officer of his state's retirement fund. The fund has always used outside advisers for the real estate allocation, and this information is clearly presented in all fund communications. Thomas Nagle, a recognized sell-side research analyst and Papis's business school classmate, recently left the investment bank he worked for to start his own asset management firm, Accessible Real Estate. Nagle is trying to build his assets under management and contacts Papis about gaining some of the retirement fund's allocation. In the previous few years, the performance of the retirement fund's real estate investments was in line with the fund's benchmark but was not extraordinary. Papis decides to help out his old friend and also to seek better returns by moving the real estate allocation to Accessible. The only notice of the change in adviser appears in the next annual report in the listing of associated advisers.

>   *Comment*: Papis's actions highlight the need for supervision and review at all levels in an organization. His responsibilities may include the selection of external advisers, but the decision to change advisers appears arbitrary. Members and candidates should ensure that their firm has appropriate policies and procedures in place to detect inappropriate actions, such as the action taken by Papis.
>
>   See also Standard V(A)–Diligence and Reasonable Basis, Standard V(B)–Communication with Clients and Prospective Clients, and Standard VI(A)–Disclosure of Conflicts.

Example 8 (Supervising Research Activities):

Mary Burdette was recently hired by Fundamental Investment Management (FIM) as a junior auto industry analyst. Burdette is expected to expand the social media presence of the firm because she is active with various networks, including Facebook, LinkedIn, and Twitter. Although Burdette's supervisor, Joe Graf, has never used social media, he encourages Burdette to explore opportunities to increase FIM's online presence and ability to share content, communicate, and broadcast information to clients. In response to Graf's encouragement, Burdette is working on a proposal detailing the advantages of getting FIM onto Twitter in addition to launching a company Facebook page.

As part of her auto industry research for FIM, Burdette is completing a report on the financial impact of Sun Drive Auto Ltd.'s new solar technology for compact automobiles. This research report will be her first for FIM, and she believes Sun Drive's technology could revolutionize the auto industry. In her excitement, Burdette sends a quick tweet to FIM Twitter followers summarizing her "buy" recommendation for Sun Drive Auto stock.

Comment: Graf has violated Standard IV(C) by failing to reasonably supervise Burdette with respect to the contents of her tweet. He did not establish reasonable procedures to prevent the unauthorized dissemination of company research through social media networks. Graf must make sure all employees receive regular training about FIM's policies and procedures, including the appropriate business use of personal social media networks.

See Standard III(B) for additional guidance.

Example 9 (Supervising Research Activities):

Chen Wang leads the research department at YYRA Retirement Planning Specialists. Chen supervises a team of 10 analysts in a fast-paced and understaffed organization. He is responsible for coordinating the firm's approved process to review all reports before they are provided to the portfolio management team for use in rebalancing client portfolios.

One of Chen's direct reports, Huang Mei, covers the banking industry. Chen must submit the latest updates to the portfolio management team tomorrow morning. Huang has yet to submit her research report on ZYX Bank because she is uncomfortable providing a "buy" or "sell" opinion of ZYX on the basis of the completed analysis. Pressed for time and concerned that Chen will reject a "hold" recommendation, she researches various websites and blogs on the banking sector for whatever she can find on ZYX. One independent blogger provides a new interpretation of the recently reported data Huang has analyzed and concludes with a strong "sell" recommendation for ZYX. She is impressed by the originality and resourcefulness of this blogger's report.

Very late in the evening, Huang submits her report and "sell" recommendation to Chen without any reference to the independent blogger's report. Given the late time of the submission and the competence of Huang's prior work, Chen compiles this report with the recommendations from each of the other analysts and meets with the portfolio managers to discuss implementation.

Comment: Chen has violated Standard IV(C) by neglecting to reasonably and adequately follow the firm's approved review process for Huang's research report. The delayed submission and the quality of prior work do not remove Chen's requirement to uphold the designated review process. A member or candidate with supervisory responsibility must make reasonable efforts to see that appropriate procedures are established, documented, communicated to covered personnel, and followed.

STANDARD V: INVESTMENT ANALYSIS, RECOMMENDATIONS, AND ACTIONS

Standard V(A) Diligence and Reasonable Basis

Members and Candidates must:

1 Exercise diligence, independence, and thoroughness in analyzing investments, making investment recommendations, and taking investment actions.

2 Have a reasonable and adequate basis, supported by appropriate research and investigation, for any investment analysis, recommendation, or action.

Guidance

Highlights:

- *Defining Diligence and Reasonable Basis*
- *Using Secondary or Third-Party Research*
- *Using Quantitatively Oriented Research*
- *Developing Quantitatively Oriented Techniques*
- *Selecting External Advisers and Subadvisers*
- *Group Research and Decision Making*

The application of Standard V(A) depends on the investment philosophy the member, candidate, or firm is following, the role of the member or candidate in the investment decision-making process, and the support and resources provided by the member's or candidate's employer. These factors will dictate the nature of the diligence and thoroughness of the research and the level of investigation required by Standard V(A).

The requirements for issuing conclusions based on research will vary in relation to the member's or candidate's role in the investment decision-making process, but the member or candidate must make reasonable efforts to cover all pertinent issues when arriving at a recommendation. Members and candidates enhance transparency by providing or offering to provide supporting information to clients when recommending a purchase or sale or when changing a recommendation.

Defining Diligence and Reasonable Basis

Every investment decision is based on a set of facts known and understood at the time. Clients turn to members and candidates for advice and expect these advisers to have more information and knowledge than they do. This information and knowledge is the basis from which members and candidates apply their professional judgment in taking investment actions and making recommendations.

At a basic level, clients want assurance that members and candidates are putting forth the necessary effort to support the recommendations they are making. Communicating the level and thoroughness of the information reviewed before the member or candidate makes a judgment allows clients to understand the reasonableness of the recommended investment actions.

As with determining the suitability of an investment for the client, the necessary level of research and analysis will differ with the product, security, or service being offered. In providing an investment service, members and candidates typically use a variety of resources, including company reports, third-party research, and results from quantitative models. A reasonable basis is formed through a balance of these resources appropriate for the security or decision being analyzed.

The following list provides some, but definitely not all, examples of attributes to consider while forming the basis for a recommendation:

- global, regional, and country macroeconomic conditions,
- a company's operating and financial history,
- the industry's and sector's current conditions and the stage of the business cycle,
- a mutual fund's fee structure and management history,
- the output and potential limitations of quantitative models,
- the quality of the assets included in a securitization, and
- the appropriateness of selected peer-group comparisons.

Even though an investment recommendation may be well informed, downside risk remains for any investment. Members and candidates can base their decisions only on the information available at the time decisions are made. The steps taken in developing a diligent and reasonable recommendation should minimize unexpected downside events.

Using Secondary or Third-Party Research

If members and candidates rely on secondary or third-party research, they must make reasonable and diligent efforts to determine whether such research is sound. Secondary research is defined as research conducted by someone else in the member's or candidate's firm. Third-party research is research conducted by entities outside the member's or candidate's firm, such as a brokerage firm, bank, or research firm. If a member or candidate has reason to suspect that either secondary or third-party research or information comes from a source that lacks a sound basis, the member or candidate must not rely on that information.

Members and candidates should make reasonable enquiries into the source and accuracy of all data used in completing their investment analysis and recommendations. The sources of the information and data will influence the level of the review a member or candidate must undertake. Information and data taken from internet sources, such as personal blogs, independent research aggregation websites, or social media websites, likely require a greater level of review than information from more established research organizations.

Criteria that a member or candidate can use in forming an opinion on whether research is sound include the following:

- assumptions used,
- rigor of the analysis performed,
- date/timeliness of the research, and
- evaluation of the objectivity and independence of the recommendations.

A member or candidate may rely on others in his or her firm to determine whether secondary or third-party research is sound and use the information in good faith unless the member or candidate has reason to question its validity or the processes and procedures used by those responsible for the research. For example, a portfolio manager may not have a choice of a data source because the firm's senior managers

Standard V: Investment Analysis, Recommendations, and Actions

conducted due diligence to determine which vendor would provide services; the member or candidate can use the information in good faith assuming the due diligence process was deemed adequate.

A member or candidate should verify that the firm has a policy about the timely and consistent review of approved research providers to ensure that the quality of the research continues to meet the necessary standards. If such a policy is not in place at the firm, the member or candidate should encourage the development and adoption of a formal review practice.

Using Quantitatively Oriented Research

Standard V(A) applies to the rapidly expanding use of quantitatively oriented research models and processes, such as computer-generated modeling, screening, and ranking of investment securities; the creation or valuation of derivative instruments; and quantitative portfolio construction techniques. These models and processes are being used for much more than the back testing of investment strategies, especially with continually advancing technology and techniques. The continued broad development of quantitative methods and models is an important part of capital market developments.

Members and candidates need to have an understanding of the parameters used in models and quantitative research that are incorporated into their investment recommendations. Although they are not required to become experts in every technical aspect of the models, they must understand the assumptions and limitations inherent in any model and how the results were used in the decision-making process.

The reliance on and potential limitations of financial models became clear through the investment crisis that unfolded in 2007 and 2008. In some cases, the financial models used to value specific securities and related derivative products did not adequately demonstrate the level of associated risks. Members and candidates should make reasonable efforts to test the output of investment models and other pre-programed analytical tools they use. Such validation should occur before incorporating the process into their methods, models, or analyses.

Although not every model can test for every factor or outcome, members and candidates should ensure that their analyses incorporate a broad range of assumptions sufficient to capture the underlying characteristics of investments. The omission from the analysis of potentially negative outcomes or of levels of risk outside the norm may misrepresent the true economic value of an investment. The possible scenarios for analysis should include factors that are likely to have a substantial influence on the investment value and may include extremely positive and negative scenarios.

Developing Quantitatively Oriented Techniques

Individuals who create new quantitative models and services must exhibit a higher level of diligence in reviewing new products than the individuals who ultimately use the analytical output. Members and candidates involved in the development and oversight of quantitatively oriented models, methods, and algorithms must understand the technical aspects of the products they provide to clients. A thorough testing of the model and resulting analysis should be completed prior to product distribution.

Members and candidates need to consider the source and time horizon of the data used as inputs in financial models. The information from many commercially available databases may not effectively incorporate both positive and negative market cycles. In the development of a recommendation, the member or candidate may need to test the models by using volatility and performance expectations that represent scenarios outside the observable databases. In reviewing the computer models or the resulting output, members and candidates need to pay particular attention to the assumptions used in the analysis and the rigor of the analysis to ensure that the model incorporates a wide range of possible input expectations, including negative market events.

Selecting External Advisers and Subadvisers

Financial instruments and asset allocation techniques continue to develop and evolve. This progression has led to the use of specialized managers to invest in specific asset classes or diversification strategies that complement a firm's in-house expertise. Standard V(A) applies to the level of review necessary in selecting an external adviser or subadviser to manage a specifically mandated allocation. Members and candidates must review managers as diligently as they review individual funds and securities.

Members and candidates who are directly involved with the use of external advisers need to ensure that their firms have standardized criteria for reviewing these selected external advisers and managers. Such criteria would include, but would not be limited to, the following:

- reviewing the adviser's established code of ethics,
- understanding the adviser's compliance and internal control procedures,
- assessing the quality of the published return information, and
- reviewing the adviser's investment process and adherence to its stated strategy.

Codes, standards, and guides to best practice published by CFA Institute provide members and candidates with examples of acceptable practices for external advisers and advice in selecting a new adviser. The following guides are available at the CFA Institute website (www.cfainstitute.org): Asset Manager Code of Professional Conduct, Global Investment Performance Standards, and Model Request for Proposal (for equity, credit, or real estate managers).

Group Research and Decision Making

Commonly, members and candidates are part of a group or team that is collectively responsible for producing investment analysis or research. The conclusions or recommendations of the group report represent the consensus of the group and are not necessarily the views of the member or candidate, even though the name of the member or candidate is included on the report. In some instances, a member or candidate will not agree with the view of the group. If, however, the member or candidate believes that the consensus opinion has a reasonable and adequate basis and is independent and objective, the member or candidate need not decline to be identified with the report. If the member or candidate is confident in the process, the member or candidate does not need to dissociate from the report even if it does not reflect his or her opinion.

Recommended Procedures for Compliance

Members and candidates should encourage their firms to consider the following policies and procedures to support the principles of Standard V(A):

- Establish a policy requiring that research reports, credit ratings, and investment recommendations have a basis that can be substantiated as reasonable and adequate. An individual employee (a supervisory analyst) or a group of employees (a review committee) should be appointed to review and approve such items prior to external circulation to determine whether the criteria established in the policy have been met.

- Develop detailed, written guidance for analysts (research, investment, or credit), supervisory analysts, and review committees that establishes the due diligence procedures for judging whether a particular recommendation has a reasonable and adequate basis.

Standard V: Investment Analysis, Recommendations, and Actions

- Develop measurable criteria for assessing the quality of research, the reasonableness and adequacy of the basis for any recommendation or rating, and the accuracy of recommendations over time. In some cases, firms may consider implementing compensation arrangements that depend on these measurable criteria and that are applied consistently to all related analysts.
- Develop detailed, written guidance that establishes minimum levels of scenario testing of all computer-based models used in developing, rating, and evaluating financial instruments. The policy should contain criteria related to the breadth of the scenarios tested, the accuracy of the output over time, and the analysis of cash flow sensitivity to inputs.
- Develop measurable criteria for assessing outside providers, including the quality of information being provided, the reasonableness and adequacy of the provider's collection practices, and the accuracy of the information over time. The established policy should outline how often the provider's products are reviewed.
- Adopt a standardized set of criteria for evaluating the adequacy of external advisers. The policy should include how often and on what basis the allocation of funds to the adviser will be reviewed.

Application of the Standard

Example 1 (Sufficient Due Diligence):

Helen Hawke manages the corporate finance department of Sarkozi Securities, Ltd. The firm is anticipating that the government will soon close a tax loophole that currently allows oil-and-gas exploration companies to pass on drilling expenses to holders of a certain class of shares. Because market demand for this tax-advantaged class of stock is currently high, Sarkozi convinces several companies to undertake new equity financings at once, before the loophole closes. Time is of the essence, but Sarkozi lacks sufficient resources to conduct adequate research on all the prospective issuing companies. Hawke decides to estimate the IPO prices on the basis of the relative size of each company and to justify the pricing later when her staff has time.

> *Comment*: Sarkozi should have taken on only the work that it could adequately handle. By categorizing the issuers by general size, Hawke has bypassed researching all the other relevant aspects that should be considered when pricing new issues and thus has not performed sufficient due diligence. Such an omission can result in investors purchasing shares at prices that have no actual basis. Hawke has violated Standard V(A).

Example 2 (Sufficient Scenario Testing):

Babu Dhaliwal works for Heinrich Brokerage in the corporate finance group. He has just persuaded Feggans Resources, Ltd., to allow his firm to do a secondary equity financing at Feggans Resources' current stock price. Because the stock has been trading at higher multiples than similar companies with equivalent production, Dhaliwal presses the Feggans Resources managers to project what would be the maximum production they could achieve in an optimal scenario. Based on these numbers, he is able to justify the price his firm will be asking for the secondary issue. During a sales pitch to the brokers, Dhaliwal then uses these numbers as the base-case production levels that Feggans Resources will achieve.

> *Comment*: When presenting information to the brokers, Dhaliwal should have given a range of production scenarios and the probability of Feggans Resources achieving each level. By giving the maximum production level

as the likely level of production, he has misrepresented the chances of achieving that production level and seriously misled the brokers. Dhaliwal has violated Standard V(A).

Example 3 (Developing a Reasonable Basis):

Brendan Witt, a former junior sell-side technology analyst, decided to return to school to earn an MBA. To keep his research skills and industry knowledge sharp, Witt accepted a position with On-line and Informed, an independent internet-based research company. The position requires the publication of a recommendation and report on a different company every month. Initially, Witt is a regular contributor of new research and a participant in the associated discussion boards that generally have positive comments on the technology sector. Over time, his ability to manage his educational requirements and his work requirements begin to conflict with one another. Knowing a recommendation is due the next day for On-line, Witt creates a report based on a few news articles and what the conventional wisdom of the markets has deemed the "hot" security of the day.

> *Comment*: Witt's knowledge of and exuberance for technology stocks, a few news articles, and the conventional wisdom of the markets do not constitute, without more information, a reasonable and adequate basis for a stock recommendation that is supported by appropriate research and investigation. Therefore, Witt has violated Standard V(A).
>
> See also Standard IV(C)–Responsibilities of Supervisors because it relates to the firm's inadequate procedures.

Example 4 (Timely Client Updates):

Kristen Chandler is an investment consultant in the London office of Dalton Securities, a major global investment consultant firm. One of her UK pension funds has decided to appoint a specialist US equity manager. Dalton's global manager of research relies on local consultants to cover managers within their regions and, after conducting thorough due diligence, puts their views and ratings in Dalton's manager database. Chandler accesses Dalton's global manager research database and conducts a screen of all US equity managers on the basis of a match with the client's desired philosophy/style, performance, and tracking-error targets. She selects the five managers that meet these criteria and puts them in a briefing report that is delivered to the client 10 days later. Between the time of Chandler's database search and the delivery of the report to the client, Chandler is told that Dalton has updated the database with the information that one of the firms that Chandler has recommended for consideration lost its chief investment officer, the head of its US equity research, and the majority of its portfolio managers on the US equity product—all of whom have left to establish their own firm. Chandler does not revise her report with this updated information.

> *Comment*: Chandler has failed to satisfy the requirement of Standard V(A). Although Dalton updated the manager ratings to reflect the personnel turnover at one of the firms, Chandler did not update her report to reflect the new information.

Example 5 (Group Research Opinions):

Evelyn Mastakis is a junior analyst who has been asked by her firm to write a research report predicting the expected interest rate for residential mortgages over the next six months. Mastakis submits her report to the fixed-income investment committee of her firm for review, as required by firm procedures. Although some committee members support Mastakis's conclusion, the majority of the committee disagrees with

Standard V: Investment Analysis, Recommendations, and Actions

her conclusion, and the report is significantly changed to indicate that interest rates are likely to increase more than originally predicted by Mastakis. Should Mastakis ask that her name be taken off the report when it is disseminated?

> *Comment*: The results of research are not always clear, and different people may have different opinions based on the same factual evidence. In this case, the committee may have valid reasons for issuing a report that differs from the analyst's original research. The firm can issue a report that is different from the original report of an analyst as long as there is a reasonable and adequate basis for its conclusions.
>
> Generally, analysts must write research reports that reflect their own opinion and can ask the firm not to put their name on reports that ultimately differ from that opinion. When the work is a group effort, however, not all members of the team may agree with all aspects of the report. Ultimately, members and candidates can ask to have their names removed from the report, but if they are satisfied that the process has produced results or conclusions that have a reasonable and adequate basis, members and candidates do not have to dissociate from the report even when they do not agree with its contents. If Mastakis is confident in the process, she does not need to dissociate from the report even if it does not reflect her opinion.

Example 6 (Reliance on Third-Party Research):

Gary McDermott runs a two-person investment management firm. McDermott's firm subscribes to a service from a large investment research firm that provides research reports. McDermott's firm makes investment recommendations on the basis of these reports.

> *Comment*: Members and candidates can rely on third-party research but must make reasonable and diligent efforts to determine that such research is sound. If McDermott undertakes due diligence efforts on a regular basis to ensure that the research produced by the large firm is objective and reasonably based, McDermott can rely on that research when making investment recommendations to clients.

Example 7 (Due Diligence in Submanager Selection):

Paul Ostrowski's business has grown significantly over the past couple of years, and some clients want to diversify internationally. Ostrowski decides to find a submanager to handle the expected international investments. Because this will be his first subadviser, Ostrowski uses the CFA Institute model "request for proposal" to design a questionnaire for his search. By his deadline, he receives seven completed questionnaires from a variety of domestic and international firms trying to gain his business. Ostrowski reviews all the applications in detail and decides to select the firm that charges the lowest fees because doing so will have the least impact on his firm's bottom line.

> *Comment*: The selection of an external adviser or subadviser should be based on a full and complete review of the adviser's services, performance history, and cost structure. In basing the decision on the fee structure alone, Ostrowski may be violating Standard V(A).
>
> See also Standard III(C)–Suitability because it relates to the ability of the selected adviser to meet the needs of the clients.

Example 8 (Sufficient Due Diligence):

Michael Papis is the chief investment officer of his state's retirement fund. The fund has always used outside advisers for the real estate allocation, and this information is clearly presented in all fund communications. Thomas Nagle, a recognized sell-side research analyst and Papis's business school classmate, recently left the investment bank he worked for to start his own asset management firm, Accessible Real Estate. Nagle is trying to build his assets under management and contacts Papis about gaining some of the retirement fund's allocation. In the previous few years, the performance of the retirement fund's real estate investments was in line with the fund's benchmark but was not extraordinary. Papis decides to help out his old friend and also to seek better returns by moving the real estate allocation to Accessible. The only notice of the change in adviser appears in the next annual report in the listing of associated advisers.

> *Comment*: Papis violated Standard V(A). His responsibilities may include the selection of the external advisers, but the decision to change advisers appears to have been arbitrary. If Papis was dissatisfied with the current real estate adviser, he should have conducted a proper solicitation to select the most appropriate adviser.
> See also Standard IV(C)–Responsibilities of Supervisors, Standard V(B)–Communication with Clients and Prospective Clients, and Standard VI(A)–Disclosure of Conflicts.

Example 9 (Sufficient Due Diligence):

Andre Shrub owns and operates Conduit, an investment advisory firm. Prior to opening Conduit, Shrub was an account manager with Elite Investment, a hedge fund managed by his good friend Adam Reed. To attract clients to a new Conduit fund, Shrub offers lower-than-normal management fees. He can do so because the fund consists of two top-performing funds managed by Reed. Given his personal friendship with Reed and the prior performance record of these two funds, Shrub believes this new fund is a winning combination for all parties. Clients quickly invest with Conduit to gain access to the Elite funds. No one is turned away because Conduit is seeking to expand its assets under management.

> *Comment*: Shrub violated Standard V(A) by not conducting a thorough analysis of the funds managed by Reed before developing the new Conduit fund. Shrub's reliance on his personal relationship with Reed and his prior knowledge of Elite are insufficient justification for the investments. The funds may be appropriately considered, but a full review of their operating procedures, reporting practices, and transparency are some elements of the necessary due diligence.
> See also Standard III(C)–Suitability.

Example 10 (Sufficient Due Diligence):

Bob Thompson has been doing research for the portfolio manager of the fixed-income department. His assignment is to do sensitivity analysis on securitized subprime mortgages. He has discussed with the manager possible scenarios to use to calculate expected returns. A key assumption in such calculations is housing price appreciation (HPA) because it drives "prepays" (prepayments of mortgages) and losses. Thompson is concerned with the significant appreciation experienced over the previous five years as a result of the increased availability of funds from subprime mortgages. Thompson insists that the analysis should include a scenario run with –10% for Year 1, –5% for Year 2, and then (to project a worst-case scenario) 0% for Years 3 through 5. The manager replies that these assumptions are too dire because there has never been a time in their available database when HPA was negative.

Standard V: Investment Analysis, Recommendations, and Actions

Thompson conducts his research to better understand the risks inherent in these securities and evaluates these securities in the worst-case scenario, a less likely but possible environment. Based on the results of the enhanced scenarios, Thompson does not recommend the purchase of the securitization. Against the general market trends, the manager follows Thompson's recommendation and does not invest. The following year, the housing market collapses. In avoiding the subprime investments, the manager's portfolio outperforms its peer group that year.

> *Comment*: Thompson's actions in running the scenario test with inputs beyond the historical trends available in the firm's databases adhere to the principles of Standard V(A). His concerns over recent trends provide a sound basis for further analysis. Thompson understands the limitations of his model, when combined with the limited available historical information, to accurately predict the performance of the funds if market conditions change negatively.
> See also Standard I(B)–Independence and Objectivity.

Example 11 (Use of Quantitatively Oriented Models):

Espacia Liakos works in sales for Hellenica Securities, a firm specializing in developing intricate derivative strategies to profit from particular views on market expectations. One of her clients is Eugenie Carapalis, who has become convinced that commodity prices will become more volatile over the coming months. Carapalis asks Liakos to quickly engineer a strategy that will benefit from this expectation. Liakos turns to Hellenica's modeling group to fulfill this request. Because of the tight deadline, the modeling group outsources parts of the work to several trusted third parties. Liakos implements the disparate components of the strategy as the firms complete them.

Within a month, Carapalis is proven correct: Volatility across a range of commodities increases sharply. But her derivatives position with Hellenica returns huge losses, and the losses increase daily. Liakos investigates and realizes that although each of the various components of the strategy had been validated, they had never been evaluated as an integrated whole. In extreme conditions, portions of the model worked at cross-purposes with other portions, causing the overall strategy to fail dramatically.

> *Comment*: Liakos violated Standard V(A). Members and candidates must understand the statistical significance of the results of the models they recommend and must be able to explain them to clients. Liakos did not take adequate care to ensure a thorough review of the whole model; its components were evaluated only individually. Because Carapalis clearly intended to implement the strategy as a whole rather than as separate parts, Liakos should have tested how the components of the strategy interacted as well as how they performed individually.

Example 12 (Successful Due Diligence/Failed Investment):

Alton Newbury is an investment adviser to high-net-worth clients. A client with an aggressive risk profile in his investment policy statement asks about investing in the Top Shelf hedge fund. This fund, based in Calgary, Alberta, Canada, has reported 20% returns for the first three years. The fund prospectus states that its strategy involves long and short positions in the energy sector and extensive leverage. Based on his analysis of the fund's track record, the principals involved in managing the fund, the fees charged, and the fund's risk profile, Newbury recommends the fund to the client and secures a position in it. The next week, the fund announces that it has suffered a loss of 60% of its value and is suspending operations and redemptions until after a regulatory review. Newbury's client calls him in a panic and asks for an explanation.

Comment: Newbury's actions were consistent with Standard V(A). Analysis of an investment that results in a reasonable basis for recommendation does not guarantee that the investment has no downside risk. Newbury should discuss the analysis process with the client while reminding him or her that past performance does not lead to guaranteed future gains and that losses in an aggressive investment portfolio should be expected.

Example 13 (Quantitative Model Diligence):

Barry Cannon is the lead quantitative analyst at CityCenter Hedge Fund. He is responsible for the development, maintenance, and enhancement of the proprietary models the fund uses to manage its investors' assets. Cannon reads several high-level mathematical publications and blogs to stay informed of current developments. One blog, run by Expert CFA, presents some intriguing research that may benefit one of CityCenter's current models. Cannon is under pressure from firm executives to improve the model's predictive abilities, and he incorporates the factors discussed in the online research. The updated output recommends several new investments to the fund's portfolio managers.

Comment: Cannon has violated Standard V(A) by failing to have a reasonable basis for the new recommendations made to the portfolio managers. He needed to diligently research the effect of incorporating the new factors before offering the output recommendations. Cannon may use the blog for ideas, but it is his responsibility to determine the effect on the firm's proprietary models.

See Standard VII(B) regarding the violation by "Expert CFA" in the use of the CFA designation.

Example 14 (Selecting a Service Provider):

Ellen Smith is a performance analyst at Artic Global Advisors, a firm that manages global equity mandates for institutional clients. She was asked by her supervisor to review five new performance attribution systems and recommend one that would more appropriately explain the firm's investment strategy to clients. On the list was a system she recalled learning about when visiting an exhibitor booth at a recent conference. The system is highly quantitative and something of a "black box" in how it calculates the attribution values. Smith recommended this option without researching the others because the sheer complexity of the process was sure to impress the clients.

Comment: Smith's actions do not demonstrate a sufficient level of diligence in reviewing this product to make a recommendation for selecting the service. Besides not reviewing or considering the other four potential systems, she did not determine whether the "black box" attribution process aligns with the investment practices of the firm, including its investments in different countries and currencies. Smith must review and understand the process of any software or system before recommending its use as the firm's attribution system.

Example 15 (Subadviser Selection):

Craig Jackson is working for Adams Partners, Inc., and has been assigned to select a hedge fund subadviser to improve the diversification of the firm's large fund-of-funds product. The allocation must be in place before the start of the next quarter. Jackson uses a consultant database to find a list of suitable firms that claim compliance with the GIPS standards. He calls more than 20 firms on the list to confirm their potential

Standard V: Investment Analysis, Recommendations, and Actions

interest and to determine their most recent quarterly and annual total return values. Because of the short turnaround, Jackson recommends the firm with the greatest total return values for selection.

> *Comment*: By considering only performance and GIPS compliance, Jackson has not conducted sufficient review of potential firms to satisfy the requirements of Standard V(A). A thorough investigation of the firms and their operations should be conducted to ensure that their addition would increase the diversity of clients' portfolios and that they are suitable for the fund-of-funds product.

Example 16 (Manager Selection):

Timothy Green works for Peach Asset Management, where he creates proprietary models that analyze data from the firm request for proposal questionnaires to identify managers for possible inclusion in the firm's fund-of-funds investment platform. Various criteria must be met to be accepted to the platform. Because of the number of respondents to the questionnaires, Green uses only the data submitted to make a recommendation for adding a new manager.

> *Comment*: By failing to conduct any additional outside review of the information to verify what was submitted through the request for proposal, Green has likely not satisfied the requirements of Standard V(A). The amount of information requested from outside managers varies among firms. Although the requested information may be comprehensive, Green should ensure sufficient effort is undertaken to verify the submitted information before recommending a firm for inclusion. This requires that he go beyond the information provided by the manager on the request for proposal questionnaire and may include interviews with interested managers, reviews of regulatory filings, and discussions with the managers' custodian or auditor.

Example 17 (Technical Model Requirements):

Jérôme Dupont works for the credit research group of XYZ Asset Management, where he is in charge of developing and updating credit risk models. In order to perform accurately, his models need to be regularly updated with the latest market data.

Dupont does not interact with or manage money for any of the firm's clients. He is in contact with the firm's US corporate bond fund manager, John Smith, who has only very superficial knowledge of the model and who from time to time asks very basic questions regarding the output recommendations. Smith does not consult Dupont with respect to finalizing his clients' investment strategies.

Dupont's recently assigned objective is to develop a new emerging market corporate credit risk model. The firm is planning to expand into emerging credit, and the development of such a model is a critical step in this process. Because Smith seems to follow the model's recommendations without much concern for its quality as he develops his clients' investment strategies, Dupont decides to focus his time on the development of the new emerging market model and neglects to update the US model.

After several months without regular updates, Dupont's diagnostic statistics start to show alarming signs with respect to the quality of the US credit model. Instead of conducting the long and complicated data update, Dupont introduces new codes into his model with some limited new data as a quick "fix." He thinks this change will address the issue without needing to complete the full data update, so he continues working on the new emerging market model.

Several months following the quick "fix," another set of diagnostic statistics reveals nonsensical results and Dupont realizes that his earlier change contained an error. He quickly corrects the error and alerts Smith. Smith realizes that some of the prior trades he performed were due to erroneous model results. Smith rebalances the portfolio to remove the securities purchased on the basis of the questionable results without reporting the issue to anyone else.

> *Comment*: Smith violated standard V(A) because exercising "diligence, independence, and thoroughness in analyzing investments, making investment recommendations, and taking investment actions" means that members and candidates must understand the technical aspects of the products they provide to clients. Smith does not understand the model he is relying on to manage money. Members and candidates should also make reasonable enquiries into the source and accuracy of all data used in completing their investment analysis and recommendations.
>
> Dupont violated V(A) even if he does not trade securities or make investment decisions. Dupont's models give investment recommendations, and Dupont is accountable for the quality of those recommendations. Members and candidates should make reasonable efforts to test the output of pre-programed analytical tools they use. Such validation should occur before incorporating the tools into their decision-making process.
>
> See also Standard V(B)–Communication with Clients and Prospective Clients.

Standard V(B) Communication with Clients and Prospective Clients

Members and Candidates must:

1. Disclose to clients and prospective clients the basic format and general principles of the investment processes they use to analyze investments, select securities, and construct portfolios and must promptly disclose any changes that might materially affect those processes.

2. Disclose to clients and prospective clients significant limitations and risks associated with the investment process.

3. Use reasonable judgment in identifying which factors are important to their investment analyses, recommendations, or actions and include those factors in communications with clients and prospective clients.

4. Distinguish between fact and opinion in the presentation of investment analyses and recommendations.

Guidance

Highlights:

- *Informing Clients of the Investment Process*
- *Different Forms of Communication*
- *Identifying Risk and Limitations*
- *Report Presentation*
- *Distinction between Facts and Opinions in Reports*

Standard V: Investment Analysis, Recommendations, and Actions

Standard V(B) addresses member and candidate conduct with respect to communicating with clients. Developing and maintaining clear, frequent, and thorough communication practices is critical to providing high-quality financial services to clients. When clients understand the information communicated to them, they also can understand exactly how members and candidates are acting on their behalf, which gives clients the opportunity to make well-informed decisions about their investments. Such understanding can be accomplished only through clear communication.

Standard V(B) states that members and candidates should communicate in a recommendation the factors that were instrumental in making the investment recommendation. A critical part of this requirement is to distinguish clearly between opinions and facts. In preparing a research report, the member or candidate must present the basic characteristics of the security(ies) being analyzed, which will allow the reader to evaluate the report and incorporate information the reader deems relevant to his or her investment decision-making process.

Similarly, in preparing a recommendation about, for example, an asset allocation strategy, alternative investment vehicle, or structured investment product, the member or candidate should include factors that are relevant to the asset classes that are being discussed. Follow-up communication of significant changes in the risk characteristics of a security or asset strategy is required. Providing regular updates to any changes in the risk characteristics is recommended.

Informing Clients of the Investment Process

Members and candidates must adequately describe to clients and prospective clients the manner in which they conduct the investment decision-making process. Such disclosure should address factors that have positive and negative influences on the recommendations, including significant risks and limitations of the investment process used. The member or candidate must keep clients and other interested parties informed on an ongoing basis about changes to the investment process, especially newly identified significant risks and limitations. Only by thoroughly understanding the nature of the investment product or service can a client determine whether changes to that product or service could materially affect his or her investment objectives.

Understanding the basic characteristics of an investment is of great importance in judging the suitability of that investment on a standalone basis, but it is especially important in determining the impact each investment will have on the characteristics of a portfolio. Although the risk and return characteristics of a common stock might seem to be essentially the same for any investor when the stock is viewed in isolation, the effects of those characteristics greatly depend on the other investments held. For instance, if the particular stock will represent 90% of an individual's investments, the stock's importance in the portfolio is vastly different from what it would be to an investor with a highly diversified portfolio for whom the stock will represent only 2% of the holdings.

A firm's investment policy may include the use of outside advisers to manage various portions of clients' assets under management. Members and candidates should inform the clients about the specialization or diversification expertise provided by the external adviser(s). This information allows clients to understand the full mix of products and strategies being applied that may affect their investment objectives.

Different Forms of Communication

For purposes of Standard V(B), communication is not confined to a written report of the type traditionally generated by an analyst researching a security, company, or industry. A presentation of information can be made via any means of communication, including in-person recommendation or description, telephone conversation, media broadcast, or transmission by computer (e.g., on the internet).

Computer and mobile device communications have rapidly evolved over the past few years. Members and candidates using any social media service to communicate business information must be diligent in their efforts to avoid unintended problems because these services may not be available to all clients. When providing information to clients through new technologies, members and candidates should take reasonable steps to ensure that such delivery would treat all clients fairly and, if necessary, be considered publicly disseminated.

The nature of client communications is highly diverse—from one word ("buy" or "sell") to in-depth reports of more than 100 pages. A communication may contain a general recommendation about the market, asset allocations, or classes of investments (e.g., stocks, bonds, real estate) or may relate to a specific security. If recommendations are contained in capsule form (such as a recommended stock list), members and candidates should notify clients that additional information and analyses are available from the producer of the report.

Identifying Risks and Limitations

Members and candidates must outline to clients and prospective clients significant risks and limitations of the analysis contained in their investment products or recommendations. The type and nature of significant risks will depend on the investment process that members and candidates are following and on the personal circumstances of the client. In general, the use of leverage constitutes a significant risk and should be disclosed.

Members and candidates must adequately disclose the general market-related risks and the risks associated with the use of complex financial instruments that are deemed significant. Other types of risks that members and candidates may consider disclosing include, but are not limited to, counterparty risk, country risk, sector or industry risk, security-specific risk, and credit risk.

Investment securities and vehicles may have limiting factors that influence a client's or potential client's investment decision. Members and candidates must report to clients and prospective clients the existence of limitations significant to the decision-making process. Examples of such factors and attributes include, but are not limited to, investment liquidity and capacity. Liquidity is the ability to liquidate an investment on a timely basis at a reasonable cost. Capacity is the investment amount beyond which returns will be negatively affected by new investments.

The appropriateness of risk disclosure should be assessed on the basis of what was known at the time the investment action was taken (often called an *ex ante* basis). Members and candidates must disclose significant risks known to them at the time of the disclosure. Members and candidates cannot be expected to disclose risks they are unaware of at the time recommendations or investment actions are made. In assessing compliance with Standard V(B), it is important to establish knowledge of a purported significant risk or limitation. A one-time investment loss that occurs after the disclosure does not constitute a pertinent factor in assessing whether significant risks and limitations were properly disclosed. Having no knowledge of a risk or limitation that subsequently triggers a loss may reveal a deficiency in the diligence and reasonable basis of the research of the member or candidate but may not reveal a breach of Standard V(B).

Report Presentation

Once the analytical process has been completed, the member or candidate who prepares the report must include those elements that are important to the analysis and conclusions of the report so that the reader can follow and challenge the report's reasoning. A report writer who has done adequate investigation may emphasize certain areas, touch briefly on others, and omit certain aspects deemed unimportant. For instance,

Standard V: Investment Analysis, Recommendations, and Actions

a report may dwell on a quarterly earnings release or new-product introduction and omit other matters as long as the analyst clearly stipulates the limits to the scope of the report.

Investment advice based on quantitative research and analysis must be supported by readily available reference material and should be applied in a manner consistent with previously applied methodology. If changes in methodology are made, they should be highlighted.

Distinction between Facts and Opinions in Reports

Standard V(B) requires that opinion be separated from fact. Violations often occur when reports fail to separate the past from the future by not indicating that earnings estimates, changes in the outlook for dividends, or future market price information are *opinions* subject to future circumstances.

In the case of complex quantitative analyses, members and candidates must clearly separate fact from statistical conjecture and should identify the known limitations of an analysis. Members and candidates may violate Standard V(B) by failing to identify the limits of statistically developed projections because such omission leaves readers unaware of the limits of the published projections.

Members and candidates should explicitly discuss with clients and prospective clients the assumptions used in the investment models and processes to generate the analysis. Caution should be used in promoting the perceived accuracy of any model or process to clients because the ultimate output is merely an estimate of future results and not a certainty.

Recommended Procedures for Compliance

Because the selection of relevant factors is an analytical skill, determination of whether a member or candidate has used reasonable judgment in excluding and including information in research reports depends heavily on case-by-case review rather than a specific checklist.

Members and candidates should encourage their firms to have a rigorous methodology for reviewing research that is created for publication and dissemination to clients.

To assist in the after-the-fact review of a report, the member or candidate must maintain records indicating the nature of the research and should, if asked, be able to supply additional information to the client (or any user of the report) covering factors not included in the report.

Application of the Standard

Example 1 (Sufficient Disclosure of Investment System):

Sarah Williamson, director of marketing for Country Technicians, Inc., is convinced that she has found the perfect formula for increasing Country Technicians' income and diversifying its product base. Williamson plans to build on Country Technicians' reputation as a leading money manager by marketing an exclusive and expensive investment advice letter to high-net-worth individuals. One hitch in the plan is the complexity of Country Technicians' investment system—a combination of technical trading rules (based on historical price and volume fluctuations) and portfolio construction rules designed to minimize risk. To simplify the newsletter, she decides to include only each week's top five "buy" and "sell" recommendations and to leave out details of the valuation models and the portfolio structuring scheme.

> *Comment*: Williamson's plans for the newsletter violate Standard V(B). Williamson need not describe the investment system in detail in order to implement the advice effectively, but she must inform clients of Country

Technicians' basic process and logic. Without understanding the basis for a recommendation, clients cannot possibly understand its limitations or its inherent risks.

Example 2 (Providing Opinions as Facts):

Richard Dox is a mining analyst for East Bank Securities. He has just finished his report on Boisy Bay Minerals. Included in his report is his own assessment of the geological extent of mineral reserves likely to be found on the company's land. Dox completed this calculation on the basis of the core samples from the company's latest drilling. According to Dox's calculations, the company has more than 500,000 ounces of gold on the property. Dox concludes his research report as follows: "Based on the fact that the company has 500,000 ounces of gold to be mined, I recommend a strong BUY."

> *Comment*: If Dox issues the report as written, he will violate Standard V(B). His calculation of the total gold reserves for the property based on the company's recent sample drilling is a quantitative opinion, not a fact. Opinion must be distinguished from fact in research reports.

Example 3 (Proper Description of a Security):

Olivia Thomas, an analyst at Government Brokers, Inc., which is a brokerage firm specializing in government bond trading, has produced a report that describes an investment strategy designed to benefit from an expected decline in US interest rates. The firm's derivative products group has designed a structured product that will allow the firm's clients to benefit from this strategy. Thomas's report describing the strategy indicates that high returns are possible if various scenarios for declining interest rates are assumed. Citing the proprietary nature of the structured product underlying the strategy, the report does not describe in detail how the firm is able to offer such returns or the related risks in the scenarios, nor does the report address the likely returns of the strategy if, contrary to expectations, interest rates rise.

> *Comment*: Thomas has violated Standard V(B) because her report fails to describe properly the basic characteristics of the actual and implied risks of the investment strategy, including how the structure was created and the degree to which leverage was embedded in the structure. The report should include a balanced discussion of how the strategy would perform in the case of rising as well as falling interest rates, preferably illustrating how the strategies might be expected to perform in the event of a reasonable variety of interest rate and credit risk–spread scenarios. If liquidity issues are relevant with regard to the valuation of either the derivatives or the underlying securities, provisions the firm has made to address those risks should also be disclosed.

Example 4 (Notification of Fund Mandate Change):

May & Associates is an aggressive growth manager that has represented itself since its inception as a specialist at investing in small-cap US stocks. One of May's selection criteria is a maximum capitalization of US$250 million for any given company. After a string of successful years of superior performance relative to its peers, May has expanded its client base significantly, to the point at which assets under management now exceed US$3 billion. For liquidity purposes, May's chief investment officer (CIO) decides to lift the maximum permissible market-cap ceiling to US$500 million and change the firm's sales and marketing literature accordingly to inform prospective clients and third-party consultants.

Comment: Although May's CIO is correct about informing potentially interested parties as to the change in investment process, he must also notify May's existing clients. Among the latter group might be a number of clients who not only retained May as a small-cap manager but also retained mid-cap and large-cap specialists in a multiple-manager approach. Such clients could regard May's change of criteria as a style change that distorts their overall asset allocations.

Example 5 (Notification of Fund Mandate Change):

Rather than lifting the ceiling for its universe from US$250 million to US$500 million, May & Associates extends its small-cap universe to include a number of non-US companies.

Comment: Standard V(B) requires that May's CIO advise May's clients of this change because the firm may have been retained by some clients specifically for its prowess at investing in US small-cap stocks. Other changes that require client notification are introducing derivatives to emulate a certain market sector or relaxing various other constraints, such as portfolio beta. In all such cases, members and candidates must disclose changes to all interested parties.

Example 6 (Notification of Changes to the Investment Process):

RJZ Capital Management is an active value-style equity manager that selects stocks by using a combination of four multifactor models. The firm has found favorable results when back testing the most recent 10 years of available market data in a new dividend discount model (DDM) designed by the firm. This model is based on projected inflation rates, earnings growth rates, and interest rates. The president of RJZ decides to replace its simple model that uses price to trailing 12-month earnings with the new DDM.

Comment: Because the introduction of a new and different valuation model represents a material change in the investment process, RJZ's president must communicate the change to the firm's clients. RJZ is moving away from a model based on hard data toward a new model that is at least partly dependent on the firm's forecasting skills. Clients would likely view such a model as a significant change rather than a mere refinement of RJZ's process.

Example 7 (Notification of Changes to the Investment Process):

RJZ Capital Management loses the chief architect of its multifactor valuation system. Without informing its clients, the president of RJZ decides to redirect the firm's talents and resources toward developing a product for passive equity management—a product that will emulate the performance of a major market index.

Comment: By failing to disclose to clients a substantial change to its investment process, the president of RJZ has violated Standard V(B).

Example 8 (Notification of Changes to the Investment Process):

At Fundamental Asset Management, Inc., the responsibility for selecting stocks for addition to the firm's "approved" list has just shifted from individual security analysts to a committee consisting of the research director and three senior portfolio managers. Eleanor Morales, a portfolio manager with Fundamental Asset Management, thinks this change is not important enough to communicate to her clients.

Comment: Morales must disclose the process change to all her clients. Some of Fundamental's clients might be concerned about the morale and motivation among the firm's best research analysts after such a change. Moreover, clients might challenge the stock-picking track record of the portfolio managers and might even want to monitor the situation closely.

Example 9 (Sufficient Disclosure of Investment System):

Amanda Chinn is the investment director for Diversified Asset Management, which manages the endowment of a charitable organization. Because of recent staff departures, Diversified has decided to limit its direct investment focus to large-cap securities and supplement the needs for small-cap and mid-cap management by hiring outside fund managers. In describing the planned strategy change to the charity, Chinn's update letter states, "As investment director, I will directly oversee the investment team managing the endowment's large-capitalization allocation. I will coordinate the selection and ongoing review of external managers responsible for allocations to other classes." The letter also describes the reasons for the change and the characteristics external managers must have to be considered.

Comment: Standard V(B) requires the disclosure of the investment process used to construct the portfolio of the fund. Changing the investment process from managing all classes of investments within the firm to the use of external managers is one example of information that needs to be communicated to clients. Chinn and her firm have embraced the principles of Standard V(B) by providing their client with relevant information. The charity can now make a reasonable decision about whether Diversified Asset Management remains the appropriate manager for its fund.

Example 10 (Notification of Changes to the Investment Process):

Michael Papis is the chief investment officer of his state's retirement fund. The fund has always used outside advisers for the real estate allocation, and this information is clearly presented in all fund communications. Thomas Nagle, a recognized sell-side research analyst and Papis's business school classmate, recently left the investment bank he worked for to start his own asset management firm, Accessible Real Estate. Nagle is trying to build his assets under management and contacts Papis about gaining some of the retirement fund's allocation. In the previous few years, the performance of the retirement fund's real estate investments was in line with the fund's benchmark but was not extraordinary. Papis decides to help out his old friend and also to seek better returns by moving the real estate allocation to Accessible. The only notice of the change in adviser appears in the next annual report in the listing of associated advisers.

Comment: Papis has violated Standard V(B). He attempted to hide the nature of his decision to change external managers by making only a limited disclosure. The plan recipients and the fund's trustees need to be aware when changes are made to ensure that operational procedures are being followed.
See also Standard IV(C)–Responsibilities of Supervisors, Standard V(A)–Diligence and Reasonable Basis, and Standard VI(A)–Disclosure of Conflicts.

Example 11 (Notification of Errors):

Jérôme Dupont works for the credit research group of XYZ Asset Management, where he is in charge of developing and updating credit risk models. In order to perform accurately, his models need to be regularly updated with the latest market data.

Standard V: Investment Analysis, Recommendations, and Actions

Dupont does not interact with or manage money for any of the firm's clients. He is in contact with the firm's US corporate bond fund manager, John Smith, who has only very superficial knowledge of the model and who from time to time asks very basic questions regarding the output recommendations. Smith does not consult Dupont with respect to finalizing his clients' investment strategies.

Dupont's recently assigned objective is to develop a new emerging market corporate credit risk model. The firm is planning to expand into emerging credit, and the development of such a model is a critical step in this process. Because Smith seems to follow the model's recommendations without much concern for its quality as he develops his clients' investment strategies, Dupont decides to focus his time on the development of the new emerging market model and neglects to update the US model.

After several months without regular updates, Dupont's diagnostic statistics start to show alarming signs with respect to the quality of the US credit model. Instead of conducting the long and complicated data update, Dupont introduces new codes into his model with some limited new data as a quick "fix." He thinks this change will address the issue without needing to complete the full data update, so he continues working on the new emerging market model.

Several months following the quick "fix," another set of diagnostic statistics reveals nonsensical results and Dupont realizes that his earlier change contained an error. He quickly corrects the error and alerts Smith. Smith realizes that some of the prior trades he performed were due to erroneous model results. Smith rebalances the portfolio to remove the securities purchased on the basis of the questionable results without reporting the issue to anyone else.

> *Comment*: Smith violated V(B) by not disclosing a material error in the investment process. Clients should have been informed about the error and the corrective actions the firm was undertaking on their behalf.
>
> See also Standard V(A)–Diligence and Reasonable Basis.

Example 12 (Notification of Risks and Limitations):

Quantitative analyst Yuri Yakovlev has developed an investment strategy that selects small-cap stocks on the basis of quantitative signals. Yakovlev's strategy typically identifies only a small number of stocks (10–20) that tend to be illiquid, but according to his backtests, the strategy generates significant risk-adjusted returns. The partners at Yakovlev's firm, QSC Capital, are impressed by these results. After a thorough examination of the strategy's risks, stress testing, historical back testing, and scenario analysis, QSC decides to seed the strategy with US$10 million of internal capital in order for Yakovlev to create a track record for the strategy.

After two years, the strategy has generated performance returns greater than the appropriate benchmark and the Sharpe ratio of the fund is close to 1.0. On the basis of these results, QSC decides to actively market the fund to large institutional investors. While creating the offering materials, Yakovlev informs the marketing team that the capacity of the strategy is limited. The extent of the limitation is difficult to ascertain with precision; it depends on market liquidity and other factors in his model that can evolve over time. Yakovlev indicates that given the current market conditions, investments in the fund beyond US$100 million of capital could become more difficult and negatively affect expected fund returns.

Alan Wellard, the manager of the marketing team, is a partner with 30 years of marketing experience and explains to Yakovlev that these are complex technical issues that will muddy the marketing message. According to Wellard, the offering material should focus solely on the great track record of the fund. Yakovlev does not object because the fund has only US$12 million of capital, very far from the US$100 million threshold.

Comment: Yakovlev and Wellard have not appropriately disclosed a significant limitation associated with the investment product. Yakovlev believes this limitation, once reached, will materially affect the returns of the fund. Although the fund is currently far from the US$100 million mark, current and prospective investors must be made aware of this capacity issue. If significant limitations are complicated to grasp and clients do not have the technical background required to understand them, Yakovlev and Wellard should either educate the clients or ascertain whether the fund is suitable for each client.

Example 13 (Notification of Risks and Limitations):

Brickell Advisers offers investment advisory services mainly to South American clients. Julietta Ramon, a risk analyst at Brickell, describes to clients how the firm uses value at risk (VaR) analysis to track the risk of its strategies. Ramon assures clients that calculating a VaR at a 99% confidence level, using a 20-day holding period, and applying a methodology based on an *ex ante* Monte Carlo simulation is extremely effective. The firm has never had losses greater than those predicted by this VaR analysis.

Comment: Ramon has not sufficiently communicated the risks associated with the investment process to satisfy the requirements of Standard V(B). The losses predicted by a VaR analysis depend greatly on the inputs used in the model. The size and probability of losses can differ significantly from what an individual model predicts. Ramon must disclose how the inputs were selected and the potential limitations and risks associated with the investment strategy.

Example 14 (Notification of Risks and Limitations):

Lily Smith attended an industry conference and noticed that John Baker, an investment manager with Baker Associates, attracted a great deal of attention from the conference participants. On the basis of her knowledge of Baker's reputation and the interest he received at the conference, Smith recommends adding Baker Associates to the approved manager platform. Her recommendation to the approval committee included the statement "John Baker is well respected in the industry, and his insights are consistently sought after by investors. Our clients are sure to benefit from investing with Baker Associates."

Comment: Smith is not appropriately separating facts from opinions in her recommendation to include the manager within the platform. Her actions conflict with the requirements of Standard V(B). Smith is relying on her opinions about Baker's reputation and the fact that many attendees were talking with him at the conference. Smith should also review the requirements of Standard V(A) regarding reasonable basis to determine the level of review necessary to recommend Baker Associates.

Standard V(C) Record Retention

Members and Candidates must develop and maintain appropriate records to support their investment analyses, recommendations, actions, and other investment-related communications with clients and prospective clients.

Standard V: Investment Analysis, Recommendations, and Actions

Guidance

Highlights:

- *New Media Records*
- *Records Are Property of the Firm*
- *Local Requirements*

Members and candidates must retain records that substantiate the scope of their research and reasons for their actions or conclusions. The retention requirement applies to decisions to buy or sell a security as well as reviews undertaken that do not lead to a change in position. Which records are required to support recommendations or investment actions depends on the role of the member or candidate in the investment decision-making process. Records may be maintained either in hard copy or electronic form.

Some examples of supporting documentation that assists the member or candidate in meeting the requirements for retention are as follows:

- personal notes from meetings with the covered company,
- press releases or presentations issued by the covered company,
- computer-based model outputs and analyses,
- computer-based model input parameters,
- risk analyses of securities' impacts on a portfolio,
- selection criteria for external advisers,
- notes from clients from meetings to review investment policy statements, and
- outside research reports.

New Media Records

The increased use of new and evolving technological formats (e.g., social media) for gathering and sharing information creates new challenges in maintaining the appropriate records and files. The nature or format of the information does not remove a member's or candidate's responsibility to maintain a record of information used in his or her analysis or communicated to clients.

Members and candidates should understand that although employers and local regulators are developing digital media retention policies, these policies may lag behind the advent of new communication channels. Such lag places greater responsibility on the individual for ensuring that all relevant information is retained. Examples of non-print media formats that should be retained include, but are not limited to,

- e-mails,
- text messages,
- blog posts, and
- Twitter posts.

Records Are Property of the Firm

As a general matter, records created as part of a member's or candidate's professional activity on behalf of his or her employer are the property of the firm. When a member or candidate leaves a firm to seek other employment, the member or candidate cannot take the property of the firm, including original forms or copies of supporting records of the member's or candidate's work, to the new employer without the express consent of the previous employer. The member or candidate cannot use historical recommendations or research reports created at the previous firm because the supporting documentation is unavailable. For future use, the member or candidate must re-create the supporting records at the new firm with information gathered through public sources or directly from the covered company and not from memory or sources obtained at the previous employer.

Local Requirements

Local regulators often impose requirements on members, candidates, and their firms related to record retention that must be followed. Firms may also implement policies detailing the applicable time frame for retaining research and client communication records. Fulfilling such regulatory and firm requirements satisfies the requirements of Standard V(C). In the absence of regulatory guidance or firm policies, CFA Institute recommends maintaining records for at least seven years.

Recommended Procedures for Compliance

The responsibility to maintain records that support investment action generally falls with the firm rather than individuals. Members and candidates must, however, archive research notes and other documents, either electronically or in hard copy, that support their current investment-related communications. Doing so will assist their firms in complying with requirements for preservation of internal or external records.

Application of the Standard

Example 1 (Record Retention and IPS Objectives and Recommendations):

One of Nikolas Lindstrom's clients is upset by the negative investment returns of his equity portfolio. The investment policy statement for the client requires that the portfolio manager follow a benchmark-oriented approach. The benchmark for the client includes a 35% investment allocation in the technology sector. The client acknowledges that this allocation was appropriate, but over the past three years, technology stocks have suffered severe losses. The client complains to the investment manager for allocating so much money to this sector.

> *Comment*: For Lindstrom, having appropriate records is important to show that over the past three years, the portion of technology stocks in the benchmark index was 35%, as called for in the IPS. Lindstrom should also have the client's IPS stating that the benchmark was appropriate for the client's investment objectives. He should also have records indicating that the investment has been explained appropriately to the client and that the IPS was updated on a regular basis. Taking these actions, Lindstrom would be in compliance with Standard V(C).

Example 2 (Record Retention and Research Process):

Malcolm Young is a research analyst who writes numerous reports rating companies in the luxury retail industry. His reports are based on a variety of sources, including interviews with company managers, manufacturers, and economists; on-site company visits; customer surveys; and secondary research from analysts covering related industries.

> *Comment*: Young must carefully document and keep copies of all the information that goes into his reports, including the secondary or third-party research of other analysts. Failure to maintain such files would violate Standard V(C).

Example 3 (Records as Firm, Not Employee, Property):

Martin Blank develops an analytical model while he is employed by Green Partners Investment Management, LLP (GPIM). While at the firm, he systematically documents the assumptions that make up the model as well as his reasoning behind the assumptions. As a result of the success of his model, Blank is hired to be the head of the research department of one of GPIM's competitors. Blank takes copies of the records supporting his model to his new firm.

> *Comment*: The records created by Blank supporting the research model he developed at GPIM are the records of GPIM. Taking the documents with him to his new employer without GPIM's permission violates Standard V(C). To use the model in the future, Blank must re-create the records supporting his model at the new firm.

STANDARD VI: CONFLICTS OF INTEREST

Standard VI(A) Disclosure of Conflicts

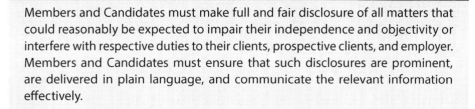

Members and Candidates must make full and fair disclosure of all matters that could reasonably be expected to impair their independence and objectivity or interfere with respective duties to their clients, prospective clients, and employer. Members and Candidates must ensure that such disclosures are prominent, are delivered in plain language, and communicate the relevant information effectively.

Guidance

Highlights:

- *Disclosure of Conflicts to Employers*
- *Disclosure to Clients*
- *Cross-Departmental Conflicts*
- *Conflicts with Stock Ownership*
- *Conflicts as a Director*

Best practice is to avoid actual conflicts or the appearance of conflicts of interest when possible. Conflicts of interest often arise in the investment profession. Conflicts can occur between the interests of clients, the interests of employers, and the member's or candidate's own personal interests. Common sources for conflict are compensation structures, especially incentive and bonus structures that provide immediate returns for members and candidates with little or no consideration of long-term value creation.

Identifying and managing these conflicts is a critical part of working in the investment industry and can take many forms. When conflicts cannot be reasonably avoided, clear and complete disclosure of their existence is necessary.

Standard VI(A) protects investors and employers by requiring members and candidates to fully disclose to clients, potential clients, and employers all actual and potential conflicts of interest. Once a member or candidate has made full disclosure, the member's or candidate's employer, clients, and prospective clients will have the information needed to evaluate the objectivity of the investment advice or action taken on their behalf.

To be effective, disclosures must be prominent and must be made in plain language and in a manner designed to effectively communicate the information. Members and candidates have the responsibility of determining how often, in what manner, and in what particular circumstances the disclosure of conflicts must be made. Best practices dictate updating disclosures when the nature of a conflict of interest changes materially—for example, if the nature of a conflict of interest worsens through the introduction of bonuses based on each quarter's profits as to opposed annual profits. In making and updating disclosures of conflicts of interest, members and candidates should err on the side of caution to ensure that conflicts are effectively communicated.

Disclosure of Conflicts to Employers

Disclosure of conflicts to employers may be appropriate in many instances. When reporting conflicts of interest to employers, members and candidates must give their employers enough information to assess the impact of the conflict. By complying with employer guidelines, members and candidates allow their employers to avoid potentially embarrassing and costly ethical or regulatory violations.

Reportable situations include conflicts that would interfere with rendering unbiased investment advice and conflicts that would cause a member or candidate to act not in the employer's best interest. The same circumstances that generate conflicts to be reported to clients and prospective clients also would dictate reporting to employers. Ownership of stocks analyzed or recommended, participation on outside boards, and financial or other pressures that could influence a decision are to be promptly reported to the employer so that their impact can be assessed and a decision on how to resolve the conflict can be made.

The mere appearance of a conflict of interest may create problems for members, candidates, and their employers. Therefore, many of the conflicts previously mentioned could be explicitly prohibited by an employer. For example, many employers restrict personal trading, outside board membership, and related activities to prevent situations that might not normally be considered problematic from a conflict-of-interest point of view but that could give the appearance of a conflict of interest. Members and candidates must comply with these restrictions. Members and candidates must take reasonable steps to avoid conflicts and, if they occur inadvertently, must report them promptly so that the employer and the member or candidate can resolve them as quickly and effectively as possible.

Standard VI(A) also deals with a member's or candidate's conflicts of interest that might be detrimental to the employer's business. Any potential conflict situation that could prevent clear judgment about or full commitment to the execution of a member's or candidate's duties to the employer should be reported to the member's or candidate's employer and promptly resolved.

Disclosure to Clients

Members and candidates must maintain their objectivity when rendering investment advice or taking investment action. Investment advice or actions may be perceived to be tainted in numerous situations. Can a member or candidate remain objective if, on behalf of the firm, the member or candidate obtains or assists in obtaining fees for services? Can a member or candidate give objective advice if he or she owns stock in the company that is the subject of an investment recommendation or if the member or candidate has a close personal relationship with the company managers? Requiring members and candidates to disclose all matters that reasonably could be expected to impair the member's or candidate's objectivity allows clients and prospective clients to judge motives and possible biases for themselves.

Standard VI: Conflicts of Interest

Often in the investment industry, a conflict, or the perception of a conflict, cannot be avoided. The most obvious conflicts of interest, which should always be disclosed, are relationships between an issuer and the member, the candidate, or his or her firm (such as a directorship or consultancy by a member; investment banking, underwriting, and financial relationships; broker/dealer market-making activities; and material beneficial ownership of stock). For the purposes of Standard VI(A), members and candidates beneficially own securities or other investments if they have a direct or indirect pecuniary interest in the securities, have the power to vote or direct the voting of the shares of the securities or investments, or have the power to dispose or direct the disposition of the security or investment.

A member or candidate must take reasonable steps to determine whether a conflict of interest exists and disclose to clients any known conflicts of the member's or candidate's firm. Disclosure of broker/dealer market-making activities alerts clients that a purchase or sale might be made from or to the firm's principal account and that the firm has a special interest in the price of the stock.

Additionally, disclosures should be made to clients regarding fee arrangements, subadvisory agreements, or other situations involving nonstandard fee structures. Equally important is the disclosure of arrangements in which the firm benefits directly from investment recommendations. An obvious conflict of interest is the rebate of a portion of the service fee some classes of mutual funds charge to investors. Members and candidates should ensure that their firms disclose such relationships so clients can fully understand the costs of their investments and the benefits received by their investment manager's employer.

Cross-Departmental Conflicts

Other circumstances can give rise to actual or potential conflicts of interest. For instance, a sell-side analyst working for a broker/dealer may be encouraged, not only by members of her or his own firm but by corporate issuers themselves, to write research reports about particular companies. The buy-side analyst is likely to be faced with similar conflicts as banks exercise their underwriting and security-dealing powers. The marketing division may ask an analyst to recommend the stock of a certain company in order to obtain business from that company.

The potential for conflicts of interest also exists with broker-sponsored limited partnerships formed to invest venture capital. Increasingly, members and candidates are expected not only to follow issues from these partnerships once they are offered to the public but also to promote the issues in the secondary market after public offerings. Members, candidates, and their firms should attempt to resolve situations presenting potential conflicts of interest or disclose them in accordance with the principles set forth in Standard VI(A).

Conflicts with Stock Ownership

The most prevalent conflict requiring disclosure under Standard VI(A) is a member's or candidate's ownership of stock in companies that he or she recommends to clients or that clients hold. Clearly, the easiest method for preventing a conflict is to prohibit members and candidates from owning any such securities, but this approach is overly burdensome and discriminates against members and candidates.

Therefore, sell-side members and candidates should disclose any materially beneficial ownership interest in a security or other investment that the member or candidate is recommending. Buy-side members and candidates should disclose their procedures for reporting requirements for personal transactions. Conflicts arising from personal investing are discussed more fully in the guidance for Standard VI(B).

Conflicts as a Director

Service as a director poses three basic conflicts of interest. First, a conflict may exist between the duties owed to clients and the duties owed to shareholders of the company. Second, investment personnel who serve as directors may receive the securities or options to purchase securities of the company as compensation for serving on the board, which could raise questions about trading actions that might increase the value of those securities. Third, board service creates the opportunity to receive material nonpublic information involving the company. Even though the information is confidential, the perception could be that information not available to the public is being communicated to a director's firm—whether a broker, investment adviser, or other type of organization. When members or candidates providing investment services also serve as directors, they should be isolated from those making investment decisions by the use of firewalls or similar restrictions.

Recommended Procedures for Compliance

Members or candidates should disclose special compensation arrangements with the employer that might conflict with client interests, such as bonuses based on short-term performance criteria, commissions, incentive fees, performance fees, and referral fees. If the member's or candidate's firm does not permit such disclosure, the member or candidate should document the request and may consider dissociating from the activity.

Members' and candidates' firms are encouraged to include information on compensation packages in firms' promotional literature. If a member or candidate manages a portfolio for which the fee is based on capital gains or capital appreciation (a performance fee), this information should be disclosed to clients. If a member, a candidate, or a member's or candidate's firm has outstanding agent options to buy stock as part of the compensation package for corporate financing activities, the amount and expiration date of these options should be disclosed as a footnote to any research report published by the member's or candidate's firm.

Application of the Standard

Example 1 (Conflict of Interest and Business Relationships):

Hunter Weiss is a research analyst with Farmington Company, a broker and investment banking firm. Farmington's merger and acquisition department has represented Vimco, a conglomerate, in all of Vimco's acquisitions for 20 years. From time to time, Farmington officers sit on the boards of directors of various Vimco subsidiaries. Weiss is writing a research report on Vimco.

> *Comment*: Weiss must disclose in his research report Farmington's special relationship with Vimco. Broker/dealer management of and participation in public offerings must be disclosed in research reports. Because the position of underwriter to a company entails a special past and potential future relationship with a company that is the subject of investment advice, it threatens the independence and objectivity of the report writer and must be disclosed.

Example 2 (Conflict of Interest and Business Stock Ownership):

The investment management firm of Dover & Roe sells a 25% interest in its partnership to a multinational bank holding company, First of New York. Immediately after the sale, Margaret Hobbs, president of Dover & Roe, changes her recommendation for First of New York's common stock from "sell" to "buy" and adds First of New York's commercial paper to Dover & Roe's approved list for purchase.

Standard VI: Conflicts of Interest

> *Comment*: Hobbs must disclose the new relationship with First of New York to all Dover & Roe clients. This relationship must also be disclosed to clients by the firm's portfolio managers when they make specific investment recommendations or take investment actions with respect to First of New York's securities.

Example 3 (Conflict of Interest and Personal Stock Ownership):

Carl Fargmon, a research analyst who follows firms producing office equipment, has been recommending purchase of Kincaid Printing because of its innovative new line of copiers. After his initial report on the company, Fargmon's wife inherits from a distant relative US$3 million of Kincaid stock. He has been asked to write a follow-up report on Kincaid.

> *Comment*: Fargmon must disclose his wife's ownership of the Kincaid stock to his employer and in his follow-up report. Best practice would be to avoid the conflict by asking his employer to assign another analyst to draft the follow-up report.

Example 4 (Conflict of Interest and Personal Stock Ownership):

Betty Roberts is speculating in penny stocks for her own account and purchases 100,000 shares of Drew Mining, Inc., for US$0.30 a share. She intends to sell these shares at the sign of any substantial upward price movement of the stock. A week later, her employer asks her to write a report on penny stocks in the mining industry to be published in two weeks. Even without owning the Drew stock, Roberts would recommend it in her report as a "buy." A surge in the price of the stock to the US$2 range is likely to result once the report is issued.

> *Comment*: Although this holding may not be material, Roberts must disclose it in the report and to her employer before writing the report because the gain for her will be substantial if the market responds strongly to her recommendation. The fact that she has only recently purchased the stock adds to the appearance that she is not entirely objective.

Example 5 (Conflict of Interest and Compensation Arrangements):

Samantha Snead, a portfolio manager for Thomas Investment Counsel, Inc., specializes in managing public retirement funds and defined benefit pension plan accounts, all of which have long-term investment objectives. A year ago, Snead's employer, in an attempt to motivate and retain key investment professionals, introduced a bonus compensation system that rewards portfolio managers on the basis of quarterly performance relative to their peers and to certain benchmark indexes. In an attempt to improve the short-term performance of her accounts, Snead changes her investment strategy and purchases several high-beta stocks for client portfolios. These purchases are seemingly contrary to the clients' investment policy statements. Following their purchase, an officer of Griffin Corporation, one of Snead's pension fund clients, asks why Griffin Corporation's portfolio seems to be dominated by high-beta stocks of companies that often appear among the most actively traded issues. No change in objective or strategy has been recommended by Snead during the year.

> *Comment*: Snead has violated Standard VI(A) by failing to inform her clients of the changes in her compensation arrangement with her employer, which created a conflict of interest between her compensation and her clients' IPSs. Firms may pay employees on the basis of performance, but pressure by Thomas Investment Counsel to achieve short-term performance goals is in basic conflict with the objectives of Snead's accounts.

See also Standard III(C)–Suitability.

Example 6 (Conflict of Interest, Options, and Compensation Arrangements):

Wayland Securities works with small companies doing IPOs or secondary offerings. Typically, these deals are in the US$10 million to US$50 million range, and as a result, the corporate finance fees are quite small. To compensate for the small fees, Wayland Securities usually takes "agent options"—that is, rights (exercisable within a two-year time frame) to acquire up to an additional 10% of the current offering. Following an IPO performed by Wayland for Falk Resources, Ltd., Darcy Hunter, the head of corporate finance at Wayland, is concerned about receiving value for her Falk Resources options. The options are due to expire in one month, and the stock is not doing well. She contacts John Fitzpatrick in the research department of Wayland Securities, reminds him that he is eligible for 30% of these options, and indicates that now would be a good time to give some additional coverage to Falk Resources. Fitzpatrick agrees and immediately issues a favorable report.

> *Comment*: For Fitzpatrick to avoid being in violation of Standard VI(A), he must indicate in the report the volume and expiration date of agent options outstanding. Furthermore, because he is personally eligible for some of the options, Fitzpatrick must disclose the extent of this compensation. He also must be careful to not violate his duty of independence and objectivity under Standard I(B).

Example 7 (Conflict of Interest and Compensation Arrangements):

Gary Carter is a representative with Bengal International, a registered broker/dealer. Carter is approached by a stock promoter for Badger Company, who offers to pay Carter additional compensation for sales of Badger Company's stock to Carter's clients. Carter accepts the stock promoter's offer but does not disclose the arrangements to his clients or to his employer. Carter sells shares of the stock to his clients.

> *Comment*: Carter has violated Standard VI(A) by failing to disclose to clients that he is receiving additional compensation for recommending and selling Badger stock. Because he did not disclose the arrangement with Badger to his clients, the clients were unable to evaluate whether Carter's recommendations to buy Badger were affected by this arrangement. Carter's conduct also violated Standard VI(A) by failing to disclose to his employer monetary compensation received in addition to the compensation and benefits conferred by his employer. Carter was required by Standard VI(A) to disclose the arrangement with Badger to his employer so that his employer could evaluate whether the arrangement affected Carter's objectivity and loyalty.

Example 8 (Conflict of Interest and Directorship):

Carol Corky, a senior portfolio manager for Universal Management, recently became involved as a trustee with the Chelsea Foundation, a large not-for-profit foundation in her hometown. Universal is a small money manager (with assets under management of approximately US$100 million) that caters to individual investors. Chelsea has assets in excess of US$2 billion. Corky does not believe informing Universal of her involvement with Chelsea is necessary.

> *Comment*: By failing to inform Universal of her involvement with Chelsea, Corky violated Standard VI(A). Given the large size of the endowment at Chelsea, Corky's new role as a trustee can reasonably be expected to be time consuming, to the possible detriment of Corky's portfolio responsibilities with Universal. Also, as a trustee, Corky may become involved in

the investment decisions at Chelsea. Therefore, Standard VI(A) obligates Corky to discuss becoming a trustee at Chelsea with her compliance officer or supervisor at Universal before accepting the position, and she should have disclosed the degree to which she would be involved in investment decisions at Chelsea.

Example 9 (Conflict of Interest and Personal Trading):

Bruce Smith covers eastern European equities for Marlborough Investments, an investment management firm with a strong presence in emerging markets. While on a business trip to Russia, Smith learns that investing in Russian equities directly is difficult but that equity-linked notes that replicate the performance of underlying Russian equities can be purchased from a New York–based investment bank. Believing that his firm would not be interested in such a security, Smith purchases a note linked to a Russian telecommunications company for his own account without informing Marlborough. A month later, Smith decides that the firm should consider investing in Russian equities by way of the equity-linked notes. He prepares a write-up on the market that concludes with a recommendation to purchase several of the notes. One note he recommends is linked to the same Russian telecom company that Smith holds in his personal account.

> *Comment*: Smith has violated Standard VI(A) by failing to disclose his purchase and ownership of the note linked to the Russian telecom company. Smith is required by the standard to disclose the investment opportunity to his employer and look to his company's policies on personal trading to determine whether it was proper for him to purchase the note for his own account. By purchasing the note, Smith may or may not have impaired his ability to make an unbiased and objective assessment of the appropriateness of the derivative instrument for his firm, but Smith's failure to disclose the purchase to his employer impaired his employer's ability to decide whether his ownership of the security is a conflict of interest that might affect Smith's future recommendations. Then, when he recommended the particular telecom notes to his firm, Smith compounded his problems by not disclosing that he owned the notes in his personal account—a clear conflict of interest.

Example 10 (Conflict of Interest and Requested Favors):

Michael Papis is the chief investment officer of his state's retirement fund. The fund has always used outside advisers for the real estate allocation, and this information is clearly presented in all fund communications. Thomas Nagle, a recognized sell-side research analyst and Papis's business school classmate, recently left the investment bank he worked for to start his own asset management firm, Accessible Real Estate. Nagle is trying to build his assets under management and contacts Papis about gaining some of the retirement fund's allocation. In the previous few years, the performance of the retirement fund's real estate investments was in line with the fund's benchmark but was not extraordinary. Papis decides to help out his old friend and also to seek better returns by moving the real estate allocation to Accessible. The only notice of the change in adviser appears in the next annual report in the listing of associated advisers.

> *Comment*: Papis has violated Standard VI(A) by not disclosing to his employer his personal relationship with Nagle. Disclosure of his past history with Nagle would allow his firm to determine whether the conflict may have impaired Papis's independence in deciding to change managers.

See also Standard IV(C)–Responsibilities of Supervisors, Standard V(A)–Diligence and Reasonable Basis, and Standard V(B)–Communication with Clients and Prospective Clients.

Example 11 (Conflict of Interest and Business Relationships):

Bob Wade, trust manager for Central Midas Bank, was approached by Western Funds about promoting its family of funds, with special interest in the service-fee class. To entice Central to promote this class, Western Funds offered to pay the bank a service fee of 0.25%. Without disclosing the fee being offered to the bank, Wade asked one of the investment managers to review the Western Funds family of funds to determine whether they were suitable for clients of Central. The manager completed the normal due diligence review and determined that the funds were fairly valued in the market with fee structures on a par with their competitors. Wade decided to accept Western's offer and instructed the team of portfolio managers to exclusively promote these funds and the service-fee class to clients seeking to invest new funds or transfer from their current investments. So as to not influence the investment managers, Wade did not disclose the fee offer and allowed that income to flow directly to the bank.

Comment: Wade is violating Standard VI(A) by not disclosing the portion of the service fee being paid to Central. Although the investment managers may not be influenced by the fee, neither they nor the client have the proper information about Wade's decision to exclusively market this fund family and class of investments. Central may come to rely on the new fee as a component of the firm's profitability and may be unwilling to offer other products in the future that could affect the fees received.

See also Standard I(B)–Independence and Objectivity.

Example 12 (Disclosure of Conflicts to Employers):

Yehudit Dagan is a portfolio manager for Risk Management Bank (RMB), whose clients include retirement plans and corporations. RMB provides a defined contribution retirement plan for its employees that offers 20 large diversified mutual fund investment options, including a mutual fund managed by Dagan's RMB colleagues. After being employed for six months, Dagan became eligible to participate in the retirement plan, and she intends to allocate her retirement plan assets in six of the investment options, including the fund managed by her RMB colleagues. Dagan is concerned that joining the plan will lead to a potentially significant amount of paperwork for her (e.g., disclosure of her retirement account holdings and needing preclearance for her transactions), especially with her investing in the in-house fund.

Comment: Standard VI(A) would not require Dagan to disclose her personal or retirement investments in large diversified mutual funds, unless specifically required by her employer. For practical reasons, the standard does not require Dagan to gain preclearance for ongoing payroll deduction contributions to retirement plan account investment options.

Dagan should ensure that her firm does not have a specific policy regarding investment—whether personal or in the retirement account—for funds managed by the company's employees. These mutual funds may be subject to the company's disclosure, preclearance, and trading restriction procedures to identify possible conflicts prior to the execution of trades.

Standard VI(B) Priority of Transactions

Investment transactions for clients and employers must have priority over investment transactions in which a Member or Candidate is the beneficial owner.

Guidance

Highlights:

- *Avoiding Potential Conflicts*
- *Personal Trading Secondary to Trading for Clients*
- *Standards for Nonpublic Information*
- *Impact on All Accounts with Beneficial Ownership*

Standard VI(B) reinforces the responsibility of members and candidates to give the interests of their clients and employers priority over their personal financial interests. This standard is designed to prevent any potential conflict of interest or the appearance of a conflict of interest with respect to personal transactions. Client interests have priority. Client transactions must take precedence over transactions made on behalf of the member's or candidate's firm or personal transactions.

Avoiding Potential Conflicts

Conflicts between the client's interest and an investment professional's personal interest may occur. Although conflicts of interest exist, nothing is inherently unethical about individual managers, advisers, or mutual fund employees making money from personal investments as long as (1) the client is not disadvantaged by the trade, (2) the investment professional does not benefit personally from trades undertaken for clients, and (3) the investment professional complies with applicable regulatory requirements.

Some situations occur where a member or candidate may need to enter a personal transaction that runs counter to current recommendations or what the portfolio manager is doing for client portfolios. For example, a member or candidate may be required at some point to sell an asset to make a college tuition payment or a down payment on a home, to meet a margin call, or so on. The sale may be contrary to the long-term advice the member or candidate is currently providing to clients. In these situations, the same three criteria given in the preceding paragraph should be applied in the transaction so as to not violate Standard VI(B).

Personal Trading Secondary to Trading for Clients

Standard VI(B) states that transactions for clients and employers must have priority over transactions in securities or other investments for which a member or candidate is the beneficial owner. The objective of the standard is to prevent personal transactions from adversely affecting the interests of clients or employers. A member or candidate having the same investment positions or being co-invested with clients does not always create a conflict. Some clients in certain investment situations require members or candidates to have aligned interests. Personal investment positions or transactions of members or candidates or their firm should never, however, adversely affect client investments.

Standards for Nonpublic Information

Standard VI(B) covers the activities of members and candidates who have knowledge of pending transactions that may be made on behalf of their clients or employers, who have access to nonpublic information during the normal preparation of research recommendations, or who take investment actions. Members and candidates are prohibited from conveying nonpublic information to any person whose relationship to the member or candidate makes the member or candidate a beneficial owner of the person's securities. Members and candidates must not convey this information to any other person if the nonpublic information can be deemed material.

Impact on All Accounts with Beneficial Ownership

Members or candidates may undertake transactions in accounts for which they are a beneficial owner only after their clients and employers have had adequate opportunity to act on a recommendation. Personal transactions include those made for the member's or candidate's own account, for family (including spouse, children, and other immediate family members) accounts, and for accounts in which the member or candidate has a direct or indirect pecuniary interest, such as a trust or retirement account. Family accounts that are client accounts should be treated like any other firm account and should neither be given special treatment nor be disadvantaged because of the family relationship. If a member or candidate has a beneficial ownership in the account, however, the member or candidate may be subject to preclearance or reporting requirements of the employer or applicable law.

Recommended Procedures for Compliance

Policies and procedures designed to prevent potential conflicts of interest, and even the appearance of a conflict of interest, with respect to personal transactions are critical to establishing investor confidence in the securities industry. Therefore, members and candidates should urge their firms to establish such policies and procedures. Because investment firms vary greatly in assets under management, types of clients, number of employees, and so on, each firm should have policies regarding personal investing that are best suited to the firm. Members and candidates should then prominently disclose these policies to clients and prospective clients.

The specific provisions of each firm's standards will vary, but all firms should adopt certain basic procedures to address the conflict areas created by personal investing. These procedures include the following:

- *Limited participation in equity IPOs*: Some eagerly awaited IPOs rise significantly in value shortly after the issue is brought to market. Because the new issue may be highly attractive and sought after, the opportunity to participate in the IPO may be limited. Therefore, purchases of IPOs by investment personnel create conflicts of interest in two principal ways. First, participation in an IPO may have the appearance of taking away an attractive investment opportunity from clients for personal gain—a clear breach of the duty of loyalty to clients. Second, personal purchases in IPOs may have the appearance that the investment opportunity is being bestowed as an incentive to make future investment decisions for the benefit of the party providing the opportunity. Members and candidates can avoid these conflicts or appearances of conflicts of interest by not participating in IPOs.

    Reliable and systematic review procedures should be established to ensure that conflicts relating to IPOs are identified and appropriately dealt with by supervisors. Members and candidates should preclear their participation in IPOs, even in situations without any conflict of interest between a member's or candidate's participation in an IPO and the client's interests. Members and

Standard VI: Conflicts of Interest

candidates should not benefit from the position that their clients occupy in the marketplace—through preferred trading, the allocation of limited offerings, or oversubscription.

- *Restrictions on private placements*: Strict limits should be placed on investment personnel acquiring securities in private placements, and appropriate supervisory and review procedures should be established to prevent noncompliance.

    Firms do not routinely use private placements for clients (e.g., venture capital deals) because of the high risk associated with them. Conflicts related to private placements are more significant to members and candidates who manage large pools of assets or act as plan sponsors because these managers may be offered special opportunities, such as private placements, as a reward or an enticement for continuing to do business with a particular broker.

    Participation in private placements raises conflict-of-interest issues that are similar to issues surrounding IPOs. Investment personnel should not be involved in transactions, including (but not limited to) private placements, that could be perceived as favors or gifts that seem designed to influence future judgment or to reward past business deals.

    Whether the venture eventually proves to be good or bad, managers have an immediate conflict concerning private placement opportunities. If and when the investments go public, participants in private placements have an incentive to recommend the investments to clients regardless of the suitability of the investments for their clients. Doing so increases the value of the participants' personal portfolios.

- *Establish blackout/restricted periods*: Investment personnel involved in the investment decision-making process should establish blackout periods prior to trades for clients so that managers cannot take advantage of their knowledge of client activity by "front-running" client trades (trading for one's personal account before trading for client accounts).

    Individual firms must decide who within the firm should be required to comply with the trading restrictions. At a minimum, all individuals who are involved in the investment decision-making process should be subject to the same restricted period. Each firm must determine specific requirements related to blackout and restricted periods that are most relevant to the firm while ensuring that the procedures are governed by the guiding principles set forth in the Code and Standards. Size of firm and type of securities purchased are relevant factors. For example, in a large firm, a blackout requirement is, in effect, a total trading ban because the firm is continually trading in most securities. In a small firm, the blackout period is more likely to prevent the investment manager from front-running.

- *Reporting requirements*: Supervisors should establish reporting procedures for investment personnel, including disclosure of personal holdings/beneficial ownerships, confirmations of trades to the firm and the employee, and preclearance procedures. Once trading restrictions are in place, they must be enforced. The best method for monitoring and enforcing procedures to eliminate conflicts of interest in personal trading is through reporting requirements, including the following:
    - **Disclosure of holdings in which the employee has a beneficial interest**. Disclosure by investment personnel to the firm should be made upon commencement of the employment relationship and at least annually thereafter. To address privacy considerations, disclosure of personal holdings should be handled in a confidential manner by the firm.

- **Providing duplicate confirmations of transactions**. Investment personnel should be required to direct their brokers to supply to firms duplicate copies or confirmations of all their personal securities transactions and copies of periodic statements for all securities accounts. The duplicate confirmation requirement has two purposes: (1) The requirement sends a message that there is independent verification, which reduces the likelihood of unethical behavior, and (2) it enables verification of the accounting of the flow of personal investments that cannot be determined from merely looking at holdings.
- **Preclearance procedures**. Investment personnel should examine all planned personal trades to identify possible conflicts prior to the execution of the trades. Preclearance procedures are designed to identify possible conflicts before a problem arises.

■ *Disclosure of policies*: Members and candidates should fully disclose to investors their firm's policies regarding personal investing. The information about employees' personal investment activities and policies will foster an atmosphere of full and complete disclosure and calm the public's legitimate concerns about the conflicts of interest posed by investment personnel's personal trading. The disclosure must provide helpful information to investors; it should not be simply boilerplate language, such as "investment personnel are subject to policies and procedures regarding their personal trading."

Application of the Standard

Example 1 (Personal Trading):

Research analyst Marlon Long does not recommend purchase of a common stock for his employer's account because he wants to purchase the stock personally and does not want to wait until the recommendation is approved and the stock is purchased by his employer.

> *Comment*: Long has violated Standard VI(B) by taking advantage of his knowledge of the stock's value before allowing his employer to benefit from that information.

Example 2 (Trading for Family Member Account):

Carol Baker, the portfolio manager of an aggressive growth mutual fund, maintains an account in her husband's name at several brokerage firms with which the fund and a number of Baker's other individual clients do a substantial amount of business. Whenever a hot issue becomes available, she instructs the brokers to buy it for her husband's account. Because such issues normally are scarce, Baker often acquires shares in hot issues but her clients are not able to participate in them.

> *Comment*: To avoid violating Standard VI(B), Baker must acquire shares for her mutual fund first and acquire them for her husband's account only after doing so, even though she might miss out on participating in new issues via her husband's account. She also must disclose the trading for her husband's account to her employer because this activity creates a conflict between her personal interests and her employer's interests.

Example 3 (Family Accounts as Equals):

Erin Toffler, a portfolio manager at Esposito Investments, manages the retirement account established with the firm by her parents. Whenever IPOs become available, she first allocates shares to all her other clients for whom the investment is appropriate;

only then does she place any remaining portion in her parents' account, if the issue is appropriate for them. She has adopted this procedure so that no one can accuse her of favoring her parents.

> *Comment*: Toffler has violated Standard VI(B) by breaching her duty to her parents by treating them differently from her other accounts simply because of the family relationship. As fee-paying clients of Esposito Investments, Toffler's parents are entitled to the same treatment as any other client of the firm. If Toffler has beneficial ownership in the account, however, and Esposito Investments has preclearance and reporting requirements for personal transactions, she may have to preclear the trades and report the transactions to Esposito.

Example 4 (Personal Trading and Disclosure):

Gary Michaels is an entry-level employee who holds a low-paying job serving both the research department and the investment management department of an active investment management firm. He purchases a sports car and begins to wear expensive clothes after only a year of employment with the firm. The director of the investment management department, who has responsibility for monitoring the personal stock transactions of all employees, investigates and discovers that Michaels has made substantial investment gains by purchasing stocks just before they were put on the firm's recommended "buy" list. Michaels was regularly given the firm's quarterly personal transaction form but declined to complete it.

> *Comment*: Michaels violated Standard VI(B) by placing personal transactions ahead of client transactions. In addition, his supervisor violated Standard IV(C)–Responsibilities of Supervisors by permitting Michaels to continue to perform his assigned tasks without having signed the quarterly personal transaction form. Note also that if Michaels had communicated information about the firm's recommendations to a person who traded the security, that action would be a misappropriation of the information and a violation of Standard II(A)–Material Nonpublic Information.

Example 5 (Trading Prior to Report Dissemination):

A brokerage's insurance analyst, Denise Wilson, makes a closed-circuit TV report to her firm's branches around the country. During the broadcast, she includes negative comments about a major company in the insurance industry. The following day, Wilson's report is printed and distributed to the sales force and public customers. The report recommends that both short-term traders and intermediate investors take profits by selling that insurance company's stock. Seven minutes after the broadcast, however, Ellen Riley, head of the firm's trading department, had closed out a long "call" position in the stock. Shortly thereafter, Riley established a sizable "put" position in the stock. When asked about her activities, Riley claimed she took the actions to facilitate anticipated sales by institutional clients.

> *Comment*: Riley did not give customers an opportunity to buy or sell in the options market before the firm itself did. By taking action before the report was disseminated, Riley's firm may have depressed the price of the calls and increased the price of the puts. The firm could have avoided a conflict of interest if it had waited to trade for its own account until its clients had an opportunity to receive and assimilate Wilson's recommendations. As it is, Riley's actions violated Standard VI(B).

Standard VI(C) Referral Fees

> Members and Candidates must disclose to their employer, clients, and prospective clients, as appropriate, any compensation, consideration, or benefit received from or paid to others for the recommendation of products or services.

Guidance

Standard VI(C) states the responsibility of members and candidates to inform their employer, clients, and prospective clients of any benefit received for referrals of customers and clients. Such disclosures allow clients or employers to evaluate (1) any partiality shown in any recommendation of services and (2) the full cost of the services. Members and candidates must disclose when they pay a fee or provide compensation to others who have referred prospective clients to the member or candidate.

Appropriate disclosure means that members and candidates must advise the client or prospective client, before entry into any formal agreement for services, of any benefit given or received for the recommendation of any services provided by the member or candidate. In addition, the member or candidate must disclose the nature of the consideration or benefit—for example, flat fee or percentage basis, one-time or continuing benefit, based on performance, benefit in the form of provision of research or other noncash benefit—together with the estimated dollar value. Consideration includes all fees, whether paid in cash, in soft dollars, or in kind.

Recommended Procedures for Compliance

Members and candidates should encourage their employers to develop procedures related to referral fees. The firm may completely restrict such fees. If the firm does not adopt a strict prohibition of such fees, the procedures should indicate the appropriate steps for requesting approval.

Employers should have investment professionals provide to the clients notification of approved referral fee programs and provide the employer regular (at least quarterly) updates on the amount and nature of compensation received.

Application of the Standard

Example 1 (Disclosure of Referral Arrangements and Outside Parties):

Brady Securities, Inc., a broker/dealer, has established a referral arrangement with Lewis Brothers, Ltd., an investment counseling firm. In this arrangement, Brady Securities refers all prospective tax-exempt accounts, including pension, profit-sharing, and endowment accounts, to Lewis Brothers. In return, Lewis Brothers makes available to Brady Securities on a regular basis the security recommendations and reports of its research staff, which registered representatives of Brady Securities use in serving customers. In addition, Lewis Brothers conducts monthly economic and market reviews for Brady Securities personnel and directs all stock commission business generated by referral accounts to Brady Securities.

Willard White, a partner in Lewis Brothers, calculates that the incremental costs involved in functioning as the research department of Brady Securities are US$20,000 annually.

Referrals from Brady Securities last year resulted in fee income of US$200,000 for Lewis Brothers, and directing all stock trades through Brady Securities resulted in additional costs to Lewis Brothers' clients of US$10,000.

Diane Branch, the chief financial officer of Maxwell Inc., contacts White and says that she is seeking an investment manager for Maxwell's profit-sharing plan. She adds, "My friend Harold Hill at Brady Securities recommended your firm without qualification, and that's good enough for me. Do we have a deal?" White accepts the new account but does not disclose his firm's referral arrangement with Brady Securities.

> *Comment*: White has violated Standard VI(C) by failing to inform the prospective customer of the referral fee payable in services and commissions for an indefinite period to Brady Securities. Such disclosure could have caused Branch to reassess Hill's recommendation and make a more critical evaluation of Lewis Brothers' services.

Example 2 (Disclosure of Interdepartmental Referral Arrangements):

James Handley works for the trust department of Central Trust Bank. He receives compensation for each referral he makes to Central Trust's brokerage department and personal financial management department that results in a sale. He refers several of his clients to the personal financial management department but does not disclose the arrangement within Central Trust to his clients.

> *Comment*: Handley has violated Standard VI(C) by not disclosing the referral arrangement at Central Trust Bank to his clients. Standard VI(C) does not distinguish between referral payments paid by a third party for referring clients to the third party and internal payments paid within the firm to attract new business to a subsidiary. Members and candidates must disclose all such referral fees. Therefore, Handley is required to disclose, at the time of referral, any referral fee agreement in place among Central Trust Bank's departments. The disclosure should include the nature and the value of the benefit and should be made in writing.

Example 3 (Disclosure of Referral Arrangements and Informing Firm):

Katherine Roberts is a portfolio manager at Katama Investments, an advisory firm specializing in managing assets for high-net-worth individuals. Katama's trading desk uses a variety of brokerage houses to execute trades on behalf of its clients. Roberts asks the trading desk to direct a large portion of its commissions to Naushon, Inc., a small broker/dealer run by one of Roberts' business school classmates. Katama's traders have found that Naushon is not very competitive on pricing, and although Naushon generates some research for its trading clients, Katama's other analysts have found most of Naushon's research to be not especially useful. Nevertheless, the traders do as Roberts asks, and in return for receiving a large portion of Katama's business, Naushon recommends the investment services of Roberts and Katama to its wealthiest clients. This arrangement is not disclosed to either Katama or the clients referred by Naushon.

> *Comment*: Roberts is violating Standard VI(C) by failing to inform her employer of the referral arrangement.

Example 4 (Disclosure of Referral Arrangements and Outside Organizations):

Alex Burl is a portfolio manager at Helpful Investments, a local investment advisory firm. Burl is on the advisory board of his child's school, which is looking for ways to raise money to purchase new playground equipment for the school. Burl discusses a plan with his supervisor in which he will donate to the school a portion of his service fee from new clients referred by the parents of students at the school. Upon getting the approval from Helpful, Burl presents the idea to the school's advisory board and directors. The school agrees to announce the program at the next parent event and asks Burl to provide the appropriate written materials to be distributed. A week following the distribution of the flyers, Burl receives the first school-related referral. In establishing the client's investment policy statement, Burl clearly discusses the school's referral and outlines the plans for distributing the donation back to the school.

> *Comment*: Burl has not violated Standard VI(C) because he secured the permission of his employer, Helpful Investments, and the school prior to beginning the program and because he discussed the arrangement with the client at the time the investment policy statement was designed.

Example 5 (Disclosure of Referral Arrangements and Outside Parties):

The sponsor of a state employee pension is seeking to hire a firm to manage the pension plan's emerging market allocation. To assist in the review process, the sponsor has hired Thomas Arrow as a consultant to solicit proposals from various advisers. Arrow is contracted by the sponsor to represent its best interest in selecting the most appropriate new manager. The process runs smoothly, and Overseas Investments is selected as the new manager.

The following year, news breaks that Arrow is under investigation by the local regulator for accepting kickbacks from investment managers after they are awarded new pension allocations. Overseas Investments is included in the list of firms allegedly making these payments. Although the sponsor is happy with the performance of Overseas since it has been managing the pension plan's emerging market funds, the sponsor still decides to have an independent review of the proposals and the selection process to ensure that Overseas was the appropriate firm for its needs. This review confirms that, even though Arrow was being paid by both parties, the recommendation of Overseas appeared to be objective and appropriate.

> *Comment*: Arrow has violated Standard VI(C) because he did not disclose the fee being paid by Overseas. Withholding this information raises the question of a potential lack of objectivity in the recommendation of Overseas by Arrow; this aspect is in addition to questions about the legality of having firms pay to be considered for an allocation.
>
> Regulators and governmental agencies may adopt requirements concerning allowable consultant activities. Local regulations sometimes include having a consultant register with the regulatory agency's ethics board. Regulator policies may include a prohibition on acceptance of payments from investment managers receiving allocations and require regular reporting of contributions made to political organizations and candidates. Arrow would have to adhere to these requirements as well as the Code and Standards.

STANDARD VII: RESPONSIBILITIES AS A CFA INSTITUTE MEMBER OR CFA CANDIDATE

Standard VII(A) Conduct as Participants in CFA Institute Programs

> Members and Candidates must not engage in any conduct that compromises the reputation or integrity of CFA Institute or the CFA designation or the integrity, validity, or security of CFA Institute programs.

Guidance

Highlights:

- *Confidential Program Information*
- *Additional CFA Program Restrictions*
- *Expressing an Opinion*

Standard VII(A) covers the conduct of CFA Institute members and candidates involved with the CFA Program and prohibits any conduct that undermines the public's confidence that the CFA charter represents a level of achievement based on merit and ethical conduct. There is an array of CFA Institute programs beyond the CFA Program that provide additional educational and credentialing opportunities, including the Certificate in Investment Performance Measurement (CIPM) Program and the CFA Institute Investment Foundations™ Program. The standard's function is to hold members and candidates to a high ethical criterion while they are participating in or involved with any CFA Institute program. Conduct covered includes but is not limited to

- giving or receiving assistance (cheating) on any CFA Institute examinations;
- violating the rules, regulations, and testing policies of CFA Institute programs;
- providing confidential program or exam information to candidates or the public;
- disregarding or attempting to circumvent security measures established for any CFA Institute examinations;
- improperly using an association with CFA Institute to further personal or professional goals; and
- misrepresenting information on the Professional Conduct Statement or in the CFA Institute Continuing Education Program.

Confidential Program Information

CFA Institute is vigilant about protecting the integrity of CFA Institute programs' content and examination processes. CFA Institute program rules, regulations, and policies prohibit candidates from disclosing confidential material gained during the exam process.

Examples of information that cannot be disclosed by candidates sitting for an exam include but are not limited to

- specific details of questions appearing on the exam and
- broad topical areas and formulas tested or not tested on the exam.

All aspects of the exam, including questions, broad topical areas, and formulas, tested or not tested, are considered confidential until such time as CFA Institute elects to release them publicly. This confidentiality requirement allows CFA Institute to maintain the integrity and rigor of exams for future candidates. Standard VII(A) does not prohibit candidates from discussing nonconfidential information or curriculum material with others or in study groups in preparation for the exam.

Candidates increasingly use online forums and new technology as part of their exam preparations. CFA Institute actively polices blogs, forums, and related social networking groups for information considered confidential. The organization works with both individual candidates and the sponsors of online or offline services to promptly remove any and all violations. As noted in the discussion of Standard I(A)–Knowledge of the Law, candidates, members, and the public are encouraged to report suspected violations to CFA Institute.

Additional CFA Program Restrictions

The CFA Program rules, regulations, and policies define additional allowed and disallowed actions concerning the exams. Violating any of the testing policies, such as the calculator policy, personal belongings policy, or the Candidate Pledge, constitutes a violation of Standard VII(A). Candidates will find all of these policies on the CFA Program portion of the CFA Institute website (www.cfainstitute.org). Exhibit 2 provides the Candidate Pledge, which highlights the respect candidates must have for the integrity, validity, and security of the CFA exam.

Members may participate as volunteers in various aspects of the CFA Program. Standard VII(A) prohibits members from disclosing and/or soliciting confidential material gained prior to or during the exam and grading processes with those outside the CFA exam development process.

Examples of information that cannot be shared by members involved in developing, administering, or grading the exams include but are not limited to

- questions appearing on the exam or under consideration,
- deliberation related to the exam process, and
- information related to the scoring of questions.

Members may also be asked to offer assistance with other CFA Institute programs, including but not limited to the CIPM and Investment Foundations programs. Members participating in any CFA Institute program should do so with the same level of integrity and confidentiality as is required of participation in the CFA Program.

Expressing an Opinion

Standard VII(A) does *not* cover expressing opinions regarding CFA Institute, the CFA Program, or other CFA Institute programs. Members and candidates are free to disagree and express their disagreement with CFA Institute on its policies, its procedures, or any advocacy positions taken by the organization. When expressing a personal opinion, a candidate is prohibited from disclosing content-specific information, including any actual exam question and the information as to subject matter covered or not covered in the exam.

Exhibit 2	Sample of CFA Program Testing Policies
Candidate Pledge	As a candidate in the CFA Program, I am obligated to follow Standard VII(A) of the CFA Institute Standards of Professional Conduct, which states that members and candidates must not engage in any conduct that compromises the reputation or integrity of CFA Institute or the CFA designation or the integrity, validity, or security of the CFA exam.

- Prior to this exam, I have not given or received information regarding the content of this exam. During this exam, I will not give or receive any information regarding the content of this exam.

- After this exam, I will not disclose **ANY** portion of this exam and I will not remove **ANY** exam materials from the testing room in original or copied form. I understand that all exam materials, including my answers, are the property of CFA Institute and will not be returned to me in any form.

- I will follow **ALL** rules of the CFA Program as stated on the CFA Institute website and the back cover of the exam book. My violation of any rules of the CFA Program will result in CFA Institute voiding my exam results and may lead to suspension or termination of my candidacy in the CFA Program.

Application of the Standard

Example 1 (Sharing Exam Questions):

Travis Nero serves as a proctor for the administration of the CFA examination in his city. In the course of his service, he reviews a copy of the Level II exam on the evening prior to the exam's administration and provides information concerning the exam questions to two candidates who use it to prepare for the exam.

Comment: Nero and the two candidates have violated Standard VII(A). By giving information about the exam questions to two candidates, Nero provided an unfair advantage to the two candidates and undermined the integrity and validity of the Level II exam as an accurate measure of the knowledge, skills, and abilities necessary to earn the right to use the CFA designation. By accepting the information, the candidates also compromised the integrity and validity of the Level II exam and undermined the ethical framework that is a key part of the designation.

Example 2 (Bringing Written Material into Exam Room):

Loren Sullivan is enrolled to take the Level II CFA examination. He has been having difficulty remembering a particular formula, so prior to entering the exam room, he writes the formula on the palm of his hand. During the afternoon section of the exam, a proctor notices Sullivan looking at the palm of his hand. She asks to see his hand and finds the formula.

Comment: Because Sullivan wrote down information from the Candidate Body of Knowledge (CBOK) and took that written information into the exam room, his conduct compromised the validity of his exam performance and violated Standard VII(A). Sullivan's conduct was also in direct contradiction with the rules and regulations of the CFA Program, the Candidate Pledge, and the CFA Institute Code and Standards.

Example 3 (Writing after Exam Period End):

At the conclusion of the morning section of the Level I CFA examination, the proctors announce, "Stop writing now." John Davis has not completed the exam, so he continues to randomly fill in ovals on his answer sheet. A proctor approaches Davis's desk and reminds him that he should stop writing immediately. Davis, however, continues to complete the answer sheet. After the proctor asks him to stop writing two additional times, Davis finally puts down his pencil.

> *Comment*: By continuing to complete his exam after time was called, Davis has violated Standard VII(A). By continuing to write, Davis took an unfair advantage over other candidates, and his conduct compromised the validity of his exam performance. Additionally, by not heeding the proctor's repeated instructions, Davis violated the rules and regulations of the CFA Program.

Example 4 (Sharing Exam Content):

After completing Level II of the CFA exam, Annabelle Rossi posts on her blog about her experience. She posts the following: "Level II is complete! I think I did fairly well on the exam. It was really difficult, but fair. I think I did especially well on the derivatives questions. And there were tons of them! I think I counted 18! The ethics questions were really hard. I'm glad I spent so much time on the Code and Standards. I was surprised to see there were no questions at all about IPO allocations. I expected there to be a couple. Well, off to celebrate getting through it. See you tonight?"

> *Comment*: Rossi did not violate Standard VII(A) when she wrote about how difficult she found the exam or how well she thinks she may have done. By revealing portions of the CBOK covered on the exam and areas not covered, however, she did violate Standard VII(A) and the Candidate Pledge. Depending on the time frame in which the comments were posted, Rossi not only may have assisted future candidates but also may have provided an unfair advantage to candidates yet to sit for the same exam, thereby undermining the integrity and validity of the Level II exam.

Example 5 (Sharing Exam Content):

Level I candidate Etienne Gagne has been a frequent visitor to an internet forum designed specifically for CFA Program candidates. The week after completing the Level I examination, Gagne and several others begin a discussion thread on the forum about the most challenging questions and attempt to determine the correct answers.

> *Comment*: Gagne has violated Standard VII(A) by providing and soliciting confidential exam information, which compromises the integrity of the exam process and violates the Candidate Pledge. In trying to determine correct answers to specific questions, the group's discussion included question-specific details considered to be confidential to the CFA Program.

Example 6 (Sharing Exam Content):

CFA4Sure is a company that produces test-preparation materials for CFA Program candidates. Many candidates register for and use the company's products. The day after the CFA examination, CFA4Sure sends an e-mail to all its customers asking them to share with the company the hardest questions from the exam so that CFA4Sure can better prepare its customers for the next exam administration. Marisol Pena e-mails a summary of the questions she found most difficult on the exam.

Standard VII: Responsibilities as a CFA Institute Member or CFA Candidate

> *Comment*: Pena has violated Standard VII(A) by disclosing a portion of the exam questions. The information provided is considered confidential until publicly released by CFA Institute. CFA4Sure is likely to use such feedback to refine its review materials for future candidates. Pena's sharing of the specific questions undermines the integrity of the exam while potentially making the exam easier for future candidates.
>
> If the CFA4Sure employees who participated in the solicitation of confidential CFA Program information are CFA Institute members or candidates, they also have violated Standard VII(A).

Example 7 (Discussion of Exam Grading Guidelines and Results):

Prior to participating in grading CFA examinations, Wesley Whitcomb is required to sign a CFA Institute Grader Agreement. As part of the Grader Agreement, Whitcomb agrees not to reveal or discuss the exam materials with anyone except CFA Institute staff or other graders. Several weeks after the conclusion of the CFA exam grading, Whitcomb tells several colleagues who are candidates in the CFA Program which question he graded. He also discusses the guideline answer and adds that few candidates scored well on the question.

> *Comment*: Whitcomb violated Standard VII(A) by breaking the Grader Agreement and disclosing information related to a specific question on the exam, which compromised the integrity of the exam process.

Example 8 (Compromising CFA Institute Integrity as a Volunteer):

Jose Ramirez is an investor-relations consultant for several small companies that are seeking greater exposure to investors. He is also the program chair for the CFA Institute society in the city where he works. Ramirez schedules only companies that are his clients to make presentations to the society and excludes other companies.

> *Comment*: Ramirez, by using his volunteer position at CFA Institute to benefit himself and his clients, compromises the reputation and integrity of CFA Institute and thus violates Standard VII(A).

Example 9 (Compromising CFA Institute Integrity as a Volunteer):

Marguerite Warrenski is a member of the CFA Institute GIPS Executive Committee, which oversees the creation, implementation, and revision of the GIPS standards. As a member of the Executive Committee, she has advance knowledge of confidential information regarding the GIPS standards, including any new or revised standards the committee is considering. She tells her clients that her Executive Committee membership will allow her to better assist her clients in keeping up with changes to the Standards and facilitating their compliance with the changes.

> *Comment*: Warrenski is using her association with the GIPS Executive Committee to promote her firm's services to clients and potential clients. In defining her volunteer position at CFA Institute as a strategic business advantage over competing firms and implying to clients that she would use confidential information to further their interests, Warrenski is compromising the reputation and integrity of CFA Institute and thus violating Standard VII(A). She may factually state her involvement with the Executive Committee but cannot infer any special advantage to her clients from such participation.

Standard VII(B) Reference to CFA Institute, the CFA Designation, and the CFA Program

> When referring to CFA Institute, CFA Institute membership, the CFA designation, or candidacy in the CFA Program, Members and Candidates must not misrepresent or exaggerate the meaning or implications of membership in CFA Institute, holding the CFA designation, or candidacy in the CFA Program.

Guidance

Highlights:

- *CFA Institute Membership*
- *Using the CFA Designation*
- *Referring to Candidacy in the CFA Program*

Standard VII(B) is intended to prevent promotional efforts that make promises or guarantees that are tied to the CFA designation. Individuals must not exaggerate the meaning or implications of membership in CFA Institute, holding the CFA designation, or candidacy in the CFA Program.

Standard VII(B) is not intended to prohibit factual statements related to the positive benefit of earning the CFA designation. However, statements referring to CFA Institute, the CFA designation, or the CFA Program that overstate the competency of an individual or imply, either directly or indirectly, that superior performance can be expected from someone with the CFA designation are not allowed under the standard.

Statements that highlight or emphasize the commitment of CFA Institute members, CFA charterholders, and CFA candidates to ethical and professional conduct or mention the thoroughness and rigor of the CFA Program are appropriate. Members and candidates may make claims about the relative merits of CFA Institute, the CFA Program, or the Code and Standards as long as those statements are implicitly or explicitly stated as the opinion of the speaker. Statements that do not express opinions have to be supported by facts.

Standard VII(B) applies to any form of communication, including but not limited to communications made in electronic or written form (such as on firm letterhead, business cards, professional biographies, directory listings, printed advertising, firm brochures, or personal resumes) and oral statements made to the public, clients, or prospects.

CFA Institute Membership

The term "CFA Institute member" refers to "regular" and "affiliate" members of CFA Institute who have met the membership requirements as defined in the CFA Institute Bylaws. Once accepted as a CFA Institute member, the member must satisfy the following requirements to maintain his or her status:

- remit annually to CFA Institute a completed Professional Conduct Statement, which renews the commitment to abide by the requirements of the Code and Standards and the CFA Institute Professional Conduct Program, and
- pay applicable CFA Institute membership dues on an annual basis.

Standard VII: Responsibilities as a CFA Institute Member or CFA Candidate

If a CFA Institute member fails to meet any of these requirements, the individual is no longer considered an active member. Until membership is reactivated, individuals must not present themselves to others as active members. They may state, however, that they were CFA Institute members in the past or refer to the years when their membership was active.

Using the CFA Designation

Those who have earned the right to use the Chartered Financial Analyst designation are encouraged to do so but only in a manner that does not misrepresent or exaggerate the meaning or implications of the designation. The use of the designation may be accompanied by an accurate explanation of the requirements that have been met to earn the right to use the designation.

"CFA charterholders" are those individuals who have earned the right to use the CFA designation granted by CFA Institute. These people have satisfied certain requirements, including completion of the CFA Program and required years of acceptable work experience. Once granted the right to use the designation, individuals must also satisfy the CFA Institute membership requirements (see above) to maintain their right to use the designation.

If a CFA charterholder fails to meet any of the membership requirements, he or she forfeits the right to use the CFA designation. Until membership is reactivated, individuals must not present themselves to others as CFA charterholders. They may state, however, that they were charterholders in the past.

Given the growing popularity of social media, where individuals may anonymously express their opinions, pseudonyms or online profile names created to hide a member's identity should not be tagged with the CFA designation.

Use of the CFA designation by a CFA charterholder is governed by the terms and conditions of the annual Professional Conduct Statement Agreement, entered into between CFA Institute and its membership prior to commencement of use of the CFA designation and reaffirmed annually.

Referring to Candidacy in the CFA Program

Candidates in the CFA Program may refer to their participation in the CFA Program, but such references must clearly state that an individual is a *candidate* in the CFA Program and must not imply that the candidate has achieved any type of partial designation. A person is a candidate in the CFA Program if

- the person's application for registration in the CFA Program has been accepted by CFA Institute, as evidenced by issuance of a notice of acceptance, and the person is enrolled to sit for a specified examination or
- the registered person has sat for a specified examination but exam results have not yet been received.

If an individual is registered for the CFA Program but declines to sit for an exam or otherwise does not meet the definition of a candidate as described in the CFA Institute Bylaws, then that individual is no longer considered an active candidate. Once the person is enrolled to sit for a future examination, his or her CFA Program candidacy resumes.

CFA Program candidates must never state or imply that they have a partial designation as a result of passing one or more levels or cite an expected completion date of any level of the CFA Program. Final award of the charter is subject to meeting the CFA Program requirements and approval by the CFA Institute Board of Governors.

If a candidate passes each level of the exam in consecutive years and wants to state that he or she did so, that is not a violation of Standard VII(B) because it is a statement of fact. If the candidate then goes on to claim or imply superior ability by obtaining the designation in only three years, however, he or she is in violation of Standard VII(B).

Exhibit 3 provides examples of proper and improper references to the CFA designation.

Exhibit 3 Proper and Improper References to the CFA Designation

Proper References	Improper References
"Completion of the CFA Program has enhanced my portfolio management skills."	"CFA charterholders achieve better performance results."
"John Smith passed all three CFA Program examinations in three consecutive years."	"John Smith is among the elite, having passed all three CFA examinations in three consecutive attempts."
"The CFA designation is globally recognized and attests to a charterholder's success in a rigorous and comprehensive study program in the field of investment management and research analysis."	"As a CFA charterholder, I am the most qualified to manage client investments."
"The credibility that the CFA designation affords and the skills the CFA Program cultivates are key assets for my future career development."	"As a CFA charterholder, Jane White provides the best value in trade execution."
"I enrolled in the CFA Program to obtain the highest set of credentials in the global investment management industry."	"Enrolling as a candidate in the CFA Program ensures one of becoming better at valuing debt securities."
"I passed Level I of the CFA Program."	"CFA, Level II"
"I am a 2010 Level III candidate in the CFA Program."	"CFA, Expected 2011"
"I passed all three levels of the CFA Program and may be eligible for the CFA charter upon completion of the required work experience."	"CFA, Expected 2011" "John Smith, Charter Pending"

Recommended Procedures for Compliance

Misuse of a member's CFA designation or CFA candidacy or improper reference to it is common by those in a member's or candidate's firm who do not possess knowledge of the requirements of Standard VII(B). As an appropriate step to reduce this risk, members and candidates should disseminate written information about Standard VII(B) and the accompanying guidance to their firm's legal, compliance, public relations, and marketing departments (see www.cfainstitute.org).

For materials that refer to employees' affiliation with CFA Institute, members and candidates should encourage their firms to create templates that are approved by a central authority (such as the compliance department) as being consistent with Standard VII(B). This practice promotes consistency and accuracy in the firm of references to CFA Institute membership, the CFA designation, and CFA candidacy.

Standard VII: Responsibilities as a CFA Institute Member or CFA Candidate

Application of the Standard

Example 1 (Passing Exams in Consecutive Years):

An advertisement for AZ Investment Advisors states that all the firm's principals are CFA charterholders and all passed the three examinations on their first attempt. The advertisement prominently links this fact to the notion that AZ's mutual funds have achieved superior performance.

> *Comment*: AZ may state that all principals passed the three examinations on the first try as long as this statement is true, but it must not be linked to performance or imply superior ability. Implying that (1) CFA charterholders achieve better investment results and (2) those who pass the exams on the first try may be more successful than those who do not violates Standard VII(B).

Example 2 (Right to Use CFA Designation):

Five years after receiving his CFA charter, Louis Vasseur resigns his position as an investment analyst and spends the next two years traveling abroad. Because he is not actively engaged in the investment profession, he does not file a completed Professional Conduct Statement with CFA Institute and does not pay his CFA Institute membership dues. At the conclusion of his travels, Vasseur becomes a self-employed analyst accepting assignments as an independent contractor. Without reinstating his CFA Institute membership by filing his Professional Conduct Statement and paying his dues, he prints business cards that display "CFA" after his name.

> *Comment*: Vasseur has violated Standard VII(B) because his right to use the CFA designation was suspended when he failed to file his Professional Conduct Statement and stopped paying dues. Therefore, he no longer is able to state or imply that he is an active CFA charterholder. When Vasseur files his Professional Conduct Statement, resumes paying CFA Institute dues to activate his membership, and completes the CFA Institute reinstatement procedures, he will be eligible to use the CFA designation.

Example 3 ("Retired" CFA Institute Membership Status):

After a 25-year career, James Simpson retires from his firm. Because he is not actively engaged in the investment profession, he does not file a completed Professional Conduct Statement with CFA Institute and does not pay his CFA Institute membership dues. Simpson designs a plain business card (without a corporate logo) to hand out to friends with his new contact details, and he continues to put "CFA" after his name.

> *Comment*: Simpson has violated Standard VII(B). Because he failed to file his Professional Conduct Statement and ceased paying dues, his membership has been suspended and he has given up the right to use the CFA designation. CFA Institute has procedures, however, for reclassifying a member and charterholder as "retired" and reducing the annual dues. If he wants to obtain retired status, he needs to file the appropriate paperwork with CFA Institute. When Simpson receives his notification from CFA Institute that his membership has been reclassified as retired and he resumes paying reduced dues, his membership will be reactivated and his right to use the CFA designation will be reinstated.

Example 4 (Stating Facts about CFA Designation and Program):

Rhonda Reese has been a CFA charterholder since 2000. In a conversation with a friend who is considering enrolling in the CFA Program, she states that she has learned a great deal from the CFA Program and that many firms require their employees to be CFA charterholders. She would recommend the CFA Program to anyone pursuing a career in investment management.

> *Comment*: Reese's comments comply with Standard VII(B). Her statements refer to facts: The CFA Program enhanced her knowledge, and many firms require the CFA designation for their investment professionals.

Example 5 (Order of Professional and Academic Designations):

Tatiana Prittima has earned both her CFA designation and a PhD in finance. She would like to cite both her accomplishments on her business card but is unsure of the proper method for doing so.

> *Comment*: The order of designations cited on such items as resumes and business cards is a matter of personal preference. Prittima is free to cite the CFA designation either before or after citing her PhD. Multiple designations must be separated by a comma.

Example 6 (Use of Fictitious Name):

Barry Glass is the lead quantitative analyst at CityCenter Hedge Fund. Glass is responsible for the development, maintenance, and enhancement of the proprietary models the fund uses to manage its investors' assets. Glass reads several high-level mathematical publications and blogs to stay informed on current developments. One blog, run by Expert CFA, presents some intriguing research that may benefit one of CityCenter's current models. Glass is under pressure from firm executives to improve the model's predictive abilities, and he incorporates the factors discussed in the online research. The updated output recommends several new investments to the fund's portfolio managers.

> *Comment*: "Expert CFA" has violated Standard VII(B) by using the CFA designation inappropriately. As with any research report, authorship of online comments must include the charterholder's full name along with any reference to the CFA designation.
>
> See also Standard V(A), which Glass has violated for guidance on diligence and reasonable basis.

PRACTICE PROBLEMS

Unless otherwise stated in the question, all individuals in the following questions are CFA Institute members or candidates in the CFA Program and, therefore, are subject to the CFA Institute Code of Ethics and Standards of Professional Conduct.

1 Smith, a research analyst with a brokerage firm, decides to change his recommendation for the common stock of Green Company, Inc., from a "buy" to a "sell." He mails this change in investment advice to all the firm's clients on Wednesday. The day after the mailing, a client calls with a buy order for 500 shares of Green Company. In this circumstance, Smith should:
   A Accept the order.
   B Advise the customer of the change in recommendation before accepting the order.
   C Not accept the order because it is contrary to the firm's recommendation.

2 Which statement about a manager's use of client brokerage commissions violates the Code and Standards?
   A A client may direct a manager to use that client's brokerage commissions to purchase goods and services for that client.
   B Client brokerage commissions should be used to benefit the client and should be commensurate with the value of the brokerage and research services received.
   C Client brokerage commissions may be directed to pay for the investment manager's operating expenses.

3 Jamison is a junior research analyst with Howard & Howard, a brokerage and investment banking firm. Howard & Howard's mergers and acquisitions department has represented the Britland Company in all of its acquisitions for the past 20 years. Two of Howard & Howard's senior officers are directors of various Britland subsidiaries. Jamison has been asked to write a research report on Britland. What is the best course of action for her to follow?
   A Jamison may write the report but must refrain from expressing any opinions because of the special relationships between the two companies.
   B Jamison should not write the report because the two Howard & Howard officers serve as directors for subsidiaries of Britland.
   C Jamison may write the report if she discloses the special relationships with the company in the report.

4 Which of the following statements clearly *conflicts* with the recommended procedures for compliance presented in the CFA Institute *Standards of Practice Handbook*?
   A Firms should disclose to clients the personal investing policies and procedures established for their employees.
   B Prior approval must be obtained for the personal investment transactions of all employees.
   C For confidentiality reasons, personal transactions and holdings should not be reported to employers unless mandated by regulatory organizations.

5 Bronson provides investment advice to the board of trustees of a private university endowment fund. The trustees have provided Bronson with the fund's financial information, including planned expenditures. Bronson receives a phone call on Friday afternoon from Murdock, a prominent alumnus,

requesting that Bronson fax him comprehensive financial information about the fund. According to Murdock, he has a potential contributor but needs the information that day to close the deal and cannot contact any of the trustees. Based on the CFA Institute Standards, Bronson should:

A Send Murdock the information because disclosure would benefit the client.

B Not send Murdock the information to preserve confidentiality.

C Send Murdock the information, provided Bronson promptly notifies the trustees.

6 Miller heads the research department of a large brokerage firm. The firm has many analysts, some of whom are subject to the Code and Standards. If Miller delegates some supervisory duties, which statement best describes her responsibilities under the Code and Standards?

A Miller's supervisory responsibilities do not apply to those subordinates who are not subject to the Code and Standards.

B Miller no longer has supervisory responsibility for those duties delegated to her subordinates.

C Miller retains supervisory responsibility for all subordinates despite her delegation of some duties.

7 Willier is the research analyst responsible for following Company X. All the information he has accumulated and documented suggests that the outlook for the company's new products is poor, so the stock should be rated a weak "hold." During lunch, however, Willier overhears a financial analyst from another firm whom he respects offer opinions that conflict with Willier's forecasts and expectations. Upon returning to his office, Willier releases a strong "buy" recommendation to the public. Willier:

A Violated the Standards by failing to distinguish between facts and opinions in his recommendation.

B Violated the Standards because he did not have a reasonable and adequate basis for his recommendation.

C Was in full compliance with the Standards.

8 An investment management firm has been hired by ETV Corporation to work on an additional public offering for the company. The firm's brokerage unit now has a "sell" recommendation on ETV, but the head of the investment banking department has asked the head of the brokerage unit to change the recommendation from "sell" to "buy." According to the Standards, the head of the brokerage unit would be permitted to:

A Increase the recommendation by no more than one increment (in this case, to a "hold" recommendation).

B Place the company on a restricted list and give only factual information about the company.

C Assign a new analyst to decide if the stock deserves a higher rating.

9 Albert and Tye, who recently started their own investment advisory business, have registered to take the Level III CFA examination. Albert's business card reads, "Judy Albert, CFA Level II." Tye has not put anything about the CFA designation on his business card, but promotional material that he designed for the business describes the CFA requirements and indicates that Tye participates in the CFA Program and has completed Levels I and II. According to the Standards:

A Albert has violated the Standards, but Tye has not.

B Tye has violated the Standards, but Albert has not.

C Both Albert and Tye have violated the Standards.

10 Scott works for a regional brokerage firm. He estimates that Walkton Industries will increase its dividend by US$1.50 a share during the next year. He realizes that this increase is contingent on pending legislation that would, if enacted, give Walkton a substantial tax break. The US representative for Walkton's home district has told Scott that, although she is lobbying hard for the bill and prospects for its passage are favorable, concern of the US Congress over the federal deficit could cause the tax bill to be voted down. Walkton Industries has not made any statements about a change in dividend policy. Scott writes in his research report, "We expect Walkton's stock price to rise by at least US$8.00 a share by the end of the year because the dividend will increase by US$1.50 a share. Investors buying the stock at the current time should expect to realize a total return of at least 15% on the stock." According to the Standards:

A Scott violated the Standards because he used material inside information.

B Scott violated the Standards because he failed to separate opinion from fact.

C Scott violated the Standards by basing his research on uncertain predictions of future government action.

11 Which one of the following actions will help to ensure the fair treatment of brokerage firm clients when a new investment recommendation is made?

A Informing all people in the firm in advance that a recommendation is to be disseminated.

B Distributing recommendations to institutional clients prior to individual accounts.

C Minimizing the time between the decision and the dissemination of a recommendation.

12 The mosaic theory holds that an analyst:

A Violates the Code and Standards if the analyst fails to have knowledge of and comply with applicable laws.

B Can use material public information and nonmaterial nonpublic information in the analyst's analysis.

C Should use all available and relevant information in support of an investment recommendation.

13 Jurgen is a portfolio manager. One of her firm's clients has told Jurgen that he will compensate her beyond the compensation provided by her firm on the basis of the capital appreciation of his portfolio each year. Jurgen should:

A Turn down the additional compensation because it will result in conflicts with the interests of other clients' accounts.

B Turn down the additional compensation because it will create undue pressure on her to achieve strong short-term performance.

C Obtain permission from her employer prior to accepting the compensation arrangement.

14 One of the discretionary accounts managed by Farnsworth is the Jones Corporation employee profit-sharing plan. Jones, the company president, recently asked Farnsworth to vote the shares in the profit-sharing plan in favor of the slate of directors nominated by Jones Corporation and against the directors sponsored by a dissident stockholder group. Farnsworth does not want to lose this account because he directs all the account's trades to a brokerage firm that provides Farnsworth with useful information about tax-free investments. Although this information is not of value in managing the Jones Corporation account, it does help in managing several other accounts. The brokerage firm providing this information also offers the lowest commissions for trades and provides best execution. Farnsworth investigates the director issue, concludes that the management-nominated slate is better for the long-run performance of the company than the dissident group's slate, and votes accordingly. Farnsworth:

A Violated the Standards in voting the shares in the manner requested by Jones but not in directing trades to the brokerage firm.

B Did not violate the Standards in voting the shares in the manner requested by Jones or in directing trades to the brokerage firm.

C Violated the Standards in directing trades to the brokerage firm but not in voting the shares as requested by Jones.

15 Brown works for an investment counseling firm. Green, a new client of the firm, is meeting with Brown for the first time. Green used another counseling firm for financial advice for years, but she has switched her account to Brown's firm. After spending a few minutes getting acquainted, Brown explains to Green that she has discovered a highly undervalued stock that offers large potential gains. She recommends that Green purchase the stock. Brown has committed a violation of the Standards. What should she have done differently?

A Brown should have determined Green's needs, objectives, and tolerance for risk before making a recommendation of any type of security.

B Brown should have thoroughly explained the characteristics of the company to Green, including the characteristics of the industry in which the company operates.

C Brown should have explained her qualifications, including her education, training, and experience and the meaning of the CFA designation.

16 Grey recommends the purchase of a mutual fund that invests solely in long-term US Treasury bonds. He makes the following statements to his clients:

I. "The payment of the bonds is guaranteed by the US government; therefore, the default risk of the bonds is virtually zero."

II. "If you invest in the mutual fund, you will earn a 10% rate of return each year for the next several years based on historical performance of the market."

Did Grey's statements violate the CFA Institute Code and Standards?

A Neither statement violated the Code and Standards.

B Only statement I violated the Code and Standards.

C Only statement II violated the Code and Standards.

17 Anderb, a portfolio manager for XYZ Investment Management Company—a registered investment organization that advises investment firms and private accounts—was promoted to that position three years ago. Bates, her supervisor, is responsible for reviewing Anderb's portfolio account transactions and her required monthly reports of personal stock transactions. Anderb has been using Jonelli, a broker, almost exclusively for brokerage transactions for the portfolio account. For securities in which Jonelli's firm makes a market, Jonelli has been giving Anderb lower prices for personal purchases and higher prices for personal sales than Jonelli gives to Anderb's portfolio accounts and other investors. Anderb has been filing monthly reports with Bates only for those months in which she has no personal transactions, which is about every fourth month. Which of the following is *most likely* to be a violation of the Code and Standards?

A Anderb failed to disclose to her employer her personal transactions.

B Anderb owned the same securities as those of her clients.

C Bates allowed Anderb to use Jonelli as her broker for personal trades.

Practice Problems

18 Which of the following is a correct statement of a member's or candidate's duty under the Code and Standards?
   A In the absence of specific applicable law or other regulatory requirements, the Code and Standards govern the member's or candidate's actions.
   B A member or candidate is required to comply only with applicable local laws, rules, regulations, or customs, even though the Code and Standards may impose a higher degree of responsibility or a higher duty on the member or candidate.
   C A member or candidate who trades securities in a securities market where no applicable local laws or stock exchange rules regulate the use of material nonpublic information may take investment action based on material nonpublic information.

19 Ward is scheduled to visit the corporate headquarters of Evans Industries. Ward expects to use the information he obtains there to complete his research report on Evans stock. Ward learns that Evans plans to pay all of Ward's expenses for the trip, including costs of meals, hotel room, and air transportation. Which of the following actions would be the *best* course for Ward to take under the Code and Standards?
   A Accept the expense-paid trip and write an objective report.
   B Pay for all travel expenses, including costs of meals and incidental items.
   C Accept the expense-paid trip but disclose the value of the services accepted in the report.

20 Which of the following statements is *correct* under the Code and Standards?
   A CFA Institute members and candidates are prohibited from undertaking independent practice in competition with their employer.
   B Written consent from the employer is necessary to permit independent practice that could result in compensation or other benefits in competition with a member's or candidate's employer.
   C Members and candidates are prohibited from making arrangements or preparations to go into a competitive business before terminating their relationship with their employer.

21 Smith is a financial analyst with XYZ Brokerage Firm. She is preparing a purchase recommendation on JNI Corporation. Which of the following situations is *most likely* to represent a conflict of interest for Smith that would have to be disclosed?
   A Smith frequently purchases items produced by JNI.
   B XYZ holds for its own account a substantial common stock position in JNI.
   C Smith's brother-in-law is a supplier to JNI.

22 Michelieu tells a prospective client, "I may not have a long-term track record yet, but I'm sure that you'll be very pleased with my recommendations and service. In the three years that I've been in the business, my equity-oriented clients have averaged a total return of more than 26% a year." The statement is true, but Michelieu only has a few clients, and one of his clients took a large position in a penny stock (against Michelieu's advice) and realized a huge gain. This large return caused the average of all of Michelieu's clients to exceed 26% a year. Without this one investment, the average gain would have been 8% a year. Has Michelieu violated the Standards?
   A No, because Michelieu is not promising that he can earn a 26% return in the future.

B No, because the statement is a true and accurate description of Michelieu's track record.

C Yes, because the statement misrepresents Michelieu's track record.

23 An investment banking department of a brokerage firm often receives material nonpublic information that could have considerable value if used in advising the firm's brokerage clients. In order to conform to the Code and Standards, which one of the following is the best policy for the brokerage firm?

A Permanently prohibit both "buy" and "sell" recommendations of the stocks of clients of the investment banking department.

B Establish physical and informational barriers within the firm to prevent the exchange of information between the investment banking and brokerage operations.

C Monitor the exchange of information between the investment banking department and the brokerage operation.

24 Stewart has been hired by Goodner Industries, Inc., to manage its pension fund. Stewart's duty of loyalty, prudence, and care is owed to:

A The management of Goodner.

B The participants and beneficiaries of Goodner's pension plan.

C The shareholders of Goodner.

25 Which of the following statements is a stated purpose of disclosure in Standard VI(C)–Referral Fees?

A Disclosure will allow the client to request discounted service fees.

B Disclosure will help the client evaluate any possible partiality shown in the recommendation of services.

C Disclosure means advising a prospective client about the referral arrangement once a formal client relationship has been established.

26 Rose, a portfolio manager for a local investment advisory firm, is planning to sell a portion of his personal investment portfolio to cover the costs of his child's academic tuition. Rose wants to sell a portion of his holdings in Household Products, but his firm recently upgraded the stock to "strong buy." Which of the following describes Rose's options under the Code and Standards?

A Based on his firm's "buy" recommendation, Rose cannot sell the shares because he would be improperly prospering from the inflated recommendation.

B Rose is free to sell his personal holdings once his firm is properly informed of his intentions.

C Rose can sell his personal holdings but only when a client of the firm places an order to buy shares of Household.

27 A former hedge fund manager, Jackman, has decided to launch a new private wealth management firm. From his prior experiences, he believes the new firm needs to achieve US$1 million in assets under management in the first year. Jackman offers a $10,000 incentive to any adviser who joins his firm with the minimum of $200,000 in committed investments. Jackman places notice of the opening on several industry web portals and career search sites. Which of the following is *correct* according to the Code and Standards?

A A member or candidate is eligible for the new position and incentive if he or she can arrange for enough current clients to switch to the new firm and if the member or candidate discloses the incentive fee.

B A member or candidate may not accept employment with the new firm because Jackman's incentive offer violates the Code and Standards.

Practice Problems

    C A member or candidate is not eligible for the new position unless he or she is currently unemployed because soliciting the clients of the member's or candidate's current employer is prohibited.

28 Carter works for Invest Today, a local asset management firm. A broker that provides Carter with proprietary research through client brokerage arrangements is offering a new trading service. The broker is offering low-fee, execution-only trades to complement its traditional full-service, execution-and-research trades. To entice Carter and other asset managers to send additional business its way, the broker will apply the commissions paid on the new service toward satisfying the brokerage commitment of the prior full-service arrangements. Carter has always been satisfied with the execution provided on the full-service trades, and the new low-fee trades are comparable to the fees of other brokers currently used for the accounts that prohibit soft dollar arrangements.

    A Carter can trade for his accounts that prohibit soft dollar arrangements under the new low-fee trading scheme.

    B Carter cannot use the new trading scheme because the commissions are prohibited by the soft dollar restrictions of the accounts.

    C Carter should trade only through the new low-fee scheme and should increase his trading volume to meet his required commission commitment.

29 Rule has worked as a portfolio manager for a large investment management firm for the past 10 years. Rule earned his CFA charter last year and has decided to open his own investment management firm. After leaving his current employer, Rule creates some marketing material for his new firm. He states in the material, "In earning the CFA charter, a highly regarded credential in the investment management industry, I further enhanced the portfolio management skills learned during my professional career. While completing the examination process in three consecutive years, I consistently received the highest possible scores on the topics of Ethics, Alternative Investments, and Portfolio Management." Has Rule violated Standard VII(B)–Reference to CFA Institute, the CFA Designation, and the CFA Program in his marketing material?

    A Rule violated Standard VII(B) in stating that he completed the exams in three consecutive years.

    B Rule violated Standard VII(B) in stating that he received the highest scores in the topics of Ethics, Alternative Investments, and Portfolio Management.

    C Rule did not violate Standard VII(B).

30 Stafford is a portfolio manager for a specialized real estate mutual fund. Her firm clearly describes in the fund's prospectus its soft dollar policies. Stafford decides that entering the CFA Program will enhance her investment decision-making skill and decides to use the fund's soft dollar account to pay the registration and exam fees for the CFA Program. Which of the following statements is *most likely* correct?

    A Stafford did not violate the Code and Standards because the prospectus informed investors of the fund's soft dollar policies.

    B Stafford violated the Code and Standards because improving her investment skills is not a reasonable use of the soft dollar account.

    C Stafford violated the Code and Standards because the CFA Program does not meet the definition of research allowed to be purchased with brokerage commissions.

31 Long has been asked to be the keynote speaker at an upcoming investment conference. The event is being hosted by one of the third-party investment managers currently used by his pension fund. The manager offers to cover all conference and travel costs for Long and make the conference registrations free for three additional members of his investment management team. To ensure that the conference obtains the best speakers, the host firm has arranged for an exclusive golf outing for the day following the conference on a local championship-caliber course. Which of the following is *least likely* to violate Standard I(B)?

   A Long may accept only the offer to have his conference-related expenses paid by the host firm.

   B Long may accept the offer to have his conference-related expenses paid and may attend the exclusive golf outing at the expense of the hosting firm.

   C Long may accept the entire package of incentives offered to speak at this conference.

32 Andrews, a private wealth manager, is conducting interviews for a new research analyst for his firm. One of the candidates is Wright, an analyst with a local investment bank. During the interview, while Wright is describing his analytical skills, he mentions a current merger in which his firm is acting as the adviser. Andrews has heard rumors of a possible merger between the two companies, but no releases have been made by the companies concerned. Which of the following actions by Andrews is *least likely* a violation of the Code and Standards?

   A Waiting until the next day before trading on the information to allow time for it to become public.

   B Notifying all investment managers in his firm of the new information so none of their clients are disadvantaged.

   C Placing the securities mentioned as part of the merger on the firm's restricted trading list.

33 Pietro, president of Local Bank, has hired the bank's market maker, Vogt, to seek a merger partner. Local is currently not listed on a stock exchange and has not reported that it is seeking strategic alternatives. Vogt has discussed the possibility of a merger with several firms, but they have all decided to wait until after the next period's financial data are available. The potential buyers believe the results will be worse than the results of prior periods and will allow them to pay less for Local Bank.

   Pietro wants to increase the likelihood of structuring a merger deal quickly. Which of the following actions would *most likely* be a violation of the Code and Standards?

   A Pietro could instruct Local Bank to issue a press release announcing that it has retained Vogt to find a merger partner.

   B Pietro could place a buy order for 2,000 shares (or four times the average weekly volume) through Vogt for his personal account.

   C After confirming with Local's chief financial officer, Pietro could instruct Local to issue a press release reaffirming the firm's prior announced earnings guidance for the full fiscal year.

34 ABC Investment Management acquires a new, very large account with two concentrated positions. The firm's current policy is to add new accounts for the purpose of performance calculation after the first full month of management. Cupp is responsible for calculating the firm's performance returns. Before the end of the initial month, Cupp notices that one of the significant holdings of the new accounts is acquired by another company, causing the value of the investment to double. Because of this holding, Cupp decides to account for the new portfolio as of the date of transfer, thereby allowing ABC Investment to reap the positive impact of that month's portfolio return.

Practice Problems

    A Cupp did not violate the Code and Standards because the GIPS standards allow composites to be updated on the date of large external cash flows.

    B Cupp did not violate the Code and Standards because companies are allowed to determine when to incorporate new accounts into their composite calculation.

    C Cupp violated the Code and Standards because the inclusion of the new account produces an inaccurate calculation of the monthly results according to the firm's stated policies.

35 Cannan has been working from home on weekends and occasionally saves correspondence with clients and completed work on her home computer. Because of worsening market conditions, Cannan is one of several employees released by her firm. While Cannan is looking for a new job, she uses the files she saved at home to request letters of recommendation from former clients. She also provides to prospective clients some of the reports as examples of her abilities.

    A Cannan violated the Code and Standards because she did not receive permission from her former employer to keep or use the files after her employment ended.

    B Cannan did not violate the Code and Standards because the files were created and saved on her own time and computer.

    C Cannan violated the Code and Standards because she is prohibited from saving files on her home computer.

36 Quinn sat for the Level III CFA exam this past weekend. He updates his resume with the following statement: "In finishing the CFA Program, I improved my skills related to researching investments and managing portfolios. I will be eligible for the CFA charter upon completion of the required work experience."

    A Quinn violated the Code and Standards by claiming he improved his skills through the CFA Program.

    B Quinn violated the Code and Standards by incorrectly stating that he is eligible for the CFA charter.

    C Quinn did not violate the Code and Standards with his resume update.

37 During a round of golf, Rodriguez, chief financial officer of Mega Retail, mentions to Hart, a local investment adviser and long-time personal friend, that Mega is having an exceptional sales quarter. Rodriguez expects the results to be almost 10% above the current estimates. The next day, Hart initiates the purchase of a large stake in the local exchange-traded retail fund for her personal account.

    A Hart violated the Code and Standards by investing in the exchange-traded fund that included Mega Retail.

    B Hart did not violate the Code and Standards because she did not invest directly in securities of Mega Retail.

    C Rodriguez did not violate the Code and Standards because the comments made to Hart were not intended to solicit an investment in Mega Retail.

38 Park is very frustrated after taking her Level II exam. While she was studying for the exam, to supplement the curriculum provided, she ordered and used study material from a third-party provider. Park believes the additional material focused her attention on specific topic areas that were not tested while ignoring other areas. She posts the following statement on the provider's discussion board: "I am very dissatisfied with your firm's CFA Program Level II material. I found the exam extremely difficult and myself unprepared for specific questions after using your product. How could your service provide such limited instructional resources on the analysis of inventories and taxes when the exam had multiple questions about them? I will not recommend your products to other candidates."

- **A** Park violated the Code and Standards by purchasing third-party review material.
- **B** Park violated the Code and Standards by providing her opinion on the difficulty of the exam.
- **C** Park violated the Code and Standards by providing specific information on topics tested on the exam.

39 Paper was recently terminated as one of a team of five managers of an equity fund. The fund had two value-focused managers and terminated one of them to reduce costs. In a letter sent to prospective employers, Paper presents, with written permission of the firm, the performance history of the fund to demonstrate his past success.

- **A** Paper did not violate the Code and Standards.
- **B** Paper violated the Code and Standards by claiming the performance of the entire fund as his own.
- **C** Paper violated the Code and Standards by including the historical results of his prior employer.

40 Townsend was recently appointed to the board of directors of a youth golf program that is the local chapter of a national not-for-profit organization. The program is beginning a new fund-raising campaign to expand the number of annual scholarships it provides. Townsend believes many of her clients make annual donations to charity. The next week in her regular newsletter to all clients, she includes a small section discussing the fund-raising campaign and her position on the organization's board.

- **A** Townsend did not violate the Code and Standards.
- **B** Townsend violated the Code and Standards by soliciting donations from her clients through the newsletter.
- **C** Townsend violated the Code and Standards by not getting approval of the organization before soliciting her clients.

The following information relates to Questions 41–46

Prudent Investment Associates (PIA) is a small-cap equity investment management company that uses fundamental equity analysis in its investment decision-making process. All portfolio managers at PIA manage both discretionary and non-discretionary accounts. Kevin Danko, CFA, is PIA's owner and chief investment officer and supervises May Chau, a recently hired portfolio manager. PIA has adopted the CFA Institute Code of Ethics and Standards of Professional Conduct.

Chau is enrolled to sit for the Level III CFA® examination. In its marketing brochure, PIA states: "May Chau is a Level III candidate in the CFA Program." A colleague tells Chau this presentation may be incorrect according to the CFA Institute Code and Standards and suggests the following change: "May Chau has passed Level II of the CFA examination."

PIA has established a relationship with Fair Trading Incorporated (FTI), a regional investment bank and broker/dealer. FTI provides clients with access to research and analysts' recommendations via a user-registered website. This access is available on the condition that clients not forward any of the research and recommendations to any other parties. In exchange for this access and after concluding that FTI provides best execution, Danko directs to FTI most of his trade orders.

FTI also provides to a select group of brokerage clients, including PIA, information regarding several of its investment banking customers. This information includes the customers' own earnings projections. FTI instructs this select group of brokerage clients not to disseminate these earnings projections to the public until released by the investment banking customers. On a regular basis, Danko reviews the list of "strong buys" on FTI's website to see if there have been any new "buy" recommendations. Danko quickly places orders for discretionary client accounts to purchase shares of any company for which the investment recommendation has been changed to a "strong buy." He takes this action so discretionary account clients do not miss any price appreciation. After each purchase, he instructs Chau to perform the appropriate fundamental analysis on these companies within five business days so the research file is adequately documented.

From time to time, PIA receives initial public offering (IPO) allocations from FTI. Danko allocates these IPOs to those discretionary accounts that normally participate in IPOs. If the IPO is oversubscribed, he excludes his wife's discretionary non-fee paying account so that he is not accused of bias when allocating the oversubscribed IPOs.

During a recent presentation, Danko and Chau are asked what procedures PIA uses to ensure employees do not benefit from information prior to executing trades in client accounts. Danko responds that PIA has the following Trading Procedures:

Procedure 1   Investment personnel are not permitted to trade securities for five business days prior to trades executed in discretionary client accounts.

Procedure 2   Each quarter a randomly selected group of investment personnel must provide duplicate trade confirmations to the PIA compliance officer.

Procedure 3   Investment personnel must receive prior approval for personal trades only for those trades greater than $5,000.

41 Does the reference to Chau's participation in the CFA Program, as presented in the marketing brochure, or in the suggested change, violate the Standards of Professional Conduct?

   A No.
   B The marketing brochure is a violation, but the suggested change is not a violation.
   C The suggested change is a violation, but the marketing brochure is not a violation.

42 Does Danko violate the Standards when he directs trades to FTI?

   A No.
   B Yes, because by trading with FTI, Danko is putting PIA's interests ahead of his clients'.
   C Yes, because Danko has a duty to provide FTI's research to PIA's clients before executing trades.

43 According to the Standards, which of the following actions is the *most* appropriate for Danko to take with respect to the use of the earnings projections? Danko should:

   A disclose the information to the public.
   B terminate PIA's relationship with FTI.
   C keep the information confidential and not use it in his analysis.

44 Does Danko's decision to purchase shares that are recommended as a "strong buy" violate the Standards?

   A No.
   B Yes, because Danko must have a reasonable and adequate basis prior to purchasing the shares.
   C Yes, because Danko must give non-discretionary accounts the opportunity to purchase equities at the same time he purchases equities in the discretionary accounts.

45 Does Danko violate the Standards when he allocates over-subscribed IPO issues?

   A No.
   B Yes, because he should allocate the over-subscribed IPOs across all discretionary accounts.
   C Yes, because he should treat his wife's account the same as other discretionary accounts and include it in the over-subscribed IPO allocations.

46 Which of PIA's Trading Procedures is most consistent with the Standards?

   A Procedure 1
   B Procedure 2
   C Procedure 3

The following information relates to Questions 47–51

Elias Nano, a recent MBA graduate and a CFA® Level II candidate, is an unpaid summer intern with Patriarch Investment Counsel and expects to be offered a full-time paid position in the fall. Through his efforts, he is able to convince some family members and friends to become clients of the firm, and he now assists with the management of their accounts. His supervisor congratulates him and states: "These clients are the foundation from which you will be able to build your career as an investment advisor." After working hard all summer, Nano is told that Patriarch will not be able to offer him a paid position.

Nano interviews with a number of firms, and tells each one about the accounts that he is managing and expects to be able to bring with him. Because he was merely an intern at Patriarch, he does not think he owes any particular loyalty to Patriarch. He gains further assurance that he can keep the clients from the fact that his former supervisor implied that these were Nano's clients.

Nano subsequently joins Markoe Advisors as an assistant director with supervisory responsibilities. Markoe Advisors is an investment management firm that advertises that it provides customized portfolio solutions for individual and institutional clients. As a matter of policy, Markoe does not reject as a client any individual meeting the account minimum size. Markoe has two strategies—aggressive growth equity and growth equity—and is always fully invested. Nano asks his family and friends to transfer their accounts from Patriarch to Markoe.

As the first CFA candidate to be employed by Markoe, Nano has been asked to head a team that is reviewing the firm's compliance policies and procedures, which Nano considers inadequate and incomplete. He states his concerns to President Markoe: "Although Markoe Advisors, as a firm, cannot adopt the CFA Institute Code of Ethics and Standards of Professional Conduct, the firm can adopt the CFA Institute Asset Manager Code of Professional Conduct." President Markoe tells Nano that the firm is considering acquiring another advisory firm that has similar compliance policies and procedures. Markoe says: "We are not going to consider any compliance changes at this time."

Nano decides to draft a model compliance document to guide discussions about compliance issues at the firm in the future. Nano's initial draft includes the following components of a compliance policy statement:

1 Performance Presentation

Performance data must be documented for each of Markoe Advisors' active accounts, be disclosed upon request, and be compared with the firm's composite, which is composed of active accounts only. Performance data must be presented on a before-tax basis to all clients, with the disclosure that all performance data are presented gross of fees.

2 Suitability of Investments

Markoe Advisors, to maintain consistency of performance, assigns each client to one of the firm's two portfolios. Both of these portfolios are sufficiently broadly diversified to meet the investment objectives of all of our clients.

3 Disclosures of Conflicts

Markoe Advisors encourages its staff to be involved in the business and civic community. Only business or civic interests that relate to current portfolio holdings need to be reported to the firm.

4 Violations

Any violation of the Markoe Advisors compliance policy statement will be reported to the president, and employees will receive an official warning.

5 Compensation

All staff members of Markoe Advisors will discuss with their supervisor all outside compensation that they are receiving or may receive.

47 Does Nano comply with the Standards of Professional Conduct when he asks his clients to transfer their accounts to Markoe Advisors?
 A No.
 B Yes, because he contacted the clients after leaving Patriarch.
 C Yes, because he was an intern and not a paid employee of Patriarch.

48 According to the Code and Standards, what action should Nano take after discussing the firm's compliance policy with President Markoe? Nano should:
 A resign from the firm.
 B notify the board of directors.
 C decline to accept supervisory responsibilities.

49 Does Nano's draft compliance policy statement conform to the Code and Standards with respect to performance presentation?
 A No, because terminated accounts are excluded.
 B No, because performance is reported to all clients gross of fees.
 C No, because performance data are presented on a before-tax basis.

50 Does Nano's draft compliance policy statement conform to the Code and Standards with respect to:

	Suitability of Investments	Disclosure of Conflicts
A	No	No
B	No	Yes
C	Yes	No

51 Does Nano's draft compliance policy statement conform to the Code and Standards with respect to:

	Violations	Compensation
A	No	No
B	No	Yes
C	Yes	No

The following information relates to Questions 52–56

Patricia Jollie, CFA, is the fixed-income analyst and portfolio manager at Mahsud Financial Corporation, a small investment firm.

On 5 April, a friend who works for a bond-rating agency mentions to Jollie that a bond the agency is analyzing will experience a rating change. That bond also happens to be in Mahsud Financial's portfolios. Not wanting to trade ahead of the rating change announcement, Jollie decides to wait for distribution of the information through her friend's scheduled interview on a business television program the afternoon of 8 April. On the morning of 8 April, the information is released on a worldwide financial news service. Jollie immediately changes her mind about waiting for the interview and trades the bonds in Mahsud Financial's portfolios.

On 8 April, Jollie also trades a second bond to rebalance one of Mahsud Financial's portfolios. Jollie knows before executing her transaction that the bond is thinly traded. Although Jollie's trade will materially affect the bond's market price, it is not her intention to create price movement. A colleague witnesses the trade and large bond price change and says, "What a market overreaction; the bond price appears to be distorted now!" The colleague also points out to Jollie that Mahsud Financial's policy on market manipulation states: "Mahsud Financial employees must refrain from making transactions that distort security prices or volume with the intent to mislead market participants."

In conducting fixed-income research, Jollie believes that insight into prospective corporate bond returns can be derived from information that is also relevant to a company's stock. She spends several hours a week in equity investment chat rooms on the Internet, and she pays particular attention to the research reports posted by Jill Dean, CFA, a self-employed analyst, on www.Jill Dean the Independent Analyst.com. Prior to writing each report, Dean is paid a flat fee by the companies whose stocks she researches, but she does not reveal this fact to readers of her reports. She produces reports only for those companies whose stocks she can legitimately give "buy" recommendations after conducting a thorough analysis. Otherwise, she returns the flat fee. Investors have come to recognize all her "buy" ratings as having a sound and reasonable basis.

Jollie considers Dean's summaries and forecasts to be very well-crafted. Dean has given Jollie written permission to use her summaries and forecasts, word for word and without attribution, in her own bond analysis reports. On occasion, Jollie has done so. In Dean's other Internet postings, she reports the results of relevant academic finance

Practice Problems

studies. Once Jollie learns of a study by reading Dean's postings, she often reads the original study and mentions the results in her own reports. Jollie always cites the original study only and does not reveal that she learned of the study through Dean.

Mahsud Financial occasionally sponsors seminars on ethics. In the most recent seminar, the main speaker made statements about potential sources of conflict of interest for research analysts. The seminar speaker's statements were:

Statement 1   For situations in which conflicts of interest cannot be avoided, Mahsud Financial's written compliance policy should include the following component: "For unavoidable conflicts of interest that the employee judges to be material, employees must disclose the conflicts of interest to clients prominently, and in plain language."

Statement 2   On the matter of gifts that might impair employees' objectivity, Mahsud Financial's written compliance policy should also include the following component: "Employees must disclose to Mahsud Financial all client gifts regardless of value."

52 Does Jollie violate the Standards of Professional Conduct by trading on the news of the bond rating change?
   A   No.
   B   Yes, only because she possessed material non-public information.
   C   Yes, only because she should have waited to trade until after her friend's television interview took place.

53 Are Jollie's 8 April trade of the second bond and Mahsud Financial's policy on market manipulation, respectively, consistent with the Standards on market manipulation?

	Jollie's 8 April Trade	Mahsud Financial's Policy
A	Yes	Yes
B	No	Yes
C	Yes	No

54 Does Dean violate the Standards in preparing and disseminating her equity reports?
   A   No.
   B   Yes, only by misrepresenting her recommendations as independent.
   C   Yes, only by accepting payment from the companies on which she produces reports.

55 In preparing investment reports, does Jollie violate the Standards with respect to her:

	use of Dean's summaries and forecasts?	citation of studies found in Dean's Internet postings?
A	No	Yes
B	Yes	No
C	Yes	Yes

56 Are the seminar speaker's statements #1 and #2, respectively, sufficient to meet the requirements of the related Standards?

	Statement #1	Statement #2
A	No	No
B	No	Yes
C	Yes	No

The following information relates to Questions 57–62

A. J. Vinken, CFA, manages the Stonebridge Fund at Silk Road Capital Management. He develops a growth-stock selection model which produces highly favorable simulated performance results. He would like to employ the model in managing the Stonebridge Fund, a large-capitalization equity fund. He drafts a letter for distribution to all shareholders. In it, he discusses in detail his approach to equity selection using the model. He includes both the actual and simulated performance results of the Stonebridge Fund for the past three years as seen in Exhibit 1:

Exhibit 1 Stonebridge Fund Annual Returns

Year	Stonebridge Fund (Simulated)	Stonebridge Fund (Actual)
1	10.71%	9.22%
2	2.83%	−4.13%
3	22.23%	22.23%
Average annual return	11.92%	9.11%

Vinken writes, "Using the proprietary selection model for the past three years, the Stonebridge Fund would have earned an average annual return of almost 300 basis points in excess of the fund's actual return. Based on these simulated results, I am confident that employing the model will yield better performance results in the future; however, Silk Road Capital Management can make no statement of assurances or guarantee regarding future investment returns."

D.S. Khadri, CFA, is also a portfolio manager at Silk Road. She recently assumed management of the small-cap Westlake Fund from Vinken.

Khadri implements an electronic record-retention policy when she becomes the Westlake manager. In accordance with her policy, all records for the fund, including investment analyses, transactions, and investment-related communications with clients and prospective clients, are scanned and electronically stored. Vinken maintained the same records in hard-copy format for the five years that he managed the Westlake Fund. Khadri has begun the process of scanning all of the past records of the Westlake Fund; however, Vinken complains that Khadri is wasting company resources by scanning old records. Vinken insists that he will continue to maintain only hard-copy records for the Stonebridge Fund for the five years required by regulators.

Khadri writes a performance review of the Westlake Fund for its quarterly newsletter. She reports that Silk Road Capital Management is moving toward compliance with the Global Investment Performance Standards (GIPS). She states, "The Westlake Fund is already partially GIPS compliant. We expect to be fully compliant with the GIPS standards within the next 12 months."

In the quarterly newsletter, Khadri makes the following statements:

Practice Problems

Statement 1 "China's pegging of the yuan to the US dollar will end within the next 12 months which will lead to the yuan increasing in value by more than 40%, supporting our overweighting of Chinese-related stocks in the Westlake Fund."

Statement 2 "Increased geo-political uncertainty around the globe should keep oil prices above 3-year levels and supports our recommendation for an over-weighting of equities in the small-cap energy sector."

Khadri also reports:

"The quarterly return of the Westlake Fund was 4.07%. The quarterly return exceeded the performance of its benchmark, the Russell 2000 Index by .16%. Investors should not expect this type of performance to continue into the foreseeable future.*

* Additional detailed information available upon request."

After the quarterly newsletter is distributed, a client contacts Khadri claiming that the Westlake Fund actually underperformed the benchmark during the quarter. After researching the issue, Khadri confirms that the client is correct and sends him a letter in which she provides the corrected results. In her letter to the client, she blames the discrepancy—which was the result of a human typographical error—on a computer programming error.

57 In his letter regarding the stock-selection model, does Vinken violate any CFA Institute Standards of Professional Conduct?
  A No.
  B Yes, because he uses simulated performance results.
  C Yes, because he claims that the new model will yield better performance results.

58 Are the record-retention policies of both Khadri and Vinken consistent with CFA Institute Standards?
  A Yes.
  B No, Khadri's policy is not consistent.
  C No, Vinken's policy is not consistent.

59 Are Khadri's statements regarding compliance with the Global Investment Performance Standards consistent with CFA Institute Standards?
  A Yes.
  B No, because Khadri may not claim partial compliance.
  C No, because Khadri fails to disclose the areas of noncompliance.

60 Are Khadri's statements in the quarterly newsletter consistent with CFA Institute Standards?
  A Yes.
  B No, because Statement 1 is opinion, not fact.
  C No, because Statement 2 is opinion, not fact.

61 Are Khadri's newsletter comments regarding returns consistent with CFA Institute Standards?
  A Yes.
  B No, because Khadri used an inappropriate benchmark.
  C No, because Khadri did not disclose whether the performance results are before or after fees.

62 When responding to the client complaint regarding Westlake's performance, Khadri *least likely* violates the Standard relating to:
   A misconduct.
   B misrepresentation.
   C performance presentation.

SOLUTIONS

1 The correct answer is B. This question involves Standard III(B)–Fair Dealing. Smith disseminated a change in the stock recommendation to his clients but then received a request contrary to that recommendation from a client who probably had not yet received the recommendation. Prior to executing the order, Smith should take additional steps to ensure that the customer has received the change of recommendation. Answer A is incorrect because the client placed the order prior to receiving the recommendation and, therefore, does not have the benefit of Smith's most recent recommendation. Answer C is also incorrect; simply because the client request is contrary to the firm's recommendation does not mean a member can override a direct request by a client. After Smith contacts the client to ensure that the client has received the changed recommendation, if the client still wants to place a buy order for the shares, Smith is obligated to comply with the client's directive.

2 The correct answer is C. This question involves Standard III(A)–Loyalty, Prudence, and Care and the specific topic of soft dollars or soft commissions. Answer C is the correct choice because client brokerage commissions may not be directed to pay for the investment manager's operating expenses. Answer B describes how members and candidates should determine how to use brokerage commissions—that is, if the use is in the best interests of clients and is commensurate with the value of the services provided. Answer A describes a practice that is commonly referred to as "directed brokerage." Because brokerage is an asset of the client and is used to benefit the client, not the manager, such practice does not violate a duty of loyalty to the client. Members and candidates are obligated in all situations to disclose to clients their practices in the use of client brokerage commissions.

3 The correct answer is C. This question involves Standard VI(A)–Disclosure of Conflicts. The question establishes a conflict of interest in which an analyst, Jamison, is asked to write a research report on a company that is a client of the analyst's employer. In addition, two directors of the company are senior officers of Jamison's employer. Both facts establish that there are conflicts of interest that must be disclosed by Jamison in her research report. Answer B is incorrect because an analyst is not prevented from writing a report simply because of the special relationship the analyst's employer has with the company as long as that relationship is disclosed. Answer A is incorrect because whether or not Jamison expresses any opinions in the report is irrelevant to her duty to disclose a conflict of interest. Not expressing opinions does not relieve the analyst of the responsibility to disclose the special relationships between the two companies.

4 The correct answer is C. This question asks about compliance procedures relating to personal investments of members and candidates. The statement in answer C clearly conflicts with the recommended procedures in the *Standards of Practice Handbook*. Employers should compare personal transactions of employees with those of clients on a regular basis regardless of the existence of a requirement by any regulatory organization. Such comparisons ensure that employees' personal trades do not conflict with their duty to their clients, and the comparisons can be conducted in a confidential manner. The statement in answer A does not conflict with the procedures in the *Handbook*. Disclosure of such policies will give full information to clients regarding potential conflicts of interest on the part of those entrusted to manage their money. Answer B is incorrect because firms are encouraged to establish policies whereby employees clear their personal holdings and transactions with their employers.

5 The correct answer is B. This question relates to Standard III(A)–Loyalty, Prudence, and Care and Standard III(E)–Preservation of Confidentiality. In this case, the member manages funds of a private endowment. Clients, who are, in this case, the trustees of the fund, must place some trust in members and candidates. Bronson cannot disclose confidential financial information to anyone without the permission of the fund, regardless of whether the disclosure may benefit the fund. Therefore, answer A is incorrect. Answer C is incorrect because Bronson must notify the fund and obtain the fund's permission before publicizing the information.

6 The correct answer is C. Under Standard IV(C)–Responsibilities of Supervisors, members and candidates may delegate supervisory duties to subordinates but such delegation does not relieve members or candidates of their supervisory responsibilities. As a result, answer B is incorrect. Moreover, whether or not Miller's subordinates are subject to the Code and Standards is irrelevant to her supervisory responsibilities. Therefore, answer A is incorrect.

7 The correct answer is B. This question relates to Standard V(A)–Diligence and Reasonable Basis. The opinion of another financial analyst is not an adequate basis for Willier's action in changing the recommendation. Answer C is thus incorrect. So is answer A because, although it is true that members and candidates must distinguish between facts and opinions in recommendations, the question does not illustrate a violation of that nature. If the opinion overheard by Willier had sparked him to conduct additional research and investigation that justified a change of opinion, then a changed recommendation would be appropriate.

8 The correct answer is B. This question relates to Standard I(B)–Independence and Objectivity. When asked to change a recommendation on a company stock to gain business for the firm, the head of the brokerage unit must refuse in order to maintain his independence and objectivity in making recommendations. He must not yield to pressure by the firm's investment banking department. To avoid the appearance of a conflict of interest, the firm should discontinue issuing recommendations about the company. Answer A is incorrect; changing the recommendation in any manner that is contrary to the analyst's opinion violates the duty to maintain independence and objectivity. Answer C is incorrect because merely assigning a new analyst to decide whether the stock deserves a higher rating will not address the conflict of interest.

9 The correct answer is A. Standard VII(B)–Reference to CFA Institute, the CFA Designation, and the CFA Program is the subject of this question. The reference on Albert's business card implies that there is a "CFA Level II" designation; Tye merely indicates in promotional material that he is participating in the CFA Program and has completed Levels I and II. Candidates may not imply that there is some sort of partial designation earned after passing a level of the CFA exam. Therefore, Albert has violated Standard VII(B). Candidates may communicate that they are participating in the CFA Program, however, and may state the levels that they have completed. Therefore, Tye has not violated Standard VII(B).

10 The correct answer is B. This question relates to Standard V(B)–Communication with Clients and Prospective Clients. Scott has issued a research report stating that he expects the price of Walkton Industries stock to rise by US$8 a share "because the dividend will increase" by US$1.50 per share. He has made this statement knowing that the dividend will increase only if Congress enacts certain legislation, an uncertain prospect. By stating that the dividend will increase, Scott failed to separate fact from opinion.

The information regarding passage of legislation is not material nonpublic information because it is conjecture, and the question does not state whether the US representative gave Scott her opinion on the passage of the legislation in confidence. She could have been offering this opinion to anyone who asked. Therefore, statement A is incorrect. It may be acceptable to base a recommendation, in part, on an expectation of future events, even though they may be uncertain. Therefore, answer C is incorrect.

11 The correct answer is C. This question, which relates to Standard III(B)–Fair Dealing, tests the knowledge of the procedures that will assist members and candidates in treating clients fairly when making investment recommendations. The step listed in C will help ensure the fair treatment of clients. Answer A may have negative effects on the fair treatment of clients. The more people who know about a pending change, the greater the chance that someone will inform some clients before the information's release. The firm should establish policies that limit the number of people who are aware in advance that a recommendation is to be disseminated. Answer B, distributing recommendations to institutional clients before distributing them to individual accounts, discriminates among clients on the basis of size and class of assets and is a violation of Standard III(B).

12 The correct answer is B. This question deals with Standard II(A)–Material Nonpublic Information. The mosaic theory states that an analyst may use material public information and nonmaterial nonpublic information in creating a larger picture than shown by any individual piece of information and the conclusions the analyst reaches become material only after the pieces are assembled. Answers A and C are accurate statements relating to the Code and Standards but do not describe the mosaic theory.

13 The correct answer is C. This question involves Standard IV(B)–Additional Compensation Arrangements. The arrangement described in the question— whereby Jurgen would be compensated beyond the compensation provided by her firm, on the basis of an account's performance—is not a violation of the Standards as long as Jurgen discloses the arrangement in writing to her employer and obtains permission from her employer prior to entering into the arrangement. Answers A and B are incorrect; although the private compensation arrangement could conflict with the interests of other clients and lead to short-term performance pressures, members and candidates may enter into such agreements as long as they have disclosed the arrangements to their employer and obtained permission for the arrangement from their employer.

14 The correct answer is B. This question relates to Standard III(A)–Loyalty, Prudence, and Care—specifically, a member's or candidate's responsibility for voting proxies and the use of client brokerage. According to the facts stated in the question, Farnsworth did not violate Standard III(A). Although the company president asked Farnsworth to vote the shares of the Jones Corporation profit-sharing plan a certain way, Farnsworth investigated the issue and concluded, independently, the best way to vote. Therefore, even though his decision coincided with the wishes of the company president, Farnsworth is not in violation of his responsibility to be loyal and to provide care to his clients. In this case, the participants and the beneficiaries of the profit-sharing plan are the clients, not the company's management. Had Farnsworth not investigated the issue or had he yielded to the president's wishes and voted for a slate of directors that he had determined was not in the best interest of the company, Farnsworth would have violated his responsibilities to the beneficiaries of the plan. In addition, because the brokerage firm provides the lowest commissions and best execution for securities transactions, Farnsworth has met his obligations to the client in using this brokerage firm. It does not matter that the brokerage firm also

provides research information that is not useful for the account generating the commission because Farnsworth is not paying extra money of the client's for that information.

15   The correct answer is A. In this question, Brown is providing investment recommendations before making inquiries about the client's financial situation, investment experience, or investment objectives. Brown is thus violating Standard III(C)–Suitability. Answers B and C provide examples of information members and candidates should discuss with their clients at the outset of the relationship, but these answers do not constitute a complete list of those factors. Answer A is the best answer.

16   The correct answer is C. This question involves Standard I(C)–Misrepresentation. Statement I is a factual statement that discloses to clients and prospects accurate information about the terms of the investment instrument. Statement II, which guarantees a specific rate of return for a mutual fund, is an opinion stated as a fact and, therefore, violates Standard I(C). If statement II were rephrased to include a qualifying statement, such as "in my opinion, investors may earn . . .," it would not be in violation of the Standards.

17   The correct answer is A. This question involves three of the Standards. Anderb, the portfolio manager, has been obtaining more favorable prices for her personal securities transactions than she gets for her clients, which is a breach of Standard III(A)–Loyalty, Prudence, and Care. In addition, she violated Standard I(D)–Misconduct by failing to adhere to company policy and by hiding her personal transactions from her firm. Anderb's supervisor, Bates, violated Standard IV(C)–Responsibilities of Supervisors; although the company had requirements for reporting personal trading, Bates failed to adequately enforce those requirements. Answer B does not represent a violation because Standard VI(B)–Priority of Transactions requires that personal trading in a security be conducted after the trading in that security of clients and the employer. The Code and Standards do not prohibit owning such investments, although firms may establish policies that limit the investment opportunities of members and candidates. Answer C does not represent a violation because the Code and Standards do not contain a prohibition against employees using the same broker for their personal accounts that they use for their client accounts. This arrangement should be disclosed to the employer so that the employer may determine whether a conflict of interest exists.

18   The correct answer is A because this question relates to Standard I(A)–Knowledge of the Law—specifically, global application of the Code and Standards. Members and candidates who practice in multiple jurisdictions may be subject to various securities laws and regulations. If applicable law is more strict than the requirements of the Code and Standards, members and candidates must adhere to applicable law; otherwise, members and candidates must adhere to the Code and Standards. Therefore, answer A is correct. Answer B is incorrect because members and candidates must adhere to the higher standard set by the Code and Standards if local applicable law is less strict. Answer C is incorrect because when no applicable law exists, members and candidates are required to adhere to the Code and Standards, and the Code and Standards prohibit the use of material nonpublic information.

19   The correct answer is B. The best course of action under Standard I(B)–Independence and Objectivity is to avoid a conflict of interest whenever possible. Therefore, for Ward to pay for all his expenses is the correct answer. Answer C details a course of action in which the conflict would be disclosed, but the solution is not as appropriate as avoiding the conflict of interest.

Answer A would not be the best course because it would not remove the appearance of a conflict of interest; even though the report would not be affected by the reimbursement of expenses, it could appear to be.

20 The correct answer is B. Under Standard IV(A)–Loyalty, members and candidates may undertake independent practice that may result in compensation or other benefit in competition with their employer as long as they obtain consent from their employer. Answer C is not consistent with the Standards because the Standards allow members and candidates to make arrangements or preparations to go into competitive business as long as those arrangements do not interfere with their duty to their current employer. Answer A is not consistent with the Standards because the Standards do not include a complete prohibition against undertaking independent practice.

21 The correct answer is B. This question involves Standard VI(A)–Disclosure of Conflicts—specifically, the holdings of an analyst's employer in company stock. Answers A and C do not describe conflicts of interest that Smith would have to disclose. Answer A describes the use of a firm's products, which would not be a required disclosure. In answer C, the relationship between the analyst and the company through a relative is so tangential that it does not create a conflict of interest necessitating disclosure.

22 The correct answer is C. This question relates to Standard I(C)–Misrepresentation. Although Michelieu's statement about the total return of his clients' accounts on average may be technically true, it is misleading because the majority of the gain resulted from one client's large position taken against Michelieu's advice. Therefore, this statement misrepresents the investment performance the member is responsible for. He has not taken steps to present a fair, accurate, and complete presentation of performance. Answer B is thus incorrect. Answer A is incorrect because although Michelieu is not guaranteeing future results, his words are still a misrepresentation of his performance history.

23 The correct answer is B. The best policy to prevent violation of Standard II(A)–Material Nonpublic Information is the establishment of firewalls in a firm to prevent exchange of insider information. The physical and informational barrier of a firewall between the investment banking department and the brokerage operation prevents the investment banking department from providing information to analysts on the brokerage side who may be writing recommendations on a company stock. Prohibiting recommendations of the stock of companies that are clients of the investment banking department is an alternative, but answer A states that this prohibition would be permanent, which is not the best answer. Once an offering is complete and the material nonpublic information obtained by the investment banking department becomes public, resuming publishing recommendations on the stock is not a violation of the Code and Standards because the information of the investment banking department no longer gives the brokerage operation an advantage in writing the report. Answer C is incorrect because no exchange of information should be occurring between the investment banking department and the brokerage operation, so monitoring of such exchanges is not an effective compliance procedure for preventing the use of material nonpublic information.

24 The correct answer is B. Under Standard III(A)–Loyalty, Prudence, and Care, members and candidates who manage a company's pension fund owe these duties to the participants and beneficiaries of the pension plan, not the management of the company or the company's shareholders.

25 The correct answer is B. Answer B gives one of the two primary reasons listed in the *Handbook* for disclosing referral fees to clients under Standard VI(C)–Referral Fees. (The other is to allow clients and employers to evaluate the full cost of the services.) Answer A is incorrect because Standard VI(C) does not require members or candidates to discount their fees when they receive referral fees. Answer C is inconsistent with Standard VI(C) because disclosure of referral fees, to be effective, should be made to prospective clients before entering into a formal client relationship with them.

26 The correct answer is B. Standard VI(B)–Priority of Transactions does not limit transactions of company employees that differ from current recommendations as long as the sale does not disadvantage current clients. Thus, answer A is incorrect. Answer C is incorrect because the Standard does not require the matching of personal and client trades.

27 Answer C is correct. Standard IV(A)–Loyalty discusses activities permissible to members and candidates when they are leaving their current employer; soliciting clients is strictly prohibited. Thus, answer A is inconsistent with the Code and Standards even with the required disclosure. Answer B is incorrect because the offer does not directly violate the Code and Standards. There may be out-of-work members and candidates who can arrange the necessary commitments without violating the Code and Standards.

28 Answer A is correct. The question relates to Standard III(A)–Loyalty, Prudence, and Care. Carter believes the broker offers effective execution at a fee that is comparable with those of other brokers, so he is free to use the broker for all accounts. Answer B is incorrect because the accounts that prohibit soft dollar arrangements do not want to fund the purchase of research by Carter. The new trading scheme does not incur additional commissions from clients, so it would not go against the prohibitions. Answer C is incorrect because Carter should not incur unnecessary or excessive "churning" of the portfolios (excessive trading) for the purpose of meeting the brokerage commitments of soft dollar arrangements.

29 Answer B is correct according to Standard VII(B)–Reference to CFA Institute, the CFA Designation, and the CFA Program. CFA Program candidates do not receive their actual scores on the exam. Topic and subtopic results are grouped into three broad categories, and the exam is graded only as "pass" or "fail." Although a candidate may have achieved a topical score of "above 70%," she or he cannot factually state that she or he received the highest possible score because that information is not reported. Thus, answer C is incorrect. Answer A is incorrect as long as the member or candidate actually completed the exams consecutively. Standard VII(B) does not prohibit the communication of factual information about completing the CFA Program in three consecutive years.

30 Answer C is correct. According to Standard III(A)–Loyalty, Prudence, and Care, the CFA Program would be considered a personal or firm expense and should not be paid for with the fund's brokerage commissions. Soft dollar accounts should be used only to purchase research services that directly assist the investment manager in the investment decision-making process, not to assist the management of the firm or to further education. Thus, answer A is incorrect. Answer B is incorrect because the reasonableness of how the money is used is not an issue; the issue is that educational expense is not research.

31 Answer A is correct. Standard I(B)–Independence and Objectivity emphasizes the need for members and candidates to maintain their independence and objectivity. Best practices dictate that firms adopt a strict policy not to accept compensation for travel arrangements. At times, however, accepting paid travel would not compromise one's independence and objectivity. Answers B and C are incorrect because the added benefits—free conference admission for additional staff members and an exclusive golf retreat for the speaker—could be viewed as inducements related to the firm's working arrangements and not solely related to the speaking engagement. Should Long wish to bring other team members or participate in the golf outing, he or his firm should be responsible for the associated fees.

32 Answer C is correct. The guidance to Standard II(A)–Material Nonpublic Information recommends adding securities to the firm's restricted list when the firm has or may have material nonpublic information. By adding these securities to this list, Andrews would uphold this standard. Because waiting until the next day will not ensure that news of the merger is made public, answer A is incorrect. Negotiations may take much longer between the two companies, and the merger may never happen. Andrews must wait until the information is disseminated to the market before he trades on that information. Answer B is incorrect because Andrews should not disclose the information to other managers; no trading is allowed on material nonpublic information.

33 Answer B is correct. Through placing a personal purchase order that is significantly greater than the average volume, Pietro is violating Standard IIB–Market Manipulation. He is attempting to manipulate an increase in the share price and thus bring a buyer to the negotiating table. The news of a possible merger and confirmation of the firm's earnings guidance may also have positive effects on the price of Local Bank, but Pietro's actions in instructing the release of the information does not represent a violation through market manipulation. Announcements of this nature are common and practical to keep investors informed. Thus, answers A and C are incorrect.

34 Answer C is correct. Cupp violated Standard III(D)–Performance Presentations when he deviated from the firm's stated policies solely to capture the gain from the holding being acquired. Answer A is incorrect because the firm does not claim GIPS compliance and the GIPS standards require external cash flows to be treated in a consistent manner with the firm's documented policies. Answer B is incorrect because the firm does not state that it is updating its composite policies. If such a change were to occur, all cash flows for the month would have to be reviewed to ensure their consistent treatment under the new policy.

35 Answer A is correct. According to Standard V(C)–Record Retention, Cannan needed the permission of her employer to maintain the files at home after her employment ended. Without that permission, she should have deleted the files. All files created as part of a member's or candidate's professional activity are the property of the firm, even those created outside normal work hours. Thus, answer B is incorrect. Answer C is incorrect because the Code and Standards do not prohibit using one's personal computer to complete work for one's employer.

36 Answer B is correct. According to Standard VII(B)–Reference to CFA Institute, the CFA Designation, and the CFA Program, Quinn cannot claim to have finished the CFA Program or be eligible for the CFA charter until he officially learns that he has passed the Level III exam. Until the results for the most recent exam are released, those who sat for the exam should continue to refer to themselves as "candidates." Thus, answer C is incorrect. Answer A is incorrect because members and candidates may discuss areas of practice in which they believe the CFA Program improved their personal skills.

37 Answer A is correct. Hart's decision to invest in the retail fund appears directly correlated with Rodriguez's statement about the successful quarter of Mega Retail and thus violates Standard II(A)–Material Nonpublic Information. Rodriguez's information would be considered material because it would

influence the share price of Mega Retail and probably influence the price of the entire exchange-traded retail fund. Thus, answer B is incorrect. Answer C is also incorrect because Rodriguez shared information that was both material and nonpublic. Company officers regularly have such knowledge about their firms, which is not a violation. The sharing of such information, however, even in a conversation between friends, does violate Standard II(A).

38 Answer C is correct. Standard VII(A)–Conduct as Members and Candidates in the CFA Program prohibits providing information to candidates or the public that is considered confidential to the CFA Program. In revealing that questions related to the analysis of inventories and analysis of taxes were on the exam, Park has violated this standard. Answer B is incorrect because the guidance for the standard explicitly acknowledges that members and candidates are allowed to offer their opinions about the CFA Program. Answer A is incorrect because candidates are not prohibited from using outside resources.

39 Answer B is correct. Paper has violated Standard III(D)–Performance Presentation by not disclosing that he was part of a team of managers that achieved the results shown. If he had also included the return of the portion he directly managed, he would not have violated the standard. Thus, answer A is incorrect. Answer C is incorrect because Paper received written permission from his prior employer to include the results.

40 Answer A is correct. Townsend has not provided any information about her clients to the leaders or managers of the golf program; thus, she has not violated Standard III(E)–Preservation of Confidentiality. Providing contact information about her clients for a direct-mail solicitation would have been a violation. Answer B is incorrect because the notice in the newsletter does not violate Standard III(E). Answer C is incorrect because the golf program's fund-raising campaign had already begun, so discussing the opportunity to donate was appropriate.

41 The correct answer is A. Both the first and second presentations are consistent with the Code and Standards. According to the Standards a candidate may reference their participation in the CFA Program as long as they are active but cannot imply a partial designation. A statement about the level of the exam successfully passed or a level of the exam upcoming is appropriate whereas indicating or implying a partial designation or citing a future date of expected completion of a level in the CFA Program is prohibited.

42 The correct answer is A. Danko directs his trading with FTI only after taking into account FTI's ability to provide best execution. There is no indication that FTI requires a certain amount of trading for access to the website only that access is provided in exchange for orders…this is arrangement for trading in return for research services discussed in the Guidance to the Standards under Standard III.A.

43 C is correct because the information that Danko received is material non-public information. Disclosing the information to the public is not his role; further earning gains for his clients does not excuse the violation and is not a justifiable reason for taking action on the material nonpublic information. The only entities that should release the information are the corporations or another entity with their permission, perhaps FTI.

44 B is correct because investment decision making due to speed or based on third party research alone is insufficient for meeting the standard set by Standard V.A.

45 The correct answer is A because when an issue is oversubscribed allocations cannot be made to accounts where members and candidates have beneficial interest; client orders must be filled first.

Solutions

46 The correct answer is A because a Blackout period is appropriate for investment decision making personnel so that managers do not take advantage of their knowledge of trading activity and 'front run' the trade. The actual detail of the blackout period is not specified in the Standards only that one should exist.

47 B is correct. Standard IV(A) prohibits employees from soliciting the clients of employers prior to, but not subsequent to, their departure.

48 C is correct. Standard IV (C) states that the member or candidate should decline in writing to accept supervisory responsibility until the firm adopts reasonable procedures to allow them to adequately exercise such responsibility.

49 The correct answer is A. Standard III (D) states that both terminated and active accounts must be included as part of the performance history.

50 The correct answer is A. By placing all clients in one of the two specialized portfolios it operates, Markoe Advisors is not giving adequate consideration to the individual needs, circumstances, and objectives of each client as required by the Standards. In addition, the Standards require that members and candidates disclose all actual and potential conflicts of interest, not just those that relate to current portfolio holdings.

51 The correct answer is A. Standard IV (C) deals with violations of applicable laws, rules, regulations, and the Code and Standards. The Guidance of that standard, under Compliance Procedures, reads as follows: "Reporting the misconduct up to the chain of command and warning the employee to cease the activity are also not enough. Pending the outcome of the investigation, a supervisor should take steps to insure that the violation will not be repeated, such as placing limits on the employee's activities or increasing the monitoring of the employee's activity."

Standard IV (B) deals with additional compensation arrangements and states that members and candidates must not accept additional compensation unless they obtain written consent from all parties involved. The Guidance of that standard specifies that the party offering the additional compensation must confirm the arrangement.

52 The correct answer is A. Jollie did not act on the material non-public information she possessed but waited until it became public. According to the Standards of Practice Handbook, "It is not necessary ... to wait for the slowest methods of delivery."

53 The correct answer is A. Jollie's transaction is a legitimate market order in a thinly-traded security, and Mahsud Financial's policy statement is consistent with the Standards relating to the Integrity of Capital Markets.

54 B is correct. It is not a violation to accept compensation from an issuer in exchange for research, but such arrangements must be disclosed prominently and in plain language.

55 B is correct. Receiving Dean's written permission does not absolve Jollie of her responsibility to provide attribution. Because Jollie uses the results of the research studies and does not use Dean's interpretation of the studies, it is appropriate to cite the original authors only.

56 B is correct. Statement 1 is incorrect. The disclosure of a conflict should be made—prominently and in plain language—regardless of whether the member views the conflict as material, so the client can determine the materiality of the conflict. Gifts (the $100 threshold is no longer applicable) from clients should be disclosed to the employer, which is responsible for determining whether the gift could affect the employee's independence and objectivity. Statement 2 is in compliance with the Standards. The Mahsud Financial disclosure requirement exceeds, and therefore meets, the Standards.

57 A is correct. Vinken does not violate any CFA Standards of Professional Conduct in his letter. In accordance with Standard III(D)—Performance Presentation, he presents fair, accurate, and complete information when he identifies actual and simulated performance results. Also in accordance with the Standard, he does not guarantee superior future investment returns. In accordance with Standard V(B)—Communication with Clients and Prospective Clients, Vinken describes to his clients and prospective clients the process and logic of the new investment model. By providing the basic details of the model, Vinken provides his clients the basis for understanding the limitations or inherent risks of the investment strategy.

58 A is correct. The policies of both Khadri and Vinken are consistent with Standard V(C)—Record Retention, which states that members and candidates must develop and maintain appropriate records to support their investment analyses, recommendation, actions, performance and other communications with clients and prospective clients. The records required to support recommendations and/or investment actions depend on the role of the member or candidate in the investment decision-making process. Records can be maintained either in hard copy or electronic form. Even though they use different methods, Khadri and Vinken each maintain the appropriate records and have adequate systems of record control.

59 B is correct. Khadri is in violation of Standard III(D). When claiming compliance with GIPS, firms must meet all the requirements. GIPS standards, while voluntary, only apply on a firm-wide basis. Neither a firm nor a fund can claim partial compliance with GIPS standards.

60 B is correct. Standard V(B)—Communication with Clients and Prospective Clients requires the member or candidate to separate and distinguish "facts from opinions" in the presentation of analyses and investment recommendations. Statement 1 in the newsletter states that "China's pegging of the yuan to the US dollar *will* end within the next 12 months which *will* lead to the yuan increasing in value by more than 40%, supporting our over-weighting of Chinese-related stocks in the portfolio." Khadri does not clearly differentiate between opinion and fact. The statement about the future of oil pricing is not as questionable because Khadri uses the term "should" which helps clients understand that this is an opinion and not a certainty. Members may communicate opinions, estimates, and assumptions about future values and possible events but they must take care to differentiate fact from opinion.

61 C is correct. Khadri violates the Standard relating to Performance Presentation because he does not disclose whether the performance results are before or after fees. Standard III(D) requires that members make reasonable efforts to ensure that investment performance information is "fair, accurate, and complete." According to the guidance provided in the *Standards of Practice Handbook*, members should include disclosures that fully explain the performance results (for example, whether the performance is gross of fees, net of fees, or after tax).

62 C is correct. As Khadri provides the corrected information in her letter to the client, she is least likely to violate the Standard relating to performance presentation. She is more likely to violate the Standards relating to Misconduct and Misrepresentation because she knowingly misrepresents the cause of the error. Standard I(D)—Misconduct requires that members not engage in any professional conduct involving dishonesty. Standard I(C) prohibits members from knowingly making any misrepresentation relating to investment actions and professional activities.

Performance Evaluation

Measurement, Attribution, and Appraisal

STUDY SESSIONS

Study Session 2   Performance Measurement
Study Session 3   Performance Attribution
Study Session 4   Performance Appraisal
Study Session 5   Manager Selection

TOPIC LEVEL LEARNING OUTCOME

The candidate should be able to explain and apply methodologies for calculating returns of portfolios that contain futures and options and returns of multicurrency portfolios; explain the factors that enter benchmark selection decisions; calculate and evaluate commonly used performance appraisal risk measures; conduct performance attribution analyses of equity and fixed-income portfolios and interpret the results; and explain performance appraisal and manager selection processes.

© 2020 CFA Institute. All rights reserved.

PERFORMANCE EVALUATION
STUDY SESSION

2

Performance Measurement

The CIPM Level I curriculum presented the calculation of time-weighted and money-weighted rates of return, including methods for estimating time-weighted returns for periods in which external cash flows occur. This study session reviews certain relatively advanced topics.

The first reading in this study session addresses the measurement of portfolio returns in several practically important cases; specifically, when portfolios contain short positions or make use of derivatives contracts, or when positions are held in multiple currencies other than the base currency. The second reading sets out considerations involved in ensuring that the data being used in the calculation of returns provides a consistent and reliable basis for this measurement.

READING ASSIGNMENTS

3   Topics in Return Measurement
    by Carl R. Bacon, CIPM, Bruce J. Feibel, CFA, and Bernd R. Fischer, PhD
4   Topics in Data Integrity
    by Marc. A. Wright, CFA

© 2020 CFA Institute. All rights reserved.

READING
3

Topics in Return Measurement

by Carl R. Bacon, CIPM, Bruce J. Feibel, CFA, and Bernd R. Fischer, PhD

Carl R. Bacon, CIPM, is at StatPro and the University of Manchester (United Kingdom). Bruce J. Feibel, CFA, is at State Street (USA). Bernd R. Fischer, PhD (Germany).

LEARNING OUTCOME STATEMENTS

Mastery	The candidate should be able to:
☐	a. calculate and interpret rates of return of long–short, short extension, and market-neutral investment portfolios;
☐	b. determine the effects on portfolio return of specified positions in forwards, futures, swaps, and options;
☐	c. define economic (notional) exposure and notional return;
☐	d. describe the notional market value approach to calculating returns to portfolios including forwards, futures, swaps, or options;
☐	e. calculate and interpret economic exposures and notional returns of portfolios including forwards, futures, swaps, or options;
☐	f. calculate and interpret the returns to unhedged and partially hedged multicurrency portfolios;
☐	g. describe the problem of zero or near-zero market value denominators (e.g., in currency overlay portfolios).

INTRODUCTION

1

In the case of investing in traditional domestic assets, the measurement of returns is typically for long positions denominated in a domestic currency. However, investors also use short positions and derivative contracts and invest globally. In each situation, the measurement of returns requires a treatment different from that of long-only domestic investments. The purpose of this reading is to describe the return calculations that each of these situations require.

Short positions can be combined with long positions to create long–short, short extension, and market-neutral portfolios. In these cases, the performance analyst must determine how to weight and calculate returns for both the long and the short positions. When derivative contracts such as forwards, futures, swaps, and options are used, the calculation and weighting of returns is complicated because the cash invested does not represent the economic exposure. To capture the essence of the portfolio's economic exposures, the performance analyst must calculate notional

© 2016 CFA Institute. All rights reserved.

weights and returns. The calculation of returns on asset positions denominated in a foreign currency is complicated because the returns must be converted to the domestic currency. Derivative contracts can be used to hedge the positions in foreign currency assets, which requires return calculations distinct from those applied to domestic currency assets. In all cases, the goal is to estimate the investor's returns, which can then be used for performance evaluation. A subsequent reading will discuss how to use the return measurement to determine return attribution for these same positions.

This reading is organized as follows. Section 2 discusses the measurement of returns for portfolios containing short positions. Section 3 examines the measurement of portfolio returns when derivative contracts are used, and Section 4 discusses the measurement of portfolio returns when an asset is denominated in a foreign currency. Section 5 provides a conclusion and summary.

2. LONG–SHORT PERFORMANCE MEASUREMENT

Active investors have two ways to act on a view on the current value of a security and potentially earn a return:

1 If the view is that the security is undervalued, *purchase it* and earn a gain if it goes *up* in value.

2 If the view is that the security is overvalued, *sell it short* and earn a gain if it goes *down* in value.

Often, a portfolio contains positions with both views represented. Short positions and the combination of long and short strategies in a portfolio present special challenges in return measurement, which we cover below.

2.1 Short Selling

Short selling is used by investors to profit from a negative view on a stock. Although not all instruments can be sold short and shorting is restricted in some markets, strategies using short selling are of great interest to many investors. Performance measurement of strategies that sell securities short presents both mathematical and conceptual challenges to the performance analyst. This reading provides an overview of short selling mechanics, describes the types of portfolios engaging in short selling, and finally shows how to calculate returns and contributions to return for portfolios that go short and the securities held within them.

2.2 Long–Short Portfolio Construction

How does short selling work in a portfolio context? A **short sale** is the sale of a security that the seller does not own at the time of the sale. How does one sell something one does not yet own? In order to sell a security short, the seller first must borrow it from an existing holder who is willing to lend the security for this purpose. Assume that the investor has $1,000 and wants to use a strategy that attempts to add value by identifying both under- and overvalued securities. Exhibit 1 illustrates the process of establishing this portfolio.

Long–Short Performance Measurement

Exhibit 1 Creating a Portfolio That Goes both Long and Short

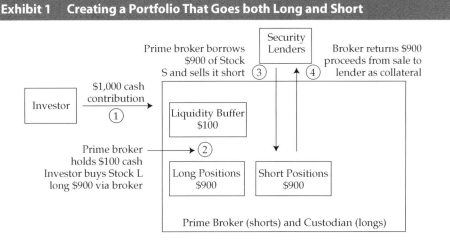

The following describes the transactions depicted in Exhibit 1:

1. The investor creates an account with a prime broker and deposits $1,000 cash. Prime brokers provide services required to create the short segment of a portfolio. The prime broker facilitates short selling by identifying long owners who are willing to lend their securities. The prime broker may be affiliated with the custodian bank holding the investor's long securities and cash, or it may be a separate firm.

2. A portion of the deposited cash—in this case, $900—is used to purchase Stock L, which the investor expects to increase in value. The investor now has a long position in Stock L. The rest of the cash, $100, is held as a liquidity buffer because the prime broker is aware of the investor's intention to hold a short position. The liquidity buffer or margin is available to cover margin calls if the value of the short securities goes up instead of down. Margin is required because a short position has theoretically unlimited loss potential. As the value of a short security goes up, the prime broker will demand additional cash collateral from the short seller in the form of periodic **margin calls**.

3. The prime broker identifies holders of the securities that the investor wants to sell short and in this case borrows $900 worth of Stock S. The investor now has a short position in Stock S. In this example, Stock S does not pay a dividend while it is held short. If a stock were to pay a dividend while held short, then the short seller would be responsible for paying the dividend to the lender. (In this case the calculation of the return on the short position would account for the cost of reimbursing the dividend to the lender.)

4. The broker then sells the stocks, with the short sale proceeds going to the lender or the lender's agent (typically a bank) as collateral. This also motivates the short seller to return the borrowed securities. Long investors who choose to lend their securities do so in order to earn a small incremental return on their long position. When short positions are collateralized with cash, the broker invests the cash collateral. A percentage of the interest earned on the invested collateral is returned to the borrower as a **fee rebate**. The difference between the income on the cash collateral and the income rebated to the borrower is shared between the lender and the lending agent. When securities, rather than cash, are accepted as collateral, the borrower pays a fee that is split between broker and lender. Collateral is carefully managed, because in exchange for the income from reinvested collateral, the lender and the broker assume the risks of

lending securities. Risks to the security lender include (1) that the value of the collateral declines and does not cover the value of the securities and (2) that the borrower does not return the securities.

At this point, the investor has a long position of $900 in Security L, a $900 short position in Security S, $100 in cash, and $900 cash on collateral. Exhibit 2 shows what happens to the investor's position, assuming success in both the long and the short positions—in other words, assuming that the prices of the stocks held long increase *and* the prices of the stocks held short decrease.

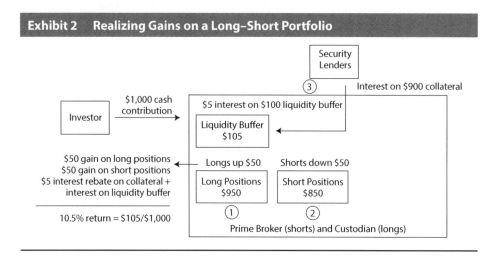

Exhibit 2 Realizing Gains on a Long–Short Portfolio

1. The long securities increase in value from $900 to $950, registering a $50 gain.
2. The short securities decrease in value from $900 to $850, registering another $50 gain.
3. The cash and collateral accrue interest. In practice, the interest on the collateral will be split between the borrower, the lender, and the lender's agent. Here we assume an incremental $5 interest credit comprising a rebate on the interest earned on the collateral plus interest earned on a liquidity buffer.

The portfolio as a whole achieved a 10.5% ($105/$1,000) return over the period. When the investor wants to exit the short position, the prime broker, at the investor's request, purchases the securities previously sold short. The broker closes out the short position for the investor and then returns the shares to the lender to close out the security loan. Note that if the portfolio had losses on the long or short position, the presence of the liquidity buffer would help cover these losses at the portfolio level.

2.3 Strategies Using Short Selling

Any portfolio that uses both long positions and short selling can be called a **long–short portfolio**. A portfolio may sell securities in a limited way to hedge a particular position or risk exposure. There are also several investment strategies that systematically use short selling as a core component of the strategy.

In the previous example, the portfolio held an equal amount in long and short positions. Long–short strategies that match long and short risk exposures are called **market-neutral strategies**. They are labeled "market-neutral" because they intend to eliminate exposure to the market and earn gains only by exploiting security- or sector-specific factors. Market-neutral strategy returns are theoretically uncorrelated with the market; in other words, they should have a beta close to zero.

Another common strategy using short selling is a **short extension** strategy (which may also be referred to as a long–short extension or long extension strategy). Such strategies are identified by the ratio of their long exposure to their short exposure. For example, a 130/30 strategy is leveraged on the long side to 130% of the market exposure, and this is offset by short positions worth 30% of the gross portfolio exposure. If the portfolio is worth $100, then there are approximately $130 in long positions and $30 in short positions. This strategy, in effect, generates $160 exposure to the manager's stock-picking ability with a $100 net market exposure.

Performance measurement techniques used for long-only strategies need to be modified to accommodate short positions. The next section describes this process.

2.4 Return Calculation

The first step in performance measurement is to take portfolio valuations as inputs and then calculate single- and multi-period returns. When short positions are present, we need to consider the following:

1 Return calculation for long positions in segments and securities (**segments** are groups of securities within a portfolio—e.g., countries, sectors, or industries)

2 Return calculation for short positions in segments and securities

First, consider the calculation of return for a particular *security*. If the price for a stock starts at $10 and moves to $11, then the *security return* for the period is 10%. If we were asked how the security performed in the marketplace, without reference to whether the security was held long or short, we would reply that it increased in value by 10%. As you will see, it is important to use a convention for describing performance in the presence of short positions. Our convention is to report

- a return on the underlying asset as positive if the asset increases in value, *regardless of whether it is held long or short*, and
- a return on the underlying asset as negative if the asset decreases in value, *regardless of whether it is held long or short*.

The next step is to communicate performance taking into account whether the security is held long or short in the portfolio. Using the previous example, if the portfolio had a long position in the security, then the portfolio enjoyed a positive contribution due to the 10% return in the underlying security asset.

Conversely, if the security was held short and the underlying security went up in value, *the return we use, per our convention, is still positive*. This convention may seem counterintuitive because there is a $1 position-level loss; the security will need to be purchased at the current price of $11 and was previously short sold for $10. We use the positive return because, as we will show in the next section, it is the *position* (represented by market value or weight) that creates the negative impact of the security gain on portfolio return. The negative portfolio position multiplied by the positive underlying security return will give us the correct negative impact of the position on portfolio performance. Note that in the portfolio valuation inputs to return calculations, *short positions are tracked using negative market values*.

The preceding discussion describes the single-period return calculation. Multi-period returns must be calculated to understand a position's return over time. When there are short positions, a security or segment may transition from a long to a short position, or vice versa. This is sometimes called *crossing through zero*. Special consideration, beyond the scope of this reading, is required when a position crosses through zero.

2.5 Contribution to Portfolio Return

Analysts want to know whether long–short managers add value by shorting. This section shows how contributions to portfolio return can be calculated for four different long–short portfolios: a portfolio using a short extension strategy, a portfolio using a long–short strategy that includes cash, a portfolio using a long–short strategy that also uses leverage, and a portfolio using a market-neutral strategy. Contribution analysis quantifies the impact of each position and the relative impact of the long versus short positions on total portfolio performance.

Exhibit 3 illustrates the performance of a short extension portfolio using contribution-to-return analysis ($m equals 1 million US dollars).

Exhibit 3   Short Extension Portfolio Contribution to Return

Position	Market Values ($m)			Contribution Analysis		
	BMV	Gain/Loss	EMV	Beginning Weight	Underlying Return	Contribution
Long	130	0	130	130%	0%	0%
Short	−30	5	−25	−30%	−16.7%	5%
Total	100	5	105	100%	5%	5%

Here we have a portfolio with a beginning market value (BMV) of $100m. In this example, a stock is bought for $130m and remains at this price as shown by its ending market value (EMV). Another stock is sold short at $30m and is later priced at $25m, generating a potential profit of $5m. The total portfolio value at the end of the period is $105m, which is the long position net of the short position.

The presence of short positions means that the calculation of contributions to return requires special consideration:

- First, the weights need to be calculated such that they add up to 100%. To do this, we sum the portfolio values—long positions with positive signs and short positions with negative signs.

- Then, market values are converted into weights by dividing each position value by the total portfolio market value. Because there are short positions, the long position weights will exceed 100%.

- Next, again assuming a convention of negative weights representing short positions and security returns representing the return on the underlying security, contribution to return is calculated as weight times return. The underlying security held short fell in value by −16.7% which, multiplied by the beginning weight of −30%, leads to a positive contribution of 5% at the portfolio level. In this example, the value of the portfolio increased from $100 to $105 over the period, and the entire gain is made up of the positive contribution to return from the short segment.

In our next example, we examine a portfolio that has long and short equity positions as well as cash. Exhibit 4 illustrates the performance of a short extension fund that includes cash ($m equals 1 million US dollars).

Exhibit 4 Long–Short Portfolio (Including Cash) Contribution to Return

	Market Values ($m)			Contribution Analysis		
Position	BMV	Gain/Loss	EMV	Beginning Weight	Underlying Return	Contribution
Long US equities	120	14.4	134.4	120%	12.0%	14.4%
Short US equities	–30	–2.7	–32.7	–30%	9.0%	–2.7%
Cash	10	0.3	10.3	10%	3.0	0.3%
Total	100	12.0	112	100%	12.0%	12.0%

Here we have a portfolio with a BMV of $100m. In this example, the value of the long US equities at the beginning of the period is $120m and the value at the end of the period is $134.4m. The value of the short US equities at the beginning of the period is $30m and the value at the end of the period is $32.7m. There is also $10m cash in the portfolio. Interest on this cash over the period amounted to $0.3m, providing an EMV of $10.3m in cash. The total portfolio value at the end of the period is $112m.

- The total return on the portfolio is (112/100) – 1 = 12%.
- The beginning weight of the long US equities represents 120/100 = 120% of the overall portfolio. The return on the long US equities is 14.4/120 = 12%. The contribution to overall return, however, is 120% × 12% = 14.4%, or 14.4/100 = 14.4%. The contribution is greater than the return because the value of the long US equities is greater than the overall value of the portfolio.
- The portfolio manager is able to create a leveraged weight of more than 100% in long US equities because of the short US equity position. The value of the short US equities at the beginning of the period is $30m; and because they are short, the negative sign is used to calculate the percentage weight as –30/100 = –30%. In this example, the underlying stocks have increased in value but because they have been shorted, the result is a loss. The return on the short US equities is –2.7/–30 = 9.0%. The contribution to overall return, however, is –30% × 9.0% = –2.7%, or –2.7/100 = –2.7%. The return of the underlying assets is positive because the price of these assets has appreciated; there is, of course, a negative contribution because the weight is negative.
- The beginning value of cash is $10m representing 10/100 = 10% of the overall portfolio. The return on cash is 0.3/10 = 3.0%, and the contribution from cash is 10% × 3.0% = 0.3%, or 0.3/100 = 0.3%.

In our third example, we examine a long–short portfolio that is using leverage. Exhibit 5 illustrates the analysis of a short extension portfolio that uses borrowed funds as represented by a short cash position ($m equals 1 million US dollars).

Exhibit 5 Long–Short Portfolio (Using Leverage) Contribution to Return

	Market Values ($m)			Contribution Analysis		
Position	BMV	Gain/Loss	EMV	Beginning Weight	Underlying Return	Contribution
Long US equities	140	16.8	156.8	140%	12.0%	16.8%
Short US equities	–30	–2.7	–32.7	–30%	9.0%	–2.7%

(continued)

Exhibit 5 (Continued)

Position	Market Values ($m)			Contribution Analysis		
	BMV	Gain/Loss	EMV	Beginning Weight	Underlying Return	Contribution
Cash	−10	−0.4	−10.4	−10%	4.0	−0.4%
Total	100	13.7	113.7	100%	13.7%	13.7%

Here we have a portfolio with a BMV of $100m. In this example, the value of the long US equities at the beginning of the period is $140m and the value at the end of the period is $156.8m. The value of the short US equities at the beginning of the period is $30m and the value at the end of the period is $32.7m. There is also a short $10m cash position in the portfolio that, in part (together with short US equities), is funding the leverage in the long US equities. The interest cost on this borrowing[1] over the period amounts to $0.4m and thus results in an EMV of −$10.4m in cash. The total portfolio value at the end of the period is $113.7m.

- The total return on the portfolio is (113.7/100) − 1 = 13.7%.
- The beginning weight of the long US equities represents 140/100 = 140% of the overall portfolio. The return on the long US equities is 16.8/140 = 12%. The contribution to overall return, however, is 140% × 12% = 16.8%, or 16.8/100 = 16.8%.
- The value of the short US equities at the beginning of the period is $30m; and because they are short, the negative sign is used to calculate the percentage weight as −30/100 = −30%. The return on the short US equities is −2.7/−30 = 9.0%. The contribution to overall return, however, is −30% × 9% = −2.7%, or −2.7/100 = −2.7%.
- The beginning weight of cash is −$10m, representing −10/100 = −10% of the overall portfolio. The return on cash reflecting borrowing costs is −0.4/−10 = 4.0%, and the contribution from cash is −10% × 4% = −0.4%, or −0.4/100 = −0.4%. The return on cash is still shown as a positive 4.0% because of the fact that the cash is being borrowed, or short causes the negative weight and hence the negative contribution to return. In this example, the cost of leveraging the portfolio is applied to only the cash return, not to the long or short segments. Despite these higher borrowing costs, the return on the portfolio in Exhibit 5 is higher than the return on the portfolio in Exhibit 4 because the portfolio is leveraged in a rising market. This return is true even though the long and short segments have the same returns in Exhibits 4 and 5.

In our final example, we examine a portfolio with a near zero exposure to the equity market. Exhibit 6 illustrates the analysis of a market-neutral portfolio.

Exhibit 6 Market-Neutral Portfolio Contribution to Return

Position	Beginning Weight	Underlying Return	Contribution
US equities			
Long	50%	16%	8.0%
Short	−50%	6%	−3.0%
Canadian equities			

---

[1] Borrowing costs are probably greater than the interest that can be earned on cash.

Long–Short Performance Measurement

Exhibit 6 (Continued)

Position	Beginning Weight	Underlying Return	Contribution
Long	50%	−8%	−4.0%
Short	−40%	−10%	4.0%
Cash	90%	2.0%	1.8%
Total	100%	6.8%	6.8%

The portfolio has offsetting long and short positions in US equities, theoretically eliminating exposure to the US market, and a net 10% long exposure to Canadian equities and is therefore not entirely market neutral with a 90% exposure to cash. A truly market-neutral portfolio is focused on leveraging the manager's skill by selecting securities to buy or short. Here we use the same convention as in the previous examples, where short positions are represented with a negative weight and negative returns on the underlying will result in gains on short positions.

Note in this example that the long US equities significantly outperformed the short US equities, therefore despite offsetting weights, the overall contribution from US equities was 8% − 3% = 5%. Although the Canadian long and short weights did not offset because the Canadian short equities underperformed the Canadian long equities, the contributions to return did offset. The basic aim of market-neutral portfolios is to have little or no exposure to markets, in this case the portfolio is 90% exposed to cash, contributing 1.8% to the return. Clearly, in low interest rate environments, this type of strategy is less attractive.

These examples illustrate some key insights an analyst looks for when reviewing the performance of long–short portfolios: Does the manager add value by being able to go both long and short? Short selling has higher risks and costs[2] than going long, so the isolation of long and short performance is of interest to the analyst. Other interesting insights can be obtained from a contribution analysis. For example, does a global equity manager add value by shorting US stocks but not exhibit skill by shorting global stocks? If the manager holds himself out as having the skills to analyze stocks globally, the contribution analysis would be an interesting discussion point with the manager. Does the manager short stocks well in poorly performing markets but not do as well on the short side during periods when the market as a whole is rising? Knowing these facts could enrich the conversation with the manager.

EXAMPLE 1

Portfolios with Short Positions

1. Which of these factors is **not** a consideration when calculating the return on a portfolio that includes short positions?

   A Securities lending fee rebate

   B The probability of a margin call

   C Interest on the collateral supporting the short positions

2. A portfolio has the following transactions:

---

[2] These higher costs might be reflected in a lower cash return (for cash weights that are positive) or higher borrowing costs (for cash weights that are negative) or adversely affect the contribution from the shorted segment. The treatment depends on where the expenses of the stock lending program are allocated.

- The portfolio manager purchases 10 shares of Security A at $5.00 per share and 10 shares of Security B at $5.00 per share.
- The portfolio manager shorts 10 shares of Security C at $1.50 per share and 10 shares of Security D at $1.50 per share.
- $1 of interest accrues on the cash collateral posted to cover the short positions.
- The following are the end-of-period per-share prices:
  - Security A: $6.00
  - Security B: $4.00
  - Security C: $1.60
  - Security D: $1.30

The portfolio return is *closest* to:

A   −2.00%.

B   1.00%.

C   2.00%.

3 Which of the following is *most* accurate regarding a portfolio using a 130/30 short extension strategy?

A   The portfolio is market-neutral.

B   The portfolio has a net 130% long exposure to its given market.

C   The strategy allows managers to add value by identifying both assets that are expected to perform well and assets that are expected to perform poorly in a given market.

4 Which of the following is *most likely* a reason for a long–short equity portfolio to establish ready access to cash?

A   To pay for new short positions

B   To reimburse the lender of a security for dividends

C   If the prices of stocks held short go down, the broker may ask for an increase in collateral.

Solution to 1:

B is correct. The probability of a margin call is not considered in the calculation of portfolio return. The securities lending fee rebate is included because any lending fees that are shared by the portfolio count as income over the period. The interest on collateral supporting the short positions is explicitly included in the portfolio return calculation because the interest is income earned on the positions in the portfolio over the period.

Solution to 2:

C is correct. The return is 2% because the total value of the portfolio increased from $100 to $102. There is $30 in collateral to cover $30 in short positions [(10 × 1.50) + (10 × 1.50)]. The beginning value of $100 is calculated using the prices and positions of the four securities plus the collateral: (10 × 5.00) + (10 × 5.00) − (10 × 1.50) − (10 × 1.50) + 30. The ending value of $102 is calculated as (10 × 6.00) + (10 × 4.00) − (10 × 1.60) − (10 × 1.30) + $30 cash + $1 of interest.

> **Solution to 3:**
>
> C is correct. The 130/30 short extension strategy can go both long and short, enabling the manager to profit from the ability to identify in advance assets that are going to over- or underperform others. A market-neutral strategy would have equal long and short exposures neutralizing its exposure to the underlying market. A 130/30 portfolio is in net 100% exposed to the underlying market.
>
> **Solution to 4:**
>
> B is correct. Having ready access to cash facilitates the reimbursement of dividends to the lender of a shorted security (ready cash also helps in meeting margin calls if a stock held short goes up in value and the broker asks for additional collateral). The establishment of a short position generates cash: To create the position, the manager borrows securities and then sells the borrowed securities for cash.

DERIVATIVES PERFORMANCE MEASUREMENT

The use of derivative products has grown rapidly since the 1980s. There are numerous reasons for the increase in their use in investment portfolios. Derivatives usually allow a portfolio manager to implement investment strategies with relatively low transaction costs. Derivatives also offer potential leverage, which decreases the capital needed to achieve a desired target return.

There are two main classes of derivatives: forward commitments (futures, forwards, and swaps) and contingent claims (options). Forward commitments are commitments or promises to buy or sell an asset at some specified future date. Options give the owner the right, but not the obligation, to buy or sell an asset. Derivatives can be traded on an exchange or over the counter (OTC). Although different, the basic principles of performance measurement apply to the various types of derivatives.

In studying the treatment of derivatives in performance measurement, the standard formulas for return calculation (time-weighted rate of return, unit price method)[3] are still valid. However, analysts must know how to apply these formulas in a meaningful way in this context and to which (combination of) assets they should be applied.

Of course, it is impossible to cover all types of derivative instruments here. However, the basic concepts introduced by means of the most basic instrument types also apply to many other categories of derivatives that are not explicitly discussed in this reading.

The use of futures, for example, shows that it is meaningless to consider the performance of an instrument in isolation because the derivative return depends on the return to the underlying. Unlike stocks or bonds, futures do not have a market value; rather, they have a "net realizable value."[4] This value is the profit or loss resulting from the change in the futures price each day. Because futures prices are marked to market—which means that profits and losses are realized at the end of each trading day by an addition or subtraction to a cash account—net unrealized value equals zero after the mark to market at the end of a trading day. In order to assess the return to this type of instrument, one needs to take the profits and losses booked in a cash account

---

[3] Fischer and Wermers (2012).
[4] Stannard (1996, p. 28).

into consideration. In addition, for performance measurement in accordance with the principles of this reading, the use of futures requires the consideration of the notional derivative amount and not just the associated cash profit/loss and margin positions.[5]

3.1 The Notional Value of a Derivative and Futures Return Calculation

The concept of an associated cash position is closely linked to the concept of the notional market value (or exposure) of a derivative, representing the market risk of the derivative.

Although it seems like a simple concept, it is not straightforward to define notional exposure in general terms. As an approximation, one can say that the notional market value is the value of the underlying security where changes in the market value of the underlying security would equal changes in the combination of futures and the cash position. We use the following definition: The **notional market value** (also known as **notional exposure**, or NE) of a futures contract is defined as the value of an underlying security that would cause (approximately) the same change in net realizable value for a given (infinitesimal) change in the price of the underlying security as the change in the combination of futures and the associated cash position. The purpose of calculating the notional exposure is to estimate the **economic exposure**—that is, the risk of the loss that one experiences if one invests in an asset class.

3.1.1 Valuation and Notional Value of Futures Contracts

A futures contract is a standardized binding contract traded on an exchange between two parties to exchange a specified asset of standardized quantity and quality for a price agreed today with delivery occurring at a specified future date.[6] Valuation approaches for futures contracts are based on a consideration of the **cost of carry**.[7] This term comes from the trading of commodities, such as resources (e.g., oil and gold) and agricultural products (e.g., orange juice, wheat, cattle). In these cases, holding the commodities generates non-negligible costs, such as rents, costs for the storage and insurance of the commodities, and the costs of financing such holdings. In the following sections, only futures where the underlying is a financial instrument, such as a stock, an equity index, or a bond, will be considered. In these cases, physical storage and insurance costs are of very limited relevance. Nevertheless, the term *cost of carry* is also used for these contracts. In such cases, the cost of carry includes the net income (a benefit) from purchasing the underlying in a spot transaction and holding it until the maturity of the futures contract. Thus, the income derived from the underlying (interest payments, dividends, etc.) and the cost of financing the spot purchase are netted to determine the futures price.[8] Under the assumption that there

---

[5] This situation is actually not radically different from the situation with stocks and bonds. If one computes the return (especially the money-weighted rate of return) for these instruments, then one needs to include all cash flows (dividends, interest) over the computation period.
[6] This section is based on Section 15.2 in Fischer and Wermers (2012).
[7] The valuation of futures instruments will be described in more detail than for the other instruments, the purpose being to introduce important concepts that are relevant for other derivative types as well.
[8] Here, the case of a futures long position is implicitly considered. In the case of short positions, the opposite holds.

are no arbitrage opportunities, the investment in the underlying must deliver the same return as the investment in a futures contract and a cash position corresponding to the notional value of the underlying.[9] Thus, the following conceptual relationship holds:

$$\text{Futures price} = \text{Spot price} + \underbrace{\text{Cost of financing} - \text{Net Income from underlying}}_{\text{Cost of carry}} \quad (1)$$

If the cost of financing exceeds the net income of the underlying, the futures price is expected to be greater than the spot price, and vice versa. A more precise expression for the price of a futures contract with delivery date T at t ($t < T$) is given by[10]

$$F_t = \left(B_t - \frac{E}{\left(1 + r_{fin}\right)^{\tilde{t}-t}} \right)\left(1 + r_{fin}\right)^{T-t} \quad (2)$$

where

F_t = Futures price according to the cost-of-carry approach at t
B_t = Price of the underlying at t
r_{fin} = Cost of financing on an annual basis
E = Income of the underlying (e.g., dividends)
$\tilde{t}$ = Date of the cash flow

At the transaction date when a futures contract is entered into, a margin account needs to be set up (initial margin). The position is valued daily, and gains and losses are settled on each exchange trading day. If losses reduce the margin account to a pre-specified level, the investor will receive a margin call and needs to transfer more cash (or bonds of a high credit quality) to the margin account to avoid having the position closed. Because the invested capital in the margin account is much smaller than the notional position of the underlying, the use of a futures contract results in leverage. The value of a (long) futures transaction at t_1 entered into at t_0 is given by $F_{t_1} - F_{t_0}$.

We define the notional exposure of futures contracts as

$$\text{NE} = \text{Sign} \times \text{Number of contracts} \\ \times \text{Contract value multiplier} \times \text{Price underlying} \quad (3)$$

where Sign equals +1 for long positions and –1 for short positions. Notice that the price of the underlying is used instead of the futures price. This corresponds to the basic relationship shown in Equation 1. In practice, however, the futures price is often used instead of the underlying price owing to the availability of data.[11] Sometimes it is difficult to obtain all the required data (i.e., the prices of the underlying of the futures contracts) for performance measurement systems. Consider the example of a performance measurement firm that analyzes a variety of funds on behalf of a client. Assume that the necessary holding and transaction data are provided by the custodian of the funds. If the interface does not include explicit information on the underlying of the futures, then the performance measurement firm needs to either establish an interface to an additional source or work with specific assumptions (such as using the futures prices). There are also other reasons why it might be difficult to use the price of the underlying (see the discussion of interest rate futures). For most applications, however, the resulting differences are small, especially if interest rates are low.

---

9 The difference between the position in the physical underlying and the futures/cash position results from the fact that dividends/interest and funding cost may arise for the former but not for the latter.
10 In the performance attribution literature, this relationship is occasionally presented in a highly simplified form: $F_{t_0} = B_{t_0}(1 + r_{fin} - r_e)$, where r_{fin} and r_e represent, respectively, the periodic cost of financing and the income of the underlying. See, for example, Stannard (1996) and LIFFE (1992).
11 LIFFE (1992, Section 2.6).

There are a wide variety of instruments that can serve as the underlying. The underlying for stock futures can be formed by equity indexes or single stocks. The underlying for bond futures is more complicated.

3.1.2 Interest Rate Futures

Interest rate futures are futures contracts with an interest-bearing instrument as the underlying asset. For an exposure analysis, interest rate futures can be mapped to the notional bond named in the contract. Alternatively, the mapping can be based on a real bond from the basket of deliverable bonds specified by the exchange. Because the price of an interest rate futures contract is closely linked to the price of the cheapest-to-deliver (CTD) bond, choosing this specific bond provides another option for the mapping. From a basket of deliverable bonds, the **CTD bond** is the one that—based on the then-prevailing price, the level of short-term financing rates, and the pre-specified conversion factor—has the lowest cost to deliver upon expiry of the contract. The bond expected to be cheapest to deliver may vary frequently over the life of the futures contract. The following are examples of interest rate futures contracts.

A US Treasury futures: In the case of *US Treasury bond futures*, the notional bond is a (hypothetical) treasury bond with varying standards. At the time of writing, US Treasury futures have a conversion factor based on a notional 6% yield, and deliverable bonds must have maturities between 15 and 25 years as of the delivery date.[12]

B Euro Bund futures: *Euro Bund futures* are futures contracts on an obligation of the German government with a coupon rate of 6%. The term range of the deliverable bonds is 8.5–10.5 years; the contract value is €100,000. Only bonds issued by the German government with a nominal value of at least €5 billion are eligible for delivery.[13] Because the notional bond for these futures contracts is not uniquely defined, there are choices in the mapping of these contracts. For the purpose of exposure analysis, the notional bond may, for instance, be defined as a (hypothetical) federal bond with a time to maturity of 9.5 years and a coupon rate of 6%—that is, with regard to the remaining term the bond will be placed in the middle of the spectrum. The advantage of this fixation is that one realizes a constant mapping (with respect to the target) over the course of time. If one realizes the mapping via the CTD bond, then the mapping must be adjusted for each change in the CTD bond. If this task is considered too tedious for an application in practice, then there is the further option of mapping the futures contract to a fixed bond in the basket of deliverable bonds.[14]

These examples demonstrate that futures on interest-bearing instruments are quite different from stock futures. In particular, the term *physical security* in the definition of the notional exposure requires interpretation because of the mapping of the futures contract to the underlying. In spite of these differences, bond futures are treated in the exposure analysis in a similar way as equity index futures.

3.1.3 Examples Using Specific Futures Contracts

DAX Futures Consider the case where the underlying is the DAX, a German large-cap equity index. DAX futures have a contract value of 25 "DAX stocks" (25 is called the "contract value multiplier"). The expiration dates of the DAX contracts fall on the third Friday of the delivery months. The delivery months are March, June, September,

---

12 CME Group (2015).
13 See Eurex (2015).
14 On the delivery date, the seller of the Euro Bund futures has the obligation to deliver bonds corresponding to the notional value of the contract. The basket of bonds with which this obligation can be fulfilled is defined by Eurex Clearing AG. These baskets (including the required conversion factors) are made public.

and December. Each contract has a lifespan at inception of roughly nine months. A contract issued in March will expire in December, and so on. Gains or losses are settled in cash in the delivery month (cash settlement).

We consider a (long) DAX futures contract with an expiration date in December and a price of €8,650 as of 30 September. The price of the underlying DAX index is €8,630.

Exhibit 7 Prices of the DAX and DAX Futures

	9/30	10/31
DAX	8,630	8,651
DAX Futures	8,650	8,670

The notional exposure for one long contract is then calculated as[15]

NE = Sign × Number of contracts × Contract value multiplier × Price underlying
  = +1 × 1 × 25 × €8,630 = €215,750

This is also the maximum risk (maximum loss in the theoretical case of the DAX going to zero) at the purchase of this long contract position. The associated cash position is equal to the notional value of the futures contract.

Assume that a portfolio currently has a long position in German equities of €1m (where m equals 1 million) and €0.3m in cash. If the manager wishes to increase equity exposure through the purchase of a single DAX futures contract, then the portfolio exposures change as shown in Exhibit 8.

Exhibit 8 Effective Portfolio Exposure

Asset class	Actual Holdings (€m)	Exposure Due to Futures (€m)	Associated Economic Exposure (€m)	Percentage of Portfolio
German equities	1.0	0.216	1.216	93.5
Cash	0.3	−0.216	0.084	6.5
Total	**1.3**	**0.000**	**1.300**	**100.00**

The portfolio has an initial net asset value (NAV) of €1.3m, allocated between German equities (€1.0m) and cash (€0.3m). By buying a futures position, the equity exposure is increased by €0.216m (the rounded value of €215,750) to €1.216m, the "associated economic exposure." There is a corresponding decrease in the cash position of €0.216m and its associated economic exposure. The percentage of the portfolio is calculated on the basis of these economic exposures—for example, 93.5% = 1.216/1.3.

Here we adjusted the portfolio cash, which includes the cash earmarked as margin for the futures contract. We assume that the same interest rate applies to both positions, which allows for their aggregation.

---

15 Note that we are calculating the notional exposure and not the price of the futures contract. Therefore, we do not need to consider the cost of carry (net income and financing costs).

As noted previously, in practice, the futures price is often used for the exposure calculation. If the futures price trades at a premium (i.e., the price is higher than the spot price), the equity exposure will be slightly overestimated. If the futures price is less than the spot price, the exposure will be slightly underestimated.

Next, we will compute the return of the notional equity position generated by the DAX futures for the month of October. The return of the notional stock position over a period is equal to the total margin receipt plus the notional income. The exposure to the underlying stock position is formed by the futures (which is measured using the spot price), as reflected in the associated notional cash position of €215,750. Assume that the cash position would have earned income at a monthly rate of 0.1%.

We will assign a portion of the income from cash to the equity segment. As €215,750 of notional exposure was added to the equity, we assign cash income of €215,750 × 0.1% = €215.75 to the position. Note that in this performance measurement calculation, we use the actual economic exposure in the denominator as measured using the spot price, whereas in the numerator, we use the profit on the futures position. The return of the notional stock position is then given by

$$\begin{aligned}\text{Notional return} &= \frac{25 \times (€8{,}670 - €8{,}650) + €215.75}{€215{,}750} \\ &= \frac{25 \times €20 + €215.75}{€215{,}750} \\ &= \frac{€715.75}{€215{,}750} \\ &= 0.332\%\end{aligned} \qquad (4)$$

In general, the interest rate applied to the notional cash position (implicitly defined by the futures contract) and the physical cash positions will differ. In this example, for the sake of simplicity, the return for both notional and physical cash is assumed to be 0.1%

At the beginning of the period, the futures price is above the price of the DAX, which reflects the positive financing costs. Dividend payments do not play a role because the DAX is a total return index (or performance index).[16,17]

Exhibit 9 shows the returns of the various components of the German equity portfolio. We will assume that the return of the investor's physical stock position is 0.40%. As shown before, the return of the notional stock position (generated by the futures position) is equal to 0.33%, which led to a total return of 0.39% for the combined equity position:

$$\frac{1 \times 0.40\% + 0.216 \times 0.33\%}{1.216} = 0.39\%$$

---

[16] Changes in both a spot investment in and a futures contract on the DAX correspond to changes in the index level. Therefore, spot and futures investments do not differ in how dividends affect their value. This is a feature of all futures or forwards on total return indexes.

[17] The FTSE futures contract is based on a price index; therefore, the futures price might be lower than the price of the FTSE index if the FTSE dividend yield is greater than the positive financing costs.

Derivatives Performance Measurement

Exhibit 9 Portfolio Holdings: Long Equity Futures Performance Measurement

Asset Class	Associated Economic Exposure (€m)	Percentage of Portfolio	Return (%)
German equities (notional)	0.216	16.60	0.33
German equities (stocks)	1.000	76.92	0.40
German equities (total)	**1.216**	**93.52**	**0.39**
Cash (physical)	0.300	23.08	0.10
Cash (notional)	−0.216	−16.60	0.10
Cash (netted)	**0.084**	**6.48**	**0.10**
Total	**1.300**	**100.00**	**0.37**

The netted cash position of 0.084 is equal to the cash position after the deduction of the notional cash position (0.300 − 0.216). The total associated economic exposure is a sum of German equities (total) and cash (netted). The total return of 0.37% that follows is a weighted sum of the return for these classes. It is calculated as (1.216/1.30) × 0.39% + (0.084/1.30) × 0.10% = 0.37%.

Suppose that, instead of a long position in the DAX futures contract, the manager took a short position in the contract to decrease exposure to German equities. In that case, the notional equities position would be negative, thereby reducing the total equities position to less than €1m. Similarly, the cash position would increase to be above €0.3m as shown in Exhibit 10.

Exhibit 10 Portfolio Holdings: Short Equity Futures Performance Measurement

Asset Class	Associated Economic Exposure (€m)	Percentage of Portfolio	Return (%)
German equities (notional)	−0.216	−16.60	0.33
German equities (stocks)	1.000	76.92	0.40
German equities (total)	**0.784**	**60.32**	**0.42**
Cash (physical)	0.300	23.08	0.10
Cash (notional)	0.216	16.60	0.10
Cash (netted)	**0.516**	**39.68**	**0.10**
Total	**1.300**	**100.00**	**0.29**

The notional exposure for one short contract is then calculated as

NE = Sign × Number of contracts × Contract value multiplier × Price underlying

NE = −1 × 1 × 25 × €8,630 = −€215,750

The portfolio has an initial NAV of €1.3m, allocated between German equities (€1.0m) and cash (€0.3m). By selling a futures position, the equity exposure is decreased by €0.216m (the rounded value of −€215,750) to €0.784m, the associated economic exposure. There is a corresponding increase in the cash position of €0.216m and its associated economic exposure. The percentage of the portfolio is calculated on the basis of these economic exposures—for example, 0.784/1.3 = 60.32%.

The return of the notional stock position is exactly as calculated previously; the fact that we now have a short position does not alter the return on the underlying instrument.

The total return on the combined equity position is now 0.42%:

$$\frac{1 \times 0.40\% - 0.216 \times 0.33\%}{1.0 - 0.216} = 0.42\%$$

Relative to the long futures position in Exhibit 9, the return on the total equities position here is higher because the lower return futures position (0.33%) is shorted.

The netted cash position of 0.516 is equal to the cash position after the addition of the notional cash position (0.300 + 0.216). The total associated economic exposure is a sum of German equities (total) and cash (netted). The total return of 0.29% that follows is a weighted sum of the return for these classes and is calculated as (0.784/1.30) × 0.42% + (0.516/1.30) × 0.10% = 0.29%. Relative to the long futures position in Exhibit 9, the portfolio return here of 0.29% is lower because the short futures position creates a greater weight (39.68%) in the low return (0.10%) cash position.

Now, consider a portfolio that includes physical German equities of €1m and French equities of €1m and no physical cash. Assume the manager wants to increase the exposure to German equities using the same DAX futures contract as shown in the previous example and to decrease the French equities exposure by selling CAC futures contracts with the following prices:

Exhibit 11   Prices of the CAC and CAC Futures

	9/30	10/31
CAC	4,143	4,300
CAC Futures	4,134	4,282

The manager is long one DAX futures contract and short five CAC futures contracts. The contract value multiplier for CAC futures contracts is 10. The notional exposure for five short CAC contracts is

NE = Sign × Number of contracts × Contract value multiplier × Price underlying
NE = –1 × 5 × 10 × €4,143 = –€207,150

Exhibit 12   Effective Portfolio Exposure

Asset class	Actual Holdings (€m)	Exposure Due to Futures (€m)	Associated Economic Exposure (€m)	Percentage of Portfolio (%)
German equities	1.0	0.216	1.216	60.8
French equities	1.0	–0.207	0.793	39.7
Cash	0.0	–0.009	–0.009	–0.5
Total	2.0	0.000	2.000	100.00

The return calculation on the notional German equities is identical to that in Exhibits 9 and 10 because the underlying data are the same:

$$\text{Notional return} = \frac{25 \times (€8{,}670 - €8{,}650) + €215.75}{€215{,}750}$$

$$= \frac{25 \times €20 + €215.75}{€215{,}750}$$

$$= \frac{€715.75}{€215{,}750}$$

$$= 0.332\%$$

The income on the futures position on the notional equities position is per contract: $10 \times 4{,}143 \times 0.1\% = €41.43$. The per-contract return on the notional French equities is then calculated as

$$\text{Notional return} = \frac{10 \times (€4{,}282 - €4{,}134) + €41.43}{10 \times €4{,}143}$$

$$= \frac{10 \times €148 + €41.43}{€41{,}430} = \frac{€1{,}521.43}{€41{,}430} = 3.672\%$$

Exhibit 13 Portfolio Holdings: Equity Futures Performance Measurement

Asset Class	Associated Economic Exposure (€m)	Percentage of Portfolio (%)	Return (%)
German equities (notional)	0.216	10.80	0.33
German equities (stocks)	1.000	50.00	0.40
German equities (total)	**1.216**	**60.80**	**0.39**
French equities (notional)	−0.207	−10.35	3.67
French equities (stocks)	1.000	50.00	4.00
French equities (total)	**0.793**	**39.65**	**4.09**
Cash (physical)	0.000	0.00	0.10
Cash (notional)	−0.009	−0.45	0.10
Cash (netted)	**−0.009**	**−0.45**	**0.10**
Total	2.000	100.00	1.86

Exhibit 13 shows the return components of various segments of the entire portfolio. The combined German equity performance, as before, is

$$\frac{1 \times 0.40\% + 0.216 \times 0.33\%}{1.216} = 0.39\%$$

Assuming the return on the investor's French equity position is 4.00%, the combined French equity performance is

$$\frac{1 \times 4.0\% - 0.207 \times 3.67\%}{0.793} = 4.09\%$$

The net cash position of −0.009 represents a small amount of leverage resulting from the addition of notional cash from the short CAC futures contracts of 0.207 plus the deduction of notional cash from the long DAX futures contract of −0.216. There is no physical cash to add in this example. The total return of 1.86% that follows is a weighted sum of the return for these classes. It is calculated as (1.216/2.0 × 0.39%) + (0.793/2.0 × 4.09%) − (0.009/2.0 × 0.1%) = 1.86%.

Euro Bund Futures   We will now consider the effect of a futures position on a fixed-income portfolio. The portfolio consists of positions in euro-denominated bonds with a time to maturity between 4 and 10 years and a cash position. The initial net asset value of the portfolio is €7.3m. The allocation among the three maturity classes is shown in the second column in Exhibit 14.

Assume the portfolio manager wishes to increase the duration of the portfolio and does so by purchasing 10 Euro Bund futures contracts, which have maturities of 8–10 years. The futures price is 105% and the contract multiplier is 100,000.[18] For practical reasons, the notional exposure is calculated using the futures price rather than the price of the underlying.[19] The notional exposure is then given by

$$\begin{aligned} \text{NE} &= \text{Sign} \times \text{Number of contracts} \times \text{Contract value multiplier} \times \text{Futures price} \\ &= 1 \times 10 \times 100{,}000 \times \text{€}(105/100) \\ &= \text{€}1.05\text{m} \end{aligned}$$

Exhibit 14 shows how this derivative position affects the exposure of the various asset classes. It provides an example for a portfolio that includes—among other investments—the previously described Euro Bund futures contract. The first three rows provide the positions in fixed-income investments in the respective maturity bands. Row 3 shows a €1.0m position in actual fixed-income investments and an increase in exposure due to the purchase of Euro Bund futures. The cash position and the corresponding reduction in exposure due to the purchase of Euro Bund futures is shown in Row 4.[20] The net exposure due to futures is zero, which corresponds to the real effect of the investment in the futures on a portfolio level.

The use of the futures contract increases the exposure of the 8–10 year maturity band, reduces the cash position, and increases the duration of the portfolio.

Exhibit 14   Portfolio Holdings: Bond/Futures Performance Measurement

Asset Class/Maturity	Actual Holdings (€m)	Percentage of Portfolio Based on Actual Holding	Exposure Due to Futures (€m)	Associated Economic Exposure (€m)	Percentage of Portfolio
4–6 years	2.0	27.40		2.00	27.40
6–8 years	3.0	41.10		3.00	41.10
8–10 years	1.0	13.70	1.05	2.05	28.08
Cash	1.3	17.81	−1.05	0.25	3.42
Total	**7.3**	**100.00**	**0.00**	**7.30**	**100.00**

---

18 Note that the futures price is a percentage figure, so we need to divide by 100 to calculate the notional exposure.
19 The alternative choices are described in Section 3.1.1. The use of, for example, the CTD bond would in practice require frequent adjustments because the bond expected to be cheapest to deliver can vary considerably over the life of a futures contract.
20 The intuition behind the reduction of the cash position by the notional exposure from the futures contract is that the cash has been "transformed" to a bond by the futures contract. Viewed in another light, the return on this portfolio should be measured on an equivalent basis to a portfolio (without futures) where cash was used to buy the underlying. Thus, cash is reduced by the amount that would have been used to purchase the underlying in the spot market.

Derivatives Performance Measurement

The exposure in the 8–10 year sector increased from 13.70% to 28.08% (2.05/7.30). The cash exposure changed accordingly from 17.81% to 3.42% (0.25/7.30).

These exposure considerations are also important for an analysis of the return contributions of the various management decisions. The return calculation for the Euro Bund futures position is analogous to the calculation for the DAX futures contract.

In the following example, we will compute the return for the 8–10 year position based on the economic exposure of 2.05. Assume that the futures price has increased to 106% and that the value of the actual 8–10 year bonds in the portfolio has increased from €1m to €1.03m. The €1.03m reflects the price change of the bonds as well as accrued and paid interest (total return).

The cash return associated with the notional exposure of the bond futures is attributed to the 8–10 year maturity (not the cash maturity) because, as the cost-of-carry relationship in Equation 1 shows, a futures position is composed of the spot asset plus the interest cost of financing. The return of the cash position was 0.1% over the observation period, so the income allocated to the 8–10 year futures position equals

€1.05m × 0.1% = €0.00105m

The return, R, of the total 8–10 year position is then equal to

$$R = \frac{(1.03 - 1.0) + (1.06 - 1.05) + 0.00105}{2.05}$$

$$= \frac{0.04105}{2.05}$$

$$= 2.00\%$$

3.2 The Notional Market Value Approach for Other Derivatives

In addition to futures contracts, performance analysts may also be faced with portfolios containing forwards, options, and swaps. We next discuss the appropriate return measurements for portfolios containing these derivatives.

3.2.1 Forwards

The methodology for futures can be applied to forwards, which are similar to futures. A forward contract (or **forward**) is a non-standardized (and non-exchange-traded) contract between two parties to buy or sell an asset at a specified future time at a price agreed upon today. At the transaction date, the valuation of forwards and futures with similar terms leads to identical results. Generally, forwards are not traded on margin and settlement occurs at the delivery date; the economic risk may, however, be eliminated by means of a suitable countertrade.[21]

The pricing formula (Equation 1) is the same for futures and forwards. A key difference between futures and forwards is that in the case of futures the unrealized daily profit and loss and the related cash flow are reflected in the margin account, whereas in the case of forwards the cash flow occurs at maturity. Therefore, when calculating the value of a forward investment, the gains and losses need to be discounted using discount rate r_{fin}. The value of a (long) forward investment at time t_1 with forward contract maturity T and price change between t_0 and t_1 is[22]

$$\left(F_{t_1} - F_{t_0}\right)\frac{1}{\left(1 + r_{fin}\right)^{(T-t_1)}} \quad (5)$$

---

[21] For the differences in the valuation of futures and forwards, see the Appendix to this reading, "A Primer on Derivatives."
[22] The discount rate should be expressed consistent with the time exponent in the formula. For example, if the discount rate is an annual rate, then $T - t_1$ should be the number of years (or partial years) to maturity.

DAX Forwards To illustrate the difference between forwards and futures, let us revisit the DAX futures example. Instead of a futures contract, the portfolio manager chooses to use a forward contract with a multiplier of 25 on the DAX. There are 50 days remaining until maturity.

We use the market convention of a 360-day year and a 30-day month. Given that the *monthly* rate is 0.1% and that there are 50 days left until the maturity of the forward, the notional return of the equity position reflected in the forward position is

$$\text{Notional return} = \frac{25 \times (€8{,}670 - €8{,}650)(1 + 0.1\%)^{-(50/30)} + €215.75}{€215{,}750}$$

$$= \frac{€500 \times 0.9983 + €215.75}{€215{,}750}$$

$$= \frac{€499.17 + €215.75}{€215{,}750}$$

$$= 0.331\%$$

(6)

The term $(1 + 0.1\%)^{-(50/30)}$ follows from Equation 5. If we interpret r_{fin} as the monthly rate, then the exponent corresponds to the number of months to maturity (50/30).

Compared with the return of 0.332% in Equation 4, the discounting of the future gain or loss has only a minimal impact on the return of 0.331% in Equation 6.

3.2.2 Options

The analysis of futures positions can be adapted to the case of options. There are two major differences to note. First, options are highly non-linear (or asymmetric) instruments. Second, options have a non-zero market value (the option premium value) over their lifespan. A call option behaves very differently depending on its **moneyness**. A deep in-the-money option is more sensitive to the underlying's price than a deeply out-of-the-money option. The price relationship between the option and the underlying can be approximately expressed by the **option delta**, which is a change in the value of the call for a unit change in the value of the underlying.[23] For a deep in-the-money call option, the delta (δ) is close to 1, which means that a change in the underlying will cause a change in option price of the same magnitude. The delta of a deeply out-of-the-money call option is close to zero, which means that a change in the price of the underlying will have almost no effect on the option price. When the stock price is near the strike price of the option, delta is typically close to 0.5.

Given that options have a non-zero market value, one way to measure the performance of an option is to simply calculate the (time-weighted) return based on the change in the market value. Because options have a (non-zero) weight, one can then calculate the contributions (return times weight) to the return of a position or a portfolio.[24] This is a perfectly acceptable (and very common) approach in practice.

As in the case of the simplified treatment of futures contributions, however, this methodology does not reflect the underlying economic exposure in the reporting and return analysis. This is especially important for attribution analyses.

The relevant economic exposures can be determined using a method similar to the procedure for futures. The notional exposure assumes the following form:

$$\text{NE} = \text{Sign} \times \delta \times \text{Number of contracts}$$
$$\times \text{Contract value multiplier} \times \text{Price of underlying}$$

(7)

---

[23] Here we will implicitly consider the most basic forms of options (e.g., American-type call options). These considerations are in principle also applicable to other, more complex forms (such as Bermudan-type options); the actual computations become more complex.

[24] This calculation would yield a contribution analysis similar to the simplified approach in the case of futures.

Derivatives Performance Measurement

The sign is +1 for a long position in the underlying and −1 for a short position in the underlying.

It is important to note that this formula is a reasonable approximation for only small changes in the underlying. It should also in general be applied only for short time intervals. The delta (δ) must be recalculated for each period. In this case, it does not make sense to use the price of the option instead of the price of the underlying. This holds for all non-linear instruments.

Call Option on the DAX   Previously, we discussed how the use of a futures contract can change equity exposure and return. Now we assume that the portfolio manager chooses to increase equity exposure using call options on the DAX rather than futures. The option has a strike price of €8,700 and a maturity of December 2013. The delta equals 0.45, reflecting the fact that the option is near the money. The portfolio manager buys 10 contracts. The price of one option is €400 and the contract multiplier is 5, so the market value (cost) of the option position equals €20,000 (10 × €400 × 5 = €0.02m).[25] If the underlying index value is €8,630, the notional exposure is

$$NE = +1 \times 0.45 \times 10 \times 5 \times €8{,}630$$
$$= €194{,}175$$

The option contracts change the exposure as shown in Exhibit 15.

Exhibit 15   Effective Portfolio Exposure with Long Call Options

Asset Class	Actual Holdings (€m)	Exposure Due to Options (€m)	Associated Economic Exposure (€m)	Percentage of Portfolio (exposure)
German equities	1.00	0.19	1.19	91.54
Options	0.02	−0.02		
Cash	0.28	−0.17	0.11	8.46
Total	1.30	0.00	1.30	100.00

Note that when we examine the effective portfolio exposures for the use of options, we must record them separately from those of the underlying equities to account for their value.

As in Section 3.1.3, the initial total net asset value is €1.3m, part of which (€0.02m) is invested in stock options on the DAX index, leaving €0.28m in cash. The option position creates an exposure of €0.19m (the rounded value of €194,175), so the overall exposure to German equities increases to €1.19m. The corresponding net cash balance amounts to €0.11m on an exposure basis.

Note that the option is converted to increase equity exposure (€0.19m; third column in Exhibit 15) with a decrease in notional cash position due to the difference between the cost and notional exposure of the options. The offset in the cash balance reflects the full economic exposure of the option, €0.19m. Because the option cost was €0.02m and is reflected in cash, the cash position is reduced by an additional €0.17m (row 3).

---

[25] The multiplier of the DAX option refers to the number of DAX indexes that one option contract represents. Note that the price of the option in this example is somewhat unrealistic given the relation between the strike price and the actual DAX level. This choice was made in order to emphasize the effect.

Cash earned a return of 0.1%, resulting in a gain of €0.17m × 0.1% = €0.00017m = €170. Over the period, the portfolio's holding of German equities increased by 0.4%. As a result of increases in the value of the DAX, the market value of the options rose from €0.02m to €0.025m. The return of the notional equities position resulting from the use of the options is then

$$\text{Notional return} = \frac{(0.025 - 0.02) + 0.00017}{0.19} = 2.72\%$$

Exhibit 16 shows returns for the individual positions (including the actual stock position) and the total portfolio.

Exhibit 16 Portfolio Holdings: Equity/Long-Call-Option Performance Measurement

Asset Class	Associated Economic Exposure (€m)	Percentage of Portfolio	Return (%)
German equities (notional from options)	0.19	14.62	2.72
German equities (stocks)	1.00	76.92	0.40
German equities (total)	**1.19**	**91.54**	**0.77**
Cash (actual)	0.28	21.54	0.10
Cash (notional)	−0.17	−13.08	0.10
Cash (effective)	**0.11**	**8.46**	**0.10**
*Total**	*1.30*	*100.00*	*0.71*

* The total return of the portfolio is a weighted sum of the segment return.

For the cash position, the return is 0.10%. The actual stock holdings of the portfolio achieved a return of 0.40%, and the German equity position due to the exposure created by the options had a return of 2.72%. The combined return on the total equities position is 0.77%:

$$\frac{0.19 \times 2.72\% + 1 \times 0.40\%}{1.19} = 0.77\%$$

The effective cash position is the cash position after the addition for the notional cash associated with the options. The overall portfolio return is then calculated as follows:

$$\frac{1.19 \times 0.77\% + 0.11 \times 0.10\%}{1.30} = 0.71\%$$

The portfolio return can also be calculated using the portfolio percentages: 0.9154 × 0.77% + 0.0846 × 0.10% = 0.71%.

Now, we examine the case where a manager's use of options decreases, instead of increases, equity exposure. Using the previous example, assume that the portfolio manager enters a short position in the call options; in other words, he sells the option contracts to another investor. This other investor has the right to "purchase" the DAX at a level of 8,700. Exercising the option makes sense only if the DAX reaches a level above 8,700. In this transaction, the portfolio manager receives the option premium

Derivatives Performance Measurement

of €0.02m upfront. Also, in this case an initial margin has to be provided.[26] If the level of the DAX increases further, more cash must be transferred to the margin account. Exhibit 17 shows the account statement in this case.

Exhibit 17 Effective Portfolio Exposure with Written Call Options

Asset Class	Actual Holdings (€m)	Exposure Due to Options (€m)	Associated Economic Exposure (€m)	Percentage of Portfolio (exposure)
German equities	1.00	−0.19	0.81	62.31
Options	−0.02	0.02	—	—
Cash	0.32	0.17	0.49	37.69
Total	1.30	0.00	1.30	100.00

Note that the notional exposure representation, in a strict sense, holds only for (infinitesimally) small changes in the price of the underlying. The exposure of −€0.19m corresponds approximately to a short position in the underlying; that is, it will create approximately the same effect as the underlying position (for small changes).[27]

In this case, the overall portfolio assumes the form shown in Exhibit 18.

Exhibit 18 Portfolio Holdings: Equity/Written-Call-Option Performance Measurement

Asset Class	Associated Economic Exposure (€m)	Percentage of Portfolio	Return (%)
German equities (notional from options)	−0.19	−14.62	2.72
German equities (stocks)	1.00	76.92	0.40
German equities (total)	**0.81**	**62.31**	**−0.14**
Cash (physical)	0.32	24.62	0.10
Cash (notional)	0.17	13.07	0.10
Cash (effective)	**0.49**	**37.69**	**0.10**
Total	*1.30*	*100.00*	*−0.05*

The return of the notional equities position is calculated as follows:

$$\frac{0.025 - 0.02 + 0.00017}{0.19} = 2.72\%$$

Recognizing the short options position with a negative sign, the return of the total equities position is then given by

$$\frac{(-0.19) \times 2.72\% + 1.00 \times 0.40\%}{0.81} = -0.14\%$$

---

26 For simplicity, we assume that this margin is part of the cash component.
27 Note that because the deltas will fluctuate, the exposure will change accordingly.

The overall portfolio return is

$$\frac{0.81 \times (-0.14\%) + 0.49 \times 0.10\%}{1.30} = -0.05\%$$

3.2.3 Swaps

A **swap** is an instrument in which counterparties exchange cash flows; the cash flows of one party's financial instrument are exchanged for the cash flows of the other party's financial instrument. An example is a swap involving two bonds where the counterparties agree to exchange the two cash flows. Often, one of the bonds is a fixed-rate bond and the other a floating-rate note. In theory, there are no limitations to the types of cash flows that can be swapped.

Again, we will not discuss valuation issues in detail, because doing so is not really required for a discussion of performance effects.[28] The valuation can be summarized quite simply: A swap can be regarded as a long position in Instrument 1 and a short position in Instrument 2, and the market value of the swap is simply equal to the difference of the market values of these instruments. The respective exposures can thus be directly derived from the market values of the individual instruments:[29]

Exposure to Instrument 1 = Market value of Instrument 1
Exposure to Instrument 2 = −Market value of Instrument 2

For the sake of simplicity, we consider only instruments in the base currency of a portfolio. The market value of the instruments refers to the actual cash flows only.

Fixed vs. Floating Swap A portfolio consists of US$-denominated bonds with maturities between zero and six years and a cash position. The net asset value of the portfolio equals US$38.5m. The portfolio manager enters a swap agreement in which he agrees to pay six months Libor in exchange for receiving an annual payment of 3% fixed on a notional value of US$10m. The swap has a remaining life of two years. If the value of the fixed instrument equals US$10.25m and that of the floating instrument equals US$9.88m, the exposures are

- Exposure in the fixed-rate position with the two-year maturity: +US$10.25m
- Exposure in the floating-rate position: −US$9.88m

In Exhibit 19, we consider this swap in a portfolio context to demonstrate its impact on portfolio exposures at initiation of the swap, t_0.

Exhibit 19 Portfolio Holdings at t_0: US Bonds/Receive Fixed Swap Performance Measurement

Asset Class/Maturity	Actual Holdings (US$m)	Exposure Due to Swaps (US$m)	Associated Economic Exposure (US$m)	Percentage of Portfolio
Cash	0.50	−0.37	0.13	0.34
0–1 years	12.00	−9.88	2.12	5.51
1–2 years	8.00	10.25	18.25	47.40
2–4 years	12.00		12.00	31.17

---

28 For details, see Hull (2006, Chapter 7).
29 See Cubilié (2007, p 261).

Exhibit 19 (Continued)

Asset Class/Maturity	Actual Holdings (US$m)	Exposure Due to Swaps (US$m)	Associated Economic Exposure (US$m)	Percentage of Portfolio
4–6 years	6.00		6.00	15.58
Total	38.50	0.00	38.50	100.00

The values of the bond holdings and swaps contain the accrued interest. The second column shows the value of the actual bond position of the portfolio and the cash balance. The figures in the third column show the change in exposure that is caused by the use of the swap. The use of the swap leads to a decrease in the exposure of the 0–1 year segment of –US$9.88m and an increase for the 1–2 year segment of US$10.25m. At the initiation of the swap transaction, an upfront fee of US$0.37m (the market value of the swap) has to be paid from the long fixed position (valued at US$10.25m) to the long floating-rate position (valued at US$9.88m) to make the positions equal. This fee payment reduces cash from US$0.50m to US$0.13m for the portfolio with the long fixed position. The net asset value of the portfolio still equals US$38.5m.

With this swap, the portfolio manager has increased the portfolio's exposure to bonds with a 1–2 year term.

We now consider changes in the portfolio's value over time. Exhibit 20 shows changes in the portfolio value six months after t_0 due to changes in the value of the positions and interest on the bonds and swaps.

Exhibit 20   Portfolio Holdings at t_1: US Bonds/Receive Fixed Swap Performance Measurement

Asset Class/Maturity	Actual Holdings (US$m)	Exposure Due to Swaps (US$m in t_1)	Interest Payment on Bonds (US$m)	Interest Payment Swaps (US$m)
Cash	0.60		0.00	
0–1 years	11.90	–9.81	0.12	–0.10
1–2 years	8.10	10.30	0.10	0.15
2–4 years	12.15		0.13	
4–6 years	6.05		0.07	
Total	38.80	0.49	0.42	0.05

We assume that no further transactions have taken place. The total net asset value of the portfolio has grown to US$39.29m (US$38.80m + US$0.49m) from US$38.50m. This increase stems from the appreciation of the bonds (from US$38m to US$38.2m), the appreciation of the swap value (from US$0.37m to US$0.49m) and the total interest payments (reflected in the cash balance of $0.60m). In Exhibit 20, the bond interest payments, the interest payments of the swap, and the upfront fee are included in the cash balance, which grew from US$0.50m to US$0.60m as a result of the total bond interest payments and swap interest payments, including the initial upfront fee (0.60 = 0.50 – 0.37 + 0.42 + 0.05).

The returns of the various positions can now be computed. For the 1–2 year bond position, we obtain

$$\text{Return}_{1-2\,years} = \frac{(8.10 - 8.00) + (10.30 - 10.25) + 0.10 + 0.15}{8.00 + 10.25} = 2.19\%$$

The numerator includes the gain from the actual holdings (8.1 − 8.0), the gain from the swap (10.30 − 10.25), and the interest payment of the bonds and the swap (respectively, 0.10 and 0.15). The returns for the other positions are calculated similarly. For the other positions, we obtain

$$\text{Return}_{0-1\,years} = \frac{(11.90 - 12.00) + [-9.81 - (-9.88)] + 0.12 - 0.10}{12.00 - 9.88} = -0.47\%$$

$$\text{Return}_{2-4\,years} = \frac{(12.15 - 12.00) + 0.13}{12.00} = 2.33\%$$

$$\text{Return}_{4-6\,years} = \frac{(6.05 - 6.00) + 0.07}{6.00} = 2.00\%$$

For the cash position, we obtain a return of 0%:

$$\text{Return}_{Cash} = \frac{(0.60 - 0.42 - 0.05) - (0.50 - 0.37)}{0.13} = 0\%$$

It should be noted that to avoid double counting, we subtracted out the total interest payments on the bonds and swap (0.42 and 0.05, respectively) from the ending cash balance of 0.60 because these payments have already been attributed to the other maturity segments of the portfolio.

The overall return of the portfolio is then given by

$$\text{Return}_{Portfolio} = 0.34\% \times 0\% + 5.51 \times (-0.47\%) + 47.40\% \times 2.19\% + 31.17\% \times 2.33\% + 15.58\% \times 2.00\%$$
$$= 2.05\%$$

EXAMPLE 2

Portfolios with Forwards, Futures, and Options

1 Assume that the net income derived from an underlying stock index is less than the cost of financing the spot purchase. If one uses the futures price in the calculation of the notional exposure from the index future, then one would:

   A overestimate the exposure.

   B underestimate the exposure.

   C estimate the exposure accurately.

2 All else being equal, the notional return of a forward contract is *most likely* different from the futures contract notional return because:

   A forwards are usually traded on margin.

   B futures are not traded on a stock exchange.

   C cash flows of the forward occur at contract maturity.

3 Assume that a portfolio manager sold five contracts of EURO STOXX 50 Index Futures. The contract value multiplier for such instruments is 10. On 6 February, the index had a price of €3,393. The portfolio has

a position in the underlying European stocks of €170,000. The portfolio manager in trading these futures in regard to the overall position in European stocks is *most likely* intending to:

A increase exposure.

B create a neutral portfolio position.

C create a short position in terms of economic exposure.

4 Consider a long position in 10 DAX futures contracts. The contract value multiplier of the DAX futures is 25. The following are the values at close:

	31 Dec.	31 Jan.
DAX	9,805	10,694
DAX Futures	9,986	10,708

Given a return on an associated cash position of 0.04%, the notional return of the futures contract position is *closest* to:

A 7.36%.

B 7.40%.

C 9.11%.

5 A portfolio manager buys 10 call options on the EURO STOXX 50 to obtain a long position on European equities. On that day, the underlying index has a value of €3,404. The strike price of the option is €3,500 and the contract multiplier is 5. If the delta of the option is 0.4 and the price of the option is €80, the notional exposure of this position is *closest* to:

A €1,600.

B €68,080.

C €170,200.

Solution to 1:

A is correct. With the net income from the underlying stock index being less than the cost of financing, the futures price is higher than the underlying stock index price. The use of the futures price, rather than the price of the underlying, in the calculation of the notional exposure would overestimate the exposure.

Solution to 2:

C is correct. Because the cash flow occurs at maturity, it needs to be discounted in the valuation. Therefore, returns will in general be different. Forwards do not usually require margin, and futures are traded on exchanges.

Solution to 3:

B is correct. The notional exposure created by the short position in the futures is given by NE = −1 × 5 × 10 × €3,393 = −€169,650. Thus, the net economic exposure in the European stock segment is given by €350 (€170,000 − €169,650), which is close to zero. The net equity position is approximately neutral.

Solution to 4:

B is correct. The initial notional exposure of this position is NE = 10 × 25 × €9,805 = €2,451,250. The notional income is €2,451,250 × 0.04% = €980.5. Thus the notional return is

$$\frac{10 \times 25 \times (10{,}708 - 9{,}986) + 980.5}{2{,}451{,}250} = 7.40\%$$

> Response A omits the interest on the cash position. Response C uses the change in the price of the underlying instead of that for the futures prices.
>
> **Solution to 5:**
>
> B is correct: NE = 5 × 10 × €3,404 × 0.4 = €68,080.

4. MULTICURRENCY PERFORMANCE MEASUREMENT

So far in our discussion of portfolios, we have assumed that the portfolio was denominated in a single currency. Because investors look globally for investment opportunities, portfolios are likely to contain several currency exposures. We next examine return measurement in these cases.

4.1 Returns on Unhedged Portfolios

A domestic asset is an asset that trades in the investor's domestic currency. Foreign assets (or non-domestic assets) are assets denominated in currencies other than the investor's domestic currency. The **domestic currency** (also called the **base currency**) is the currency in which the portfolio is valued for return calculations.

Suppose an investor holds a foreign asset and the asset goes up in value by 10%. From the investor's perspective, 10% is the asset's return in foreign currency terms. This return is often called the *local currency return* or simply the *local return*. The investor can restate the local return in base currency terms. The base currency return would reflect the local return and any currency exchange gain or losses over the holding period. Local, currency, and base returns for a portfolio of assets denominated in US dollars (USD) reported in a base currency of British pounds (GBP) are shown in Example 3. In this example, a British investor has invested in USD-denominated assets.

> **EXAMPLE 3**
>
> ### Portfolios with Exchange Rate Exposure
>
> Calculate the local, currency, and base returns given the data in Exhibit 21. The base currency is GBP. Throughout this reading, the notation USD/GBP is used to indicate the **spot exchange rate** for the amount of USD that one GBP is worth.
>
> **Exhibit 21 Market Value in Local (USD) Currency and Prevailing Spot Currency Exchange Rates**
>
> | Period | Market Value in USD (m) | USD/GBP Spot Exchange Rate | GBP/USD Spot Exchange Rate |
> |---|---|---|---|
> | Start | 100 | 1.5 | 0.66667 |
> | End of Month 1 | 100 | 1.6 | 0.62500 |
> | End of Month 2 | 110 | 1.65 | 0.60606 |
> | End of Month 3 | 115 | 1.4 | 0.71429 |
> | End of Month 4 | 105 | 1.3 | 0.76923 |

Exhibit 21 (Continued)

Period	Market Value in USD (m)	USD/GBP Spot Exchange Rate	GBP/USD Spot Exchange Rate
End of Month 5	95	1.4	0.71429
End of Month 6	90	1.4	0.71429

Note: The USD/GBP spot exchange rate is the amount of USD that one GBP is worth.

Local (USD) returns are calculated as

Month 1 local return: $\dfrac{100}{100} - 1 = 0\%$

Month 2 local return: $\dfrac{110}{100} - 1 = 10\%$

Month 3 local return: $\dfrac{115}{110} - 1 = 4.55\%$

Month 4 local return: $\dfrac{105}{115} - 1 = -8.7\%$

Month 5 local return: $\dfrac{95}{105} - 1 = -9.52\%$

Month 6 local return: $\dfrac{90}{95} - 1 = -5.26\%$

The **currency spot return** for Month t is $(S_t/S_{t-1}) - 1$ where S_t is the spot exchange rate at time t.

Therefore, the Month 1 currency spot return for USD versus GBP is $(S_1/S_0) - 1 = (0.625/0.66667) - 1 = -6.25\%$. The British pound bought more dollars at the end of Month 1 than at the start, so the British pound has appreciated and the US dollar has depreciated, relative to one another.

Note that the Month 1 currency spot return for GBP versus USD is 1.6/1.5 − 1 = 6.67%; expressed as a wealth ratio, 1 + 6.67% is the reciprocal of 1 − 6.25%, not the opposite of 6.67%. There are always two ways to express currency movements from either perspective. In the context of this example from the perspective of a GBP investor with assets denominated in USD, we are concerned with the US dollar performance against the British pound. By investing in US assets, the British investor is taking a position in both the asset itself and the US dollar. Just as with any other investment, if the US dollar appreciates, the British investor benefits.

Currency Spot Returns USD vs. GBP

Month 2: $\dfrac{S_2}{S_1} - 1 = \dfrac{0.60606}{0.625} - 1 = -3.03\%$

Month 3: $\dfrac{S_3}{S_2} - 1 = \dfrac{0.71429}{0.60606} - 1 = 17.86\%$

Month 4: $\dfrac{S_4}{S_3} - 1 = \dfrac{0.76923}{0.71429} - 1 = 7.69\%$

(continued)

> **(Continued)**
>
> Month 5 $\quad \dfrac{S_5}{S_4} - 1 = \dfrac{0.71429}{0.76923} - 1 = -7.14\%$
>
> Month 6 $\quad \dfrac{S_6}{S_5} - 1 = \dfrac{0.71429}{0.71429} - 1 = 0\%$

To calculate the base currency returns, we convert the USD portfolio values into GBP terms. For example, the Month 0 portfolio value in GBP terms is

$$\dfrac{\text{USD}100}{1.5} = \text{GBP}66.67$$

The returns in the base currency can be calculated as follows for each month:

[(End-of-month market value converted to the base currency at the rate in effect at the end of the month)/(Beginning-of-month market value converted to the base currency at the rate in effect at the beginning of the month)] – 1.

The base currency returns are as follows.

Month 1 base currency return: $\dfrac{100/1.6}{100/1.5} - 1 = \dfrac{62.5}{66.67} - 1 = -6.25\%$

In Month 1, there is no change in the local market value; therefore, the base currency return is entirely the result of the currency spot return. Equivalently, to obtain the base currency return, we can compound the asset's return in local currency and the change in the spot rate: $(1 + 0\%) \times (1 - 6.25\%) - 1 = -6.25\%$.

Month 2 base currency return: $\dfrac{110/1.65}{100/1.6} - 1 = \dfrac{66.67}{62.5} - 1 = 6.67\%$ or
$(1 + 10\%) \times (1 - 3.03\%) - 1 = 6.67\%$.

In Month 2, there is a positive change in the local market value and a smaller negative change in spot currency return, leading to a combined positive return overall.

Month 3 base currency return: $\dfrac{115/1.4}{110/1.65} - 1 = \dfrac{82.14}{66.67} - 1 = 23.21\%$, or
$(1 + 4.55\%) \times (1 + 17.86\%) - 1 = 23.21\%$

In Month 3, there is both a positive change in the local market value and a positive change in spot currency return, leading to a combined total return of 23.2%.

Month 4 base currency return: $\dfrac{105/1.3}{115/1.4} - 1 = \dfrac{80.77}{82.14} - 1 = -1.67\%$, or
$(1 - 8.7\%) \times (1 + 7.69\%) - 1 = -1.67\%$

In Month 4, there is a negative change in the local market value and a smaller positive change in spot currency return, leading to a small combined negative return of –1.67%.

Month 5 base currency return: $\dfrac{95/1.4}{105/1.3} - 1 = \dfrac{67.86}{80.77} - 1 = -15.99\%$, or
$(1 - 9.52\%) \times (1 - 7.14\%) - 1 = -15.99\%$

In Month 5, both the local market return and the spot currency return are negative, leading to a combined negative return of −15.99%.

Month 6 base currency return: $\frac{90/1.4}{95/1.4} - 1 = \frac{64.29}{67.86} - 1 = -5.26\%$, or

$(1 - 5.26\%) \times (1 - 0.0\%) - 1 = -5.26\%$

In Month 6, there is no change in currency exchange rates; therefore, the entire return of −5.26% is the result of the change in the local market value.

The total base currency return for the portfolio over the six-month period uses the beginning value of GBP66.67 and the ending value of GBP64.29: $(64.29/66.67) - 1 = -3.57\%$, or $(1 - 6.25\%) \times (1 + 6.67\%) \times (1 + 23.21\%) \times (1 - 1.67\%) \times (1 - 15.99\%) \times (1 - 5.26\%) - 1 = -3.57\%$.

The total local return for the portfolio in USD over the six-month period is $(90/100) - 1 = -10.00\%$, or $(1 + 0.0\%) \times (1 + 10.0\%) \times (1 + 4.55\%) \times (1 - 8.7\%) \times (1 - 9.52\%) \times (1 - 5.26\%) - 1 = -10.00\%$.

The total spot currency return for the USD over the six-month period is $(S_6/S_0) - 1 = (0.71429/0.66667) - 1 = 7.14\%$, or $(1 - 6.25\%) \times (1 - 3.03\%) \times (1 + 17.86) \times (1 + 7.69\%) \times (1 - 7.14\%) \times (1 + 0.0\%) - 1 = 7.14\%$.

The compounded local return for six months, in turn, compounds with the total spot currency return for six months to produce the total return in base currency for six months of −3.57% [= $(1 - 10.0\%) \times (1 + 7.14\%) - 1$]. These returns are summarized in Exhibit 22:

Exhibit 22 Impact of Local and Currency Returns

Period	Market Value in USD (m)	USD/GBP Spot Rate	Local Return (USD)	Currency Return	Base Return (GBP)
Start	100	1.5			
End of Month 1	100	1.6	0.00%	−6.25%	−6.25%
End of Month 2	110	1.65	10.0%	−3.03%	6.67%
End of Month 3	115	1.4	4.55%	17.86%	23.21%
End of Month 4	105	1.3	−8.70%	7.69%	−1.67%
End of Month 5	95	1.4	−9.52%	−7.14%	−15.99%
End of Month 6	90	1.4	−5.26%	0.0%	−5.26%
			−10.0%	**7.14%**	**−3.57%**

Note: The USD/GBP spot exchange rate is the amount of USD that one GBP is worth.

4.2 The Cost and Benefits of Hedging Currency Risk

Investors may decide that although they are content with the risk of holding the underlying asset, they are not content with the additional uncertainty of foreign currency exposure. Consequently, they may decide to hedge their currency risk. The purpose of currency hedging is to reduce or eliminate currency exposure. Investors can hedge their currency risk using forward currency contracts, currency futures contracts, currency options, and currency swaps.

Forward currency contracts are relatively simple derivative instruments. They are contracts between two parties for the exchange of an agreed amount of currency at a fixed exchange rate on a fixed date in the future. The two currencies are not actually exchanged until the future date or value date is reached, but the rate is agreed to on the date when the trade is initially executed, known as the trade date.[30] The exchange rate for a forward currency contract can be established using the spot exchange rate and the interest rates of the two currencies involved, as shown in Example 4.

EXAMPLE 4

Currency Forward Contracts

- Assume a current spot rate of GBP/USD 0.66667 or USD/GBP 1.5
- Assume an annual rate of interest in GBP of 4%
- Assume an annual rate of interest in USD of 2%

Calculate the one-month forward rate of USD against the GBP and the one-month forward rate of GBP against the USD.

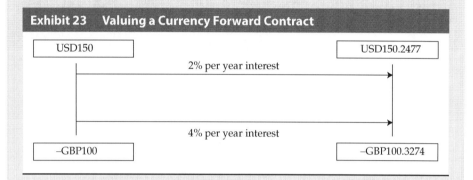

Exhibit 23 Valuing a Currency Forward Contract

At today's spot rate, GBP100 would buy GBP100 × 1.5 = USD150. Borrowing GBP100 at an annualized interest rate of 4% for one month would cost 100 × $(1.04)^{1/12}$ = 100.3274. Investing USD 150 at an annualized rate of 2% for one month would yield 150 × $(1.02)^{1/12}$ = 150.2477. The forward value of USD against the GBP in one month's time is, therefore,

USD150.2477 = GBP100.3274
USD1 = (100.3274/150.2477) = GBP0.66775

The one-month forward rate (the currency exchange rate today for conversion in one month's time) is therefore GBP/USD 0.66775.

Or expressed as the GBP against the USD, the forward rate for delivery in one month's time is therefore:

GBP100.3274 = USD150.2477
GBP1 = (150.2477/100.3274) = USD1.497574

If the forward rate did not reflect relative interest rates, then an arbitrageur could borrow in one country, invest in another, and cover the future repayment of the loan without currency risk using a forward contract. The potential for this covered interest arbitrage results in a relationship known as **covered interest rate parity**, which states that the forward rate will be a function of the spot rate and relative interest rates in the two countries. More formally,

$$F_0 = S_0 \frac{1 + r_{FC}}{1 + r_{DC}}$$

---

[30] Note that non-deliverable forward contracts are settled in cash and do not require physical settlement.

Multicurrency Performance Measurement

where

F_0 = forward exchange rate at time $t = 0$ for future currency delivery[31]
S_0 = spot exchange rate at time $t = 0$
r_{FC} = interest rate in the foreign currency at time $t = 0$
r_{DC} = interest rate in the domestic currency at time $t = 0$

Applying the formula to our example, we obtain

$$F_0 = \frac{\text{USD}1.50}{\text{GBP}} \times \frac{(1+0.02)^{1/12}}{(1+0.04)^{1/12}} = \frac{\text{USD}1.497574}{\text{GBP}}$$

The application of the formula results in the same forward rate as that previously obtained, which is no accident because the covered interest rate parity formula is based on the potential for arbitrage from borrowing in one currency, investing in another, and converting currencies using the spot and forward rates.

The return on a forward currency contract is not the same as the spot currency return (unless the interest rates of both currencies are identical). The return on the forward currency contract is known as the forward currency return (or simply the forward return or currency surprise).[32]

The currency forward return for period t is $\dfrac{S_{t+1}}{F_t} - 1$

where

S_{t+1} = spot exchange rate at time $t + 1$
F_t = forward exchange rate at time t for conversion at time $t + 1$

The forward return using the forward rate in Example 4 and assuming a spot rate of GBP/USD of 0.625 at the end of the month, USD versus GBP is $(S_1/F_0) - 1 = (0.625/0.66775) - 1 = -6.40\%$. In this example, the forward return is worse than the spot currency return of $(S_1/S_0) - 1 = (0.625/0.66667) - 1 = -6.25\%$ because interest rates in GBP are higher than interest rates in USD.

In addition to the forward and spot returns, we also define the forward premium. The forward currency premium for period t is $(F_t/S_t) - 1$. The forward currency premium reflects the interest differential between the two currencies involved and can be either a discount or a premium.

The forward discount for the GBP against the USD at $t = 0$ is $(F_0/S_0) - 1 = (1.497574/1.5) - 1 = -0.16\%$.

Notionally to gain exposure to US dollars and hedge British pounds currency risk, cash must be borrowed in British pounds at a higher rate of interest than can then be reinvested in US dollars. This is called the **cost of hedging**. *Ex ante*, this cost may be accepted by risk-averse investors to reduce their currency exposure.

In contrast, for an investor who wishes to hedge USD assets into GBP, the forward return of GBP versus USD is $(S_1/F_0) - 1 = (1.6/1.497574) - 1 = 6.84\%$.[33] In this case, the forward return is better than the currency spot return of GBP versus USD of $(S_1/S_0) - 1 = (1.6/1.5) - 1 = 6.67\%$ because notionally, US dollars are being borrowed at lower rates of interest and are subsequently reinvested in British pounds at a higher rate of interest. In this case, there is a **benefit of hedging**. The investor benefits from reduced currency risk and a forward premium.

---

31 The forward rate and spot rate used in the formula are quoted as indirect quotes, where the domestic currency is in the denominator and the foreign currency is in the numerator. If direct quotes (domestic currency in the numerator) are used, the interest rate ratio is simply inverted to be consistent with the currency quotes.
32 The term "currency surprise" is used because this is the element of the return that is unknown.
33 Note that $(1 + 6.84\%)$ is the reciprocal of $(1 - 6.40\%)$.

The forward premium for the USD against the GBP is $(F_0/S_0) - 1 = (0.66775/0.66667) - 1 = 0.16\%$.

4.3 Portfolio Returns Using a Currency Overlay Strategy

The local returns in Example 3 are unobtainable for a GBP-based investor; the only returns that are obtainable are either the local returns converted to GBP or returns hedged back into GBP. Unless interest rates in both currencies are the same, there will be a cost or benefit associated with hedging.

To hedge the USD exposure in Example 3, we can use forward currency contracts—in effect, shorting the US dollar and gaining exposure to the British pound. We can trade these forward contracts using a **currency overlay** strategy. The strategy can be executed by hiring a currency overlay manager to trade the forward contracts in a separate currency overlay portfolio, or the forwards can be traded within the current portfolio. Example 5 demonstrates the hedged returns from the use of a currency overlay portfolio.[34]

Gains and losses from the overlay portfolio arise from currency movements and are used to provide a hedge of the currency risk of the underlying portfolio. In Example 5, the overlay manager will be using a forward contract hedge, where the manager must deliver USD to the counterparty and in exchange receives GBP. The short USD position in the hedge reduces the risk of the underlying long USD position from the USD portfolio. At the beginning of each month, the overlay manager will contract with a counterparty, such as a bank, to deliver USD in one month in the amount of the beginning-of-month USD portfolio value.

At the end of each month, the manager will buy USD in the spot market to satisfy the required delivery of USD in the forward contract. The forward contract requires delivery of USD at the end of the month. At that time, the overlay manager will sell GBP to buy USD in the spot market. The manager then delivers the USD to the counterparty in the forward contract. If USD can be bought cheaply in the spot market, then a profit is recorded for the overlay strategy. "Cheaply" is defined as paying less GBP for USD in the spot than the rate in the forward contract. If, however, the manager must pay more GBP to buy the USD in the spot than the rate in the forward contract, a loss is recorded for the overlay strategy. The overlay return is then added to the underlying portfolio's return in the base currency (here, GBP) to arrive at the **hedged return**.

EXAMPLE 5

Forward Rate Calculations

Using the same spot rates in Example 3 and assuming no change in interest rates, the USD/GBP one-month forward rates are calculated for each month as demonstrated in Example 4 and are shown in Exhibit 24.

---

[34] One usually thinks of an overlay portfolio as a currency hedging strategy managed separately from the underlying portfolio by another firm or in a different portfolio. Regardless of whether the currency position is hedged within or outside the portfolio, however, the process of calculating the resulting returns is the same.

Multicurrency Performance Measurement

Exhibit 24 Comparison of Spot and One-Month Forward Currency Exchange Rates

Period	Market Value in USD (m)	USD/GBP Spot Rate	USD/GBP One-Month Forward Rate
Start	100	1.5	1.497574
End of Month 1	100	1.6	1.597413
End of Month 2	110	1.65	1.647332
End of Month 3	115	1.4	1.397736
End of Month 4	105	1.3	1.297898
End of Month 5	95	1.4	1.397736
End of Month 6	90	1.4	1.397736

Note: The USD/GBP spot exchange rate is the amount of USD that one GBP is worth.

To hedge the USD exposure of the portfolio in Month 1 of Example 3 requires the sale of USD100m into GBP at a forward rate of 1.497574, with the forward hedge entered at $t = 0$.

At the end of Month 1, the profit in GBP on this contract is

$(100/1.497574) - (100/1.6) = 66.7747 - 62.5 = $ GBP4.2747m

The logic of the calculation is as follows. At the USD/GBP forward rate of 1.497574, the investor would have had to pay GBP66.7747m. But at a USD/GBP currency spot rate of 1.6, the British investor needs to pay only GBP62.5m to deliver USD100m and satisfy the forward contract. Thus, there is a profit of GBP4.2747m because it is cheaper to buy the USD in the spot market, relative to the forward contract rate.

Using the starting GBP value of the portfolio of $(100/1.5) = $ GBP66.67m, this results in a base currency return of $(4.2747/66.67) = 6.41\%$.

It is not required for this example, but note that the profit in USD is $4.2747 \times 1.6 = 6.8395$, which in turn is equivalent to a return in USD of $(6.8395/100) = 6.84\%$—the same as the currency forward return, $(S_1/F_0) - 1 = (1.6/1.497574) - 1 = 6.84\%$.

In Example 3, the US portfolio's return in the GBP base currency using spot currency rates at Month 0 and Month 1 was

$$\frac{100/1.6}{100/1.5} - 1 = \frac{62.5}{66.67} - 1 = -6.25\%$$

Adding the currency overlay return in Month 1 to the base currency return of the portfolio in Month 1 provides the hedged return:

$-6.25\% + 6.41\% = 0.16\%$

The base currency return of the underlying assets is −6.25% but the currency hedge contributes 6.41%, so the total hedged return is 0.16%. Because in local USD terms there was no change in asset market value, the 0.16% represents the benefit of hedging.

Recall that the asset's value was constant from Month 0 to Month 1, at USD100m. Therefore, the hedge required to eliminate currency risk in Month 2 is the sale of USD100m into GBP at a forward rate of 1.597413 at the beginning of Month 2.

At the end of Month 2, the profit on this contract is

$(100/1.597413) - (100/1.65) = 62.6012 - 60.6061 = $ GBP1.99516m

Using the GBP value of the start of the month of 100/1.6 = GBP62.5m, this profit results in a return of

(1.99516/62.50) = 3.19%

The base return of the portfolio from Example 3 is 6.67% and 3.19% is the contribution from the hedge, giving a total hedged return in Month 2 of 6.67% + 3.19% = 9.86%.

The hedge required in Month 3 is the sale of USD110m into GBP at a forward rate of 1.647332. At the end of Month 3, the profit in GBP on this contract is

(110/1.647332) − (110/1.4) = 66.7746 − 78.5714 = −GBP11.7968m

In this case, notice that there is a loss from the hedge because, at the spot rate, the investor must sell GBP78.5714m (110/1.4) to satisfy the forward contract. Under the forward contract, however, the investor would have had to make delivery of only GBP66.7746m (110/1.647332).

Using the GBP value at the start of the month of (110/1.65) = GBP66.67m results in a return of

(−11.7968/66.67) = −17.70%

The base return of the portfolio from Example 3 is 23.21%. The hedged return in Month 3 is therefore 23.21% − 17.70% = 5.51%.

The hedge required in Month 4 is the sale of USD115m into GBP at a forward rate of 1.397736. At the end of Month 4, the profit in GBP on this contract is

(115/1.397736) − (115/1.3) = 82.2759 − 88.4615 = −GBP6.18565m

Using the GBP value of the start of the month of (115/1.4) = GBP82.14m, this results in a return of

(−6.18565/82.14) = −7.53%

The hedged return in Month 4 is therefore −1.67% − 7.53% = −9.20%.

The hedge required in Month 5 is the sale of USD105m into GBP at a forward rate of 1.297898. At the end of Month 5, the profit in GBP on this contract is

(105/1.297898) − (105/1.4) = 80.9000 − 75.0000 = GBP5.90004m

Using the GBP value of the start of the month of 105/1.3 = GBP80.77m, this results in a return of

(5.90004/80.77) = 7.30%

The hedged return in Month 5 is therefore −15.99% + 7.30% = −8.69%.

The hedge required in Month 6 is the sale of USD95m into GBP at a forward rate of 1.397736. At the end of Month 6, the profit in GBP on this contract is

(95/1.397736) − (95/1.4) = 67.9671 − 67.8571 = GBP0.10991m

Using the GBP value of the start of the month of 95/1.4 = GBP67.86m, this results in a return of

(0.10991/67.86) = 0.16%

The hedged return in Month 6 is therefore −5.26% + 0.16% = −5.10%.

Because there is no change in the spot exchange rate, there is no contribution from any unhedged residual currency exposure and the difference between the local market return of −5.26% and the −5.10% hedged return is the familiar benefit of hedging of 0.16%. Because in this example interest rates are assumed to have not changed, the same benefit of hedging is present in all six months.

The total hedged return over the six-month period is (1 + 0.16%) × (1 + 9.86%) × (1 + 5.51%) × (1 − 9.20%) × (1 − 8.69%) × (1 − 5.10%) − 1 = −8.65%. These returns are summarized in Exhibit 25.

Exhibit 25   Hedged Portfolio Returns in Base Currency (GBP)

Period	USD/GBP Spot Rate	USD/GBP 1-Month Forward Rate	Base Return	Currency Overlay Return	Hedged Return
Start	1.5	1.497574			
End of Month 1	1.6	1.597413	−6.25%	6.41%	0.16%
End of Month 2	1.65	1.647332	6.67%	3.19%	9.86%
End of Month 3	1.4	1.397736	23.21%	−17.70%	5.51%
End of Month 4	1.3	1.297898	−1.67%	−7.53%	−9.20%
End of Month 5	1.4	1.397736	−15.99%	7.30%	−8.69%
End of Month 6	1.4	1.397736	−5.26%	0.16%	−5.10%
			−3.57%	**na**	**−8.65%**

na = not applicable.

4.4 Hedged vs. Perfectly Hedged Returns

The Month 1 hedged return in Example 5 is slightly positive even though the local return is 0.0% and the initial currency exposure is fully hedged. This outcome is caused by the benefit of implicitly borrowing USD at low rates of interest and investing in GBP with higher rates of interest. This benefit (or forward premium) can be derived directly from the interest rates of 4% per year in GBP and 2% per year in USD, as follows:

$$\frac{(1.04)^{1/12}}{(1.02)^{1/12}} - 1 = 0.16\%$$

Note that in the hedged return calculation in Example 5, only the initial currency position is hedged. During the period under analysis, the currency exposure will change with the underlying market movements of the assets. In Month 1, there is no local market movement and therefore no impact, but in Month 2, the underlying local market return is 10% leading to net unhedged USD exposure in the period. From the perspective of a currency overlay manager, unless informed differently,[35] he will be unaware of these residual currency exposures caused by underlying local market movements. If these residual positions are perfectly hedged, then the only difference between the local return and the hedged return will be due to the interest rate differential (as reflected in the forward premium/discount between the respective currencies).

The theoretically perfectly hedged returns are, therefore,

Month 1: (1 + 0.0%) × (1 + 0.16%) − 1 = 0.16%

Month 2: (1 + 10.0%) × (1 + 0.16%) − 1 = 10.18%

Month 3: (1 + 4.55%) × (1 + 0.16%) − 1 = 4.71%

Month 4: (1 − 8.70%) × (1 + 0.16%) − 1 = −8.55%

Month 5: (1 − 9.52%) × (1 + 0.16%) − 1 = −9.38%

Month 6: (1 − 5.26%) × (1 + 0.16%) − 1 = −5.11%

---

35 In practice, this means being informed more frequently. Currency overlay managers are best advised to manage against the currency exposures they are aware of, rather than assumptions of currency exposures based on the impact of market movements.

The hedged returns resulting from currency overlay and the perfectly hedged returns are summarized in Exhibit 26.

Exhibit 26   Hedged vs. Perfectly Hedged Returns

Period	Hedged Return	Perfectly Hedged Return
End of Month 1	0.16%	0.16%
End of Month 2	9.86%	10.18%
End of Month 3	5.51%	4.71%
End of Month 4	−9.20%	−8.55%
End of Month 5	−8.69%	−9.38%
End of Month 6	−5.10%	−5.11%
	−8.65%	**−9.12%**

The hedged return of 9.86% in Month 2 is less than the perfectly hedged return of 10.18% because there is residual unhedged USD exposure caused by the underlying portfolio's positive return combined with the USD falling against GBP during the month. Specifically, the portfolio rose in value from USD100m to USD110m during this month, and the USD fell in value from 1.60 to 1.65 per GBP (it took more dollars to buy a pound because the dollar was weaker). In the hedged case, USD10m of exposure is unhedged and converted at a spot rate that is detrimental to the investor, relative to using the forward rate.

The hedged return in Month 3 of 5.51% is greater than the perfectly hedged return of 4.71% because the portfolio rose in value from $110m to $115m and the dollar rose in value from 1.65 to 1.4 per GBP (it took fewer dollars to buy a pound because the dollar was stronger). As a result, the unhedged exposure of USD5m was converted at a higher exchange rate relative to the initial forward rate.

The hedged return of −9.20% in Month 4 is less than the perfectly hedged return of −8.55% because the fall in the portfolio's USD value leads to an overhedged position that combined with the USD rising in value against the GBP from 1.40 to 1.30 per GBP. Specifically, the portfolio fell in value from USD115m to USD105m. In the hedged case, the investor would have to purchase USD10m more dollars at an appreciated value to satisfy the forward contract at the end of Month 4.

The hedged return of −8.69% in Month 5 is greater than the perfectly hedged return of −9.38% because a further fall in portfolio value again leads to an overhedged position, but in this month, the USD is now falling in value against the GBP. A hedged return should, of course, be close to the local return of the portfolio (in this case, −10%). The difference between the perfectly hedged return and the local return is the "benefit of hedging" from the interest rate differential between USD and GBP.

4.5 Additional Measurement Considerations Regarding Currency Overlay Portfolios

The six months of currency overlay returns in Exhibit 25 are not linked in the same manner as the portfolio base currency returns or the combined hedged returns. Currency overlay is not an asset as such; you cannot invest in a currency overlay portfolio and receive returns that geometrically link through time. In effect, currency overlay is a source of excess return with no or little capital allocation leading to zero or near-zero market value denominators (or negative market values in the event of net negative unrealized losses). In practice, a small amount of capital may be allocated to currency overlay portfolios to fund realized losses, but the majority of assets are normally held in a separate underlay portfolio. The overlay manager is informed periodically of the value of assets to be overlaid. Clearly, if the underlaid and overlay portfolios are separate, the profits (or losses) of each are not reinvested in the other.[36]

It is thus inappropriate to calculate the return of the currency overlay portfolio using traditional methods. The investment decisions of the currency overlay portfolio are taken in context of the underlaid assets, not the small amount of allocated capital. In fact, in the event of unrealized losses on long-term forward currency contracts, the total allocated capital may in effect be negative. The investor and currency overlay manager must determine the value of the underlaid assets at various points in time, and it is this value that is used in the denominator of the return calculation. It is a minor point as to whether the value of the allocated capital (positive or negative) should be added to the value of underlaid assets. It probably should be, but it should also be recognized that the value of underlaid assets is constantly changing and never accurately available to the currency overlay manager. Therefore, for simplicity, using the notional value in the overlay return calculation is acceptable.

There are two types of overlay strategies:

- Those designed to reduce (or hedge) existing currency exposures
- Those designed to generate excess return from active currency management

In any event, to calculate the added value of the currency overlay manager, a benchmark currency overlay return must be calculated. This benchmark return is calculated in a manner similar to that for the currency overlay return. The benchmark return is calculated by notionally creating forward currency contracts (including the costs and benefits of hedging) that achieve the benchmark currency exposures required. In this sense, the currency overlay returns in Exhibit 25 represent the benchmark returns of a 100% hedged overlay. There is no doubt that in an active strategy, the portfolio manager will seek to add value by varying the size of the forward contracts in the actual overlay portfolio.

4.6 Total Portfolio Returns

In Exhibit 22, we examined portfolio returns when currency risk was unhedged. In Exhibit 25, we evaluated the returns when a currency overlay strategy is added to an unhedged position. Now, we examine total portfolio returns over time. Here, the gains and losses from hedging from one period to the next are cumulated in the return calculation, as shown in Example 6. The cumulative gains or losses from hedging are added to the underlaid portfolio to provide the combined, total portfolio returns over time.

EXAMPLE 6

Multi-Period Currency Returns

Calculate the combined base currency return of the underlaid portfolio in Exhibit 22 and the currency overlay portfolio in Exhibit 25.

$$\text{Combined portfolio return in Month 1: } \frac{62.50 + 4.27}{66.67} - 1 = 0.16\%$$

---

[36] "Underlaid" assets in this context are the assets that are "overlaid" by the overlay portfolio.

The combined portfolio value at the end of Month 1 results from the market value of the underlaid portfolio at the current spot rate, 100/1.6 = 62.50, together with the gains in the overlay portfolio of GBP4.27m already calculated in Example 5.[37]

For Month 2, the combined portfolio return is $\dfrac{66.67 + 2.00 + 4.27}{66.77} - 1 = 9.23\%$

The combined portfolio value at the end of Month 2 results from the market value of the underlaid portfolio at the current spot rate, 110/1.65 = 66.67, together with the Month 2 overlay hedging gain of GBP2.0m (the rounded value of GBP1.99516) and the cumulative gains in the overlay portfolio of GBP4.27m—again, previously calculated in Example 5. We divide through using a base value determined from the previous-period portfolio value of 66.77.

Likewise, for the Month 3 through Month 6 return, we add the value of the current portfolio at current spot rates to the cumulative gains from the previous period and the hedging gain from the current month.

Combined portfolio return in Month 3:
$$\frac{82.14 - 11.80 + 6.27}{72.94} - 1 = 5.04\%$$
Combined portfolio return in Month 4:
$$\frac{80.77 - 6.19 - 5.53}{76.62} - 1 = -9.87\%$$
Combined portfolio return in Month 5:
$$\frac{67.86 + 5.90 - 11.71}{69.06} - 1 = -10.15\%$$
Combined portfolio return in Month 6:
$$\frac{64.29 + 0.11 - 5.81}{62.04} - 1 = -5.58\%$$

The cumulative combined return over six months is (1 + 0.16%) × (1 + 9.23%) × (1 + 5.04%) × (1 − 9.87%) × (1 − 10.15%) × (1 − 5.58%) − 1 = −12.13%. Alternatively, the cumulative combined return over six months is

$$\frac{64.29 + 0.11 - 5.81}{66.67} - 1 = -12.13\%$$

These returns are summarized in Exhibit 27.

Exhibit 27 Combined Base Currency Return of Underlaid Portfolio and Currency Overlay

Period	Market Value in GBP (m)	Currency Overlay Gains and Losses	Cumulative Overlay Gains and Losses	Combined Portfolio Value	Combined Portfolio Return
Start	66.67			66.67	
End of Month 1	62.50	4.27	4.27	66.77	0.16%
End of Month 2	66.67	2.00	6.27	72.94	9.23%
End of Month 3	82.14	−11.80	−5.53	76.62	5.04%
End of Month 4	80.77	−6.19	−11.71	69.06	−9.87%

---

[37] The final calculations in this section round the intermediate values from Example 5 and, as such, may differ slightly from those using the presented values.

Exhibit 27 (Continued)

Period	Market Value in GBP (m)	Currency Overlay Gains and Losses	Cumulative Overlay Gains and Losses	Combined Portfolio Value	Combined Portfolio Return
End of Month 5	67.86	5.90	−5.81	62.04	−10.15%
End of Month 6	64.29	0.11	−5.70	58.58	−5.58%
					−12.13%

The combined portfolio returns in Exhibit 27 and the overlay hedged returns in Exhibit 26 are summarized for comparison in Exhibit 28.

Exhibit 28 Hedged vs. Combined Portfolio Returns

Period	Hedged Return	Combined Portfolio Return
Start		
End of Month 1	0.16%	0.16%
End of Month 2	9.86%	9.23%
End of Month 3	5.51%	5.04%
End of Month 4	−9.20%	−9.87%
End of Month 5	−8.69%	−10.15%
End of Month 6	−5.10%	−5.58%
	−8.65%	**−12.13%**

The returns in Month 1 are identical because the same asset base is used. But the combined portfolio return in Month 2 of 9.23% is dampened because of the inclusion of the gains in the currency overlay portfolio in the asset base in Month 1. The combined portfolio return in Month 3 of 5.04% is also slightly dampened because of the smaller cumulative gain, but in Month 4, the negative return of −9.87% is leveraged because of the inclusion of cumulative currency overlay losses. The negative returns in both Month 5 and Month 6 are leveraged (to a greater extent in Month 5) by continued cumulative currency overlay losses. The difference between the −8.64% six-month hedged return and the −12.13% combined return is simply the difference in the asset base size. The combined portfolio includes the cumulative losses (in later months) of the currency overlay, which in effect leverages to a greater extent the losses in the later months. The unrealized profits and losses on the currency forwards serve as a notional cash balance that either dampens (positive balance) or leverages (negative balance) the physical portfolio, depending on whether it is showing a profit or loss.

4.7 Hedged and Partially Hedged Benchmarks

Index providers of international benchmarks generally supply three types of return for each constituent country within the index:

- Local

- Base
- 100% hedged back to base currency[38]

Typical monthly index data for a USD-based index are shown in Exhibit 29. The weights are customized.

Exhibit 29   Index Returns in Local Currency, in Base Currency, and Hedged to Base Currency

Country	Initial Weight	Local Returns	Base Returns (USD)	Hedged Returns
Australia	10%	0.81%	6.28%	0.33%
Japan	15%	2.68%	6.23%	2.85%
Switzerland	5%	0.47%	3.89%	0.55%
UK	30%	−2.03%	−1.63%	−2.19%
US	40%	−0.74%	−0.74%	−0.74%
Total	100%	−0.40%	0.97%	−0.46%

The total return for each version of the index is simply the sum product of the initial weight and the appropriate return. The hedged return represents the 100% hedged return with no currency risk[39] and is close to the local return, but in this example, it includes a small cost of hedging. The base return is unhedged (or 0% hedged). Investors might wish to have some currency exposure and choose not to be fully hedged and apply a hedge ratio between 0% and 100%, in which case the benchmark would be described as **partially hedged**.

Using the data in Exhibit 29, a 60% partially hedged index is calculated by taking 40% of the unhedged index return and 60% of the hedged index return as follows:

40% × 0.97% + 60% × −0.46% = 0.11%

Although this index is described as 60% partially hedged into USD, the actual currency exposure to USD is greater than 60% because there is USD exposure in the unhedged part of the index, which arises from the index's 40% exposure to US securities. The actual USD exposure can be derived from the following equation:

$h \times 100\% + (1 - h) \times w_\$$

where

h = the partial hedge rate (or hedge ratio)
$w_\$$ = the weight of USD exposure in the unhedged index

Hence, the total exposure to USD in a 60% partially hedged index is 60% × 100% + 40% × 40% = 76%.

To achieve 60% USD exposure, the hedge ratio needs to be 33.33%. If 33.33% of the index value is hedged into USD, then 1 − 0.3333 = 66.67% is left unhedged. In this case, the USD currency exposure is 33.33% × 100% + 66.67% × 40% = 60%. The hedged part of the index provides 33.33% exposure to the USD, and the unhedged part provides 26.67% direct exposure to the USD.

---

38 Base currency returns are typically available for the major currencies.
39 Ignoring the fact that a perfectly hedged index is difficult to achieve. Index vendors' methodologies will vary with resulting differing amounts of residual currency risk.

Multicurrency Performance Measurement

EXAMPLE 7

Return Calculations

1. The start value of a portfolio in Australian dollars (AUD) is AUD135m, and the end value is AUD160m. The currency spot exchange rate is 2.0 AUD/GBP at the start of the period and 1.8 AUD/GBP at the end of the period. The base currency return of the portfolio in British pounds (GBP) is *closest* to:
   - A   6.67%.
   - B   29.63%.
   - C   31.69%.

2. Which of the following types of returns are **not** achievable for investors in a different reporting currency?
   - A   Base
   - B   Local
   - C   Hedged

3. The return on a forward currency contract is known as the:
   - A   local return.
   - B   currency surprise.
   - C   spot currency return.

4. Assume a current spot rate of 0.8 EUR/USD

   Assume an annual rate of interest in USD of 1%

   Assume an annual rate of interest in EUR of 3%

   The one-month forward rate of USD against the EUR is *closest* to:
   - A   0.7987.
   - B   0.8013.
   - C   0.8158.

5. Which of the following statements is incorrect? Currency overlay:
   - A   portfolio values can be positive or negative.
   - B   portfolio returns must be linked geometrically.
   - C   portfolios can be used to generate excess return from active currency management.

6. In an international benchmark, hedged index returns are:
   - A   lower than local returns.
   - B   higher than local returns.
   - C   can be either lower or higher than local returns.

Solution to 1:

C is correct: $\dfrac{160/1.8}{135/2.0} - 1 = \dfrac{88.89}{67.5} - 1 = 31.69\%$

Solution to 2:

B is correct. Local returns (returns denominated in the local currency) are unachievable for investors with a different reporting or base currency. Hedged and base currency returns are achievable.

Solution to 3:

B is correct. The return on a forward contract is known as the forward return or currency surprise because it is the element of the return that is unknown.

Solution to 4:

B is correct. At the current spot rate, EUR100 would buy EUR100 × 1.25 = USD125. Borrowing EUR100 at an annualized interest rate of 3% for one month would cost $100 \times (1.03)^{1/12} = 100.2466$.

Investing USD125 at an annualized rate of 1% for one month would yield $125 \times (1.01)^{1/12} = 125.1037$.

The forward value of USD against the EUR in one month's time is, therefore, USD125.1037 = EUR100.2466;

$$USD1 = \frac{100.2466}{125.1037} = 0.8013$$

Solution to 5:

The answer is B. Currency overlay is not an asset; you cannot invest in a currency overlay portfolio and receive returns that are geometrically linked over time.

Solution to 6:

C is correct. The difference between the local and hedged index returns represents the interest rate differential between the two currencies concerned, which could result in either a "cost" or "benefit" of hedging.

5. CONCLUSION AND SUMMARY

Performance analysts must be able to extend generic performance measurement techniques to provide insights into the unique performance drivers of particular asset classes and strategies. In this reading, we covered the key concepts required to analyze performance for long–short, derivative, and multi-currency portfolios. The reading makes several key points:

- Short selling is an investment tool that allows a manager to profit from the ability to identify securities likely to fall in value in the future.
- Long–short investing is a generic term for strategies allowed to go short. There are several basic variations of investment strategies that use short selling. Short extension strategies, such as 130/30 funds, use short positions but are net 100% exposed to the underlying market.
- Market-neutral strategies have offsetting long and short positions, making them (at least theoretically) unexposed to the fortunes of the underlying market and 100% exposed to the security selection skills of the manager.
- A manager has achieved a gain for a short position when a security held short decreases in value. Other components of the return specific to short positions include a portion of the interest earned on the collateral held for margin calls.
- There are many types of financial derivatives, such as forwards, futures, options, and swaps. To determine derivatives' effects on portfolio return, the analyst must be able to identify the return-impacting components of these contracts and adjust portfolio exposures.
- Key to understanding the impact of a derivative on portfolio exposures are the concepts of economic (notional) exposure and notional return. These concepts are derived from the specific techniques used to determine the value of

Conclusion and Summary

a derivative contract. Valuation of derivatives is driven by economic insights, such as the fact that a futures or forward contract should be worth the same amount that it would cost to borrow money and then invest it in the underlying. Notional return and portfolio exposure to the underlying originate from an understanding of these concepts.

- A single futures contract can be broken into two pieces: a long notional exposure to the underlying and a short "financing instrument" representing the (theoretical) amount borrowed to finance the position. By isolating the components and calculating a return on each, the analyst can calculate returns reflecting the intended use of the derivative in the portfolio.

- Portfolios holding assets denominated in foreign currencies require the calculation of multicurrency returns. The analyst will be interested in isolating the drivers of return: local market performance, the impact of exchange rate shifts, the impact of interest rate differentials, and the impact of any hedges intended to mute the impact of changing exchange rates. An unhedged portfolio is exposed to exchange rate moves, whereas a partially or fully hedged portfolio is somewhat protected, but at a potential cost. The analyst uses base and local market values to derive these returns.

- Hedges are not always present in the portfolio being hedged. Sometimes two different organizations are responsible for investing in the underlying market and providing a currency overlay to that portfolio. Currency overlay portfolios experience gains and losses like the underlying portfolio, but they need to be compared with the underlying portfolio or notional portfolio value in order to determine the return impact.

A PRIMER ON DERIVATIVES

by Adam Schwartz, PhD, CFA

Lexington, VA, USA

1 Introduction to Derivatives

This appendix introduces derivatives. In investments, a derivative is defined as follows:

> A **derivative**[40] is a financial instrument that derives its performance from the performance of an underlying asset.

A derivative is a financial instrument that is created as a contract between two parties: the buyer and the seller. Derivatives trade in markets around the world, including organized exchanges where highly standardized and regulated versions exist, and over-the-counter markets where customized and more lightly regulated versions trade. The basic characteristics of derivatives that influence pricing are not particularly related to where the derivatives trade, but are critically dependent on the types of derivatives.

The two basic types of derivatives are options and forwards. Options give the owner the right, but not the obligation, to buy or sell something. A forward contract (or forward) is a commitment or promise to buy or sell an asset at some specified future date. Options and forwards may be based on a variety of underlying financial assets such as shares of stocks, stock indexes, and currencies. In these cases, the value of the underlying financial asset serves as a reference for the value of the derivative. An option on Google stock derives its value from the current market price of a Google share. Underlying assets are not limited to financial assets. Prices of physical assets such as gold, gasoline, or corn also have traded derivatives. A gold futures contract derives its value from the current market price of gold. As the price of gold or Google changes, so does the value of their respective derivative contracts. A bond price can serve as the underlying asset, as can an interest rate on a bond. The underlying asset can be even more complex: A futures option is a derivative (an option) based on another derivative (a futures price) as the underlying asset.

Understanding derivative assets is made easier by knowing that options are rights and forwards are obligations. With an option, the buyer has the right to buy or sell an asset. With a forward contract, the buyer makes a commitment to buy or sell the underlying asset. More exotic financial derivatives, such as swaps and futures options, can usually be decomposed into option-based and forward-based components. We begin with an introduction to the basic option types: calls and puts. Next, we will cover the three types of forward commitments: forwards, futures, and swaps.

1.1 Fundamentals of Options

Options give the owner the right, but not the obligation, to buy or sell something. This right is a financial contract whose value is contingent on the price of the underlying asset. Options are sometimes called contingent claims for this reason. The definition of an option is as follows:

---

[40] Many of the definitions and all the equations in this Primer have been taken verbatim from Don Chance, "Derivative Markets and Instruments," in the CFA Program curriculum. These borrowings are not individually footnoted but are acknowledged here.

An **option** is a derivative contract in which one party, the buyer, pays a sum of money to the other party, the seller or writer, and receives the right to either buy or sell an underlying asset at a fixed price either on a specific expiration date or at any time prior to the expiration date.

The right to buy an asset at a fixed price is a *call* option; the right to sell an asset at a fixed price is a *put* option.

1.1.1 *Characteristics of Call Options*

A call option gives the holder (or buyer) the right to buy the underlying asset at the *strike price* (or *exercise price*), denoted X, on or before the expiration date. Depending on the market price of the underlying asset, the buyer may wish to use (exercise) the call or discard it. The right to buy at X may be worth exercising if X is lower than the market price. Prior to expiration, the buyer may also sell the unexercised option to another person.

Options on stocks and stock indexes are sold on organized exchanges all over the world. Underlying assets, strike prices, and expirations are selected by the exchange to meet the needs of their clients. The options offered by an exchange have standardized features to facilitate listing. For example, an equity call option contract will allow the owner to buy a standard quantity (such as 100 shares of the underlying stock) on or before a certain expiration date (such as the third Friday of the expiration month) at a fixed strike price. The standardized contract features are set according to the rules of the exchange. Financial institutions, such as big banks, may trade options over-the-counter (OTC). These private transactions can have quantity, expiration, and other features customized to meet the exact needs of the two parties.

Options are traded in everyday life as well. Any time a right is bought and sold, an option transaction has taken place. The purchase of a football ticket from a friend is an example of a call option transaction. The buyer pays a price (or premium) for the right to go to the game. The ticket holder may go (exercise their right), discard the ticket, or even resell it. As with most options positions, a sports ticket may be terminated one of three ways: used (exercised), sold, or discarded (if worthless at expiration). It is important to point out that options, like sports tickets, can be sold or exercised. When an option is sold, the new buyer obtains the rights. Once an option (or a sports ticket) is used, it cannot be resold.

Options have two main exercise types: American and European. These names have nothing to do with the location of trading; American and European options trade everywhere. The names refer to when the right to buy or sell can be exercised. A European option can be exercised only on the expiration date. An American option can be exercised on the expiration date, or at any time before. Therefore, an American option is the equal of the European option plus the option to exercise early. If a European call matures on 15 July, the right to buy the asset can only be exercised on that date. An American call with the same maturity date would allow the holder to buy the underlying asset on *or before* 15 July. At expiration, an American option is worth the same as the equivalent European option. Before expiration, the option to exercise early may be valuable (priced) for some calls on dividend paying stocks and for some puts. It is safe to say that an American option is always worth at least as much as (and in some cases, slightly more then) the equivalent European option. We will use the following notation for explaining the basic concepts of options.

We start by assuming that today is time 0, and the option expires at time T. The underlying is an asset currently priced at S_0, and at time T, its price is S_T. Of course, we do not know S_T until we get to the expiration. The option has an exercise or strike price of X. The symbols we use are as follows:

For calls,

c_0 = value (price) of European call today
c_T = value (price) of European call at expiration

For puts,

p_0 = value (price) of European put today
p_T = value (price) of European put at expiration

1.1.2 Call Payoffs and Profit Functions

The owner of a call option pays a price (or premium) to acquire the option, but they receive something in return. The option owner has the right to buy the underlying asset for the strike price, X. This right is described mathematically by the payoff function. The payoff of a call option at expiration depends upon the value of the underlying asset at expiration, S_T. Once we know the final value of the underlying asset on expiration, the call payoff is given as:

Payoff to the call buyer = c_T = $Max(0, S_T - X)$

This is read as "the maximum of 0 and $S_T - X$ (the difference between the underlying asset price at expiration and the strike price). The Max function picks the largest value from a list of values. Max(0,5) = 5 because 5 is larger than 0. If the stock price increases above X, the call option will have a positive payoff value. If S_T is below the strike price at expiration, the $S_T - X$ will be negative and to exercise the call would lose money: In this case, the call holder will not exercise but will let the call expire unexercised. In that case, the Max function will choose zero because the option turned out to be worthless. The zero in the Max function highlights the appeal of the call in having the right but not the obligation to exercise.

Consider a call option on a share of a stock with an X = $30 per share. If the underlying stock price (S_T) is 35 at expiration, the call value will be Max($0,$35 − $30) = $5. The option will enable its owner to buy the stock for a price $5 less than the market price. If the underlying stock price (S_T) is $2 at expiration, the call payoff will be Max($0,$2 − $30) = Max($0, −$28) = $0. The option holder will have the right to buy the stock at $30, but will not use it. Because the stock is available at a price of $2 in the market, the owner would buy at $2 instead of $30. Thus, the call owner has the right to take only the winning side of strike price.

Initially, the option is sold in exchange for a price, or premium. The option seller (or writer) knows a call is potentially valuable and will price it accordingly. The call buyer gets the benefit of the payoff function and pays the premium, so that:

Profit to the call buyer = Π = $Max(0, S_T - X) - c_0$

In words, the profit on a call is the payoff minus the cost. Exhibit A1 shows the payoff and profit to the buyer of a call option. The call payoff is zero below the strike price, and $S_T - X$ above the strike price. The profit graph simply subtracts the option cost from the payoff value. At terminal stock values at or below the strike price, the premium (c_0) is lost. The loss for an option buyer is limited to the premium. The gain for a call buyer can be unlimited, because S_T can go infinitely high (in theory).

Exhibit A1 Payoff and Profit from Buying a Call Option

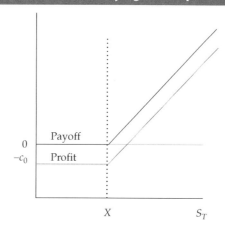

The call buyer is said to be long the call. The term "long" is associated with buying or owning an asset. The call seller has the opposite "short" position. When the price of an asset increases, the long (short) position in a call increases (decreases) in value. It is important to remember that the call option gives the buyer a right, and confers on the seller an obligation to satisfy that right if the call buyer exercises the option. When a seller writes the option, the seller must be prepared to offer the stock at the strike price if "called" to do so. The payoff to the call seller is:

Payoff to the call seller = $C_T = -\text{Max}(0, S_T - X)$

The payoff to the call seller can be negative. If they must offer shares of stock at X which cost more than X in the market, the seller will experience a loss (a negative payoff). If the seller offers the right to buy shares at an exercise price of X = $20 and the current price is $32, the payoff to the seller will be $-\text{Max}(\$0, \$32 - \$20) = -\$12$. The seller would need to buy shares at $32 to make good the obligation to sell shares at $20. If the seller offers the right to buy shares at $20 and the underlying price is $9 when the call expires, the payoff is $-\text{Max}(0, \$9 - \$20) = \$0$. In this case the buyer will not exercise the option to buy at $20 and the seller will not have to buy the shares in the market.

The profit to the call seller is given as:

Profit to the call seller = $\Pi = -\text{Max}(0, S_T - X) + c_0$

Exhibit A2 shows the payoff and profit on a short call position. When the asset price remains below the strike price, the payoff from the call is $0. In the case of $S_T < X$, the call writer keeps the entire premium, c_0. However, if the price of a share increases above X, a payoff must be made and losses may result. Losses on short call positions may be high, because there is no upper bound on the price of a share of the underlying. Upon exercise, the call writer must purchase the underlying at the market price, S_T, if they don't already own shares (are not "covered").

Exhibit A2 Payoff and Profit from Selling a Call Option

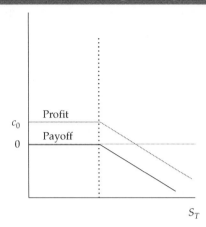

1.1.3 Characteristics of Put Options

A put option gives the holder (or buyer) the right to sell the underlying asset at the strike price on or before the expiration date. The right to sell an asset can become valuable if the asset price drops. Similar to a call, a put option transaction also involves a buyer and a writer. The buyer has the right to "put" the underlying asset to the writer, who must stand ready to buy the underlying asset at the strike price. Puts can be used to provide a kind of insurance that the value of the position in an asset will not fall below a given level. An auto insurance policy can be thought of as a type of put option. The car owner purchases the policy from the option writer (the insurance company). In exchange for the price (or policy premium), the owner has the right to recover up to the policy value if the value of their car drops for a covered reason. Financial put options are used to provide similar insurance for portfolio managers. If the underlying asset decreases below the strike price, the put holder is entitled to sell the asset for the strike price. Put options also provide income for sellers willing to assume the risk of an asset price decline.

1.1.4 Put Payoffs and Profit Functions

The payoff to the buyer of a put option at expiration is given as:

Payoff to the put buyer = p_T = Max$(0, X - S_T)$

A put is a right to sell an asset at X, and will only pay if the price of the asset S_T falls below X at expiration. If S_T = \$26 and X = \$20, the payoff from the put will be Max(\$0, \$20 − \$26) = Max(0, −\$6) = \$0. In that case, the put is worthless, because the asset can be sold for a better price in the market. If the exercise price is greater than the market price, the put will have a positive payoff value. If S_T = \$12 and X = \$20, the payoff from the put will be Max(\$0, \$20 − \$12) = Max(0, \$8) = \$8. The put holder has the right to sell an asset currently worth \$12 for a price of \$20, an \$8 improvement. The payoff to the put seller is the opposite of the buyer's payoff, so:

Payoff to the put seller = p_T = −Max$(0, X - S_T)$

The payoff to the seller is at best zero and may be negative. The put seller must buy the asset at the strike price even if the asset is worthless at expiration (S_T = 0). The maximum payment a put seller must make is −Max$(0, X - 0)$ = −X. The put seller will not have to make a payoff as long as the asset price at expiration is above X.

The put buyer receives the payoff function and pays the premium p_0. The profit to the put buyer is equal to the payoff received at expiration minus the cost of the put. So we have:

Profit to the put buyer = $\Pi = \text{Max}(0, X - S_T) - p_0$

If a put is purchased for $3 and the payoff at expiration is only $2, the position will result in a $1 loss to the buyer. Exhibit A3 shows the payoff and profit to the buyer of a put option. The zero point on the vertical axis represents a breakeven point on the put position; this happens when $\Pi = 0$ at $S_T = X - p_0$. For example, a put option costing $3 and struck at a $20 exercise price will break even at a terminal stock price of $17. The payoff from an option at breakeven is exactly equal to the option cost. The put payoff is zero above the strike price and $X - S_T$ below the strike price. As with the long call profit graph, the long put profit simply subtracts the option cost from the payoff value. At terminal stock values above the strike price, the premium (p_0) is lost. The loss for an option buyer is limited to the premium (p_0). The *maximum* profit for a put buyer occurs if the terminal stock price (S_T) goes to 0. In that case, the profit is $\Pi = \text{Max}(0, X - 0) - p_0 = X - p_0$.

Exhibit A3   Payoff and Profit from Buying a Put Option

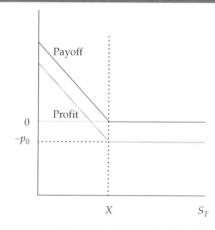

The profit to the put seller is given as:

Profit to the put seller = $\Pi = -\text{Max}(0, X - S_T) + p_0$

Exhibit A4 shows the payoff and profit to the put seller. When the asset price rises above the strike price, the payoff from the put is $0. As shown in Exhibit A4, if $S_T > X$, the put writer keeps the entire premium, p_0, as a profit. However, if the price of the asset falls below X, the writer must be prepared to purchase the asset for the strike price. The breakeven point for the put seller is the same as for the put buyer. The profit is zero when the put payoff is enough to cover the premium, or $\Pi = 0$ at $S_T = X - p_0$.

Exhibit A4 Payoff and Profit from Selling a Put Option

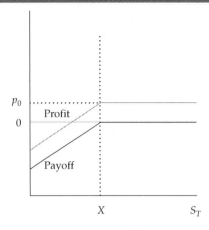

1.1.5 Intrinsic and Time Value of Options

The value of an option has two components: intrinsic value and time value. The intrinsic value of an option is the value that would result from its immediate exercise.[41] If the current stock price is $47, a three-month call option with a strike price of $50 will not be exercised early. The stock could be bought in the market for a price of $47, so exercise at $50 does not make sense. This does not mean that the call is worthless. It may sell for a price of $1 or more, because of the possibility of a payoff over the next three months. The part of an option value that accounts for the probability of a future payoff is called the time value, so that

Option value = Intrinsic value + Time value

In the case of an American call, the intrinsic value (IV) is simply the immediate exercise value given as:

$IV_{call} = Max(0, S_0 - X)$

Notice that the subscript for S now refers to the price of an underlying share today (at time 0) rather than at expiration (time T). For example, an American call option with a strike price of X = £40 a share is trading at a price of £12. The underlying stock is currently trading at S_0 = £50 a share. The intrinsic value of this call is Max(£0, £50 − £40) = £10. The remaining £2 of the option value is the time value. Call buyers may pay more than the option intrinsic value, because the asset price may further increase in the time remaining before expiration. Of course, the time value decreases as the option approaches exercise. The concept is the same for American puts except the intrinsic value is:

$IV_{put} = Max(0, X - S_0)$

The right to sell at a price of X can have significant exercise value if the current price S_0 falls low enough. Consider an American put option with a current price of $305. The option is struck at an exercise price of X = $600, and the stock is currently trading at S_0 = $300/share. The intrinsic value of the put is Max($0, $600 − $300) = $300. The remaining $5 of the option's price is explained by the time value. As with the call, the time value of an American put will decrease as the option approaches expiration. At expiration, the option value of a put or call is just equal to the intrinsic value, and the time value at expiration decays to zero.

---

[41] Because only American options can be exercised before expiration, the concept of intrinsic value is strictly correct only for American options.

1.1.6 Moneyness of Options

A concept related to intrinsic and time value is the idea of an option's moneyness. The moneyness of an option refers to its relationship to the exercise price. The terms in-the-money, at-the-money, and out-of-the-money are part of the everyday vocabulary of option traders. If a put or call has a positive intrinsic value, it is said to be in-the-money. An in-the-money call option has $S_0 > X$. It represents the right to buy a stock at a price cheaper than the current market price. So, if the current market price (S_0) of the underlying stock is $25, the X = $20 call is in-the-money. This in-the-money call allows the holder the valuable right to buy a $25 stock for only $20. For puts, in-the-money describes a right to sell at a price higher than the current market price, or $X > S_0$. For example, if the price of the underlying stock S_0 is currently $33, a put struck at X = $40 is in-the-money. In this case, the put holder would be able to sell their shares for $7 more than the current market price. Some options have so much exercise value they are given the description "deep-in-the-money" options. The right to sell shares at $100 when the current market price is only $10 is a deep-in-the-money put.

An at-the-money option has a strike price which is approximately equal to the current market price. For either puts or calls, the option is at-the-money if $S_0 \approx X$. The range is loosely used in practice, so an option that is slightly in- or out-of-the-money may be also described as at-the-money. A put or call option struck at X = $50 is at-the-money if the current market price S_0 is within a percent or two of $50.

Out-of-the-money describes an option that has no current intrinsic (exercise) value. Such an option may still be valuable, but the price is entirely explained by the time value. Exhibit A5 shows the moneyness of selected option contracts on Microsoft stock. The price of Microsoft stock in this example is $32.50. The X = $30 and $28 strikes are in-the-money for calls and out-of-the-money for puts. For example, at X = $28 the call has intrinsic value of Max($0, $32.50 − $28) = $4.50. This call sells for more than that, the remainder explained by a time value of $0.22. The X = $28 put is out-of-the-money, so the put price of $0.08 is explained entirely by time value. The X = $32 strike is the closest to the current price of Microsoft stock, so it may be termed at-the-money for both puts and calls. Strikes of $34 and $36 are out-of-the-money for calls and in-the-money for puts.

Exhibit A5 Moneyness of Selected Microsoft Options (S_0 = $32.50)

Strike Price X	American Call Price	Call Moneyness	American Put Price	Put Moneyness
$28	$4.72	In-the-money with IV = $4.50 and TV = $0.22	$0.08	Out-of-the-money, IV = $0, TV = $0.08
$30	$2.71	In-the-money	$0.22	Out-of-the-money
$32	$1.21	At-the-money	$0.75	At-the-money
$34	$0.42	Out-of-the-money IV = $0 and TV = $0.42	$1.96	In-the-money, IV = $1.50 and TV = $0.46
$36	$0.13	Out-of-the-money IV = $0 and TV = $0.13	$3.66	In-the-money, IV = $3.50 and TV = $0.16

Notes: Options have 42 days to expiration; the price of Microsoft stock was adjusted to reflect dividends. Values from Yahoo! Finance, August 2013.

1.2 Fundamentals of Forward Contracts

The basic types of derivatives are options and forwards. Whereas an option represents a *right* to buy or sell an asset, a forward contract is a *commitment* or *promise* to buy or sell an asset. In a forward agreement, both parties commit to the terms of a transaction to be undertaken at a later date in the spot (or cash) market. A spot market transaction involves paying today for immediate delivery of an asset. There are three types of forward commitments: forward contracts, futures contracts, and swap contracts (to be discussed later). These contracts may be referred to more simply as forwards, futures, and swaps. A formal definition of a forward contract is:

> A **forward contract** is an over-the-counter derivative contract in which two parties agree that one party, the buyer, will purchase an underlying asset from the other party, the seller, at a later date at a fixed price they agree upon when the contract is signed.

So a forward contract is nothing more than a buyer and seller promising to trade an asset at a later date for a price set today. A forward transaction can be tailored to meet the needs of the buyer and seller. A high degree of customization is a characteristic of private or over-the-counter transactions. A futures contract is the same idea as a forward, but futures contracts trade on an organized exchange. The futures trader gives up some flexibility in contract design for the ability to trade assets quickly and at a low cost in the futures market.

> A **futures contract** is a standardized derivative contract created and traded on a futures exchange in which two parties agree that one party, the buyer, will purchase an underlying asset from the other party, the seller, at a later date at a price agreed upon by the two parties when the contract is initiated and in which there is a daily settling of gains and losses and a credit guarantee by the futures exchange through its clearinghouse.

1.2.1 Characteristics of Futures and Forward Contracts

Forward contracts are present in our daily lives as well as in financial markets. A delivery order for a $10 pizza with pineapple on top is a forward contract. The price of $10, the delivery timeframe, and the customized asset are all characteristics of a forward contract. When the seller (or short) delivers the pizza, the buyer (or long party) inspects the pizza, pays the agreed upon price, and takes delivery. Unlike an option, no premium is required at the outset of a forward contract. Both parties are under obligation, so they only need to agree to the terms of the future sale. Sometimes a deposit (or margin) is required to guarantee that both parties will be able to meet their obligation. In the case of the pizza, both parties trust that the transaction will take place without a problem. Actual forward contracts are for transactions that can take place from a few days to several years after the initial agreement is made. The forward transaction will specify among other things a delivery time frame and a price. The forward price may be different from the spot price of an asset. The *spot price* (or cash price) is the price of an asset for immediate delivery. For example, a jeweler may be able to buy gold today at a cash price of $1200 per ounce, while a forward-based agreement to buy the same gold in six months may be priced at $1210 per ounce.

As we have seen, the definition of an exchange-traded futures contract is very similar to that of an OTC forward contract. Traders in the futures and forward markets establish prices for transactions to be undertaken at a later date. The price and terms of a forward contract are negotiated between buyer and seller. Although futures traders agree on a contract price, most of the other terms in a futures transaction are specified by the exchange. Some of the important differences between forwards and futures are highlighted in Exhibit A6.

A Primer on Derivatives

Exhibit A6 Differences between Forward and Futures Contracts

	Forward Contract	Futures Contract
Delivery date	Customized by counterparties	Delivery calendar is standardized by the Exchange
Contract size	Customized by counterparties	Quantity is standardized by the Exchange
Asset specifications	Customized by counterparties	Acceptable assets for delivery are standardized by the exchange
Underlying assets	Customized by counterparties	Selected for trading by the exchange
Regulation	Less	More
Daily settlement	No	Yes
Margin required	No	Yes
Default risk	Yes, a counterparty may default	Probably not. The transaction may be guaranteed a clearinghouse

A major difference between futures and forwards involves the daily settlement process. To lower the risk of default, futures contracts are settled daily in a process called marking-to-market. To trade on the futures exchange, a deposit or margin account must be maintained by both buyer and seller. This deposit guarantees that the funds will be available for both parties to honor their initial commitment to trade. Margin requirements are set by the exchange to reflect the volatility of the underlying asset and the contract size. At the close of daily trading, a settlement price for each futures contract is determined by the exchange. The margin accounts of all traders are adjusted to reflect the day's changes in contract price. For example, if a trader agrees to buy gold at $1200 an ounce in March and the futures price increases to $1220, the long position profits $20. This $20 gain is added to the margin account of the long party at the end of the day. A new contract to buy March gold at $1220 an ounce effectively takes the place of the old contract and the process starts over the next day. Those who agreed to sell March gold at $1200 would have their margin account decreased to reflect a $20 loss, and would now have an agreement to sell March gold at $1220. When losses to the futures position reduce the margin accounts funds below a certain level, the exchange will issue a "margin call." The minimum level of funds required for the margin account is set by the exchange for each contract and is called the "maintenance margin." Upon receiving a margin call, the trader must add funds to their account or risk having the position closed by the exchange. Daily settlement helps to reduce risk in a futures transaction. As the price changes daily, the losing party may have to put up additional funds to stay in the trade. Forward contracts do not have a daily settlement feature, so losses can accumulate over time resulting in a greater risk that the losing party may default.

Almost any underlying asset may be traded in the forward market, but the futures exchange selects assets to meet client needs. For example, US Treasury bond and Eurodollar futures contracts allow traders to manage long- and short-term interest rate risk. Stock index futures help portfolio managers control equity risk. Energy contracts (such as oil and gasoline futures), agricultural contracts (such as corn, oats, and soybeans futures), and metals contracts (such as gold and silver futures) can provide a cost effective way to manage commodity price risk.

1.2.2 Payoff for Forward Contracts

A forward is an agreement to buy or sell an asset at a later date at a price set at the start of the contract. The risk of buying an asset later is similar to the risk of buying today. A buyer in the spot or forward market stands to gain if the asset price increases, and lose if the asset price drops. The forward price $F_0(T)$ is the price set at the beginning of the contract. If the spot price of the underlying asset at expiration is given as S_T, the value (or payoff) of the long forward contract at expiration, $V_T(T)$, is given by:

$$V_T(T) = S_T - F_0(T)$$

In words:

> The value of a forward contract at expiration is the spot price of the underlying minus the forward price agreed to in the contract.

Here is a simple example. On 1 April, a refiner agrees to take delivery of a quantity of oil on 10 July at a price of $95 [$F_0(T) = \$95$] a barrel. Assume the spot price of oil on 10 July (time T) is $110 a barrel ($S_T = \$110$). In this case, the refiner has locked in a lower price than currently available in the market, so the forward contract has a positive value. The value of the long forward contract at expiration is

$$V_T(T) = S_T - F_0(T) = \$110 - \$95 = \$15$$

If the terminal asset price had decreased to $S_T = \$82$ a barrel, the refiner would have taken a $13 loss on the agreement to buy at $F_0(T) = \$95$. Whereas the long forward contract establishes a purchase price for an asset, a short forward contract establishes a sale price [$F_0(T)$]. So the profit on a short forward contract is given as:

$$V_T(T) = F_0(T) - S_T$$

So if a gold mine agrees to sell gold at a price of $1300 an ounce in three months and the price (at T) falls to $1250 an ounce, the value of their forward agreement is:

$$V_T(T) = F_0(T) - S_T = \$1300 - \$1250 = \$50$$

The forward contract allowed the gold mine to lock in a better sale price than that currently offered in the market. If the terminal price of gold had increased to $1340, the value of the agreement would have been given as $V_T(T) = \$1300 - \$1340 = -\$40$. The mine would have agreed to sell at a price lower than the current market price.

A graph of the payoff for a forward contract is shown in Exhibit A7. When the terminal price of an asset increases above the initial forward price, the long party benefits and the short party loses. When prices decrease, short forward contracts increase in value and long forward positions decrease in value.

Exhibit A7 Terminal Value of Forward Contracts

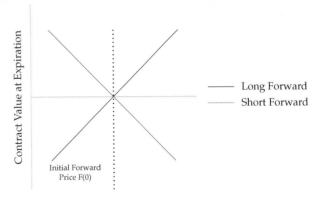

> **EXAMPLE A1**
>
> **Forward Contracts**
>
> 1. An investor enters a long forward contract to buy one ounce of gold in April at a price of $1200/ounce. If the price of gold in April is $1320/ounce, the value of the long forward contract is *closest* to:
>   A −$120.
>   B +$120.
>   C +$1320.
> 2. The gold mine interested in locking in a sale price for their output without default risk would *most likely* consider a:
>   A long forward contract.
>   B long futures contract.
>   C short futures contract.
>
> **Solution to 1:**
>
> B is correct: $V_T = S_T - F_0(T) = \$1320 - \$1200 = \$120$. A is incorrect because locking in a purchase price of $1200 will result in a gain if prices increase above $1200. C is incorrect because $1320 is the value of the asset at maturity, not the value of the long forward contract.
>
> **Solution to 2:**
>
> C is correct. A gold mine would want to sell futures (go short) to guarantee the sale price of their output. The futures clearinghouse will guarantee that the gold mine will get the agreed upon price at expiration with no default risk. A is incorrect; a long forward contract is an agreement to buy from a counterparty. The counterparty in a forward contract may also have default risk. B is incorrect; a gold mine wishing to sell would not seek to lock in a purchase price for gold by going long in the futures market.

1.3 Swaps

A third type of forward commitment is swaps. Whereas a forward contract is used to manage a single-period risk, a swap is designed with multi-period risk in mind. A swap is equivalent to a series of forward contracts. The most common type of swap is a "plain vanilla" interest rate swap. This swap contract is an over-the-counter derivative contract in which two parties agree to exchange a series of cash flows, whereby one party pays a variable interest rate and the other party pays a fixed interest rate.

For example, concerned that bond prices may increase, an investor may use a forward contract to lock in a favorable price for a planned bond purchase. That is an example of a single-period risk. The same investor may have an existing loan which requires quarterly payments for five years tied to a floating interest rate, such as Libor. If the Libor rate increases, the investor will be required to make higher interest rate payments. This position is an example of an on-going or multi-period risk. The investor enters into a swap exchanging a fixed interest rate, such as 5%, for a floating interest rate, such as Libor. The swap contract defines the series of cash flows to be exchanged as well as the base (or notional) amount on which the exchange is based. For example, a fixed rate of 5% will be exchanged for 90-day Libor quarterly for the next five years based on a notional principal equal to the loan amount. If the Libor rate increases above the fixed rate, the investor will receive a payment from the swap to offset higher interest costs for the existing floating-rate loan. If the Libor rate drops below the fixed rate, the investor will benefit from lower costs on the existing loan, but will also have to make a swap payment. The end result for the investor is that the floating payment received from the swap will offset the floating loan payment, and the ongoing cost of the loan will be converted to a fixed rate. This is an example of a fixed-for-floating, or plain vanilla interest-rate swap.

Interest rate swaps help investors concerned with multi-period interest rate risk, but other swaps exist to manage other types of reoccurring risk. A currency swap may help handle ongoing exchange rate risk. Equity swaps may be set up to exchange a fixed rate of interest for a rate tied to the returns of an equity index, such as the quarterly returns on the S&P 500. A commodity swap could provide a customized framework for a commodity producer or consumer to manage a price exposure to commodities such as gold, oil or corn. These swap agreements are simply a portfolio of forward agreements used to manage multi-period risk.

2 Option Pricing Models

The value of an option at expiration is given by the payoff function. The value before expiration is more difficult to calculate. If the price of a share of stock is $61, the expiration value of a call option struck at $50 is Max($0,$61 − $50) = $11. In words, the right to buy a stock at $50 is worth $11 if the stock price is currently $61. Remember that before the options expires, the option price reflects both time value and intrinsic (or exercise) value. Pricing models such as Black–Scholes–Merton attempt to value options before they expire.

2.1 The Black–Scholes–Merton Model

Intuition tells us that the value of an option should converge to its exercise value as the maturity date approaches. The exercise value of a call or put is easy to compute and requires only two inputs: the terminal stock price, S_T, and the strike price, X. The Black–Scholes–Merton option pricing model provides insight into the process of valuing an option before maturity. To find the value of an option before expiration, the Black–Scholes–Merton model requires five inputs. Four of the inputs are intuitive and easy to look up in the financial media: the current price of the underlying asset, S_0; the strike price of the option, X; the time remaining to expiration of the option, (T); and the risk-free interest rate, R_F. The last input, the volatility (σ_i) of the underlying asset, must be computed. To find the volatility input, the standard deviation of the underlying's returns may be determined from historical return data, or the input may be implied from the market price of traded options.[42] So, we can say the Black–Scholes–Merton price of a European call option is a function of five inputs,[43] or $c_0 = f(S_0, X, R_F, T, \sigma_i)$. The Black–Scholes–Merton model can also price a European put (p_0) as a function of the same five input variables. Once the five input variables are plugged into the Black–Scholes–Merton formula, the formula outputs an option price. Exhibit A8 summarizes how an increase in any of the five inputs affects European call and put prices.

---

[42] The implied volatility is calculated by finding the volatility input that gives a Black–Scholes–Merton option price equal to the current market price of a traded option. Computing the implied volatility is usually done with the help of a computer.

[43] The Black–Scholes–Merton model prices a European put or call option on a stock with no dividends. If the underlying stock pays a dividend before the option expires, an adjustment may be made to the model. Models are also available to price American options.

Exhibit A8	Change in Black–Scholes–Merton Model Price to *Increases* in Select Input Variables	
Variable	European Call	European Put
S_0	Increases	Decreases
X	Decreases	Increases
T	Usually increases	Usually increases
R_F	Increases	Decreases
σ_i	Increases	Increases

Intuition for some of the option price changes is easy. When the price of the underlying asset increases, the right to buy the asset (at a fixed price) becomes more valuable. An increase in the price of the underlying asset will decrease the value of a put. If the market price increases above X, a put option struck at X is worthless at expiration. As the strike price X increases, the value of a call should decrease. A call is the right to buy at X, and buyers like low prices. The value of a put will increase as the strike price increases. After all, sellers like high prices, and a put is the right to sell at X.

Both put and call prices increase as volatility increases. As volatility increases, the chance of a big payoff increases along with it. Because options are rights to take this payoff, an increase in volatility will increase the chance of a profitable price change. Consider a one-year call option struck at $100 on a low volatility stock currently priced at $100. The stock price can increase in price by $5 or decrease by $5 with equal probability over the next year. If the price of the stock increases to $105, the call will be worth Max($0,$105 − $100) or $5. If the price drops to $95, the call will expire worthless because Max($0,$95 − $100) = $0. The value of a 50% chance to get $5 and a 50% chance to get $0 is worth $2.50 in one year and the present value of that amount now. Now consider a call with the same strike price and expiration on a high volatility stock currently priced at $100. This stock can increase in price by $150 or decrease to $50 with equal probability. If the price of the stock increases to $150, the call will be worth Max($0,$150 − $100) or $50. If the price drops to $50, the call will expire worthless because Max($0,$50 − $100) = $0. The value of a 50% chance to get $50 and a 50% chance to get nothing is worth $25 in one year, or ten times as much as the low volatility example. The same argument can be used for puts. Volatility increases the chance of a highly profitable in-the-money finish.

Changes in interest rates have a small but intuitive impact on option prices. Calls represent a right to buy at a strike price X paid later. An increase in interest rates lowers the present value of the strike price to be paid later. Buyers like low prices, even in present value terms, so increases in the risk-free rate will increase (all other things equal) the price of a call option. Because a put is the right to sell for a strike price X to be received later, an increase in rates will lower the present value of the money to be received later. Sellers do not like to receive low prices. So an increase in interest rates will make the price of a put option decrease.

Increases in time to expiration, all else equal, will increase the *American* option prices. In most cases, the Black–Scholes–Merton price of European puts and calls is usually higher for longer maturity options, all else equal. There are some special cases in which increases in time to expiration would not benefit the holders of some European puts or calls. For example, after a dividend is paid, the price of the stock may drop to reflect the amount of the dividend. Extending the expiration of a European call to the day after a large dividend may not increase its value, because the ex-dividend price decrease could decrease call value. Deep-in-the-money European puts may not benefit from added time to expiration. If the stock price is currently $0.01, a European put option struck at $50 and expiring in one day will soon be worth $49.99. The European put value would not be improved if the expiration date is increased to one year. The present value of whatever amount is received in one year is likely to be lower than $49.99 received tomorrow, and the stock price cannot drop too far below $0.01.

The effect of changing stock price and maturity can also be seen in a graph of the Black–Scholes–Merton option price. Exhibit A9A shows the Black–Scholes–Merton price as a function of stock price and time for an exercise price of X = 100 call option on a non-dividend-paying stock. The Black–Scholes–Merton price for an exercise price of X = 100 put option on the same stock as a function of current stock price and time is shown in Exhibit A9B.

- For both options, the Black–Scholes–Merton option price converges to the expiration payoff value as the option approaches maturity.
- As the stock price increases, the call price increases and the put price decreases.
- As time increases, so does the call and put price.

Exhibit A9A Decay of Black–Scholes–Merton Call Price to Intrinsic Value (X = 100, R = 1%, σ = 0.2)

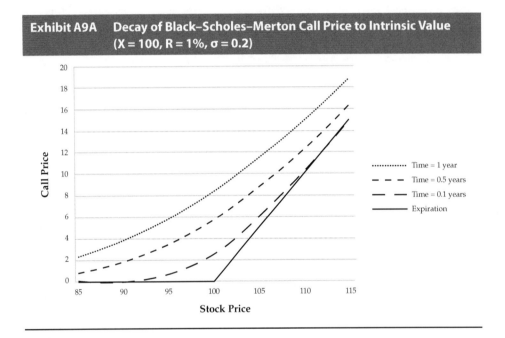

Exhibit A9B Decay of Black–Scholes–Merton Put Price to Intrinsic Value (X = 100, R = 1%, σ = 0.2)

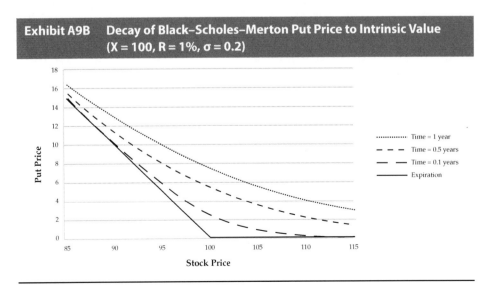

> **EXAMPLE A2**
>
> **Black–Scholes–Merton Variables**
>
> 1. A call option has a strike price of $100 and sells for a price of $5 and has three months to expire. If the price of the asset decreases to $99, all else equal the call value will *most likely*:
>   A decrease.
>   B not change.
>   C increase.
> 2. All else equal, an increase in volatility will cause call and put prices to:
>   A decrease.
>   B not change.
>   C increase.
>
> **Solution to 1:**
>
> A is correct. If none of the other variables change, a decrease in the underlying asset price will cause the call price to decrease. B is incorrect because call prices are sensitive to changes in the price of the underlying asset. C is incorrect because the call price should only increase if the asset price increases, all else equal.
>
> **Solution to 2:**
>
> C is correct. If none of the other variables change, an increase in the underlying asset price volatility will cause both put and call prices to increase. A is incorrect because the call and put price will decrease only if volatility decreases, all else equal. B is incorrect because both call and put prices are sensitive to changes in the volatility of the underlying asset.

2.2 Sensitivities of the Black–Scholes–Merton Model: The "Greeks"

Traders know that changes in the underlying asset will impact the value of derivatives based on those assets. For example, a change in the price or volatility of Microsoft stock will affect the price of Microsoft calls and puts. The sensitivities of the Black–Scholes–Merton option price to changes in the input variables are collectively known as the "Greeks." The term comes from the Greek letters [delta (Δ), gamma (Γ), theta (θ), rho (ρ), and vega (ν)[44]] traditionally used to represent option price sensitivity. Values for each of the Greeks can be calculated for individual option positions and aggregated for portfolios of underlying assets and multiple derivative positions.

Each Greek letter has its own formula which approximates the change in the Black–Scholes–Merton option price for small changes in the input variables.[45] Although the computation of the Black–Scholes–Merton formula will not be presented here, intuition for how changes in the input variables affect option prices can be developed.

---

[44] Unlike the other Greeks, vega is not a letter in the Greek alphabet. Vega represents the sensitivity of the option price to changes in the underlying's volatility.
[45] The Greeks are calculated by taking partial derivatives. These approximations work best for small changes to only one underlying variable, with the other Black–Scholes–Merton variables held constant.

2.2.1 *Option Price Sensitivity to Changes Underlying Asset Price: Delta*

Changes in the price of the underlying asset drive changes in option prices, and this relationship is captured by delta (Δ). Any of the Greeks can be estimated by noting the change in the price of an option given the change in the input variable. In particular, delta can be estimated as a ratio of the change in the option price to the change in the underlying asset price. For a stock option the formula for delta is:

$$\Delta_c = \frac{\text{Change in call price}}{\text{Change in stock price}} \quad \text{(A1)}$$

Consider a few simple examples. A call option with an exercise price of X = $100 and one year before expiration is currently priced at $8.916 and has a delta of +0.579 as shown in Exhibit A10. The underlying stock is currently priced at $100, so the call option is at-the-money. If the price of the underlying stock increases by $0.10 to $100.10, then Δ should approximate the call price change as follows:

$$\Delta_c = \frac{\text{Change in call price}}{+\$0.10} = +0.579$$

A delta of +0.579 implies that a $0.10 increase (decrease) in the price of the underlying stock will result in an increase (decrease) of approximately $0.0579 in the call price. It is important to note that delta changes with the moneyness of the option, so the approximation only works for small changes. For example, if the price of the underlying stock is $120, the X = 100 call option is now deep-in-the-money with a delta of 0.867 and valued at $23.742, as shown in Exhibit A10.

Exhibit A10 Black–Scholes–Merton Call Values, Deltas, and Moneyness (X = 100, R = 2%, σ = 0.20, T = 1 year)

Stock Price	Call Price	Call Delta	Moneyness
120	$23.742	0.867	Deep in the money
110	$15.609	0.751	In the money
100	$8.916	0.579	At the money
90	$4.148	0.372	Out of the money
80	$1.427	0.180	Deep out of the money

A call option becomes more sensitive to stock price increases as it moves in-the-money. The higher delta of 0.867 reflects the fact that the option is now more sensitive to changes in the underlying stock price. If the price of the underlying stock increases by $0.10 to $120.10, the price of the call option should increase by $0.0867 to approximately $23.8287 [23.742 + (0.1 × 0.867)].

Another way to think of delta is:

> Delta is the change in the value of an option, given a $1 change in the price of the underlying asset.

For a call, a $1 change in the underlying price will never cause the option price to change more than $1, all else equal. When the call option is deep-in-the-money, delta approaches its limiting value of 1. Assume that the price of the underlying stock in the previous examples jumps to $150. The same exercise price of X = 100 call option is deep-in-the-money and priced at $52.12. If the price of the underlying stock increases by another $1 to $151.00, the price of the option increases by $0.99 to $53.11. Delta has now almost reached its limit of 1 as confirmed by our calculation:

$$\Delta_c = \frac{+\$0.99}{+\$1} = +0.99$$

Once calculated, we can use delta to estimate changes in the option price as the price of the underlying asset changes. For example, a trader owns a call option priced at $4.00 on a stock currently trading for $50/share. If $\Delta_c = +0.75$ and the price of the underlying stock increases by $0.16, what is the updated call price?

Updated call price ≈ Old call price + Change in call price

where:

Change in call price = Δ_c × Change in stock price

Updated call price ≈ $4 + (0.75 × $0.16) = $4.12

The delta for a put option can be easily computed in the same manner as the call option. However, the value of a put option will decrease as the asset price increases, so put option deltas are less than or equal to 0.

$$\Delta_p = \frac{\text{Change in put price}}{\text{Change in stock price}} \quad \text{(A2)}$$

Consider a put option struck at an exercise price of X = $100 with prices and deltas shown in Exhibit A11.

Exhibit A11 Black–Scholes–Merton Put Values, Deltas, and Moneyness (X = 100, R = 2%, σ = 0.20, T = 1 year)

	Put Price	Put Delta	Moneyness
120	$1.762	−0.133	Deep out of the money
110	$3.629	−0.249	Out of the money
100	$6.936	−0.421	At the money
90	$12.167	−0.628	In the money
80	$19.447	−0.820	Deep in the money

Assume the underlying stock is currently priced at $100, the put option is at-the-money and currently sells for $6.936. If the price of the underlying stock drops by $0.10 to $99.90, the put option price increase should be approximated by the formula:

$$\Delta_p = \frac{\text{Change in put price}}{-\$0.10} = -0.421$$

So the $0.10 decrease in the stock price will cause the put price to increase by about $0.421. Solving for the updated put price:

Updated put price ≈ Old put price + Δ_P × Change in stock price

≈ 6.936 + (−0.421) × (−0.10) = $6.9781

We can also observe changes in stock and option prices and imply the put delta. For example, if a $0.25 increase in the stock price causes the put price to drop by $0.20, this implies a put delta of:

$$\Delta_p = \frac{-\$0.20}{+\$0.25} = -0.8$$

At a delta of −0.8, a $1 increase (decrease) in the price of the underlying stock will cause the put option price to decrease (increase) by approximately $0.80. Similar to the call, a put option also becomes more sensitive to stock price increases as it moves in-the-money. Eventually the put option delta will approach a limit of −1, as it moves more in the money.

EXAMPLE A3

Calculation of Option Delta

1. An at-the-money call option with an exercise price of X = 30 and 0.1 years to expiration is priced at $0.50. If the stock price increases from $30 to $30.25 and the call price increases to $0.64, which of the following is *closest* to the call's delta?

   A $\Delta = -0.16$

   B $\Delta = +0.14$

   C $\Delta = +0.56$

2. The current price of Synotec Corporation stock is $51 and a put option with an exercise price of X = 50 is currently priced at $2.00. If the delta of the Synotec put option is −0.4 and the stock price increases to $51.20, which of the following is the *best* approximation for the updated put value?

   A p = $1.60

   B p = $1.92

   C p = $2.08

3. A deep-in-the-money call option and a deep-in-the-money put option will:

   A both have a delta ≈ 0.0.

   B both have a delta ≈ +1.0.

   C have different delta values.

Solution to 1:

C is correct. The ratio of the call price change to the stock price change is $0.14/$0.25 = 0.56. A is incorrect because a call delta can't be negative. B is the call price change, not the delta.

Solution to 2:

B is correct, because $2 + (−0.4) × (+0.20) = $1.92. A is incorrect because it simply subtracts the put delta from the original put price. C is incorrect because an increase in the stock price will cause the put price to fall.

Solution to 3:

C is correct. A deep-in-the-money put option will have a delta which approaches −1.0, whereas a deep-in-the-money call will have a delta which approaches +1.0. A is incorrect because a zero delta would be characteristic of a deep-out-of-the-money put or call. B is incorrect because a put delta should always be negative.

Properties of delta can be illustrated by referring to Exhibits A12A and A12B:

- Delta changes with moneyness for both calls and puts. This fact is expected from the cases presented in Exhibit A10 (for calls) and 11 (for puts).

A Primer on Derivatives

- Delta changes most rapidly for puts and calls when the current stock price is close to the strike price of the option (at-the-money).
- The delta of a call Δ_c is non-negative and bounded by $0 \leq \Delta_c \leq 1$. Consider the graph of delta in Exhibit A12A. When the call option is deep-out-of-the-money (for example, S = $50), delta is close to 0. A $1 increase in the stock price (from $50 to $51) will not appreciably change the call value. When the option is deep-in-the-money, delta approaches 1. A delta of 1 means that as the stock moves up $1, so does the option price. As the stock moves from $149 to $150, the value of the option increases by about $1.
- The delta of a put Δ_p is non-positive and bounded by $-1 \leq \Delta_p \leq 0$. A graph of Δ_p is shown in Exhibit A12B. As the put gets deeper in-the-money, the delta of the put approaches -1. A deep-out-of-the-money put will not be very sensitive to movements in the stock and will have a delta that approaches zero.

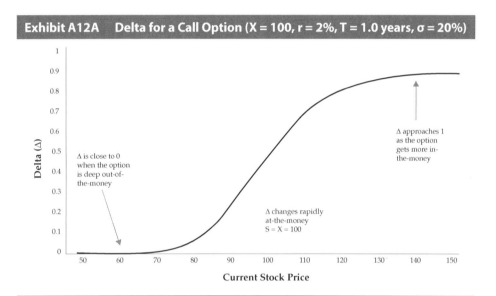

Exhibit A12A   Delta for a Call Option (X = 100, r = 2%, T = 1.0 years, σ = 20%)

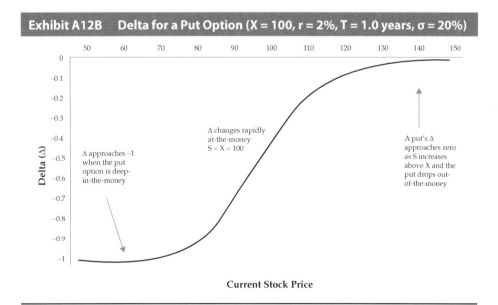

Exhibit A12B   Delta for a Put Option (X = 100, r = 2%, T = 1.0 years, σ = 20%)

2.2.2 Delta Sensitivity to Changes in the Underlying Asset Price: Gamma

The change in delta shown in Exhibits A12A and A12B is well known to option traders. They know that the sensitivity of their positions to moves in the underlying price will vary with moneyness. This change in delta is described by gamma.[46] Away from the money (both deep in-the-money and deep out-of-the-money), as delta approaches its limits, there is very little change in delta. Referring to Exhibit A12A, the call delta is 0 at S = $50 and remains 0 at S = $51. A trader will not get very excited about the right to buy a stock at $100 when the price is $50, and that opinion won't change much at $51. The change in delta (gamma) at that price is low, so gamma is also low. Gamma increases as delta starts to change. Gamma peaks for both puts and calls at (or close to) the money when the change in delta is greatest. As a call gets deep-in-the-money, delta approaches 1 and remains there. In Exhibit A12A for calls, we see delta is 1 at S = 149 and delta is 1 at S = 150. Because delta is not changing at that point, gamma, the sensitivity of delta to changes in S, will be zero.

2.2.3 Option Price Sensitivity to Changes in Underlying Asset Volatility: Vega

As mentioned previously, option prices increase as volatility increases. The rate of change in the option price as volatility changes is given by vega. Once vega is estimated, the effect of changing volatility on an option price or a derivative portfolio can be understood. For equivalent puts and calls (same strike price and expiration date) on the same stock, the Black–Scholes–Merton vega will be the same.

2.2.4 Option Price Sensitivity to Changes in the Risk-free Rate: Rho

All else equal, Black–Scholes–Merton put and call prices on most underlying assets are not very sensitive to the small changes in the risk-free interest rates usually encountered in the market. The option price sensitivity to changes in the risk-free rate can still be calculated and is referred to by the Greek letter rho.

2.2.5 Option Price Sensitivity to Time: Theta

The decay rate in value of Black–Scholes–Merton option prices is approximated by theta. Traders follow this Greek with great interest, as it indicates the rate at which option prices decline as the date of expiration approaches.

3 Managing Portfolio Risk with Derivatives

In finance, a portfolio is a collection of assets. Portfolio assets can include mutual funds, stock index funds, stocks, bonds, commodities, and cash. Derivatives can also be an important part of a portfolio because they can be used to gain or reduce exposure to a particular underlying asset. We now examine how derivatives may be used to manage portfolio risk and return.

For some investors, derivatives are a significant part of their portfolio. Executives granted call options as part of their compensation package know that derivatives make up a large share of their personal wealth. Other investors may buy calls to participate in a potential increase in the price of the underlying asset. If the asset price increases, they will profit as previously shown in Exhibit A1. The other side of the call is taken by the call seller (writer). The premiums collected from writing calls are a valuable source of income, but the losses can be considerable if the price of the underlying asset increases (see Exhibit A2). Selling or writing a call involves risk. The seller must be ready to offer the shares at the strike price if called to do so. A call writer may wish

---

46 Gamma is the partial derivative of delta with respect to the stock price and the second partial derivative of the call price with respect to the stock price.

to own the underlying shares as part of their portfolio, so if the shares are "called" they are "covered." A covered call position involves both owning a stock and writing calls against it. When added to a stock portfolio (shown as the solid line in Exhibit A13), a short call position (shown as the dotted line) will add the option premium to portfolio profits. Above the strike price, payoffs to short call position are offset by equivalent gains in the stock price. The covered call portfolio trades potential upside gains for the income collected from the call premium.

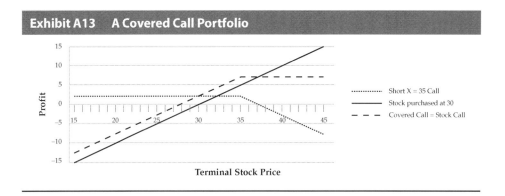

Exhibit A13 A Covered Call Portfolio

Put options may also be used to manage portfolio risk and returns. For example, exposure to a single stock or stock index may pose a significant risk. Owning a put option in a portfolio provides a measure of protection if the asset price falls. A "protective put" allows the investor to benefit if their shares increase, while limiting losses if prices decline. Exhibit A14 illustrates the addition of an S&P 500 put option struck at 1450 to a portfolio containing a long position in the S&P 500 Index initiated at a level of 1500. Below the strike price, gains in the put position offset losses in the stock portfolio, as shown along the dashed line. Of course, the protection offered by a put comes at a price and lasts for only a finite time period.

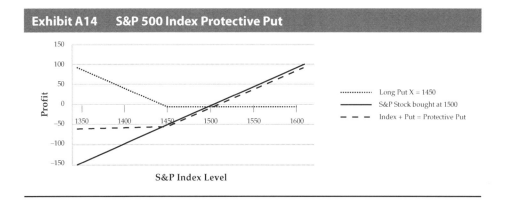

Exhibit A14 S&P 500 Index Protective Put

4 Replication with Derivatives

We have seen that the addition of a put to a stock portfolio can reduce downside losses and the addition of a short call position can reduce upside gains. If a put and a short call are added to an underlying stock, it is possible to reduce the risk of the stock position to zero. This is shown in Exhibit A15. After the derivatives are combined with the stock position, the resulting combination of assets is given by the horizontal line (shown with dashes and dots). This line represents a constant payoff that is independent of the asset price and is risk-free. The payoff represents the return that would be earned from buying a stock and a put and selling a call option with the same strike price and expiration as the put option. The return on this three-asset portfolio should be equal to the return on a risk-free bond requiring the same investment as the portfolio.[47]

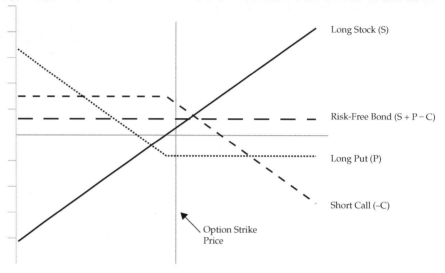

Exhibit A15 A Risk-Free Bond made from an Asset and Two Derivatives: Bond = Stock + Put − Call

Because a risk-free asset can be created from the combination of a derivative and an asset, other combinations are possible. This point is shown in Exhibit A16, a process referred to as *replication*. Replication is the creation of an asset or portfolio from another asset, portfolio, and/or derivative. Exhibit A16 shows first that an asset plus the derivative can replicate the risk-free asset. Similarly, we see that an asset minus the risk-free asset (meaning to borrow at the risk-free rate) is equivalent to the opposite position in the derivative, and a derivative minus the risk-free asset is equivalent to the opposite position in the asset.

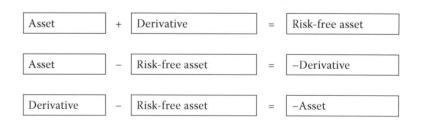

Exhibit A16 Replication and Derivatives

Derivatives mixed with other derivatives can form new derivatives. Exhibit A17 shows the payoff which results from the combination of a call and a short put. The call requires a premium be paid, but pays off if the underlying price increases. Although the put sale recovers a premium (assumed to be equal to the cost of the call in this

---

47 If a risk-free asset does not return the risk-free rate, arbitrage may be possible.

example), it will require a payoff be made if the price of the asset decreases below X. Taken together, these two derivative positions result in a payoff similar to that of a forward contract (shown in Exhibit A7).

Exhibit A17 A Forward Contract Created from a Long Call and a Short Put: Long Forward = Call − Put

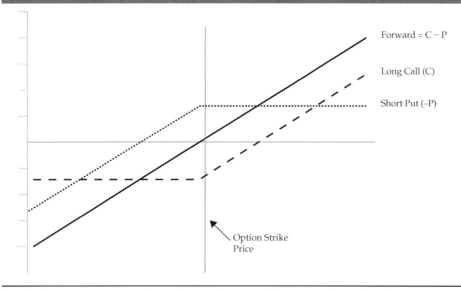

Investors normally buy a stock initially (go long) and hope to profit by selling later at a higher price. A short stock position takes the opposite view; they sell upfront. *In a short sale, an asset such as a share of stock is borrowed and sold in the hope that the asset may be replaced later at a cheaper price.* For example, a hedge fund may borrow shares of Facebook stock and sell them at a market price of $74. If the market price increases by $10, the short must pay $84 to replace the borrowed shares. The short would incur a loss of $10 on the trade. However, if the price of Facebook shares falls from $74 to $58, the short may replace the shares at $58 and keep a profit of $16. The same payoff can be replicated using derivatives as shown in Exhibit A18. In the exhibit, a long put position provides some of the downside payoff received from a short stock position. Above the strike price, a short call reproduces the loss from a short asset position. The bond needed to complete the picture is not shown in Exhibit A18, but is subtracted to arrive at the final portfolio.

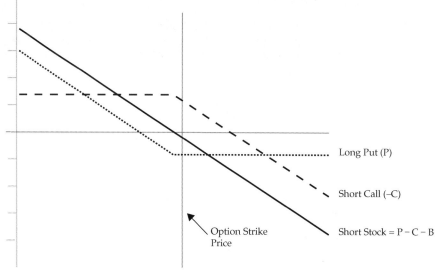

EXAMPLE A4

Replication of a Call

An investor seeking to reproduce the payoff of a call option with a strike price X would *most likely*:

A buy the underlying asset, sell a put option struck at X, and lend an amount equal to X.

B sell the underlying asset, buy a put option struck at X, and lend an amount equal to X.

C buy the underlying asset, buy a put option struck at X, and borrow an amount equal to X.

Solution:

C is correct. Buying the asset will provide the same upside as the call, and adding a put will limit losses if the underlying price falls below X. A position of minus a bond (from Exhibit A18) means to borrow at the risk-free rate. A is incorrect because the loss on a call is limited to the premium in the event of decreasing asset prices, a long position in the underlying asset will not be restricted without a long (protective) put. B is incorrect because a short position in the underlying asset and a long position in a put will not reproduce the upside potential of a call if the underlying asset prices increases.

Summary

- A long call option grants the holder the right to buy an underlying asset (such as a share of stock) at a fixed price (referred to as the strike price) for a finite period of time. The option will require the buyer to pay an initial cost called the premium.

- At expiration, a call option value is equal to the difference between the asset price at expiration and the strike price, or zero, whichever is greater. If the asset price is below the strike price, the call will expire with a zero value and the buyer will lose the premium.
- The profit on a long call option position at expiration is equal to the long call value at expiration minus the call's initial purchase price. The profit on a call option can be theoretically unlimited, but the loss can never exceed the purchase price.
- A short call option allows the seller to collect the option premium. In return, the call seller must provide the right to buy the underlying asset to the call buyer at a fixed price for a finite period of time. The maximum gain on a short call position is limited to the call premium. The maximum loss on a short call position can be theoretically unlimited.
- A long put option grants the holder the right to sell an underlying asset (such as a share of stock) at a fixed price (referred to as the strike price) for a finite period of time. The put option also requires the buyer to pay an initial cost called the premium.
- At expiration, a put option value is equal to the difference between the strike price at expiration and the asset price, or zero, whichever is greater. If the asset price is above the strike price, the put will expire with a zero value.
- The profit on a long put option position at expiration is equal to the put value at expiration minus the put's initial purchase price. If the underlying asset price is above the option strike price at expiration, the buyer of the put option will lose the premium paid.
- The put option seller collects the initial put premium and must be able to purchase the underlying asset from the put holder for an amount equal to the strike price.
- A call (put) option is in-the-money when the underlying asset price is greater (less) than the strike price.
- A call or put option is at-the-money when the underlying asset price is approximately equal to the strike price.
- A call (put) option is out-of-the-money when the underlying asset price is less (greater) than the strike price.
- A long forward/futures contract is an agreement to buy an underlying asset at a fixed price at some later date.
- A short forward/futures contract is an agreement to sell an underlying asset at a fixed price at some later date.
- Forward and futures contracts have important differences. A futures contract is exchange-traded and standardized in features such as delivery date, margin requirement, contract size, and asset description. Forward contracts can be customized.
- The performance of a futures contract is guaranteed by a clearinghouse. A forward contract is subject to the risk of a default by the counterparty.
- The value of a long forward contract at expiration is equal to the spot asset price minus the forward price. The value of a long forward contract will be positive (negative) if the asset value at expiration is greater (less) than the initial forward price.
- A forward/futures contact can be used to hedge single-period risk. A swap can be viewed as a portfolio of forward contracts, and may be used to hedge multi-period risk.

- Whereas the value of an option at expiration is easy to determine using pay-off functions, the value of an option prior to expiration requires the use of an option pricing model such as the Black–Scholes–Merton model.
- The Black–Scholes–Merton model calculates the call or put value prior to expiration as a function of five variables: the current price of the underlying asset, the volatility of the underlying asset, the strike price, the risk-free interest rate, and time to maturity.
- The sensitivity of an option price to changes in the price of the underlying asset is given by the options delta.
  - For a call, $0 \leq \Delta \leq 1$
  - For a put, $-1 \leq \Delta \leq 0$
- Delta approaches +1 (–1) as a call (put) option gets deeper in-the-money.
- Delta approaches 0 as a put or call option gets deeper out-of-the-money.
- The change in delta as the underlying asset price changes is captured by gamma.
- Calls and puts can be combined with their underlying assets to create an investor's desired payoffs or payoffs which replicate those of other assets.

END OPTIONAL SEGMENT

REFERENCES

Cubilié, M. 2007. "Derivative Products in Performance Attribution." Ch. 8 in *Advanced Portfolio Attribution Analysis*. Edited by C. Bacon. London: Risk Books.

Eurex. 2015. "Contract Specifications for Futures Contracts and Options Contracts at Eurex Deutschland and Eurex Zürich" (www.eurexchange.com/exchange-en/resources/rules-regulations/Specifications-for-Futures-Contracts-and-Options-Contracts-/136774; accessed 4 August).

Fischer, B., and R. Wermers. 2012. *Performance Evaluation and Attribution of Security Portfolios*. Waltham, MA: Academic Press.

Group, CME. 2015. "U.S. Treasury Bond Futures Contract Specs" (www.cmegroup.com/trading/interest-rates/us-treasury/30-year-us-treasury-bond_contract_specifications.html; accessed 13 February).

Hull, J.C. 2006. *Options, Futures, and Other Derivatives*, 6th ed. Upper Saddle River, NJ: Prentice Hall.

LIFFE. 1992. "The Reporting and Performance Measurement of Financial Futures and Options in Investment Portfolios."

Stannard, J.C. 1996. "Measuring Investment Returns of Portfolios Containing Futures and Options." *Journal of Performance Measurement*, Fall: 27–33.

PRACTICE PROBLEMS

The following information relates to Questions 1–5

A fixed-income portfolio manager with the EUR as its base currency invests in Japanese government bonds, US Treasury bonds, and German government bonds (bunds), as shown in Exhibit 1. The time horizon is six months.

Exhibit 1 Portfolio Holdings and Weights, as of Beginning of 20X7

Asset Class (Currency)	Beginning of Period Portfolio Values (millions)	Expected End of Period Portfolio Values (millions)	Beginning of Period Base Currency Portfolio Weights (%)
US treasury bonds (USD)	25	28	53
German government bunds (EUR)	10	9	23
Japanese government bonds (JPY)	742	742	12
Cash (EUR)	5	5	12
Total			100

The bunds have a two-year maturity and a yield that is equal to the Libor rate of 1%.

Interest Rate Hedge

At the beginning of 20X7, the manager expected that over the next six months, the general level of interest rates would increase in Germany and decline in the United States and that these changes would cause the EUR to appreciate against the USD. The manager considered selling 20 EUR bund interest rate futures contracts to partially hedge the portfolio's German bund exposure. In his valuation, the manager assumed that all market values were inclusive of accrued interest and that cash accounts would constantly earn 0.1% during the period. The contract value multiplier for the EUR bund interest rate futures was EUR100,000. Data for the German Government bund and futures are provided in Exhibit 2.

Exhibit 2 Maturity Range and Prices of Bund and Futures

Asset Class	Maturity Range (years)	Beginning of Period Price (% of par)	End of Period Price (% of par)
German government bunds	2	100	97
EUR bund interest rate futures	8.5 to 10.5	100	97

Currency Hedge

The manager also considered entering into a forward contract with a notional value of USD25 million to hedge the expected depreciation of the USD relative to the EUR. The forward contract under consideration was to expire at the end of the period. Exhibit 3 provides information on the relevant exchange rates.

Exhibit 3 Exchange Rates		
	EUR/JPY	EUR/USD
Beginning of period spot exchange rate	0.0067	0.91
End of period spot exchange rate	0.0064	0.77

At the beginning of the period, interest rates were 3% in the United States and 1% in Germany.

1 The notional exposure of the manager's interest rate hedge is *best* calculated using the price of:
   A the underlying bund.
   B cheapest-to-deliver US Treasury bond.
   C a broad international fixed-income index.

2 Using the data in Exhibit 2, if at the beginning of 20X7 the manager entered into the interest rate hedge, the notional exposure of the manager's bund futures contract position would be:
   A –EUR2.00 million.
   B –EUR1.94 million.
   C EUR2.00 million.

3 If at the beginning of 20X7 the manager entered into the bund futures hedge, using the futures contract as the price of the underlying, the notional return for the German bund futures contract over the observation period would be *closest* to:
   A –2.9%.
   B –3.0%.
   C –3.1%.

4 Given the data in Exhibits 1 and 3, as of the beginning of 20X7, the portfolio's base currency return on an unhedged basis is expected to be *closest* to:
   A –6.7%.
   B –5.7%.
   C 0.3%.

5 Assuming the manager enters into the forward contract hedge at the beginning of 20X7, the return of the forward currency contract for the period is *closest* to:
   A –16.2%.
   B 17.0%.
   C 18.2%.

Practice Problems

The following information relates to Problems 6–12

Newbern Asset Management is a US-based money manager that manages assets for domestic clients. Newbern restricts its investments to equities of the 500 largest traded companies domiciled in the United States, derivative instruments, and cash. Newbern uses primarily a market-neutral investment strategy but will occasionally adjust its exposures with derivatives for its enhanced strategy.

Newbern manages its equity in two allocations: a value segment and a growth segment. The weights and two-month returns for the market neutral strategy are provided in Exhibit 1. The beginning cash position of the portfolio was $2,000,000.

Exhibit 1 Market Neutral Portfolio Weights and Two-Month Returns

Position	Beginning Weight (%)	Underlying Return (%)
Value segment		
Long	60	–0.10
Short	–60	–0.20
Growth segment		
Long	40	–0.50
Short	–40	–0.40

For the two-month period ending 30 June, in order to adjust its exposure to the market, the fund established a long position using 10 E-mini futures contracts on the S&P 500 Index. The beginning and ending values of the futures contracts and the underlying S&P 500 are summarized in Exhibit 2.

Exhibit 2 Prices of the S&P 500 and the E-Mini S&P 500 Futures

	30 April ($)	30 June ($)
S&P 500	2,105	2,084
E-mini S&P 500 futures	2,093	2,076

One E-mini S&P 500 futures contract has a contract value multiplier of $50. Returns for notional cash positions and physical cash positions associated with the investments were 0.1% per month (0.2% over the two-month period).

At the time of establishing the futures position for the fund, Newbern also considered using forward contracts expiring 30 August for the same purpose. Jon Raifer, Newbern's portfolio manager, asked about the differences in notional exposure between the two types of contracts, and received the following opinions:

Opinion 1: The notional exposure would be significantly lower for the forward position because the fund would not need to put down margin.

Opinion 2: The notional exposure would be similar for the forward and futures positions because the economic exposure is similar.

Opinion 3: There will be no notional exposure for forwards because the cash flows for forward contracts occur at maturity.

In addition to the analyses with futures and forward contracts, Newbern also investigated the purchase of call options to achieve its objective. The options contracts they considered have a contract value multiplier of $50 for each option. The fund's policy is to use out-of-the-money call options.

6 Which of the following statements is correct regarding Newbern's primary strategy? The fund's returns:

   A   are independent of manager stock-selection skills.

   B   will be closely aligned with those of the S&P 500.

   C   can be positive even when all segments have negative returns.

7 Based on Exhibit 1 and ignoring the return on cash, the equity return on Newbern's market-neutral strategy was *closest* to:

   A   −58%.

   B   −54%.

   C   0.02%.

8 Based on Exhibit 2, the notional exposure for the futures contracts used by Newbern was *closest* to:

   A $1,046,500.

   B $1,052,500.

   C $1,054,605.

9 Based on Exhibit 2, the return generated on the notional stock position using the futures contracts was *closest* to:

   A   −0.808%.

   B   −0.798%.

   C   −0.608%.

10 Which opinion received by Newbern's portfolio manager regarding notional exposure is *most* accurate?

   A   Opinion 1

   B   Opinion 2

   C   Opinion 3

11 If Newbern had used the forward contract in place of the futures contracts, the notional return for the forward contract would have been:

   A   lower than the notional return on the futures contracts.

   B   the same as the notional return on the futures contracts.

   C   higher than the notional return on the futures contracts.

12 In using options contracts to achieve the same level of notional exposure as in the 10 futures contracts, Newbern would need to purchase:

   A   fewer than 10 option contracts.

   B   10 option contracts.

   C   more than 10 option contracts.

Practice Problems

The following information relates to questions 13–21

Hamelia Investments LLC is an asset management firm based in the USA, and the base currency of its funds is in USD. Hamelia manages an equity fund (the "Fund"), which invests in eurozone stocks denominated in EUR. The Fund uses the MSCI Euro Index as its benchmark.

Eric Tai is a portfolio manager of the Fund. After the market close on 31 December 20X4, Tai compiles monthly portfolio market values in local currency and currency exchange rates as shown in Exhibit 1:

Exhibit 1	Portfolio Market Values in Local Currency and Spot Currency Exchange Rates		
End Date	Market Value in EUR (millions)	EUR/USD Spot Exchange Rate	USD/EUR Spot Exchange Rate
30 Sep 20X4	100.00	0.79161	1.26325
31 Oct 20X4	98.17	0.79815	1.25290
30 Nov 20X4	101.30	0.80215	1.24665
31 Dec 20X4	98.90	0.82641	1.21005

Tai proposes to use forward currency contracts to hedge the currency risk of the Fund in 20X5. Tai researches the currency market and collects the information shown in Exhibit 2:

Exhibit 2	Interest Rates and EUR/USD Spot Rate on 31 December 20X4
Annual interest rate of USD	0.20%
Annual interest rate of EUR	0.10%
EUR/USD spot exchange rate	0.82641

Hamelia's bank sets the 3-month quote of its EUR/USD forward contracts based on the principles of covered interest rate parity. Tai finds the following statements on covered interest rate parity in an online forum on currency hedging:

Statement 1 "Covered interest rate parity is a condition in which the relationship between interest rates and the spot rate and forward currency rates of two countries is in equilibrium."

Statement 2 "Covered interest rate parity refers to the situation in which interest rate arbitrage opportunities using forward currency contracts exist between two currencies."

Upon Tai's suggestion, Hamelia's management team hires Kevin Hurley, a currency overlay manager, to implement a 100% currency hedge to USD for the Fund. Hamelia allocates USD1 million to Hurley's currency overlay portfolio to fund any potential loss. Tai agrees to update Hurley monthly on the underlying portfolio market value. Between 31 December 20X4 and 30 June 20X5, there are no interest rate changes for USD and EUR. The portfolio market values, spot rates, and one-month forward rates as of each month-end in the period from 31 December 20X4 to 30 June 20X5 are shown in Exhibit 3:

Exhibit 3   Portfolio Market Values and EUR/USD Spot Currency Exchange Rates

End Date	Market Value in EUR (millions)	EUR/USD Spot Exchange Rate	EUR/USD One-Month Forward Rate
31 Dec 20X4	98.90	0.82641	0.82634
31 Jan 20X5	106.06	0.88617	0.88610
28 Feb 20X5	113.41	0.89154	0.89147
31 Mar 20X5	115.42	0.93110	0.93102
30 Apr 20X5	115.56	0.89242	0.89235
31 May 20X5	117.40	0.91212	0.91204
30 Jun 20X5	112.01	0.89750	0.89743

In July 20X5, Hurley sends Tai a report of portfolio base returns, currency overlay returns, portfolio hedged returns, and perfectly hedged returns.

Hurley asks Tai to implement a partially hedged strategy that will be benchmarked against the return of the MSCI Euro Index 70% hedged to the USD. Exhibit 4 presents the returns of the MSCI Euro Index in EUR and USD (with unhedged currency exposure) and the MSCI Euro Hedge Index in USD (with fully hedged currency exposure) for the month of August 2015.

Exhibit 4   Return of MSCI Euro Index and MSCI Euro Hedge Index, August 20X5

End Date	MSCI Euro Index in EUR	MSCI Euro Index in USD	MSCI Euro Hedge Index in USD
31 Aug 20X5	0.12%	4.46%	−0.11%

13 Based on Exhibit 1, the portfolio return in local currency for 20X4 Q4 is *closest* to:

   A   −5.27%.

   B   −4.21%.

   C   −1.10%.

14 Based on Exhibit 1, the currency return of the portfolio for 20X4 Q4 is *closest* to:

   A   −5.27%.

   B   −4.21%.

   C   4.40%.

15 Based on Exhibit 1, the portfolio return in base currency for December 20X4 is *closest* to:

   A   −5.24%.

   B   −2.37%.

Practice Problems

    C   −1.10%.

16 The bank's 3-month forward rate quote that satisfies the conditions of covered interest rate parity on 31 December 20X4 is *closest* to:

    A   0.82559.

    B   0.82620.

    C   0.82662.

17 Which of the following statement(s) regarding covered interest rate parity is (are) correct?

    A   Statement 1 only

    B   Statement 2 only

    C   Both Statement 1 and Statement 2

18 Based on Exhibit 3, the Fund's 100% hedged return in base currency for the month of March 20X5 is *closest* to:

    A   1.59%.

    B   1.70%.

    C   4.25%.

19 Based on Exhibit 3, the hedged portfolio return of the Fund in USD for May 20X5 is:

    A   less than the perfectly hedged portfolio return in USD.

    B   equal to the perfectly hedged portfolio return in USD.

    C   greater than the perfectly hedged portfolio return in USD.

20 Which of the following is the *most appropriate* asset base used as the denominator of the currency overlay portfolio return calculation in May 20X5?

    A   USD1 million.

    B   EUR98.90 million.

    C   EUR115.56 million.

21 Based on Exhibit 4, the August 20X5 target return of Tai's strategy in USD is closest to:

    A   −0.04%.

    B   1.26%.

    C   3.09%.

The following information relates to questions 22–27

Pierre Grégoire, a private wealth manager in Lyon, France, is reviewing the performance of two large-cap equity funds. The two portfolios are actively managed by Isabelle Fabré and invest in eurozone stocks and derivatives.

    Portfolio A follows a leveraged long/short strategy. Grégoire prepares a contribution-to-return analysis of Portfolio A based on the 31 December 20X5 market value information presented in Exhibit 1.

Exhibit 1 Portfolio A (€ millions)

Position	Beginning Market Value 1 January 20X5	Gain/Loss Year 20X5	Ending Market Value 31 December 20X5
Long eurozone equities	300.0	31.4	331.4
Short eurozone equities	−40.0	3.7	−36.3
Cash	−60.0	−0.8	−60.8
Total	200.0	34.3	234.3

Fabré uses equity options and futures contracts to adjust Portfolio A's equity market exposure. She makes the following statements to Grégoire regarding the futures contracts used in Portfolio A:

Statement 1 Futures have no market value over their lifespan.

Statement 2 Delta is used in calculating the notional exposure of futures.

Statement 3 The notional exposure formula provides a reasonable approximation for large changes in the price of the underlying.

Portfolio B implements a long stock/call option strategy. As of 1 January 20X5, Portfolio B consists of €5,000,000 in eurozone equities and €880,000 in cash.

Fabré informs Grégoire that at the close of trading on 31 December 20X5, she used call options on the EURO STOXX 50 Index to increase the exposure of Portfolio B to eurozone equities by €750,000. Exhibit 2 presents selected information about the EURO STOXX 50 Index call options.

Exhibit 2 EURO STOXX 50 Index Call Options, 31 December 20X5

Contract value multiplier	10
Delta	0.50
Value	3,275

One year after Fabré's call option strategy was implemented, Grégoire assembles the market value and performance information on Portfolio B listed in Exhibit 3.

Exhibit 3 Portfolio B

Asset Class	Actual Holdings (€) 31 December 20X5	Gain/Loss (€) 20X6
Eurozone equities	5,000,000	20,000
Call options	100,000	490

Practice Problems

Exhibit 3 (Continued)

Asset Class	Actual Holdings (€) 31 December 20X5	Gain/Loss (€) 20X6
Cash	780,000	780
Total	5,880,000	21,270

22 Based on Exhibit 1, the contribution to the overall portfolio return of the short eurozone equities position in Portfolio A is *closest* to:
 A −9.25%.
 B 1.85%.
 C 9.25%.

23 Based on Exhibit 1, the contribution to the overall portfolio return from cash in Portfolio A is *closest* to:
 A −0.40%.
 B −0.35%.
 C 1.33%.

24 Which of the following statements made by Fabré concerning futures is correct?
 A Statement 1
 B Statement 2
 C Statement 3

25 Based on Exhibit 2, the number of call option contracts on the EURO STOXX 50 Index that Fabré used to adjust the equity market exposure of Portfolio B is *closest* to:
 A 23.
 B 46.
 C 458.

26 Based on Exhibit 3, the return on the notional equities position resulting from the use of options in Portfolio B is *closest* to:
 A 0.07%.
 B 0.15%.
 C 0.17%.

27 Based on Exhibit 3, the amount of effective cash after considering the effect of options in Portfolio B is *closest* to:
 A €130,000.
 B €650,000.
 C €780,000.

The following information relates to Questions 28–34

Paul North, a fund manager, oversees three portfolios, A, B, and C, with the help of junior analyst Mike Smith. The three portfolios have the US dollar as their base currency.

North reviews last month's performance of Portfolio A, which uses a 120/20 short extension strategy. He notes that the net market exposure of the portfolio increased from $2 million to $2.2 million, with no change in the market value for securities held short.

North has a positive outlook for gold stocks and discusses with Smith the merits of using forwards or futures contracts in Portfolio B to increase exposure to the gold sector. Smith tells North the following:

Statement 1   The valuation of forwards and futures with the same terms leads to identical results at initiation.

Statement 2   Forward contracts offer potential leverage, which increases the capital required to achieve a desired target return.

Statement 3   The value of the forward is the difference in spot prices between the forward and the underlying asset, discounted to contract maturity.

North contacts a large institutional client to discuss adding gold forward contracts to Portfolio B. The client asks North how the addition of forwards would affect Portfolio B's total associated economic exposure at forward initiation.

North purchases one HUI forward contract for Portfolio B at a price of $1,247. The contract, which tracks the NYSE Arca Gold BUGS Index of companies involved in gold mining, expires in six months and has a contract value multiplier of 50. The index price is $1,254, and the current monthly discount rate on cash is 0.2%.

One month later, North evaluates the performance of the notional equity position generated by the forward contract when the forward price is $1,277 and the index level is $1,275.

Portfolio C consists of global metals and mining stocks. Two years ago, North entered into a two-year swap in Portfolio C in which he agreed to pay the return on a $5 million position in the Global Silver Miners ETF and receive the return on a $5 million position in the Global Gold Miners ETF.

At the initiation of the swap, Portfolio C had a net asset value of $41 million. The net asset value (NAV) increased by $3.4 million in Year 1 and by $4.3 million in Year 2. Returns for the two exchange-traded funds (ETFs) over the last two years are presented in Exhibit 1.

Exhibit 1   Performance for ETFs since Swap Initiation

Exchange-Traded Fund	Year 1	Year 2
Global Gold Miners	2.35%	4.79%
Global Silver Miners	−1.59%	0.85%

North wants to limit the currency risk that Portfolio C has in Brazilian stocks. The beginning market value of Brazilian stocks in Portfolio C is R$24 million (R$ = Brazilian real). He hires a currency overlay manager to trade forward contracts in a separate portfolio to hedge Brazilian real exposure. One month after initiation of the currency overlay strategy, the market value of the Brazilian stocks is R$26 million. North gathers the information on the spot and one-month forward currency exchange rates presented in Exhibit 2.

Practice Problems

Exhibit 2	Spot and One-Month Forward Currency Exchange Rates	
Period	BRL/USD Spot Rate	BRL/USD One-Month Forward Rate
Start of Month	3.1250	3.1155
End of Month	3.2550	3.2650

28 Last month's return on the long positions in Portfolio A was *closest* to:
  A 7.14%.
  B 8.33%.
  C 10.00%.

29 Which of Smith's statements regarding forwards and futures contracts is correct?
  A Statement 1
  B Statement 2
  C Statement 3

30 North's *most likely* response to the institutional client's question about the use of gold forward contracts is that the total associated economic exposure of Portfolio B would:
  A decrease.
  B not change.
  C increase.

31 The one-month return of the notional equity position generated by the HUI forward contract in Portfolio B is *closest* to:
  A 2.37%.
  B 2.57%.
  C 2.59%.

32 Based on Exhibit 1, the swap's contribution to Portfolio C's Year 1 return is *closest* to:
  A 0.10%.
  B 0.48%.
  C 0.76%.

33 Based on Exhibit 1, the swap's contribution to Portfolio C's return by the swap to Portfolio C is:
  A higher in Year 1.
  B higher in Year 2.
  C the same in both years.

34 Based on Exhibit 2, the total hedged return on Brazilian stocks for the month is:
  A less than the perfectly hedged return.
  B equal to the perfectly hedged return.
  C greater than the perfectly hedged return.

SOLUTIONS

1. A is correct. Although it is acceptable to use the futures price instead of the underlying price when there is a lack of pricing data, the price of the underlying bund is provided and thus should be used.

2. A is correct. The notional exposure is defined as:

   Notional exposure = Sign × Number of contracts × Contract value multiplier × Price of the underlying.

   The underlying is priced at par at the beginning of the observation period. Thus,

   Notional exposure = –1 × 20 × 100,000 × (100/100) = –2,000,000.

   Because the manager is hedging the exposure by selling contracts, the sign is negative.

3. A is correct. The bund futures contract position value is calculated as follows:

   20 × 100,000 × (100/100) = 2,000,000.

   Interest earned on the cash due to the futures position = 2,000,000 × 0.001 = 2,000. The bund futures have declined in total by = (0.97 – 1.00) × (2,000,000) = –60,000. Thus, the notional return is calculated as follows:

   $$\text{Notional return} = \frac{-60{,}000 + 2{,}000}{2{,}000{,}000} = -2.9\%.$$

   Note that when the total return on the portfolio (consisting of the underlying bunds, bund futures, and cash) is calculated, the short position in the bund futures contract will be reflected by a negative economic exposure of –2,000,000 and a corresponding negative weight in the portfolio (similar to the short futures position example shown in Exhibit 10). The negative weight times the return of –2.9% will result in a positive contribution to the portfolio return.

4. B is correct. The first step is to convert the local currency portfolio values into the base currency by using beginning-of-period values:

   $$\frac{\text{USD}25}{1.098901} = \text{EUR}\,22.75000$$

   $$\frac{\text{JPY}742}{149.253731} = \text{EUR}\,4.971400$$

   The next step is to convert the local currency portfolio values into the base currency by using end-of-period values:

   28 × .77 = 21.5600

   742 × 0.0064 = 4.7488

   The total beginning market value in EUR = 22.75 + 4.971400 + 10 + 5 = 42.7214.

The total ending market value in EUR = 21.56 + 4.7488 + 9 + 5 = 40.2888.

$$\text{The base currency return} = \frac{\text{Ending base currency market value}}{\text{Beginning base currency market value}} - 1$$

$$= \frac{40.2888}{42.721400} - 1 = 0.943059 - 1$$

$$= -0.056941, \text{ or } -5.7\%$$

5. B is correct. The manager is selling (going short) USD and buying (going long) EUR to reduce the risk of the long underlying USD position. The base currency is the EUR and the foreign currency is the USD. The USD hedge requires the sale of USD25 million into EUR in time period $t = 0$ at a forward rate, F_0, of

$$F_0 = \frac{\text{USD}1.098901}{\text{EUR}} \times \frac{(1 + 0.03)^{6/12}}{(1 + 0.01)^{6/12}} = \frac{\text{USD}1.109727}{\text{EUR}}$$

The spot rate at time $t + 1$ is given in Exhibit 3:

$$S_1 = \frac{1}{0.77} = 1.298701$$

The forward contract return, also known as the forward currency return, would be

$$\text{Forward contract return} = \frac{S_1}{F_0} - 1 = \frac{1.298701}{1.109727} - 1 = 0.170289 \text{ or } 17.0\%.$$

A is incorrect because the forward rate is calculated in terms of USD instead of EUR. Also, the spot rate for EUR/USD is used instead of the spot rate for USD/EUR.

$$F_0 = \frac{\text{EUR}0.91}{\text{USD}} \times \frac{1.03}{1.01} = \frac{\text{EUR}0.928020}{\text{USD}}$$

$$S_1 = 0.77$$

$$\text{Forward contract return} = \frac{0.77}{0.928020} - 1 = -0.170277, \text{ or } -17.0\%.$$

C is incorrect because the spot currency return is calculated instead of the forward currency contract return.

$$\text{Spot currency return} = \frac{S_1}{S_0} - 1 = \frac{1.298701}{1.098901} - 1 = 0.181818 = 18.2\%.$$

6. C is correct. A market-neutral portfolio is focused on leveraging the manager's skill by selecting securities to buy or to short. Short positions are profitable when returns are negative and can outweigh the effect of negative returns in long segments.

7. C is correct. The return is calculated as follows:

r = (60% × −0.10%) + (−60% × −0.20%) + (40% × −0.50%) + (−40% × −0.40%)
= 0.02%.

8 B is correct. The notional exposure (NE) for the contracts is calculated by using the price on the S&P 500 as follows:

NE = Sign × Number of contracts × Contract value multiplier × Price underlying

= +1 × 10 × 50 × $2,105

= $1,052,500.

9 C is correct. The exposure to the underlying stock position is reflected in the associated notional exposure of $1,052,500 (calculated in Question 8). Based on the monthly rate of 0.1%, the cash position would have earned an income of 0.2% × $2,000,000 = $4,000. A portion of the income on cash is applied to the equity segment, which amounts to

$$\$4{,}000 \times \frac{\$1{,}052{,}500}{\$2{,}000{,}000} = \$2{,}105$$

The return of the notional stock position is then given by the following:

$$= \frac{10 \times 50 \times (\$2{,}076 - \$2{,}093) + 2{,}105}{\$1{,}052{,}500}$$

$$= \frac{-\$8{,}500 + \$2{,}105}{\$1{,}052{,}500}$$

$$= \frac{-\$6{,}395}{\$1{,}052{,}500} = -0.608\%$$

10 B is correct. The methodology for futures can be applied to forwards, which leads to identical results.

11 C is correct. The result can be calculated as follows using 60 as the number of days from 30 June to the end of the forward contract on 30 August (see Equation 6 in the reading):

$$= \frac{10 \times 50 \times (\$2{,}076 - \$2{,}093)(1.001)^{-(60/30)} + \$2{,}105}{\$1{,}052{,}500}$$

$$= \frac{-\$8{,}483 + \$2{,}105}{\$1{,}052{,}500}$$

$$= \frac{-\$6{,}378}{\$1{,}052{,}500} = -0.606\%$$

The return for the futures contract is −0.608%, calculated as follows:

$$= \frac{10 \times 50 \times (\$2{,}076 - \$2{,}093) + 2{,}105}{\$1{,}052{,}500}$$

$$= \frac{-\$8{,}500 + \$2{,}105}{\$1{,}052{,}500}$$

$$= \frac{-\$6{,}395}{\$1{,}052{,}500} = -0.608\%$$

The forward contract had a higher return as a result of the discounting seen in the numerator.

Alternatively, logic can be applied to augment the result for the notional stock position on the futures contracts. Note that the loss of $17 = ($2,076 − $2,093) per contract will be discounted in finding the notional return for the forward contract. In this case, a loss being discounted will be lower in magnitude (less negative), resulting in a higher return than in the case of the futures contracts (−0.606% > −0.608%).

Solutions

12 C is correct.

For options, the notional exposure (NE) assumes the following form:

NE = Sign × δ × Number of contracts × Contract value multiplier × Price underlying.

For the futures contracts, the notional exposure is determined as follows:

NE = Sign × Number of contracts × Contract value multiplier × Price underlying

= +1 × 10 × 50 × $2,105

= $1,052,500.

To accomplish the same notional exposure with a delta of 1 would require 10 contracts. Because the delta is less than 1 (most likely between 0 and 0.50), based on the fund policy to buy out-of-the-money call options, it would require more than 10 contracts.

13 C is correct. The 20X4 Q4 portfolio return in local currency (EUR) is

$$\frac{EURMV_{Dec}}{EURMV_{Sep}} - 1 = \frac{98.9}{100} = -1.10\%$$

14 B is correct. The local currency of the portfolio is in EUR, and the base currency is in USD. From 30 Sep 20X4 to 31 Dec 20X4, EUR1 depreciated from USD1.26325 to USD1.21005 (i.e., the foreign currency depreciated relative to the base currency). So, the currency return of the portfolio in 20X4 Q4 is:

$$\frac{USD/EUR_{Dec}}{USD/EUR_{Sep}} - 1 = \frac{1.21005}{1.26325} - 1 = -4.21\%$$

15 A is correct. The portfolio return in base currency (USD) for December 20X4 is

$$\frac{USDMV_{Dec}}{USDMV_{Nov}} - 1 = \frac{98.9 \times 1.21005}{101.3 \times 1.24665} - 1 = -5.24\%$$

or

(1 + Local return) × (1 + Currency return) –

$$1 = \left(1 + \frac{98.9}{101.3} - 1\right) \times \left(1 + \frac{1.21005}{1.24665} - 1\right) - 1 = -5.24\%$$

16 B is correct. The 3-month interest rate of USD is

$$(1 + 0.20\%)^{3/12} = 1.0005$$

The 3-month interest rate of EUR is

$$(1 + 0.10\%)^{3/12} = 1.00025$$

To satisfy covered interest rate parity, the forward quote must satisfy

$$F_0 = S_0 \times \frac{1 + r_{FC}}{1 + r_{DC}} = 0.82641 \times \frac{1 + 0.025\%}{1 + 0.05\%} = 0.82620$$

17 A is correct. Covered interest rate parity states that the forward rate will be a function of the spot rate and relative interest rates in the two countries. More formally: $F_0 = S_0 \times [(1 + r_{FC})/1 + r_{DC})]$. If the forward rate did not reflect relative interest rates, arbitrage trades would bring it back to equilibrium in the market. Therefore, Statement 1 is correct. Statement 2, however, is not correct because interest rate parity refers to a situation in which the potential for covered interest arbitrage is eliminated.

18 B is correct.

The portfolio's base currency return for March 20X5 is

$$\frac{\text{USDMV}_{\text{Mar}}}{\text{USDMV}_{\text{Feb}}} - 1 = \frac{115.42/0.93110}{113.41/0.89154} - 1 = -2.55\%$$

The profit of the forward contract in EUR

$$\frac{\text{EURMV}_{\text{Feb}}}{\frac{\text{EUR}}{\text{USD}}\text{FebForwardRate}} - \frac{\text{EURMV}_{\text{Feb}}}{\frac{\text{EUR}}{\text{USD}}\text{MarSpotRate}} = \begin{array}{l}(113.41/0.89147)\\ -(113.41/0.93110)\end{array}$$

$$= \text{USD5.41 million}$$

Currency overlay return

5.41/(113.41/0.89154) = 4.25%

Hedged return = −2.55% + 4.25% = 1.70%

19 A is correct. From 30 April 20X5 to 31 May 20X5, the portfolio rose in value from EUR115.56 million to EUR117.40 million, while the EUR/USD spot rate rose in value (i.e., USD appreciated against EUR). Thus, the unhedged local currency (EUR) gain would be converted at a higher rate (i.e., 0.91212) to less USD as compared to the forward rate (i.e., 0.89235) in the perfectly hedged case, which leads to less currency gain in the hedged return calculation.

This conclusion is demonstrated by the following calculations:

In the hedged return calculation, the unhedged local currency gain of EUR1.84 million (117.40 million − 115.56 million) would be converted at the spot rate (i.e., 0.91212) to USD1.84 million/0.91212 = USD2.02 million.

In the perfectly hedged return calculation, the same EUR gain is considered to have been fully hedged. Therefore, it would be converted at the forward rate (i.e., 0.89235) to USD1.84 million/0.89235 = USD2.06 million.

So, the hedged portfolio return in USD is less than the perfectly hedged portfolio return in USD.

20 C is correct. The investor and currency overlay manager must determine the value of the underlaid assets at various points in time, and it is the value that is used in the denominator of the return calculation. In the case of Hamelia, Tai gave Hurley monthly updates. The value of the underlying assets as of 30 April 20X5 (namely, EUR115.56 million) should be used as the denominator of the currency overlay portfolio calculation for the month of May 20X5.

21 B is correct. 70% hedged into USD means that 70% of the USD exposure is hedged and only 30% exposure to USD is retained. So, the partially hedged index is a combination of 70% of MSCI Euro Hedge Index (100% hedged to USD) and 30% of unhedged MSCI Euro Index in USD. The monthly return of the partially hedged index in April 20X5 is:

70% × (−0.11%) + 30% × 4.46% = 1.26%

22 B is correct. The formula for the underlying return of the short eurozone equities position is:

(Ending market value/Beginning market value − 1)

From Exhibit 1: (−€36.3/−€40.0) − 1 = −9.25%

Solutions

Contribution to return is calculated as weight times return. Negative weights are used to represent short positions, and the security return is the return on the underlying security.

The formula for the contribution to the overall portfolio return of the short eurozone equities position is (Position beginning market value/Portfolio beginning market value) × Underlying return

From Exhibit 1: (−€40.0/€200.0) × (−9.25%) = 1.85%

23 A is correct. The beginning weight of cash is −€60.0 million, representing −€60.0 million/€200.0 million = −30% of the overall portfolio. The return on cash reflecting borrowing costs is −€0.8 million/−€60.0 million = 1.33%. The contribution to the overall portfolio return of cash, including borrowing costs, is −30% × 1.33% = −0.40%.

24 A is correct. Unlike stocks or bonds, futures do not have a market value; rather, they have a "net realizable value." This value is the profit or loss resulting from the change in the futures price each day. Because futures prices are marked to market—which means that profits and losses are realized at the end of each trading day by an addition or subtraction to a cash account—net unrealized value equals zero after the mark to market at the end of the trading day.

25 B is correct. The formula for calculating notional exposure is:

Notional exposure (NE) = Sign × δ × Number of contracts × Contract value multiplier × Price of underlying.

The NE of one call option contract on the EURO STOXX 50 Index on 31 December 20X5 was:

NE = +1 × 0.50 × 1 × 10 × 3,275 = 16,375

Dividing €750,000 by 16,375 yields 45.80 contracts required to increase equity exposure by €750,000.

26 B is correct. The formula to calculate the return on the notional equities position resulting from the use of the options in Portfolio B is:

Notional return = [(Option EMV − Option BMV) + Gain in cash]/Exposure due to options

The return on cash is: €780/€780,000 = 0.10%. The notional cash associated with the option is: €750,000 − €100,000 = €650,000. Thus, the notional cash generates a €650,000 × 0.10% = €650 gain. From Exhibit 3, the gain in the value of the call options is: €490.

For Portfolio B, the return on the notional equities position resulting from the use of call options is:

(€490 + €650)/€750,000 = 0.15%

27 A is correct. The effective cash position is the cash position after the addition for the notional cash associated with the options.

Exposure due to options can be broken down as follows:

0.00 = Notional exposure − Market value of the options − Notional cash associated with the options

= €750,000 − €100,000 − €650,000 = 0.00.

The amount of effective cash is:

Actual cash − Notional cash associated with the options = €780,000 − €650,000 = €130,000.

28 B is correct. The market value of the short positions did not change, so all of Portfolio A's gain was generated by the long positions. The 120/20 short extension strategy with a beginning net market exposure of $2 million implies a beginning long position of $2.4 million (= 120% × $2 million), an ending long position of $2.6 million (= $2.4 million + $0.2 million), and a short position of $0.4 million (= 20% × $2 million).

Therefore, the return on the long positions is calculated as follows:

Return on Portfolio A's long positions = ($2.6 million − $2.4 million)/$2.4 million

= 8.33%.

29 A is correct. On the transaction date, the valuation of forwards and futures with the same terms leads to identical results.

30 B is correct. The total associated economic exposure at the initiation of the contract does not change. The total associated economic exposure in Portfolio B is a sum of equities (total) and cash (netted). Before the addition of the long forward contract, the total economic exposure is calculated as Total economic exposure = Equities (stocks) + Physical cash.

After the addition of the long forward contract, the total economic exposure is calculated as

Total economic exposure = [Equities (stocks) + Equities (notional)] + (Physical cash − Notional cash).

At initiation, the notional equity is equal to the cash notional, so Total economic exposure = Equities (stocks) + Physical cash.

31 B is correct. The return on the notional equity position generated by the forward position in Portfolio B is calculated as follows:

Step 1. Compute the notional exposure (NE):

NE = Sign × Number of contracts × Contract value multiplier × Price underlying

= +1 × 1 × 50 × $1,254

= $62,700

Step 2. Compute the cash income:

Cash income = $62,700 × 0.2%

= $125.40

Step 3. Compute the notional return:

$$\frac{\text{Multiplier} \times \begin{pmatrix} \text{End} & \text{Beginning} \\ \text{contract} - \text{contract} \\ \text{price} & \text{price} \end{pmatrix} \times \left(1 + \text{Discount rate}\right)^{-\begin{pmatrix} \text{Number of} \\ \text{periods to} \\ \text{maturity} \end{pmatrix}} + \left(\text{Notional cash} \times \text{Discount rate}\right)}{\text{Notional exposure}}$$

Discount rate is a monthly rate with 5 months to maturity (= 6 months − 1 month).

$$\text{Notional return} = \frac{50 \times (\$1,277 - \$1,247) \times (1 + 0.2\%)^{-5} + \$125.40}{\$62,700}$$

= 2.57%

Solutions

32 B is correct. Contribution to return is calculated as follows:

$$\text{Contribution to return} = \left(\frac{\text{Position value}}{\text{Total portfolio market value}}\right) \times \text{Underlying return}$$

The contribution of the long Global Gold Miners ETF instrument is calculated as

Contribution of Global Gold Miners ETF = $5 million/$41 million × 2.35% = 0.29%.

The contribution of the short Global Silver Miners ETF instrument is calculated as

Contribution of Global Silver Miners ETF = –$5 million/$41 million × (–1.59%) = 0.19%.

The swap's contribution to return is the sum of the contributions of its long and short instruments: Total contribution = 0.29% + 0.19% = 0.48%.

33 A is correct. The swap's overall contribution to return is the sum of the contributions of its individual long and short instruments.

In both years, returns are based on $5 million instruments, but the net asset value is different:

At swap initiation, the portfolio had an NAV of $41 million.

$$\text{Year 1 contribution} = \frac{\$5 \text{ million} \times 2.35\% + (-5 \text{ million} \times -1.59\%)}{\$41 \text{ million}}$$

$$= 0.48\%$$

Smith computes the increase in NAV at the end of Year 1 as $3.4 million, so the NAV was $44.4 million

$$\text{Year 2 contribution} = \frac{\$5 \text{ million} \times 4.79\% + (-5 \text{ million} \times 0.85\%)}{\$44.4 \text{ million}}$$

$$= 0.44\%$$

Therefore, the overall contribution to return of adding the swap to Portfolio C is greater in Year 1

34 A is correct. During the month, the local market value of Brazilian stocks increased from R$24 million to R$26 million, leading to net unhedged Brazilian real exposure.

Step 1. Compute the total hedged return:

Total hedged return = Base currency return + Overlay return

$$\text{Base currency return of Brazilian stocks} = \frac{26/3.2550}{24/3.1250} - 1 = 4.01\%$$

At the end of the month, the profit of the currency overlay in US dollars is calculated as follows:

Profit = 24/3.1155 – 24/3.2550 = 0.3301 million

Starting US dollar value of Brazilian stocks = 24/3.1250 = 7.68 million

Overlay return = 0.3301/7.68 = 4.30%

Total hedged return = 4.01% + 4.30% = 8.31%

Step 2. Compute the perfectly hedged return:

Perfectly hedged return = (1 + Local return) × (1 + Forward premium) − 1

Local return = 26/24 − 1 = 8.33%

The forward premium for the Brazilian real against the US dollar is calculated as

Forward premium = $F_0/S_0 - 1$.

The one-month forward rate (F_0) of the Brazilian real against the US dollar (USD/BRL) is

(F_0) = 1/3.1155 = 0.3210

The spot rate (S_0) of the Brazilian real against the US dollar (USD/BRL) is

(S_0) = 1/3.1250 = 0.3200

Forward premium = 0.3210/0.3200 − 1 = 0.31%

Perfectly hedged return = (1 + 8.33%) × (1 + 0.30%) − 1 = 8.67%

Step 3. Compare the total hedged return vs the perfectly hedged return:

8.31% is less than 8.67%

READING

4

Topics in Data Integrity

by Marc. A. Wright, CFA

Marc. A. Wright, CFA, is at Russell Investments (USA).

LEARNING OUTCOMES	
Mastery	*The candidate should be able to:*
☐	a. explain common causes of performance discrepancies between the investment manager and the custodian;
☐	b. explain common causes of performance discrepancies between NAV-based performance and end-of-day time-weighted performance;
☐	c. describe best practices for maintaining composite data in order to ensure the composite provides a reliable representation of the investment strategy.

INTRODUCTION

Given their exposure to questions of performance and analytics, CIPM candidates understand that calculating returns involves approximation. "Upstream" data flows come in different varieties, and their nature affects how the performance of funds and fund managers are ultimately represented. True performance can be elusive for even the most diligent manager.

Professionalism calls for an understanding of the ambiguities of data, particularly within the financial data that drive performance measurement. The list of issues we cover here is not exhaustive; hundreds of decisions and approximations come into play. By building an awareness of these data dependencies and their impact, we may boost our analytical expertise. Sometimes the data pitfalls are evident, allowing us to be transparent with investors and other consumers of our investment performance metrics. Other times the challenges are not explicit, requiring us to approach performance results with increased caution.

We start by examining discrepancies between the performance calculated by the investment manager and the performance calculated by the custodian; often, the discrepancies are legitimate and inform how we communicate returns. We then turn to discrepancies between NAV-based performance and end-of-day time-weighted performance. Finally, we examine the data issues that arise in the management of and reporting on composites, and we describe best practices for maintaining composite data.

© 2020 CFA Institute. All rights reserved.

2 PERFORMANCE DISCREPANCIES: INVESTMENT MANAGER VS. CUSTODIAN

Even for a given fund or portfolio, different stakeholders have their own hopes for the story that the numbers will tell. The official performance figures, however, are typically measured by a third party, frequently the investment custodian. Even if stakeholders' intentions are aligned, whenever two or more parties measure the performance of the same fund, discrepancies may arise.

Candidates should be familiar with those discrepancies and be able to elaborate on why differences in performance appear. Here we consider seven of the most common causes of discrepancies between the returns generated by investment managers and their custodians. Note that there are many other possible causes, including the choice of performance methodology and cash flow weighting, which are addressed elsewhere in the CIPM curriculum.

Exhibit 1 shows the performance numbers for a hypothetical portfolio generated by the investment manager and the custodian for the first two weeks of July. We will use this table of return discrepancies throughout our discussion as we examine possible data-driven explanations for those differences.

Exhibit 1   Performance for Portfolio ABC

Date	Investment Manager (%)	Custodian (%)	Difference (%)
1 Jul	2.40	2.46	−0.06
2 Jul	0.08	0.07	0.01
3 Jul	−0.25	−0.22	−0.03
4 Jul	−0.11	−0.12	0.01
5 Jul	−0.39	−0.37	−0.02
8 Jul	−0.90	−0.92	0.02
9 Jul	0.91	0.91	0.00
10 Jul	0.52	0.50	0.02
11 Jul	1.01	0.99	0.02
12 Jul	−2.10	−2.12	0.02

2.1 Pricing

We obtain market prices to measure the values of the individual components of a portfolio, and every security has multiple pricing sources. Even at a given point in time, different sources may offer different prices. The differences tend to be larger for less liquid securities, such as corporate bonds, structured products, and shares listed in some less developed markets.

As performance-measurement practitioners, our familiarity with the sources of our pricing information is important. We need to understand which sources are used to derive the market values of our portfolios. We also need to be sensitive to potential timing differences and to the impact of different securities' markets on those prices. A price, after all, is merely the amount that two or more parties agreed to buy or sell a particular security at a particular time. The investment manager has its own unique or non-standard pricing (choice of bid/ask/mid/end prices or broker price). In addition, pricing vendors provide prices for illiquid assets using model valuation rather than basing prices on actual trades.

In order to provide services to their various clients, investment custodians negotiate with pricing vendors for data and in turn use that data to calculate the value of their clients' holdings. These arrangements typically mean that custodians use only a few sources for pricing all of the securities in their book. Meanwhile, investment managers have their own pricing sources, which may differ from the custodian's chosen pricing vendors. Discrepancies between the performance results calculated by the investment manager and the custodian inevitably result.

Any third party the investment manager relies on for daily performance metrics will also source its own prices, of course. Let's compare the performance provided by a third-party performance provider to those of the investment manager's custodian in Exhibit 1.

If the headline portfolio performance numbers differ, a review of the pricing discrepancies in individual holdings may reveal the cause of the portfolio-level discrepancy. We know from Exhibit 1 that there is a difference of 6 basis points on 1 July between what the investment manager reported and what the custodian reported. Exhibit 2 shows us example pricing differences in three select holdings out of the more than one hundred holdings in Portfolio ABC. Differences in the reported prices of individual holdings may or may not introduce significant differences in the reported portfolio performance.

Exhibit 2   1 July Prices of Portfolio ABC Select Holdings (in $)

Security	Performance Provider	Custodian	Difference
Microsoft	135.68	135.71	−0.03
Nestlé	102.14	101.99	0.15
Toyota	125.79	125.78	0.01

The practitioner could seek to reproduce the calculations of the two providers, but that would require both an understanding of their methodologies and the processing of additional data (e.g., number of holdings, previous day prices, transactions). Rather than attempting to reproduce the performance calculated by the two different providers, a practitioner would likely ask both parties to confirm that the prices agree with their pricing policy. If a pricing data policy exists, the performance provider may be asked to change pricing to match the policy (or possibly make an exception) and recalculate performance for that day. More frequently practitioners will need to 1) understand the reasons for the discrepancy (e.g., pricing differences between the vendors, different methodologies), 2) document the discrepancy, 3) implement controls to alert to those discrepancies, and 4) communicate those discrepancies, as needed, to all consumers of the performance reports.

In Exhibit 3, we see that the custodian calculates the portfolio's ending market value to be $128,201,291, which is $72,909 higher than the investment manager's calculation. Upon investigation, the performance measurement analyst found that the source of the ending market value (EMV) discrepancy was the difference of 3 cents in the reported price of Microsoft. While the pricing discrepancy was greater for the Nestlé holding at 15 cents, the investment manager's position in Nestlé was much smaller than its holding in Microsoft (position weights not shown); thus, the contribution of the Microsoft position to the overall discrepancy at the portfolio level was much greater.

Exhibit 3   Impact of Pricing Differences on Performance for 1 July

Portfolio ABC	Investment Manager	Custodian	Difference (manager − custodian)
Beginning market value	$125,128,400	$125,127,951	$449
Ending market value	$128,128,382	$128,201,291	−$72,909
Return	2.40%	2.46%	−0.06%

Note: We assume there are no inflows or outflows from the portfolio.

2.2 Missing trades

The measurement of performance is also impacted by trading. The omission of a trade in the calculation of a position can have a significant impact on reported performance, and missing trades occur frequently. For example, custodians typically insist on daily cutoff times by which they must receive all trade data from the manager in order to be included in that day's performance calculations. If certain trades come in too late, those trades will not be included in the performance calculations.

Consider the example where a fund manager hires a sub-adviser to manage part or all of the fund. The sub-adviser typically sends all of their trades to both the custodian and the investment manager. In this example, the sub-adviser prepares different trade feeds, one to match the custodian's required format and the other to meet the requirements of the fund managers. Two separate feeds—and processes to generate those feeds—introduce the possibility that trades (or other data) provided in one are missing from the other.

In both of these examples, missing trades affect the calculation of performance return. The impact may be non-material, but a discrepancy will be introduced nonetheless.

Referring to Exhibit 1, we know there's a return discrepancy of 1 basis point at the portfolio level on 4 July. Upon investigation, the performance analyst learns that a single trade was not reported to the custodian that day, as shown in Exhibit 4. The custodian missed a purchase of a security (one of many transactions that took place that day) in the amount of $223,569, impacting both the amount of trades as well as the change in the cash balance. The asset in question increased in value after it was bought, so the value reflected in the custodian's book was lower at the EMV as the custodian was unaware the trade had taken place. As such, the EMV calculated by the custodian was lower than the EMV calculated by the investment manager by $19,569. The impact to the portfolio return was 1 basis point lower: 0.12% for the custodian versus 0.11% for the investment manager.

In practice, the trade was likely processed by the custodian the following day and backdated so that performance could be recalculated and the discrepancy resolved.

Exhibit 4   Trade Not Reported

Portfolio ABC	Investment Manager	Custodian	Difference (manager − custodian)
Beginning market value	$130,128,119	$130,128,101	$18
Trades	$2,551,678	$2,328,109	$223,569
Cash	−$2,551,678	−$2,328,109	−$223,569

Exhibit 4 (Continued)

Portfolio ABC	Investment Manager	Custodian	Difference (manager − custodian)
Ending market value	$129,984,978	$129,965,409	$19,569
Return	−0.11%	−0.12%	0.01%

Notes: We assume there are no inflows or outflows from the portfolio. Numbers are rounded.

2.3 Missing and mistimed cash flows

Custodians record all movements of cash into and out of the fund. Tracking cash flow underpins the fund accounting services that custodians often provide and their role in holding the **Accounting Book of Record (ABOR)** for those funds. ABOR is an official accounting record, as explained later.

Because custodians typically manage the flows of cash with investors and other parties, it is not uncommon for an investment manager to miss a flow in or out of the fund; operational shortfalls, technological errors, and poor documentation may also come into play. Performance numbers are affected by missed cash flows in a manner proportional to the size of the missed flow.

Timing differences are frequently the source of discrepancies. The custodian and investment manager may record cash flows on different dates, for instance, whether intentionally or not. It may be the practice of a custodian to account for the cash flow on the settlement date—when the cash is actually moved—while the investment manager records the trade and a change in the cash account on the day the trade takes place (i.e., the trade date). Responsible practitioners are aware of these timing differences and are equipped to make the relevant adjustments.

2.4 Corporate actions

Most corporate actions—including stock splits, mergers, acquisitions, spinoffs, and the issuance of dividends and bonuses—impact the calculation of performance. Any failure to track them correctly, or neglecting timing differences between the custodian and investment manager, will result in performance discrepancies.

Because custodians work with so many financial institutions, they necessarily track corporate action information for most securities. Investment managers, on the other hand, may dedicate limited resources to the costly, data-intensive process of maintaining a complete awareness of corporate actions; the official book of record, after all, is usually maintained by the custodian. Any corporate actions missed by the investment manager could lead to a discrepancy, but even if all parties recognize the corporate action when it happens, it may be processed differently or incorrectly by either party.

Consider the scenario in Exhibit 5, where a dividend is not processed by the custodian. In this instance, the custodian has missed one or more dividend payments totaling $29,882, resulting in an EMV that is lower than the investment manager's by that amount. The impact on the return is 2 basis points. Good practice calls for performance measurement staff to consider how material the impact is and to make any changes based on the investment manager firm's revision policies.

Exhibit 5	Dividend Not Processed		
Portfolio ABC	**Investment Manager**	**Custodian**	**Difference**
Beginning market value	$133,891,002	$133,890,972	$30
Trades	$5,997,284	$5,997,284	$0
Cash	−$5,465,383	−$5,495,265	$29,882
Dividends	$531,901	$502,019	$29,882
Ending market value	$131,081,225	$131,051,343	$29,882
Return	−2.10%	−2.12%	0.02%

Note: We assume there are no inflows or outflows from the portfolio.

2.5 Exchange rate data

When practitioners calculate market values or express performance metrics in different currencies, the exchange-rate differences create discrepancies. Because exchange rates change constantly, many analysts choose to use standard published rates, such as the WM/Reuters, for performance measurement and portfolio evaluation. But these standard rates, fixed at a specific time of day for a specific vendor, may introduce differences from the rates quoted by different exchanges or at different times of day.

2.6 Missing or incorrect terms and conditions

The presence of derivative securities and currency forwards in a portfolio introduces further scope for discrepancies. The terms and conditions associated with over-the-counter (OTC) derivatives are necessary for correctly valuing them and measuring exposures, but such information is often costly to obtain and not provided automatically to custodians, which limits their ability to measure the impact on performance. They must weigh the extra cost of the additional data against the extra precision they may obtain. In some circumstances, the extra precision may be required by the regulators. Currency forwards also introduce scope for discrepancies, as they are not priced by outside vendors. Instead, they are priced by internal systems that investment managers and custodians use.

2.7 Expenses and fees

Performance can be calculated net of taxes and management fees. Fees differ with each client. Here, too, we face the possibility of generating discrepancies; custodians and investment managers may specify or apply fees in divergent ways.

2.8 Summary

This section reviewed some of the possible discrepancies that may arise between the investment manager and their custodian in the calculation of performance. Practitioners, particularly fund managers, need to be aware of these discrepancies. Firms should implement controls and operational practices that alert data managers to discrepancies so that the most material differences can be addressed before asset owners review the performance figures. Written plans that address discrepancies within sensible tolerance values are an important part of best practice.

Performance Discrepancies: Investment Manager vs. Custodian

Most important, practitioners must always remember that returns are the product of multiple sets of data, any of which may give rise to discrepancies. As a result, they must be able to articulate the accuracy of the returns based on the known and potentially unknown issues.

> **EXAMPLE 1 PERFORMANCE DISCREPANCIES**
>
> Carnara Investment Management has recently hired Panos as a junior performance analyst. Panos is reviewing the past month of daily performance reports for a portfolio, with performance metrics calculated both by the custodian and Carnara. The portfolio has a buy-and-hold mandate and tends to hold some dividend paying, illiquid securities. Panos has a few questions for his manager, Roberta, who has managed the performance team at Carnara for the past eight years.
>
> Panos notices that most of the daily returns calculated internally and by the custodian are within 1 basis point of each other, except for yesterday's performance. Yesterday, Carnara calculated a return of 1.29% for the fund in question, while the custodian calculated 1.47%. Panos asks Roberta about the potential causes of the discrepancy.
>
> **Question 1**
>
> Based on the holdings of the portfolio, to help Panos identify the source of the discrepancy, Roberta should suggest that the *least likely* sources of discrepancy are:
>
> **A** corporate actions.
>
> **B** pricing differences.
>
> **C** missing trades.
>
> **Question 2**
>
> Roberta also tells Panos she just heard from the portfolio manager for a different mandate that information about one of the day's trades (a sale) was not sent to the custodian in time to be included in yesterday's performance report. What should Panos's response be?
>
> **A** Conclude the search because the missing trade should explain the difference.
>
> **B** Find out the amount of the missing trade and calculate the likely impact of the missing trade on performance to see if that trade explains the difference.
>
> **C** Base the materiality of the missing trade on the security's transaction price from the end-of-day closing price.
>
> **Question 3**
>
> Along with yesterday's performance report, a summary of corporate actions from the same day comes across Panos's desk. The summary lists stock splits and dividends for 20 different securities across the entire universe of portfolios that the firm manages. Panos asks Roberta if any of those corporate actions could impact performance, and he seeks her advice about what to do next. What is most likely to be the best advice Roberta should offer Panos regarding the corporate actions summary report?
>
> **A** Disregard the summary report because it only includes stock splits and dividends and does not impact performance.

B Obtain a list of security holdings for the portfolio in question, and reference them against the list of 20 securities on the summary report.

C Go through each security on the summary report to determine its impact on performance.

Solution to 1

C is correct. Since the mandate is a buy and hold, it is unlikely that there would be any trading that wasn't directed by the client.

A is incorrect because corporate actions may be a source of discrepancy. These securities may pay dividends, which is a corporate action.

B is incorrect because pricing differences between the manager and the custodian may arise, particularly as there are illiquid securities in the portfolio.

Solution to 2

B is correct. Given the information from Roberta, Panos should investigate whether or not the missing trade explains the difference in the performance report. If it does not, or if it does not explain it completely, Panos should continue to investigate other possible causes.

A is incorrect because the missing trade may or may not explain the difference.

C is incorrect because materiality cannot be solely based on the security's price movement. The portfolio weight of the security is also needed to judge what the impact would be.

Solution to 3

B is correct. Panos should determine if any of the securities covered by the corporate actions summary are actually held in the portfolio. If not, there is no further action to take because yesterday's corporate actions would then be irrelevant to portfolio performance. If there were corporate actions involving holdings in the portfolio, Panos should determine their impact, if any.

A is incorrect because stock splits and dividends *can* impact performance.

C is incorrect because there is no need for Panos to research corporate actions relating to securities that may not be held in the portfolio.

3. PERFORMANCE DISCREPANCIES: NAV-BASED VS. END-OF-DAY TIME-WEIGHTED PERFORMANCE

The net asset value (NAV) of a fund represents the net value, or total assets minus total liabilities, at a given point in time. Fund NAVs are usually calculated by the custodian or administrator once per day and are then used to calculate daily performance. The NAV performance is often the performance measure that is entered into a fund's book of record. NAV-based returns frequently differ from another standard measure, end-of-day time-weighted performance, as we will show. First, we need to explain the two different sets of accounting data.

3.1 ABOR vs. IBOR

Most investment managers are provided with an official set of accounting records, typically calculated by a custodian or administrator, which cover the day's activity. This **Accounting Book of Record (ABOR)** collects all the pertinent daily investment data at a single point in time, the "cutoff" time, including pricing and exchange rates. The data contained in the ABOR are used to value portfolios and to generate NAVs and NAV-based performance metrics. The calculation of risk, portfolio exposures, performance relative to benchmark, and price at which units of mutualized products are created or redeemed may also depend on the ABOR figures. ABOR figures are used for public consumption and are fed into peer group databases for comparative purposes.

Many investment managers, however, create a separate set of data for trading and portfolio-management purposes called the **Investment Book of Record (IBOR)**. The figures recorded there are typically timelier (from the perspective of the fund manager's working hours) than those found in the ABOR. If the ABOR's figures are calculated at the end of the previous day, for instance, the IBOR's figures may be updated overnight to include the latest trades, corporate actions, pricing updates, and exchange rates for a more accurate picture of the portfolio at the start of the next trading day. Alternatively, if the ABOR cutoff time is at midday, the fund managers may wish to see the end-of-day returns given by IBOR cutoff in the evening. IBOR may be calculated once or multiple times throughout the day to reflect ongoing activity and market movements. Thus, performance returns generated with ABOR data frequently differ from those generated with IBOR data. Practitioners need to be aware of these differences

3.2 NAV calculation

Consider Exhibit 6. The basic calculation of NAV involves summing the assets (securities + receivables + cash and cash equivalents + accrued income) and subtracting the sum of the liabilities (short-term + long-term + accrued expenses). The net value is then divided by the number of outstanding shares to calculate the NAV per share. Any balance-sheet item could be the source of differences between the time-weighted performance and the NAV performance figures.

Exhibit 6   Sample NAV

Portfolio ABC	29 July	30 July
Securities	$130,000,000	$124,000,000
Receivables	$4,200,000	$5,800,000
Cash and cash equivalents	$6,000,000	$7,200,000
Accrued income	$175,000	$176,000
Short-term liabilities	$11,500,000	$11,900,000
Long-term liabilities	$2,830,000	$2,900,000
Accrued expenses	$15,000	$18,000
NAV total	$126,030,000	$122,358,000
Shares outstanding	7,500,000	7,350,000
NAV per share/unit	$16.80	$16.65
NAV return		−0.89%

3.3 Timing differences

Among the most common sources for discrepancies in the reporting of ABOR-based NAV vs. the IBOR-based returns is timing. NAVs are calculated at the cutoff time—once a day—usually mandated by the regulations that apply to the fund in question (for example, at midday or 1 pm). Alternatively, in some regions the mandated cutoff time may be after markets close in the late afternoon (for example, 5pm). The difference between the cutoff times for the NAV calculation differ from the IBOR time-weighted calculation because:

- the company manages a fund that is administered or domiciled on a different region or time zone,
- the company manages a fund that is partly or fully invested in a different region or time zone, or
- it is convenient to produce IBOR time-weighted returns whose cutoff differs from the NAV cutoff time.

In fact, a whole range of circumstances may arise. Here is one such example: a US-based fund management company manages a UK-domiciled mutual fund, with MSCI World Index exposure and administered out of Luxembourg, that uses a closing time of 5pm or 6pm GMT, which is prior to the US market closing and well before the time-weighted returns are calculated by the fund manager.

If the cutoff time for NAV calculation purposes is not the same as the cutoff for time-weighted performance calculation, differences in performance arise for a number of reasons, including the following:

- Prices of portfolio holdings will change between the two points in time. For example, most prices used for a 1pm NAV calculation will be different compared to those used for a 6pm cutoff time-weighted calculation.
- Exchange rates will change between the two points in time. If exchange rates are required to calculate returns, the rates used will vary at different times of the day.
- Portfolio holdings may change. For example, if Fund ABC's mandated cutoff time is 1pm, the NAV calculations, as shown in Exhibit 7, include all portfolio trades received before that time. If time-weighted performance is computed at 6pm, it will also include trade data relating to transactions that occurred between 1pm and 6pm. That trade data was not available at the 1pm NAV cutoff time. So if the fund manager traded a particular security holding at around 2pm, the trade details could not be included in the NAV calculation for that day. The time-weighted return, calculated later in the day, *would* include the trade.

Performance Discrepancies: NAV-Based vs. End-of-Day Time-Weighted Performance

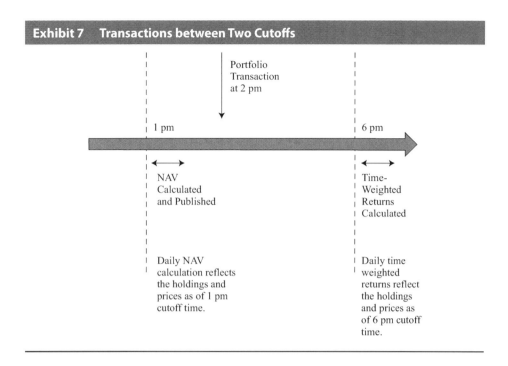

Exhibit 7   Transactions between Two Cutoffs

In addition to different prices and holdings used for return calculations at different times of the day, differences due to timing may also arise when transactions close to the cutoff times (e.g., 1pm in Exhibit 7) are not communicated to the custodian quickly enough to be captured in the NAV calculation. For example, the fund manager traded at 12:50pm, and NAV (reflecting prices and holdings at 1pm) is calculated soon after the time of the transaction; thus, the information about the trade may not reach the custodian in time to be reflected in the NAV calculation, as Exhibit 8 shows. This may happen for a variety of reasons, such as a time period of heavy trading activity.

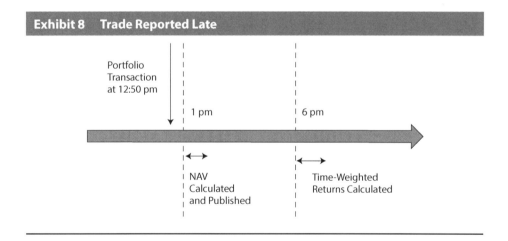

Exhibit 8   Trade Reported Late

3.4 Fees, charges, and other data points

Many data points are used to calculate NAVs as well as time-weighted returns. Although we do not go into detail here, several items that may cause discrepancies are worth noting. NAV calculations include pending receipts from debtors; management fees and, if applicable, performance fees that the investment manager charges; legal costs; operating costs and distribution charges; and foreign liabilities, such as sale proceeds pending repatriation. The timing of fees may vary between the one applied by the custodians or administrators who calculate the NAV and the fund manager calculating the time-weighted end-of-day returns. For example, the manager may not accrue management fees on a daily basis. Practitioners measuring performance will need to understand their client's particular situation and which fees and charges should be included or excluded from a particular return calculation.

EXAMPLE 2 PERFORMANCE DISCREPANCIES

Packwood Asset Management recently hired a middle-office outsourcing firm to provide IBOR time-weighted returns, calculated twice a day, to be used alongside Packwood's official NAV (based on ABOR), itself created by Packwood's custodian. All official returns for Packwood's funds are calculated from the ABOR NAVs, which are calculated at the close of business in the evening at 6pm. The middle-office outsourcing firm calculates time-weighted performance using the IBOR data at times that do not match the NAV cutoff times, one later in the day at 8pm (shown in Exhibit 9) and then another in the morning at 8am.

Pradeep, a performance analyst at Packwood, uses the following table (Exhibit 9) containing NAV-based and IBOR-based returns to explain the performance of portfolio ABC, which is invested in securities around the world, to Hannah, the portfolio manager.

Exhibit 9   Daily Returns for Portfolio ABC

Date	NAV (ABOR) Return	IBOR End-of-Day Return	Difference
1 Aug 2019	1.08	1.02	0.06
2 Aug 2019	0.97	0.98	−0.01
5 Aug 2019	−1.01	−1.21	0.20
6 Aug 2019	−0.55	−0.60	0.05
7 Aug 2019	0.39	0.25	0.14
8 Aug 2019	−1.21	−1.01	−0.20
9 Aug 2019	0.72	0.78	−0.06
12 Aug 2019	0.29	0.37	−0.08

Pradeep makes the following statement:

"Possible explanations for the observed performance discrepancies are the differences in cutoff times leading to different prices and exchange rates being used, the possibility that trades were executed after the NAV cutoff times, as well as different treatment of fees and charges."

Question 1

Is the statement correct?

A Yes.

B No, because trades that take place after the NAV is calculated do not make a difference to performance for that day.

C No. Treatment of fees and charges is agreed in advance between the two parties.

Question 2

Although the NAV performance is the official performance measure for Portfolio ABC, why might Hannah prefer to use the IBOR-based returns?

A The IBOR-based returns are based on more up-to-date information from the fund manager's perspective.

B Packwood uses end-of-day, IBOR-based, time-weighted returns as the official-book-of-record returns.

C The IBOR-based returns can be more readily compared to other funds in its universe via a peer group database.

Solution to 1

A is correct. All of the reasons mentioned in the statement could explain the discrepancies in the table. B is incorrect because trades that take place after the NAV cutoff time will still impact that day's IBOR end-of-day return. C is incorrect because the parties are likely to apply fees and charges in different ways reflecting different circumstances.

Solution to 2

A is correct. IBOR returns will include trades that are recorded after the NAV cutoff time, whereas the NAV performance is limited to a strict cutoff time. B is incorrect because Packwood uses NAV-based returns for the official book of record, not the IBOR-based returns. C is incorrect because ABOR-based returns are available to the public and are provided to peer group databases for comparison.

4. MAINTENANCE OF COMPOSITE DATA

A **composite** is an aggregation of one or more portfolios that a firm manages according to a similar investment mandate, objective, or strategy. Its design and maintenance requirements raise data-integrity challenges and issues of best practice.

4.1 Data issues affecting composites

Managing composites calls for a large volume of data that the **composite system** (the set of processes, tools, and equipment that underpins it) must be able to handle. Performance data must be available in the correct format for potentially hundreds of portfolios over many time periods. In addition, the disclosures required for reporting purposes include items that may not be automatically covered by the composite management system. For example, information about **discretion**, the ability of a firm to implement its intended strategy, needs to be provided and documented. Clients may impose a number of restrictions on what the fund managers can do, which would make the fund non-discretionary. But it is a requirement that every portfolio that is discretionary be included in a composite.

In addition to the these challenges, firms often use composites that are made up of different fund types. For example, they may include separately managed, segregated client portfolios (sometimes referred to as "segregated accounts"). The same composites may also include mutualized or pooled portfolios. Separate client accounts are often subject to performance-impacting items booked to the account. Yet those items are not the investment manager's responsibility. They might include fees paid to entities, such as custodians, or may include lending income. In addition, management fees may be treated differently in different fund types. Adjustments for all such items on each of those client portfolios are required before the portfolio returns can be included in the composite return calculation.

Data challenges with composites may be viewed with reference to certain dimensions of data integrity—namely, accuracy, completeness, conformity, and timeliness. Exhibit 10 explores these dimensions.

Exhibit 10   Data Integrity and Composites

Data Integrity Dimensions	Issues with Composites
Accuracy: Are the data valid and correct?	The system for managing composites must be able to generate all data that are required to calculate composite returns and provide disclosures. Examples: ■ The system must avoid double counting total firm assets in case fund-of-funds products are invested in the firm's own portfolios. ■ The system must accurately maintain information on discretionary and non-discretionary status of portfolios. ■ Changes made by the client to the strategy or mandate of a particular portfolio may require a change to the composite as the portfolio is moved from one composite to another. Accounting for the timing of the switch incorrectly could distort the returns reported for the two composites.
Completeness: Are the data sufficiently complete for the intended purpose?	Completeness requirements apply to both performance data and additional disclosures. Examples: ■ The performance data of all the portfolios that make up the composite should be available in the system. The standard deviation of composite returns over three years is commonly required. Missing returns on any one of the portfolios in a composite may make the disclosure of an accurate standard deviation calculation impossible. ■ Details on discretion and disclosures compose a form of information that is required but difficult to standardize. ■ A full and fair set of information must be available to explain why a portfolio is not assigned to a composite.
Conformity: Do the data conform to standards and rules?	■ The composition of composites should be covered by an appropriate allocation rule or by definitions formulated by the GIPS committee (explained later). In some cases, the setup of composites or the existing composite management system will not fulfill all GIPS requirements. A manual solution may be required.
Timeliness: Are the data available in time for use, and are they updated regularly?	■ Portfolios should be assigned to a composite in a timely manner. ■ Additional disclosures (such as those on discretion status) should be available in a timely manner.

4.2 Best practices in composite construction and maintenance

The composite construction process impacts several departments in an asset management firm, but it particularly affects the operational staff responsible for integrity and maintenance of the data that supports the composites. The needs of various stakeholders will directly inform GIPS composite construction policies, the required frequency of review, and the types and quality of data required to manage the composite membership and reporting. The GIPS standards provide a framework and rules for constructing composites. Assisted by the standards, practitioners can navigate potential conflicts of interest. The degree of flexibility and judgment allowed by the GIPS standards encourages composites designed in line with the investment strategies of the firm and the way that the firm presents itself to prospective clients. We outline the best practices next.

4.2.1 GIPS committee

Instead of seeking sign-off on composite construction from all stakeholders, best practice is to establish a GIPS committee that consists of different stakeholders. The committee should be responsible for setting out and maintaining firm policies and procedures regarding composites. Best practice includes defining a composite structure that reflects the investment strategy and the requirements of the stakeholders. Decisions around new portfolios, such as allocating them to existing composites or to setting up new ones, should be the responsibility of the GIPS committee. The committee should meet regularly to discuss composite maintenance.

The following departments would expect representation on the GIPS committee:

- portfolio accounting & administration
- performance measurement
- product management
- information technology
- risk management
- legal & compliance

The GIPS committee may include representatives from the sales & marketing team or the investment decision makers themselves, the portfolio managers. Neither the composite system nor its policies, however, should be driven by marketing needs, market conditions, or the wish to display investment performance in the best light for marketing purposes. Instead, the system is to be designed so that the composites accurately reflect the performance of the firm's investment strategies.

4.2.2 Recommended best practices

In general, practitioners will favor minimizing the amount of data required to maintain composites (all other factors being equal) and limiting how often portfolios are moved into and out of composites (unless documented changes to a portfolio's investment mandate, objective, or strategy, or the redefinition of the composite, makes switching appropriate). Best practice, in addition to having a GIPS committee in place, calls on the practitioner to:

Understand the needs of the entire organization and obtain their support. By creating composites, firms have an opportunity to create policies and procedures that clearly define how the firm generates the data that goes into the construction of composites. For example, a firm might include a policy to establish the minimum asset levels for portfolios to be included or excluded from the composites. The firm should then implement data controls to monitor those asset levels and create alerts when portfolio asset levels in composites are approaching the minimum levels. Ultimately, properly implemented controls improve the quality and timeliness of data for all stakeholders.

Avoid composite definitions that are too broad or too narrow. Composite maintenance can be onerous if definitions are not thoughtfully designed. A very narrow definition of composites (i.e., one that is necessarily very detailed because the investment process for the composite is complicated or highly customized) leads to the formation of many more composites and a lot of extra maintenance work, including moving portfolios in and out and managing all the associated data requirements. According to best practice, composites reflect actual measurable mandates that are reflective of the investment process. A definition of composites that is too broad, on the other hand, may lead to large magnitudes of return dispersion within the composite. A balance needs to be found whereby composites reflect true distinctions in the investment process without being so narrowly focused as to create additional data maintenance responsibilities and increased operational risk. Exhibit 11 illustrates such considerations in a fictitious firm.

EXHIBIT 11 ABC INVESTMENT MANAGEMENT

ABC Investment Management (ABC AM) is a global equity manager with a focus on security selection. ABC's product suite includes region-specific portfolios covering North America, EMEA, APAC, and other emerging and frontier markets. It offers products with different market capitalizations (small-cap, mid-cap, and large-cap) in each region. ABC AM has completed its initial GIPS composite definitions ahead of marketing its investment strategy to institutional clients. One composite has been labeled the Emerging Markets Composite and was defined to reflect any portfolio that holds more than 95% of its assets in emerging-market countries. Applying this definition, ABC AM calculates the following results:

Manager ABC's Emerging Markets Equities Composite

Year	Total Return (Gross of Fees)	Total Return (Net of Fees)	Composite Benchmark Return (%)	Number of Portfolios	Dispersion (%)	Total Composite Assets
2014	3.22	1.95	−2.55	347	0.89	$709,128,901
2015	2.10	−0.05	−2.22	422	0.92	$743,002,945
2016	−16.01	−17.99	−15.01	409	0.94	$751,902,811
2017	14.29	12.16	11.31	413	0.86	$702,902,694
2018	39.58	37.22	38.29	461	0.83	$797,182,981
2019	−10.11	−12.37	−14.51	444	0.90	$761,902,638

The initial composite definition results in a rather large dispersion (as shown in the "Dispersion" column and measured by the equal-weighted standard deviation of returns), indicating a large amount of variance across the portfolio returns within the composite.

In this instance, the manager finds that this broad composite definition, which focuses exclusively on what region the assets are in (emerging markets, in this case), ignores the different market-cap focus of the various portfolios, limiting the composite's usefulness. Within this composite some portfolios are weighted much more heavily to small-cap stocks, others to larger-cap stocks.

Instead, the manager tries a narrower definition, redefining the composite to differentiate for market cap. This change creates a Large-Cap Emerging Market Equities Composite. The definition stipulates that 95% of the assets are in emerging-market countries *and* 70% of its securities have a market cap greater than USD5 billion. The results for this new composite definition are shown in Exhibit 12, where we see a much lower dispersion of returns within the composite. We can expect the other composites that include the remaining portfolios, the Small-Cap Emerging Market Equities Composite and the Mid-Cap Emerging Market Equities Composite (not shown here), to also show lower amounts of dispersion.

Exhibit 12 Manager ABC's Large-Cap Emerging Market Equities Composite

Year	Total Return (Gross of Fees)	Total Return (Net of Fees)	Composite Benchmark Return (%)	Number of Portfolios	Dispersion (%)	Total Composite Assets
2014	2.81	1.89	−2.05	243	0.43	$567,303,121
2015	−1.85	−0.16	−1.82	309	0.72	$594,402,356
2016	−15.59	−17.12	−14.95	302	0.52	$601,522,249
2017	14.04	12.47	12.91	341	0.68	$562,322,155
2018	38.99	36.82	38.93	352	0.63	$637,746,385
2019	−11.08	−13.05	−14.45	376	0.59	$609,522,110

The manager thus decides to include market cap as part of the new, narrower composite definition. Although more data are required to calculate and present the results, the narrower composite definition better fits with the manager's investment process and results in lower dispersion.

Define discretion with measurable criteria. Every discretionary portfolio must be included in a composite. Note that discretion is the ability of a firm to implement its intended strategy. Client-imposed restrictions, such as a ban on purchases of certain stocks or the requirement for pre-approval on trades, may interfere with the implementation of the intended strategy. In those cases, the portfolios are not representative of the strategy and are therefore considered non-discretionary. A sensible practice, and a requirement of the GIPS standards, is for the firm's GIPS policies and procedures to include its definition of discretion. Firms need to complete discretionary reviews on a regular basis for *all* fee-paying portfolios, not only for those already included in composites. It is difficult to automate information about the discretionary/non-discretionary nature of individual portfolios. Nevertheless, such information must be available, monitored, and refreshed—requiring manual processes.

No new portfolio can be classified without review, as stated in the GIPS standards, Guidance Statement on Composite Definition: "Few of these [client-imposed] restrictions are reason to automatically classify a portfolio as non-discretionary, as the firm must determine if the restriction will significantly hinder the implementation of the intended strategy." As such, enough time should be allowed both to thoroughly review and reconcile internal records to those from custodians, administrators, or other parties—to confirm the discretionary status and thus allocate the portfolio to the appropriate composite.

Consider the future evolution of the investment process. In general, the GIPS standards recommend that changes to the investment strategy of a particular portfolio will require either creating a new composite or switching the portfolio to an existing but different composite. Where possible, practitioners should anticipate the evolution of their investment process, creating enough space in the composite definitions to allow for some change. Practitioners should also include large grace periods in their policies and procedures, specifying a workable amount of time allowed before a new portfolio must be added to a composite. Lastly, policies and processes put in place should anticipate issues that may arise in the future, and if such need arises, should allow for modifications to individual composite definitions.

> **EXAMPLE 3 COMPOSITE PORTFOLIOS**
>
> Helen, a performance analyst at Clayton Investment Management, is working with her manager, Norah, to define the composites for Clayton. Clayton manages only fixed-income portfolios, specializing in government bonds. They have 1,430 portfolios under management—900 invested in either developed or emerging markets and 530 blended with bonds from developed and emerging countries that are tailored for individual clients.
>
> ### Question 1
>
> Helen is concerned about the maintenance requirements of using too many composites. She proposes that Clayton use only two composites, one for emerging-market debt and one for developed-market bonds. Norah then tells Helen, "I will define the criteria so that all discretionary portfolios will be in one of the two composites. I may have to include portfolios with an investment process that differs from the overall composite, but I will ensure the dispersion of the performance returns is within tolerance set forth by the GIPS committee."
>
> Norah's approach is most likely incorrect because of:
>
> **A** both of her comments regarding the investment process and dispersion.
>
> **B** her comment regarding differences of investment process only.
>
> **C** her comment regarding dispersion only.
>
> ### Question 2
>
> Upon review of the performance of the two composites, Helen finds that the dispersion (calculated as the equal-weighted standard deviation of returns) of the developed-market composite is 0.82% and the dispersion of the emerging markets composite is 0.94%. If she removes the 530 blended individual client portfolios from the two composites, leaving only the 900 developed or emerging ones, the dispersion drops to a more acceptable 0.43% and 0.47%, respectively. What should Helen propose to do next?
>
> **A** Maintain the separate developed and emerging composites and create a third composite for the blended portfolios.
>
> **B** Examine the investment process for the blended portfolios to determine if there are strategies that would warrant creation of several composites into which the blended portfolios could be allocated.
>
> **C** Create separate composites for each blended portfolio.
>
> Helen and Norah then discuss the various investment strategies with the key stakeholders and organize the portfolios by strategy. They determine that the best approach for Clayton is to create one Developed Markets Debt Composite, one Emerging Markets Debt Composite, and three composites for the different blended strategies that they have identified. The Emerging Markets Debt Composite will require at least 90% portfolio allocation to emerging-market debt, while the Developed Markets Debt Composite will require at least 90% of the portfolio to be invested in developed markets debt. They have established policies on tolerances around the thresholds.

Question 3

What should Norah and Helen do to ensure that their approach continues to be appropriate?

A Having established the allocation of portfolios into the composites based on the investment strategies, they should focus on the regular measurement of dispersion.

B They should introduce in their procedures a tolerance check that specifies that if the number of portfolios in either composite exceeds 1,000, a new composite should be created.

C They should monitor the weighting of emerging-market debt held in the Emerging Markets Debt Composite portfolios and do the same with the Developed Markets Debt Composite, taking action and switching portfolios to a new or a different composite whenever the portfolios' emerging or developed holdings weights move below or above the 90% threshold.

Question 4

Several months later, Norah learns that two of the firm's clients with separate accounts that are currently part of the Developed Markets Debt Composite have imposed restrictions on fund holdings. The restrictions are determined to be of a material nature. As a result, the portfolios no longer meet the firm's definition of discretion. What course of action should Norah take?

A Broaden the definition of the composite.

B Remove the portfolio from the composite as it has become non-discretionary.

C Create a new composite for the portfolio.

Solution to 1

B is correct. Norah should ensure that the investment approach for all included portfolios is closely aligned within the composite. The types of portfolios the firm manages are too distinct to fit into just two composites. The composite definitions don't provide for the blended portfolios.

A & C are incorrect because Norah's approach is wrong for reasons other than dispersion.

Solution to 2

B is correct. Before creating another composite, Helen should work with the portfolio managers to understand the investment process in more detail.

A is incorrect because the investment process used for the client portfolios may or may not be similar. C is incorrect because creating a separate composite for each blended portfolio would result in the creation of hundreds of composites, each with a very narrow definition.

Solution to 3

C is correct. They should institute a check that signals if the 90% threshold is crossed in either direction while also implementing a clear policy (control) that outlines how changes are made based on that check.

A is incorrect because they should continue to compare the composite definition to the investment process. B is incorrect because there is no limit to the number of portfolios in a composite.

Solution to 4

B is correct. Non-discretionary portfolios should be removed from the composite.

> A is incorrect because definitions of composites should not be changed to accommodate portfolios that faces restrictions. C is incorrect because the portfolio has become non-discretionary and therefore can no longer be included in any composite.

SUMMARY

Discrepancies between the returns that the manager and custodian calculate are common and typically occur for legitimate reasons. The sources of these discrepancies should be researched, documented, and explained to performance-measurement stakeholders. The implementation of systems and controls that alert practitioners to both the sources and instances of performance discrepancies will improve the accuracy and reliability of performance returns.

- *Pricing*: Multiple pricing sources exist for every security, and prices may differ even for a given time of day. The differences tend to be larger for less liquid securities, such as corporate bonds, structured products, and foreign shares.
- *Missing trades*: This is a frequent occurrence that can have a significant impact on performance.
- *Missing and mistimed cash flows*: Discrepancies arise from missing fund inflows or outflows due to improper or overlooked operational procedures, technological flaws, or poor documentation. Discrepancies may also arise if the custodian and investment manager treat the timing of cash flows differently, with the former using the settlement date and the latter using the trade date.
- *Corporate actions*: The inconsistent treatment of or incomplete information on corporate actions may cause discrepancies between the returns reported by the custodian and investment manager.
- Other causes of discrepancies include differing exchange rates, insufficient information in the terms and conditions associated with derivatives and forwards, and the handling of fund expenses and fees in different ways.
- The most common discrepancies between NAV-based and time-weighted returns are timing differences and different approaches to fees and charges.
- NAV and time-weighted returns may be calculated at different points of the day. Because of differing cutoff points, a given trade could be accounted for by time-weighted return calculations but excluded from the NAV calculations.
- Fees and charges are paid to and received from different entities and may be treated differently by those who prepare NAV and end-of-day time-weighted performance, respectively, resulting in discrepancies.
- Furthermore, practitioners should be aware of the differences between performance based on ABOR (Accounting Book of Record) and IBOR (Investment Book of Record) and should understand the data requirements of each.
- ABOR is the official set of accounting records, typically calculated by a custodian or administrator. It is based on daily investment data at a single point in time, the "cutoff" time, including pricing and exchange rates. ABOR is used to value portfolios and generate NAVs and NAV-based performance metrics. ABOR figures are used for public consumption and are fed into peer group databases for comparative purposes.

Summary

- IBOR is a separate set of portfolio data for trading and portfolio-management purposes. The figures recorded there are typically timelier from the perspective of the fund manager's working hours than those found in the ABOR. IBOR may be calculated once or multiple times throughout the day to reflect ongoing activity and market movements.
- The use of composites poses a range of data-integrity challenges. Performance data must be available in the correct format for potentially hundreds of portfolios over many time periods. Various disclosures, including information about discretion, are required for reporting purposes. Pertinent dimensions of data integrity, which inform our handling of composites, include the following: accuracy, completeness, conformity, and timeliness.
- Composite construction is complex and must account for various stakeholders, many of whom will be represented on the GIPS committee, and include the following: portfolio accounting & administration, performance measurement, product management, IT, risk management, and legal & compliance. The GIPS committee is responsible for defining firm's policies and procedures relating to composites.
- Practitioners should avoid defining GIPS composites too narrowly or too broadly. Discretion should be carefully defined using measurable criteria. Decisions around the classifications of portfolios as discretionary or non-discretionary should be documented. GIPS composites and policies and procedures should anticipate future changes in the investment process.

PRACTICE PROBLEMS

1. The *best* explanation for why equities in developed markets tend to have smaller pricing differences among market-data vendors than stocks in less developed markets is:
   - **A** because shares in less developed markets are often less liquid than those in developed markets.
   - **B** because of the impact different securities markets have on prices.
   - **C** because stocks in developed markets have multiple pricing sources while stocks in less developed markets do not.

2. When there are pricing differences between the custodian and the investment manager's pricing vendor for individual holdings of a portfolio, the practitioner's *most likely* first step is to:
   - **A** seek to reproduce the calculations of the two providers.
   - **B** ask both parties to confirm that the prices agree with their pricing policy.
   - **C** focus on the largest pricing discrepancy since it will have the greatest contribution to the overall discrepancy at the portfolio level.

3. A performance analyst notices that a trade made by a sub-adviser two days prior appears to have been missed by the custodian. The differences between the investment manager and the custodian's trade and cash balances exactly offset each other on the day the trade in question occurred. No capital additions to or withdrawals from the portfolio occurred on that day. The *most likely* cause of this discrepancy is that the trade data:
   - **A** were never received by the custodian.
   - **B** were never received by the fund manager.
   - **C** arrived after the custodian's daily cutoff time.

4. Which of the following statements is *most* accurate?
   - **A** Calculating returns involves approximation.
   - **B** Vendors provide prices for both liquid and illiquid assets based on actual trades.
   - **C** Differences in the reported prices of individual holdings introduce significant differences in the reported portfolio performance.

5. An official transcript of all movements of cash into and out of an investment fund is maintained in the:
   - **A** GIPS composite database.
   - **B** accounting book of record.
   - **C** investment book of record.

6. Which of the following is the *least likely* cause of missing and mistimed cash flows into and out of a fund?
   - **A** Such factors as operational shortfalls, technological errors, and poor documentation may come into play for investment managers.
   - **B** Because investment firms typically manage the flows of cash with investors and other parties, it is not uncommon for a custodian to miss a flow in or out of a fund.

© 2020 CFA Institute. All rights reserved.

Practice Problems

    C The custodian accounts for the cash flow on the settlement date, while the investment manager records the trade and the change in the cash account on the trade date.

7 The presence of derivatives in a portfolio introduces further scope for discrepancies between the investment manager and the custodian because:

    A custodians must weigh the extra cost of the additional data against the extra precision they may obtain.

    B the terms and conditions of OTC derivatives are often costly to obtain and are not provided automatically to custodians.

    C Derivatives, such as currency forwards, are priced by outside vendors rather than by the investment manager's own internal systems.

8 Which of the following items is *more likely* to be missed by the custodian than by the investment manager in the calculation of performance?

    A Cash flows

    B Securities trades

    C Corporate actions

9 Which of the following funds is *least likely* to experience a discrepancy between NAV-based performance and end-of-day time-weighted performance?

    A A New York-based and administered domestic small-cap equity fund.

    B A London-based UK mid-cap equity fund administered in Hong Kong.

    C An Osaka, Japan-domiciled large-cap equity fund with holdings in German shares.

10 Assume a cutoff time of 5:00 p.m. for both the custodian's NAV calculations and the firm's IBOR time-weighted performance calculations and that both the firm and the custodian use the same pricing and exchange rate feeds. While the afternoon was a period of heavy trading activity by the portfolio manager, all trades were completed before 5:00 p.m. Later, a performance analyst notices that the NAV calculation and the IBOR time-weighted calculation differ. The *most likely* cause of the calculation discrepancy was the use of different:

    A prices.

    B holdings.

    C exchange rates.

11 Given the wide variety of investment strategies, objectives, and mandates that exist, standardizing required composite disclosures across a multi-product firm can be difficult. The data integrity dimension that *most* directly addresses this data challenge is:

    A accuracy.

    B conformity.

    C completeness.

12 Designing composite definitions that are comprehensive in scope may lead to:

    A large magnitudes of return dispersion within composites.

    B increased movement of portfolios into and out of composites.

    C extra maintenance work, including managing all the associated data requirements.

13 Which of the following statements does not reflect a best practice under the GIPS standards?

    A Firms need to complete, on a regular basis, discretionary status reviews of fee-paying portfolios that are included in composites.

B Where possible, practitioners should anticipate the evolution of their investment process, creating enough space in composite definitions to allow for some change.

C To understand the needs of the entire organization and obtain their support, a GIPS committee should be established with representatives from portfolio accounting, performance measurement, product management, information technology, risk management, and legal & compliance.

14 Decisions around new portfolios, such as allocating them to existing composites or setting up new composites, should be the responsibility of the:

A GIPS committee.

B portfolio management team.

C performance measurement team.

15 HMT Asset Management is marketing a new, actively-managed Eurozone large-cap equity product. Prospective client Abel is interested in European Union large-cap stocks and is impressed by HMT's success with other strategies, but he requires that all trades be pre-approved. Prospective client Baker is interested in Eurozone stocks, but her IPS prohibits investment in tobacco companies and weapons manufacturers. The prohibited companies typically make up less than 3% of the new strategy's benchmark. Charlie, an existing client in HMT's US large-cap strategy, would like to move his portfolio to the new Eurozone large-cap equity strategy. Assuming all three prospects invest in the new product, how should HMT comply with the requirements of the GIPS standards?

A Create a single composite for Baker's and Charlie's accounts and classify Abel's account as non-discretionary.

B Create a single composite for Charlie's account and classify Abel's and Baker's accounts as non-discretionary.

C Create three individual composites, one for Abel's account, one for Baker's account, and one for Charlie's account.

SOLUTIONS

1. A is correct. Even at a given point in time, different pricing sources may offer different prices; moreover, the differences tend to be larger for less liquid securities, such as corporate bonds, structured products, and foreign shares.

   B is incorrect. As performance-measurement practitioners, we need to understand which sources are used to derive the market values of our portfolios. We also need to be sensitive to potential timing differences and to the impact of different securities markets on those prices.

   C is incorrect because there are multiple pricing sources for every security.

2. B is correct. Rather than seeking to reproduce the performance calculated by two different providers, a practitioner would likely ask both parties to confirm that the prices agree with their pricing policy. If a pricing data policy exists, the performance provider may be asked to change pricing to match the policy and recalculate performance for that day.

   A is incorrect. Seeking to reproduce the calculations of the two providers would require both an understanding of their methodologies and the processing of a lot of additional data (e.g., number of holdings, previous day prices, transactions).

   C is incorrect. The pricing discrepancy alone does not determine the holding's contribution to the overall discrepancy at the portfolio level. The position weight of the holding must also be taken into consideration.

3. A is correct. Since the trade discrepancy was still unresolved two days after the date of the sub-adviser's trade, it is most likely that the trade data were never received by the custodian.

   B is incorrect. A sub-adviser typically sends all of their trades to both the custodian and the fund manager. The sub-adviser prepares different trade feeds—one to match the custodian's required format, and the other to meet the requirements of the fund manager. Two separate feeds, and processes to generate those feeds, introduce the possibility that trades (or other data) provided in one are missing from the other. Since the fund manager's analyst was aware of the trade by the sub-adviser, we can assume that the investment firm did receive the trade data.

   C is incorrect. If the trade feed was received after the custodian's daily cutoff time, the trade would likely have been processed by the custodian the following day and backdated so that performance could be recalculated and the discrepancy resolved. If this had occurred, the discrepancy would not have existed when the sub-adviser's trading was reviewed by the analyst two days after the trade.

4. A is correct. CIPM candidates, given their exposure to questions of performance and analytics, understand that calculating returns involves approximation. "Upstream" data flows come in different varieties, and their nature affects how the performance of funds and fund managers are ultimately represented.

   B is incorrect. Pricing vendors provide prices for illiquid assets using model valuation rather than basing prices on actual trades.

   C is incorrect. Differences in the reported prices of individual holdings may or may not introduce significant differences in the reported portfolio performance.

5. B is correct. The official record of all movements of cash into and out of a fund is maintained by the custodian in the accounting book of record.

A is incorrect. The GIPS composite system (including the database) is the set of processes, tools, and equipment used to maintain and manage GIPS composites. The system is not the official fund accounting record, however.

C is incorrect. The investment book of record is a separate set of data for trading and portfolio management purposes created by the investment manager.

6 B is correct. Because custodians (not investment managers) typically manage the flows of cash with investors and other parties, it is not uncommon for an investment manager to miss a flow in or out of a fund.

A is incorrect. It is not uncommon for an investment manager to miss a flow in or out of a fund; operational shortfalls, technological errors, and poor documentation may also come into play.

C is incorrect. The custodian and the investment manager may record cash flows on different dates, whether intentionally or not. For example, the custodian may account for the cash flow on the settlement date—when the cash is actually moved—while the investment manager records the trade and a change in the cash account on the day the trade takes place (i.e., the trade date).

7 B is correct. The terms and conditions associated with over-the-counter (OTC) derivatives are necessary for correctly valuing them and measuring exposures, but such information is often costly to obtain and not provided automatically to custodians, which limits their ability to measure the impact on performance.

A is incorrect. Custodians must weigh the extra cost of the additional data (for valuing derivatives) against the extra precision they may obtain. In some circumstances, the extra precision may be required by the regulators. The choice, however, is not a cause of discrepancies, *per se*.

C is incorrect. Currency forwards are not priced by outside vendors. Instead, they are priced by internal systems that investment managers and custodians use.

8 B is correct. The omission of a trade in the calculation of a position can have a significant impact on reported performance, and missing trades occur frequently. For example, custodians typically insist on daily cutoff times by which all trade data must be received from the manager in order to be included in that day's performance calculations. If certain trades come in too late, they will not be included in performance calculations.

A is incorrect. Custodians record all movements of cash into and out of a fund. Because custodians typically manage the flows of cash with investors and other parties, it is not uncommon for an investment manager to miss a flow in or out of a fund.

C is incorrect. Because custodians work with so many financial institutions, they necessarily track corporate action information for most securities. Investment managers, on the other hand, may dedicate limited resources to the costly, data-intensive process of maintaining a complete awareness of corporate actions.

9 A is correct. The New York-based fund, in contrast to the London and Osaka funds, is not administered or domiciled on a different continent nor is it partly or fully invested in a different geographic region. For these reasons, the New York-based fund is least likely to experience a discrepancy between NAV-based performance and end-of-day time-weighted performance relative to the other funds.

B is incorrect. The cutoff times for NAV calculation and the IBOR time-weighted calculation may differ because the company manages a fund that is administered or domiciled on a different continent.

Solutions

C is incorrect. The cutoff times for NAV calculation and the IBOR time-weighted calculation may differ because the company manages a fund that is partly or fully invested in a different geographic region.

10 B is correct. The most likely cause of the difference is a transaction occurring just prior to the cutoff time that was not communicated to the custodian quickly enough to be captured in the NAV calculation. This may happen when there is heavy trading activity near the cutoff time.

A is incorrect. The cutoff time was the same for both calculations. Since the custodian and the investment manager use the same pricing vendor, their prices should be identical.

C is incorrect. The cutoff time was the same for both calculations. Since the custodian and the investment manager use the same exchange-rate vendor, their FX rates should be identical.

11 C is correct. With respect to the GIPS standards, the data integrity dimension of completeness applies to both performance data and additional disclosures. The dimension addresses the question: Are the data sufficiently complete for the intended purpose? An example of this data dimension is: Details on discretion and disclosures compose a form of information that is required but difficult to standardize.

A is incorrect. The accuracy data integrity dimension addresses the question: Are the data valid and correct? The system for managing composites must be able to generate all data that are required to calculate composite returns and provide disclosures. An example of this data dimension is: The system must accurately maintain information on discretionary and non-discretionary status of portfolios.

B is incorrect. The conformity data integrity dimension addresses the question: Do the data conform to standards and rules? An example of this data dimension is: The composition of composites should be covered by an appropriate allocation rule or by definitions formulated by the GIPS committee.

12 A is correct. A definition of composites that is too broad may lead to large magnitudes of return dispersion within composites. Recommended best practice is to avoid composite definitions that are too broad or too narrow.

B is incorrect. A very narrow definition of composites may lead to increased movement of portfolios into and out of composites.

C is incorrect. A very narrow definition of composites may lead to a lot of extra maintenance work, including managing all the associated data requirements.

13 A is correct. A sensible practice, and a requirement of the GIPS standards, is for a firm's GIPS policies and procedures to include its definition of discretion. Firms need to complete discretionary reviews on a regular basis for *all* fee-paying portfolios, not just for those already included in composites.

B is incorrect. In general, the GIPS standards recommend that changes to the investment strategy of a particular portfolio will require either the creation of a new composite or switching the portfolio to an existing but different composite. Where possible, practitioners should anticipate the evolution of their investment process, creating enough space in the definitions to allow for some change, as a best practice.

C is incorrect. Best practice calls on the practitioner to understand the needs of the entire organization and obtain their support. A GIPS committee should be established with representatives from portfolio accounting & administration, performance measurement, product management, information technology, risk management, and legal & compliance (and possibly sales & marketing and portfolio management).

14 A is correct. Decisions around new portfolios, such as allocating them to existing composites or setting up new composites, should be the responsibility of the GIPS committee.

B is incorrect. While portfolio managers may be included on the GIPS committee, decisions around new portfolios, such as allocating them to existing composites or setting up new composites, should be the responsibility of the full GIPS committee.

C is incorrect. While representatives from the performance measurement team should be included on the GIPS committee, decisions around new portfolios, such as allocating them to existing composites or setting up new composites, should be the responsibility of the full GIPS committee.

15 A is correct. There are no restrictions on the management of Charlie's account. The restriction against investment in tobacco companies and weapons manufacturers listed in Baker's IPS is relatively minor—given that the prohibited companies typically make up less than 3% of the new strategy's benchmark—and thus unlikely to materially impact the firm's ability to implement its intended strategy.

B is incorrect. Abel's account is clearly non-discretionary due to the requirement that all trades be pre-approved. This restriction will materially impact the firm's ability to implement its intended strategy. Additionally, Abel's interest is in the European Union, which consists of significantly more countries than are included in the Eurozone. In contrast, the restriction in Baker's IPS is relatively minor and thus unlikely to materially impact the firm's ability to implement its intended strategy.

C is incorrect. Creating a separate composite for the Baker account because of the minor restriction described would go against best practice, resulting in a narrowly defined composite and extra maintenance work for the performance team. Moreover, Abel's account is clearly non-discretionary and therefore should not be included in any composite.

PERFORMANCE EVALUATION
STUDY SESSION

3

Performance Attribution

This study session addresses advanced topics in performance attribution, beginning with a reading on the use of strategy benchmarks (also known as custom benchmarks) in the evaluation of managers' investment processes. The second reading of the study session addresses return attribution in several practically important cases: portfolios with short positions, derivatives exposures, and/or multicurrency exposures. The third reading in the study session focuses on fundamental concepts in fixed-income attribution.

READING ASSIGNMENTS

5 Strategy Benchmarks: From the Investment Manager's Perspective
by David E. Kuenzi, CFA

6 Topics in Return Attribution
by Carl R. Bacon, CIPM

7 Introduction to Fixed-Income Attribution
by Claude Giguère, BScA, and Andrew Kophamel, FRM, CFA, CIPM

© 2020 CFA Institute. All rights reserved.

READING
5

Strategy Benchmarks
From the Investment Manager's Perspective

by David E. Kuenzi, CFA

David E. Kuenzi, CFA, is at AlphaSimplex Group (USA).

LEARNING OUTCOME STATEMENTS	
Mastery	The candidate should be able to:
☐	a. explain the concept of normal (neutral) weights;
☐	b. distinguish between published benchmark-centered investment disciplines and manager strategy investment disciplines;
☐	c. explain why strategy benchmarks are more appropriate for manager strategy investment disciplines;
☐	d. describe benchmark selection/creation and risk of an institutional investment process;
☐	e. describe the impact of benchmark selection on attribution analysis and the calculation of tracking error and information ratios.

Once upon a time, the use of benchmark indexes was quite limited. Managers simply compared their total returns to those of some best-fit broad market index, such as the S&P 500 for an equity manager, or the Lehman Aggregate for a fixed-income manager.[1] During the 1990s, managers began to use indexes much more rigorously—for risk comparisons, determination of the consistency of investment manager returns, portfolio risk management, and portfolio attribution analysis.

In the last ten years, this shift in the use of benchmark indexes has led to extraordinary growth among index providers, including MSCI, Frank Russell, Dow Jones, and the index groups at S&P, Salomon Smith Barney, Lehman Brothers, FTSE, and Ryan Labs, as well as to increased interest in size and style indexes. Many of these groups also create strategy benchmarks for clients on a customized basis.

---

[1] Bloomberg acquired and maintains what were the Lehman fixed-income indexes. Today, the Lehman Aggregate is known as the Bloomberg Barclays US Aggregate.

David E. Kuenzi, CFA, "Strategy Benchmarks," *Journal of Portfolio Management*, Vol. 29, No. 2 (2003). Copyright © 2003 by Institutional Investor Journals. Reprinted with permission.

While these published indexes provide good benchmarks for many investment strategies, they are not able to provide all that is needed for sophisticated investment managers using specialized investment strategies and requiring thorough analysis of their portfolios versus a benchmark. In these cases, the use of customized or strategy benchmarks is appropriate.[2]

Research on this topic has focused mostly on client needs as an impetus for the use of strategy benchmarks. I make a case instead for use of a strategy benchmark with an emphasis on the investment process. Specifically, I show that a strategy benchmark is necessary in order for the investment process to work efficiently any time the manager's strategy produces a universe of securities that differs by rule from available published indexes. I will also show the importance of a strategy benchmark to the integrity of more recently employed performance measures, such as the information ratio.

NORMAL (OR NEUTRAL) WEIGHTS

There is a large body of work suggesting that a manager's benchmark should represent "normal" or "neutral" portfolio weights. Brinson, Hood, and Beebower [1986] and Brinson, Singer, and Beebower [1991] suggest that average allocations over time represent normal portfolio weights, and Smith [2001/2002] and Ryan [2001] build on this notion. Kritzman [1987] gives guidance for creating normal portfolios and for considering where one draws the line between style and skill.

Divecha and Grinold [1989] emphasize the importance of normal portfolios in evaluating portfolio performance. Dietz and Kirschman [1990] consider normal portfolios in the more general context of portfolio performance. Most notable in this respect, however, is the work of Bailey, Richards, and Tierney [1990] and Grinold and Kahn [1995].

In Bailey, Richards, and Tierney's [1990] framework, a manager's portfolio holdings, P, are represented as:

$$P = B + (P - B) = B + A$$

where B is the benchmark, or the portfolio's normal weight. A is the active position—the portfolio exposures, P, minus the benchmark exposures, B.

Defining M as a market index (an available published index), they write:

$$P = M + (B - M) + A = M + S + A$$

where S is the style exposure of the manager, which is equal to the manager's benchmark minus some published index.

Bailey, Richards, and Tierney distinguish between the normal weights, represented by B, and a published index, represented by M. This difference is the manager strategy, S.

This final equation:

$$P = M + S + A \qquad (1)$$

provides powerful intuitions concerning the relationships among active management, a manager's strategy, and a published index. The idea is simply that the only time a strategy benchmark is unnecessary is when $B = M$, or when the manager's normal weights are equal to those of a published benchmark, so that $B - M = 0$ and $P = M + A$. If the manager's average exposures through time, B, differ from those of a published benchmark, M, then it is crucial to create a strategy benchmark, rather than use a published benchmark and just assume that $B = M$.

---

2 While many practitioners use the term, custom benchmark, I use the term, strategy benchmark—to emphasize its use in relation to a manager's peculiar strategy and universe of securities.

Grinold and Kahn [1995] suggest the use of factor exposures for describing the normal portfolio.[3] The active manager will likely always be taking on some active risk due to differences in the number of securities in the index and the number of securities in the portfolio, thus making benchmark security allocations a somewhat clumsy, if accurate, way to measure neutral exposures. In the case of equities, this would involve sector exposures as well as exposure to other factors, such as average P/E, average price momentum, or average volatility. In the case of fixed-income, this would involve exposure to sectors, maturity categories, rating categories, duration, convexity, and so on.

Both Bailey, Richards, and Tierney [1990] and Bailey [1992] support the notion that a valid benchmark should be: 1) unambiguous, 2) investible, 3) measurable, 4) appropriate, 5) reflective of current investment opinions, and 6) specified in advance. Most investors and investment managers gravitate to benchmarks that generally have these characteristics, although the fourth and fifth items are often interpreted loosely.[4]

Bailey suggests that a benchmark is appropriate if it "is consistent with the manager's investment style," and that a benchmark is reflective of current investment opinions if "the manager has current investment knowledge of the securities that make up the benchmark" [1992, p. 10]. In order for a benchmark to work well, managers and investors must interpret these requirements rigorously, and often look to a separate strategy benchmark for which the securities are truly reflective of neutral weights of the manager universe.

The relationship between neutral weights from the manager's universe and the published benchmark may differ, however, depending on the investment management discipline.

TWO TYPES OF INVESTMENT DISCIPLINES

For the purposes of benchmarking, it is helpful to think in terms of two types of investment disciplines:

1. Published benchmark-centered (PBC) disciplines begin with a well-established broad-based benchmark as the goal and are managed closely to this index on an ongoing basis. Managers targeting pension funds may be likely to have PBC disciplines. If, for instance, a pension fund benchmarks its US equity assets to the Russell 1000, it might hire two managers with PBC disciplines in growth and value. Each manager would attempt to provide returns commensurate with or in excess of those provided by the Russell 1000 Growth and Value indexes. These managers might be expected to turn over some of their portfolios at the annual rebalancing of the Russell indexes in June of each year in order to maintain exposures reflective of those of their benchmark, as minimizing tracking

---

3 Grinold and Kahn define the manager's active position as $h_{PA} = h_P - h_B$, where h_P and h_B are vectors of security weights in the portfolio and the benchmark, respectively, and h_{PA} is the active position. If the manager has no information, then the appropriate exposures are those of the benchmark ($h_P = h_B$); if the manager does have information, then $h_P \neq h_B$.

4 To the extent that the portfolio is large and market impact in trading is a concern, the requirement that an index be "investible" is also often loosely interpreted, as it may be difficult for the manager to invest in the index due to the small float of some stocks. In such cases, float-weighting of strategy benchmarks should be considered.

error to the indexes is a primary concern. In terms of Equation 1, $B = M$ so that $S = B - M = 0$, and $P = M + A$. Enhanced indexing would be the most defining example of such a strategy.

2 Manager strategy (MS) disciplines begin with an investment strategy that is meant to take advantage of a market anomaly, to exploit a particular competitive advantage of the manager, or to otherwise provide for risk-return characteristics that may not be identical to those of some well-established index. A strategy that invests in stocks with low debt and a near-term reason for an improvement in those companies' fortunes would be an example. A manager of an MS discipline might choose a best-fit benchmark (the Russell 1000 Growth, say) as an afterthought, according to the best fit with the manager's strategy. Again, using Equation 1, it is clear that $B \neq M$ so that $P = M + S + A$.

The published benchmark-centered discipline has no need of a strategy benchmark, as the method for generating returns is subjugated to the goal of tracking the stated external benchmark. This portfolio's risk exposures (or sector exposures) will differ from, say, the Russell 1000 Growth only insofar as the manager thinks that such risk-taking will lead to outperformance of the index. In this instance, the established external benchmark provides the fund manager with neutral weights.

This is not the case with the manager strategy discipline. In this case, the published index may include securities that would never be found in the portfolio. In the example, for instance, stocks with high debt-to-capital might by rule be excluded from the portfolio. The external benchmark thus does not represent neutral weights for the portfolio, and is therefore a poor benchmark for the purposes of gauging active risk, performance attribution, and insights into the portfolio management process. Over- or underperformance of the external benchmark in a particular period may be simply a function of the long-term static strategy of the manager. In this case, a strategy benchmark is appropriate.

In general, whenever the manager's strategy is such that its universe of investible securities differs from the closest-fit published index components by a quantifiable rule, or by a style preference that can be expressed with a quantifiable rule, a strategy benchmark is appropriate. My work is applicable exclusively to investment disciplines whose specialized strategies make use of a strategy benchmark appropriate.

GENERAL FRAMEWORK OF AN INSTITUTIONAL PROCESS

To establish why a strategy benchmark is crucial for this type of investment discipline, it is first important to review the basic elements of an institutional investment process.

The investment process for a long-only unleveraged active institutional investor includes a number of essential elements, as represented in Exhibit 1.[5] The four basic elements are 1) investment policy; 2) generation of alpha estimates, investment decision-making, and security/factor overweighting or underweighting; 3) execution; and 4) performance measurement and attribution.

The investment management group begins with an investment philosophy (how it intends to add value in a fairly efficient market over the intermediate to long term), client goals, benchmarks and measures to evaluate performance, and risk bands around benchmark exposures (the amount by which, say, a fixed-income portfolio could be longer or shorter than the duration of the benchmark). The investment manager then

---

[5] See, for instance, Maginn and Tuttle [1990, Ch.1], Grinold and Kahn [1995], and Agache [2001]. Thanks go to the Nuveen Investments municipal research team for help in creation of the diagram in Exhibit 1.

makes active decisions on which securities and risk factors to overweight or underweight in order to generate active returns. These decisions are then implemented and perhaps modified, depending on how easily they can be executed.

Finally, the investment management group performs attribution analysis in order to determine whether it has been able to add value along the intended dimensions. This feedback is then considered in the context of refinements to the investment process—both in the short and intermediate term for refining tactical strategies, and over the long term for the determination of appropriate policy.

In order for this process to work well, the benchmark must be reflective of appropriate neutral weights, and for a manager strategy-centered discipline, a strategy benchmark is absolutely necessary.

Investment Policy and the Strategy Benchmark

Two of the most important aspects of investment policy are the choice of the benchmark and the risk controls around benchmark factor exposures (the first box in Exhibit 1). Grinold and Kahn note that "the client bears the benchmark risk, and the active manager bears the active risk of deviating from the benchmark" [1995, p. 83]. When the manager and client identify the benchmark, they are identifying the general risk-return characteristics that the client will expect over time.

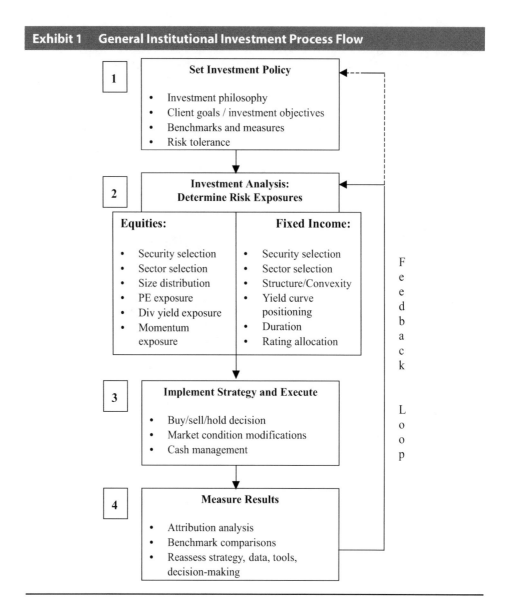

Exhibit 1 General Institutional Investment Process Flow

If the investment manager deviates from the benchmark by policy, as the result of an investment strategy that specifically excludes a large portion of the securities in the benchmark, the client is not, on average, bearing benchmark risk. The client will be exposed to a different set of risks, which may be ill defined from the client's perspective. Additionally, the concept of risk controls becomes distorted if the manager employs a benchmark that is not representative of true neutral weights.

A strategy benchmark enables the manager to accurately identify the risk-return characteristics that the investor can expect over time (which may be very different from those of the closest-fit published index), and to use risk controls more meaningfully.

An example shows this best. Suppose that an investment manager has a strategy of finding companies with low debt (a high degree of flexibility to pursue profitable projects) that the manager believes are undervalued compared to other similar firms. To this end, the manager starts with the S&P 500, removes the 350 stocks with the highest debt-to-capital ratios, and then performs bottom-up analysis on the remaining 150 companies to find the stocks most undervalued relative to other low debt-to-capital stocks in that sector. (Note that this first step could be easily applied in the creation of a strategy benchmark.)

Let's suppose further that the manager benchmarks against the S&P 500. This decision is based on the fact that at inception of the product, say, five years ago, 66% of the capitalization of the 150-stock portfolio was in the S&P 500/Barra Growth Index and 34% of the capitalization was in the S&P 500/Barra Value Index, with the number of stocks in each divided approximately evenly. Additionally, we assume that the manager sets sector risk bands at ±7.5% of the benchmark.[6]

Exhibit 2 provides some detail. Column (1) of the exhibit represents the sector weights that will be understood to be the neutral weights in the agreement between the client and the manager—the weights of the S&P 500 index. Column (2) shows how much the investment manager will be able to deviate from each of these index sector weights. Columns (3) and (4) show the minimum and maximum allocation that the manager can have to any one of these sectors. Column (5) provides the capitalization weights of the strategy universe—the 150 low debt-to-capital stocks. These are the sector weights of the stocks that the manager really has access to, given the stated strategy. Column (6) is the difference between the strategy and the S&P 500. This column shows the built-in sector underweights or overweights of the strategy universe versus the published benchmark.

The most striking element in column (5) is the zero weight in utilities. These stocks are patently excluded from consideration for investment by the manager, yet they constitute 7.28% of the S&P 500 and thus have a neutral weight of 7.28%. The manager will therefore, by policy, have a continual underweight in utilities by nearly the maximum allowable underweight.

Exhibit 2 Published Index Sector Weights/Risk Controls and Those Implied by Strategy

	(1) S&P 500 Weights	(2) Risk Limits	(3) Maximum Exposure	(4) Minimum Exposure	(5) Strategy Weight	(6) Difference Strat – S&P
Energy	3.57%	±7.5%	11.07%	0.00%	12.15%	8.58%
Materials	5.78%	±7.5%	13.28%	0.00%	1.68%	−4.10%
Industrials	11.80%	±7.5%	19.30%	4.30%	4.55%	−7.25%
Consumer Discrt	15.27%	±7.5%	22.77%	7.77%	11.75%	−3.52%
Consumer Stpls	11.65%	±7.5%	19.15%	4.15%	6.70%	−4.95%
Health Care	11.60%	±7.5%	19.10%	4.10%	22.34%	10.74%
Financials	17.02%	±7.5%	24.52%	9.52%	5.07%	−11.95%
Info Technology	12.83%	±7.5%	20.33%	5.33%	34.84%	22.00%
Telecomm Svcs	3.20%	±7.5%	10.70%	0.00%	0.92%	−2.28%
Utilities	7.28%	±7.5%	14.78%	0.00%	0.00%	−7.28%

Another observation is that technology is only 12.83% of the index but 34.84% of the strategy. At a maximum overweight, the manager can invest only 20.33% of assets in technology. Given that a good portion of the 150 stocks the manager is looking at are technology stocks (52, to be exact), it is likely that there will be a systematic overweight (close to the 20% limit) in this sector.

---

6 The S&P 500/Barra Growth and Value indexes are derived by dividing the total capitalization of the S&P 500 equally into two buckets—the first including the stocks with higher price-to-book values and the second stocks with low price-to-book values.

Generally, with strategy overweights in energy, health care, and information technology, and underweights in industrials, consumer-oriented stocks, and financials, the portfolio will likely have a higher standard deviation than the S&P 500. While the risk bands in this instance serve to reduce risk vis-à-vis the S&P 500, the investor's ongoing exposure is very different from that indicated by the S&P 500 weights. Additionally, the risk bands will largely serve to shape the true long-term sector weights rather than as extreme boundaries around a neutral weight.

The net result is that the investor is taking on more risk than expected, and the risk bands are not serving their purpose.

Alpha Generation and Risk Management

The active management process represented in the second box in Exhibit 1 is largely a process of deciding which factor exposures to overweight or underweight vis-à-vis the index. In the case of our example, the limited opportunity set (only 150 stocks) will force the manager to the outside limits of many risk controls on an ongoing basis. As the manager attempts to decide which factors to over- or underweight, the decision in many cases will already have been made by risk controls set around an inappropriate benchmark.

The question of whether to overweight technology, for instance, will be answered in a constant fashion at each portfolio review. Thus, active management is artificially constrained due to poor benchmark selection. This could be a severely damaging choice from an investment process perspective.

If the manager constructs a strategy benchmark consisting of the 150 lowest debt-to-capital stocks in the S&P 500 index, the neutral weights would be fully reflective of the manager's true opportunity set.[7] The weights and risk bands for such an index are shown in Exhibit 3. Using column (1) of Exhibit 3 as neutral weights, and risk limits of the same size, ±7.5%, the manager's neutral exposures would now be reflective of the securities that the manager has access to.

The problem with utility stocks is overcome, as the neutral weight in utilities is now zero. Technology, on the other hand, has a large neutral allocation equal to, on average, 34.84% of the portfolio. Implementing the risk bands, the manager can invest anywhere from 27.34% to 42.34% in technology. Health care exposure is also greater, with a maximum overweight of 29.84%.

These riskier neutral weights are a direct result of the manager's strategy—to buy companies with significant business risk and very little financial risk. If investors are not comfortable with this level of equity risk, they should consider a different strategy. If the investment management team is not comfortable with this level of risk, it should consider alterations to its strategy.

Exhibit 3	Strategy Neutral Weights, Risk Controls, and Number of Stocks Represented				
	(1) Strategy Benchmark	(2) Risk Limits	(3) Maximum Exposure	(4) Minimum Exposure	(5) Number of Stocks
Energy	12.15%	±7.5%	19.65%	4.65%	5
Materials	1.68%	±7.5%	9.18%	0.00%	6
Industrials	4.55%	±7.5%	12.05%	0.00%	20
Consumer Discrt	11.75%	±7.5%	19.25%	4.25%	19

---

7 For simplicity, we assume full quarterly rebalancing and capitalization-weighting of the stocks.

Exhibit 3 (Continued)

	(1) Strategy Benchmark	(2) Risk Limits	(3) Maximum Exposure	(4) Minimum Exposure	(5) Number of Stocks
Consumer Stpls	6.70%	±7.5%	14.20%	0.00%	6
Health Care	22.34%	±7.5%	29.84%	14.84%	23
Financials	5.07%	±7.5%	12.57%	0.00%	18
Info Technology	34.84%	±7.5%	42.34%	27.34%	52
Telecomm Svcs	0.92%	±7.5%	8.42%	0.00%	1
Utilities	0.00%	±7.5%	7.50%	0.00%	0

The solution is not, however, to use neutral weights, and therefore risk bands, that are not compatible with the strategy (although some times the weights of excessively large holdings or large sectors can and should be reduced in order to better reflect the strategy).[8]

It is clear, then, that the use of a strategy benchmark enables active management to take place in the rational context of decisions to overweight or underweight factor exposures versus the benchmark. Without a strategy benchmark, such decisions often don't make sense, which can lead to a general breakdown in the investment process. A strategy benchmark can thus be a crucial element of a well-honed investment process.

Decisions to overweight or underweight particular factors or securities lead to the execution phase of the investment process (the third box in Exhibit 1). The critical issues here are 1) the extent to which the ideas, information, and decisions generated in the second box of Exhibit 1 are efficiently transmitted or executed, and 2) the extent to which the factor exposures decided on in the previous step can be executed with sufficient ease, given liquidity and other constraints. Finally, we get investment results.

Performance Attribution

The last box in Exhibit 1 shows one of the most important elements of the active management process—when managers engage in self-evaluation in order to understand what's working and what they might improve.[9]

Are the factor exposures taken on by the investment team paying off? Are the quantitative models working right? Are the bottom-up analysts looking at the right information? Is the team executing on this information in an optimal fashion? What might the investment management team be missing, and how should it correct any glitches?

---

[8] The reweighting of individual holdings is particularly applicable for concentrated strategy benchmarks used by mutual fund managers. Managers must maintain compliance with regulated investment company (RIC) guidelines in order to avoid double taxation. Such guidelines require that no individual holding be greater than 25% of total assets and that no three holdings make up more than 50%. With respect to the remaining 50% of the portfolio, no holding can be greater than 5% of total assets. If the strategy benchmark violates these guidelines, the benchmark is not investible, and its weightings must be modified.

This can be accomplished by using iterative methods to reduce the weights of the largest holdings and to then spread excess weight across the remainder of the portfolio on a capweighted basis. These or similar processes can be used to reduce sector weights or to otherwise hone the strategy benchmark. Managers who tend to equally weight their portfolios, and hence have size bias, should refer to Divecha and Grinold [1989] for guidance.

[9] While this analysis is also important from the perspectives of clients and consultants, this idea is well developed in Bailey, Richards, and Tierney [1990]. Here, we choose to focus on its importance to the investment manager.

The integrity of attribution information is crucial if the manager is to make sensible and timely adjustments to the activities that determine how and when risks are taken or neutralized vis-à-vis the benchmark, and this requires a benchmark that represents true neutral weights.

Attribution analysis provides a manager with sources of return. Return-based attribution indicates the amount of the total return that can be attributed to asset allocation, timing, and security selection, and is used mainly by investors. Investment managers generally use holding-based attribution models. This analysis indicates the amount of benchmark outperformance that is attributable to various factor exposures—the portion of the outperformance attributable to exposures listed in the second box in Exhibit 1.

Attribution is highly dependent on which benchmark is used. Exhibit 4 provides an example, using the simple mechanics for attribution described in Dietz and Kirschman [1990].

Suppose the fund exposure to technology is 25%, an allocation that the manager looks at as being about average over time. If the manager is using a non-representative index, the attribution model will interpret the weight difference between the portfolio and the benchmark as an overweight, thereby attributing outperformance to this active decision. From the manager's perspective, this is not an active decision at all, and the attribution results based on technology exposure are fully anticipated each month. This colors any results concerning the overall value-added of tactical sector allocation decisions, and renders the attribution analysis almost worthless.

Exhibit 4   Attribution Example Using a Published and a Strategy Benchmark

	Using Published Benchmark	Using Strategy Benchmark
Outperformance of Technology Sector	10%	10%
Portfolio Technology Exposure	25%	25%
Benchmark Technology Exposure	15%	25%
Overweight (Portfolio Exposure – Index Exposure)	10%	0%
Outperformance Attributable to Technology Exposure*	1%	0%

* Calculated as Overweight × Outperformance.

If, however, a strategy benchmark that accurately represents neutral is used, any overweight or underweight to a particular factor is either 1) an active decision, 2) a calculated by-product of an active decision, or 3) an unanticipated by-product of an active decision and thus a failure to effectively manage risk. Attribution based on these overweights and underweights then provides valuable information to the manager concerning active investment decisions and risk management.

PERFORMANCE COMPARISONS, TRACKING ERROR, AND INFORMATION RATIO

Our analysis below, which compares the strategy benchmark to two published indexes, can be viewed in two ways. First, to the extent that we expect the manager's risk exposures to be reflected in the more narrow strategy benchmark, it drives home the notion that direct comparison of the manager's results with inappropriate benchmarks provides little useful information. Second, it provides a blueprint for the type of analysis that might be considered for evaluating a manager's strategy—separate and apart from the manager's efforts to add value around that strategy—in accordance with some published benchmark that may be of interest to the investor.

Performance comparison results can be grossly distorted if unrepresentative benchmarks are used. Looking back on five years (60 months) of performance for our low debt-to-capital strategy (April 1997 through March 2002), it is clear that style is a significant factor influencing returns and that poor benchmark selection can provide for poor comparisons.

Exhibit 5 shows the composition of the 150-stock strategy benchmark. Over time, approximately half of the stocks in the strategy were in the S&P 500/Barra Growth Index, with the other half in the S&P 500/Barra Value Index; about 68% of the capitalization of the strategy has been in growth, with the remainder in value. Given this result, it seems that one might choose either the S&P 500 or the S&P 500/Barra Growth Index as a benchmark.

In Exhibit 6, we compare the returns of our strategy benchmark, our 150-stock portfolio of low debt-to-capital stocks, rebalanced quarterly, to the returns of both the S&P 500 and the S&P 500/Barra Growth Index. Over the full five-year period, the strategy benchmark marginally outperforms both indexes, by 8 and 12 basis points, respectively. The first 36 months of the period represent the last three years of the technology bull market, while the remaining 24 months represent the market decline.

During this first three-year period, the strategy benchmark outperforms both indexes and the S&P 500 quite dramatically. This is reversed for both indexes during the subsequent two-year period.

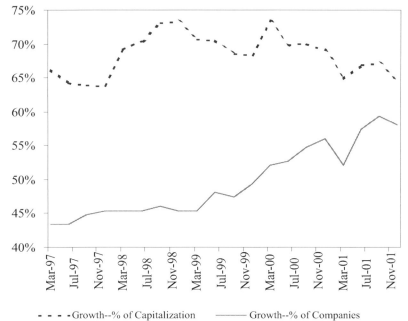

Exhibit 6 Raw Returns and Outperformance of Strategy Benchmark Against Published Indexes

	Annualized Total Return	Total Return versus S&P 500	Total Return versus S&P/Barra Growth
Full Period 4/97–3/02	10.27%	0.08%	0.12%
3 Years 4/97–3/00	37.78%	10.36%	2.02%
2 Years 4/00–3/02	−21.05%	−9.66%	−1.55%

This can be seen graphically in Exhibit 7. Assuming that the manager's portfolio tracked closely with the strategy, it is clear that comparing performance to the S&P 500, and even to what seems to be a better-fitting S&P 500/Barra Growth Index, would likely have given poor signals as to when the manager was adding value. On the simple basis of total return comparisons, the manager would have looked quite good at the market peak.[10]

Results are similar when we adjust these returns for risk. Exhibit 8 shows the returns, standard deviations, and Sharpe ratios for the two benchmarks and the strategy for both the longer period and the two subperiods.[11] Here again, given the results of the strategy benchmark, it is likely that the manager would have shown a strong risk-adjusted return at the market's peak compared to the published indexes.

---

10 Despite the inclusion of many value stocks in the strategy benchmark, the portfolio likely tracks better against the growth index because of its strategy of choosing companies with low financial risk and higher business risk. Value companies with this quality are likely to behave more like growth companies than would the overall value universe.

11 Sharpe ratios for negative excess returns are not meaningful. In this case, the lower the excess return, the higher the Sharpe ratio.

Exhibit 7 Return Comparisons—S&P 500, S&P/BARRA Growth, and Strategy Benchmark

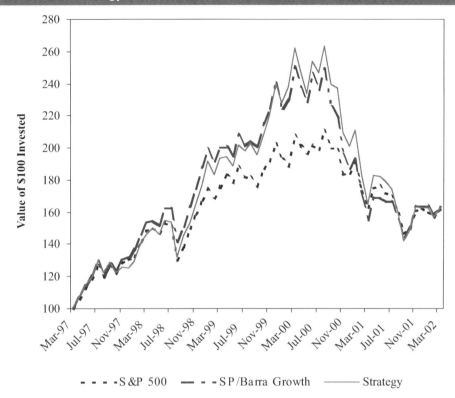

Exhibit 8 Return, Standard Deviation, and Sharpe Ratio Comparison—S&P 500, S&P/BARRA Growth, and Strategy Benchmark

(Annualized from Monthly Data)	Full Period 4/97–3/02			3 Years 4/97–3/00			2 Years 4/00–3/02		
	S&P 500	Growth	Strategy	S&P 500	Growth	Strategy	S&P 500	Growth	Strategy
Geometric Total Return	10.19%	10.15%	10.27%	27.43%	35.76%	37.78%	−11.39%	−19.50%	−21.05%
Standard Deviation	17.72%	20.55%	22.69%	17.43%	20.89%	19.42%	16.52%	20.89%	24.28%
Sharpe Ratio	0.31	0.24	0.24	1.07	1.29	1.69	NM	NM	NM

Exhibit 9 Risk, Return, and Outperformance Statistics for Strategy Benchmark Against S&P 500 and S&P/BARRA Growth Indexes

	Full Period 4/97–3/02		3 Years 4/97–3/00		2 Years 4/00–3/02	
	versus S&P 500	versus Growth	versus S&P 500	versus Growth	versus S&P 500	versus Growth
Beta	1.20	1.08	1.04	1.03	1.41	1.14
Alpha	−0.97%	−0.27%	7.27%	0.80%	−4.68%	1.69%
Total Tracking Error	8.55%	5.31%	7.12%	5.15%	9.64%	5.61%

(continued)

Exhibit 9 (Continued)

	Full Period 4/97–3/02		3 Years 4/97–3/00		2 Years 4/00–3/02	
	versus S&P 500	versus Growth	versus S&P 500	versus Growth	versus S&P 500	versus Growth
Residual Tracking Error	7.75%	5.08%	7.09%	5.13%	6.82%	4.82%
Information Ratio	−0.13	−0.05	1.03	0.16	−0.69	0.35

Now let's consider value-added against the benchmarks. Exhibit 9 shows the beta, alpha, total tracking error, residual tracking error, and information ratio for the strategy benchmark against the two published indexes for both the full period and the two subperiods.[12]

The first row shows beta coefficients. Note that during the first three years the betas are close to 1.0 and then shoot upward to 1.41 and 1.14 during the last 24 months. Using an inappropriate benchmark might lead an investor to determine that, in order to boost returns during the market downturn, the manager began taking on more market-timing risk by increasing the portfolio's beta, when in actuality this shift in beta is purely a function of a passive set of rules employed by the manager.

Second, the strategy shows a strong alpha—especially against the S&P 500—during the first three years. For an investor comparing this manager to the S&P, the peak in the market may have seemed an ideal time to increase exposure to this manager.

Perhaps most important is the tracking error. Both total tracking error and residual tracking error are very high. Using an inappropriate benchmark leads to built-in tracking error, which will in turn distort the information ratio and make evaluation of a manager much more difficult. Waring in Belden and Waring [2001] notes that:

> Using benchmarks that represent the manager's normal as closely as possible has a solid basis in theory. We want the simple, investible benchmark to "explain" in a statistical sense as much of the manager's behavior as possible....If part of the investment result that could have been explained with a more general benchmark is left in the residual, it will add tracking error...that obscures the manager's true trail [2001, p. 70].

My work here provides a compelling example of this phenomenon. All of the tracking error shown in Exhibit 9 could be eliminated by using the strategy benchmark rather than an inappropriate published benchmark.

Tracking error is also important in calculation of the information ratio. The information ratio is calculated as:

$$IR = \frac{\alpha}{\omega} \tag{2}$$

where α is the beta-adjusted benchmark outperformance, and ω is the residual risk (the portion of tracking error unrelated to benchmark timing risk).

The information ratio is used more and more frequently to evaluate both manager skill and proposed investment strategies. Equation 2 shows us that the lower the residual risk, ω, all other things equal, the higher the information ratio. Built-in

---

[12] I use the notation and definitions of Grinold and Kahn [1995]. Beta is defined as the slope of the regression $r_p(t) = \alpha_P + \beta_P r_B(t) + \varepsilon_P$. Alpha is defined from this equation as well; assuming that ε_p is, on average, equal to zero, we get $\alpha_P = r_p(t) - \beta_P r_B(t)$. Total tracking error, Ψ_p, is defined as $std\{r_p(t) - r_B(t)\}$, and residual tracking error, ω_p, as $std\{r_p(t) - \beta_P r_B(t)\}$. The information ratio, IR, is then defined as α_p/ω_p.

residual risk through the use of an inappropriate benchmark could have the impact of reducing the information ratio of a very skilled manager—an unfavorable outcome from both the manager's and the investor's perspectives.

And, all else equal, a manager outperforms if α is higher. If a strategy entails style risk against an inappropriate benchmark, a favorable environment for that style can result in a high information ratio when the supposed outperformance is really just a function of the manager's particular style being in favor.

This is clearly the case in Exhibit 9. The information ratio of the strategy benchmark is a significant 1.03 against the S&P 500 during the first three years but reverses significantly during the subsequent two-year period. Goodwin's research [1998] supports this conclusion. He finds that information ratios among managers differ by manager style. His final conclusion is that "you should always be cautious in interpreting a published information ratio, and you should discount any that uses an inappropriate benchmark" [Goodwin, 1998, p. 42].

Overall, the analysis shows that this particular strategy is not at all neutral to either published benchmark. The strategy has its own style that makes it perform differently. Given that manager style drift tends to occur in the direction of outperforming styles (see Arrington [2000]), another interpretation of Exhibit 9 is that the manager has engaged in significant style drift in order to boost returns. This confusion can be avoided through use of a strategy benchmark.

If the manager or investor were to perform the analysis using the strategy benchmark as the benchmark, the fit with the portfolio would be extraordinarily high, and the value-added of the manager—above and beyond a simple rule for narrowing down the broader universe of stocks—would be much more clear.

CONCLUSION

I have shown that in order for a benchmark to provide the investment manager with the qualities necessary for the implementation of a robust investment process, the benchmark must represent neutral or normal weights to both security and factor exposures. When there is no published index reflective of the manager's neutral, the manager must develop a strategy benchmark, either internally or with the help of a third party.

This strategy benchmark enables the investment process to maintain integrity with regard to: mean sector/factor exposures, the use of risk bands around sector/factor exposures, the process of overweighting and underweighting exposures, and attribution analysis. Without a strategy benchmark, many investment processes will tend to operate suboptimally, as the neutral weights, risk bands, overweighting, and attribution are skewed by differences between the chosen benchmark and the essential characteristics of the investment strategy.

Additionally, I have shown that some of the most useful measures—tracking error and the information ratio—can give spurious results if the benchmark used in the analysis is not truly representative of the manager's particular style.

While earlier work on this subject suggests that it is mainly in the investor's interests to use a strategy benchmark, my analysis shows that it is equally and perhaps even more important from the investment manager's perspective. Investment managers who are able to implement the framework described in Exhibit 1 around an appropriate benchmark are well positioned to continually improve their investment processes, and will thus be more likely to provide investors with superior results.

REFERENCES

Agache, Kristof. 2001. "The European Equity Investment Process." *Journal of Investing*, Winter:17–23.

Arrington, George R. 2000. "Chasing Performance Through Style Drift." *Journal of Investing*, Summer:13–17.

Bailey, Jeffery V. 1992. "Are Manager Universes Acceptable Performance Benchmarks?" *Journal of Portfolio Management*, Spring:9–13.

Bailey, Jeffery V., Thomas M. Richards, and David E. Tierney. 1990. "Benchmark Portfolios and the Manager/Plan Sponsor Relationship." In Frank J. Fabozzi and T. Dessa Fabozzi, eds., *Current Topics in Investment Management*. New York: Harper Collins, pp. 349–363.

Belden, Susan, and M. Barton Waring. 2001. "Compared to What? A Debate on Picking Benchmarks." *Journal of Investing*, Winter:66–72.

Brinson, Gary P., L. Randolph Hood, and Gilbert L. Beebower. 1986. "Determinants of Portfolio Performance." *Financial Analysts Journal*, July/August:39–44.

Brinson, Gary P., Brian D. Singer, and Gilbert L. Beebower. 1991. "Determinants of Portfolio Performance II: An Update." *Financial Analysts Journal*, May/June:40–48.

Dietz, Peter O., and Jeannette R. Kirschman. 1990. "Evaluating Portfolio Performance." In John L. Maginn and Donald L. Tuttle, eds., *Managing Investment Portfolios*. Charlottesville, VA: Warren, Gorham & Lamont, pp. 14.1–14.58.

Divecha, Arjun, and Richard C. Grinold. 1989. "Normal Portfolios: Issues for Sponsors, Managers and Consultants." *Financial Analysts Journal*, March/April:7–13.

Goodwin, Thomas H. 1998. "The Information Ratio." *Financial Analysts Journal*, July/August:34–43.

Grinold, Richard C., and Ronald N. Kahn. 1995. *Active Portfolio Management*. Chicago: Richard D. Irwin.

Kritzman, Mark. 1987. "How to Build a Normal Portfolio in Three Easy Steps." *Journal of Portfolio Management*, Summer:21–23.

Maginn, John L., and Donald L. Tuttle. 1990. "The Portfolio Management Process and Its Dynamics." In John L. Maginn and Donald L. Tuttle, eds., *Managing Investment Portfolios*. Charlottesville, VA: Warren, Gorham & Lamont, pp. 1.1–1.11.

Ryan, Timothy P. 2001. "Separating the Impact of Portfolio Management Decisions." *Journal of Performance Measurement*, Fall:29–40.

Smith, Paul. 2001/2002. "Process Attribution—Measuring the Performance of the Investment Process." *Journal of Performance Measurement*, Winter:21–28.

PRACTICE PROBLEMS

The following information relates to Questions 1–4

The investment strategy of Latrobe Capital Management's large cap value composite is to buy the common stock of non-financial corporations whose operating efficiency is higher than average. Latrobe's equity research department screens the stocks in the firm's large cap universe and identifies those with superior operating leverage and above-average returns on operating assets. The large cap value portfolio manager selects undervalued and fairly valued stocks from the resulting subset of the universe and divests any existing holdings whose operating measures have deteriorated.

For performance measurement purposes, the composite's existing benchmark is a widely-used capitalization-weighted large-cap value style index constructed in accordance with well-defined rules on the basis of the constituent stocks' fundamental characteristics. However, several clients question the appropriateness of the benchmark, and Latrobe hires Emilio Dominguez, an investment consultant, to evaluate its benchmark selection for the large cap value composite. Dominguez compares the composite's actual sector weights to the benchmark as of the beginning of the most recent measurement period. The comparison is displayed in Exhibit 1.

Exhibit 1   Composite vs. Benchmark Sector Weights

GICS® Sector*	Composite Weight	Benchmark Weight
Energy	5.0%	9.3%
Materials	8.4	3.0
Industrials	19.0	11.3
Consumer Discretionary	12.5	10.8
Consumer Staples	13.4	9.5
Health Care	9.7	13.3
Financials	0.0	21.2
Information Technology	21.2	15.1
Telecommunication Services	4.7	3.1
Utilities	6.1	3.4
Total	100.0%	100.0%

* The Global Industry Classification Standard (GICS®) was developed by and is the exclusive property of Morgan Stanley Capital International Inc. and Standard & Poor's. GICS is a service mark of MSCI and S&P and has been licensed for use by CFA Institute.

Dominguez tests the benchmark for systematic bias relative to the composite, calculates tracking error, and assesses benchmark coverage. He also examines a composite-level attribution analysis that Latrobe provides as supplemental information in its performance presentations. In the most recent period, the attribution analysis for the large cap value composite indicates that the primary contributors to Latrobe's value-added return were the firm's overweight position in the information technology sector and security selections in the consumer staples sector. Dominguez observes that the effect of the sector-weighting/security selection interaction is included in the security selection values.

1 Which one of the following statements is *most likely* to be accurate?
   A Latrobe's large cap value clients are bearing benchmark risk.
   B The benchmark reflects the risk and returns of the large cap value market.
   C The benchmark represents neutral sector weights for Latrobe's large cap value strategy.

2 The *most* accurate statement is that the attribution analysis is invalid because it:
   A is mathematically imprecise.
   B does not reflect Latrobe's active investment decisions.
   C distorts the impact of Latrobe's security selection decisions.

3 Dominguez, the consultant, recommends that Latrobe construct a strategy benchmark in accordance with the firm's specialized approach to large cap value investing. It is *most* appropriate for the strategy benchmark to include all the stocks that are contained in:
   A the published benchmark, with the exception of the Financials sector.
   B Latrobe's research universe and that meet the criteria for above-average operating efficiency.
   C Latrobe's research universe but that do not necessarily meet the criteria for above-average operating efficiency.

4 Latrobe constructs a strategy benchmark for the large cap value composite. In order to evaluate the firm's large cap value investment strategy, it is *most* appropriate to compare the:
   A composite returns to the returns of the strategy benchmark.
   B composite returns to the returns of the published large cap value index.
   C strategy benchmark returns to the returns of the published large cap value index.

The following information relates to Questions 5–14

Fund X invests in large-cap growth stocks. The manager of Fund X uses a strategy benchmark for the Fund's performance analysis. The strategy benchmark comprises Russell 1000 Growth Index constituents with both higher-than-average return on equity ratios and lower-than-average earnings variability. The portfolio manager has recently increased security holdings of companies with low debt ratios. Industrials sector weights and returns for Fund X and related indexes are presented in Exhibit 1.

Practice Problems

Exhibit 1: Fund X Industrials Sector Data for the Most Recent Annual Period

	Weight	Return
Fund X	10%	6%
Fund X Strategy Benchmark	15%	5%
Russell 1000 Growth Index	12%	1%

A performance analyst and a risk specialist for Fund X are reviewing two large-cap growth funds managed by competitors. Fund Y uses the Russell 1000 Growth Index for its benchmark, but the performance analyst recommends using a strategy benchmark. Holdings of Fund Y are selected from the benchmark's universe of equities that remain after being screened for below-average earnings yield. Fund Z is an enhanced index fund that overweights the top 10 companies with the highest forecasted earnings growth rates by 0.2% each and underweights all other holdings proportionally. Fund Z also uses the Russell 1000 Growth Index for its benchmark.

The performance analyst and the risk specialist have a conversation about the risk of Fund X that begins with the performance analyst making the following two comments:

Comment 1   The investor bears benchmark risk, and the fund manager bears the active risk of deviating from the benchmark.

Comment 2   The risk–return characteristics of Fund X are comparable to those of the Russell 1000 Growth Index.

Fund X does not limit sector exposures. The risk specialist would like to add risk bands to cap active sector exposure at 10% relative to the strategy benchmark weights. The risk specialist makes the following three statements:

Statement 1   Risk bands should have a significant impact on long-term sector weights.

Statement 2   Neutral weights should be reflective of the universe of investments from which a manager selects.

Statement 3   Risk bands should be extreme boundaries around a neutral weight.

5 What is the normal weight of the industrials sector for Fund X for the most recent annual period?
   A 10%
   B 12%
   C 15%

6 What was the style exposure of the industrials sector for Fund X for the most recent annual period?
   A −5%
   B −3%
   C 3%

7 Which of the funds has a manager strategy discipline?
   A Only Fund X
   B Only Fund Y
   C Both Fund X and Fund Y

8 Fund Z can *best* be described as:
   A requiring a strategy benchmark.

B not committed to minimizing tracking error.

C having a published benchmark–centered discipline.

9 For which manager would the calculated active risk *most likely* be misleading?

A Fund X

B Fund Y

C Fund Z

10 Which of the performance analyst's comments is correct?

A Only Comment 1

B Only Comment 2

C Both Comment 1 and Comment 2

11 Which of the risk specialist's statements is incorrect?

A Statement 1

B Statement 2

C Statement 3

12 The decision to exclude companies with high earnings variability from Fund X is *best* evaluated by analyzing the Fund's:

A active risk.

B active returns.

C investment strategy.

13 How will attribution analysis of the industrials sector of Fund X be affected by using the Russell 1000 Growth Index in place of the fund's current benchmark? The returns attributed to active security selection will be:

A understated.

B accurate.

C overstated.

14 How will the tracking risk for Fund Y be affected by using its established benchmark instead of following the performance analyst's recommendation? The calculated tracking error for Fund Y *most likely* will be:

A understated.

B accurate.

C overstated.

SOLUTIONS

1. B is correct. A widely-used capitalization-weighted style index presumably reflects the risks and returns of the large cap value market segment. A is not the best answer. Siegel writes, "If the investment manager deviates from the benchmark by policy, as the result of an investment strategy that specifically excludes a large portion of the securities in the benchmark, the client is not, on average, bearing benchmark risk." C is incorrect because Latrobe does not use benchmark sector weights as the basis for constructing large cap value portfolios.

2. B is correct. Latrobe's bottom-up large cap value decision process appears to proceed without reference to benchmark sector weights. Thus, for instance, the firm did not make an active decision to overweight the information technology sector relative to the benchmark; instead, the firm selected securities issued by companies with above-average operating efficiency, and a large percentage of the composite's market value happened to fall in the information technology sector. The underlying problem is that the published benchmark is inappropriate for Latrobe's large cap value strategy. A is not the best answer because the attribution methodology may be mathematically precise, and C is incorrect because Latrobe's combining the security selection and interaction effects (a common practice) does not render the attribution analysis invalid.

3. B is correct. The stocks that meet Latrobe's criteria for inclusion in the large cap value composite are those that are really eligible for the portfolio manager to purchase. They constitute the manager's true opportunity set. C is not the best answer because stocks that are in the research universe but have below-average operating efficiency are systematically excluded by the portfolio construction rule. A is not the best answer because simply excluding financials from the published benchmark is unlikely to produce the portfolio's true neutral weights.

4. C is correct. Comparing the returns of the strategy benchmark to those of the published index will provide useful evidence whether the firm's strategy outperforms the overall large cap value market. A is not the best answer because comparing composite (or portfolio) returns to the returns of the strategy benchmark discloses the results of the manager's decisions to deviate from the benchmark but does not show how Latrobe's strategy produces results that differ from large cap value market returns. B is not the best answer because comparing composite returns to the returns of the published index does not isolate the impact of Latrobe's strategy from the results of the portfolio manager's tactical deviations from the strategy benchmark.

5. C is correct. The benchmark should represent normal portfolio sector weights. Fund X's average exposure to market sectors over time differs from that of the Russell 1000 Growth Index, owing to the quantitative filter, so the manger created a strategy benchmark to represent normal sector weights. The industrials sector weight for the Fund X Strategy Benchmark, found in Exhibit 1, is 15%.

6. C is correct. The style exposure (S) is the difference between a manager's strategy benchmark weight (B) and the market (published) index weight (M).

    $S = B - M = 15\% - 12\% = 3\%$.

7. C is correct. Both Fund X and Fund Y are constructed with active decisions of a quantitatively filtered universe, so the risk–return characteristics will not be consistent with those of a published index and, therefore, are manager strategy disciplines. Instead of the Russell 1000 Growth Index, Fund Y should use a strategy benchmark to better track the neutral weights of the strategy.

8 C is correct. Fund Z has an enhanced index strategy, which is the defining example of a published benchmark–centered discipline. Published benchmark–centered disciplines begin with a well-established broad-based benchmark as the goal and are managed closely to this index on an ongoing basis.

9 B is correct. Fund Y is using the Russell 1000 Growth Index as the benchmark. In this case, the published index will likely include securities that would not be in the Fund. The external index does not represent the neutral weights for the portfolio, making it a poor benchmark for the purposes of gauging active risk, performance attribution, and gaining insights into the portfolio management process. The calculated active risk value *most likely* will be misleading under this scenario.

10 A is correct. Only Comment 1 is correct. The client bears the benchmark risk, and the active manager bears the risk of deviating from the benchmark. When the manager and the investor identify the benchmark, they are identifying the general risk–return characteristics that the investor will expect over time. Comment 2 is incorrect because the risk–return characteristics of the fund will be comparable to those of the strategy benchmark, not the market index.

11 A is correct. Statement 1 is incorrect. Risk bands should not have a significant impact on the long-term sector weights. They should serve as extreme boundaries around a neutral weight. If the long-term sector weights are at the risk band boundaries, then the benchmark weights may not be representative of the long-term risk and return characteristics of the strategy.

12 C is correct. Companies with high earnings variability are filtered out of the opportunity set and are not included in the strategy benchmark. Comparing the strategy benchmark with the market index will capture the impact of the decision to exclude companies with high earnings variability.

13 C is correct. The attribution analysis should be performed against the strategy benchmark in order to measure active portfolio management decisions. The return of the industrials sector, shown in Exhibit 1, was significantly higher for Fund X (6%) than for the Russell 1000 Growth Index (1%), so security selection results would be overstated if the attribution analysis used the Russell 1000 Growth Index as the benchmark.

14 C is correct. Fund Y uses the Russell 1000 Growth Index, an externally published benchmark, instead of a strategy benchmark. The use of a published index in this case is inappropriate because the index does not reflect the neutral weights of Fund Y's portfolio. Using an inappropriate benchmark leads to built-in tracking error, making it overstated.

READING
6

Topics in Return Attribution

by Carl R. Bacon, CIPM

Carl R. Bacon, CIPM, is at StatPro and the University of Manchester (United Kingdom).

LEARNING OUTCOMES	
Mastery	The candidate should be able to:
☐	a. calculate and interpret return attribution results for portfolios containing short positions;
☐	b. calculate and interpret return attribution results for portfolios containing futures or options;
☐	c. calculate and interpret the asset allocation, security selection, and currency allocation effects in a multi-currency portfolio using the Karnosky–Singer approach;
☐	d. calculate and interpret the asset allocation, security selection, and currency allocation effects in a multi-currency portfolio using a geometric methodology when returns are not continuously compounded;
☐	e. describe why interest rate differentials matter in multi-currency return attribution;
☐	f. contrast arithmetic and geometric multi-period attribution analysis;
☐	g. describe problems associated with multi-asset attribution analysis, including analysis of balanced portfolios and portfolios combining liquid and illiquid assets.

INTRODUCTION 1

This reading is an extension of the reading "Topics in Return Measurement." This reading uses the techniques described in "Topics in Return Measurement" to perform return attribution analysis on portfolios containing short positions, derivative instruments, and multiple currencies.

The reading is organized as follows. Section 2 discusses return attribution of portfolios containing short positions. Section 3 discusses attribution analysis in the case in which the portfolio contains futures contracts or option contracts. Section 4 discusses the challenging topic of multi-currency attribution and introduces the

Karnosky–Singer model and geometric models for such attribution. Section 5 describes multi-period attribution, and Section 6 discusses some problems associated with multi-asset attribution.

2. ATTRIBUTION ANALYSIS FOR PORTFOLIOS CONTAINING SHORT POSITIONS

The Brinson model for return attribution is a robust model that can be applied to many varied investment decision strategies without any specific adjustment.[1] In particular, it can be applied to strategies that include short positions, such as long–short, short extension, and market neutral strategies. In market neutral strategies, the portfolio manager offsets the risk of short positions by taking a similar sized long position so that the net risk exposure is approximately zero; this positioning suggests that the strategy's return can be benchmarked against the return to cash. Without generating market exposure, the strategy approximately doubles the exposure to the portfolio manager's stock picking ability (summing exposure on the long side and exposure on the short side). Assuming the betas of the long and short positions are the same so that the portfolio's net beta is zero, then in theory, a good stock picker should be able to generate attractive absolute returns in all market conditions, and the return attribution analysis should accurately reflect this strategy.

Market neutral strategies are examples of absolute return strategies and are typically benchmarked against a short term cash index. Benchmarks for long–short strategies are challenging, and absolute return benchmarks are not necessarily appropriate for attribution because they contain so little information (e.g., risk).[2] There are borrowing costs associated with implementing the short element of the strategy, and these can either be reflected in the return of the shorted assets or included in the cash return.

In the market neutral strategy example in Exhibit 1, the investor is simultaneously long and short both US and Canadian equities. Note that the manager has a net 10% long position in Canadian equities and hence the implementation of the strategy is not perfectly neutral. Short positions are represented by a negative weight. Cash received from the short sales is equal to the total of the short positions. The cash used to fund the portfolio has been fully allocated to long US and Canadian equities. For the offsetting long and short benchmark weights, the assumption is made that the strategy requires 120% (60% long plus 60% short) exposure to the manager's US equities stock picking expertise and 80% (40% long plus 40% short) exposure to the manager's Canadian equities stock picking expertise.[3] In Exhibit 1, benchmark returns for US and Canadian equities represent hypothetical returns to broad US and Canadian equity indexes, respectively. The portfolio and benchmark returns shown in the table are in the investor's base currency. The overall benchmark, consistent with a zero net market exposure, is a cash benchmark.

---

1 The foundations of return attribution were established in two articles written by Brinson and Fachler (1985) and Brinson, Hood, and Beebower (1986). These models are discussed in the CIPM Level I reading "Return Attribution" by Carl R. Bacon and Marc A. Wright. In this reading, we use the Brinson and Fachler analysis with the interaction effect included in the selection effect.
2 An absolute return benchmark is simply a minimum target return that the manager is expected to beat. The return may be a stated minimum (e.g., 9%), stated as a spread above a market index (e.g., Libor plus 4%), or determined from actuarial assumptions.
3 The benchmark weights in this case would arise from, for example, the client's policy allocation, the manager's policy decision, or the asset allocation committee's decision.

Attribution Analysis for Portfolios Containing Short Positions

Exhibit 1 Market Neutral Attribution

Category	Portfolio Weight (%)	Benchmark Weight (%)	Portfolio Return (%)	Benchmark Return (%)
Long US equities	50.0	60.0	16.0	10.0
Long Canadian equities	50.0	40.0	−8.0	−6.0
Short US equities	−50.0	−60.0	6.0	10.0
Short Canadian equities	−40.0	−40.0	−10.0	−6.0
Cash	90.0	100.0	2.0	3.0
Total	100.0	100.0	6.8	3.0

The total portfolio and benchmark returns in the investor's base currency are calculated as follows:

$$\text{Portfolios return } R = \sum_{i=1}^{i=n} w_i \times R_i$$

$$\text{Benchmark return } B = \sum_{i=1}^{i=n} W_i \times B_i$$

where

w_i = weight of the ith sector in the portfolio
R_i = return of the portfolio assets in the ith sector
W_i = weight of the benchmark in the ith sector
B_i = return of the benchmark in the ith sector
n = number of sectors

The total portfolio return is $R = \sum_{i=1}^{i=n} w_i \times R_i$:

$R = (50\% \times 16\%) + (50\% \times -8\%) + (-50\% \times 6\%) + (-40\% \times -10\%) + (90\% \times 2\%)$
$= 6.8\%$

The total benchmark return is $B = \sum_{i=1}^{i=n} W_i \times B_i$:

$B = (60\% \times 10\%) + (40\% \times -6\%) + (-60\% \times 10\%) + (-40\% \times -6\%) + (100\% \times 3\%)$
$= 3.0\%$

Using the standard arithmetic Brinson and Fachler (BF) attribution analysis, the total arithmetic excess return is 6.8% − 3.0% = 3.8%. This excess return is composed of both allocation and selection effects.

Allocation To calculate the allocation effect A, we use the following formula in which the manager's weight is compared with the benchmark weight, and the benchmark return for a sector is compared with the overall benchmark return:

$A_i = (w_i - W_i) \times (B_i - B)$

We will use Exhibit 1 to illustrate the formula's application, starting with the long US equities position. The manager has underweighted US equities compared with the benchmark weight. The US equities benchmark had a 10% return compared with the overall benchmark return of 3%. Because the long US equity position is underweight and the US equity market outperformed the overall benchmark return during the period, this results in an allocation effect of −0.7%:

Long US equities (50.0% − 60.0%) × (10.0% − 3.0%) = −0.7%

The long Canadian equity position is 10% overweight and the Canadian equity benchmark underperformed the overall benchmark return, resulting in an allocation effect of −0.9%:

Long Canadian equities (50.0% − 40.0%) × (−6.0% − 3.0%) = −0.9%

The short US equity position is effectively 10% overweight (not as short as the benchmark), which mirrors the 10% underweight position in the long US equities position. This results in a positive allocation effect of 0.7% because US equities outperformed in the benchmark. This positive allocation effect offsets the −0.7% allocation effect in the long US equity position.

Short US equities [−50.0% − (−60.0%)] × (10.0% − 3.0%) = 0.7%

The short Canadian equity position weighting matches the benchmark weighting; therefore, the allocation effect is 0.0%:

Short Canadian equities [−40.0% − (−40.0%)] × (−6.0% − 3.0%) = 0.0%

The cash position is 10% underweight, but because the cash benchmark and the total benchmark are identical, the allocation effect is 0.0%:

Cash (90.0% − 100.0%) × (3.0% − 3.0%) = 0.0%

The total allocation effect $A = \sum_{i=1}^{i=n} A_i$ is −0.7% − 0.9% + 0.7% + 0.0% + 0.0% = −0.9%.

Selection The selection effect measures whether the portfolio manager chooses securities that outperform the benchmark securities in each sector. The contribution to selection in the ith sector is:

$S_i = w_i \times (R_i - B_i)$

Using the data in Exhibit 1, the selection effects are calculated as follows.

For the long US equities position, the manager's very strong outperformance added 3.0% to the total excess return:

Long US equities 50.0% × (16.0% − 10.0%) = 3.0%

The manager's underperformance in long Canadian equities generated a negative contribution to excess return of −1.0%:

Long Canadian equities 50.0% × [−8.0% − (−6.0%)] = −1.0%

In the short US equity portion of the portfolio, the manager has shorted stocks that have underperformed the benchmark. Although the underlying stock return is positive because the segment underperformed on a relative basis, this negative position contributed 2.0% of excess return:

Short US equities −50.0% × (6.0% − 10.0%) = 2.0%

In the short Canadian equity portion of the portfolio, the manager shorted stocks that fell in value and underperformed the benchmark. The added value from the stock selection perspective generated an excess return of 1.6%:

Short Canadian equities −40.0% × [−10.0% − (−6.0%)] = 1.6%

Because cash represented 90% of the portfolio value, the manager's 1% underperformance resulted in a −0.9% effect:

Cash 90.0% × (2.0% − 3.0%) = −0.9%

A stock selection effect in the cash portion might be a surprise, but it is entirely possible. The underperformance in the cash sector relative to the benchmark might result from a variety of factors. These factors include underperforming cash or near cash instruments, losses as a result of currency translation, lower interest received from instruments denominated in a foreign currency, and/or the borrowing costs of implementing short positions.

The total stock selection effect $S = \sum_{i=1}^{i=n} S_i$ is 3.0% − 1.0% + 2.0% + 1.6% − 0.9% = 4.7%.

The asset allocation and stock selection effects in the sectors are summarized in Exhibit 2 below. The total arithmetic excess return is 3.8%, as previously calculated using the total portfolio and benchmark returns: 6.8% − 3.0%. Of the total arithmetic excess return, 4.7% is derived from stock selection and −0.9% from asset allocation.

Exhibit 2 Market Neutral Attribution

Category	Allocation (%)	Selection (%)
Long US equities	−0.7	3.0
Long Canadian equities	−0.9	−1.0
Short US equities	0.7	2.0
Short Canadian equities	0.0	1.6
Cash	0.0	−0.9
Total	−0.9	4.7

This attribution assumes that the short and long sides of the strategy are essentially independent but that does not need to be the case. For example, if the long element of the strategy is underweight in the oil sector, then the portfolio manager may compensate by being less short the oil sector in the short element of strategy. This weighting choice may affect the stock selection results of both the long and short positions but they offset each other. This weighting choice can either be addressed in a narrative explanation to the client when presenting the return attribution analysis or the benchmark can be explicitly adjusted[4] to reflect the underlying strategy of the portfolio manager. Provided the adjustments are mirrored in both the long and short element of the benchmark, this approach will not affect the overall strategic benchmark and will correctly reflect the stock selection effects in both the long and short elements of the portfolio. Securities could be grouped for long and short positions into country, industrial sector, market capitalization, or style segments. Even individual stocks might specifically offset each other (one stock short, the other stock long) in *pairs trading*.

Variations of the basic Brinson model are applicable to long–short strategies, including Brinson–Fachler (used earlier) or Brinson–Hood–Beebower methodologies, arithmetic or geometric approaches, and whether to include the stock selection effect in the interaction.

Other examples of strategies with short positions include short extension strategies. A short extension strategy allows the manager to go short a proportion of the long position. An example of this strategy is a 130/30 extension in which a manager goes short 30% and uses the resulting sale proceeds to make a further investment in long securities.

---

[4] For example, the index can be customized by adjusting the weight in the oil sector equally in both the long and the short elements of the benchmark.

> **EXAMPLE 1**
>
> ### Attribution for a Short Extension Fund
>
> Exhibit 3 shows data from a 130/30 fund.
>
> **Exhibit 3   US Equities 130/30 Fund**
>
> | Category | Portfolio Weight (%) | Benchmark Weight (%) | Portfolio Return (%) | Benchmark Return (%) |
> |---|---|---|---|---|
> | Long US equities | 120.0 | 130.0 | 12.0 | 10.0 |
> | Short US equities | –30.0 | –30.0 | 9.0 | 10.0 |
> | Cash | 10.0 | 0.0 | 3.0 | 3.0 |
> | Total | 100.0 | 100.0 | 12.0 | 10.0 |
>
> **1** The selection effect in short US equities is *closest* to:
> **A** –2.7%.
> **B** –0.3%.
> **C** +0.3%.
>
> **2** The total asset allocation effect is *closest* to:
> **A** –0.7%.
> **B** +0.0%.
> **C** +0.7%.
>
> **3** Market neutral strategies can be challenging to analyze *most likely* because:
> **A** the Brinson model is not appropriate.
> **B** a suitable benchmark is difficult to identify.
> **C** portfolio returns cannot be calculated for short positions.
>
> ### Solution to 1:
>
> C is correct. –30% × (9.0% – 10.0%) = 0.3%
>
> ### Solution to 2:
>
> A is correct.
>
> > Allocation in long US equities (120.0% – 130.0%) × (10.0% – 10.0%) = 0.0%
> >
> > Allocation in short US equities [–30.0% – (–30.0%)] × (10.0% – 10.0%) = 0.0%
> >
> > Allocation in cash (10.0% – 0.0%) × (3.0% – 10.0%) = –0.7%
> >
> > Total allocation 0.0% + 0.0% – 0.7% = –0.7%
>
> ### Solution to 3:
>
> B is correct. Attribution analysis can be challenging for market neutral strategies because a suitable benchmark is often difficult to identify. Absolute return benchmarks are not necessarily appropriate because they contain so little information.

ATTRIBUTION ANALYSIS FOR A PORTFOLIO CONTAINING DERIVATIVES

Derivatives can be used in asset management to transfer or hedge risk, change asset and risk allocations, synthetically replicate certain assets, and create leverage and speculate.[5] For example, UK equity futures contracts can be added to the market neutral portfolio in Exhibit 1 to gain UK equity market exposure. This section presents attribution for portfolios containing futures and/or options.

3.1 Attribution for a Portfolio Containing Futures

In Exhibit 4, the previous market neutral portfolio has been overlaid with UK equity futures to create a portfolio with UK equity market exposure while retaining exposure to the stock picking abilities of the portfolio manager in US and Canadian equities on both the long and the short side. The benchmark of the manager's UK strategy is a UK equity index that the futures contract is linked to. Because the long and short US and Canadian benchmark positions offset each other, the overall benchmark return for the manager is now that of the UK equity index.

Exhibit 4   Market Neutral Attribution plus UK Futures Overlay

Category	Portfolio Weight (%)	Benchmark Weight (%)	Portfolio Return (%)	Benchmark Return (%)
Long US equities	50.0	60.0	16.0	10.0
Long Canadian equities	50.0	40.0	−7.0	−6.0
Short US equities	−50.0	−60.0	6.0	10.0
Short Canadian equities	−40.0	−40.0	−7.0	−6.0
UK equity futures	100.0	100.0	7.9	8.0
Associated economic exposure	−100.0	0.0	2.0	3.0
Cash	90.0	0.0	2.0	3.0
Total	100.0	100.0	12.0	8.0

The Brinson–Fachler arithmetic attribution calculations are as follows:

Allocation

$A_i = (w_i - W_i) \times (B_i - B)$

Long US equities (50.0% − 60.0%) × (10.0% − 8.0%) = −0.2%

Long Canadian equities (50.0% − 40.0%) × (−6.0% − 8.0%) = −1.4%

Short US equities [−50.0% − (−60.0%)] × (10.0% − 8.0%) = 0.2%

Short Canadian equities [−40.0% − (−40.0%)] × (−6.0% − 8.0%) = 0.0%

UK Equity Futures (100.0% − 100.0%) × (8.0% − 8.0%) = 0.0%

Associated economic exposure (−100.0% − 0.0%) × (3.0% − 8.0%) = 5.0%

---

5 For a discussion on the fundamental of derivatives, see "A Primer on Derivatives," which is the appendix to the reading *Topics in Return Measurement*.

Cash (90.0% − 0.0%) × (3.0% − 8.0%) = −4.5%

Futures positions at any point in time do not change the overall value of the portfolio, rather they adjust economic exposure. Profit and loss is reflected daily in the variation margin account. Conceptually, the manager has borrowed cash at 2% interest and used that borrowed cash to invest in UK equities via the futures contract. The borrowed cash is shown as the associated economic exposure; the long UK equity futures position creates an associated economic exposure that is always equal in weight and opposite in sign. The long element of the UK futures position itself has not added any allocation value because the 8.0% benchmark return in UK futures representing the return to the underlying reference asset is the same as the total benchmark return. The associated economic exposure has added 5.0% because the portfolio manager has borrowed cash in a rising equity market. Note the 3.0% benchmark return for the associated economic exposure is the same as the physical cash benchmark used in Exhibit 1. An argument can be made to use as the benchmark the rate used to price the futures contract (2%). The correct one to use will largely depend on the actual investment process.

The physical cash position is overweight with an allocation effect of −4.5%. The associated economic exposure and cash allocation effects are often combined for presentation—described, say, as effective cash—in a manner more consistent with the portfolio manager's investment process.

Selection

$$S_i = w_i \times (R_i - B_i)$$

The selection effects for the components of the market neutral strategy are unchanged from the previous example.

Long US equities 50.0% × (16.0% − 10.0%) = 3.0%

Long Canadian equities 50.0% × [−7.0% − (−6.0%)] = −0.5%

Short US equities −50.0% × (6.0% − 10.0%) = 2.0%

Short Canadian equities −40.0% × [−7.0% − (−6.0%)] = 0.4%

Cash 90.0% × (2.0% − 3.0%) = −0.9%

The selection effect for the UK equity futures position is:

UK equity futures 100.0% × (7.9% − 8.0%) = −0.1%

Even though, in this case, the UK equity futures are benchmarked against the same index as the underlying futures contract, there is a −0.1% selection effect. The reason is that the futures contract itself may not be trading at fair value to the underlying index or, more likely, it is a timing effect. The futures contract may be traded at intraday index values that differ from the index value at the end of day. In effect, intraday values would be used to determine the return to the futures contract whereas end of day index values are used to calculate the benchmark return.

The notional return on the associated economic exposure is 2%. This is based on the interest rate used to price the futures contract, which for a UK contract is GBP Libor. For futures contracts in other countries' equity, interest rates in those currencies are used.

The 1.0% contribution to selection from the associated economic exposure reflects the lower cost of borrowing cash at 2% than the physical cash benchmark of 3%.[6]

Associated economic exposure −100.0% × (2.0% − 3.0%) = 1.0%

---

6 When we go long an equity futures contract, we are essentially borrowing cash to invest in the asset. If we went short the equity futures contract, we would be lending cash to the counterparty. Futures contracts denominated in different currencies naturally use different interest rate assumptions.

The total arithmetic excess return is 4.0%; 4.9% is derived from selection and −0.9% from allocation, which is summarized in Exhibit 5.

Exhibit 5 Market Neutral Attribution plus UK Futures Overlay: Allocation and Selection

Category	Allocation (%)	Selection (%)
Long US equities	−0.2	3.0
Long Canadian equities	−1.4	−0.5
Short US equities	0.2	2.0
Short Canadian equities	0.0	0.4
UK equity futures	0.0	−0.1
Associated economic exposure	5.0	1.0
Cash	−4.5	−0.9
Total	−0.9	4.9

Combining associated economic exposure and cash, which is consistent with the investment decision process of the portfolio manager, the completed attribution is shown in Exhibit 6.

Exhibit 6 Market Neutral Attribution plus UK Futures Overlay: Completed Attribution

Category	Portfolio Weight (%)	Benchmark Weight (%)	Portfolio Return (%)	Benchmark Return (%)	Allocation (%)	Selection (%)
Long US equities	50.0	60.0	16.0	10.0	−0.2	3.0
Long Canadian equities	50.0	40.0	−7.0	−6.0	−1.4	−0.5
Short US equities	−50.0	−60.0	6.0	10.0	0.2	2.0
Short Canadian equities	−40.0	−40.0	−7.0	−6.0	0.0	0.4
UK equity futures	100.0	100.0	7.9	8.0	0.0	−0.1
Effective cash	−10.0	0.0	2.0	3.0	0.5	0.1
Total	100.0	100.0	12.0	8.0	−0.9	4.9

3.2 Attribution for a Portfolio Containing Options

Options can be included in attribution analysis in a similar way to futures contracts because they also create an associated economic exposure. But options have a value in their own right and are instruments with highly non-linear or asymmetrical payoffs. The buyer of a European style option has the right but not the obligation to buy (call option) or sell (put option) an agreed amount of a specified asset (the underlying or reference asset) at a specified price (the exercise or strike price) on a future date (the expiry date). European options can only be exercised at expiry whereas American style options can be exercised on any business day up to and including the expiry date. The purchaser of an option pays a premium to the seller or writer of the contract. The writer receives a premium but has a potential liability in the form of a negatively valued asset (the short call or a short put position).

The performance of option contracts is measured in the same way as any other asset, but the associated economic exposure is not linear; it is convex and will change depending on how close the price of the reference asset is to the exercise price.

The total value of an option is made up of intrinsic value and time value. The intrinsic value of the option is the value that would be realized by immediately exercising the option. If no value would be realized, the intrinsic value is zero; the intrinsic value is never negative because the option holder cannot be compelled to exercise the option.

The time value reflects the possibility that the option may have a positive intrinsic value or be in the money before expiry. If the spot price of the asset is equal to the exercise price, the option is said to be at the money. For calls, the option is in the money when the spot price is more than the exercise price and out of the money when the spot price is less than the exercise price; for puts, the opposite is true.

The price sensitivities of options' values are measured by the "Greeks": delta, gamma, theta, vega, and rho:

- Delta, δ, is the change in value of an option for a small change in the underlying asset price.
- Gamma, γ, measures the rate of change of delta (equivalent to the convexity measure for bonds).
- Theta, θ, measures the option's sensitivity to time.
- Vega measures the option's sensitivity to volatility.
- Rho, ρ, measures the option's sensitivity to interest rates.

Option traders are interested in all these measures, but from a performance measurement perspective theta, vega, and rho are relatively minor selection effects. The most important measure is delta, which is used in the calculation of associated economic exposure and to arrive at a return attribution consistent with the investment decision process.

Delta can be thought of as providing information about the investor's exposure to the underlying asset. If a call option is at the money, the delta will typically be approximately 0.50, meaning for every $1 change in the underlying asset's value, the call value will change by approximately $0.50.[7] If the call option is in the money, the delta will be greater than 0.50, indicating that the option's value has a greater sensitivity to changes in the underlying asset's value. If the call option is out of the money, the delta will be less than 0.50, indicating that changes in the underlying asset value have less impact on the option value. The delta converges to 1.00 if deeply in the money and 0 if deeply out of the money. The delta for a put option will be between 0 and –1, reflecting the inverse relationship between put values and the underlying asset values.

In the attribution analysis, the value of the option provides part of the position's valuation. The remainder of the position's associated economic exposure is derived as shown in the following.[8]

$$\text{Option associated economic exposure} = \delta \times \text{Number of options} \times \text{Underlying price} \quad (1)$$

$$= \text{Option value} + \text{Notional assets} \quad (2)$$

The delta and thus the associated economic exposure is continuously changing as the underlying asset's price changes. The total option associated economic exposure is arrived at using Equation 1. This exposure is then decomposed into option value and notional assets, as shown in Equation 2.

---

[7] There are some cases in which an at-the-money call will have a delta that diverges from 0.50 (e.g., when interest rates are high and there is a long time to expiration). Additionally, delta becomes less accurate in estimating an option price change when the underlying asset price change is large, in which case the use of both delta and gamma will reduce the estimation error.

[8] Note that in general, Number of options = Number of contracts × Contract value multiplier.

Consider the portfolio shown in Exhibit 7, consisting of 3,000 shares in a US company each priced at $100, 10,000 long call options in the same company with a strike price of $100 each priced at $10, and $600,000 in cash. Attribution analysis is performed on this portfolio using a benchmark consisting of 60% in the US company stock and 40% in cash, which, for the purpose of this exercise, we shall assume is the policy allocation of the client.

Exhibit 7 Portfolio Containing Long Call Options

Asset Class	Actual Holdings (US dollars)	Percentage Exposure (%)
US company stock	300,000	30
Options	100,000	10
Physical cash	600,000	60
Total	1,000,000	100

With a strike price of $100, the options are at the money. Assume a delta of 0.5. Consistent with the portfolio manager's investment decision process, we need to calculate the associated beginning economic exposure of the option position using delta, the number of options, and the current stock price as follows:[9]

$$0.5 \times 10,000 \times \$100 = \$500,000$$

The options are already valued at $100,000 and therefore we need a further $400,000 of notional cash assets to in effect be transferred from cash to create the total economic exposure of $500,000 for the option. The total US equity position is then $300,000 + $100,000 + $400,000 = $800,000.

In this example, assume a 2% return on the US company shares, a 10% return on the options, and a 0.1% return on cash. The price change for the stock is from $100 to $102, creating a gain of $6,000 ($2 × 3,000). The price change for the options position is $1, which is the delta of 0.5 times the underlying stock price change of $2. Thus the option price changes from $10 to $11, creating a gain of $10,000 ($1 × 10,000). The gain on the cash is 0.1% × $600,000 = $600. The return on the total portfolio before the adjustment for the notional assets is:

$$\frac{(6,000 + 10,000 + 600)}{1,000,000} = 1.66\%$$

The combined return on the US equity position including options and notional assets is:

$$\frac{(6,000 + 10,000 + 400)}{(300,000 + 100,000 + 400,000)} = 2.05\%$$

The $400 in interest in the numerator is the notional cash assets of $400,000 times the interest rate of 0.1%. The remaining cash position or effective cash is $600,000 − $400,000 = $200,000, or 20% of the total portfolio position. The total portfolio return including the cash return is:

$$(80\% \times 2.05\%) + (20\% \times 0.1\%) = 1.66\%$$

The total benchmark return using its 60/40 weights, the 2% stock return, and the 0.1% cash return is:

$$(60\% \times 2.0\%) + (40\% \times 0.1\%) = 1.24\%$$

---

9 Note that the price used is the underlying reference price, not the strike price. The economic exposure is fluid and changes with the underlying stock value and the delta.

The portfolio adjusted to reflect the associated economic exposure of the options is shown in Exhibit 8.

Exhibit 8 Portfolio Exposures Assuming Long Call Option Positions

Asset Class	Actual Holdings USD	Exposure (%)	Return (%)
US company	300,000	30	2.0
Options	100,000	10	10.0
Notional assets	400,000	40	0.1
Total US	800,000	80	2.05
Physical cash	600,000	60	0.1
Notional assets	–400,000	–40	0.1
Effective cash	200,000	20	0.1
Total	1,000,000	100	1.66

The Brinson–Fachler arithmetic attribution calculations are as follows:

Allocation

$A_i = (w_i - W_i) \times (B_i - B)$

Total US equity position (80.0% – 60.0%) × (2.0% – 1.24%) = 0.152%

Effective cash (20.0% – 40.0%) × (0.10% – 1.24%) = 0.228%

Total allocation 0.152% + 0.228% = 0.38%

In terms of physical assets (the US company stock and options), the portfolio is underweight the US company stock, but after including notional assets to achieve the associated economic exposure generated by the options, the portfolio is overweight, leading to 0.152% of added value. Although overweight physical cash, the effective cash weight—after adjusting for notional cash assets—is underweight, leading to 0.228% of added value. A total of 0.38% is attributable to allocation.

Selection

$S_i = w_i \times (R_i - B_i)$

Total US equity position 80.0% × (2.05% – 2.0%) = 0.04%

Effective cash 20.0% × (0.1% – 0.1%) = 0.00%

Total selection 0.04% + 0.00% = 0.04%

The return on total US assets including options and notional cash is 2.05%, which is greater than the underlying asset return of 2.0%. The synthetically created equity position outperformed the underlying equity position and contributed 0.04% of selection. There is no selection effect in the effective cash position.[10]

Overall, the portfolio outperformed the benchmark by 0.42% (1.66% – 1.24%). Of the outperformance, 0.38% is from allocation and 0.04% is from selection.

---

10 In this example, the return on physical cash, the return on notional cash, and the benchmark return on cash are all assumed to be 0.1%. This situation is quite normal and leads to a selection effect in cash of 0.0%. Theoretically and practically, the physical return on cash may differ from the benchmark return on cash and the assumed return on the notional cash may differ from the benchmark cash return, which may generate a non-zero cash selection effect.

Attribution Analysis for a Portfolio Containing Derivatives

The attribution is summarized in Exhibit 9.

Exhibit 9 Attribution Including Long Call Options

	Portfolio Weight (%)	Benchmark Weight (%)	Portfolio Return (%)	Benchmark Return (%)	Allocation (%)	Selection (%)
Total US	80	60	2.05	2.0	0.152	0.04
Effective cash	20	40	0.1	0.1	0.228	0.00
Total	100	100	1.66	1.24	0.38	0.04

Now, consider an example in which the portfolio manager is attempting to reduce equity exposure using options, which could be achieved by shorting or "writing" call options or purchasing long put options. Using short call options, first consider the portfolio in Exhibit 10 containing 6,000 shares in the same US company used in Exhibit 7, each priced at $100; a short position of 10,000 call options in the same US company, each priced at $10 with a strike price of $100; and $500,000 in cash. Attribution analysis is also performed on this portfolio using the same benchmark as before, consisting of 60% in the US company stock and 40% in cash.

Exhibit 10 Portfolio Containing Short Call Options

Asset Class	Actual Holdings (US dollars)	Percentage Exposure (%)
US company stock	600,000	60
Options	−100,000	−10
Physical cash	500,000	50
Total	1,000,000	100

As before with a strike price of $100, the options are at the money and have a delta of approximately 0.5. Also as before, we calculate the associated beginning economic exposure of the option position using delta, the number of options, and the current stock price as follows:

$0.5 \times -10,000 \times \$100 = -\$500,000$

Because the portfolio is effectively short in options, they are already valued at −$100,000 and, therefore, we need a further $400,000 of notional cash assets to, in effect, be transferred to cash to create the total economic exposure of −$500,000 for the options. The total US equity position is then $600,000 − $100,000 − $400,000 = $100,000.

Again, assume a 2% return on the US company shares, a 10% return on the options, and a 0.1% return on cash. The price change for the stock is from $100 to $102, creating a gain of $12,000 ($2 × 6,000). The price change for the options position is from $10 to $11, creating a loss of $10,000 because the portfolio is short these options. The gain on the cash is 0.1% × $500,000 = $500. The return on the total portfolio before the adjustment for the notional assets is

$$\frac{(12,000 - 10,000 + 500)}{1,000,000} = 0.25\%$$

The combined return on the US equity position, including options and notional assets, is

$$\frac{(12,000 - 10,000 - 400)}{(600,000 - 100,000 - 400,000)} = 1.6\%$$

The –$400 in interest in the numerator is the notional cash assets of –$400,000 times the interest rate of 0.1%.

The effective cash position is now $500,000 + $400,000 = $900,000, or 90% of the total portfolio position. The total portfolio return, including the cash return, is

$(10\% \times 1.6\%) + (90\% \times 0.1\%) = 0.25\%$

The total benchmark return using its 60/40 weights, the 2% stock return, and the 0.1% cash return is

$(60\% \times 2.0\%) + (40\% \times 0.1\%) = 1.24\%$

The portfolio adjusted to reflect the associated economic exposure of the options is shown in Exhibit 11.

Exhibit 11 Portfolio Exposures assuming Short Call Option Positions

Asset Class	Actual Holdings (US dollars)	Exposure (%)	Return (%)
US company	600,000	60	2.0
Options	–100,000	–10	10.0
Notional assets	–400,000	–40	0.1
Total US	100,000	10	1.6
Physical cash	500,000	50	0.1
Notional assets	400,000	40	0.1
Effective cash	900,000	90	0.1
Total	1,000,000	100	0.25

The Brinson–Fachler arithmetic attribution calculations are as follows.

Allocation

$A_i = (w_i - W_i) \times (B_i - B)$

Total US equity position: $(10.0\% - 60.0\%) \times (2.0\% - 1.24\%) = -0.38\%$

Effective cash: $(90.0\% - 40.0\%) \times (0.10\% - 1.24\%) = -0.57\%$

Total allocation: $-0.38\% - 0.57\% = -0.95\%$

In terms of physical assets (the US company stock and options), the portfolio is slightly underweight the US company stock, but when notional assets to achieve the associated economic exposure generated by the options are included, the portfolio is significantly more underweight, leading to 0.38% of subtracted value. Physical cash, the effective cash weight, is initially slightly overweight and, after adjustments for notional cash assets is significantly overweight, leading to 0.57% of subtracted value. A total of –0.95% is attributable to allocation.

Selection

$S_i = w_i \times (R_i - B_i)$

Attribution Analysis for a Portfolio Containing Derivatives

Total US equity position: 10.0% × (1.6% − 2.0%) = −0.04%

Effective cash: 90.0% × (0.1% − 0.1%) = 0.00%

Total selection: −0.04% + 0.00% = −0.04%

The return on total US equity, including options and notional cash, is 1.6%, which is less than the underlying asset return of 2.0%. The synthetically created asset position outperformed the underlying equity, and because we are effectively short the synthetic asset in the combined US equity position, this contributed −0.04% of selection. There is no selection effect in the effective cash position.

Overall, the portfolio underperformed the benchmark by −0.99% (0.25% − 1.24%). Of the underperformance, −0.95% is from allocation and −0.04% is from selection. The attribution is summarized in Exhibit 12.

Exhibit 12 Attribution Including Short Call Options

	Portfolio Weight (%)	Benchmark Weight (%)	Portfolio Return (%)	Benchmark Return (%)	Allocation (%)	Selection (%)
Total US	10	60	1.6	2.0	−0.38	−0.04
Effective cash	90	40	0.1	0.1	−0.57	0.00
Total	100	100	0.25	1.24	−0.95	−0.04

Now, consider a similar portfolio in Exhibit 13 using long put options consisting of 6,000 shares in the same US company used in Exhibit 7, each priced at $100; a long position of 20,000 put options in the same US company, each priced at $5 with a strike price of $84; and $300,000 in cash. Attribution analysis is also performed on this portfolio using the same benchmark as before, consisting of 60% in the US company stock and 40% in cash.

Exhibit 13 Portfolio Containing Long Put Options

Asset Class	Actual Holdings (US dollars)	Percentage Exposure (%)
US company stock	600,000	60
Options	100,000	10
Physical cash	300,000	30
Total	1,000,000	100

With a strike price of $84, the options are out of the money and have a delta of approximately −0.25.[11] Consistent with the portfolio manager's investment decision process, we need to calculate the associated beginning economic exposure of the option position using delta, the number of options, and the current stock price as follows:

−0.25 × 20,000 × $100 = −$500,000

The options are valued at $100,000 already, and therefore, we need $600,000 of notional cash assets to cover this $100,000 to generate the negative economic exposure of −$500,000. The total US equity position is then $600,000 + $100,000 − $600,000 = $100,000.

---

[11] Note the negative delta for a put option.

Again, assume a 2% return on the US company shares, a −10% return on the options,[12] and a 0.1% return on cash. The price change for the stock is from $100 to $102, creating a gain of $12,000 ($2 × 6,000). The price change for the option position is from $5 to $4.50, creating a loss of $10,000. The gain on the cash is 0.1% × $300,000 = $300. The return on the total portfolio before the adjustment for the notional assets is:

$$\frac{(12{,}000 - 10{,}000 + 300)}{1{,}000{,}000} = 0.23\%$$

The combined return on the US equity position, including options and notional assets, is:

$$\frac{(12{,}000 - 10{,}000 - 600)}{(600{,}000 + 100{,}000 - 600{,}000)} = 1.4\%$$

The −$600 in interest in the numerator is the notional cash assets of −$600,000 times the interest rate of 0.1%.

The effective cash position is now $300,000 + $600,000 = $900,000, or 90% of the total portfolio position. The total portfolio return, including the cash return, is:

$$(10\% \times 1.4\%) + (90\% \times 0.1\%) = 0.23\%$$

The total benchmark return using its 60/40 weights, the 2% stock return, and the 0.1% cash return is:

$$(60\% \times 2.0\%) + (40\% \times 0.1\%) = 1.24\%$$

The portfolio adjusted to reflect the associated economic exposure of the options is shown in Exhibit 14.

Exhibit 14   Portfolio Exposures assuming Long Put Option Positions

Asset Class	Actual Holdings (US dollars)	Exposure (%)	Return (%)
US company	600,000	60	2.0
Options	100,000	10	−10.0
Notional assets	−600,000	−60	0.1
Total US	100,000	10	1.4
Physical cash	300,000	30	0.1
Notional assets	600,000	60	0.1
Effective cash	900,000	90	0.1
Total	1,000,000	100	0.23

The Brinson–Fachler arithmetic attribution calculations are as follows.

Allocation

$A_i = (w_i - W_i) \times (B_i - B)$

Total US equity position: (10.0% − 60.0%) × (2.0% − 1.24%) = −0.38%

Effective cash: (90.0% − 40.0%) × (0.10% − 1.24%) = −0.57%

---

[12] Note that because the delta is −0.25, a price change of $2 for the underlying stock leads to an approximate change in the option price of −0.25 × $2 = −$0.50 (a 10% reduction in the original price of $5).

Total allocation: −0.38% − 0.57% = −0.95%

The allocation result is identical to that described in Exhibit 12 because the effective weights and benchmark returns are the same. However, the selection impact differs.

Selection

$S_i = w_i \times (R_i - B_i)$

Total US equity position: 10.0% × (1.4% − 2.0%) = −0.06%

Effective cash: 90.0% × (0.1% − 0.1%) = 0.00%

Total selection: −0.06% + 0.00% = −0.06%

The return on total US assets, including options and notional cash, is 1.4%, which is less than the underlying asset return of 2.0%. In this particular example, the combination of a long put and notional cash, although achieving the same allocation effect as that of the short call, underperformed from a stock selection perspective, resulting in a greater selection loss of −0.06%. There is no selection effect in the effective cash position.

Overall, the portfolio underperformed the benchmark by −1.01% (0.23% − 1.24%). Of the underperformance, −0.95% is from allocation and −0.06% is from selection. The attribution is summarized in Exhibit 15.

Exhibit 15   Attribution Including Long Put Options

	Portfolio Weight (%)	Benchmark Weight (%)	Portfolio Return (%)	Benchmark Return (%)	Allocation (%)	Selection (%)
Total US	10	60	1.4	2.0	−0.38	−0.06
Effective cash	90	40	0.1	0.1	−0.57	0.00
Total	100	100	0.23	1.24	−0.95	−0.06

EXAMPLE 2

Notional Cash Assets Calculation for a Portfolio Containing Options

A portfolio contains 1,000 long call options at a current price of $10 in an underlying stock with a strike price of $100. The underlying stock price is $90, and the delta is 0.4. The value of notional cash assets that must be transferred from cash is *closest to*:

A $26,000.

B $36,000.

C $40,000.

Solution:

A is correct. The associated economic exposure is 1,000 × $90 × 0.4 = $36,000, but we already have a $10,000 value from the options; so the value of notional cash assets is $36,000 − $10,000 = $26,000.

4 MULTI-CURRENCY ATTRIBUTION

Multi-currency attribution is more complex than attribution for single-currency portfolios. If the currency decision is implicit within or a result of the asset allocation decision, then there is no requirement to attribute the currency effect separately. For genuinely multi-currency investment decision strategies, however, we must address a number of issues, including (but not limited to) the following:

- Interest rate differentials between countries
- The compounding effects of security market and currency returns
- Securities denominated in currencies other than the currency of economic exposure

4.1 Karnosky and Singer Multi-currency Attribution

Earlier papers addressed multi-currency attribution, but the 1994 paper by Karnosky and Singer is considered a definitive paper on the subject. This paper explains why managing multi-currency portfolios is sub-optimal if currency is not managed independently and also provides a framework for calculating attribution effects taking into account interest rate differentials. The compounding of local market and currency returns is conveniently resolved in Karnosky and Singer (1994) by using continuously compounded (or log) returns, which allows simple addition and subtraction of terms.[13]

In effect, Karnosky and Singer[14] defined the total return of the portfolio as:

$$R = \sum_{i=1}^{i=n} w_i \times (R_{Li} + C_i) \qquad (3)$$

where

w_i = portfolio weight of country i
R_{Li} = portfolio return in local-currency terms for country i
C_i = the spot currency return (in relation to the base currency)

Note that the local currency is that in which the security is denominated whereas the base currency is the investor's home or domestic currency. Thus, $(R_{Li} + C_i)$ represents the base-currency return for an investment in country i. The addition of local-country portfolio return and spot currency return can be used instead of multiplicative returns because the returns used are continuously compounded (or log) returns.

Equation 3 can be expanded as follows:

$$R = \sum_{i=1}^{i=n} w_i \times R_{Li} + \sum_{i=1}^{i=n} w_i \times C_i \qquad (4)$$

Introducing the interest rate of each currency i, Equation 4 can be further expanded as follows:

$$R = \sum_{i=1}^{i=n} w_i \times (R_{Li} - I_i) + \sum_{i=1}^{i=n} w_i \times (C_i + I_i) \qquad (5)$$

---

[13] Continuously compounded returns are discussed in the CIPM Level I reading *Performance Evaluation: Rate-of-Return Measurement*, by Carl R. Bacon, David R. Cariño, and Arin Stancil.
[14] Karnosky and Singer assigned a separate weight to cash.

where

I_i = interest rate in currency i
$(R_{Li} - I_i)$ = the equity premium above local interest rates in each country
$(C_i + I_i)$ = the spot currency return plus interest in each currency

The advantage of introducing interest rates for the markets the investor is exposed to is that we account for the forward premium or discount for foreign currencies, which is a function of interest rate differentials between two currencies. The interest rate differential between markets is known to managers at the time of investment, and their response to it is within their control. We therefore account for it in the attribution analysis. The first term in Equation 5 represents an equity risk premium that is used to measure the manager's asset allocation decision in each country. The second term in Equation 5 represents the foreign cash return converted to the investor's base currency and is used to measure the manager's currency performance decision in each country.

If the portfolio includes forward currency contracts, these can be included as shown in Equation 6.[15]

$$R = \sum_{i=1}^{i=n} w_i \times (R_{Li} - I_i) + \sum_{i=1}^{i=n} w_i \times (C_i + I_i) + \sum_{i=1}^{i=n} \tilde{w}_i \times (C_i + I_i) \qquad (6)$$

where $\tilde{w}_i$ = the weight in forward currency i.

Note that each forward currency contract will consist of two segments—one positive in sign and one negative. At the start of a contract, the weights of each offset to zero. Combining the last two terms of Equation 6, the return of the portfolio can be calculated as follows:[16]

$$R = \sum_{i=1}^{i=n} w_i \times (R_{Li} - I_i) + \sum_{i=1}^{i=n} (w_i + \tilde{w}_i) \times (C_i + I_i) \qquad (7)$$

This equation states that the portfolio return can be decomposed as the portfolio weight times the equity premium in each country plus the sum of the portfolio and forward weights times the currency return and interest rate in each country.

Similarly, the benchmark return is defined as follows:[17]

$$B = \sum_{i=1}^{i=n} W_i \times (B_{Li} - I_i) + \sum_{i=1}^{i=n} (W_i + \tilde{W}_i) \times (C_i + I_i) \qquad (8)$$

where

B_{Li} = benchmark return in local currency for country i
W_i = benchmark weight of country i
$\tilde{W}_i$ = benchmark weight in forward currency i

The first element of Equation 8 represents the equity premium benchmark, B_L, in local-currency terms:

$$B_L = \sum_{i=1}^{i=n} W_i \times (B_{Li} - I_i)$$

---

[15] In their paper, Karnosky and Singer (1994) referred to hedge ratios rather than weights allocated to forward currency contracts, but the calculation approach is the same.

[16] Note that the portfolio return can also be calculated as $R = \sum_{i=1}^{i=n} w_i \times (R_{Li} + C_i) + \sum_{i=1}^{i=n} \tilde{w}_i \times (C_i + I_i)$.

[17] Note that the benchmark return can also be calculated as $B = \sum_{i=1}^{i=n} W_i \times (B_{Li} + C_i) + \sum_{i=1}^{i=n} \tilde{W}_i \times (C_i + I_i)$.

The second element of Equation 8 represents the currency benchmark, C:

$$C = \sum_{i=1}^{i=n}\left(W_i + \tilde{W}_i\right) \times \left(C_i + I_i\right)$$

Subtracting Equation 8 from Equation 7, we obtain:

$$R - B = \underbrace{\sum_{i=1}^{i=n} w_i \times \left(R_{Li} - I_i\right) - \sum_{i=1}^{i=n} W_i \times \left(B_{Li} - I_i\right)}_{\text{Equity premium attribution}}$$

$$+ \underbrace{\sum_{i=1}^{i=n}\left(w_i + \tilde{w}_i\right) \times \left(C_i + I_i\right) - \sum_{i=1}^{i=n}\left(W_i + \tilde{W}_i\right) \times \left(C_i + I_i\right)}_{\text{Currency attribution}}$$

A standard Brinson–Fachler attribution can be applied to each part of this equation, attributing the equity premium and currency separately.

Applying the Brinson–Fachler approach, the allocation and selection effects are calculated in local-currency terms. The allocation effect in country i is the difference in portfolio and benchmark weights times the benchmark's country i return in excess of the interest rate and total benchmark return:

$$A_i = (w_i - W_i) \times (B_{Li} - I_i - B_L) \tag{9}$$

The selection effect in country i is the portfolio weight times the portfolio's country i return in excess of the benchmark's country i return:[18]

$$S_i = w_i \times (R_{Li} - B_{Li}) \tag{10}$$

There is no need to subtract interest rates to create an equity premium for selection because the interest rate is the same for both the portfolio and benchmark returns. In practice, the selection effect is the same, measured in local or base currency.

The two previous effects were calculated based on equity premiums. The third effect incorporates the currency component in each country. The currency attribution in currency i is the portfolio equity and forward weights in excess of the benchmark's weights times the sum of the currency return and interest in excess of the currency benchmark return:

$$CA_i = \left[\left(w_i + \tilde{w}_i\right) - \left(W_i + \tilde{W}_i\right)\right] \times \left[\left(C_i + I_i\right) - C\right] \tag{11}$$

In the basic Karnosky–Singer model, only currency allocation effects are calculated. It is assumed that spot currency and forward currency returns are the same in both the portfolio and the benchmark. Differences in currency returns would lead to a selection or "timing" effect in currency.

Exhibit 16 provides the data for a three-country, three-currency portfolio including forward currency contracts in both the portfolio and the benchmark. The base currency of this portfolio is GBP. The underlying equity exposure of the benchmark requested by the client generates exposure to AUD and USD. Although the exposure to Australian and US equities is desired, the client is more cautious about currency exposure and requests that the benchmark be hedged 50% back to GBP. This results in a net 70% exposure to GBP, 10% AUD, and 20% USD. The 30% benchmark GBP forward contract exposure results from two forward currency positions: 10% against AUD and 20% against USD.

In generating the actual currency exposures of the portfolio against the benchmark, the portfolio manager responsible for the currency process takes into account the currency exposure of both the underlying physical assets and the forward currency exposures. In Exhibit 16, the benchmark exposure to AUD is 20% from the AUD

---

18 The selection effect here includes the interaction terms, sometimes treated separately in other models.

underlying assets minus 10% forward currency, equaling 10%. The portfolio's exposure to AUD from underlying assets is 30%; therefore, a forward contract exposure of negative 15% generates a net long exposure of 15% and a 5% overweight relative to the benchmark. The benchmark exposure to USD is 40% from the underlying assets minus 20% forward currency assets, resulting in a net 20% exposure. The portfolio manager requires a net long USD position of 20% also against the GBP, and therefore, a forward contract exposure of negative 10% is required. Relative to the benchmark, the resulting portfolio is overweight 5% AUD, neutral USD, and underweight 5% GBP.

In the benchmark, the short AUD and USD forward contract positions are offset by a combined long position in GBP. For the purposes of Exhibit 16, the portfolio's short AUD and USD forward contract positions also offset, although in practice, unrealized gains and losses on these contracts might lead to a net position slightly different from zero.

Exhibit 16 A Multi-currency Portfolio

Category	Portfolio Weight, w_i (%)	Benchmark Weight, W_i (%)	Portfolio Local Return, R_{Li} (%)	Benchmark Local Return, B_{Li} (%)	Local Interest Rate, I_i (%)	Spot Currency Return, C_i (%)
UK equities	40	40	12.0	10.0	1.0	0
Australian equities	30	20	4.0	6.0	2.0	5
US equities	30	40	−6.0	−4.0	0.5	10
	$\tilde{w}_i$	$\tilde{W}_i$				
GBP forward contracts	+25	+30			1.0	0
AUD forward contracts	−15	−10			2.0	5
USD forward contracts	−10	−20			0.5	10
Total weights and base-currency returns	100	100	6.85	6.1		

The portfolio return in base currency is calculated using Equation 7 as follows:

$$R = \sum_{i=1}^{i=n} w_i \times (R_{Li} - I_i) + \sum_{i=1}^{i=n} (w_i + \tilde{w}_i) \times (C_i + I_i)$$

R = 40% × (12.0% − 1.0%) + 30% × (4.0% − 2.0%) + 30% × (−6.0% − 0.5%) +
(40% + 25%) × (0.0% + 1%) + (30% − 15%) × (5.0% + 2.0%) + (30% − 10%) ×
(10.0% + 0.5%)
= 6.85%

The benchmark return in base currency is calculated using Equation 8 as follows:

$$B = \sum_{i=1}^{i=n} W_i \times (B_{Li} - I_i) + \sum_{i=1}^{i=n} (W_i + \tilde{W}_i) \times (C_i + I_i)$$

B = 40% × (10.0% − 1.0%) + 20% × (6.0% − 2.0%) + 40% × (−4.0% − 0.5%) +
(40% + 30%) × (0.0% + 1.0%) + (20% − 10%) × (5.0% + 2.0%) + (40% − 20%)
× (10.0% + 0.5%)
= 6.10%

Total excess return: R − B = 6.85% − 6.10% = 0.75%

The equity premium benchmark is:

$$B_L = \sum_{i=1}^{i=n} W_i \times (B_{Li} - I_i)$$

B_L = 40% × (10.0% − 1.0%) + 20% × (6.0% − 2.0%) + 40% × (−4.0% − 0.5%)
= 2.6%

The currency benchmark is calculated as follows:

$$C = \sum_{i=1}^{i=n} (W_i + \tilde{W}_i) \times (C_i + I_i)$$

C = (40% + 30%) × (0.0% + 1.0%) + (20% − 10%) × (5.0% + 2.0%) + (40% − 20%) × (10.0% + 0.5%)
= 3.5%

Allocation

$A_i = (w_i - W_i) \times (B_{Li} - I_i - B_L)$

UK equities (40% − 40%) × [(10.0% − 1.0%) − 2.6%] = 0.0%

Australian equities (30% − 20%) × [(6.0% − 2.0%) − 2.6%] = 0.14%

US equities (30% − 40%) × [(−4.0% − 0.5%) − 2.6%] = 0.71%

Total asset allocation effect = 0.85%

Selection

$S_i = w_i \times (R_{Li} - B_{Li})$

UK equities 40% × (12.0% − 10.0%) = 0.8%

Australian equities 30% × (4.0% − 6.0%) = −0.6%

US equities 30% × [−6.0% − (−4.0%)] = −0.6%

Total security selection effect = −0.4%

Currency allocation

$$CA_i = \left[(w_i + \tilde{w}_i) - (W_i + \tilde{W}_i)\right] \times \left[(C_i + I_i) - C\right]$$

GBP [(40% + 25%) − (40% + 30%)] × [(0.0% + 1.0%) − 3.5%] = 0.125%

AUD [(30% − 15%) − (20% − 10%)] × [(5.0% + 2.0%) − 3.5%] = 0.175%

USD [(30% − 10%) − (40% − 20%)] × [(10.0% + 0.5%) − 3.5%] =0.0%

Total currency allocation effect = 0.3%

The sum of the allocation, selection, and currency allocation effects is 0.85% − 0.4% + 0.3% = 0.75%. This confirms the previous calculation of the excess return of 6.85% − 6.10% = 0.75%.

EXAMPLE 3

Attribution for a Multi-currency Portfolio

Exhibit 17 provides the data for a portfolio containing US, European, and Canadian equities. The base currency of the portfolio is USD.

Exhibit 17 A Multi-currency Portfolio

Category	Portfolio Weight, w_i (%)	Benchmark Weight, W_i (%)	Portfolio Local Return, R_{Li} (%)	Benchmark Local Return, B_{Li} (%)	Local Interest Rates, I_i (%)	Spot Currency Return, C_i (%)
US equities	70	60	−2.0	−4.0	0.5	0.0
European equities	20	30	3.0	2.0	1.0	−5.0
Canadian equities	10	10	−3.0	−6.0	2.0	5.0
	$\tilde{w}_i$	$\tilde{W}_i$				
USD forward contracts	+20	+40			0.5	0.0
EUR forward contracts	−20	−30			1.0	−5.0
CAD forward contracts	0	−10			2.0	5.0
Total weights and base-currency returns	100	100	−0.7	−2.7		

1 The selection effect in US equities is *closest* to:
  A 1.05%.
  B 1.40%.
  C 1.75%.

2 The allocation effect in European equities is *closest* to:
  A −0.47%.
  B −0.42%.
  C +0.04%.

3 The currency allocation effect in Canadian dollars is *closest* to:
  A −0.65%.
  B 0.0%.
  C +0.65%.

4 Karnosky and Singer resolved the compounding effect of local market and currency returns by using:
  A geometric attribution.
  B interest rate differentials.
  C continuously compounded returns.

Solution to 1:
B is correct. $S_i = w_i \times (R_{Li} - B_{Li}) = 70\% \times [-2.0\% - (-4.0\%)] = 1.4\%$.

Solution to 2:
B is correct. The equity premium benchmark is $B_L = \sum_{i=1}^{i=n} W_i \times (B_{Li} - I_i)$:

$B_L = 60\% \times (-4.0\% - 0.5\%) + 30\% \times (2.0\% - 1.0\%) + 10\% \times (-6.0\% - 2.0\%)$
$\quad = -3.2\%$

The allocation effect in European equities is $A_i = (w_i - W_i) \times (B_{Li} - I_i - B_L)$:

$(20\% - 30\%) \times [(2.0\% - 1.0\%) - (-3.2\%)] = -0.42\%$

Solution to 3:

C is correct. The currency benchmark is $C = \sum_{i=1}^{i=n}(W_i + \tilde{W}_i) \times (C_i + I_i)$. So:

$C = (60\% + 40\%) \times (0.0\% + 0.5\%) + (30\% - 30\%) \times (-5.0\% + 1.0\%) +$
$\quad (10\% - 10\%) \times (5.0\% + 2.0\%)$
$= 0.5\%$

The currency allocation in CAD is

$$CA_i = \left[(w_i + \tilde{w}_i) - (W_i + \tilde{W}_i)\right] \times \left[(C_i + I_i) - C\right]$$

$[(10\% + 0\%) - (10\% - 10\%)] \times [(5.0\% + 2.0\%) - 0.5\%] = 0.65\%$

Solution to 4:

C is correct. Karnosky and Singer used continuously compounded (or log) returns to resolve the compounding effect of local market and currency returns. Karnosky and Singer did not use a geometric approach to attribution. Karnosky and Singer used interest rate differentials but not to resolve the compounding effect of local market and currency returns.

4.2 Geometric Multi-currency Attribution

Karnosky and Singer used continuously compounded returns to resolve the compounding effect of local market and currency returns and to provide an arithmetic form of multi-currency attribution. To avoid using continuously compounded returns, which may be unfamiliar to many users, the excess return of multi-currency portfolios can be attributed using a geometric approach. In this approach, we start with a simple naive calculation ignoring interest rate differentials but implicitly including compounding effects. Then, building on this simple approach, we can add further complexity by identifying specifically any compounding effects and introducing the effect of interest differentials in an approach similar to that of Karnosky and Singer. For many, the simpler approach of naive currency attribution provides sufficient currency analysis; others may judge that the added complexity of the Karnosky and Singer approach is justified by its more complete analysis.

4.2.1 Naive Currency Attribution

The total portfolio return in the base currency is a weighted average of the base-currency returns in each country:

$$R = \sum_{i=1}^{i=n} w_i \times R_i$$

In local-currency terms, the portfolio return is:

$$R_L = \sum_{i=1}^{i=n} w_i \times R_{Li}$$

Similarly, for the benchmark, the total return in the base currency is a weighted average of the base-currency returns in each country:

$$B = \sum_{i=1}^{i=n} W_i \times B_i$$

Multi-currency Attribution

In local-currency terms, the benchmark return is:

$$B_L = \sum_{i=1}^{i=n} W_i \times B_{Li}$$

We also define a local-currency, semi-notional return using the *portfolio* weights and *benchmark* local-currency returns. The semi-notional return indicates what managers would have earned in local-currency terms if they had invested in the benchmark securities. It is determined using:

$$B_{SL} = \sum_{i=1}^{i=n} w_i \times B_{Li}$$

By definition, the currency performance of the portfolio must be the relative difference between the portfolio performance in base-currency and local-currency terms.

$$R_C = \frac{1+R}{1+R_L} - 1$$

Similarly, the currency performance of the benchmark is defined as the relative difference between the performance of the benchmark in base currency and in local currency.

$$B_C = \frac{1+B}{1+B_L} - 1$$

Naive currency attribution is the ratio of the currency return of the portfolio relative to the currency return of the benchmark:

$$\frac{1+R_C}{1+B_C} - 1 = \left[\frac{(1+R)/(1+R_L)}{(1+B)/(1+B_L)}\right] - 1 \qquad (12)$$

This equation can be re-written as follows:

$$\text{Naive currency attribution} = \left(\frac{1+R}{1+R_L}\right) \times \left(\frac{1+B_L}{1+B}\right) - 1$$

This simple version of currency attribution is described as naive because it does not take into account interest rate differentials as described by Karnosky and Singer. In this naive version of currency attribution, we calculate the attribution effects of allocation and stock selection in local currency as follows.

The allocation effect is the ratio of the semi-notional portfolio return compared with the benchmark in local-currency terms.

Allocation

$$\frac{1+B_{SL}}{1+B_L} - 1$$

Here we hold the security selection constant by using benchmark country returns. The allocation effect indicates what the manager earned relative to the benchmark by choosing portfolio weights that differ from the benchmark.

The stock selection effect is the ratio of the portfolio return in local currency relative to that of the semi-notional portfolio.

Stock selection

$$\frac{1+R_L}{1+B_{SL}} - 1$$

We can now see that the stock selection, asset allocation, and currency allocation effects compound to provide the portfolio return in excess of the benchmark return:

$$\underbrace{\left(\frac{1+R_L}{1+B_{SL}}\right)}_{\text{Selection}} \times \underbrace{\left(\frac{1+B_{SL}}{1+B_L}\right)}_{\text{Allocation}} \times \underbrace{\left(\frac{1+R}{1+R_L}\right) \times \left(\frac{1+B_L}{1+B}\right)}_{\text{Naive Currency Allocation}} - 1 = \frac{1+R}{1+B} - 1$$

Exhibit 18 provides data for a three-country, three-currency portfolio excluding any forward currency contracts for a UK-based investor with a base currency of GBP.[19]

Exhibit 18 Multi-currency Portfolio

Category	Portfolio Weight, w_i (%)	Benchmark Weight, W_i (%)	Portfolio Local Return, R_{Li} (%)	Benchmark Local Return, B_{Li} (%)	Portfolio Base Return, R_i (%)	Benchmark Base Return, B_i (%)	Currency Return, C_i (%)
UK equities	40	40	12.0	10.0	12.0	10.0	0.0
European equities	30	20	−7.0	−8.0	2.3	1.2	10.0
US equities	30	40	6.0	6.0	0.7	0.7	−5.0
Total	100	100	4.5	4.8	5.7	4.52	

The portfolio return in base currency is calculated as:

$R = (40\% \times 12.0\%) + (30\% \times 2.3\%) + (30\% \times 0.7\%) = 5.7\%$

The benchmark return in base currency is calculated as:

$B = (40\% \times 10.0\%) + (20\% \times 1.2\%) + (40\% \times 0.7\%) = 4.52\%$

Total excess return:

$$\frac{1+R}{1+B} - 1 = \frac{1.057}{1.0452} - 1 = 1.13\%$$

The portfolio local return is calculated as:

$R_L = (40\% \times 12.0\%) + [30\% \times (-7.0\%)] + (30\% \times 6.0\%) = 4.5\%$

The benchmark local return is calculated as:

$B_L = (40\% \times 10.0\%) + [20\% \times (-8.0\%)] + (40\% \times 6.0\%) = 4.8\%$

The semi-notional return is calculated as:

$B_{SL} = (40\% \times 10.0\%) + [30\% \times (-8.0\%)] + (30\% \times 6.0\%) = 3.4\%$

The stock selection effect is calculated as:

$$\frac{1+R_L}{1+B_{SL}} - 1 = \frac{1.045}{1.034} - 1 = 1.0638\%$$

The allocation effect is calculated as:

$$\frac{1+B_{SL}}{1+B_L} - 1 = \frac{1.034}{1.048} - 1 = -1.3359\%$$

---

[19] Notice that in the example here, the currency return is the same for the portfolio and benchmark. However, this is not always the case.

The actual currency performance of the portfolio is therefore:

$$R_C = \frac{1+R}{1+R_L} - 1 = \frac{1.057}{1.045} - 1 = 1.1483\%$$

The actual currency return of the benchmark is therefore:

$$B_C = \frac{1+B}{1+B_L} - 1 = \frac{1.0452}{1.048} - 1 = 0.997328 - 1 = -0.2672\%$$

The naive currency attribution effect is therefore:

$$\frac{1+R_C}{1+B_C} - 1 = \frac{1.011483}{0.997328} - 1 = 1.4193\%$$

The stock selection, allocation, and currency attribution effects compound to provide the previously calculated portfolio excess return of 1.13% [= (1.010638 × (1 − 0.013359) × 1.014193) − 1].

4.2.2 Compounding Effects

An unavoidable complication in multi-currency portfolios is the effect of changing currency exposure due to the changing market values of the underlying assets. For example, a manager may fully hedge the currency exposure of an initial foreign equity investment, but by the end of the month the investment value is often much different, leaving the currency exposure of the capital gain or loss unhedged.

When a currency overlay is used, the currency hedging strategy is typically managed separately from the underlying portfolio, either by another firm or in a different portfolio. Thus, currency overlay managers are often unaware of changing asset values (in either the portfolio or the benchmark) and are obliged to respond only when they are informed of market value changes. Therefore, if the currency exposure is independently managed, we must isolate these compounding effects.

We define an implied currency return in the benchmark to be equal to the sum product of the benchmark weights and currency returns:[20]

$$\text{Implied benchmark currency return } B'_C = \sum_{i=1}^{i=n} W_i \times C_i \quad (13)$$

Similarly, we define an implied currency return in the portfolio to be equal to the sum product of the portfolio weights and currency returns:

$$\text{Implied portfolio currency return } R'_C = \sum_{i=1}^{i=n} w_i \times C_i \quad (14)$$

Using the currency returns in Exhibit 18, the implied currency returns are calculated as follows:

$$B'_C = (40\% \times 0.0\%) + (20\% \times 10.0\%) + \left[40\% \times (-5.0\%)\right] = 0.0\%$$

$$R'_C = (40\% \times 0.0\%) + (30\% \times 10.0\%) + \left[30\% \times (-5.0\%)\right] = 1.5\%$$

The difference between implied and actual currency returns can be described as compounding or a cross-product effect. It results from the changing market value of the underlying assets changing the ultimate currency position. Clearly, it is inappropriate to allocate this effect to the managers responsible for currency exposure because it is usually impossible to predict the future value of equity exposures.

---

20 The implied currency return assumes there are no underlying changes in the asset's market value. It is "implied" in the sense that it is what one might expect the currency return to be (but is not, because the underlying asset changes in value).

The total effect of compounding within the benchmark is:

$$\frac{1 + B'_C}{1 + B_C} - 1$$

The total effect of compounding within the portfolio is:

$$\frac{1 + R_C}{1 + R'_C} - 1$$

The implied term is shown in the denominator of the portfolio compounding and in the numerator of the benchmark compounding because at a later stage we will wish to compare portfolio compounding against benchmark compounding.

The compounding effects in our sample portfolio using data from Exhibit 18 are as follows:

$$\text{Benchmark compounding } \frac{1 + B'_C}{1 + B_C} - 1 = \frac{1.00}{0.997328} - 1 = 0.27\%$$

$$\text{Portfolio compounding } \frac{1 + R_C}{1 + R'_C} - 1 = \frac{1.011483}{1.015} - 1 = -0.35\%$$

In this example, the falling value of European equities reduces the proportionate exposure to the rising EUR, resulting in a total actual currency return lower than the total implied currency return for both the portfolio and the benchmark. The very slightly increased exposure to USD from the rising value of US equities combined with the falling dollar has a negative effect.

4.2.3 Geometric Currency Allocation

Using the implied currency returns implicit in Equations 13 and 14 for the benchmark and portfolio, respectively, we can calculate currency allocation effects from the perspective of the currency overlay manager (excluding compounding effects):

$$\frac{1 + R'_C}{1 + B'_C} - 1$$

The total currency overlay attribution from Exhibit 18 in implied terms is:

$$\frac{1 + R'_C}{1 + B'_C} - 1 = \frac{1.015}{1.0} - 1 = 1.5\%$$

Note that this is similar to the previously calculated 1.42% naive currency attribution effect.

The currency allocation formula is similar to the geometric asset allocation formula,[21] where the difference in portfolio and benchmark weights is multiplied by the relative difference between the spot currency return and the overall benchmark implied currency return:

$$(w_i - W_i) \times \left(\frac{1 + C_i}{1 + B'_C} - 1 \right) \quad (15)$$

The currency allocation effects in each market in Exhibit 18 are as follows:

$$\text{GBP } (40\% - 40\%) \times \left(\frac{1 + 0\%}{1 + 0\%} - 1 \right) = 0.0\%$$

$$\text{EUR } (30\% - 20\%) \times \left(\frac{1 + 10\%}{1 + 0\%} - 1 \right) = 1.0\%$$

---

[21] It is similar in the sense that it is an allocation-type equation, not a selection-type equation.

Multi-currency Attribution

$$\text{USD } (30\% - 40\%) \times \left(\frac{1 - 5.0\%}{1 + 0.0\%} - 1 \right) = 0.5\%$$

The currency allocation effect calculated to produce the total naive currency attribution, which includes the effects of portfolio and benchmark compounding and currency overlay, is as follows:

$$\underbrace{\left(\frac{1 + R_C}{1 + R'_C}\right)}_{\text{Portfolio Compounding}} \times \underbrace{\left(\frac{1 + B'_C}{1 + B_C}\right)}_{\text{Benchmark Compounding}} \times \underbrace{\left(\frac{1 + R'_C}{1 + B'_C}\right)}_{\text{Currency Overlay}} - 1 = \left(\frac{1 + R_C}{1 + B_C}\right) - 1$$

This equation can now be expanded to include selection and allocation effects to get the attribution effects that determine the portfolio return in excess of the benchmark return:

$$\underbrace{\left(\frac{1 + R_L}{1 + B_{SL}}\right)}_{\text{Selection}} \times \underbrace{\left(\frac{1 + B_{SL}}{1 + B_L}\right)}_{\text{Allocation}} \times \underbrace{\left(\frac{1 + R'_C}{1 + B'_C}\right)}_{\text{Currency Overlay}} \times \underbrace{\left(\frac{1 + R_C}{1 + R'_C}\right) \times \left(\frac{1 + B'_C}{1 + B_C}\right)}_{\text{Compounding}} - 1 = \frac{1 + R}{1 + B} - 1$$

In summary, the attribution effects for the portfolio in Exhibit 18 are as follows:

Stock selection $\frac{1 + R_L}{1 + B_{SL}} - 1 = \frac{1.045}{1.034} - 1 = 1.0638\%$

Asset allocation $\frac{1 + B_{SL}}{1 + B_L} - 1 = \frac{1.034}{1.048} - 1 = -1.3359\%$

Currency overlay $\frac{1 + R'_C}{1 + B'_C} - 1 = \frac{1.015}{1.0} - 1 = 1.5\%$

Compounding $\left(\frac{1 + R_C}{1 + R'_C}\right) \times \left(\frac{1 + B'_C}{1 + B_C}\right) - 1 = \left(\frac{1.011483}{1.015}\right) \times \left(\frac{1.0}{1 - 0.002672}\right) - 1 = -0.08\%$

Naive currency

$$\underbrace{\left(\frac{1 + R_C}{1 + R'_C}\right)}_{\text{Portfolio Compounding}} \times \underbrace{\left(\frac{1 + B'_C}{1 + B_C}\right)}_{\text{Benchmark Compounding}} \times \underbrace{\left(\frac{1 + R'_C}{1 + B'_C}\right)}_{\text{Currency Overlay}} - 1 =$$

$$\left(\frac{1.011483}{1.015}\right) \times \left(\frac{1.0}{1 - 0.002672}\right) \times \left(\frac{1.015}{1.0}\right) - 1 = 1.42\%$$

From this decomposition, we see that the naive currency return of 1.42% (obtained by rounding the previously calculated 1.4193%) is composed of the currency overlay return of 1.50% and the portfolio and benchmark compounding effect of −0.08%. Note that the compounding effect would reflect a return beyond a currency overlay manager's control.

The previously calculated total excess portfolio return of 1.13% can also be confirmed using the stock selection, asset allocation, currency overlay, and compounding effects: $(1.010638) \times (1 - 0.013359) \times (1.015) \times (1 - 0.0008) - 1 = 1.13\%$.

4.2.4 Interest Rate Differentials

A further complicating factor in multi-currency portfolios is the exposure to the interest rate differentials between currencies implicit in currency derivative contracts. Karnosky and Singer recognized this effect by using the return premium of the local market return above local interest rates using arithmetic, continuously compounded returns. In this section, we have been using geometric returns to avoid the use of continuously compounded returns. Now, we incorporate interest rates into geometric attribution analysis using the return on forward contracts.

If a country manager decides to overweight (or underweight) a particular country, it will result in a currency exposure. The currency manager may wish to hedge the currency exposure caused by the country manager using currency forward contracts or other currency derivative instruments. The cost or benefit of hedging the currency position to neutral should be attributed to the country manager who caused the currency exposure. As in the Karnosky–Singer analysis, this should be reflected in the calculation of both asset allocation and currency allocation attribution effects.

In addition to hedging exposed positions caused by country managers or attaining the benchmarks' currency positions, the currency manager may be seeking to generate active currency positions. Whatever the case may be, these positions can be achieved only by instruments exposed to interest rate differentials.

Forward currency contracts are priced by reference to the interest rate differential between the relevant currencies.[22] Therefore, any currency manager who creates a currency exposure (overweight or underweight) using these contracts is exposed to the costs (or benefits) of these interest rate differentials. In other words, the forward return, rather than the spot currency return, should be used to measure currency allocation effects.

Assuming that any exposed currency positions as a result of country allocation decisions are notionally hedged,[23] hedged benchmark returns can be used to calculate attribution effects. The hedged benchmark return B_{Hi} in currency i is defined as the differential of the benchmark return and the forward return:

$$B_{Hi} = \frac{(1 + B_i)}{(1 + F_i)} - 1$$

where F_i = the currency forward return in currency i.

4.2.5 Revised Currency Allocation

Any overweight or underweight position created by the currency manager uses a forward currency contract (notional or actual) or other currency derivative. As a result, the forward currency rate, not the spot rate, should be used to measure the contribution of that decision. Therefore, the implied currency return in Equation 14 is adjusted for any variation from the benchmark as follows:

$$R_C'' = \sum_{i=1}^{i=n} W_i \times C_i + \sum_{i=1}^{i=n} (w_i - W_i) \times F_i$$

Equation 15 is adapted to use forward returns rather than spot returns:

$$(w_i - W_i) \times \left(\frac{1 + F_i}{1 + B_C'} - 1\right) \quad (16)$$

The data in Exhibit 19 supplement the data in Exhibit 18, adding currency forward and hedged benchmark returns.[24] Recall that there are no actual forward currency contracts in this particular example.

---

[22] The relationship between forward prices, spot prices, and relative interest rates is referred to as *covered interest rate parity* and is discussed in the "Topics in Return Measurement" reading.
[23] Notional in the sense that within the attribution calculations, we assume the cost or benefits of hedging the underlying country bet occur whether or not the actual hedge is initiated.
[24] The difference between the benchmark hedged returns in Exhibit 19 and the benchmark local returns in Exhibit 18 would reflect interest rate differentials.

Multi-currency Attribution

Exhibit 19 Currency Forward and Hedged Benchmark Returns

Category	Currency Forward Return, F_i (%)	Benchmark Hedged Return, B_{Hi} (%)
UK equities	0.0	10.0
European equities	8.91	−7.08
US equities	−5.47	6.53

The implied currency return using forward returns is now as follows:

$$R_C'' = (40\% \times 0.0\%) + (20\% \times 10.0\%) + [40\% \times (-5.0\%)] + [(40\% - 40\%) \times 0.0\%]$$
$$+ [(30\% - 20\%) \times 8.91\%] + [(30\% - 40\%) \times (-5.47\%)]$$
$$= 1.44\%$$

The revised currency allocation effects are calculated as follows using Equation 16:

$$\text{GBP } (40\% - 40\%) \times \left(\frac{1.0}{1.0} - 1\right) = 0.0\%$$

$$\text{EUR } (30\% - 20\%) \times \left(\frac{1.0891}{1.0} - 1\right) = 0.89\%$$

$$\text{USD } (30\% - 40\%) \times \left(\frac{0.9453}{1.0} - 1\right) = 0.55\%$$

Total currency allocation = $(1 + 0.0\%) \times (1 + 0.89\%) \times (1 + 0.55\%) - 1$

$$= 1.44\%, \text{ or } \frac{1 + R_C''}{1 + B_C'} - 1 = \frac{1.0144}{1.0} - 1 = 1.44\%$$

4.2.6 Revised Country Allocation

The cost or benefit of hedging currency positions caused by country allocation decisions must be attributed to the country allocator. To do this, we can use hedged indexes, rather than local indexes, to measure the true effect of the country allocator. The cost or benefit is in effect transferred from the currency overlay manager to the country allocator.

The revised semi-notional return including the cost of hedging to neutral is:

$$B_{SH} = \sum_{i=1}^{i=n} W_i \times B_{Li} + (w_i - W_i) \times B_{Hi}$$

$$B_{SH} = (40\% \times 10.0\%) + [20\% \times (-8.0\%)] + (40\% \times 6.0\%) + [(40\% - 40\%) \times 10.0\%] + [(30\% - 20\%) \times (-7.08\%)] + [(30\% - 40\%) \times 6.53\%]$$
$$= 3.44\%$$

The difference between B_{SL} and B_{SH} is subtle: The overweight or underweight position $(w_i - W_i)$ uses the hedged benchmark return rather than the local benchmark return—hence, the cost or benefit of hedging is now notionally included in the revised semi-notional return.

Asset allocation attribution is now calculated by:

$$(w_i - W_i) \times \left(\frac{1 + B_{Hi}}{1 + B_L} - 1\right) \tag{17}$$

The total revised asset allocation including the cost of hedging is:

$$\frac{1+B_{SH}}{1+B_L} - 1$$

The asset allocation attribution effects taking into account hedging of any country bets are as follows:

UK equities $(40\% - 40\%) \times \left(\frac{1.1}{1.048} - 1\right) = 0.0\%$

European equities $(30\% - 20\%) \times \left(\frac{0.9292}{1.048} - 1\right) = -1.13\%$

US equities $(30\% - 40\%) \times \left(\frac{1.0653}{1.048} - 1\right) = -0.17\%$

Total revised asset allocation $= (1 + 0.0\%) \times (1 - 1.13\%) \times (1 - 0.17\%) - 1$

$$= -1.30\%, \text{ or } \frac{1+B_{SH}}{1+B_L} - 1 = \frac{1.0344}{1.048} - 1 = -1.30\%$$

In the following, we summarize these calculations:

Stock selection $\frac{1+R_L}{1+B_{SL}} - 1 = \frac{1.045}{1.034} - 1 = 1.0638\% = 1.06\%$

Revised asset allocation $\frac{1+B_{SH}}{1+B_L} - 1 = \frac{1.0344}{1.048} - 1 = -1.30\%$

Total currency effects

$$\frac{1+B_{SL}}{1+B_{SH}} \times \frac{1+R}{1+R_L} \times \frac{1+B_L}{1+B} - 1 =$$

$$\frac{1.034}{1.0344} \times \frac{1.057}{1.045} \times \frac{1.048}{1.0452} - 1 = 1.38\%$$

These factors compound to give the total geometric excess return, as follows:

$$\underbrace{\frac{1+R_L}{1+B_{SL}}}_{\text{Selection}} \times \underbrace{\frac{1+B_{SH}}{1+B_L}}_{\text{Allocation}} \times \underbrace{\frac{1+B_{SL}}{1+B_{SH}}}_{\substack{\text{Hedging} \\ \text{Cost} \\ \text{Transferred}}} \times \underbrace{\frac{1+R}{1+R_L} \times \frac{1+B_L}{1+B}}_{\substack{\text{Naive} \\ \text{Currency} \\ \text{Attribution}}} - 1 = \frac{1+R}{1+B} - 1 \quad (18)$$

$$\underbrace{\frac{1.045}{1.034}}_{\text{Stock}} \times \underbrace{\frac{1.0344}{1.048}}_{\text{Asset}} \times \underbrace{\frac{1.034}{1.0344}}_{\substack{\text{Hedging} \\ \text{Cost} \\ \text{Transferred}}} \times \underbrace{\frac{1.057}{1.045} \times \frac{1.048}{1.0452}}_{\substack{\text{Naive} \\ \text{Currency} \\ \text{Attribution}}} - 1 = \frac{1.057}{1.0452} - 1 = 1.13\%$$

The total currency effects can be broken down further:

$$\underbrace{\frac{1+R_C''}{1+B_C'}}_{\substack{\text{Currency} \\ \text{Overlay}}} \times \underbrace{\frac{1+B_{SL}}{1+B_{SH}}}_{\substack{\text{Hedging} \\ \text{Cost} \\ \text{Transferred}}} \times \underbrace{\frac{1+R_C'}{1+R_C''}}_{\substack{\text{Hedging} \\ \text{Mismatch}}} \times \underbrace{\frac{1+R_C}{1+R_C'} \times \frac{1+B_C'}{1+B_C}}_{\text{Compounding}} - 1$$

Multi-currency Attribution

Note that an additional ratio, $(1 + R'_C)/(1 + R''_C)$, has been introduced to ensure that no residuals result from the calculation. This effect, when combined with the cost of hedging, is normally close to zero. This minor adjustment is required because the cost-of-hedging effect implicitly included in currency overlay is applied to a slightly different denominator from that of the country allocator.

The total currency effect of 1.38% in our example can be decomposed as follows:

$$\frac{1.0144}{1.0} \times \frac{1.034}{1.0344} \times \frac{1.015}{1.0144} \times \frac{1.0115}{1.015} \times \frac{1.0}{.9973} - 1 = 1.38\%$$

For simplicity, forward currency contracts have not been added to this example, but they can be easily introduced with portfolio weights representing each segment of the forward contract.

4.3 Other Currency Topics

The currency denomination of a security does not necessarily coincide with the economic exposure of a security. A classic example are Japanese warrants and convertible bonds denominated in US dollars, Swiss francs, and other currencies, which encourage international investors to buy without the need of any currency transactions. Although they are denominated in the investor's currency, their value is determined in part by the value of the yen. The prices of these instruments effectively adjust for the currency movements between the denomination currency and yen and, therefore, are economically exposed to yen. Another example of instruments with currency denominations that are not the same as the economic exposure is American Depositary Receipts (ADRs).

EXAMPLE 4

Multi-currency Attribution

1 Assuming there is a separate country and currency allocation decision process, the currency hedging cost or benefit of an overweight country position should be allocated to the:
   A stock picker.
   B country allocator.
   C currency allocator.

2 According to Karnosky and Singer, which type of return must be used to measure currency allocation effects?
   A Spot
   B Local
   C Forward

Solution to 1:

B is correct. The country allocator is responsible for the country allocation decision and must therefore bear the cost (or benefit) of hedging the currency position to neutral.

Solution to 2:

C is correct. Currency managers are exposed to interest rate differentials because they use forward currency contracts or other currency derivatives to change currency positions. Therefore, the forward currency return must be used to measure currency allocation effects.

5 MULTI-PERIOD ATTRIBUTION

The arithmetic sum of the excess return for each finite period does not typically sum to the total arithmetic excess return for the total period being analyzed:

$$R - \bar{R} \neq \sum_{t=1}^{t=T}\left(R_t - \bar{R}_t\right)$$

Therefore, over multiple periods we should not expect arithmetic attribution factors that add over single periods to add up for the total period under analysis. Nevertheless, attribution users have an expectation that attribution analysis should add up over multiple periods and that all the contributions to excess return are fully explained. In order to meet client expectations, a number of software companies have developed smoothing and linking algorithms to give the impression that multi-period attribution does indeed add up.

For example, the data from Exhibit 20 illustrate arithmetic attribution analysis for each month in a single quarter. The arithmetic excess return for the entire quarter is 9.9% − (−2.3%) = 12.2%, which is not the same as the sum of each month:

$$(10.1\% - 8.2\%) + (8.5\% - 1.0\%) + [-8.0\% - (-10.6\%)] = 12.0\%$$

Exhibit 20 Multi-period Attribution

	Portfolio Weight (%)	Benchmark Weight (%)	Portfolio Return (%)	Benchmark Return (%)	Allocation (%)	Selection (%)
Month 1						
Energy	50	50	18.0	10.0	0.0	4.0
Health care	30	20	−3.0	−2.0	−1.02	−0.3
Financials	20	30	10.0	12.0	−0.38	−0.4
Total	100	100	10.1	8.2	−1.4	3.3
Month 2						
Energy	70	40	12.0	7.0	1.8	3.5
Health care	20	30	3.0	4.0	−0.3	−0.2
Financials	10	30	−5.0	−10.0	2.2	0.5
Total	100	100	8.5	1.0	3.7	3.8
Month 3						
Energy	30	50	−30.0	−20.0	1.88	−3.0
Health care	50	40	8.0	5.0	1.56	1.5
Financials	20	10	−15.0	−26.0	−1.54	2.2
Total	100	100	−8.0	−10.6	1.9	0.7
Full quarter (simple addition of attribution effects)						
Energy	50.0	46.7	−7.5	−5.8	3.68	4.5
Health care	33.3	30.0	7.9	7.0	0.24	1.0
Financials	16.7	23.3	−11.2	−15.4	0.28	2.3
Total	100	100	9.9	−2.3	4.2	7.8

It should be noted that the portfolio and benchmark weights for the full quarter are just the simple average weight over the quarter. These weights are provided for guidance only; the attribution for the quarter period is not calculated using these weights. In order to reflect the changing weights in each period, it is crucial to use the relevant weight for each period. The full quarter return for both the portfolio and the benchmark for each sector and in total is calculated in the normal way using compounding.

Well-known smoothing algorithms include those of Cariño (1999) and Menchero (2000), which take the natural residual caused by multiple-period arithmetic attribution and redistribute the residual in a structural way between the other factors to ensure that the resulting multi-period analysis adds up without residuals. Note that extending the period of analysis naturally alters the residual, leading to a recalculation of sub-period effects and a redistribution of the residual for prior periods. The Cariño algorithm relies on the additive properties of continuously compounded returns (or logs) to work. The Menchero smoothing is optimized to ensure the minimal adjustment to each factor.

Frongello (2002) and GRAP (1997) used linking algorithms that achieve the same result. But both of these algorithms are order dependent, and the linked results will change if the order of periods is re-arranged, which does seem counter-intuitive. Overall, the linking algorithms are a little more appealing than redistributing residuals. All these solutions are typically kept confidential, and very few practitioners have any knowledge of or desire to understand the background calculations provided the output sums up. Often the choice of attribution system determines the algorithm that is employed in any particular firm. The smoothing calculations themselves are beyond the scope of this reading.[25] However, applying the four smoothing algorithms to the monthly data in Exhibit 20 generates the quarterly reports show in Exhibit 21.

Exhibit 21 Multi-period Attribution: Impact of Smoothing Algorithms

	Portfolio Weight (%)	Benchmark Weight (%)	Portfolio Return (%)	Benchmark Return (%)	Allocation (%)	Selection (%)
Simple Addition						
Energy	50.0	46.7	−7.5	−5.8	3.68	4.5
Health care	33.3	30.0	7.9	7.0	0.24	1.0
Financials	16.7	23.3	−11.2	−15.4	0.28	2.3
Total	**100**	**100**	**9.9**	**−2.3**	**4.2**	**7.8**
Cariño						
Energy	50.0	46.7	−7.5	−5.8	3.93	3.84
Health care	33.3	30.0	7.9	7.0	0.52	1.23
Financials	16.7	23.3	−11.2	−15.4	0.06	2.63
Total	**100**	**100**	**9.9**	**−2.3**	**4.50**	**7.70**
Menchero						
Energy	50.0	46.7	−7.5	−5.8	3.75	4.57
Health care	33.3	30.0	7.9	7.0	0.25	1.02
Financials	16.7	23.3	−11.2	−15.4	0.27	2.34
Total	**100**	**100**	**9.9**	**−2.3**	**4.26**	**7.94**
GRAP/Frongello						
Energy	50.0	46.7	−7.5	−5.8	4.02	3.47
Health care	33.3	30.0	7.9	7.0	0.65	1.32
Financials	16.7	23.3	−11.2	−15.4	−0.02	2.76
Total	**100**	**100**	**9.9**	**−2.3**	**4.65**	**7.55**

---

25 A detailed discussion of these smoothing and linking algorithms can be found in Bacon (2008), Chapter 8.

Exhibit 21 demonstrates that the Cariño, Menchero, and GRAP/Frongello algorithms all meet their primary objective of providing multi-period arithmetic attribution that adds up. However, they provide different answers: Note the selection effect in Energy across the different methods or the slightly negative result for the Financials allocation using GRAP/Frongello.

Multi-period geometric attribution does not suffer the same linking challenges as multi-period arithmetic attribution. Because in each period allocation, selection, and currency allocation effects compound to the total geometric excess return and because geometric excess returns compound over time, it follows that the total allocation, selection, and currency allocation effects over multiple periods must also compound to the total geometric excess return.

EXAMPLE 5

Multi-period Attribution

Which of the following methodologies is most likely to be order dependent for multi-period attribution?

A Linking algorithms

B Geometric attribution

C Smoothing algorithms

Solution:

A is correct. Linking algorithms tend to be order dependent, whereas geometric attribution and smoothing algorithms are not.

6. MULTI-ASSET AND BALANCED ATTRIBUTION ANALYSIS

A balanced investment strategy aims to balance risk and return by considering allocations to liquid asset types, such as equities, bonds, currency, derivatives, and cash, and potentially illiquid assets, such as hedge funds, real estate, private equity, venture capital, and infrastructure.[26] Balanced portfolios might consist of just equities and bonds, but portfolios with longer time horizons, such as pension and sovereign wealth funds, may allocate to "alternatives" to equities and bonds,[27] exploiting illiquid risk premiums to create multi-asset portfolios.

Typically, money-weighted methodologies are used to measure the performance of illiquid assets and time-weighted methodologies are used to measure the performance of liquid assets. This creates an issue for multi-asset portfolios that contain both liquid and illiquid assets: Which measurement methodology should be used? The answer depends to a large extent on the requirements of the client. If return attribution analysis is required, then a consistent methodology should be used to ensure that the sum of the parts reconciles to the total return to avoid unexplained residuals in the analysis.

---

[26] Note that not all hedge fund strategies are illiquid.
[27] Hence the term "alternative assets."

Another problem associated with multi-asset attribution analysis is benchmark construction. Identifying benchmarks for illiquid assets is notoriously difficult, resulting in little transparency and no visibility of the underlying risk exposures for illiquid asset classes. Security-level attribution may be available only for equity and bond asset classes for which managers have access to constituent-level benchmarks.

Even for balanced portfolios consisting of equities and bonds, the investment process for each asset type may be completely different, requiring substantially different attribution methodologies that may be difficult to combine and that are often required at different levels of analysis. The Van Breukelen and other similar weighted duration–type fixed-income methodologies fit well into balanced-type attribution analysis because the methodology is itself an adjusted version of the basic Brinson method.

To be of any value to the various stakeholders in the investment decision-making process (clients, portfolio managers, risk controllers, and senior management), return attribution must reflect the investment decision-making process of the portfolio manager. The various elements of this process, such as the use of long–short positions, the use of derivatives, independent currency decisions, and multi-asset and multi-level decisions, must be accurately reflected in return attribution to provide a thorough understanding of the investment process. For example, consider a large balanced portfolio—perhaps a sovereign wealth fund containing a wide range of liquid and illiquid assets. Given this wide range of assets, many alternative multi-level, multi-asset attribution analyses could be chosen to describe the sources of added and subtracted value. However, the attribution analysis must reflect the investment decision process used by the portfolio manager. For example, in Exhibit 22 the first-level decision is an allocation between liquid and illiquid assets. The second-level decision allocates the liquid assets between equities and bonds and the illiquid assets between private equity, real estate, infrastructure, and hedge funds. The third-level decision allocates each of these liquid assets by region and country, with perhaps the hedge funds skipping a level of the decision process to individual fund selection. The fourth level of decision is at the security, instrument, or individual asset level. Attribution effects should be calculated at each level of the decision process. The attribution results for the hierarchy demonstrated in Exhibit 22 would be very different for the attribution results of the hierarchy shown in Exhibit 23, in which there is no high-level decision to allocate between liquid and illiquid assets.

Exhibit 22 Balanced Attribution Four-Level Decision Process

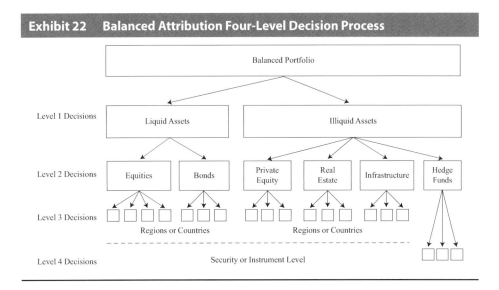

In Exhibit 23, the first-level decision is to allocate directly to the six asset classes: equities, bonds, private equity, real estate, infrastructure, and hedge funds. The second-level decision is at the regional or country level, and the third and final level of decision is at the security, instrument, or individual asset level.

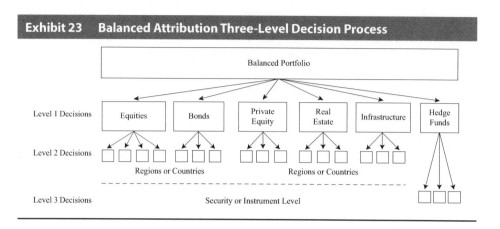

Exhibit 23   Balanced Attribution Three-Level Decision Process

Another hierarchy is illustrated in Exhibit 24, in which the first-level decision is an allocation to geographical regions. The investment decisions are made in a different order compared with the hierarchy in Exhibit 22. The second-level decision is to equities, bonds, and alternative assets within each region. The third-level decision is to countries within equities and bonds and between private equity, real estate, infrastructure, and hedge funds within alternative assets. The fourth level of decision is at the security, instrument, or individual asset level.

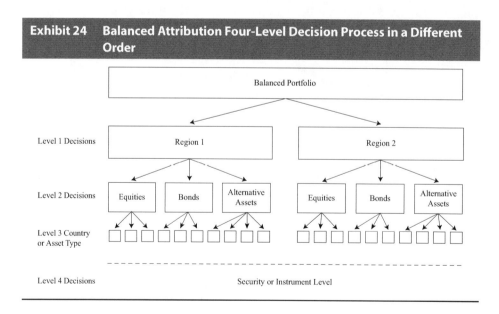

Exhibit 24   Balanced Attribution Four-Level Decision Process in a Different Order

Exhibit 25 represents a quite different two-level investment decision process in which the first and major allocation decision is a country decision and the second-level investment decision is within countries from the bottom up, in which the portfolio manager may choose any combination of liquid or illiquid asset types within specific countries.

Exhibit 25   Balanced Attribution Two-Level Decision Process

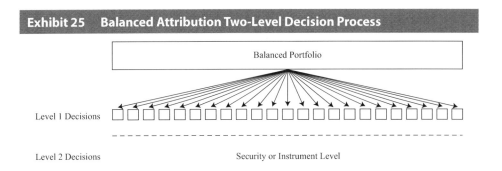

Exhibits 22–25 demonstrate the non-generic nature of attribution analysis. It is essential that the analysis is consistent with the investment decision process and meaningful for the end user. Attribution analysis is a skilled activity that requires the performance analyst to have a deep understanding of the investment process, which might be particularly complex for multi-asset portfolios. Attribution analysis provides a good starting point for a dialogue between stakeholders. The analysis may initiate a discussion on the positive and negative aspects of recent performance and help stakeholders gain an understanding of the investment decision-making process. Senior management uses return attribution analysis as a tool to control and monitor the investment process, identify outliers, and ensure value is added consistently across the firm. High-quality attribution analysis is required to support hiring, retaining, and firing decisions of portfolio managers and asset management firms.

SUMMARY

- The Brinson model for return attribution is a robust model that can be applied to long–short and short extension investment strategies.
- The usual benchmark for market neutral strategies is the return to cash under the assumption that long and short positions are established so as to have offsetting risk. A Brinson-type return attribution can be performed to measure the contributions to return of decisions to buy and short assets.
- A Brinson-type approach can also be applied to portfolios with positions in derivatives. Attribution in the case of futures and options involves determining an allocation effect that reflects the return to the associated economic exposure.
- Futures positions at any point in time do not change the overall value of the portfolio; rather, they adjust economic exposure. Each futures position requires an associated economic exposure that is equal in weight and opposite in sign.
- The performance attribution of option contracts is measured in the same way as the performance of other assets. The underlying economic exposure is influenced by the option's delta, δ.
- For options, the economic exposure is usually calculated as follows:

    Option's economic exposure = δ × Number of options × Underlying's price.

- Multi-currency attribution is more complex than attribution for single-currency portfolios. Multi-currency attribution should take account of interest rate differentials and the compounding effects of market and currency returns.

- Forward currency contracts are priced by reference to the interest rate differential between the relevant currencies. Therefore, any currency manager who wishes to take a currency allocation "bet" is exposed to the costs (or benefits) of these interest rate differentials.
- The Karnosky–Singer approach attributes portfolio excess return to equity premium effects and currency effects taking into account interest rate differentials.
- The Karnosky–Singer attribution equations are as follows:

  Allocation $A_i = (w_i - W_i) \times (B_{Li} - I_i - B_L)$

  Selection $S_i = w_i \times (R_{Li} - B_{Li})$

  Currency $CA_i = \left[(w_i + \tilde{w}_i) - (W_i + \tilde{W}_i)\right] \times \left[(C_i + I_i) - C\right]$

- An unavoidable complication in multi-currency portfolios is the effect of changing currency exposure due to the changing market values of the underlying assets.
- Naive currency attribution is described as naive because it ignores interest rate differentials. The equation for naive currency attribution includes the ratio of the currency return of the portfolio relative to the currency return of the benchmark:

$$\frac{1 + R_C}{1 + B_C} - 1 = \left[\frac{(1+R)/(1+R_L)}{(1+B)/(1+B_L)}\right] - 1$$

- If a country manager decides to overweight a particular country, it results in a currency exposure. The cost or benefit of hedging the currency position to neutral should be borne by the country manager who caused the currency exposure.
- The formula for geometric multi-currency asset allocation that adjusts for the cost or benefit of hedging is:

$$(w_i - W_i) \times \left(\frac{1 + B_{Hi}}{1 + B_L} - 1\right)$$

- The formula for geometric currency allocation that adjusts for the cost or benefit of hedging is:

$$(w_i - W_i) \times \left(\frac{1 + F_i}{1 + B'_C} - 1\right)$$

- In geometric multi-currency attribution, stock selection, asset allocation, and currency allocation effects compound to the total geometric excess return in the following equation:

$$\underbrace{\frac{1+R_L}{1+B_{SL}}}_{\text{Selection}} \times \underbrace{\frac{1+B_{SH}}{1+B_L}}_{\text{Allocation}} \times \underbrace{\frac{1+B_{SL}}{1+B_{SH}}}_{\substack{\text{Hedging} \\ \text{Cost} \\ \text{Transferred}}} \times \underbrace{\frac{1+R}{1+R_L} \cdot \frac{1+B_L}{1+B}}_{\substack{\text{Naive} \\ \text{Currency} \\ \text{Attribution}}} - 1 = \frac{1+R}{1+B} - 1$$

- The currency denomination of a security does not necessarily coincide with the economic currency exposure of that security.

- Attribution users have an expectation that attribution analysis should add up over multiple periods and that all the contributions to excess return are fully explained. In order to meet client expectations, a number of software companies have developed smoothing and linking algorithms to give the impression that multi-period attribution does indeed add up.
- Multi-period geometric attribution does not suffer the same linking challenges as multi-period arithmetic attribution.
- Different return measurement methodologies may be used for liquid and illiquid assets. This results in challenges for multi-asset portfolios that contain both liquid and illiquid assets. If return attribution analysis is required, then a consistent methodology should be used to ensure the sum of the parts reconciles to the total return to avoid unexplained residuals in the analysis.
- Attribution for portfolios consisting of multiple asset classes can be complicated by differing investment processes in managing the different asset classes.
- It is essential that the attribution analysis replicates the order and level of the investment decision process.

REFERENCES

Bacon, Carl. 2008. *Practical Portfolio Performance Measurement and Attribution*, 2nd edition. Hoboken, NJ: John Wiley & Sons.

Brinson, Gary, and Nimrod Fachler. 1985. "Measuring Non-US Equity Portfolio Performance." *Journal of Portfolio Management*, vol. 11, no. 3 (Spring): 73–76.

Brinson, Gary, Randolph Hood, and Gilbert Beebower. 1986. "Determinants of Portfolio Performance." *Financial Analysts Journal*, vol. 42, no. 4 (July–August): 39–44.

Cariño, David. 1999. "Combining Attribution Effects over Time." *Journal of Performance Measurement*, vol. 3, no. 4 (Summer): 5–14.

Frongello, Andrew. 2002. "Linking Single Period Attribution Results." *Journal of Performance Measurement*, vol. 6, no. 4 (Spring): 10–22.

GRAP. 1997. *Synthèse des Modèles d'Attribution de Performance*. Paris: Groupe de Recherche en Attribution de Performance (March).

Karnosky, Denis, and Brian Singer. 1994. *Global Asset Management and Performance Attribution*. Charlottesville, VA: Research Foundation of the Institute of Chartered Financial Analysts (February).

Menchero, Jose. 2000. "An Optimized Approach to Linking Attribution Effects over Time." *Journal of Performance Measurement*, vol. 5, no. 1 (Fall): 36–42.

PRACTICE PROBLEMS

The following information relates to questions 1–9

Joseph Patrick, an investment consultant, is evaluating the performance of two portfolios: ABC and XYZ. Both portfolios use long/short equity strategies in domestic securities. Portfolio ABC follows a short extension (150/50) strategy and uses only equity securities. Portfolio XYZ achieves its short exposure using put options.

Patrick begins his fourth-quarter evaluation by performing a Brinson–Fachler attribution analysis of Portfolio ABC using the data in Exhibit 1. He hopes to identify the reasons for Portfolio ABC's outperformance against the benchmark.

Exhibit 1 Portfolio ABC, Quarter Ending 31 December 2016

Category	Portfolio Weight (%)	Benchmark Weight (%)	Portfolio Return (%)	Benchmark Return (%)
Long value equities	80.0	75.0	9.0	6.0
Long growth equities	55.0	75.0	2.0	3.0
Short value equities	−20.0	−25.0	12.0	10.0
Short growth equities	−30.0	−25.0	−1.0	−3.0
Cash	15.0	0.0	3.0	2.5
Total	100.0	100.0	6.7	5.0

Patrick gathers the information in Exhibit 2 for Portfolio XYZ. As of 31 December 2016, Portfolio XYZ's equity holdings consist of 9,600 shares of US Corporation stock with a market price of $125 per share. The portfolio has $600,000 in cash and 32,000 long-dated put options on U.S. Corporation stock. Based on an exercise price of $102, Patrick determines that the delta value for the put options is −0.25. The put option has a current price of $6.25.

Exhibit 2 Portfolio XYZ, Quarter Ending 31 December 2016

Asset Class	Portfolio Beginning Holdings in USD	Portfolio Weight (%)	Benchmark Weight (%)	Portfolio Return (%)	Benchmark Return (%)	Portfolio Gain/Loss in USD
Equity	1,200,000	60.0	60.0	4.00	4.00	48,000
Options	200,000	10.0	—	−20.00	—	−40,000
Cash	600,000	30.0	40.0	0.15	0.15	900
Total	2,000,000	100.0	100.0	—	2.46	8,900

Practice Problems

Patrick performs an attribution analysis of Portfolio XYZ, using the data provided in Exhibit 2.

1. Based on Exhibit 1, the total allocation effect for Portfolio ABC using the Brinson–Fachler approach is *closest* to:
   A 0.43%.
   B 0.73%.
   C 1.15%.

2. Based on Exhibit 1, the total selection effect, including interaction, for Portfolio ABC using the Brinson–Fachler approach is *closest* to:
   A 0.50%.
   B 0.93%.
   C 1.65%.

3. Based on Exhibit 1, the attribution analysis of Portfolio ABC under the Brinson–Fachler approach indicates that the manager added value in the:
   A selection of short value equities.
   B allocation to short value equities.
   C selection of long growth equities.

4. The associated beginning economic exposure of Portfolio XYZ's option position is *closest* to:
   A −$300,000.
   B −$816,000.
   C −$1,000,000.

5. Based on Exhibit 2, the combined return on Portfolio XYZ's equity position including options and adjusting for notional assets is *closest* to:
   A 1.55%.
   B 3.10%.
   C 4.90%.

6. Based on Exhibit 2, the allocation effect of the total equity position in Portfolio XYZ after adjusting for the effect of the options is *closest* to:
   A −0.77%.
   B −0.62%.
   C −0.26%.

7. The selection effect of the total equity position in Portfolio XYZ after adjusting for the effect of the options is *closest* to:
   A −0.09%.
   B 0.07%.
   C 0.09%.

8. Based on Exhibit 2, the selection effect in effective cash for Portfolio XYZ is:
   A less than zero.
   B equal to zero.
   C greater than zero.

9. Based on Exhibit 2, the allocation effect in effective cash for Portfolio XYZ is *closest* to:
   A −1.16%.

B 0.00%.
C 0.23%.

The following information relates to questions 10–13

Harper Fae is a portfolio manager at World Tour Asset Management. Fae manages the firm's Global Equity Fund, for which the base currency is the US dollar (USD). During the past year, Fae has invested in the US, Chinese, and Eurozone equity markets. Fae used forward contracts to increase the fund's currency exposure to the Chinese yuan (CNY) and the euro (EUR). Exhibit 1 presents the fund's allocations to the different markets and currencies, as well as the resulting continuously compounded returns for the year.

Exhibit 1   Global Equity Fund, January 1, 20XX – December 31, 20XX

Category	Portfolio Weight, w_i (%)	Benchmark Weight, W_i (%)	Portfolio Local Return, R_{Li} (%)	Benchmark Local Return, B_{Li} (%)	Local Interest Rate, I_i (%)	Spot Currency Return, C_i (%)
US equities	80	60	10.0	12.0	0.5	0
Chinese equities	10	15	5.0	4.0	4.5	2.5
Eurozone equities	10	25	−2.0	−3.0	0.5	4.5
	$\tilde{w}_i$	$\tilde{W}_i$				
USD forward contracts	−20	−10			0.5	0
CNY forward contracts	+15	+5			4.5	2.5
EUR forward contracts	+5	+5			0.5	4.5
Total weights and base-currency returns	100	100	10.2	9.1		

Fae requests an attribution analysis of the fund's performance using Karnosky–Singer multicurrency attribution.

10 Based on Exhibit 1, the allocation effect for US equities using Karnosky–Singer multicurrency attribution is *closest* to:

  A   1.11%.

  B   1.27%.

  C   2.30%.

11 Based on Exhibit 1, the selection effect in local currency terms for Chinese equities using Karnosky–Singer multicurrency attribution is *closest* to:

  A   −0.15%.

B 0.10%.

C 0.15%.

12 Based on Exhibit 1, the currency allocation effect for the Chinese equity investments using Karnosky–Singer multicurrency attribution is *closest* to:

A −0.03%.

B 0.19%.

C 0.21%

13 Based on Exhibit 1, which of the following decisions contributed *least* favorably to fund performance?

A Selection in US equities

B Selection in Chinese equities.

C Allocation to the Eurozone market.

The following information relates to questions 14–17

An investment consultant has been monitoring the performance of Manager A's Emerging Markets Fund. This fund is described as following a market-neutral strategy with a target beta of 0. Manager A invests in long and short positions in common equities to implement the strategy. The Emerging Markets Fund's benchmark has 140% exposure (70% long and 70% short) to Asian equities, 30% exposure (15% long and 15% short) to European equities, and 30% exposure (15% long and 15% short) to Latin American equities. The consultant receives the information displayed in Exhibit 1 for the month of December 2016 for the fund and its benchmark. The fund and benchmark returns are in the fund's base currency.

Exhibit 1 Manager A, Emerging Markets Fund, December 2016				
Category	Fund Weight (%)	Benchmark Weight (%)	Fund Return (%)	Benchmark Return (%)
Long Asian equities	50.0	70.0	0.4	−1.4
Long European equities	20.0	15.0	8.3	7.2
Long Latin American equities	30.0	15.0	1.0	0.9
Short Asian equities	−50.0	−70.0	−2.8	−1.4
Short European equities	−30.0	−15.0	3.9	7.2
Short Latin American equities	−20.0	−15.0	0.1	0.9
Cash	100.0	100.0	0.1	0.1
Total	100.0	100.0	2.5	0.1

14 Based on Exhibit 1, Manager A is most likely trying to outperform the benchmark based on:

A return on cash.

- **B** stock selection.
- **C** net market exposure.

15 The return of Manager A's Emerging Markets Fund *most appropriately* is benchmarked against the return of a(n):
- **A** short-term cash index.
- **B** absolute return benchmark.
- **C** emerging markets equity index.

16 Based on Exhibit 1, the Brinson–Fachler allocation effect in short Asian equities of Manager A's Emerging Markets Fund is *closest to*:
- **A** −0.58%.
- **B** −0.30%.
- **C** 0.70%.

17 Based on Exhibit 1, the selection effect, including interaction, in short European equities of Manager A's Emerging Markets Fund in December 2016 is *closest to*:
- **A** −1.07%.
- **B** 0.50%.
- **C** 0.99%.

SOLUTIONS

1 B is correct. The total allocation effect for Portfolio ABC is closest to 0.73%. The allocation effect for each sector is calculated as $A_i = (w_i - W_i) \times (B_i - B)$,

where

w_i = weight of the ith sector in the portfolio,
W_i = weight of the benchmark in the ith sector,
B_i = return of the benchmark in the ith sector, and
B = total return of the benchmark

The allocation effect for each sector is as follows:

Long value equities: $(80.0\% - 75.0\%) \times (6.0\% - 5.0\%) = 0.05\%$
Long growth equities: $(55.0\% - 75.0\%) \times (3.0\% - 5.0\%) = 0.40\%$
Short value equities: $(-20.0\% + 25.0\%) \times (10.0\% - 5.0\%) = 0.25\%$
Short growth equities: $(-30.0\% + 25.0\%) \times (-3.0\% - 5.0\%) = 0.40\%$
Cash: $(15.0\% - 0.0\%) \times (2.5\% - 5.0\%) = -0.375\%$

The total allocation effect is calculated as follows:

$$A = \sum_{i=1}^{i=n} A_i$$

The total asset allocation effect is $A = 0.05\% + 0.40\% + 0.25\% + 0.40\% - 0.375\% = 0.725\%$.

2 B is correct. The total selection effect for Portfolio ABC is closest to 0.93%. The selection effect for each style is calculated as $S_i = w_i \times (R_i - B_i)$, where

w_i = weight of the ith sector in the portfolio,
R_i = return of the portfolio in the ith sector, and
B_i = return of the benchmark in the ith sector.

The selection effect for each style is as follows:

Long value equities: $80.0\% \times (9.0\% - 6.0\%) = 2.40\%$
Long growth equities: $55.0\% \times (2.0\% - 3.0\%) = -0.55\%$
Short value equities: $-20.0\% \times (12.0\% - 10.0\%) = -0.40\%$
Short growth equities: $-30.0\% \times (-1.0\% + 3.0\%) = -0.60\%$
Cash: $15.0\% \times (3.0\% - 2.5\%) = 0.075\%$

The total selection effect is calculated as follows:

$$S = \sum_{i=1}^{i=n} S_i$$

The total selection effect is $S = 2.40\% - 0.55\% - 0.40\% - 0.60\% + 0.075\% = 0.925\%$.

3 B is correct. The manager's successful short allocation to value equities resulted from underweighting the short positon, given that the benchmark's sector return exceeded its total return. The manager was unsuccessful in selecting value equities to short, as indicated by the portfolio's sector return exceeding the benchmark's sector return. The manager was unsuccessful in selecting growth equities in which to take a long position. The portfolio's sector return was less than the benchmark's sector return.

4 C is correct. The associated economic exposure of an option position is as follows:

$\delta \times$ Number of options $\times$ Underlying stock price

The associated economic exposure of Portfolio XYZ's option position is as follows:

$-0.25 \times 32{,}000 \times \$125 = -\$1{,}000{,}000$

5 B is correct. The combined return on Portfolio's XYZ's equity position is closest to 3.10%. The combined return on the equity position, including options and notional assets, is determined as follows:

STEP 1 Calculate the economic exposure of the option position as follows:

$\delta \times$ Number of options $\times$ Current stock price

The economic exposure of the option position is

$-0.25 \times 32{,}000 \times \$125 = -\$1{,}000{,}000$.

STEP 2 Calculate the amount of notional cash assets needed to create the total economic exposure of the option position as follows:

Economic exposure of the option position − Value of the option position

The amount of notional cash assets needed to create the total economic exposure of the option position is

$-1{,}000{,}000 - 200{,}000 = -1{,}200{,}000$.

STEP 3 Determine the gains or losses on both the equity and option positions from Exhibit 2:

The gain on the equity position was $48,000.

The loss on the option position was −$40,000.

The interest on the notional cash assets was −$1,200,000 × 0.15% = −$1,800.

STEP 4 Determine the value of the total US equity position:

Value of equity position + Value of option position − Value of notional cash assets = $1,200,000 + $200,000 − $1,200,00 = $200,000.

STEP 5 Calculate the return on the equity position, including options and notional assets: ($48,000 − $40,000 − $1,800)/$200,000 = 3.10%.

6 A is correct. The allocation effect of the US Corporation equity position, after adjusting for the options, is closest to −0.77%.

The allocation effect for each sector is $A_i = (w_i - W_i) \times (B_i - B)$, where

w_i = weight of the ith sector in the portfolio,

W_i = weight of the benchmark in the ith sector,

B_i = return of the benchmark in the ith sector, and

B = total return of the benchmark.

The allocation effect of the US Corporation equity position, after adjusting for the options, is $A_i = (10.0\% - 60.0\%) \times (4.0\% - 2.46\%) = -0.77\%$.

7 A is correct. The selection effect of the total equity position for Portfolio XYZ is closest to 0.09%.

Calculate the selection effect for each style as follows: $S_i = w_i \times (R_i - B_i)$, where

w_i = weight of the ith sector in the portfolio,

R_i = return of the portfolio in the ith sector, and

B_i = return of the benchmark in the ith sector

The selection effect for the total US Corporation equity is 10.0% × (3.10% − 4.0%) = −0.09%.

8 B is correct. The selection effect must be equal to zero because the cash return is 0.15% for both Portfolio XYZ and its benchmark.

9 A is correct. The allocation effect in effective cash for Portfolio XYZ is *closest* to −1.16%.

The allocation effect for each sector is calculated as follows: $A_i = (w_i - W_i) \times (B_i - B)$, where

w_i = weight of the ith sector in the portfolio,

W_i = weight of the benchmark in the ith sector,

B_i = return of the benchmark in the ith sector, and

B = total return of the benchmark

The allocation effect in effective cash for Portfolio XYZ is A_i = (90.0% − 40.0%) × (0.15% − 2.46%) = −1.16%.

10 A is correct.

The allocation effect is $A_i = (w_i - W_i) \times (B_{Li} - I_i - B_L)$.

First, calculate the equity premium benchmark:

$$B_L = \sum_{i=1}^{i=n} W_i \times (B_{Li} - I_i)$$

$= [60\% \times (12\% - 0.5\%)] + [0.15 \times (4\% - 4.5\%)] + [25\% \times (-3\% - 0.5\%)]$

$= 5.95\%$

The US equity allocation effect is then calculated as

A_i = (80% − 60%) × (12% − 0.5% − 5.95%) = 1.11%

11 B is correct. The selection effect is $S_i = w_i \times (R_{Li} - B_{Li})$.

The Chinese equity selection effect is calculated as S_i = 10% × (5% − 4%) = 0.10%.

12 B is correct. First, the currency benchmark is calculated as

$$C = \sum_{i=1}^{i=n} (W_i + \tilde{W}_i) \times (C_i + I_i)$$

$= [(60\% - 10\%) \times (0.5\% + 0\%)] + [(15\% + 5\%) \times (4.5\% + 2.5\%)] + [(25\% + 5\%) \times (0.5\% + 4.5\%)]$

$= 3.15\%$

The currency allocation for CNY can then be calculated as

$$CA_i = \left[(w_i + \tilde{w}_i) - (W_i + \tilde{W}_i)\right] \times \left[(C_i + I_i) - C\right]$$

$= [(10\% + 15\%) - (15\% + 5\%)] \times [(4.5\% + 2.5\%) - 3.15\%]$

$= 0.1925\%$

13 A is correct because there was a negative selection effect in US equities. The fund underperformed the benchmark in US equities (10.0% return to the fund, compared with a benchmark return of 12%), resulting in a negative selection

effect. The selection effect in Chinese equities and the allocation effect in the Eurozone market are both positive. The following table shows the allocation, selection, and currency allocation effects by market.

Market	Allocation Effect $A_i = (w_i - W_i) \times (B_{Li} - I_i - B_L)$	Selection Effect $S_i = w_i \times (R_{Li} - B_{Li})$	Currency Allocation Effect $CA_i = \left[(w_i + \tilde{w}_i) - (W_i - \tilde{W}_i)\right] \times \left[(C_i + I_i) - C\right]$
United States	(0.20)(12.0 − 0.5 − 5.95) = 1.11%	(0.8)(−2.0) = −1.60%	(0.10)(0.5 − 3.15) = −0.265%
China	(−0.50)(4.0 − 4.5 − 5.95) = 0.3225%	(0.10)(1.0) = 0.10%	(0.05)(7.0 − 3.15) = 0.1925%
Eurozone	(−0.15)(−3.0 − 0.5 − 5.95) = 1.4175%	(0.10)(1.0) = 0.10%	(−0.15)(5.0 − 3.15) = −0.2775%
Total	2.85%	−1.40%	−0.35%

The sum of the allocation, selection, and currency allocation effects is 1.10%. This number represents the difference between the 10.20% portfolio return in the base currency and the 9.10% benchmark return in the base currency.

14 B is correct because achieving higher returns through stock selection without assuming net market risk is essential to a market-neutral strategy. Without generating market exposure, the strategy approximately doubles the exposure to the portfolio manager's stock-picking ability (summing exposure on the long side and exposure on the short side). Manager A will go long in equities identified as undervalued and go short in equites identified as overvalued, maintaining a net market exposure of approximately zero. Manager A has exposures that differ from zero, but these will approximate zero over time, and the differences are not the main source of the fund's outperformance.

15 A is correct because a cash return is a suitable benchmark return when the net market exposure is zero, or nearly zero.

16 B is correct. The allocation effect in short Asian equities is closest to −0.30%. The formula for the allocation effect is as follows:

$A_i = (w_i - W_i) \times (B_i - B)$

$A_i = [-50\% - (-70\%)] \times (-1.4\% - 0.1\%) = -0.30\%$

17 C is correct. The selection effect in short European equites is closest to 0.99%. The formula for the selection effect that includes interaction is as follows:

$S_i = w_i \times (R_i - B_i)$

$S_i = -30\% \times (3.9\% - 7.2\%) = 0.99\%$

READING
7

Introduction to Fixed-Income Attribution

by Claude Giguère, BScA, and Andrew Kophamel, FRM, CFA, CIPM

Claude Giguère, BScA, is at Robust Technologies Inc. (Canada). Andrew Kophamel, FRM, CFA, CIPM (Australia).

LEARNING OUTCOMES

Mastery	The candidate should be able to:
☐	a. describe the three major approaches to fixed-income attribution (exposure decomposition—duration based, yield curve decomposition—duration based, and yield curve decomposition—full repricing);
☐	b. compare the three major approaches to fixed-income attribution in terms of associated decision-making processes, typical users, operational considerations, and limitations;
☐	c. describe and evaluate the three major approaches to fixed-income attribution in terms of their implementation, output, interpretation, and appropriate applications by various users;
☐	d. analyze and interpret the output of a fixed-income attribution analysis.

INTRODUCTION

Performance attribution is a tool that allows a performance analyst to explain the sources of any value added or subtracted by active management of a portfolio in relation to its benchmark. Returns are decomposed into terms that are commonly called attribution effects.

To be useful, performance attribution must abide by certain rules. First and foremost, the benchmark must be representative of the investment management mandate, objective, and constraints. Second, the calculation must be performed frequently enough to effectively capture the active decisions of the manager. Third, the attribution methodology must produce attribution effects that can be related directly to the investment management decisions made by the manager. If any of these criteria are not met, the fundamental purpose of attribution analysis will not be served.

The process of managing portfolios can be quite complex and differs substantially depending on the type of the investments: Domestic versus global, equity versus fixed income, cash versus derivative instruments, and long-only versus long–short hedge fund strategies will all be managed differently, and the investment decision-making process will differ for each. For example, equity managers try to predict outperforming

© 2014 CFA Institute. All rights reserved.

sectors, industries, and specific stocks, whereas fixed-income managers try to anticipate interest rate movements; changes in shapes of yield curves; and changes in the spreads of credit ratings, issuers, and issues. Indeed, the distinction between equity and fixed-income investment decision processes has pushed the investment management industry to develop attribution methodologies specific to fixed-income portfolios.

This reading is an introduction to fixed-income attribution. It provides an understanding of the philosophy (broad approach), calculations, and operational considerations pertaining to three distinct approaches of fixed-income attribution models:

1 Exposure Decomposition—Duration Based
2 Yield Curve Decomposition—Duration Based
3 Yield Curve Decomposition—Full Repricing Based

Most published and proprietary models fall into one of these three groups of models. By studying these three approaches, the reader will be prepared to interpret most fixed-income attribution analyses and to understand important considerations relevant for each. This breadth of preparation is desirable because no single fixed-income attribution model dominates the practice.

To allow the reader to appreciate concretely the similarities and differences among approaches, this reading takes an extended case study approach by showing how each group of models would typically address an attribution analysis given one common set of facts.

The reading is organized as follows: Section 2 provides an overview of each of the three approaches. Section 3 provides the data set used in the worked examples. Sections 4, 5, and 6 each address one of the three approaches in detail. Section 7 compares the various attribution analyses and the features of each. Section 8 concludes the reading. A set of references is provided at the end of the reading.

2

FIXED-INCOME ATTRIBUTION: CLASSIFICATION OF APPROACHES

Building on work by Groupe de Reflexion en Attribution de Performance, or GRAP (outlined in Giguère, 2005) and Murira and Sierra (2006, 2007), this reading classifies three distinct approaches to fixed-income attribution:

- Exposure Decomposition—Duration Based
- Yield Curve Decomposition—Duration Based
- Yield Curve Decomposition—Full Repricing Based

2.1 Exposure Decomposition—Duration Based

Exposure decomposition takes a top-down, benchmark-relative view of attribution. It focuses on explaining the active management of a portfolio relative to its benchmark, typically working a hierarchy of decisions from the top down. These often include, for example, a portfolio duration bet,[1] yield curve positioning bets, sector bets, and bond selection. The label "exposure decomposition" relates to the decomposition of portfolio risk exposures by means of grouping (sometimes called "bucketing") a portfolio's component bonds by specified characteristics (e.g., their duration or bond sector membership). The label "duration based" relates to the typical use of duration

---

[1] For the sake of brevity, this reading uses the term "bet" in the sense of "active investment decision."

to represent interest rate risk exposure decisions. Thus, portfolio duration bets are represented by grouping a portfolio's bonds into ranges (buckets) of duration covering the spectrum from short to long duration.

Models that take an exposure decomposition approach are close in spirit to the Brinson-type models commonly used in equity return attribution. Similar to Brinson-type equity attribution models, models in this approach to fixed income attribution use market value-based weights to define buckets which isolate the sources of a portfolio's overall active return. This group of models is intuitive and has comparatively simple data requirements. For these reasons, the exposure decomposition approach is often used primarily for marketing and client reports so that the users, who may not be well-versed in quantitative analysis, can understand and succinctly articulate the results of active portfolio management.

2.2 Yield Curve Decomposition—Duration Based

The yield curve decomposition—duration-based approach to fixed-income attribution can be executed either as a top-down approach focusing on portfolio-level or bucket-level (i.e., group) decisions, or built bottom-up from the security level. It seeks to estimate the return of securities, sector buckets, or years-to-maturity buckets by using the known relationship between modified duration and changes in yield to maturity (YTM):

% Total return = % Income return + % Price return

where

% Price return ≈ −Modified duration × Change in YTM

Modified duration measures the sensitivity of bond price to a change in the bond's yield to maturity. So, the percentage price return of a bond will be approximately equal to the negative of its modified duration for each 100 bp change in yields.

The **yield to maturity** represents the internal rate of return (discount factor) that must be used to make the present value of the bond's cash flows (i.e., coupons and redemption value) equal to the current market price.

The change in yield to maturity of the portfolio or instrument can be broken down into specific factors to provide additional insights. These factors represent the changes in the risk-free government curve and in the premium (spread) demanded by the market for holding riskier sectors and bonds. Combined together, and applied to the duration, a percentage price change for each can be determined.

This approach can be applied separately to portfolios and benchmarks for either specific securities or buckets to identify contributions to total return from changes in the yield to maturity. The difference between the two is identified as the effect of active portfolio management decisions. That is, an absolute attribution analysis can be executed for the portfolio and its benchmark separately with the attribution of active management based on the differences in exposures between portfolio and benchmark. In this regard, this group of models is quite different from the exposure decomposition. One consequence of this difference is that this group of models requires more data points to implement; therefore, it has better transparency, but also more operational complexity. Summary versions of this approach of attribution analysis can be used for marketing and client reports, but they tend to be better suited to the investment decision makers themselves—that is, analysts and portfolio managers.

2.3 Yield Curve Decomposition—Full Repricing

Instead of estimating price variation from duration and variation in market yields to maturity, bonds can be repriced from zero-coupon curves (spot rates). Recall that a bond consists of a number of promised cash flows whose market price equals the sum of the cash flows' present values. That is, a bond's price is the sum of its cash flows discounted at the appropriate spot rate for that cash flow's maturity.

As with the duration-based approaches, instruments can be repriced following incremental changes in spot rates, whether resulting from changes in overall interest rates, spreads, or bond-specific factors. This bottom-up security level repricing can then be translated into a contribution to a security's return and aggregated for portfolios, benchmarks, and active management.

Many attribution systems/models are built around this full repricing approach because it gives more precise pricing and it can deal with a broader range of instrument types and yield changes; it also lends itself to a greater variety of quantitative modeling outside of fixed-income attribution (e.g., *ex ante* risk). This approach is better aligned with how portfolio managers typically view the instruments. However, it requires the full capability to reprice all financial instruments in the portfolio and the benchmark. Its complex nature can make it more difficult and costly to administer operationally and the results more difficult to understand, particularly by non-investment professionals.

All three approaches can be run for either single or multi-currency portfolios. As with equity portfolios, in which there are multiple currency exposures, the separation and impact of these effects can be quantified in at least one of two ways:

- Naïve framework: The attribution is applied to the local currency return of a bond/portfolio, and the currency return/contribution arises from the translation of these local currency returns into the base currency of the portfolio.

- Karnosky–Singer-type framework: The return premium of an instrument above an appropriate risk-free rate is attributed using one of the three fixed-income attribution approaches.

The principles of fixed-income attribution are most clearly demonstrated by using a single-currency domestic portfolio, without diverging into the relative merits of these differing approaches. Therefore, the portfolio and benchmark used throughout this reading is a single-currency example.

3 SCENARIO FOR THE WORKED EXAMPLES

This reading builds on this brief introduction to these three approaches, and for each

- provides a more detailed description;
- provides a worked example, together with its typical factors and output;
- discusses the applicability of each;
- highlights some of the inherent operational compromises and limitations.

For the exposure decomposition example, only the active management is attributed. For the two yield curve decomposition approaches, a single bond is first attributed, and then aggregated with other positions into portfolio, benchmark, and active factor contributions.

Scenario for the Worked Examples

3.1 Assumed Market Conditions

Throughout this reading, the attribution calculations of the three approaches will be demonstrated by using the same set of data and market conditions. The calculations will be demonstrated at the security level for the yield curve decomposition approaches by using a hypothetical corporate bond maturing on 30 June 2018 and paying semi-annual coupons. In this case, a **plain vanilla bond** or **conventional bond** is assumed, which pays fixed rates of interest (i.e., the coupon payment does not change during the bond's life). Exhibit 1 shows the yield increase (price decrease) of the bond. On 30 June 2013, at time T with 10 coupon periods remaining to maturity, the bond is trading at a market price of 103.1997 resulting in a yield-to-maturity (YTM) of 4.28% (Circle 1). Six months later, on 31 December 2013, at time T + 1 with nine coupon periods remaining to maturity, the bond is trading at a market price of 96.2274, reflecting a YTM of 5.97% (Circle 8). The price variation is a result of the following factors (technical terms, such as duration, will be defined in Section 5):[2]

1. Passage of time: Even if the yield curve remains unchanged, bonds generate returns from coupon payments, accrued interest, price variations as a result of amortization of premium/discount, and YTM variations because of lesser time remaining to maturity.

2. Yield curve movement: Bonds are priced relative to a default-free reference curve. Most commonly, this curve is the Treasury curve. The solid and dotted lines in Exhibit 1 represent the YTM (par curve) of government (Treasury) bonds on 30 June and 31 December, respectively.

3. Spread variation: The YTM spread between the bond and its duration matched treasury.

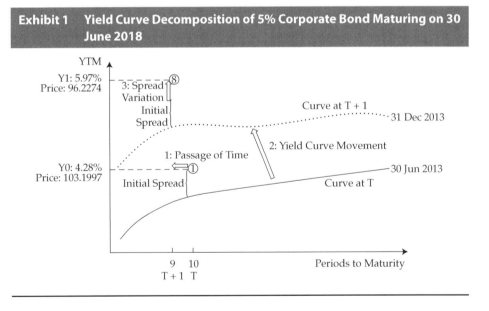

Exhibit 1 Yield Curve Decomposition of 5% Corporate Bond Maturing on 30 June 2018

The following observations about the market conditions can be made:

- The overall level of interest rates increased.
- Generally, the treasury curve flattened; that is, yields of long-term bonds increased less than yields of short-term bonds except around the five-year point (see next item).

---

2 See the appendix for an introduction to fixed-income valuation and risk measures.

- The yield increased more around the five-year maturity point (10 periods remaining to maturity on the x-axis), causing a change in the curvature of the yield curve.
- Combined, the sector- and bond-specific spread increased.

3.2 The Bonds Universe

Exhibit 2 provides information about the universe of bonds in which the portfolio and the benchmarks are invested. All bonds in the benchmark are held in the portfolio and all bonds in the portfolio are also represented in the benchmark with the exception of corporate bond (B), which is only held in the benchmark, and corporate bond (P), which is only held in the portfolio, as described following Exhibit 3.[3] The modified duration (Durat) and convexity (Conv) are shown as of 30 June. YTM and prices are shown as of 30 June and 31 December. The coupon (Cpn) column represents the semi-annual coupon interest, as a percentage of par, received on 31 December. All bonds paid coupon payments on that date. Finally, the price and total returns are shown in the last two columns. The calculations for the 5% Corporate 30 June 2018 bond (in bold) will be demonstrated in detail later in this reading.

Exhibit 2 Bonds Universe

Bond	Durat	Conv	30 June 2013 YTM	30 June 2013 Price	31 Dec. 2013 YTM	31 Dec. 2013 Price	Cpn	Rate of Return Price	Rate of Return Income	Rate of Return Total
Treasury 5% 30 June 2018	4.42	22.99	3.78%	$105.50	5.17%	$99.33	2.50%	−5.85%	2.37%	−3.48%
Treasury 7% 30 June 2023	7.47	69.31	4.35%	$121.31	5.43%	$111.55	3.50%	−8.05%	2.89%	−5.16%
Treasury 6% 30 June 2028	10.21	134.44	4.66%	$114.31	5.37%	$106.31	3.00%	−7.00%	2.62%	−4.38%
Corporate 5% 30 June 2018	**4.40**	**22.84**	**4.28%**	**$103.20**	**5.97%**	**$96.23**	**2.50%**	**−6.76%**	**2.42%**	**−4.33%**
Corporate 7% 30 June 2023	7.40	68.36	4.85%	$116.91	6.12%	$106.23	3.50%	−9.14%	2.99%	−6.14%
Corporate (B) 6% 30 June 2028	10.06	131.57	5.16%	$108.74	6.07%	$99.37	3.00%	−8.62%	2.76%	−5.86%
Corporate (P) 6% 30 June 2028	10.06	131.57	5.16%	$108.74	6.02%	$99.85	3.00%	−8.18%	2.76%	−5.42%

3.3 The Portfolio and Benchmark

The portfolio and benchmark constituents that will be used in the worked examples to illustrate the calculations of the various attribution approaches are presented in the next sections.

---

[3] As will become clear subsequently, the selection of a different bond in the portfolio generates a selection effect.

Scenario for the Worked Examples

3.3.1 Constituents

The portfolio and benchmark are invested in this universe according to the weights (Wgt) shown in Exhibit 3. Multiplying the weight by the modified duration and the total return shown in Exhibit 2 gives the contributions to duration and return. The duration and return contributions are shown for the portfolio and the benchmark.

Exhibit 3 Portfolio and Benchmark Weights

| Bond | Durat | Portfolio | | | | Benchmark | | | |
| | | Wgt | Contribution to... | | | Wgt | Contribution to ... | | |
			Durat	Conv	Return		Durat	Conv	Return
Government 5% 30 June 2018	4.42	0.10	0.44	2.30	−0.35%	0.20	0.88	4.60	−0.70%
Government 7% 30 June 2023	7.47	0.10	0.75	6.93	−0.52%	0.20	1.49	13.86	−1.03%
Government 6% 30 June 2028	10.21	0.20	2.04	26.89	−0.88%	0.15	1.53	20.17	−0.66%
Corporate 5% 30 June 2018	**4.40**	**0.10**	**0.44**	**2.28**	**−0.43%**	**0.15**	**0.66**	**3.43**	**−0.65%**
Corporate 7% 30 June 2023	7.40	0.20	1.48	13.67	−1.23%	0.15	1.11	10.25	−0.92%
Corporate (B) 6% 30 June 2028	10.06	0.00	0.00	0.00	0.00%	0.15	1.51	19.74	−0.88%
Corporate (P) 6% 30 June 2028	10.06	0.30	3.02	39.47	−1.63%	0.00	0.00	0.00	0.00%
Total		1.00	8.1679	91.55	−5.03%	1.00	7.1875	72.04	−4.83%
							Excess		−0.19%

As indicated in Exhibit 3, the manager selected a different bond in the long–corporate sector (i.e., Corporate (P) 6% 30 June 2028 in the portfolio versus Corporate (B) 6% 30 June 2028 in the benchmark.

3.3.2 Duration

Modified duration is a measure of the bond's price sensitivity to the variations of market yields to maturity. To measure the exposure of a given sector or duration bucket to such variations, calculate its modified duration. This calculation is done in three steps.

First, calculate its partial duration. The partial duration (also referred to as contribution to duration) is the product of the weightings in the portfolio or benchmark multiplied by the modified duration. For example, the Corporate 5% 30 June 2018 bond has a weight of 10% in the portfolio and a modified duration of 4.40. Its partial duration (or contribution to total portfolio duration) is 0.44:

0.44 = (10% × 4.40)

Second, sum the partial durations per bucket. For example, the partial duration of the corporate sector in the portfolio is the sum of the partial durations of its corporate bonds:

4.94 = (10% × 4.40) + (20% × 7.40) + (30% × 10.06)
4.94 = 0.44 + 1.48 + 3.02

Third, divide the partial duration of the bucket by its weight. For example, the duration of the corporate sector is 8.23:

$$8.23 = \frac{4.94}{60\%}$$

In Exhibit 4, the 8.17 duration for the total portfolio is simply the sum of the partial durations of all sectors within all duration buckets: 8.17 = 3.23 + 4.94.

Exhibit 4 and Exhibit 5 show, for the portfolio and benchmark, the weights, duration, and partial duration aggregated by sector and duration buckets. For this example, the Short, Mid, and Long duration buckets are defined as follows:

Bucket	Number of years to maturity
Short	less than or equal to 5
Mid	greater than 5 and less than or equal to 10
Long	greater than 10

Exhibit 4 Portfolio Exposures

	Weights				Duration				Partial Duration			
	Short	Mid	Long	Total	Short	Mid	Long	Total	Short	Mid	Long	Total
Government	10.0%	10.0%	20.0%	40.0%	4.42	7.47	10.21	8.08	0.44	0.75	2.04	3.23
Corporate	10.0%	20.0%	30.0%	60.0%	4.40	7.40	10.06	8.23	0.44	1.48	3.02	4.94
Total	20.0%	30.0%	50.0%	100.0%	4.41	7.42	10.12	8.17	0.88	2.23	5.06	8.17

Exhibit 5 Benchmark Exposures

	Weights				Duration				Partial Duration			
	Short	Mid	Long	Total	Short	Mid	Long	Total	Short	Mid	Long	Total
Government	20.0%	20.0%	15.0%	55.0%	4.42	7.47	10.21	7.11	0.88	1.49	1.53	3.91
Corporate	15.0%	15.0%	15.0%	45.0%	4.40	7.40	10.06	7.29	0.66	1.11	1.51	3.28
Total	35.0%	35.0%	30.0%	100.0%	4.41	7.44	10.13	7.19	1.54	2.60	3.04	7.19

The following observations about the manager's investment bets can be made:

- The manager expected the rates to fall and took a bullish position on interest rates by increasing exposure to interest rate risk. Exhibit 4 and Exhibit 5 show that the portfolio's overall duration is 8.17 compared with 7.19 for the benchmark.
- The manager over-weighted the long end of the curve by investing 50% of the portfolio compared with 30% in the benchmark.
- The manager expected credit spreads to narrow and over-weighted the corporate sector by taking a 60% position compared with 45% in the benchmark. Notice this bet increases the 4.94 partial duration of the corporate sector in the portfolio compared with the 3.28 partial duration of the benchmark. This allocation makes the portfolio more exposed to market yield fluctuations in the corporate sector.

3.3.3 Contribution to Return

The return of a given sector or duration bucket can be calculated by using the sum of contributions of its constituents. This calculation is done in three steps.

Scenario for the Worked Examples

First, calculate the return contribution of each bond as the product of the weight multiplied by the return. For example, the Corporate 5% 30 June 2018 bond has a weight of 10% in the portfolio and a return of –4.33%. Its contribution to the total portfolio return is –0.43% = (10% × –4.33%).

Second, sum the return contribution per bucket. For example, the return contribution of the corporate sector in the portfolio is the sum of the return contribution of its three corporate bonds:

–3.29% = (10% × –4.33%) + (20% × –6.14%) + (30% × –5.42%)
–3.29% = –0.43% – 1.23% – 1.63%

Third, divide the contribution to return of the bucket by its weight. For example, the return of the corporate sector is –5.48%:

$$-5.48\% = \frac{-3.29\%}{60\%}$$

The total portfolio return corresponds to the sum of the return contribution of all sectors within all duration buckets: –5.03% = –1.74% – 3.29%.

Exhibit 6 Portfolio Returns

	Weights				Return				Contribution			
	Short	Mid	Long	Total	Short	Mid	Long	Total	Short	Mid	Long	Total
Government	10.0%	10.0%	20.0%	40.0%	–3.48%	–5.16%	–4.38%	–4.35%	–0.35%	–0.52%	–0.88%	–1.74%
Corporate	10.0%	20.0%	30.0%	60.0%	–4.33%	–6.14%	–5.42%	–5.48%	–0.43%	–1.23%	–1.63%	–3.29%
Total	20.0%	30.0%	50.0%	100.0%	–3.91%	–5.82%	–5.00%	–5.03%	–0.78%	–1.74%	–2.50%	–5.03%

Exhibit 7 Benchmark Returns

	Weights				Return				Contribution			
	Short	Mid	Long	Total	Short	Mid	Long	Total	Short	Mid	Long	Total
Government	20.0%	20.0%	15.0%	55.0%	–3.48%	–5.16%	–4.38%	–4.33%	–0.70%	–1.03%	–0.66%	–2.38%
Corporate	15.0%	15.0%	15.0%	45.0%	–4.33%	–6.14%	–5.86%	–5.45%	–0.65%	–0.92%	–0.88%	–2.45%
Total	35.0%	35.0%	30.0%	100.0%	–3.84%	–5.58%	–5.12%	–4.83%	–1.35%	–1.95%	–1.54%	–4.83%

As shown in Exhibit 6, the total portfolio return is –5.03% (rounded) compared with a total benchmark return of –4.83% (rounded) for an under-performance of –0.19% (based on using unrounded numbers) over the period. Exhibit 7 shows the benchmark's returns. The purpose of performance attribution is to explain the source of this performance deviation, given the market conditions of the period being evaluated, and to quantify how each of the manager's active investment decisions added or subtracted value.

4 EXPOSURE DECOMPOSITION—DURATION BASED

Brinson-type equity attribution models provide insights to active management by quantifying the effects of overweighting (underweighting) outperforming (underperforming) buckets, with buckets defined, for example, in terms of countries, sectors, regions, or styles.

Because most analysts are familiar with this allocation–selection effect attribution paradigm, considerable research has explored the application of this type of approach to fixed-income portfolio management. These approaches do the following:

a Quantify the active management of a portfolio relative to a pre-defined benchmark. They do not generally quantify contributors/drivers to portfolio and benchmark returns independently, but can be made to do so.

b Seek to identify out- and under-performing buckets and evaluate the portfolio's active position in that bucket.

c Typically adopt a top-down hierarchical view on decision making.

If corporate bonds have out-performed government bonds and the portfolio takes an overweight position in corporates, then a positive contribution to active return is intuitively expected.

The naïve application of equity attribution models can be made to work for lower credit quality fixed-income products in which the instruments often behave with equity-like characteristics. For managers of global emerging debt portfolios, the primary concern may be sovereign risk, and then the simple allocation between countries is the primary decision factor. However, the difficulty these approaches face is to account for the decision factors more typical for developed markets and products, such as duration and yield-curve positioning, as well as sector bets, and the more sophisticated exposure decomposition models try to do exactly that.

4.1 Exposure Decomposition—Duration Based: Worked Example

Consider the subject portfolio and benchmark previously outlined. Typical decisions the portfolio manager may make could include

- taking a long or short position on duration, relative to the benchmark, in anticipation of changes in interest rates;
- placing a curve bet to take advantage of non-parallel changes in interest rates;
- over- or under-weighting corporate bonds as views on the credit markets change;
- selecting issues/issuers that are expected to perform better than those in the benchmark.

The impact of each of these decisions on active management can be quantified under the exposure decomposition framework. To do so, "bucket" the weights and returns, first by duration bucket and then by sector bucket. Exhibit 8 provides some sample bucketed data.

Exposure Decomposition—Duration Based

Exhibit 8 Portfolio and Benchmark Weights and Returns

Duration Bucket	Sector	Weight		Return	
		Portfolio	Benchmark	Portfolio	Benchmark
Short	Government	10.0%	20.0%	−3.48%	−3.48%
	Corporate	10.0%	15.0%	−4.33%	−4.33%
	Total	20.0%	35.0%	−3.91%	−3.84%
Mid	Government	10.0%	20.0%	−5.16%	−5.16%
	Corporate	20.0%	15.0%	−6.14%	−6.14%
	Total	30.0%	35.0%	−5.82%	−5.58%
Long	Government	20.0%	15.0%	−4.38%	−4.38%
	Corporate	30.0%	15.0%	−5.42%	−5.86%
	Total	50.0%	30.0%	−5.00%	−5.12%
	Total Government	40.0%	55.0%	−4.35%	−4.33%
	Total Corporate	60.0%	45.0%	−5.48%	−5.45%
Total		100%	100%	−5.03%	−4.83%
				Excess	−0.19%

Exhibit 8 provides the weights and returns for the portfolio and its benchmark, broken down by duration bucket, and within that, government and corporate sector. As an example, government securities comprise 40% of the total portfolio weight and returned −4.35%, compared with 55.0% in the government benchmark with a return of −4.33%.

Key to this example is that the portfolio has under-performed the benchmark by −0.19% [(−5.03%) − (−4.83%)] for the period, and the attribution needs to explain this performance in terms of the factors outlined earlier.

There are many different exposure decomposition models in the industry,[4] but this specific approach will explain this out-performance according to

- interest rate risk decisions, which may include
  - exposures to parallel (duration effect) yield curve changes, or
  - exposures to non-parallel (curve effect) yield curve changes;
- changes in credit spreads;
- individual bond selection.

4.1.1 Interest Rate Risk Decisions

The first decisions to quantify are the effects of duration bets and curve positioning. Recall that the price return of a bond is approximated by its negative duration multiplied by the change in yield: Longer duration bonds out-perform in a falling interest rate environment. And if the manager expects interest rates to fall, he or she will position the portfolio to take advantage of this change (described as being "long duration").

Other attribution approaches directly seek to capture the movements in yield curves. But exposure decomposition approaches infer this by grouping bonds into duration buckets and then looking at the relative returns and positioning of the portfolio relative to its benchmark.

---

[4] For example, Dynkin, Hyman, and Vankudre (1998), McLaren (2002), and Giguère (2005).

Interest rate decisions are most often associated with movements in the risk-free government curve. Therefore, in ascertaining the impact of these decisions, only the returns of the government bonds are included, and the portfolio's position exposure to the benchmark return for a government duration bucket is used. Although corporate bond returns are driven by changes in the risk-free government curve, their total return also includes the impact of changes in credit spreads, which are typically managed as a separate factor; to include them would not isolate interest rate decisions.

In Exhibit 9, the government bonds in the benchmark can be carved out by duration bucket. For example, the return of government securities with a long duration between 10 and 15 is −4.38% and the weighted average return of all government securities is −4.33%.

Exhibit 9 Government Return by Duration Bucket

Duration Bucket	Benchmark Return
Short	−3.48%
Mid	−5.16%
Long	−4.38%
Total Government	−4.33%

Recall the negative relationship between bond yields and price movements. From Exhibit 9, observe that all the returns are negative, from which can be inferred that yields have generally increased over the period.

Consider now how the portfolio was positioned relative to its benchmark, which can be determined by looking at the weights applied to each duration bucket, shown in Exhibit 10.

Exhibit 10 Duration Bucket Exposures

Duration Bucket	Weight Portfolio	Weight Benchmark	Active Bet
Short	20.0%	35.0%	−15.0%
Mid	30.0%	35.0%	−5.0%
Long	50.0%	30.0%	+20.0%
Total	100.0%	100.0%	

Exhibit 10 shows that the portfolio appears to be less exposed (i.e., under-weighted) to shorter-duration buckets (0–5/Short, 5–10/Mid) and more exposed (i.e., over-weighted) in longer duration buckets (10–15/Long) reflecting the fact that the manager has positioned the portfolio to be long duration in anticipation of decreases in (government risk-free) interest rates. However, knowing this position, and the fact that yields actually increased for the period, we can demonstrate that the manager was incorrect in this decision, and so intuitively expect to see a negative contribution to active management for the period.

Exposure Decomposition—Duration Based

To quantify this contribution, we can use the typical Brinson–Hood–Beebower[5] approach to equity attribution allocation techniques, whereby

Allocation = $(R_{b,GDB}) \times (W_{p,DB} - W_{b,DB})$

where

$R_{b,GDB}$ = Benchmark return for a government duration bucket
$W_{p,DB}$ = Weight in portfolio for the duration bucket
$W_{b,DB}$ = Weight in benchmark for the duration bucket

Applying this equation to the bond portfolio above gives the results presented Exhibit 11.

Exhibit 11 Interest Rate Allocation Effects

Duration Bucket	Weight		Benchmark Government Return	Interest Rate Allocation
	Portfolio	Benchmark		
Short	20.0%	35.0%	−3.48%	0.52%
Mid	30.0%	35.0%	−5.16%	0.26%
Long	50.0%	30.0%	−4.38%	−0.88%
Total	100.0%	100.0%	−4.33%	−0.10%

In total, the −0.10% active return was added from total interest rate allocation, with a contribution of −0.88% coming from the long bucket, calculated as follows:

(−4.38%) × (50% − 30%) = −0.88%

This negative allocation reflects the fact that the manager under-weighted the short end of the curve, (with a subsequent overweighting in the long end of the curve) in anticipation of a decrease in interest rates (and positive price returns). But, as has been shown, rates actually rose, leading to a decrease in prices (and returns) and the out-performance of the short end of the risk-free government curve. Underweighting the short end and overweighting the long end was, in hindsight, a bad decision.

4.1.2 Parallel and Non-Parallel Changes in Yield Curves

This analysis can be further refined to separate the impact of parallel changes in interest rates (duration) from non-parallel changes (curve) by using the same data.

In general, a bond's price return is approximated by an inverse linear function relating duration and yield changes. Therefore, for a parallel decline in yield curves (equal changes in yield across the curve), we would expect a long bucket to out-perform a short bucket. Graphically, Return ≈ −Duration × ΔYield is shown in Exhibit 12.

---

[5] See Brinson, Hood, and Beebower (1986). Depending on the views expressed by managers, an approach based on Brinson and Fachler (1985) may also be relevant.

Exhibit 12 Price Return per Unit of Duration

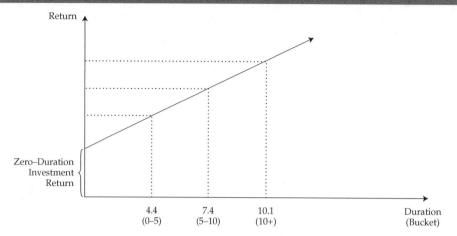

An upward sloping line demonstrates a positive return and would arise from an environment of falling yields.

Forecasting the expected return for each bucket can be achieved by using the information in the previous exhibits combined with a known zero-duration risk-free rate.

1. Estimate the duration in the benchmark for government bonds. This information may be available from vendors or can be estimated from constituent information. Exhibit 13 shows that in this example, government bonds had an overall duration of 7.11, and the 20% benchmark exposure to the short bucket (representing 20%/55% = 36% of the total benchmark government weight) contributed 1.61 to total duration.

Exhibit 13 Calculating Benchmark Government Duration

Duration Bucket	Benchmark Duration	Benchmark Weight	Adjusted Benchmark Weight	Contribution to Benchmark of Government Duration
Short	4.42	20.0%	36.4%	1.61
Mid	7.47	20.0%	36.4%	2.72
Long	10.21	15.0%	27.3%	2.78
Total		55.0%	100%	7.11

2. If we assume a zero-duration risk-free rate (RFR) of 0.15% then the benchmark government securities, with duration of 7.11, delivered an excess return of −4.48% (government benchmark return of −4.33% from Exhibit 11 minus 0.15%) over this return.

3. This performance equates to an excess return of −0.631% per year attributable to parallel movements in the risk-free government yield curve (−4.48%/7.11) for the period.

4 Knowing about the parallel movements means that the expected returns per bucket can be calculated. As an example, the Mid benchmark bucket has a total bucket duration of 7.44 (in Exhibit 5), which equates to a return attributable to parallel changes in government risk-free yields of:

Duration return = Zero-duration RFR + (Duration × Excess return per year),

Duration return$_{BM,Mid}$ = 0.15 + (7.44 × −0.631%) = −4.55%

Exhibit 14 shows price return for the Mid duration bucket; the actual benchmark return of −5.58% can be broken down into a parallel return of −4.55% and a non-parallel movement of −1.03%.

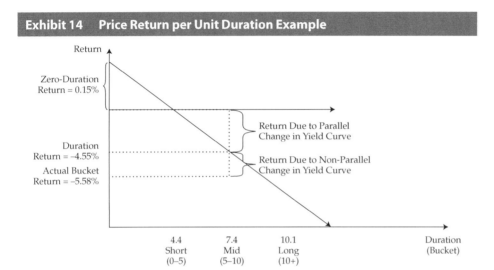

Exhibit 14 Price Return per Unit Duration Example

Duration returns for both the portfolio and the benchmark can be calculated for each bucket and then aligned with respective weights to give the contribution to return from duration for each, calculated as follows:

Duration contribution$_{p,DB}$ = Duration return$_{p,DB}$ × $W_{p,DB}$

Duration contribution$_{b,DB}$ = Duration return$_{b,DB}$ × $W_{b,DB}$

Duration effect$_{DB}$ = Duration contribution$_{p,DB}$ − Duration contribution$_{b,DB}$

where

Duration contribution$_{p,DB}$ = Duration contribution for the portfolio from duration bucket

Duration contribution$_{b,DB}$ = Duration contribution for the benchmark from duration bucket

Duration effect$_{DB}$ = Contribution to active return from duration bucket attributable to parallel changes in risk-free government curve

Exhibit 15 provides the duration effects for the sample portfolio and benchmark.

Exhibit 15 Contribution to Active Return from Duration

Duration Bucket	Portfolio				Benchmark				Duration Effect
	Weight	Duration	Duration Return	Duration Contribution	Weight	Duration	Duration Return	Duration Contribution	
Short	20.0%	4.41	−2.63%	−0.53%	35.0%	4.41	−2.63%	−0.92%	0.40%
Mid	30.0%	7.42	−4.54%	−1.36%	35.0%	7.44	−4.55%	−1.59%	0.23%
Long	50.0%	10.12	−6.24%	−3.12%	30.0%	10.13	−6.24%	−1.87%	−1.24%
Total	100.0%	8.17		−5.00%		7.19		−4.39%	−0.62%

Continuing the example with the Mid duration bucket, the expected return for the benchmark, given its duration of 7.44 and the excess return per year of −0.631, is −4.55%, which with an allocation of 35%, gives a duration contribution of −1.59% (−4.55% × 35%). The portfolio contribution from the Mid bucket, with its marginally shorter duration of 7.42 and smaller allocation (30%), is −1.36% (−4.54 × 30%). The duration effect from the Mid bucket is the contribution to active management, which is the difference between the portfolio and benchmark duration contribution, and is 0.23%.

Bucket contributions can be aggregated for an overall total duration effect of −0.62%, interpreted as the contribution to active management from being long duration as yields increased.

Non-parallel changes in the yield curve, which might also be called curve allocation, and collectively comprise slope and curvature changes, can then be calculated as the difference between these duration (parallel) effects and the total interest rate allocation effect calculated in Exhibit 11. For example, if it is known that the total interest rate allocation for the short bucket was 0.52% and duration contributed 0.40%, then the difference (0.52% − 0.40%) = 0.13% must be because of non-parallel curve movements.[6] Exhibit 16 shows the results by duration bucket.

Exhibit 16 Calculating Curve Effects

Duration Bucket	Total	Duration Effect	Curve Effect
Short	0.52%	0.40%	0.13%
Mid	0.26%	0.23%	0.03%
Long	−0.88%	−1.24%	0.37%
Total	−0.10%	−0.62%	0.52%

In this case, in total, the manager has lost 0.62% in active management from their long duration position as yields have increased, but gained 0.52% as a result of non-parallel changes in the changes to the yield curve.

---

6 Differences are the result of rounding.

4.1.3 Credit Spreads

Of course, a portfolio manager can make investments in instruments other than government bonds. In this case, they may make an active allocation to corporate bonds if they believe that they are likely to out-perform government bonds—that is, credit spreads will tighten. This decision can be taken independently of the interest rate decisions mentioned earlier and is evaluated separately.

For our portfolio, the manager has taken a positive view on credit, investing 60% of the portfolio in corporate bonds, compared with the benchmark's 45% split. The long end of the curve is particularly notable, with 30% of the portfolio invested in long corporate bonds alone versus 15% in the benchmark.

As with interest rate decisions, variance attribution techniques can be used to quantify the impact of these decisions by considering active returns and active weights. Exhibit 17 shows that the overall corporate bond benchmark returned −5.45%, underperforming the overall government bond benchmark return of −4.33% because of, on average, spreads widening.

Exhibit 17: Sector Performance by Duration Bucket

Duration Bucket	Sector	Benchmark
Short	Government	−3.48%
	Corporate	−4.33%
	Difference	−0.86%
Mid	Government	−5.16%
	Corporate	−6.14%
	Difference	−0.98%
Long	Government	−4.38%
	Corporate	−5.86%
	Difference	−1.48%
Total Government		−4.33%
Total Corporate		−5.45%

The underperformance increased gradually as duration buckets increased. From this result can be inferred that spreads had both parallel and non-parallel changes.

Although this market knowledge is informative and adds depth to the interpretation of the attribution, one of the advantages of exposure decomposition is that yield changes are not necessary in quantifying the impact on active management. Instead, and consistent with equity attribution, we can again look at the active weights in each bucket to determine the basis point impact of the active management decisions.

Exhibit 18: Sector Allocation

| Duration Bucket | Sector | Weight | | | Return | | Sector Allocation |
		Portfolio	Benchmark	Active	Benchmark	Active	
Short	Corporate	10.0%	15.0%	−5.0%	−4.33%	−0.86%	0.04%
Mid	Corporate	20.0%	15.0%	5.0%	−6.14%	−0.98%	−0.05%
Long	Corporate	30.0%	15.0%	15.0%	−5.86%	−1.48%	−0.22%
Total		60.0%	45.0%				−0.23%

Consider the long duration bucket in Exhibit 18, in which corporate bonds have underperformed government bonds by –1.48%. This bucket was also the one in which the manager decided to invest 30% of the portfolio, for an over-weight position of 15%. The product of these two generates a –0.22% negative impact for active management. More generally,

$$\text{Sector allocation} = (W_{ps} - W_{bs}) \times (R_{b,SDB} - R_{b,GDB})$$

where

$R_{b,GDB}$ = Benchmark return for a government duration bucket
$R_{b,SDB}$ = Benchmark return for a corporate sector duration bucket
W_{ps} = Sector weight in portfolio for the duration bucket
W_{bs} = Sector weight in benchmark for the duration bucket

4.1.4 Bond Selection

Finally, the manager may earn additional active management returns from choosing better performing issues or issuers than those contained in the benchmark—that is, a selection decision. Again, consistent with equity attribution, this selection decision can be quantified by looking at the relative performance within a bucket.[7] Specifically,

$$\text{Bond selection} = W_{ps} \times (R_{p,SDB} - R_{b,SDB})$$

where

$R_{p,SDB}$ = Portfolio return for a corporate sector duration bucket
$R_{b,SDB}$ = Benchmark return for a corporate sector duration bucket
W_{ps} = Sector weight in portfolio for the duration bucket

Exhibit 19 Bond Selection Effect

Duration Bucket	Sector	Weights Portfolio	Returns Portfolio	Returns Benchmark	Active	Selection
Short	Government	10.0%	–3.48%	–3.48%	0.00%	0.00%
	Corporate	10.0%	–4.33%	–4.33%	0.00%	0.00%
	Total	20.0%	–3.91%	–3.84%		0.00%
Mid	Government	10.0%	–5.16%	–5.16%	0.00%	0.00%
	Corporate	20.0%	–6.14%	–6.14%	0.00%	0.00%
	Total	30.0%	–5.82%	–5.58%		0.00%
Long	Government	20.0%	–4.38%	–4.38%	0.00%	0.00%
	Corporate	30.0%	–5.42%	–5.86%	0.44%	0.13%
	Total	50.0%	–5.00%	–5.12%		0.13%
Total		100.0%				0.13%

As shown in Exhibit 19, an additional 0.13% of return was contributed by active management in bond selection by picking better performing corporate bonds in the long end of the curve (10+ years).

4.1.5 Bringing It All Together

Combining these effects provides the output shown in Exhibit 20.

---

[7] In this example, interaction has been included in selection via the use of portfolio weight in the calculations.

Exhibit 20 Final Exposure Decomposition Attribution

Duration Bucket	Sector	Duration Effect	Curve Effect	Total Interest Rate Allocation	Sector Allocation	Bond Selection	Total
Short	Government					0.00%	0.00%
	Corporate				0.04%	0.00%	0.04%
	Total	0.40%	0.13%	0.52%	0.04%	0.00%	0.56%
Mid	Government					0.00%	0.00%
	Corporate				−0.05%	0.00%	−0.05%
	Total	0.23%	0.03%	0.26%	−0.05%	0.00%	0.21%
Long	Government					0.00%	0.00%
	Corporate				−0.22%	0.13%	−0.09%
	Total	−1.24%	0.37%	−0.88%	−0.22%	0.13%	−0.97%
Total*		−0.62%	0.52%	−0.10%	−0.23%	0.13%	−0.19%

* Differences may appear because of rounding.

4.1.6 Interpreting the Results

Interpreting this attribution, we can show that for the whole portfolio that

- the portfolio under-performed its benchmark for the period by −0.19% (based on using unrounded numbers);
- −0.62% was lost from taking a long duration position as the government risk-free yields increased;
- 0.52% was gained as the yield curve reshaped because the manager over-weighted the long end of the curve and slope flattened;
- credit spreads widened, and the portfolio's overweight position subtracted −0.23%; and
- issue selection added 0.13%.

4.2 Appropriate Uses

The comparatively simple and intuitive nature of the calculations lends itself less to stakeholders concerned with modeling individual cash flows and risk factors and more to reporting the results of active decisions to a more generalized audience. This form of attribution is used most for client reports and marketing teams, for example, and is most effective for vanilla portfolios and investment strategies.

4.3 Operational Considerations and Limitations

The strength of these approaches is that they are comparatively easy to calculate, understand, and interpret. They also tend to be easier to administer operationally because the data requirements are generally less than the other approach.

4.3.1 Portfolio Data

Exposure decomposition attribution requires only portfolio weights, by duration/sector bucket. Most corporate systems have this information readily available for portfolio management and compliance purposes.

The methodology applied to calculate bucket returns and thus attribution effects, such as Modified Dietz or daily time weighted rate of return (TWRR), can also be aligned with the overall reported performance return. This alignment is not always possible if dedicated and separate fixed-income attribution systems, perhaps using the buy-hold approach found in many yield curve decomposition approaches detailed later in Sections 5 and 6, are used. Exposure decomposition approaches can also fully capture, at a security level, the impact of intra-period trading decisions, which may become material depending on the security type, specific security, and market conditions.

All of these mean that less operational effort may be required to ensure the integrity and accuracy of the data and returns across systems from this group of approaches.

4.3.2 Benchmark Data

As with portfolios, the only requirement is for a benchmark to be broken down into duration/sector buckets, possibly supplemented with a government curve if that is not part of the benchmark. This benchmark is comparatively simple to produce, and does not require the maintenance of index data at the constituent bond level, which with some numbering in the thousands of constituents, can be particularly troublesome to maintain accurately.[8]

4.3.3 Calculations

The fewer calculations used in the exposure decomposition approach generally makes it easy and quick to run reports compared with other, more computationally intensive approaches. The more portfolios that are required to be supported, the greater the priority this becomes.

4.3.4 Portfolio Manager/Portfolio Management Applicability

The comparative simplicity of the exposure decomposition approaches does, however, lead to some limitations. The simplifications made in exposure decomposition approaches can limit their ability to reflect accurately a bond portfolio manager's investment discipline and decision-making processes. Consider fixed-income portfolios managed in an asset/liability matching framework. The aim may not be to out-perform a given benchmark, but rather to match the portfolio characteristics (duration, convexity, etc.) and cash flows to those of the liability stream. In this instance, perhaps the transparency over individual instruments and cash flows found in some of the yield curve decomposition approaches may be more appropriate.

4.3.5 Requirement to Source a Government Curve

Sector decisions are typically evaluated as excess returns (spreads) against comparable government securities. If the portfolio's benchmark does not include a government sector, it will still typically need to be sourced to allow sector returns to be separated between changes in the risk-free government curve and sector-specific spreads. Fortunately, though, these are usually the most liquid and easily available.

4.3.6 Crude Separation of Parallel and Non-Parallel Changes in Interest Rates

The method of separating parallel and non-parallel changes in interest rates, shown earlier, is comparatively crude. Depending on how narrowly the duration buckets are defined, the aggregate benchmark duration figures may not be fully accurate. Nor is there any further separation of the non-parallel movements between slope and curvature, typically found in some of the more refined term-structure models used in the

---

[8] It should be acknowledged that having constituent level benchmark data does provide an organization with increased flexibility in constructing duration or sector buckets, albeit at operational and financial costs.

yield curve decomposition approaches. Finally, although the impact of non-parallel movements can be quantified, the attribution, in isolation, gives no real indication as to what these non-parallel movements actually were. The materiality of these must be considered against the costs of implementation.

4.3.7 Aligning Benchmark and Portfolio Analytics

Common to all three approaches to fixed-income attribution, many systems and reports can lose clarity because of data differences between the portfolio and benchmark. Examples would include durations, pricing sources, and sector definitions. The additional difficulty, however, with exposure decomposition approaches is that the simplistic nature of the benchmark data, and its limited transparency, makes identifying and quantifying these differences much more difficult than other approaches. This difficulty can be significant when markets and pricing are highly variable.

4.3.8 Duration Buckets and Interest Rate Risk Exposures

The approach used in this section deliberately groups securities by duration buckets, predicated on the assumption that securities with similar durations will perform in-line once adjusted for sector spreads. That is, all government securities with a Mid duration bucket grouping should perform broadly the same and differences between government and corporate securities in the Mid bucket are solely down to spread changes. It is important to remember that duration exposure, when combined with a market value–based weight, provides a contribution to duration, which is also known as a partial duration. It is partial duration that is actually the interest rate risk exposure for that bucket.

The exposure decomposition approach can break down if securities are bucketed without a duration bucket—for example, by country and then sector. Using this example, duration differences within each country–sector bucket are not captured, possibly generating misleading results.

YIELD CURVE DECOMPOSITION—DURATION BASED

The second approach to fixed-income attribution is based on repricing bonds by using duration. Given a known change in the yield to maturity and a bond's duration, the total return of a bond can be estimated. The change in YTM can then be broken down into components, each used to successively reprice the instrument by using duration, which provides a breakdown of a return into contributing factors.

5.1 Background Concepts

In the following, concepts used in this approach are given nontechnical descriptions.

5.1.1 Duration and Convexity

Modified duration[9] is a measure that allows the estimation of the percentage price change of a bond given a small variation in its market YTM. In other words, it measures the sensitivity of bond price to small changes in market rates. The minus sign in the following formula reflects the inverse relationship between bond price and yield:

$$\Delta P/P \approx -D \times \Delta Y$$

where

$\Delta P/P$ = Percentage price change
D = Modified duration as of the beginning of the period
ΔY = Change in YTM

In addition to modified duration, a second level of approximation of the price change can be obtained by using convexity. Convexity, denoted C in the following formula, attempts to capture non-linearities in the relationship between bond price and changes in yield. Thus, the following estimate of price change approximation would be more accurate:

$$\Delta P/P \approx -D \times \Delta Y + \frac{1}{2} \times C \times \Delta Y^2$$

5.1.2 Roll Down

In normal market conditions, bonds with longer maturities trade at higher yields than those with shorter maturities.[10] This result reflects the compensation investors expect to receive when lending money for a longer period of time.

Roll down reflects the term structure of the yield curve at the beginning of the measurement period. In Exhibit 21, bonds with shorter maturity usually trade at lower YTM. Even if market yields remain stable, as time goes by, the bond will naturally trade at a lower YTM as it approaches maturity. The percentage price variation attributable to yield variation is referred to as the *roll-down effect*.

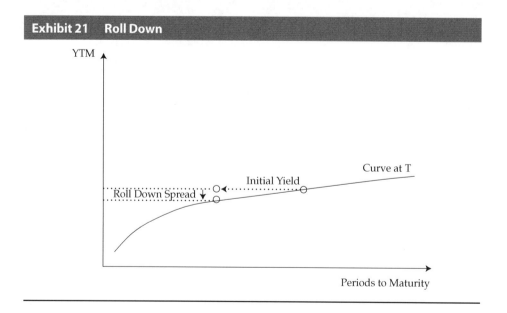

Exhibit 21 Roll Down

---

9 Modified duration assumes that the expected future cash flows are constant, which is not the case for securities with embedded options or with redemption features, such as extendible and retractable bonds. Effective duration should be used for securities with embedded options or redemption features.
10 This result is in normal market conditions when the yield curve is not inverted.

Yield Curve Decomposition—Duration Based

The roll-down factor represents the performance contribution resulting from the percentage price variation of a bond as it moves closer to maturity, at which point the reference yield curve remains constant. The steeper the yield curve at the beginning of the period, the greater the roll-down return will be.

5.1.3 Initial Yield

Fixed-income instruments earn a return even when their YTM remains constant. Generally, it is the coupon paid. In addition, with the amortization of instruments priced at anything other than par, there is also a "pull to par" that occurs with time. These components are wrapped up into the YTM of a bond. With knowledge of the YTM at the beginning of the period and the number of days being evaluated, the performance contribution can be estimated by using the following formula:

Yield = $Y \times \Delta t$

where

Yield = Initial yield effect
Y = Initial bond yield expressed on an annual basis
Δt = Number of days in period/365[11]

5.1.4 Yield Curve Movements; Shift, Slope, and Curvature

Bond portfolio managers try to predict changes in the level and shape of the yield curve. Yield curve decomposition attribution requires a technique to decompose the movement of, typically, risk-free government yield curves into elementary movements, such as shift, slope, and curvature. Most frequently, yield curves movements are expressed as one or more type of shape change.

- Parallel Movements or yield curve "shifts" are movements in the yield curve as if every point on the curve moved by the same amount, as shown in Exhibit 22.

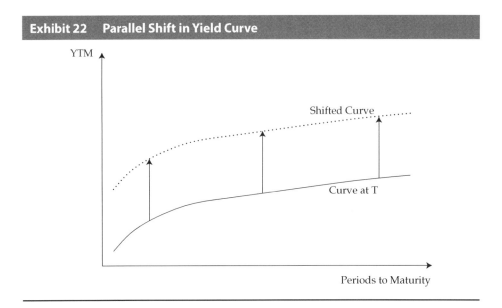

Exhibit 22 Parallel Shift in Yield Curve

- Slope movements are movements in the yield curve at some pivot point, frequently used to express the notion of the long and short end performing differently, as shown in Exhibit 23.

---

11 Or 360, depending on the assumed number of days in a year for the accrued interest day count method.

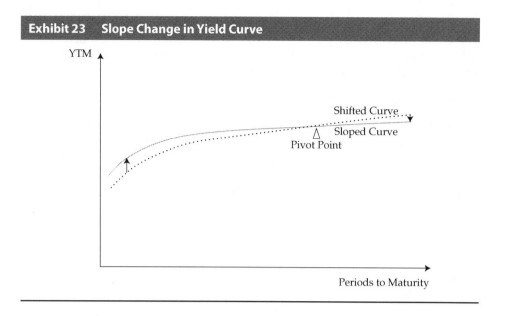

- Curvature is movements in the mid-points of the yield curve whereby it bulges, as shown in Exhibit 24.

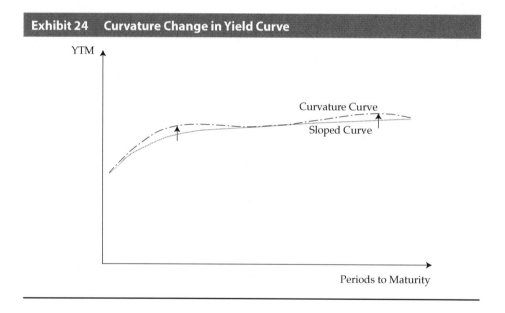

Most importantly, different systems and models use different terminology to calculate and describe these movements and some will bundle slope and curvature movements under the generic heading of non-parallel or *shape* changes.

Various techniques can be used to decompose the yield curve movement into elementary movements. For example, some use an arbitrary point (e.g., 10 year maturity) as the pivot point on the curve to determine the shift and the slope. Others may use the average yield variation of all maturity points. More elaborate techniques use polynomial regression or principal components methods to best fit the curve and, by extension, its changes. Understanding precisely how these techniques work is outside the scope of this reading,[12] but it is important to understand that different assumptions and techniques to decompose yield curve movements will lead to different attribution results and interpretations.

5.1.5 Spreads

Government (Treasury) bonds are generally considered default free. Corporate bonds, however, are riskier than government bonds. The yield difference between riskier corporate bonds and their maturity-equivalent government bond[13] is called the spread. Spreads are affected by market conditions and will widen or narrow for various reasons and vary differently for different sectors, industries, or credit quality ratings. The spread can be inherent to the general credit market (called systematic spread) and defined further by sectors and credit quality ratings. The spread specific to a particular bond is referred as the specific spread (or idiosyncratic or non-systematic spread). Managers anticipate spread variations and should select sectors, credit quality ratings, and bonds for which spreads are expected to increase the least or decrease the most. Exhibit 25 shows the spread variations.

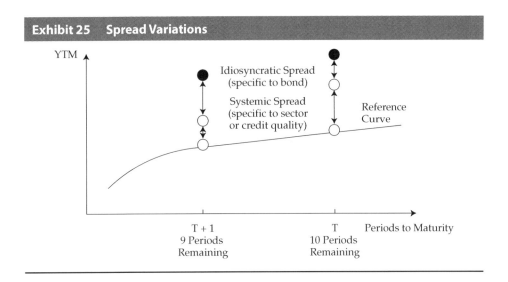

Exhibit 25 Spread Variations

5.1.6 Summary of Factors

Exhibit 26 illustrates how the YTM variation of the bond from 4.28% at time T to 5.97% at time T + 1 can be decomposed into a series of elementary yield variations illustrated with the following data points:

1. *Begin* YTM: 4.28%
2. Begin YTM but *lesser time* to maturity: 4.28%
3. YTM after *roll-down* adjustment: 4.19%
4. YTM after parallel *shift* adjustment: 5.19%
5. YTM after *slope* adjustment: 5.42%
6. YTM after *curvature* adjustment: 5.67%
7. YTM after *systematic* spread adjustment: 5.87%
8. YTM after *specific* spread adjustment: 5.97%

---

12 See, for example, Choudhry (2004) for more information.
13 Some attribution methodologies use term structures based on duration instead of maturity. In this case, a duration-equivalent Treasury bond is used.

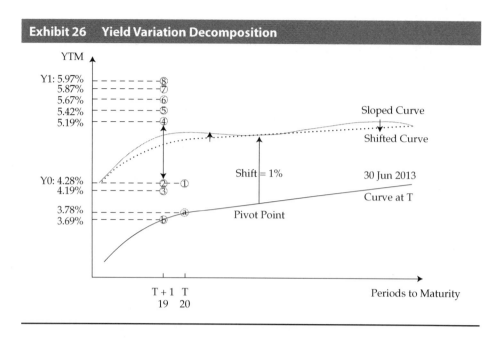

Exhibit 26 Yield Variation Decomposition

Exhibit 27 shows the factors that will be assumed to drive bond returns.

Exhibit 27 Yield Curve Decomposition: Definitions

Factors	Movement	Duration	Convexity
Passage of time			
Initial yield	1 → 2	$Y \times \Delta t$	
Roll down	2 → 3	$-D \times \Delta Y^{Roll}$	$½ \times C \times (\Delta Y^{Roll})^2$
Curve variation			
Shift	3 → 4	$-D \times \Delta Y^{Shift}$	$½ \times C \times (\Delta Y^{Shift})^2$
Slope	4 → 5	$-D \times \Delta Y^{Slope}$	$½ \times C \times (\Delta Y^{Slope})^2$
Curvature	5 → 6	$-D \times \Delta Y^{Shape}$	$½ \times C \times (\Delta Y^{Shape})^2$
Spread variations			
Sector	6 → 7	$-D \times \Delta Y^{Systematic}$	$½ \times C \times (\Delta Y^{Systematic})^2$
Specific	7 → 8	$-D \times \Delta Y^{Specific}$	$½ \times C \times (\Delta Y^{Specific})^2$

Duration-based models can be applied at any level of aggregation, from security level to bucket level to total assets, and is typically calculated independently for portfolios and benchmarks. Furthermore, because of the repricing of instruments, this group of models is often closely aligned with portfolio manager decision making.

There are many different examples of yield curve decomposition using duration-based models available in the industry,[14] but this particular approach quantifies contributions to performance according to the following attribution factors:

- Passage of time
  - Yield
  - Roll down
- Curve variations

---

[14] See Campisi (2000), Lord (1997), and Colin (2005).

Yield Curve Decomposition—Duration Based

- Shift
- Slope
- Curvature
■ Spread variations
  - Sector
  - Bond specific

5.2 Yield Curve Decomposition—Duration Based: Worked Example

The calculations are first applied to individual bonds and then aggregated upward to sector, maturity, and total portfolio and then to the benchmark. The calculations for the period of 30 June 2013 to 31 December 2013 are demonstrated in following sections using the *Corporate 5% 30 June 2018* bond (highlighted in **bold** in Exhibit 2). This bond has the following characteristics:

■ The bond matures on 30 June 2018, is a plain vanilla bond, and is paying a fixed 5% annual coupon with interest paid semi-annually.

■ For simplicity, we assume both evaluation dates are on coupon anniversaries, so there is no accrued interest to capture.

■ Assume that on 30 June, with 10 remaining coupon payment periods, the bond was trading at 4.28% YTM, priced at 103.1997, and has a modified duration of 4.4009 as of the beginning of the period.

■ At 31 December, with nine remaining coupon payment periods, the bond is trading at 5.97% YTM and priced at 96.2274.

■ The price return of the bond is 96.2274/103.1997 − 1 = −6.76%.

■ The income return of the bond is 2.50/103.1997 = 2.42%.

■ The total return of the bond is (96.2274 + 2.50)/103.1997 − 1 = −4.33%.

5.2.1 Initial Yield

Knowing the current YTM at the beginning of the period and the number of days being evaluated, the performance contribution attributable to the passage of time can be estimated. This effect arises from both an income component and any amortization in the bond price.

The opening YTM of this instrument is 4.2823%, therefore, the yield return over the reporting time period is calculated as follows:

Yield = $Y \times \Delta t$

$$4.2823\% \times \left(\frac{31\ \text{Dec} - 30\ \text{June}}{365}\right) = 2.1587\%$$

This yield return does not contain any roll-down factor because it uses the same yield as of the beginning of the period (i.e., 4.2823%) and only the number of days in the period is taken into account.

5.2.2 Roll Down

Assume a government bond located on yield curve at time T + 1 with nine periods remaining to maturity trades at 3.69%, which is −0.09% lower than at time T with 10 periods (3.78%).

This 0.09% difference is referred to as the *roll-down spread*. *Using the modified duration of the bond as of the beginning of the period, we can estimate* the percentage price variation attributable to the roll-down effect. Assuming a yield variation of −0.09% attributable to roll down,

Roll down^D = −D × ΔY^{Roll} = −4.4009 × −0.09% = 0.3961%

Using the convexity, we can refine the estimated percentage price variation attributable to the roll-down effect:

Roll down^C = ½ × C × $(\Delta Y^{Roll})^2$ = ½ × 22.8351 × $(-0.09\%)^2$ = 0.0009%

Roll down^T = Roll down^D + Roll down^C = 0.3961% + 0.0009%

These are shown graphically in Exhibit 28.

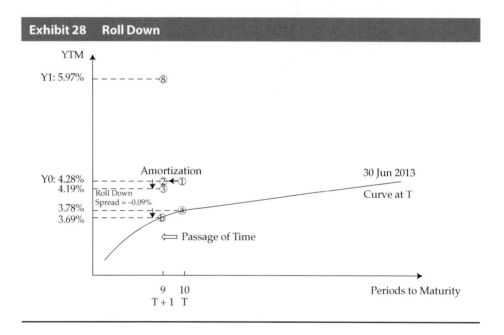

Exhibit 28 Roll Down

5.2.3 Yield Curve Movements

Assume the following curve movements:

Shift: + 1.0000%

Slope: + 0.2300%

Curvature: + 0.2461%

These are shown graphically in Exhibits 29, 30, and 31, respectively.

Yield Curve Decomposition—Duration Based

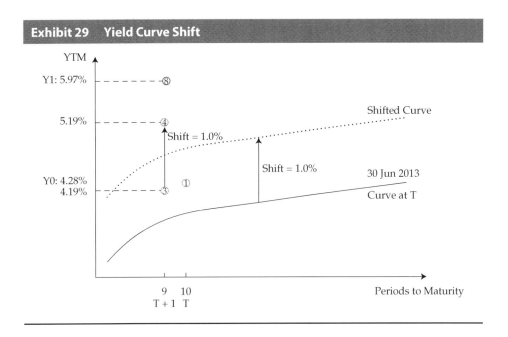

Exhibit 29 Yield Curve Shift

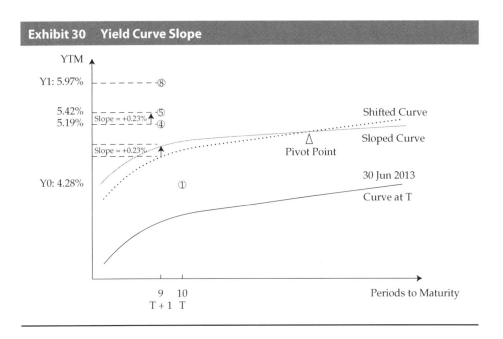

Exhibit 30 Yield Curve Slope

Exhibit 31 Curvature

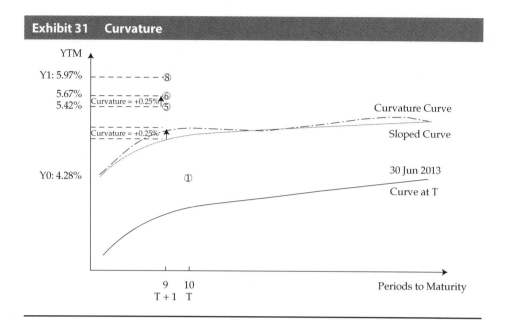

Having quantified the change in the yield curve into the various factors, we can estimate the percentage price variation attributable to various elementary yield curve movements, shown in Exhibit 32.

Exhibit 32 Curve Variation using Duration

		Curve Variation
Shift	$= -D \times \Delta Y^{Shift}$	$= -4.4009 \times 1.00\% = -4.4009\%$
Slope	$= -D \times \Delta Y^{Slope}$	$= -4.4009 \times 0.23\% = -1.0122\%$
Curvature	$= -D \times \Delta Y^{Curve}$	$= -4.4009 \times 0.2461\% = -1.0829\%$

Using the convexity, we can further estimate the bond's percentage price change attributable to yield curve movements, shown in Exhibit 33.

Exhibit 33 Curve Variation using Convexity

		Curve Variation
Shift	$= \frac{1}{2} \times C \times (\Delta Y^{Shift})^2$	$= \frac{1}{2} \times 22.8351 \times (1.00\%)^2 = 0.1142\%$
Slope	$= \frac{1}{2} \times C \times (\Delta Y^{Slope})^2$	$= \frac{1}{2} \times 22.8351 \times (0.23\%)^2 = 0.0060\%$
Curvature	$= \frac{1}{2} \times C \times (\Delta Y^{Curve})^2$	$= \frac{1}{2} \times 22.8351 \times (0.2462\%)^2 = 0.0069\%$

Percentage price variations estimated from duration and convexity calculations can then be added to calculate a total bond price change.

5.2.4 Spread

Spread can be decomposed into systematic and specific spreads.

Exhibit 34 Spread Changes

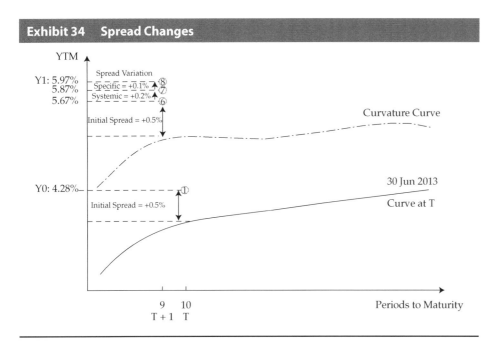

As shown in Exhibit 34, the initial spread of the bond was 0.5% and the ending spread 0.8%. In this example, we assumed a change of 0.2% in the systematic spread and 0.1% in the specific spread. Yield curves that represent the credit market and specific sectors or credit quality ratings are normally used to separate specific from systematic spread.

5.2.4.1 Systematic Spread

Using the duration of the bond, we can estimate the percentage price variation attributable to the spread effect:

$$\text{Spread}^D = -D \times \Delta Y^{Spread} = -4.4009 \times +0.20\% = -0.8802\%$$

Using the convexity, we can further refine the percentage price variation attributable to the spread effect:

$$\text{Spread}^C = \tfrac{1}{2} \times C \times (\Delta Y^{Spread})^2 = \tfrac{1}{2} \times 22.8351 \times (+0.20\%)^2 = 0.0046\%$$

$$\text{Spread}^T = \text{Spread}^D + \text{Spread}^C = -0.8802\% + 0.0046\% = -0.8756\%$$

5.2.4.2 Specific Spread

$$\text{Spread}^D = -D \times \Delta Y^{Spread} = -4.4009 \times 0.10\% = -0.4401\%$$

$$\text{Spread}^C = \tfrac{1}{2} \times C \times (\Delta Y^{Spread})^2 = \tfrac{1}{2} \times 22.8351 \times (0.10\%)^2 = 0.0011\%$$

$$\text{Spread}^T = \text{Spread}^D + \text{Spread}^C = -0.4401\% + 0.0011\% = -0.4389\%$$

5.2.5 Bringing It All Together

5.2.5.1 Single Bond

Exhibit 35 summarizes the attribution factors for this individual bond based on the calculations just presented.

Exhibit 35 Yield Curve Decomposition—Duration Based: Single Bond

		4.4009	22.8351	
Factors	Yield	Duration	Convexity	Contribution
Passage of time	4.19%			2.56%
Initial yield	4.28%			2.16%

(continued)

Exhibit 35 (Continued)

Factors	Yield	4.4009 Duration	22.8351 Convexity	Contribution
Roll down	−0.09%	0.3961%	0.0009%	0.40%
Curve variation	*1.48%*			*−6.37%*
Shift	1.00%	−4.4009%	0.1142%	−4.29%
Slope	0.23%	−1.0122%	0.0060%	−1.01%
Curvature	0.25%	−1.0829%	0.0069%	−1.08%
Spread variations	*0.30%*			*−1.31%*
Systematic	0.20%	−0.8802%	0.0046%	−0.88%
Specific	0.10%	−0.4401%	0.0011%	−0.44%
Ending yield	5.97%			−5.13%
Actual total return				−4.33%
Residual				0.79%

In Exhibit 36, the yield increase from 4.28% at the beginning of the measurement period to 5.97% at the end of the period is decomposed into successive yield variations grouped into passage of time, curve variations, and spread variations.

Exhibit 36   Yield Variations

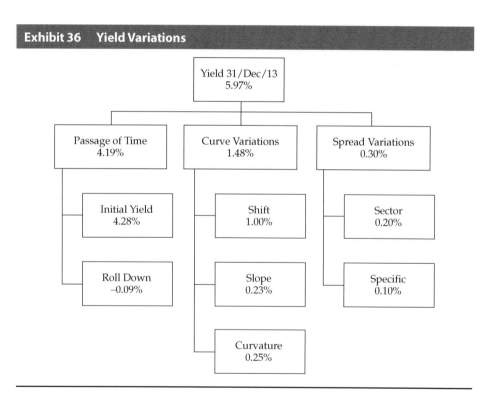

Using modified duration, convexity, and the yield variations, the estimated return attributable to each factor are aggregated, as shown in Exhibit 37.

Yield Curve Decomposition—Duration Based

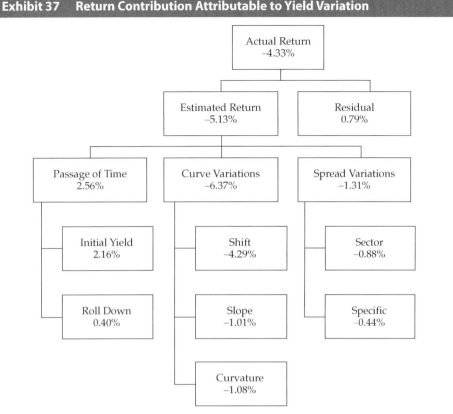

Exhibit 37 Return Contribution Attributable to Yield Variation

The total return is estimated to be –5.13%. The difference of 0.79% between the estimated return and the actual return of –4.33% is known as the *residual*. The residual is probably one of the greatest drawbacks of the duration-based yield curve decomposition approach: duration only estimates yield changes, and depending on the instrument type and market conditions, these unexplained residuals may become significant.[15]

5.2.5.2 Portfolio and Benchmark   Generally, the calculation of the factors is carried out at the constituent level of the portfolio and the benchmark independently, with active management computed as the difference between the two.

Constituent factors can also be summed at aggregated levels, such as total portfolio, total benchmark, years-to-maturity buckets, sectors, credit rating, and so on, although it is technically possible to do the calculation directly at the aggregate levels as long as duration and yield measures are available.

Recall from Exhibit 3 that the portfolio and benchmark returned –5.03% and –4.83%, respectively, for an under-performance of –0.19%. Applying the principles explained earlier to each bond in the investment universe, and assuming the yield variations in Exhibit 38, then

Yield = YTM × Δt

---

[15] The purpose of this reading is to demonstrate, using a common dataset, that some attribution models show residuals and to explain their source. The residual in this example is atypically high as a result of the large data boundaries used in this example. Residual size in this example should not be interpreted here as an indication of the value of this approach in general.

Exhibit 38 Yield Variations

Bond	Durat	Conv	YTM	Price	Begin YTM	Roll	Shift	Slope	Curvature	Spread	Specific
Government 5% 30 June 2018	4.42	22.99	3.78%	105.50	5.17%	−0.09%	1.00%	0.23%	0.25%	0.00%	0.00%
Government 7% 30 June 2023	7.47	69.31	4.35%	121.31	5.43%	−0.04%	1.00%	0.06%	0.06%	0.00%	0.00%
Government 6% 30 June 2028	10.21	134.44	4.66%	114.31	5.37%	−0.02%	1.00%	−0.10%	−0.17%	0.00%	0.00%
Corporate 5% 30 June 2018	**4.40**	**22.84**	**4.28%**	**103.20**	**5.97%**	**−0.09%**	**1.00%**	**0.23%**	**0.25%**	**0.20%**	**0.10%**
Corporate 7% 30 June 2023	7.40	68.36	4.85%	116.91	6.12%	−0.04%	1.00%	0.06%	0.06%	0.20%	0.00%
Corporate (B) 6% 30 June 2028	10.06	131.57	5.16%	108.74	6.07%	−0.02%	1.00%	−0.10%	−0.17%	0.20%	0.00%
Corporate (P) 6% 30 June 2028	10.06	131.57	5.16%	108.74	6.02%	−0.02%	1.00%	−0.10%	−0.17%	0.20%	−0.05%

We can then combine duration and convexity as follows:

Factor return = $-D \times \Delta Y^{Factor} + \frac{1}{2} \times C \times (\Delta Y^{Factor})^2$

Combining the information just presented, we can calculate the return factors for each of the bonds in the portfolio and the benchmark, as shown in Exhibit 39:

Exhibit 39 Return Factors

Bond	Yield	Roll	Shift	Slope	Shape	Spread	Specific	Residual	Total
Government 5% 30 June 2018	1.91%	0.40%	−4.30%	−1.01%	−1.08%	0.00%	0.00%	0.61%	−3.48%
Government 7% 30 June 2023	2.19%	0.30%	−7.12%	−0.45%	−0.44%	0.00%	0.00%	0.35%	−5.16%
Government 6% 30 June 2028	2.35%	0.20%	−9.54%	1.03%	1.80%	0.00%	0.00%	−0.23%	−4.38%
Corporate 5% 30 June 2018	**2.16%**	**0.40%**	**−4.29%**	**−1.01%**	**−1.08%**	**−0.88%**	**−0.44%**	**0.79%**	**−4.33%**
Corporate 7% 30 June 2023	2.44%	0.30%	−7.06%	−0.44%	−0.44%	−1.47%	0.00%	0.52%	−6.14%

Yield Curve Decomposition—Duration Based

Exhibit 39 (Continued)

Bond	Yield	Roll	Shift	Slope	Shape	Spread	Specific	Residual	Total
					Return Factors				
Corporate (B) 6% 30 June 2028	2.60%	0.20%	−9.40%	1.01%	1.73%	−1.99%	0.00%	−0.02%	−5.86%
Corporate (P) 6% 30 June 2028	2.60%	0.20%	−9.40%	1.01%	1.73%	−1.99%	0.50%	−0.08%	−5.42%

With the portfolio and benchmark being constructed from the weights in Exhibit 3, the portfolio and benchmark contribution factors at the constituent level can be calculated as the weight multiplied by the return factors. For example, with a 10% weight for the Corporate 5% 30 June 2018 in the portfolio, the return factors are computed as follows:

C^{Yield} = Weight × Yield = 0.10 × 2.16% = 0.22%

C^{Roll} = Weight × Roll = 0.10 × 0.40% = 0.04%

C^{Shift} = Weight × Shift = 0.10 × −4.29% = −0.43%

C^{Slope} = Weight × Slope = 0.10 × −1.01% = −0.10%

$C^{Curvature}$ = Weight × Curvature = 0.10 × −1.08% = −0.11%

$C^{Systematic}$ = Weight × Systematic = 0.10 × −0.88% = −0.09%

$C^{Specific}$ = Weight × Specific = 0.10 × −0.44% = −0.04%

$C^{Residual}$ = Weight × Residual = 0.10 × 0.79% = 0.08%

for a total of

$C^{Yield} + C^{Roll} + C^{Shift} + C^{Slope} + C^{Curvature} + C^{Systematic} + C^{Specific} + C^{Residual}$

0.22% + 0.04% − 0.43% − 0.10% − 0.11% − 0.09% − 0.04% + 0.08% = −0.43%

Portfolio and benchmark contributions to total return are shown in Exhibit 40 and Exhibit 41, respectively, with active management computed as the difference between the two shown in Exhibit 42.

Exhibit 40 Portfolio Return Factor Contributions

Bond	Wgt	Yield	Roll	Shift	Slope	Curvature	Spread	Specific	Residual	Total
				Portfolio Return Factors Contribution						
Government 5% 30 June 18	0.10	0.19%	0.04%	−0.43%	−0.10%	−0.11%	0.00%	0.00%	0.06%	−0.35%
Government 7% 30 June 23	0.10	0.22%	0.03%	−0.71%	−0.04%	−0.04%	0.00%	0.00%	0.04%	−0.52%
Government 6% 30 June 28	0.20	0.47%	0.04%	−1.91%	0.21%	0.36%	0.00%	0.00%	−0.05%	−0.88%
Corporate 5% 30 June 18	**0.10**	**0.22%**	**0.04%**	**−0.43%**	**−0.10%**	**−0.11%**	**−0.09%**	**−0.04%**	**0.08%**	**−0.43%**
Corporate 7% 30 June 23	0.20	0.49%	0.06%	−1.41%	−0.09%	−0.09%	−0.29%	0.00%	0.10%	−1.23%
Corporate (B) 6% 30 June 28	0.00	0.00%	0.00%	0.00%	0.00%	0.00%	0.00%	0.00%	0.00%	0.00%

(continued)

Exhibit 40 (Continued)

Bond	Wgt	Portfolio Return Factors Contribution								
		Yield	Roll	Shift	Slope	Curvature	Spread	Specific	Residual	Total
Corporate (P) 6% 30 June 28	0.30	0.78%	0.06%	−2.82%	0.30%	0.52%	−0.60%	0.15%	−0.02%	−1.63%
Total	1.00	2.36%	0.27%	−7.71%	0.17%	0.53%	−0.98%	0.11%	0.21%	−5.03%

Exhibit 41 Benchmark Return Factor Contributions

Bond	Wgt	Benchmark Return Factors Contribution								
		Yield	Roll	Shift	Slope	Curvature	Spread	Specific	Residual	Total
Government 5% 30 June 18	0.20	0.38%	0.08%	−0.86%	−0.20%	−0.22%	0.00%	0.00%	0.12%	−0.70%
Government 7% 30 June 23	0.20	0.44%	0.06%	−1.42%	−0.09%	−0.09%	0.00%	0.00%	0.07%	−1.03%
Government 6% 30 June 28	0.15	0.35%	0.03%	−1.43%	0.15%	0.27%	0.00%	0.00%	−0.03%	−0.66%
Corporate 5% 30 June 18	**0.15**	**0.32%**	**0.06%**	**−0.64%**	**−0.15%**	**−0.16%**	**−0.13%**	**−0.07%**	**0.12%**	**−0.65%**
Corporate 7% 30 June 23	0.15	0.37%	0.04%	−1.06%	−0.07%	−0.07%	−0.22%	0.00%	0.08%	−0.92%
Corporate (B) 6% 30 June 28	0.15	0.39%	0.03%	−1.41%	0.15%	0.26%	−0.30%	0.00%	0.00%	−0.88%
Corporate (P) 6% 30 June 28	0.00	0.00%	0.00%	0.00%	0.00%	0.00%	0.00%	0.00%	0.00%	0.00%
Total	1.00	2.25%	0.30%	−6.83%	−0.20%	0.00%	−0.65%	−0.07%	0.35%	−4.83%

Exhibit 42 Active Return Factor Contribution

Bond	Added Value								
	Yield	Roll	Shift	Slope	Curvature	Spread	Specific	Residual	Total
Government 5% 30 June 18	−0.19%	−0.04%	0.43%	0.10%	0.11%	0.00%	0.00%	−0.06%	0.35%
Government 7% 30 June 23	−0.22%	−0.03%	0.71%	0.04%	0.04%	0.00%	0.00%	−0.04%	0.52%
Government 6% 30 June 28	0.12%	0.01%	−0.48%	0.05%	0.09%	0.00%	0.00%	−0.01%	−0.22%
Corporate 5% 30 June 18	**−0.11%**	**−0.02%**	**0.21%**	**0.05%**	**0.05%**	**0.04%**	**0.02%**	**−0.04%**	**0.22%**
Corporate 7% 30 June 23	0.12%	0.01%	−0.35%	−0.02%	−0.02%	−0.07%	0.00%	0.03%	−0.31%
Corporate (B) 6% 30 June 28	−0.39%	−0.03%	1.41%	−0.15%	−0.26%	0.30%	0.00%	0.00%	0.88%

Exhibit 42 (Continued)

Bond	Added Value								
	Yield	Roll	Shift	Slope	Curvature	Spread	Specific	Residual	Total
Corporate (P) 6% 30 June 28	0.78%	0.06%	−2.82%	0.30%	0.52%	−0.60%	0.15%	−0.02%	−1.63%
Total	0.11%	−0.03%	−0.88%	0.38%	0.53%	−0.33%	0.17%	−0.14%	−0.19%
	Time	0.08%	Curve Movement		0.03%				

5.2.6 Interpreting the Results

For this period, the following comments could be made about the attribution effects:

- Yield: The portfolio over-weighted corporate bonds and longer-term maturities relative to the benchmark, which generally offer higher yield than governments bonds and short-term maturities, generating a positive effect of +0.11%.
- Roll: The portfolio over-weighted longer maturities. Notice in Exhibit 28 that bonds with longer maturities sit on a flatter roll decline than short maturities, in this case subtracting 0.03%.
- Shift: The portfolio overall duration of 8.17 is greater than the benchmark duration of 7.19, which, given the increase in yield of +1%, reduced portfolio return by 0.88%.
- Slope: The slope flattening caused the long-term yields to increase less than yields on shorter terms to maturity. The manager over-weighted the long end of the curve. This decision added +0.38% to the excess return.
- Curvature: The reshape of the yield curve reflects a higher yield increase at the five-year maturity point. The manager under-weighted that part of the yield curve. This decision added +0.53% to the active return.
- Spread: The manager over-weighted the corporate sector, costing −0.33% in active return because corporate spreads widened.
- Specific Spread: Looking at the specific spreads in Exhibit 38, the manager selected the Corporate 5% 30 June 2018 bond for which the specific yield decreased by −0.05% (as well as the Corporate (P) 6% 30 June 2028 versus the Corporate (B) 6% 30 June 2028 in the benchmark). This decision added value for a total of 0.17% to active return.
- Residual: A residual of −0.14% is unaccounted for because duration and convexity can estimate only the percentage price variation. It is not an accurate measure of the true price variation. The residual is more important during large yield variation, which is the case here with a +1% yield shift.

5.3 Appropriate Uses

The change in focus toward security repricing, and its focus on duration and yield curves, make this group of attribution models most used by portfolio managers. But the fact that it does not rely on the full repricing models and instead relies on duration and its ability to group securities into categories or buckets, means that reasonably concise and intuitive reports can still be assembled for other stakeholders, such as client reporting or marketing departments.

5.4 Operational Considerations and Limitations

Along with the additional level of information details, this group of approaches is a step up in terms of operational complexity.

5.4.1 Data Requirements—Portfolio and Benchmark

Not only are portfolio and benchmark security weights and returns required, but durations and YTMs are also needed.

As with exposure decomposition approaches, this data could be sourced at the constituent level, with the advantage of being able to group securities dynamically. Or, alternatively, it could be supplied by corporate systems and index providers, simplifying data collection and calculation, but possibly limiting flexibility.

5.4.2 Data Requirements—Curve Data

Yield curves and yield changes also need to be considered. Requirements are not only for a default free term structure, typically built from government issues, but also interim curves from which spread and selection effects are derived.

Most investment managers managing fixed-income portfolios would typically have this data available to them. But it might involve an effort to turn the data points into a meaningful curve (e.g., bootstrapping market rates into a spot curve) and getting these data into the relevant performance attribution systems.

Some system vendors provide this information within their package, which may simplify things, but this shortcut can cause unintended attribution effects if the curve data provided differ from the source actually used to price the instruments themselves. Unusual residual effects may arise because of using different yield curves for attribution compared with those used by external pricing providers, and these effects are most likely to be evident in thinly traded markets where pricing discrepancies between vendors may be larger.

5.4.3 Holdings Based vs. Transactional Based

Unlike exposure decomposition approaches, yield curve decomposition, whether duration or repricing based, are typically based on a set of exposures held over a period—known as a buy-and-hold or holdings-based approach. This characteristic has two implications.

First, the holding period needs to be sufficiently small to make the numbers meaningful. In anything other than portfolios with marginal turnover, this period will be at least monthly and possibly daily. Maintaining accurate daily data in performance attribution systems can itself be costly and an operational challenge.

Second, even daily based buy-and-hold returns and attributions cannot pick up the effects of intraday trading and securities purchased or sold at anything other than an end-of-day price. The impact of this issue can be treated as some form of residual effect, but it can be difficult to incorporate it at a security level. The magnitude of this trading effect and its significance to the portfolio will depend on market volatility, the size of trades being entered into, and, of course, the importance of this effect as a form of active management for the portfolio.

5.4.4 Duration as an Approximation

Use of modified duration and yield changes to approximate price returns works best for plain vanilla bonds and small changes in yield. But as a linear approximation, it can break down where instruments have, for example, embedded options and/or large movements in market yields.

Use of effective duration instead of modified duration to account for this break down, as well as including convexity as a second order effect, mitigates this issue somewhat but is still an approximation. It also adds to the calculations required. Empirically testing this approach and the magnitude of the residuals prior to building solutions would typically be prudent.

YIELD CURVE DECOMPOSITION—FULL REPRICING

Full repricing attribution methodologies rely on the ability to recalculate bonds prices based on bond pricing expressions. This approach is more precise than duration-based methodologies because instead of prices being estimated by using duration and convexity, full pricing models are used to (re)price the bond from their constituent cash flows. But it is important to recognize that bond pricing can be quite complex and requires pricing models, as well as knowledge of such characteristics, for example, as the instrument's coupon rate, payment frequency, time remaining to maturity, first or last short or long coupon periods.

The price of a bond equals the present value of its future cash flows. The discount rate to compute the present value depends on the yields offered on the market for comparable securities and represents the required yield an investor expects to receive for holding that investment. In practice, each cash flow is discounted at a rate from the spot curve corresponding to the time the cash flow will be received.[16]

$$P_0 = \frac{CF_1}{(1+r_1)^1} + \frac{CF_2}{(1+r_2)^2} + \cdots \frac{CF_N}{(1+r_n)^N}$$

where r_n represents various zero-coupon rates at maturities corresponding to the coupon payments.

The spot curve represents how yield on bonds vary by maturity. Assuming the spot rates in Exhibit 43,[17] the price of the bond is the sum of the present value of the future cash flows discounted at those rates.

It is important to note that these rates, along with the characteristics of the instrument, drive the price of the bond. Therefore, modelling these spot rates, and the changes in them, is crucial to attributing the return of that instrument. As with the duration-based yield curve decomposition approach, any instrument can be successively repriced for modelled changes in spot rates, and the percentage change between these prices can be used to attribute its return. Aggregating these constituents into portfolios and benchmarks is then straightforward.

6.1 Yield Curve Decomposition—Full Repricing: Worked Example

Continuing with the corporate bond example used in Section 5, the price at the beginning of the measurement period (T) is computed using the spot rates at that time, as shown in Exhibit 43.

---

16 The **spot curve** is the yield curve that shows the discount rates for various bond maturities that apply to bonds with a single cash flow.
17 These spot rates are adjusted by the corporate systematic spread and bond-specific spread.

Exhibit 43 Bond Price using Initial Spot Rates

(Corporate spot rate at T: 30 June 2013)

Period	Flow	Spot Rate	Present Value	
1	2.50	2.170%	2.47	$2.5 \times \left(1 + \frac{2.17\%}{2}\right)^{-1}$
2	2.50	2.820%	2.43	$2.5 \times \left(1 + \frac{2.82\%}{2}\right)^{-2}$
3	2.50	3.200%	2.38	$2.5 \times \left(1 + \frac{3.20\%}{2}\right)^{-3}$
4	2.50	3.470%	2.33	$2.5 \times \left(1 + \frac{3.47\%}{2}\right)^{-4}$
5	2.50	3.680%	2.28	$2.5 \times \left(1 + \frac{3.68\%}{2}\right)^{-5}$
6	2.50	3.850%	2.23	$2.5 \times \left(1 + \frac{3.85\%}{2}\right)^{-6}$
7	2.50	4.000%	2.18	$2.5 \times \left(1 + \frac{4.00\%}{2}\right)^{-7}$
8	2.50	4.130%	2.12	$2.5 \times \left(1 + \frac{4.13\%}{2}\right)^{-8}$
9	2.50	4.240%	2.07	$2.5 \times \left(1 + \frac{4.24\%}{2}\right)^{-9}$
10	102.50	4.340%	82.70	$102.5 \times \left(1 + \frac{4.34\%}{2}\right)^{-10}$
Begin price (T)			103.1997	

The corporate curve plus the corporate systematic and bond-specific spreads at the end of the period (T + 1) are used to compute the ending price, as shown in Exhibit 44.

Exhibit 44 Bond Price using Ending Spot Rates

(Corporate spot rate at T + 1: 31 December 2013)

Period	Flow	Spot Rate*	Present Value	
1	2.50	3.85%	2.45	$2.5 \times \left(1 + \frac{3.85\%}{2}\right)^{-1}$
2	2.50	4.51%	2.39	$2.5 \times \left(1 + \frac{4.51\%}{2}\right)^{-2}$

Yield Curve Decomposition—Full Repricing

Exhibit 44   (Continued)

(Corporate spot rate at T + 1: 31 December 2013)

Period	Flow	Spot Rate*	Present Value	
3	2.50	4.91%	2.32	$2.5 \times \left(1 + \dfrac{4.91\%}{2}\right)^{-3}$
4	2.50	5.19%	2.26	$2.5 \times \left(1 + \dfrac{5.19\%}{2}\right)^{-4}$
5	2.50	5.41%	2.19	$2.5 \times \left(1 + \dfrac{5.41\%}{2}\right)^{-5}$
6	2.50	5.60%	2.12	$2.5 \times \left(1 + \dfrac{5.60\%}{2}\right)^{-6}$
7	2.50	5.76%	2.05	$2.5 \times \left(1 + \dfrac{5.76\%}{2}\right)^{-7}$
8	2.50	5.90%	1.98	$2.5 \times \left(1 + \dfrac{5.90\%}{2}\right)^{-8}$
9	102.50	6.03%	78.47	$102.5 \times \left(1 + \dfrac{6.03\%}{2}\right)^{-9}$
End price (T + 1)			96.2274	

* Spot rate adjusted for systematic and specific spreads of bond: 0.10%.

Full repricing yield curve decomposition attribution methodologies decompose total return into return factors similar to duration-based methodologies. Some authors or software vendors may define different factors, but for the purpose of this reading, we will calculate the following:

- Passage of time
  - Coupon
  - Amortization
  - Roll down
- Yield curve movements
  - Shift
  - Slope
  - Curvature
- Spread variation
  - Systematic (credit market in general, sector)
  - Specific (idiosyncratic)

6.1.1 Coupon

The coupon (sometimes referred to as income return) is computed as the ratio of the coupon received plus changes in accrued interest over the price at the beginning. For the sample bond,

$$\frac{2.5}{103.1997} = 2.42\%$$

6.1.2 Amortization

The amortization factor represents the price variation attributable to the passage of time, keeping the spot rates constant. This factor is like shifting the curve in time (or moving the curve horizontally to the left) without applying the roll down, as shown in Exhibit 45.

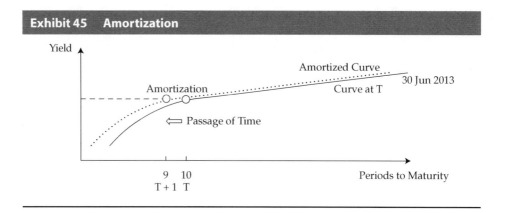

Exhibit 45 Amortization

The bond is valued by using the same set of spot rates as of the beginning of the period (T) but with less time to maturity. This intermediary curve is called the "amortized curve," and the price derived from it is the "amortized price," as shown in Exhibit 46.

Exhibit 46 Amortized Price

Period	Flow	Spot Rate	Present Value
1	2.50	2.820%	2.47
2	2.50	3.200%	2.42
3	2.50	3.470%	2.37
4	2.50	3.680%	2.32
5	2.50	3.850%	2.27
6	2.50	4.000%	2.22
7	2.50	4.130%	2.17
8	2.50	4.240%	2.11
9	102.50	4.340%	84.49
Amortized price			102.8502

Notes: Evaluation date is 31 December 2013 using corporate spot rate at T of 30 June 2013. Curve is shifted horizontally.

Yield Curve Decomposition—Full Repricing

This **amortized price** is used to compute the return factor attributable to amortization:

$$\frac{\text{Price}_{Amort} - \text{Price}_T}{\text{Price}_T} = \frac{102.8502 - 103.1997}{103.1997} = -0.34\%$$

Exhibit 47 summarizes the changes made.

Exhibit 47 Price Return Attributable to Amortization

Price	Curve Used		Curve as of	Change Applied to Curve	Evaluation Date	Periods Remaining	Price	Return
Begin (T)	Corp	T	30 June 2013	None	30 June 2013	10	103.1997	
Amortized	Corp	T	30 June 2013	Shifted horizontal	31 Dec 2013	9	102.8502	−0.34%

6.1.3 Roll Down

The roll-down factor represents the percentage price variation that results from spots rates declining as bonds get closer to maturity.[18] The bond is valued by using the same set of spot rates as of the beginning of the period (T) but with less time to maturity and consideration of the lower discount rates. This intermediary curve is called the "rolled-down curve," and the price derived from it is the "rolled-down price," as shown in Exhibit 48.

Exhibit 48 Roll-Down Price

Period	Flow	Spot Rate	Present Value
1	2.50	2.170%	2.47
2	2.50	2.820%	2.43
3	2.50	3.200%	2.38
4	2.50	3.470%	2.33
5	2.50	3.680%	2.28
6	2.50	3.850%	2.23
7	2.50	4.000%	2.18
8	2.50	4.130%	2.12
9	102.50	4.240%	84.86
Rolled-down price			103.2974

Notes: Evaluation date is 31 December 2013 using corporate spot rate at T of 30 June 2013.

As with amortization, the return factor attributable to roll down is computed as the difference between the roll-down price and the previous intermediary price (amortized price), as a percentage of the initial price:

$$\frac{\text{Price}_{Roll} - \text{Price}_{Amort}}{\text{Price}_T} = \frac{103.2974 - 102.8502}{103.1997} = +0.43\%$$

Exhibit 49 summarizes the changes made.

---

[18] This occurs when the yield curve is upward sloping. Rates get higher when the curve is inverted.

Exhibit 49 Price Return Attributable to Roll Down

Price	Curve Used		Curve as of	Change Applied to Curve	Evaluation Date	Periods Remaining	Price	Return
Amortized	Corporate	T	30 June 2013	Shifted horizontal	31 Dec 2013	9	102.8502	
Rolled down	Corporate	T	30 June 2013	None	31 Dec 2013	9	103.2974	0.43%

6.1.4 Shift

The shift effect measures the impact of the general change in risk-free rates, typically determined from changes in government curves. As with the duration-based yield curve decomposition example, the parallel increase in the curve of 1.0%[19] has been applied to the corporate spot curve and is shown in Exhibit 50.

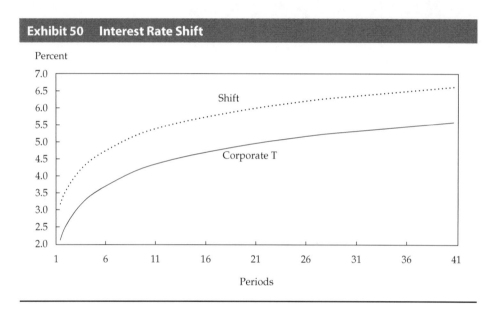

Exhibit 50 Interest Rate Shift

The bond is valued by using the rolled-down curve rates, but this time applying the 1.0% shift in the risk-free government rates. This intermediary curve is called the "shifted curve," and the price derived from it is called the "shifted price," shown in Exhibit 51.

Exhibit 51 Shift Price

Period	Flow	Spot Rate	Present Value
1	2.50	3.170%	2.46
2	2.50	3.820%	2.41
3	2.50	4.200%	2.35
4	2.50	4.470%	2.29

---

[19] Various techniques can be used to determine the amount of shift and slope and curvature. Some use elaborate polynomial regression or principal components methods to best fit the curve, others may use a simpler approach, such as taking an arbitrary point on the curve. In this example, we assumed the shift of 100 bps occurs at the 10-year maturity point (20 periods remaining).

Yield Curve Decomposition—Full Repricing

Exhibit 51 (Continued)

Period	Flow	Spot Rate	Present Value
5	2.50	4.680%	2.23
6	2.50	4.850%	2.17
7	2.50	5.000%	2.10
8	2.50	5.130%	2.04
9	102.50	5.240%	81.21
Shifted price			99.2573

Note: Evaluation date is 31 December 2013 using corporate spot rate at T of 30 June 2013. Curve is shifted vertically.

As with the roll-down price return, the change in price from shift is calculated by comparing the recalculated shift price to the previous intermediary price (roll down), as a percentage of the initial price:

$$\frac{\text{Price}_{Shift} - \text{Price}_{Roll}}{\text{Price}_T} = \frac{99.2573 - 103.2974}{103.1997} = -3.91\%$$

Exhibit 52 summarizes the changes made.

Exhibit 52 Price Return Attributable to Shift in Default-Free Curve

Price	Curve Used		Curve as of	Change Applied to Curve	Evaluation Date	Periods Remaining	Price	Return
Rolled down	Corp	T	30 June 2013	None	31 Dec 2013	9	103.2974	
Shifted	Corp	T	30 June 2013	Shifted vertical	31 Dec 2013	9	99.2573	−3.91%

6.1.5 *Slope*

The slope effect measures the impact of the change in steepness of the risk-free government yield curve. Continuing the example, Exhibit 53 shows a change in slope in the curve.[20]

---

[20] This example assume the curve is "tilted" at the 10 year point (20 remaining periods to maturity) to best fit the actual curve of the end of the period. Describing the various techniques to generate yield curves is outside the scope of this reading.

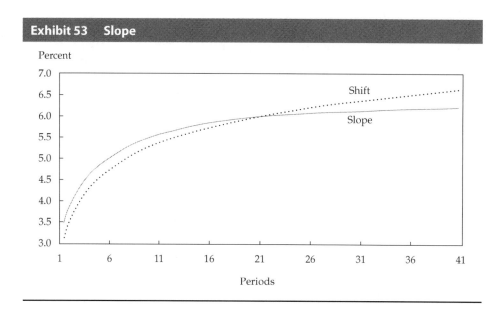

Exhibit 53 Slope

Applying these revised spot rates to discount the future cash flows, a slope price can be calculated, as shown in Exhibit 54.

Exhibit 54 Slope Price

Period	Flow	Spot Rate	Present Value
1	2.50	3.550%	2.46
2	2.50	4.180%	2.40
3	2.50	4.540%	2.34
4	2.50	4.790%	2.27
5	2.50	4.980%	2.21
6	2.50	5.130%	2.15
7	2.50	5.260%	2.08
8	2.50	5.370%	2.02
9	102.50	5.460%	80.44
Sloped price			98.3674

Notes: Evaluation date is 31 December 2013 using corporate spot rate at T of 30 June 2013. Curve is adjusted for slope variation.

The return factor attributable to the change in the slope is then computed as follows:

$$\frac{Price_{Slope} - Price_{Shift}}{Price_T} = \frac{98.3674 - 99.2573}{103.1997} = -0.86\%$$

Exhibit 55 summarizes the changes made.

Yield Curve Decomposition—Full Repricing

Exhibit 55 Price Return Attributable to a Change in Slope in the Default-Free Curve

Price	Curve Used		Curve as of	Change Applied to Curve	Evaluation Date	Periods Remaining	Price	Return
Shifted	Corporate	T	30 June 2013	Shifted vertical	31 Dec 2013	9	99.2573	
Sloped	Corporate	T	30 June 2013	Sloped	31 Dec 2013	9	98.3674	−0.86%

6.1.6 Curvature

The curvature effect measures the impact of the changes in the shape of the default-free curve apart from a change in slope.[21] In this example, we are evaluating a bond with 4.5 years remaining to maturity, and the maturity is on the curve at a point when the rates increased more than short- and long-term maturities. This intermediary curve is called the "curvature curve," shown in Exhibit 56, and the price derived from it is called the "curvature price," shown in Exhibit 57.

Exhibit 56 Curvature

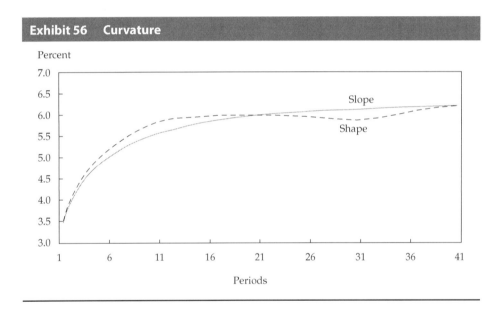

Exhibit 57 Curvature Price

Period	Flow	Spot Rate	Present Value
1	2.50	3.550%	2.46
2	2.50	4.213%	2.40
3	2.50	4.607%	2.33
4	2.50	4.890%	2.27
5	2.50	5.113%	2.20
6	2.50	5.297%	2.14
7	2.50	5.460%	2.07
8	2.50	5.603%	2.00

(continued)

---

21 To be more specific, the short-term and long-term segments rise while the middle-term segment falls, or vice versa.

Exhibit 57 (Continued)

Period	Flow	Spot Rate	Present Value
9	102.50	5.727%	79.50
Curvature price			97.3763

Notes: Evaluation date is 31 December 2013 using corporate spot rate at T of 30 June 2013. Curve is adjusted for curvature variation.

The return factor attributable to the change in the curvature of the curve is then computed as follows:

$$\frac{Price_{Curvature} - Price_{Slope}}{Price_T} = \frac{97.3763 - 98.3674}{103.1997} = -0.96\%$$

Exhibit 58 summarizes the changes made.

Exhibit 58 Price Return Attributable to a Change in Shape of the Default-Free Curve

Price	Curve Used	Curve as of	Change Applied to Curve	Evaluation Date	Periods Remaining	Price	Return
Sloped	Corporate T	30 June 2013	Sloped	31 Dec 2013	9	98.3674	
Curvature	Corporate T	30 June 2013	Curvature as of T + 1	31 Dec 2013	9	97.3763	−0.96%

6.1.7 Sector Spread

Using the same example, we assume the spread increased evenly by 0.20% along the curve. Exhibits 59 and 60 depict the spread between the corporate and Treasury curves at the beginning and end of the period, respectively.

Exhibit 59 Initial Systematic Spreads

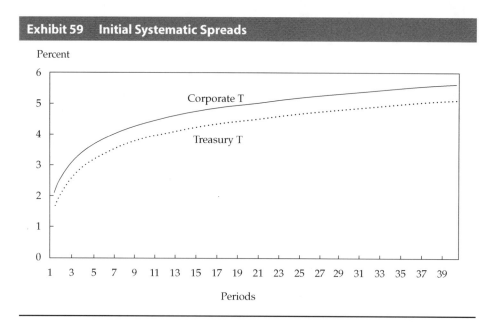

Exhibit 60 Ending Systematic Spreads

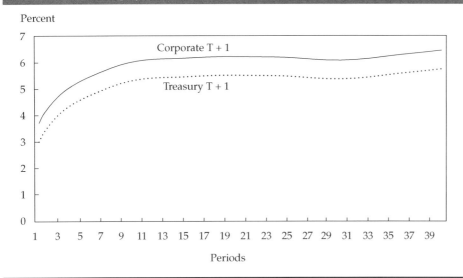

The Spread effect measures the impact on the price of the bond attributable to the change in the spread. The bond is valued by using the actual corporate curve as of the end of the period (T + 1) without any bond specific spreads (only the systematic spread is applied). Exhibit 61 shows the spread price.

Exhibit 61 Systematic Spread Price

(Corporate spot rate at T + 1: 31 December 2013)

Period	Flow	Spot Rate	Present Value
1	2.50	3.750%	2.45
2	2.50	4.413%	2.39
3	2.50	4.807%	2.33
4	2.50	5.090%	2.26
5	2.50	5.313%	2.19
6	2.50	5.497%	2.12
7	2.50	5.660%	2.06
8	2.50	5.803%	1.99
9	102.50	5.927%	78.81
Systematic spread price			96.6086

Notes: Evaluation date is 31 December 2013 using corporate spot rate at T of 30 June 2013. Curve is adjusted for systematic spread variation.

The return factor attributable to the spread variation of the curve is computed as follows:

$$\frac{\text{Price}_{Systematic} - \text{Price}_{Curvature}}{\text{Price}_T} = \frac{96.6086 - 97.3763}{103.1997} = -0.74\%$$

Exhibit 62 summarizes the changes made.

Exhibit 62 Price Return Attributable to a Change in the Systematic Spread

Price	Curve Used	Curve as of		Change Applied to Curve	Evaluation Date	Periods Remaining	Price	Return
Shaped	Corporate	T	30 June 2013	Curvature as of T + 1	31 Dec 2013	9	97.3763	
Systematic Spread	Corporate	T + 1	31 Dec. 2013	None	31 Dec 2013	9	96.6086	−0.74%

6.1.8 Specific Spread

Following the same example, we assume the corporate bond-specific spread increased by 0.10%. The spread-specific effect measures the return impact of such changes. The corporate bond is valued by using the actual corporate curve as of the end of the period (T + 1) with adjustments for bond-specific spreads. Exhibit 63 shows the specific spread price.

Exhibit 63 Specific Spread Price

(Corporate spot rate* at T + 1: 31 December 2013)

Period	Flow	Spot Rate*	Present Value
1	2.50	3.85%	2.45
2	2.50	4.51%	2.39
3	2.50	4.91%	2.32
4	2.50	5.19%	2.26
5	2.50	5.41%	2.19
6	2.50	5.60%	2.12
7	2.50	5.76%	2.05
8	2.50	5.90%	1.98
9	102.50	6.03%	78.47
End price (T + 1)			96.2274

* Spot rate adjusted for specific spread of bond: 0.10%.

The return factor attributable to the specific spread variation of the curve is computed as follows:

$$\frac{Price_{T+1} - Price_{Systematic}}{Price_T} = \frac{96.2274 - 96.6086}{103.1997} = -0.37\%$$

Exhibit 64 summarizes the changes made.

Yield Curve Decomposition—Full Repricing

Exhibit 64 Price Return Attributable to a Change in Systematic Spread

Price	Curve Used		Curve as of	Change Applied to Curve	Evaluation Date	Periods Remaining	Price	Return
Systematic Spread	Corporate	T + 1	31 Dec. 2013	None	31 Dec 2013	9	96.6086	
End (T + 1)	Corporate	T + 1	31 Dec. 2013	+ Specific spread	31 Dec 2013	9	96.2274	−0.37%

Exhibit 65 summarizes how intermediary curves are used successively to derive intermediary prices, which in turn are used to compute the attribution factors.

Exhibit 65 Summary of Price Return Factors

Price	Movement	Curve Used		Curve as of	Change Applied to Curve	Evaluation Date	Periods Remaining	Price	Return
Begin (T)	1	Corp	T	30 June 2013	None	30 June 2013	10	103.1997	
Amortized	1 → 2	Corp	T	30 June 2013	Shifted horizontal	31 Dec 2013	9	102.8502	−0.34%
Rolled down	2 → 3	Corp	T	30 June 2013	None	31 Dec 2013	9	103.2974	0.43%
Shifted	3 → 4	Corp	T	30 June 2013	Shifted vertical	31 Dec 2013	9	99.2573	−3.91%
Sloped	4 → 5	Corp	T	30 June 2013	Sloped	31 Dec 2013	9	98.3674	−0.86%
Curvature	5 → 6	Corp	T	30 June 2013	Curvature as of T + 1	31 Dec 2013	9	97.3763	−0.96%
Systematic spread	6 → 7	Corp	T + 1	31 Dec. 2013	None	31 Dec 2013	9	96.6086	−0.74%
End (T + 1)	7 → 8	Corp	T + 1	31 Dec. 2012	+ Specific spread	31 Dec 2012	9	96.2274	−0.37%
								Price return	−6.76%
								Coupon return	2.42%
								Total return	−4.33%

6.1.9 Bringing It All Together

6.1.9.1 Single Bond
Combining all of these factors, we obtain the actual return of the bond, as outlined in Exhibit 66.

Exhibit 66 Single Bond Return Attribution based on Factors and Full Repricing

Passage of time	2.52%
Coupon	2.42%
Amortization	−0.34%
Roll down	0.43%
Curve variation	−5.74%

(continued)

Exhibit 66	(Continued)
Shift	−3.91%
Slope	−0.86%
Curvature	−0.96%
Spread variations	−1.11%
Sector	−0.74%
Specific	−0.37%
Total	−4.33%
Actual total return	−4.33%
Residual	0.00%

Notice that there is no residual because the actual price of the bond has been recalculated rather than estimated from its duration and convexity.

6.1.9.2 Portfolio and Benchmark The calculation must be carried out at the constituent level of the portfolio and the benchmark with active management computed as the difference between the two. Of course, constituent factors can be summed up at aggregated levels, such as total portfolio or benchmark years-to-maturity buckets, sectors, credit rating, and so on.

Continuing our sample data, attribution effects for all sample bonds can be calculated by using the full repricing methodology to provide the results shown in Exhibit 67.

Exhibit 67 Return Factors

Bond	Cpn	Amort	Roll	Shift	Slope	Curvature	Spread	Specific	Total
Government 5% 30 June 18	2.37%	−0.53%	0.43%	−3.92%	−0.86%	−0.96%			−3.48%
Government 7% 30 June 23	2.89%	−0.85%	0.45%	−6.81%	−0.39%	−0.44%			−5.16%
Government 6% 30 June 28	2.62%	−0.48%	0.42%	−9.25%	0.85%	1.46%			−4.38%
Corporate 5% 30 June 18	**2.42%**	**−0.34%**	**0.43%**	**−3.91%**	**−0.86%**	**−0.96%**	**−0.74%**	**−0.37%**	**−4.33%**
Corporate 7% 30 June 23	2.99%	−0.72%	0.44%	−6.76%	−0.39%	−0.44%	−1.27%	0.00%	−6.14%
Corporate (B) 6% 30 June 28	2.76%	−0.38%	0.42%	−9.13%	0.82%	1.41%	−1.77%	0.00%	−5.86%
Corporate (P) 6% 30 June 28	2.76%	−0.38%	0.42%	−9.13%	0.82%	1.41%	−1.77%	0.44%	−5.42%

Note: Cpn is coupon and amort is amortization.

Assuming the portfolio and the benchmark invest in each bond as described in Section 3, the factor contributions to return are again calculated as

$$C^{Factor} = W \times Factor$$

Exhibit 68, Exhibit 69, and Exhibit 70 again show the breakdown of portfolio, benchmark, and active returns by factor.

Yield Curve Decomposition—Full Repricing

Exhibit 68 Portfolio Contributions to Return

Bond	Wgt	Portfolio Return Factors Contribution								
		Cpn	Amort	Roll	Shift	Slope	Curvature	Spread	Specific	Total
Government 5% 30 June 18	0.10	0.24%	−0.05%	0.04%	−0.39%	−0.09%	−0.10%	0.00%	0.00%	−0.35%
Government 7% 30 June 23	0.10	0.29%	−0.09%	0.04%	−0.68%	−0.04%	−0.04%	0.00%	0.00%	−0.52%
Government 6% 30 June 28	0.20	0.52%	−0.10%	0.08%	−1.85%	0.17%	0.29%	0.00%	0.00%	−0.88%
Corporate 5% 30 June 18	**0.10**	**0.24%**	**−0.03%**	**0.04%**	**−0.39%**	**−0.09%**	**−0.10%**	**−0.07%**	**−0.04%**	**−0.43%**
Corporate 7% 30 June 23	0.20	0.60%	−0.14%	0.09%	−1.35%	−0.08%	−0.09%	−0.25%	0.00%	−1.23%
Corporate (B) 6% 30 June 28	0.00	0.00%	0.00%	0.00%	0.00%	0.00%	0.00%	0.00%	0.00%	0.00%
Corporate (P) 6% 30 June 28	0.30	0.83%	−0.11%	0.13%	−2.74%	0.25%	0.42%	−0.53%	0.13%	−1.63%
Total	1.00	2.72%	−0.53%	0.43%	−7.41%	0.13%	0.39%	−0.85%	0.09%	−5.03%

Note: Wgt is weight, cpn is coupon, and amort is amortization.

Exhibit 69 Benchmark Contributions to Return

Bond	Wgt	Benchmark Return Factors Contribution								
		Cpn	Amort	Roll	Shift	Slope	Curvature	Spread	Specific	Total
Government 5% 30 June 18	0.20	0.47%	−0.11%	0.09%	−0.78%	−0.17%	−0.19%	0.00%	0.00%	−0.70%
Government 7% 30 June 23	0.20	0.58%	−0.17%	0.09%	−1.36%	−0.08%	−0.09%	0.00%	0.00%	−1.03%
Government 6% 30 June 28	0.15	0.39%	−0.07%	0.06%	−1.39%	0.13%	0.22%	0.00%	0.00%	−0.66%
Corporate 5% 30 June 18	**0.15**	**0.36%**	**−0.05%**	**0.07%**	**−0.59%**	**−0.13%**	**−0.14%**	**−0.11%**	**−0.06%**	**−0.65%**
Corporate 7% 30 June 23	0.15	0.45%	−0.11%	0.07%	−1.01%	−0.06%	−0.07%	−0.19%	0.00%	−0.92%
Corporate (B) 6% 30 June 28	0.15	0.41%	−0.06%	0.06%	−1.37%	0.12%	0.21%	−0.27%	0.00%	−0.88%
Corporate (P) 6% 30 June 28	0.00	0.00%	0.00%	0.00%	0.00%	0.00%	0.00%	0.00%	0.00%	0.00%
Total	1.00	2.67%	−0.56%	0.43%	−6.51%	−0.19%	−0.06%	−0.57%	−0.06%	−4.83%

Note: Wgt is weight, cpn is coupon, and amort is amortization.

Exhibit 70 Added Value (Attribution Effects)

Bond	Weight		Added Value								
	Portf	Bench	Cpn	Amort	Roll	Shift	Slope	Shape	Spread	Specific	Total
Treasury 5% 30 June 2018	10%	20%	−0.24%	0.05%	−0.04%	0.39%	0.09%	0.10%	0.00%	0.00%	0.35%
Treasury 7% 30 June 2023	10%	20%	−0.29%	0.09%	−0.04%	0.68%	0.04%	0.04%	0.00%	0.00%	0.52%

(continued)

Exhibit 70 (Continued)

Bond	Weight		Added Value								
	Portf	Bench	Cpn	Amort	Roll	Shift	Slope	Shape	Spread	Specific	Total
Treasury 6% 30 June 2028	20%	15%	0.13%	−0.02%	0.02%	−0.46%	0.04%	0.07%	0.00%	0.00%	−0.22%
Corporate 5% 30 June 2018	**10%**	**15%**	**−0.12%**	**0.02%**	**−0.02%**	**0.20%**	**0.04%**	**0.05%**	**0.04%**	**0.02%**	**0.22%**
Corporate 7% 30 June 2023	20%	15%	0.15%	−0.04%	0.02%	−0.34%	−0.02%	−0.02%	−0.06%	0.00%	−0.31%
Corporate (B) 6% 30 June 2028	0%	15%	−0.41%	0.06%	−0.06%	1.37%	−0.12%	−0.21%	0.27%	0.00%	0.88%
Corporate (P) 6% 30 June 2028	30%	0%	0.83%	−0.11%	0.13%	−2.74%	0.25%	0.42%	−0.53%	0.13%	−1.63%
Total			0.05%	0.04%	−0.002%	−0.90%	0.31%	0.45%	−0.29%	0.15%	−0.19%
			Passage of time		0.09%	Curve Movement		−0.14%			

Note: Portf is portfolio, bench is the benchmark, cpn is coupon, and amort is amortization.

6.1.10 Interpreting the Results

For this period, the following commentary could be added for the attribution effects:

- Coupon: The portfolio is over-weighted in higher coupon bonds, generating a positive coupon effect of +0.05%.
- Amortization: All bonds are priced at a premium (i.e., above 100 par value) at the beginning of the period because their coupon rates are higher than market rates. As time goes by, their prices converge toward par value. This natural drop in price negatively affects the return. The higher the premium, the greater the impact will be. Because the portfolio is under-weighted in bonds with the highest premium, a positive amortization effect of +0.04% is generated.
- Roll: The portfolio over-weighted longer maturities, which by nature sit on a flatter roll decline than short maturities.
- Shift: The overall portfolio duration of 8.17 is greater than the benchmark duration of 7.19, which, given the increase in yield of +1%, relatively disadvantaged the portfolio by −0.90%.
- Slope: The slope flattened, causing the long-term yields to increase less than shorter-term yields. The manager over-weighted bonds at the long end of the curve and under-weighted bonds at the short end. This decision added +0.31%.
- Curvature: The reshape of the yield curve caused greater rate increase around the five year maturity point. The portfolio is under-weighted in that part of the yield curve. This decision added +0.45%.
- Systematic Spread: The portfolio is over-weighted in the corporate sector, costing −0.29% of active return as corporate spreads widened.
- Specific Spread: Exhibit 38 shows that the yield increased by an additional 0.10% for the Corporate 5% 30 June 2018 bond. The portfolio under-weighted that bond, (10% versus 15% in the benchmark). Underweighting a bond for which the specific yield increased was a good decision and added 0.02%.

Yield Curve Decomposition—Full Repricing

Also, for the Corporate (P) 30 June 2028 bond, the yield increased by 0.05%. Overweighting a bond for which the yield increased less is a good decision and added 0.13%.

6.2 Appropriate Uses

The ability to dissect portfolios and benchmarks down to individual cash flows, and to aggregate upward to instruments, strategies, portfolios, and benchmarks is extremely powerful. Primarily, this form of attribution is most useful to fixed-income investment managers, particularly those managing to liability targets and for whom matching cash inflows and outflows is important.

Other stakeholders, such as clients or marketing departments, may need information to be summarized for non-technical audiences, which is possible if detail is available. If the only purpose of attribution, however, is to serve these stakeholders, then the additional instrument/cash-flow level detail provided by this form of attribution may not warrant the additional operational efforts compared with other approaches.

6.3 Operational Considerations and Limitations

Understanding a portfolio's and a benchmark's constituent cash flows is a significant undertaking, and with it comes commensurate operational effort. Perhaps unsurprisingly, attribution results using this form of attribution are highly sensitive to data inputs.

6.3.1 Static Data

The full repricing approaches require detailed information about the securities characteristics in order to recalculate prices from yield curves. Whether held in the portfolio or in the benchmark, such information about securities includes coupon rate, coupon dates, odd first or last coupon periods, accrual day count convention, and so on. This information may be readily available for most bonds, but others with embedded option features, such as retractable and extendible bonds, mortgage backed securities (MBS), and such derivative instruments as futures, options, interest rate swaps, and credit default swaps introduce significant challenges and complexities for calculating their prices accurately. Getting reliable information for recalculating prices for all types of instruments is the key for a successful implementation of a full repricing fixed-income attribution approach.

6.3.2 Benchmark Constituents

Because this form of attribution is built up from constituent level, even more so than the duration-based yield curve decomposition approach, it requires constituent level security data to be executed. Having this data does bring with it flexibility, and may on occasion be provided by system vendors, but the sourcing of this data, and all the required static data to go with it, may be a significant operational effort. It needs to be sourced, checked, validated, and reconciled before attribution analysis can be accurately and reliably performed. Many benchmarks, particularly municipal bonds and international fixed-income indexes, may have thousands of constituents.

6.3.3 Pricing Models

Each instrument that is in either the portfolio or the benchmark must have a relevant pricing model associated with it. This model, together with the static data items mentioned previously, provides a map of cash flows to be discounted and used in the (re)pricing of that security, given yield changes.

Obtaining a pricing model for vanilla, fixed-coupon securities may be straightforward. But it becomes increasingly difficult with more exotic instrument types. For example,

- valuing embedded options,
- understanding how MBS prices include pre-payment assumptions, or
- determining how inflation-linked annuities price in securities account for breakeven rates.

Not only must the attribution system have an appropriate pricing model for each security type under consideration, but this pricing model must also be consistent with that used by the pricing vendor, typically a third-party provider, who is supplying prices into the organization for use in such things as valuation, accounting, record-keeping, and compliance monitoring. Furthermore, these pricing models must be fully documented and developed in the attribution system for all new instrument types before investing if the instruments require attribution, form a significant part of the portfolio, or cannot be approximated by using alternative pricing models.

6.3.4 Computational Speed

Repricing portfolio and benchmark constituents, which may be large in number, for yield changes can be computationally intensive; and system speed, resources, and constraints must be considered when evaluating this approach.

6.3.5 Build or Buy

Most organizations considering using a full repricing approach to attribution may have limited system choices available to them. The data requirements outlined earlier, mean that few organizations will have the scale and resources for in-house system development.

One potential upside of developing (and buying) a system with pricing models and portfolio and benchmark constituent level static data is that they typically lend themselves to uses beyond fixed-income attribution, and many systems will also offer services, such as *ex ante* risk modeling, compliance checking, and cash-flow forecasting.

7 COMPARISON OF ATTRIBUTION RESULTS

Exhibits 71, 72, and 73 summarize the attribution results computed using the methodologies described in this reading.

Exhibit 71 Exposure Decomposition—Duration Based

	Duration	Curve	Sector	Selection	Total
Short	0.40%	0.13%	0.04%	0.00%	0.56%
Governments				0.00%	
Corporates				0.00%	
Mid	0.23%	0.03%	−0.05%	0.00%	0.21%
Governments				0.00%	
Corporates				0.00%	
Long	−1.24%	0.37%	−0.22%	0.13%	−0.97%
Governments				0.00%	

Comparison of Attribution Results

Exhibit 71 (Continued)

	Duration	Curve	Sector	Selection	Total
Corporates				0.13%	
Total	−0.62%	0.52%	−0.23%	0.13%	−0.19%

Exhibit 72 Yield Curve Decomposition—Duration Based

	Yield	Roll	Shift	Slope	Curvature	Spread	Specific	Residual	Total
Short	−0.30%	−0.06%	0.64%	0.15%	0.16%	0.04%	0.02%	−0.10%	0.56%
Governments	−0.19%	−0.04%	0.43%	0.10%	0.11%	0.00%	0.00%	−0.06%	0.35%
Corporates	−0.11%	−0.02%	0.21%	0.05%	0.05%	0.04%	0.02%	−0.04%	0.22%
Mid	−0.10%	−0.02%	0.36%	0.02%	0.02%	−0.07%	0.00%	−0.01%	0.21%
Governments	−0.22%	−0.03%	0.71%	0.04%	0.04%	0.00%	0.00%	−0.04%	0.52%
Corporates	0.12%	0.01%	−0.35%	−0.02%	−0.02%	−0.07%	0.00%	0.03%	−0.31%
Long	0.51%	0.04%	−1.89%	0.20%	0.35%	−0.30%	0.15%	−0.03%	−0.97%
Governments	0.12%	0.01%	−0.48%	0.05%	0.09%	0.00%	0.00%	−0.01%	−0.22%
Corporates	0.39%	0.03%	−1.41%	0.15%	0.26%	−0.30%	0.15%	−0.02%	−0.75%
Total	0.11%	−0.03%	−0.88%	0.38%	0.53%	−0.33%	0.17%	−0.14%	−0.19%

Exhibit 73 Yield Curve Duration—Full Repricing

	Cpn	Amort	Roll	Shift	Slope	Curvature	Spread	Specific	Total
Short	−0.36%	0.07%	−0.07%	0.59%	0.13%	0.14%	0.04%	0.02%	0.56%
Governments	−0.24%	0.05%	−0.04%	0.39%	0.09%	0.10%	0.00%	0.00%	0.35%
Corporates	−0.12%	0.02%	−0.02%	0.20%	0.04%	0.05%	0.04%	0.02%	0.22%
Mid	−0.14%	0.05%	−0.02%	0.34%	0.02%	0.02%	−0.06%	0.00%	0.21%
Governments	−0.29%	0.09%	−0.04%	0.68%	0.04%	0.04%	0.00%	0.00%	0.52%
Corporates	0.15%	−0.04%	0.02%	−0.34%	−0.02%	−0.02%	−0.06%	0.00%	−0.31%
Long	0.55%	−0.08%	0.08%	−1.83%	0.17%	0.28%	−0.27%	0.13%	−0.97%
Governments	0.13%	−0.02%	0.02%	−0.46%	0.04%	0.07%	0.00%	0.00%	−0.22%
Corporates	0.41%	−0.06%	0.06%	−1.37%	0.12%	0.21%	−0.27%	0.13%	−0.75%
Total	0.05%	0.04%	0.00%	−0.90%	0.31%	0.45%	−0.29%	0.15%	−0.19%

Note: Cpn is coupon and amort is amortization.

Notice how all three attribution approaches explain the 19 bps underperformance and tell a similar story. That is, that the portfolio was negatively affected from being over-weighted long duration bonds as yields rose, but benefitted from a reshaping of the yield curve. The over-exposure to the credit market cost the portfolio return, but was outweighed somewhat by issue selection.

There are philosophical differences between the approaches. Exposure decomposition approaches solely explain the relative return from active management of a portfolio. Both yield curve decomposition approaches, however, break down returns into contributions or drivers of those returns, which can then be assembled to reflect specific investment decision-making processes. Passage of time, for example, is not a decision by itself, instead, it is a contributing factor to the performance of bonds.

Furthermore, although the attribution explanation presented in each of the models is similar, examining the comparative numbers reveals differences in the magnitudes. The reason is because of differences in assumptions, calculation methodologies, and the specific, possibly extreme, example used. Indeed, the magnitude of these differences will vary with the types of instruments being modelled, length of time, and volatility of the markets, and evaluating these alongside the operational considerations and user requirements will drive which approach is most appropriate for an organization.

Aside from the specifics of this illustrative example, Exhibit 74 compares the three approaches with respect to how they break down returns, the typical factors used, and operational factors, such as data requirements, return type, and primary audience.

Exhibit 74 Comparison of Three Fixed-Income Attribution Approaches

	Exposure Decomposition—Duration Based	Yield Curve Decomposition—Duration Based	Yield Curve Decomposition—Full Repricing Based
Executed as	Top-down hierarchical view on decision making	Top-down approach focusing on portfolio or bucket-level decisions, or built bottom-up from security level	Bottom-up from security level
Contribution to	Generally active return only	■ Portfolio return ■ Benchmark return ■ Active return	■ Portfolio return ■ Benchmark return ■ Active return
Typical factors	Duration, curve, sector, selection	Yield, roll, shift, slope, curvature, spread, specific	Coupon, amortization, roll, shift, slope, curvature, spread, specific
Calculation	Straightforward based on active bucket exposure and relative bucket returns	More involved based on duration (and convexity) and yield change	Detailed, security-specific pricing models required; can be very intensive computationally
Return type	Generally transactional	Generally buy-and-hold.	Generally buy-and-hold
Data requirements	Comparatively simple requirements at duration-bucket level	Security- or bucket-level modified durations, weights, and returns.	Full security level static data, weights, and returns

Exhibit 74 (Continued)

	Exposure Decomposition—Duration Based	Yield Curve Decomposition—Duration Based	Yield Curve Decomposition—Full Repricing Based
Primary audience/users	▪ Client reporting ▪ Marketing ▪ Some investment management insights	▪ Client reporting ▪ Marketing ▪ Investment managers	▪ Investment managers
Selected published models	McLaren (2002) GRAP (2005) van Breukelen (2000)	Campisi (2000), (2011) Lord (1997) Colin (2005) van Breukelen (2000)	Many commercial systems

Note: Authors' placement of selected published models represents their judgment. In some cases, various placements might be argued. For example, G. van Breukelen[22] considers his model an example of the second approach, whereas some analysts would place it in the first approach.

SUMMARY

This reading has outlined several key aspects of fixed-income attribution. It has shown that the naïve application of equity attribution approaches to fixed income is not always appropriate and that consideration must be given to the specific nature of many fixed-income products, instruments, and management decisions when designing or considering attribution models.

Against this backdrop, three fixed-income attribution approaches were introduced, namely exposure decomposition, duration-based, and full repricing–based examples of yield curve decomposition. For each approach, a worked example was presented, but also operational considerations and limitations discussed. Among the points made by the reading are the following:

- Fixed-income attribution models can be grouped into three approaches: Exposure Decomposition—Duration Based, Yield Curve Decomposition—Duration Based, and Yield Curve Decomposition—Full Repricing Based

- Exposure Decomposition—Duration Based involves calculating active weights in duration and sector buckets, identifying active positions taken by the investment manager, and quantifying the impact of these in terms of relative returns. It is the simplest of the approaches, as well as intuitive and possibly easier to implement.

- Yield Curve Decomposition—Duration Based uses the known relationship between price movements and modified duration (and convexity). By breaking down yield movements into factors, such as movement in government curves

---

22 Communication of 23 May 2014.

or sector spreads, changes in price can then be estimated. It is more complex in its implementation, but possibly more flexible and intuitive to investment managers.

- Yield Curve Decomposition—Full Repricing Based involves the application of full security pricing models to known changes in yields across the yield curve, providing very detailed and accurate attribution at a cost of significant operational effort.

Importantly, a sample output has been provided for each approach and interpreted in terms of active management decisions and the market conditions that were experienced. Many performance analysts will, after all, be charged not only with the calculation of attribution effects but also their presentation to key stakeholders.

REFERENCES

Brinson, G., and N. Fachler. 1985. "Measuring Non-US Equity Portfolio Performance." *Journal of Portfolio Management*, vol. 11, no. 3 (Spring).

Brinson, G., L.R. Hood, and G.L. Beebower. 1986. "Determinants of Portfolio Performance." *Financial Analysts Journal*, vol. 42, no. 4 (July/August).

Campisi, S. 2000. "Primer on Fixed Income Performance Attribution." *Journal of Performance Measurement*, vol. 4, no. 4 (Summer).

Choudhry, M. 2004. *Analysing and Interpreting the Yield Curve*. Hoboken, NJ: John Wiley & Sons.

Colin, A. 2005. *Fixed Income Attribution*. Hoboken, NJ: John Wiley & Sons.

Dynkin, L., J. Hyman, and P. Vankudre. 1998. "Attribution of Portfolio Performance Relative to an Index," Lehman Brothers Fixed Income Research (March).

Giguère, C. 2005. "Thinking Through Fixed income Attribution – Reflections from a Group of French Practitioners." *Journal of Performance Measurement*, vol. 9, no. 4 (Summer).

Lord, T. 1997. "The Attribution of Portfolio and Index Returns in Fixed Income." *Journal of Performance Measurement*, vol. 2, no. 1 (Fall).

McLaren, A. 2002. "A Framework for Multi-Currency Fixed Income Attribution." *Journal of Performance Measurement*, vol. 6, no. 4 (Summer).

Murira, B., and H. Sierra. 2006. "Fixed Income Attribution: A Unified Framework – Part 1." *Journal of Performance Measurement*, vol. 11, no. 1 (Fall).

Murira, B., and H. Sierra. 2007. "Fixed Income Attribution: A Unified Framework – Part 2." *Journal of Performance Measurement*, vol. 11, no. 2 (Winter).

van Breukelen, G. 2000. "Fixed Income Attribution." *Journal of Performance Measurement*, vol. 4, no. 4 (Summer).

FIXED INCOME FUNDAMENTALS

by John D. Stowe, PhD, CFA

1 Introduction

This reading[23] provides an overview of basic concepts and techniques of fixed income analysis. Major focuses include the characteristics of bonds, the basic formula for bond pricing, measures of interest rate risk, and how various term structures of interest rates are defined and related to each other. (An *interest rate term structure* indicates the level of market interest rates at various maturities; the graphical plot of an interest rate term structure is called a *yield curve*.)

Section 2 reviews the basics of bond pricing. The focus is on bonds with a fixed interest rate and no embedded options, called "vanilla" bonds (the analogy is that vanilla is one of the most basic flavors). Section 3 reviews established measures of a bond's interest rate risk, duration, and convexity, and shows how these measures are interpreted. Section 4 discusses the term structure of interest rates. The section contrasts four measures of bond yield that are used in term structure analysis: the yield-to-maturity, the par yield, the spot yield, and the forward yield. A summary of key points concludes the reading.

2 What Bonds Are and How They Are Priced

Bonds represent loans to the bond issuer (the business or government that issued the bonds). The position of the bondholder (buyer of the bond) is that of a lender, and the position of the issuer is that of a borrower. The promised payments on a bond typically consist of interest payments (known as "coupons") and the repayment of the principal amount of the bond—the amount of borrowing that the bond represents. These promised payments are contractual obligations of the issuer and must be met before any distributions can be made to any ownership interests, in particular investors in common shares when the issuer is a business. Common share investors as owners are interested in earnings net of interest payments and taxes—net earnings—the residual that remains after lenders and tax authorities receive what is owed them. Thus, common share values are driven by factors, such as earnings growth, that are of special concern to owners. By contrast, changes in bond values are driven primarily by changes in market interest rates, changes in issuer *credit risk* (the risk that the issuer will miss making a promised payment), and changes in investors' required compensation for bearing credit risk. Bond values typically rise when interest rates fall and decline when interest rates rise. This exposure to interest rate movements is called *interest rate risk*. Other factors that affect bond values include the liquidity of the bond issue (investors will pay for the ability to sell a bond quickly at close to its fair value) and the bond's tax status.

The value of a bond can be expressed as the present value of the coupon interest and principal payments, with each cash flow discounted by a market discount rate, r:

$$PV^{Full} = \frac{PMT}{(1+r)^{1-t/T}} + \frac{PMT}{(1+r)^{2-t/T}} + \cdots + \frac{PMT + FV}{(1+r)^{N-t/T}} \tag{1}$$

---

[23] This reading draws extensively from four CFA Institute readings: "Introduction to Fixed-Income Valuation" and "Understanding Fixed-Income Risk and Return" by James F. Adams and Donald J. Smith, "The Term Structure and Interest Rate Dynamics" by Thomas S.Y. Ho, Sang Bin Lee, and Stephen E. Wilcox, and "Yield Curve Construction, Trading Strategies, and Risk Analysis" by Bernd Hanke and Gregory G. Seals.

where

PV^{Full} = the present value of future cash flows, including accrued interest
t = the number of days from the last coupon payment to the settlement date
T = the number of days in the coupon period
t/T = the fraction of the coupon period that has gone by since the last payment
PMT = the coupon payment per period
FV = the future value paid at maturity, known as the par value or principal value of the bond
r = the yield-to-maturity, or the market discount rate, per period
N = the number of evenly spaced payment periods to maturity as of the beginning of the current period

Example 1 illustrates the use of the bond valuation formula, Equation 1, to find the yield-to-maturity on a bond.

EXAMPLE 1

Valuation of an Annual Pay Bond

Assume that an investor initially buys a 10-year, 8% annual coupon payment bond at a price of 85.503075 per 100 units of par value. The investor buys the bond immediately after a coupon payment, so $t/T = 0$. The investor receives a coupon payment of $PMT = 8$ each year for ten years plus the principal amount at maturity of $FV = 100$. The bond's yield-to-maturity, found using a spreadsheet or financial calculator, is 10.40%.

$$85.503075 = \frac{8}{(1+r)^1} + \frac{8}{(1+r)^2} + \frac{8}{(1+r)^3} + \frac{8}{(1+r)^4} + \frac{8}{(1+r)^5} + \frac{8}{(1+r)^6} + \frac{8}{(1+r)^7} + \frac{8}{(1+r)^8} + \frac{8}{(1+r)^9} + \frac{108}{(1+r)^{10}}, \quad r = 0.1040$$

The bond's yield-to-maturity (YTM) is the discount rate that makes the present value of the future payments equal to the bond's price. The YTM for this bond is 10.40%. The YTM at the time of purchase is a rough estimate of the investor's rate of return. The estimate should be exact when three conditions are fulfilled: (1) The investor holds the bond to maturity, (2) there is no default by the issuer, and (3) the coupon interest payments are reinvested at that same rate of interest.

In this reading, we illustrate many of the basics of bond analysis using a traditional, option-free bond.[24] In practice, various option-like bond features complicate the basic valuation model. Such features include (but are not limited to):

- *Callability*, which describes a feature of bonds for which the issuer has the right to retire some or all of the bond issue at a specific price before the bond's scheduled maturity. Bonds are frequently called to replace the bond issue with a lower cost issue when interest rates have dropped or to escape onerous bond covenants.

- *Sinking fund provisions*, which require the issuer to retire certain amounts of the outstanding bond issue each year.

---

24 Callable bonds are discussed in Section 3.4.

Fixed Income Fundamentals

- *Put provisions*, which grant bondholders the right to sell the bond issue back to the issuer on designated dates.
- *Convertibility*. A convertible bond can be exchanged for specified amounts of common shares in the issuing firm.

An investor in a fixed-rate bond has three sources of return: (1) receipt of the promised coupon and principal payments on the scheduled dates, (2) reinvestment of coupon payments, and (3) potential capital gains or losses on the sale of the bond prior to maturity. This assumes, of course, that the issuer makes the coupon and principal payments as scheduled. This reading focuses primarily on interest rate risk, which affects the reinvestment of coupon payments and the market price if the bond is sold prior to maturity.

When a bond is purchased at a discount or a premium, the bond is amortized towards its par value. Such a trajectory is shown in Exhibit A1 for a 10-year, 8% annual payment bond purchased at a price of 85.503075 per 100 monetary units of par value. A point on the trajectory represents the *carrying value* of the bond at that time. The carrying value is the purchase price plus the amortized amount of the discount if the bond is purchased at a price below par value. If the bond is purchased at a price above par value, the carrying value is the purchase price minus the amortized amount of the premium.

Exhibit A1 Constant-Yield Price Trajectory for a 10-Year, 8% Annual Payment Bond

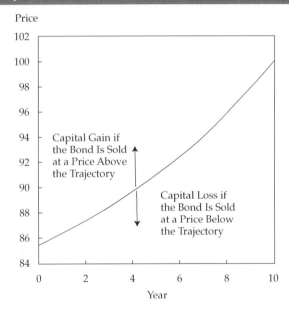

Note: Price is price per 100 of par value.

The amortized amount for each year is the change in the price between two points on the trajectory. The initial price of the bond is 85.503075 per 100 of par value. Its price (the carrying value) after one year is 86.393394, calculated using the original YTM of 10.40%. When market yields change, the bond price will not fall on the constant-yield price trajectory. Capital gains arise if a bond is sold at a price above its constant-yield price trajectory and capital losses occur if a bond is sold at a price below its constant-yield price trajectory.

When an investor purchases a bond between coupon payments, the buyer must pay the interest on the bond that has accrued since the last coupon payment. The *full price* is the total amount the buyer pays. The *flat price* is the full price minus the accrued interest. By contrast, there is no such adjustment for dividends on common shares. If bought before the shares go ex dividend, the common stock buyer will get the whole dividend payment.

3 Interest Rate Risk of Fixed-Interest-Rate Bonds

This section covers two commonly used measures of interest rate risk: duration and convexity. The *duration* of a bond measures the sensitivity of the bond's full price (including accrued interest) to changes in the bond's YTM or to changes in benchmark interest rates. Duration estimates the changes in the bond price assuming that all variables other than the YTM or benchmark rates are held constant. Most importantly, the time-to-maturity is unchanged. Therefore, duration measures the *instantaneous* (or at least same-day) change in the bond price. The accrued interest is the same, so it is the flat price that goes up or down when the full price changes. Duration is a useful measure because it represents the approximate amount of time a bond would have to be held for the market discount rate at purchase to be realized if there is a single change in interest rate. If the bond is held for the duration period, an increase from reinvesting coupons is offset by a decrease in price if interest rates increase, and a decrease from reinvesting coupons is offset by an increase in price if interest rates decrease.

There are two major types of bond duration measures: yield duration measures and curve duration measures. *Yield duration measures* capture the sensitivity of the bond price with respect to the bond's own YTM. *Curve duration measures* capture the sensitivity of the bond price (or more generally, the market value of a financial asset or liability) with respect to changes in the benchmark yield curve. In this reading, we limit the analysis to yield durations. Two yield duration measures used in fixed-income analysis are Macaulay duration and modified duration. Effective duration and key rate durations are curve duration measures.

3.1 Yield Duration Measures: Macaulay and Modified Duration

Named after an economist who first wrote about the measure in 1938,[25] *Macaulay duration* is a weighted average of the time to receipt of the bond's promised payments, where the weights are the shares of the full price that correspond to each of the bond's promised future payments (this becomes especially clear in Equation 3 below).

Equation 2 is a general formula to calculate the Macaulay duration (MacDur) of a traditional fixed interest rate bond.

$$\text{MacDur} = \left[\frac{\frac{(1-t/T) \times PMT}{(1-r)^{1-t/T}} + \frac{(2-t/T) \times PMT}{(1+r)^{2-t/T}} + \cdots + \frac{(N-t/T) \times (PMT+FV)}{(1+r)^{N-t/T}}}{\frac{PMT}{(1+r)^{1-t/T}} + \frac{PMT}{(1+r)^{2-t/T}} + \cdots + \frac{PMT+FV}{(1+r)^{N-t/T}}} \right] \quad (2)$$

---

[25] Frederick R. Macaulay, *Some Theoretical Problems Suggested by the Movements of Interest Rates, Bond Yields and Stock Prices in the United States since 1856* (New York: National Bureau of Economic Research, 1938).

where

t = the number of days from the last coupon payment to the settlement date
T = the number of days in the coupon period
t/T = the fraction of the coupon period that has gone by since the last payment
PMT = the coupon payment per period
FV = the future value paid at maturity, or the par value of the bond
r = the YTM, or the market discount rate, per period
N = the number of evenly spaced periods to maturity as of the beginning of the current period

The denominator in Equation 2 is the full price (PV^{Full}) of the bond including accrued interest as represented in Equation 1.

Equation 3 combines Equations 1 and 2 to reveal that a bond's Macaulay duration is equal to its weighted-average time to maturity:

$$\text{MacDur} = \left\{ (1 - t/T) \left[\frac{\frac{PMT}{(1+r)^{1-t/T}}}{PV^{Full}} \right] + (2 - t/T) \left[\frac{\frac{PMT}{(1+r)^{2-t/T}}}{PV^{Full}} \right] + \cdots + (N - t/T) \left[\frac{\frac{PMT + FV}{(1+r)^{N-t/T}}}{PV^{Full}} \right] \right\} \quad (3)$$

The time to receipt of cash flow measured in terms of time periods are $1 - t/T$, $2 - t/T$, ..., $N - t/T$. The weights are the present values of the cash flows divided by the full price. Therefore, Macaulay duration is measured in terms of time periods. Some examples will clarify this calculation.

EXAMPLE 2

Calculating a Macaulay Duration

This example shows the calculation of Macaulay duration for two bonds. The first is an annual-pay bond purchased immediately after a coupon payment, and the second is a semiannual-pay bond purchased between coupon dates.

Consider first the 10-year, 8% annual coupon payment bond used in Example 1. The bond's YTM is 10.40%, and its price is 85.503075 per 100 of par value. This bond has 10 evenly spaced periods to maturity. Settlement is on a coupon payment date so that $t/T = 0$. Exhibit A2 illustrates the calculation of the bond's Macaulay duration.

Exhibit A2 Macaulay Duration of a 10-Year, 8% Annual Payment Bond

Period	Cash Flow	Present Value	Weight	Period × Weight
1	8	7.246377	0.08475	0.0847
2	8	6.563747	0.07677	0.1535
3	8	5.945423	0.06953	0.2086
4	8	5.385347	0.06298	0.2519

(continued)

(Continued)

Period	Cash Flow	Present Value	Weight	Period × Weight
5	8	4.878032	0.05705	0.2853
6	8	4.418507	0.05168	0.3101
7	8	4.002271	0.04681	0.3277
8	8	3.625245	0.04240	0.3392
9	8	3.283737	0.03840	0.3456
10	108	40.154389	0.46963	4.6963
		85.503075	1.00000	7.0029

Note: Rounding may cause apparent small discrepancies in numbers in this and other exhibits.

The first column of Exhibit A2 shows the number of periods to the receipt of the cash flow; the second column shows the amount of the payment per 100 of par value; the third column is the present value of the cash flow. For example, the final payment is 108 (the last coupon payment plus the redemption of principal) and its present value is 40.154389.

$$\frac{108}{(1.1040)^{10}} = 40.154389$$

The sum of the present values is the full price of the bond. The fourth column, weight, is the proportion of the bond's total market value that each cash flow represents. For example, the final payment of 108 per 100 of par value is 46.963% of the bond's market value.

$$\frac{40.154389}{85.503075} = 0.46963$$

The sum of the weights is 1.00000. The fifth column is the number of periods to the receipt of the cash flow (the first column) multiplied by the weight (the fourth column). The sum of that column is 7.0029, which is the Macaulay duration of this 10-year, 8% annual coupon payment bond. This statistic is sometimes reported as 7.0029 *years*, although the time frame is not needed in most applications.

Now consider an example of a bond purchased *between* coupon payment dates. A 6% semiannual payment corporate bond that matures on 14 February 2022 is purchased for settlement on 11 April 2014. The coupon payments are 3 per 100 of par value, paid on 14 February and 14 August of each year. The YTM is 6.00% quoted on a street-convention semiannual bond basis.[26] The full price of this bond comprises the flat price plus accrued interest. The flat price for the bond is 99.990423 per 100 of par value. The accrued interest is calculated using the 30/360 method to count days. This settlement date is 57 days into the 180-day semiannual period, so $t/T = 57/180$. The accrued interest is 0.950000 (= 57/180 × 3) per 100 of par value. The full price for the bond is 100.940423 (= 99.990423 + 0.950000). Exhibit A3 shows the calculation of the bond's Macaulay duration.

---

[26] In the United States, semiannual coupon payments predominate, whereas annual coupons are most common elsewhere.

Fixed Income Fundamentals

Exhibit A3 Macaulay Duration of an Eight-Year, 6% Semiannual Payment Bond Priced to Yield 6.00%

Period	Time to Receipt	Cash Flow	Present Value	Weight	Time × Weight
1	0.6833	3	2.940012	0.02913	0.019903
2	1.6833	3	2.854381	0.02828	0.047601
3	2.6833	3	2.771244	0.02745	0.073669
4	3.6833	3	2.690528	0.02665	0.098178
5	4.6833	3	2.612163	0.02588	0.121197
6	5.6833	3	2.536080	0.02512	0.142791
7	6.6833	3	2.462214	0.02439	0.163025
8	7.6833	3	2.390499	0.02368	0.181959
9	8.6833	3	2.320873	0.02299	0.199652
10	9.6833	3	2.253275	0.02232	0.216159
11	10.6833	3	2.187645	0.02167	0.231536
12	11.6833	3	2.123927	0.02104	0.245834
13	12.6833	3	2.062065	0.02043	0.259102
14	13.6833	3	2.002005	0.01983	0.271389
15	14.6833	3	1.943694	0.01926	0.282740
16	15.6833	103	64.789817	0.64186	10.066535
			100.940423	1.00000	12.621268

There are 16 semiannual periods to maturity between the last coupon payment date of 14 February 2014 and maturity on 14 February 2022. The time to receipt of cash flow in semiannual periods is in the second column: 0.6833 = 1 − 57/180, 1.6833 = 2 − 57/180, etc. The cash flow for each period is in the third column. The annual YTM is 6.00%, so the yield per semiannual period is 3.00%. When that yield is used to get the present value of each cash flow, the full price of the bond is 100.940423, the sum of the fourth column. The weights, which are the proportions of the full price corresponding to each cash flow, are in the fifth column. The Macaulay duration is the sum of the items in the sixth column, which is the weight multiplied by the time to receipt of each cash flow. The result, 12.621268, is the Macaulay duration on an eight-year, 6% semiannual payment bond for settlement on 11 April 2014 measured in *semiannual periods*. Similar to coupon rates and yields-to-maturity, duration statistics are generally annualized in practice. Therefore, the Macaulay duration typically is reported as 6.310634 *years* (= 12.621268/2).[27]

---

[27] Microsoft Excel users can obtain the Macaulay duration using the DURATION financial function: DURATION ("4/11/2014," "2/14/2022," 0.06, 0.06, 2, 0). The inputs are the settlement date, maturity date, annual coupon rate as a decimal, annual yield-to-maturity as a decimal, periodicity, and the code for the day count (0 for 30/360, 1 for actual/actual).

Modified duration is more frequently used than Macaulay duration. The calculation of the modified duration (ModDur) statistic of a bond requires a simple adjustment to Macaulay duration. It is the Macaulay duration statistic divided by one plus the yield per period.

$$\text{ModDur} = \frac{\text{MacDur}}{1+r} \quad (4)$$

By assuming that a given shift in yield to maturity is applied to all bond payments regardless of their maturity, modified duration, similar to Macaulay duration, essentially assumes shifts in the yield curve are parallel (the same at all maturities).

The modified duration of the 10-year, 8% annual payment bond for which Macaulay duration was previously calculated is 6.3432.

$$\text{ModDur} = \frac{7.0029}{1.1040} = 6.3432$$

The modified duration of the 6% semiannual payment bond maturing on 14 February 2022 is 12.253658 semiannual periods.

$$\text{ModDur} = \frac{12.621268}{1.0300} = 12.253658$$

The annualized modified duration (AnnModDur) of the 6% semiannual payment bond is 6.126829 (= 12.253658/2).[28]

The importance of modified duration is that it provides an estimate of the percentage price change for a bond given a change in its YTM.

$$\%\Delta PV^{Full} \approx -\text{AnnModDur} \times \Delta\text{Yield} \quad (5)$$

The percentage price change refers to the full price, including accrued interest. The AnnModDur term in Equation 5 is, as noted above, the *annual* modified duration, and the ΔYield term is the change in the *annual* YTM. The $\approx$ sign indicates that this calculation is an estimation. The minus sign indicates that bond prices and yields-to-maturity move inversely.

If the annual yield on the 6% semiannual payment bond that matures on 14 February 2022 rises by 100 bps, from 6.00% to 7.00%, the estimated loss in value for the bond is 6.1268%.

$$\%\Delta PV^{Full} \approx -6.126829 \times 0.0100 = -0.061268$$

If the YTM were to drop by 100 bps to 5.00%, the estimated gain in value is also 6.1268%.

$$\%\Delta PV^{Full} \approx -6.126829 \times -0.0100 = 0.061268$$

Modified duration provides a *linear* estimate of the percentage price change. In terms of absolute value, the change is the same for either an increase or decrease in the YTM. Later in this reading (Equation 7), a "convexity adjustment" to duration is introduced which improves the accuracy of this estimate, especially when a large change in YTM (such as 100 bps) is considered.

The modified duration statistic for a fixed-rate bond is easily obtained if the Macaulay duration is already known. An alternative approach is to *approximate* modified duration directly by changing YTM up and down by the same small amount ΔYield. Then the bond prices given the new yields-to-maturity are calculated. The price when the yield is increased is denoted PV_+. The price when the YTM is reduced

---

[28] Microsoft Excel users can obtain the modified duration using the MDURATION financial function: MDURATION ("4/11/2014," "2/14/2022," 0.06, 0.06, 2, 0). The inputs are the same as for the Macaulay duration in Footnote 5.

is denoted PV_-. The original price is PV_0. These prices are the full prices, including accrued interest. With these inputs, the approximate value of modified duration stated on an annual basis is:

$$\text{ApproxModDur} = \frac{(PV_-) - (PV_+)}{2 \times (\Delta \text{Yield}) \times (PV_0)} \qquad (6)$$

Consider the 6% semiannual coupon payment corporate bond maturing on 14 February 2022. For settlement on 11 April 2014, the full price (PV_0) is 100.940423 given that the YTM is 6.00%.

$$PV_0 = \left[\frac{3}{(1.03)^1} + \frac{3}{(1.03)^2} + \ldots + \frac{103}{(1.03)^{16}} \right] \times (1.03)^{57/180} = 100.940423$$

Raise the annual YTM by five bps, from 6.00% to 6.05%. This increase corresponds to an increase in the YTM per semiannual period of 2.5 bps, from 3.00% to 3.025% per period. The new full price (PV_+) is 100.631781.

$$PV_+ = \left[\frac{3}{(1.03025)^1} + \frac{3}{(1.03025)^2} + \ldots + \frac{103}{(1.03025)^{16}} \right] \times (1.03025)^{57/180} = 100.631781$$

Lower the annual YTM by five bps, from 6.00% to 5.95%. This decrease corresponds to a decrease in the YTM per semiannual period of 2.5 bps, from 3.00% to 2.975% per period. The new full price (PV_-) is 101.250227.

$$PV_- = \left[\frac{3}{(1.02975)^1} + \frac{3}{(1.02975)^2} + \ldots + \frac{103}{(1.02975)^{16}} \right] \times (1.02975)^{57/180} = 101.250227$$

Enter these results into Equation 6 for the 5 bps change in the annual YTM, or ΔYield = 0.0005:

$$\text{ApproxModDur} = \frac{101.250227 - 100.631781}{2 \times 0.0005 \times 100.940423} = 6.126842$$

The "exact" annual modified duration for this bond is 6.126829 and the approximate annual modified duration (calculated above) is 6.126842—virtually identical results.

In summary, the Macaulay and modified duration measures for a fixed-rate bond depend primarily on the coupon rate, YTM, and time-to-maturity. A higher coupon rate or a higher YTM are associated with a lower duration measure. Duration, and thus interest rates sensitivity, *usually* increases with increases in the time-to-maturity. A longer time-to-maturity usually leads to a higher duration, and *always* does so for a bond priced at a premium or at par value. But if the bond is priced at a discount, it is possible that a longer time-to-maturity could result in a *lower* duration. That relationship would only occur if the coupon rate is low (but not zero) relative to the yield and the time-to-maturity is long. These facts are proven in more advanced treatments of the subject and are beyond the scope of this reading.

3.2 Convexity: Adding to the Information Given by Modified Duration

Estimates of price sensitivity to a change in yield can be made more precise by considering convexity in addition to modified duration. Modified duration measures the primary effect on a bond's percentage price change given a change in the YTM. A secondary effect is measured by the convexity statistic, which is illustrated in Exhibit A4 for a traditional (option-free) fixed-rate bond.

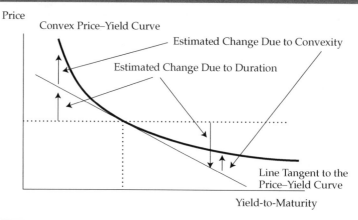

Exhibit A4 Convexity of a Traditional (Option-Free) Fixed-Rate Bond

The true relationship between the bond price and the YTM is the curved (convex) line shown in Exhibit A4. This curved line shows the actual bond price given its market discount rate. Duration estimates the change in the bond price along the straight line that is tangent to the curved line. For small YTM changes, there is little difference between the lines. But for larger changes, the difference becomes significant.

The *convexity measure* for the bond is used to improve the estimate of the percentage price change provided by modified duration alone. Equation 7 is the convexity-adjusted estimate of the percentage change in the bond's full price.

$$\%\Delta PV^{Full} \approx (-\text{AnnModDur} \times \Delta \text{Yield}) + \left[\frac{1}{2} \times \text{AnnConvexity} \times (\Delta \text{Yield})^2\right] \quad (7)$$

The calculation of annual convexity (AnnConvexity) is somewhat complex and beyond the scope of this appendix. But suppose (annual) convexity is 700 and (annual) modified duration is 9. Consider a predicted 10 basis point (0.0010) increase in yield. Then, bond value would be predicted to decline by about 87 basis points:

$$\%\Delta PV^{Full} \approx (-9 \times 0.0010) + \left[\frac{1}{2} \times 700 \times (0.0010)^2\right] = (-0.009) + (0.00035) = -0.00865$$

Taking convexity into account, the decline in bond value is somewhat less than the 90 basis point effect predicted by modified duration alone, using Equation 5. This result is typical for traditional (option-free) fixed-rate bonds. For the same increase in YTM, the more convex bond *depreciates less* in price. For the same decrease in YTM, the more convex bond *appreciates more* in price. The conclusion is that the more convex bond outperforms the less convex bond in both bull (falling interest rates) and bear (rising interest rates) markets. This conclusion assumes, however, that this positive attribute of convexity is not "priced into" the bond. To the extent that it is included, the more convex bond would have a higher price (and lower YTM).

The factors that lead to greater convexity are the same that lead to higher duration. A fixed-rate bond with a longer time-to-maturity, a lower coupon rate, and a lower YTM has greater convexity than a bond with a shorter time-to-maturity, a higher coupon rate, and a higher YTM. Another factor is the dispersion of cash flows, meaning the degree to which payments are spread out over time. If two bonds have the same duration, the one that has the greater dispersion of cash flows has the greater convexity.

3.3 Effects of Yield Volatility on Interest Rate Risk

The importance of yield volatility in measuring interest rate risk is that bond price changes are products of two factors: (1) the price impact *per* basis-point change in the YTM, and (2) the *number* of basis points in the YTM change. The first factor is duration or the combination of duration and convexity, and the second factor is the yield volatility. For example, consider a five-year bond with a modified duration of 4.5 and a 30-year bond with a modified duration of 18.0. Clearly, for a *given* change in YTM, the 30-year bond represents more much more interest rate risk to an investor who has a short-term horizon. In fact, the 30-year bond appears to have *four times* the risk given the ratio of the modified durations. But that assumption neglects the possibility that the 30-year bond might have half the yield volatility of the five-year bond.

Example 3 shows that the percentage price change for three bonds depends on their durations, convexities, and the change in the yield. In this example, the yield change is not the same for all of the bonds.

EXAMPLE 3

Yield Volatility

A fixed-income analyst is asked to rank three bonds in terms of interest rate risk. Here, interest rate risk means the potential price decrease on a percentage basis given a sudden change in financial market conditions. The increases in the yields-to-maturity represent the "worst case" for the scenario being considered.

Bond	Modified Duration	Convexity	ΔYield
A	3.72	12.1	25 bps
B	5.81	40.7	15 bps
C	12.39	158.0	10 bps

The modified duration and convexity statistics are annualized. ΔYield is the increase in the annual YTM. Rank the bonds in terms of interest rate risk.

Solution:

Calculate the estimated percentage price change for each bond using Equation 7:

$$\%\Delta PV^{Full} \approx (-\text{AnnModDur} \times \Delta \text{Yield}) + \left[\frac{1}{2} \times \text{AnnConvexity} \times (\Delta \text{Yield})^2\right]$$

Bond A: $(-3.72 \times 0.0025) + \left[\frac{1}{2} \times 12.1 \times (0.0025)^2\right] = -0.009262$

Bond B: $(-5.81 \times 0.0015) + \left[\frac{1}{2} \times 40.7 \times (0.0015)^2\right] = -0.008669$

Bond C: $(-12.39 \times 0.0010) + \left[\frac{1}{2} \times 158.0 \times (0.0010)^2\right] = -0.012311$

Based on these assumed changes in the YTM and the modified duration and convexity risk measures, Bond C has the highest degree of interest rate risk (a potential loss of 1.2311%), followed by Bond A (a potential loss of 0.9262%) and Bond B (a potential loss of 0.8669%).

3.4 Curve Duration Measures: Effective Duration and Key Rate Duration

The effective duration of a bond is the sensitivity of the bond's price to a change in a benchmark yield curve. Equation 8 is the formula for calculating effective duration (EffDur).

$$\text{EffDur} = \frac{(PV_-) - (PV_+)}{2 \times (\Delta \text{Curve}) \times (PV_0)} \tag{8}$$

Note that the denominator of Equation 8 uses the change in the benchmark yield curve, ΔCurve. Effective duration is essential to the measurement of the interest rate risk of bonds with embedded options. For such bonds, one cannot use modified duration based on the effect of a change in yield to maturity, because the bond's cash flows are contingent on the level of YTM. For example, for a callable bond, a change in the level of yield to maturity might cause the bond to be called, so the assumption that cash flows are fixed would not hold. Stated another way, the YTM for callable bonds is not well-defined because future cash flows are uncertain.

Exhibit A5 illustrates the impact of the change in the benchmark yield curve (ΔCurve) on the price of a callable bond price compared with that on a comparable non-callable bond. The two bonds have the same credit risk, coupon rate, payment frequency, and time-to-maturity. The vertical axis is the bond price. The horizontal axis is a particular benchmark yield—for instance, a point on the par curve for government bonds, which we will discuss in Section 4.3.

Exhibit A5   Interest Rate Risk Characteristics of a Callable Bond

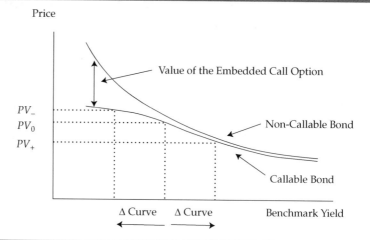

As shown in Exhibit A5, the price of the non-callable bond is always greater than that of the callable bond with otherwise identical features. The difference is the value of the embedded call option. Recall that the call option is an option to the issuer and not the holder of the bond. When interest rates are high compared with the coupon rate, the value of the call option is low. When rates are low, the value of the call option is much greater because the issuer is more likely to exercise the option to refinance the debt at a lower cost of funds. The investor bears the "call risk" because if the bond is called, the investor must reinvest the proceeds at a lower interest rate.

Exhibit A5 shows that when benchmark yields are high, the effective durations of the callable and non-callable bonds are very similar. The slopes of the lines tangent to the price–yield curve are about the same in such a situation. But when interest rates are low, the effective duration of the callable bond is lower than that of the otherwise comparable non-callable bond. That is because the callable bond price does not increase as much when benchmark yields fall. The presence of the call option limits price appreciation.

Another kind of curve duration measure is key rate duration. Effective duration assumes that all yields on the yield curve change by the same amount. An alternative curve duration measure, key rate duration measures the sensitivity of the bond price to changes in the yield at a specific maturity. A set of key rate durations for various maturities allow us to identify "shaping risk" for bonds, the bonds' sensitivity to changes in the shape of the yield curve, not only its level. Note that if we use key rate duration and shift the yield curve up or down by the same amount, the indication concerning the effect on bond price will be the same as for effective duration.

4 Yield Curve Construction

The term structure of interest rates—market interest rates at various maturities—is a vital input into the valuation of many financial products. Exhibit A6 shows a yield curve for government bonds; the exhibit breaks out for separate illustration that part of the yield curve that applies to the money market (fixed-income securities with maturities of one year or less).

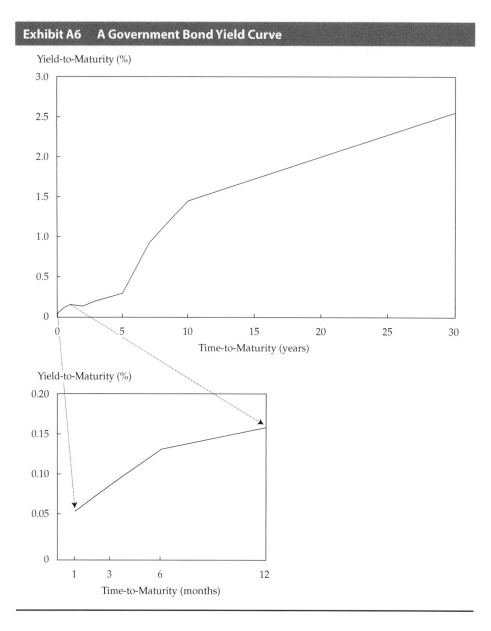

Exhibit A6 A Government Bond Yield Curve

The goal of this section is to explain the various types of yield curves. The YTM of a bond is the discount rate that makes the sum of the discounted future cash flows equal to its market price. One of the most commonly used yield curves is that for Treasury bonds, which should have little credit risk and are highly liquid. Unfortunately, the YTM is probably the least useful yield measure for a yield curve. Yield curves are calculated for measures such as (1) the YTM, (2) the par yield, (3) the spot yield, and (4) forward yields. We contrast the nature of each of these four yield measures and demonstrate the relationships between these measures.

4.1 Yield Curves from Yield-to-Maturity and Par Yield

The biggest drawback of the YTM is that it assumes that a bond's cash flows are reinvested at the YTM. Furthermore, bonds with the same maturity and different coupons can have differing YTM. These bonds will sell for a discount (or premium) if their coupons are less than (greater than) the YTM. Just considering interest rate risk, these bonds (with the same maturity) can have differing YTM because low (high) coupon bonds will have a higher (lower) duration and thus higher (lower) interest rate risk.

Fixed Income Fundamentals

Consequently, investors often use a par yield to construct the yield curve. The par yield is the yield on a hypothetical or real bond with a price equal to par value. The par yield would be the coupon rate required for a bond to sell for par. Generally, the most recently issued bonds ("on-the-run" issues) trade at prices close to par because their coupon rates were set close to the current level of interest rates. This avoids the problems associated with bonds selling for discounts or premiums, but the reinvestment assumption still remains.

Interest rates are both a barometer of the economy and an instrument for its control. The term structure of interest rates is a vital input into the valuation of many financial products. Even though the yield curve is commonly presented using yields-to-maturity or par yields, yield curves based on spot rates or forward rates are more useful for many applications. A spot interest rate (in this reading, "spot rate") is a rate of interest on a security that makes a single payment at a future point in time. The forward rate is the rate of interest set today for a single-payment security to be issued at a future date. The next section introduces these two rates.

4.2 Spot and Forward Rates: The Forward Rate Model

Spot rates are used to address problems with the YTM and the par yield. The spot rate can be thought of as the yield on a zero-coupon bond for a given maturity. There are no issues with the reinvestment assumption because there are no cash flows between the time the zero-coupon bond is issued and the maturity date (and hence no cash flows to reinvest). Spot rates can be considered the pure term structure of interest rates.

In this section, we will first explain the relationships among spot rates, forward rates, YTM, and par rates with the shape of the yield curve.

The YTM of the payment is called a *spot rate*, denoted by $r(T)$. The spot rate, $r(T)$, for a range of maturities in years $T > 0$ is called the *spot yield curve* (or, more simply, *spot curve*). The spot curve represents the term structure of interest rates at any point in time.

The spot curve shows, for various maturities, the annualized return on an option-free and default-risk-free *zero-coupon bond* (*zero* for short) with a single payment of principal at maturity. The spot rate as a yield concept avoids the complications associated with the need for a reinvestment rate assumption for coupon-paying securities. Because the spot curve depends on the market pricing of these option-free zero-coupon bonds at any point in time, the shape and level of the spot yield curve are dynamic—that is, continually changing over time.

Thus, the yield on a zero-coupon bond maturing in year T is regarded as the most accurate representation of the T-year interest rate.

A *forward rate* is an interest rate that is determined today for a loan that will be initiated in a future time period. The term structure of forward rates for a loan made on a specific initiation date is called the *forward curve*. Forward rates and forward curves can be mathematically derived from the current spot curve. This section uses the forward rate model to establish that when the spot curve is upward sloping, the forward curve will lie above the spot curve, and that when the spot curve is downward sloping, the forward curve will lie below the spot curve.

$$[1 + r(T^* + T)]^{(T^*+T)} = [1 + r(T^*)]^{T^*}[1 + f(T^*,T)]^T \tag{9}$$

Denote the forward rate of a loan initiated T^* years from today with tenor (further maturity) of T years by $f(T^*,T)$. Thus, the spot rate for $T^* + T$, which is $r(T^* + T)$, and the spot rate for T^*, which is $r(T^*)$, imply a value for the T-year forward rate at T^*, $f(T^*, T)$. Equation 9 is important because it shows how forward rates can be extrapolated from spot rates; that is, they are implicit in the spot rates at any given point in time.

Example 4 addresses forward rates and the relationship between spot and forward rates.

EXAMPLE 4

Spot and Forward Prices and Rates

The spot rates for three hypothetical zero-coupon bonds (zeros) with maturities of one, two, and three years are given in the following table:

Maturity (T)	1	2	3
Spot rates	$r(1) = 9\%$	$r(2) = 10\%$	$r(3) = 11\%$

1. Calculate the forward rate for a one-year zero issued one year from today, $f(1,1)$.
2. Calculate the forward rate for a one-year zero issued two years from today, $f(2,1)$.
3. Calculate the forward rate for a two-year zero issued one year from today, $f(1,2)$.
4. Based on your answers to 1 and 2, describe the relationship between the spot rates and the implied one-year forward rates.

Solution to 1:

$f(1,1)$ is calculated as follows (using Equation 9):

$$[1 + r(2)]^2 = [1 + r(1)]^1 [1 + f(1,1)]^1$$
$$(1 + 0.10)^2 = (1 + 0.09)^1 [1 + f(1,1)]^1$$
$$f(1,1) = \frac{(1.10)^2}{1.09} - 1 = 11.01\%$$

Solution to 2:

$f(2,1)$ is calculated as follows:

$$[1 + r(3)]^3 = [1 + r(2)]^2 [1 + f(2,1)]^1$$
$$(1 + 0.11)^3 = (1 + 0.10)^2 [1 + f(2,1)]^1$$
$$f(2,1) = \frac{(1.11)^3}{(1.10)^2} - 1 = 13.03\%$$

Solution to 3:

$f(1,2)$ is calculated as follows:

$$[1 + r(3)]^3 = [1 + r(1)]^1 [1 + f(1,2)]^2$$
$$(1 + 0.11)^3 = (1 + 0.09)^1 [1 + f(1,2)]^2$$
$$f(1,2) = \sqrt[2]{\frac{(1.11)^3}{1.09}} - 1 = 12.01\%$$

Solution to 4:

The upward-sloping zero-coupon yield curve is associated with an upward-sloping forward curve (a series of increasing one-year forward rates because 13.03% is greater than 11.01%). This point is explained further in the following paragraphs.

Fixed Income Fundamentals

The analysis of the relationship between spot rates and one-period forward rates is a logical extension of Equation 9:

$$[1+r(T)]^T = [1+r(1)][1+f(1,1)][1+f(2,1)][1+f(3,1)]\cdots[1+f(T-1,1)]$$

$$r(T) = \{[1+r(1)][1+f(1,1)][1+f(2,1)][1+f(3,1)]\cdots[1+f(T-1,1)]\}^{(1/T)} - 1 \quad (10)$$

Equation 10 shows that the spot rate for a security with a maturity of $T > 1$ can be expressed as a geometric mean of the spot rate for a security with a maturity of $T = 1$ and a series of $T - 1$ forward rates.

These relationships are illustrated in Exhibit A7. The spot rates for US Treasuries as of 31 July 2013 are represented by the lowest curve in the exhibit, which was constructed using interpolation between the data points, shown in the table following the exhibit. Note that the spot curve is upward sloping. The spot curve and the forward curves for the end of July 2014, July 2015, July 2016, and July 2017 are also presented in Exhibit A7. Because the yield curve is upward sloping, the forward curves lie above the spot curve and increasing the initiation date results in progressively higher forward curves. The highest forward curve is that for July 2017. Note that the forward curves in Exhibit A7 are progressively flatter at later start dates because the spot curve flattens at the longer maturities.

Exhibit A7 Spot Curve vs. Forward Curves, 31 July 2013

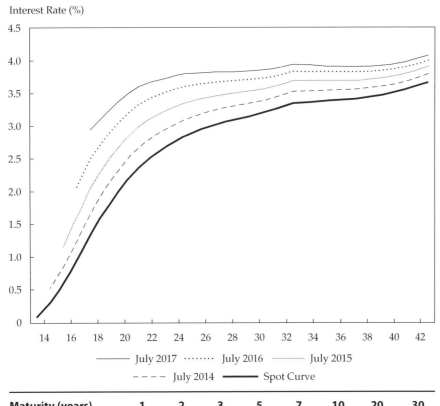

Maturity (years)	1	2	3	5	7	10	20	30
Spot rate (%)	0.11	0.33	0.61	1.37	2.00	2.61	3.35	3.66

When the spot yield curve is downward sloping (instead of upward sloping), the forward yield curve will be below the spot yield curve. Spot rates for US Treasuries as of 31 December 2006 are presented in the table following Exhibit A8. We used linear interpolation to construct the spot curve based on these data points. The yield curve data were also somewhat modified to make the yield curve more downward sloping for illustrative purposes. The spot curve and the forward curves for the end of December 2007, 2008, 2009, and 2010 are presented in Exhibit A8.

Exhibit A8 Spot Curve vs. Forward Curves, 31 December 2006 (Modified for Illustrative Purposes)

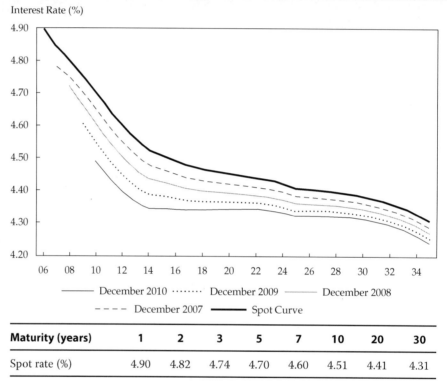

Maturity (years)	1	2	3	5	7	10	20	30
Spot rate (%)	4.90	4.82	4.74	4.70	4.60	4.51	4.41	4.31

The highest curve is the spot yield curve, and it is downward sloping. The results show that the forward curves are lower than the spot curve. Postponing the initiation date results in progressively lower forward curves. The lowest forward curve is that dated December 2010.

An important point that can be inferred from Exhibit A7 and Exhibit A8 is that forward rates do not extend any further than the furthest maturity on today's yield curve. For example, if yields extend to 30 years on today's yield curve, then three years hence, the most we can model prospectively is a bond with 27 years to final maturity. Similarly, four years hence, the longest maturity forward rate would be $f(4,26)$.

In summary, when the spot curve is upward sloping, the forward curve will lie above the spot curve. Conversely, when the spot curve is downward sloping, the forward curve will lie below the spot curve. This relationship is a reflection of the basic mathematical truth that when the average is rising (falling), the marginal data point

Fixed Income Fundamentals

must be above (below) the average. In this case, the spot curve represents an average over a whole time period and the forward rates represent the marginal changes between future time periods.[29]

4.3 Spot Rates and Par Rates

Let us return to the government par curve and establish its relation to the spot curve. The *par curve* represents the yields to maturity on coupon-paying government bonds, priced at par, over a range of maturities. In practice, recently issued bonds are typically used to create the par curve because new issues are typically priced at or close to par.

The par curve is important for valuation in that it can be used to construct a zero-coupon (spot) yield curve. The process makes use of the fact that a coupon-paying bond can be viewed as a portfolio of zero-coupon bonds. The zero-coupon rates are determined by using the par yields and solving for the zero-coupon rates one by one, in order from earliest to latest maturities, via a process of forward substitution known as *bootstrapping*. This bootstrapping process to derive spot rates from given par rates is demonstrated in Example 5.

EXAMPLE 5

Finding Spot Rates from Par Rates with Bootstrapping

The practical details of deriving the zero-coupon yield are outside the scope of this reading. But the meaning of bootstrapping can be grasped with a numerical illustration. Suppose the following yields are observed for annual coupon sovereign debt:

Par Rates for Years 1 through 4:

One-year par rate = 5%, Two-year par rate = 5.97%, Three-year par rate = 6.91%, Four-year par rate = 7.81%. From these we can bootstrap zero-coupon rates.

Zero-Coupon Rates:

The one-year zero-coupon rate is the same as the one-year par rate because, under the assumption of annual coupons, it is effectively a one-year pure discount instrument. However, the two-year bond and later-maturity bonds have coupon payments before maturity and are distinct from zero-coupon instruments.

The process of deriving zero-coupon rates begins with the two-year maturity. The two-year zero-coupon rate is determined by solving the following equation in terms of one monetary unit of current market value, using the information that $r(1) = 5\%$:

$$1 = \frac{0.0597}{(1.05)} + \frac{1 + 0.0597}{[1 + r(2)]^2}$$

In the equation, 0.0597 and 1.0597 represent payments from interest and from principal and interest, respectively, per one unit of principal value. Solving for the equation, we find that $r(2) = 6\%$. We have bootstrapped the two-year spot rate. Continuing with forward substitution, the three-year zero-coupon rate can be bootstrapped by solving the following equation, using the derived values of the one-year and two-year spot rates of 5% and 6%:

$$1 = \frac{0.0691}{(1.05)} + \frac{0.0691}{(1.06)^2} + \frac{1 + 0.0691}{[1 + r(3)]^3}$$

---

[29] Extending this discussion, one can also conclude that when a spot curve rises and then falls, the forward curves will also rise and then fall.

Thus, $r(3) = 7\%$. Finally the four-year zero-coupon rate is determined to be 8% by using

$$1 = \frac{0.0781}{(1.05)} + \frac{0.0781}{(1.06)^2} + \frac{0.0781}{(1.07)^3} + \frac{1 + 0.0781}{[1 + r(r)]^4}$$

In summary, $r(1) = 5\%$, $r(2) = 6\%$, $r(3) = 7\%$, and $r(4) = 8\%$.

4.4 Yield-to-Maturity in Relation to Spot Rates

The YTM is perhaps the most familiar pricing concept in bond markets. In this section, our goal is to clarify how it is related to spot rates and a bond's expected and realized returns.

How is the YTM related to spot rates? In bond markets, most bonds outstanding have coupon payments and many have various options, such as a call provision. The YTM of these bonds with maturity T would not be the same as the spot rate at T. But the YTM should be mathematically related to the spot curve. Because the principle of no arbitrage shows that a bond's value is the sum of the present values of payments discounted by their corresponding spot rates, the YTM of the bond should be some weighted average of spot rates used in the valuation of the bond. Example 6 addresses the relationship between spot rates and YTM.

EXAMPLE 6

Spot Rate and YTM

Recall from Example 4 the spot rates were $r(1) = 9\%$, $r(2) = 10\%$, and $r(3) = 11\%$. Let $y(T)$ be the yield to maturity.

1 Calculate the price of a two-year annual coupon bond using the spot rates. Assume the coupon rate is 6% and the face value is $1,000. Next, state the formula for determining the price of the bond in terms of its yield to maturity. Is $r(2)$ greater than or less than $y(2)$? Why?

2 Calculate the price of a three-year annual coupon-paying bond using the spot rates. Assume the coupon rate is 5% and the face value is £100. Next, write a formula for determining the price of the bond using the yield to maturity. Is $r(3)$ greater or less than $y(3)$? Why?

Solution to 1:

Using the spot rates,

$$\text{Price} = \frac{\$60}{(1 + 0.09)^1} + \frac{\$1,060}{(1 + 0.10)^2} = \$931.08$$

Using the YTM,

$$\text{Price} = \frac{\$60}{[1 + y(2)]^1} + \frac{\$1,060}{[1 + y(2)]^2} = \$931.08$$

Note that $y(2)$ is used to discount both the first- and second-year cash flows. Because the bond can have only one price, it follows that $r(1) < y(2) < r(2)$ because $y(2)$ is a weighted average of $r(1)$ and $r(2)$ and the yield curve is upward sloping. Using a calculator, one can calculate the YTM $y(2) = 9.97\%$, which is less than $r(2) = 10\%$ and greater than $r(1) = 9\%$, just as we would expect. Note that $y(2)$ is much closer to $r(2)$ than to $r(1)$ because the bond's largest cash flow occurs in Year 2, thereby giving $r(2)$ a greater weight than $r(1)$ in the determination of $y(2)$.

Solution to 2:

Using the spot rates,

$$\text{Price} = \frac{£5}{(1+0.09)^1} + \frac{£5}{(1+0.10)^2} + \frac{£105}{(1+0.11)^3} = £85.49$$

Using the YTM,

$$\text{Price} = \frac{£5}{[1+y(3)]^1} + \frac{£5}{[1+y(3)]^2} + \frac{£105}{[1+y(3)]^3} = £85.49$$

Note that $y(3)$ is used to discount all three cash flows. Because the bond can have only one price, $y(3)$ must be a weighted average of $r(1)$, $r(2)$, and $r(3)$. Given that the yield curve is upward sloping in this example, $y(3) < r(3)$. Using a calculator to compute the YTM, $y(3) = 10.93\%$, which is less than $r(3) = 11\%$ and greater than $r(1) = 9\%$, just as we would expect because the weighted YTM must lie between the highest and lowest spot rates. Note that $y(3)$ is much closer to $r(3)$ than it is to $r(2)$ or $r(1)$ because the bond's largest cash flow occurs in Year 3, thereby giving $r(3)$ a greater weight than $r(2)$ and $r(1)$ in the determination of $y(3)$.

Is the YTM the expected return on a bond? In general, it is not, except under extremely restrictive assumptions. The expected rate of return is the return one anticipates earning on an investment. The YTM is the expected rate of return for a bond that is held until its maturity, assuming that all coupon and principal payments are made in full when due and that coupons are reinvested at the original YTM. However, the assumption regarding reinvestment of coupons at the original YTM typically does not hold. The YTM can provide a poor estimate of expected return if (1) interest rates are volatile; (2) the yield curve is steeply sloped, either upward or downward; (3) there is significant risk of default; or (4) the bond has one or more embedded options (e.g., put, call, or conversion). If either (1) or (2) is the case, reinvestment of coupons would not be expected to be at the assumed rate (YTM). Case (3) implies that actual cash flows may differ from those assumed in the YTM calculation, and in case (4), the exercise of an embedded option would, in general, result in a holding period that is shorter than the bond's original maturity.

5 Summary

This appendix covers fundamentals of bond pricing, bond risk measures, and term structure analysis. Among the points made in the reading are the following:

- Changes in bond values are primarily driven by changes in interest rate, credit risk, and the market required compensation for bearing credit risk.
- The present value of a bond is the present value of its promised future cash flows. The relevant inputs to a bond valuation equation are the market discount rate, maturity or par value, coupon payment, number of days in the coupon period, the number of days since the last payment, and the number of remaining periods.
- The three sources of return on a fixed-rate are (1) receipt of the promised coupon and principal payments on the scheduled dates, (2) reinvestment of coupon payments, and (3) potential capital gains, as well as losses, on the sale of the bond prior to maturity.
- The carrying value of a bond includes the amortization of the discount (premium) if the bond is purchased at a price below (above) par value. The carrying value is any point on the constant-yield price trajectory.

- Bond duration, in general, measures the sensitivity of the full price (including accrued interest) to a change in interest rates.
- Yield duration statistics measuring the sensitivity of a bond's full price to the bond's own YTM include the Macaulay duration and modified duration.
- Macaulay duration is the weighted average of the time to receipt of coupon interest and principal payments, in which the weights are the proportion of the full price corresponding to each payment. This statistic is annualized by dividing by the periodicity (number of coupon payments or compounding periods in a year).
- Modified duration provides a linear estimate of the percentage price change for a bond given a change in its YTM.
- Effective duration provides an estimate of the percentage price change for a bond for a given change in the benchmark yield curve.
- Bonds with embedded options do not have a meaningful internal rate of return because future cash flows are contingent on interest rates. Therefore, effective duration is the appropriate interest rate risk measure, not modified duration.
- Macaulay and modified durations are inversely related to the coupon rate and the YTM, holding all else constant. Time-to-maturity and Macaulay and modified durations are *usually* positively related.
- The presence of an embedded call option reduces a bond's effective duration compared with that of an otherwise comparable non-callable bond. The reduction in the effective duration is greater when interest rates are low because the issuer is more likely to exercise the call option.
- When the yield changes, the percentage price change of a bond is a function of its duration and its convexity.
- Modified duration is the primary, or first-order, effect on a bond's percentage price change given a change in the YTM. Convexity is the secondary, or second-order, effect.
- Convexity is a positive attribute for a bond. Other things being equal, a more convex bond appreciates in price more than a less convex bond when yields fall, and depreciates less when yields rise.
- Yield curves are a plot of the yield versus maturity. The yield can be a YTM, par yield, spot rate, or forward yield.
- The spot rate for a given maturity can be expressed as a geometric average of the short-term rate and a series of forward rates.
- Forward rates are above (below) spot rates when the spot curve is upward (downward) sloping, whereas forward rates are equal to spot rates when the spot curve is flat.
- The par curve is based on the yields-to-maturity on coupon-paying government bonds priced at par over a range of maturities.
- Spot rates can be derived from a par yield curve by using a technique called bootstrapping.
- The YTM and spot rates for a bond are related because either applied to discount future cash flows to the present gives a present value equal to the bond price.
- Spot rates provide the purest form of yield curve because the rate at each maturity is the return of a zero coupon bond of that maturity.

END OPTIONAL SEGMENT

PRACTICE PROBLEMS

The following information relates to Questions 1–4

Robert Thornton, CIPM, is the lead performance analyst with Xenone Asset Management. Xenone recently launched a new fixed income product based on complex interest rate strategies. A substantial portion of the portfolio consists of mortgage backed securities (MBS) for which cash flows (interest and principal payments) are sensitive to the level of interest rates. Thornton is in the process of selecting a dedicated fixed-income attribution system capable of balancing the needs of portfolio managers and of retail clients.

Thornton coordinates a discussion with key stakeholders: Jim Howard, CIO; Elizabeth Goodall, head of client relations; and Pete Strong, vice president of product development. During the meeting, Thornton outlines three approaches to fixed-income attribution: exposure decomposition—duration based, yield curve decomposition—duration based, and yield curve decomposition—full repricing.

Howard states:

> "Our portfolio managers require a comprehensive attribution approach to provide input into the decision making process for these complex strategies; therefore, the preferred approach is yield curve decomposition with full repricing. Full repricing approaches appropriately capture changes in individual complex cash flows and reflect interest rate movements with greater precision than a duration estimation method. By contrast, attribution approaches based on the use of modified duration will likely have significant limitations. In using a full repricing approach, we will incorporate a model that predicts how changes in interest rates affect MBS cash flows; we will use that model to assure that repricing is accurate."

Goodall comments:

> "Client relations staff confirmed that their existing Brinson-type equity attribution system functions with the new fixed-income portfolio data. We tested the equity system by entering fixed-income data which initially produced both a selection and sector allocation effect. Further, we grouped the weights and returns, first by duration bucket and then by sector bucket. We prefer simple to understand client reports for our retail clients. As a result, the client reporting staff recommends maintaining the existing equity attribution system and using it for client reporting on the new complex fixed-income products."

Thornton remarks:

> "Exposure decomposition approaches break down returns into contributions or drivers of both portfolio and benchmark returns, which can then be assembled to reflect specific investment decision-making processes. Both yield curve decomposition approaches, however, explain only the relative return from active management of a portfolio."

Strong concludes:

"Only the yield curve decomposition—duration based approach would be able to separate the parallel and non-parallel changes to the risk-free government curves."

1 Does Howard's statement support the use of a full repricing approach for the new fixed income product?
   A Yes.
   B No, duration-based approaches provide greater precision.
   C No, exposure-decomposition approaches are preferred for complex strategies.

2 Does Goodall's comment support using the Brinson-type equity approach for the new fixed income product?
   A Yes.
   B No, a bottom-up approach is more relevant for client reporting.
   C No, yield curve decomposition approach is more relevant for retail client reporting.

3 Is Thornton's remark on fixed income attribution approaches accurate?
   A Yes.
   B No, exposure decomposition approaches explain only the relative return from active management of a portfolio.
   C No, only the yield curve decomposition—full repricing approach explains only the relative return from active management of a portfolio.

4 Is Strong's conclusion on fixed income attribution approaches accurate?
   A Yes.
   B No, both yield curve decomposition approaches can separate parallel and non-parallel movements in the risk-free yield curve.
   C No, both yield curve decomposition approaches and exposure decomposition approaches can separate parallel and non-parallel movements in the risk-free yield curve.

The following information relates to Questions 5–8

Tom Sharpen, head of marketing at GIX Asset Management, is tasked with summarizing the key reasons that GIX recently acquired new fixed income attribution software. The software, ExpPro, is based on an exposure decomposition—duration based approach. Sharpen drafts a memo giving the following reasons for acquiring ExpPro:

Statement 1   It offers a good compromise between providing useful insights for our portfolio managers and being understandable by clients, for the basic fixed income portfolios offered by GIX.

Statement 2   It is able to separate parallel and non-parallel changes in the risk-free government yield curve.

Statement 3   The software reprices each fixed instrument from individual cash flows.

Practice Problems

Sharpen then asked Katy Bligh, a senior performance analyst, to prepare the most recent month-end attribution report for the GIX Bond Portfolio. The portfolio consists of risk-free government bonds and conventional corporate bonds. The portfolio seeks to add value by placing bets to take advantage of changes in interest rates, by taking a long or short benchmark relative duration position, by over- or under-weighting corporate bonds as views on the credit markets change, and by selecting issues/issuers that are expected to perform better than those in the benchmark.

Bligh generated performance and attribution reports from the ExpPro software shown in Exhibits 1 and 2. (Exhibit numbers may reflect rounding discrepancies.)

Exhibit 1 GIX Bond Portfolio Performance, Month Ending 31 December

Duration Bucket	Sector	Weight Portfolio	Weight Benchmark	Duration Portfolio	Duration Benchmark	Return Portfolio	Return Benchmark
Short	Government	5.0%	15.0%			2.50%	2.50%
	Corporate	5.0%	5.0%			2.40%	2.80%
	Total	10.0%	20.0%			2.45%	2.58%
Mid	Government	10.0%	20.0%			3.00%	3.00%
	Corporate	20.0%	10.0%			2.73%	3.25%
	Total	30.0%	30.0%			2.82%	3.08%
Long	Government	40.0%	40.0%			3.20%	3.20%
	Corporate	20.0%	10.0%			3.17%	3.50%
	Total	60.0%	50.0%			3.19%	3.26%
	Total Government	55.0%	75.0%	9.12	8.27	3.10%	3.01%
	Total Corporate	45.0%	25.0%	8.30	7.91	2.89%	3.26%
Total		100.0%	100.0%	8.75	8.18	3.01%	3.07%
Excess return						−0.07%	

Exhibit 2 GIX Bond Portfolio Performance, Month Ending 31 December

Duration Bucket	Sector	Duration Effect	Curve Effect	Total Interest Rate Allocation	Sector Allocation	Bond Selection	Total
Short	Government					0.00%	0.00%
	Corporate				0.00%	−0.02%	−0.02%
	Total	−0.17%	0.22%	0.05%	0.00%	−0.02%	0.03%
Mid	Government					0.00%	0.00%
	Corporate				0.03%	−0.10%	−0.08%
	Total	0.00%	0.00%	0.00%	0.03%	−0.10%	−0.08%
Long	Government					0.00%	0.00%
	Corporate				0.03%	−0.07%	−0.04%
	Total	0.37%	−0.35%	0.02%	0.03%	−0.07%	−0.02%
Total		0.20%	−0.13%	0.07%	0.06%	−0.19%	−0.07%

The portfolio underperformed its benchmark by 7 bps for the period.

5 Which of Sharpen's statements *least* accurately aligns with the exposure decomposition—duration based approach?
   A Statement 1.
   B Statement 2.
   C Statement 3.

6 Based on Exhibits 1 and 2, the portfolio's long duration position *most likely* bet on a:
   A rising interest rate environment, which resulted in a positive contribution from active management.
   B falling interest rate environment, which resulted in a negative contribution from active management.
   C falling interest rate environment, which resulted in a positive contribution from active management.

7 Based on Exhibits 1 and 2, the change in the risk-free government yields in the benchmark is *closest* to:
   A +0.07%.
   B −0.13%.
   C −0.36%.

8 Based on Exhibits 1 and 2, the portfolio's overweight position in corporate bonds *most likely* added value of 6 bps in the sector allocation because the:
   A credit spreads widened.
   B credit spreads tightened.
   C government yield curve shifted downward.

The following information relates to Questions 9–14

Assume the following hypothetical one-bond portfolio and benchmark. The portfolio is invested only in a corporate bond maturing on 30 June 2028 (in 15 years as of 2013) which pays 3% semi-annual coupons (6% annually). The benchmark is invested only in a treasury bond maturing on 30 June 2023 (in 10 years as of 2013) which pays 3.5% semi-annual coupons (7% annually).

Exhibit 1 shows the attribution analysis obtained from a yield curve decomposition—full repricing approach. The measurement period spans six months, ending 31 December 2013. At the beginning of the period, the modified duration of the benchmark is 7.47 and 10.12 for the portfolio.

Practice Problems

Exhibit 1 Yield Curve Decomposition—Full Repricing Approach, Six Months Ending 31 December 2013

Portfolio (P) and Benchmark (B)	Duration	Added Value								
		Coupon	Amort	Roll	Shift	Slope	Curvature	Systematic	Specific	Total
P: Corporate 6% June 30, 2028	10.12	2.70%	−0.42%	0.42%	−4.74%	0.91%	0.00%	−0.19%	0.00%	−1.30%
B: Treasury 7% June 30, 2023	7.47	2.89%	−0.85%	0.45%	−3.48%	−0.40%	0.00%	0.00%	0.00%	−1.40%
		−0.18%	0.44%	−0.02%	−1.26%	1.31%	0.00%	−0.19%	0.00%	0.10%
		Passage of time		0.24%	Curve Movement		0.05%	Spread	−0.19%	

Note: Apparent small discrepancies in addition reflect the effects of rounding error.

Use the information in Exhibit 1 to infer any movements of the treasury yield curve and corporate credit spread for the period ending 31 December 2013.

9 Which of the following statements *best* describes the general change of interest rates over the period and its effect on the portfolio manager's added value? The market interest rates generally:
   A increased and had a positive effect on value added.
   B increased and had a negative effect on value added.
   C decreased and had a negative effect on value added.

10 Which of the following statements *best* describes the change of the shape of the treasury yield curve and its effect on the portfolio manager's added value? The slope of the curve:
   A flattened and had a positive effect on value added.
   B flattened and had a negative effect on value added.
   C steepened and had a positive effect on value added.

11 Which of the following statements *best* describes the change of the spread between the corporate bond and the treasury curve and its effect on the portfolio added value? The spread:
   A increased and had a positive effect on value added.
   B increased and had a negative effect on value added.
   C decreased and had a negative effect on value added.

12 Which of the following statements is *most* accurate? The positive amortization effect is primarily due to the fact that, compared with the bond in the benchmark, at the start of the period, the portfolio holds a bond that is priced at a:
   A smaller discount.
   B smaller premium.
   C greater premium.

13 Which of the following statements is *most* accurate about the roll effect? The negative roll effect is primarily due to the fact that, at the beginning of the period, compared with the 15 years maturity point, the yield curve at the 10 years maturity point is:
   A flatter.
   B steeper.

C inverted.

14 Which of the following statements about the coupon effect is *most* accurate? The negative coupon effect is primarily due to the fact that, at the start of the period, compared with the bond in the benchmark, the bond in the portfolio has a lower:

A price.

B coupon rate.

C yield to maturity.

The following information relates to Questions 15–20

Diana Bolton is a new analyst hired by Neubert Capital to calculate the performance and conduct an attribution analysis of Neubert's fixed income portfolios. Bolton's manager, Gary Isaac, tells Bolton that her first assignment is to analyze the performance of the Neubert Bond Fund. Isaac notes that previous analysts performed an attribution analysis of the bond fund using the exposure decomposition—duration based approach. Bolton explains that she will base her attribution of the fund on the yield curve decomposition—duration based approach instead. She gives the following description of that approach:

> "The yield curve decomposition—duration based approach estimates the return on individual securities by repricing bonds using the relationship between modified duration and changes in yield to maturity."

Isaac then asks Bolton to describe the advantages and limitations of using the yield curve decomposition—duration based approach. In reply, Bolton states:

Statement 1 The yield curve decomposition—duration based approach is easy to calculate.

Statement 2 The yield curve decomposition—duration based approach is typically used for portfolios that contain securities with embedded options.

Statement 3 The yield curve decomposition—duration based approach is less appropriate when there are large movements in market yields.

Bolton prepares Exhibit 1 below, indicating that the Neubert Bond Fund and its benchmark each contain two government bonds and three corporate bonds. All of the bonds held in the fund and the benchmark are identical, with the exceptions of corporate bond B and corporate bond P. At the beginning of 2015, the yield curve was upward sloping.

Exhibit 1	Fund and Benchmark Weights as of 1 January 2015	
Bond	Fund (%)	Bench (%)
Government 3% 30 Jun 19	10	25
Government 4% 30 Jun 24	30	25
Corporate 5% 30 Jun 21	30	25
Corporate B 7% 30 Jun 24	0	25

Exhibit 1 (Continued)

Bond	Fund (%)	Bench (%)
Corporate P 6% 30 Jun 24	30	0
Total	100	100

Bolton notes that by overweighting the longer duration bonds the fund had a longer duration than the benchmark at the beginning of 2015. Next, Bolton prepares the Active Return Factor Contribution analysis of the fund (covering the first quarter of 2015) in Exhibit 2.

Exhibit 2 Active Return Factor Contribution, First Quarter of 2015 (in %)

Bond	Yield	Roll	Shift	Slope	Curvature	Spread	Specific	Residual	Total
Govt 3% 30 Jun 19	−0.09	−0.08	−0.06	0.12	0.00	0.00	0.00	−0.01	−0.12
Govt 4% 30 Jun 24	0.08	0.01	0.09	0.08	0.00	0.00	0.00	0.01	0.27
Corp 5% 30 Jun 21	0.10	0.03	0.06	0.02	0.00	0.05	0.08	−0.02	0.32
Corp B 7% 30 Jun 24	−0.31	−0.02	−0.25	−0.31	0.00	−0.25	−0.24	−0.01	−1.39
Corp P 6% 30 Jun 24	0.28	0.02	0.34	0.45	0.00	0.28	0.15	−0.02	1.50
Total	0.06	−0.04	0.18	0.36	0.00	0.08	−0.01	−0.05	0.58

15 Neubert's approach to fixed income attribution prior to 2015 is *most appropriate* for reports to:
   A clients.
   B analysts.
   C portfolio managers.

16 Is Bolton's description of the yield curve decomposition—duration based approach to fixed income attribution accurate?
   A Yes.
   B No, because this approach reprices securities from zero coupon curves.
   C No, because each security must be repriced in buckets, not individually.

17 Which of Bolton's three statements on the advantages and limitations of the yield curve decomposition—duration based approach is accurate?
   A Statement 1
   B Statement 2
   C Statement 3

18 Based on Exhibits 1 and 2, during the first quarter of 2015 the yield curve *most likely*:
   A shifted lower and flattened.
   B shifted lower and steepened.
   C shifted higher and flattened.

19 Based on Exhibit 2, during the first quarter of 2015 the Neubert Bond Fund's relative performance benefited the *most* from factors associated with:
   A curve variations.

B spread variations.

C the passage of time.

20 Based on the data for corporate bond P in Exhibit 2, during the first quarter of 2015 corporate spreads *most likely*:

A narrowed.

B stayed the same.

C widened.

SOLUTIONS

1. A is correct. His assertions that a full repricing approach is most accurate for the type of fixed income product being considered are accurate. B is incorrect because duration-based models may be inaccurate for the complex fixed income product described. C is incorrect because exposure decomposition models may be inaccurate for the complex fixed income product described.

2. A is correct. The exposure decomposition—duration based approach is the fixed-income counterpart to Brinson-type equity attribution. Exposure decomposition is often used primarily for client reports so that the users, who may not be well-versed in quantitative analysis, can understand and succinctly articulate the results of active portfolio management. B is incorrect; full repricing is a bottom-up approach and is less useful for client reporting, because it is too detailed. C is incorrect; both yield curve decomposition approaches are less relevant than an exposure decomposition approach as known as a Brinson-type approach.

3. B is correct. Exposure decomposition approaches explain only the relative return from active management of a portfolio. Both yield curve decomposition approaches, however, break down returns into contributions or drivers of both portfolio and benchmark returns, which can then be assembled to reflect specific investment decision-making processes. A and C are incorrect.

4. C is correct. Exposure decomposition—duration based, yield curve decomposition—duration based, and yield curve decomposition—full repricing approaches can separate parallel and non-parallel movements in the risk-free yield curve. A and B are incorrect.

5. C is correct. The exposure decomposition models use market-value based weights and returns, in buckets, to determine exposures, and bucket returns to evaluate relative performance. Exposure decomposition models do not sequentially reprice instruments at a cash-flow level, whereas yield curve decomposition—full repricing models do.

   A is incorrect. Exposure decomposition models are simple based models which are useful for attribution in the case of basic fixed income portfolios, and provide a compromise between client considerations and management insights. B is incorrect because exposure decomposition models can separate parallel and non-parallel changes in the risk free curve.

6. C is correct. The portfolio is long duration with 8.75 for the portfolio and 8.18 for the benchmark. Because the duration effect contribution from active management is positive at 20 bps, the bet on falling rates was successful.

   A is incorrect. A rise in risk free yields and a long duration position would have seen a loss from duration. B is incorrect. A fall in risk free yields and a long duration position would have seen a gain, not a loss from duration.

7. C is correct. The relationship is % Price return ≈ –Modified duration × Change in YTM; therefore, the benchmark return of 3.01% ≈ Benchmark modified duration of –8.27 × Change in YTM. Solving for the change in YTM, 3.01%/–8.27 = –0.36%. A is incorrect because +0.07 is the portfolio total interest rate allocation effect; B is incorrect because –0.13 is the portfolio curve effect.

8. B is correct. The portfolio has an overweight position in corporate bonds and credit has out-performed governments (hence, the positive contribution). Therefore, in general and all else being equal, spreads must have tightened.

A is incorrect because an overweight to credit with widening spreads would have led to a negative contribution to active return (all else being equal). C is incorrect because the impact from credit sector allocation is quantified after removing effects from movements of the government yield curve.

9 B is correct. The shift effect reflects the impact of general interest rate movements. The added value related to the shift effect is the shift contribution to the portfolio minus the shift contribution to the benchmark for each security. Because there is only one distinctive security invested in the portfolio and the benchmark, it is easy to infer the shift effect for the portfolio and the benchmark. The shift effect for the portfolio is −4.74% which implies an increase in interest rates. The shift effect for the benchmark is −3.48%. Thus, P − B = −4.74% − (−3.48%) = −1.26%, indicating a negative effect on value added. The portfolio manager placed a bet that interest rates would decline (as portfolio duration of 10.12 exceeded the benchmark duration of 7.47), but interest rates actually increased.

A is incorrect; the general increase in rates was not in favor of the portfolio because the portfolio had a higher duration than the benchmark (10.12 versus 7.47). C is incorrect because the interest rates generally increased, not decreased.

10 A is correct. The slope effect reflects the effect of the change in the slope of the treasury curve. The added value related to the slope effect is the slope contribution to the portfolio minus the slope contribution to the benchmark for each security. The slope effect for the portfolio is positive 0.91%. The slope effect for the benchmark is −0.40%. Thus, 0.91% − (−0.40%) = 1.31% and slope changes had a positive effect on value added. From this result we can infer that rates increased less at the 15-year maturity point than the 10-year maturity point. This implies that the yield curve flattened.

B is incorrect. Although the slope of the curve got flatter, the portfolio invested at the long end of the curve; therefore, it was not favorable for the portfolio. C is incorrect. The slope of the treasury curve did not get steeper, it got flatter.

11 B is correct. The spread effect reflects the effect of the change in the spreads between the corporate yield curve and the treasury curve. The added value related to the spread effect is the spread contribution to the portfolio minus the spread contribution to the benchmark for each security. Under the column "systematic" we see that the spread effect was −0.19%. From these facts we can infer that the spread increased and had a negative effect on value added.

A is incorrect. Although the spread increased, it was not in favor of the portfolio because the portfolio over weighted the corporate sector compared with the benchmark. The spread increase had a negative effect on value added. C is incorrect. The spread increased—not decreased.

12 B is correct. A bond will generate a negative amortization contribution when it is priced at premium. The convergence from the premium price towards the par value subtracts performance. Given that the amortization effect for the portfolio is −0.42%, this suggests that the bond is priced at a premium but at a smaller premium than the benchmark with an amortization effect of −0.85%. A is incorrect. The bond in the portfolio is not priced at discount at the start of the period. C is incorrect. The premium price of the portfolio is less than that of the benchmark.

13 B is correct. The bond in the benchmark has fewer years to maturity (10 compared with 15 for the portfolio). The bond in the benchmark has a greater roll effect compared with the portfolio (0.45% versus 0.42%), which suggests that the curve is steeper around the 10-year point than at the 15-year point.

A is incorrect. The curve is not flatter at the 10-year point compared with the 15-year point. C is incorrect. When the curve is inverted, the roll effect is negative because bonds trade at higher yields as they get closer to maturity. In this case the roll effect is positive; therefore the curve cannot be inverted.

14 B is correct. The coupon effect results purely from the coupon rates of the bonds. The fact that the benchmark holds a higher coupon bond (7% compared with a 6% coupon bond in the portfolio) generates a negative coupon effect.

A is incorrect. The fact that the bond is priced lower is not the driver for the coupon effect; only the coupon rate affects the coupon effect. C is incorrect. The fact that the bond has a different yield to maturity is not the main driver for the coupon effect; only the coupon rate affects the coupon effect.

15 A is correct. Neubert traditionally used the exposure decomposition—duration based approach, which is easier to understand compared to yield curve decomposition (duration based or full repricing) and is best suited to produce client reports and marketing materials.

16 A is correct. The yield curve decomposition—duration based approach reprices securities or buckets using the known relationship between modified duration and yield to maturity where: % Price Return ≈ −Modified Duration × Change in YTM. Therefore, Bolton's description is correct.

17 C is correct. The yield curve decomposition—duration based approach does not perform well in environments where market yields experience large changes.

18 A is correct. The securities in which the fund is overweight generated a positive effect from "shift", while those securities in which the fund is underweight generated a negative effect from shift. The curve must have shifted down during this period and provided an overall benefit to bondholders. In addition, this shift effect was more pronounced for longer duration bonds. This indicates that the long end of the curve fell more than the short end of the curve; that is, the curve flattened. This flattening is also confirmed by the positive impact of "slope" on the portfolio, as the fund's higher exposure to the long-end of the curve generated a positive effect.

19 A is correct. The fund added the most value through variations in the yield curve. The "shift", "slope", and "curvature" factors generated a positive effect of 0.18% + 0.36% + 0.00% = 0.54%.

20 A is correct. The spread effect for corporate bond P, which was held in the fund but not the benchmark, is 0.28%. This number is positive because during this period corporate spreads narrowed. Corporate bond investors normally benefit when spreads narrow and are hurt when spreads widen.

Glossary

Accounting Book of Record (ABOR) It is the official fund accounting record, produced by custodians or administrators. The data contained in the ABOR are used to value portfolios and to generate NAVs and NAV-based performance metrics.

Active share A measure, ranging from 0% to 100%, of how similar a portfolio is to its benchmark. The measure is based on the differences in a portfolio's holdings and weights relative to its benchmark's holdings and their weights. A manager who precisely replicates the benchmark will have an active share of zero; a manager with no holdings in common with the benchmark will have an active share of one.

Advisory-Only Assets Assets for which the firm provides investment recommendations but has no control over implementation of investment decisions and no trading authority.

Amortized price The historical cost (initially recognized cost) of an asset, adjusted for the allocation of a premium (amortization) or discount (accretion) until the asset's maturity.

Autocorrelation When regression errors are correlated across observations; see serial correlation.

Base currency See *domestic currency*.

Batting average A measure of investment performance consistency that reports (a) the percentage of investment decisions that result in a profit divided by the total number of investment decisions, or (b) the percentage of positive return periods relative to the benchmark or peers divided by the total number of return periods.

Benchmark Description Must include the key features of the benchmark or the name of the benchmark for a readily recognized index.

Benefit of hedging In the case of currency forward contracts, the condition where using the forward rate results in a higher return than the current spot rate.

Broad Distribution Pooled Fund A pooled fund that is regulated under a framework that would permit the general public to purchase or hold the pooled fund's shares and is not exclusively offered in one-on-one presentations.

Capture ratio A measure of the manager's gain or loss relative to the gain or loss of the benchmark.

Carried interest A performance-based fee that reflects a share of the profits receivable by the manager.

Carve-Out Defined in the GIPS Glossary as a portion of a portfolio that is by itself representative of a distinct investment strategy.

Committed Capital Defined in the GIPS Glossary as pledges of capital to an investment vehicle by investors (limited partners and the general partner) or the firm.

Composite Aggregation of one or more portfolios that a firm manages according to a similar investment mandate, objective, or strategy.

Composite Creation Date The date on which the firm first grouped one or more portfolios to form the composite.

Composite Definition Detailed criteria that determine the assignment of portfolios to composites.

Composite Description General information regarding the investment mandate, objective, or strategy of the composite.

Composite Inception Date The initial date of the composite's track record.

Composite System The set of processes, tools, and equipment used to maintain and manage the composites.

Confidence interval The expected range of a statistic's value.

Conventional bond See *plain vanilla bond*.

Cost of carry The net of the costs and benefits of holding, storing, or "carrying" an asset.

Cost of hedging In the case of currency forward contracts, the condition where using the forward rate results in a lower return than the current spot rate.

Covered interest rate parity Relationship which states that the forward rate will be a function of the spot rate and relative interest rates in the two countries.

CTD bond The bond which, based on the then-prevailing price, financing rates, and conversion factor, is the lowest cost to deliver upon expiry of a futures contract.

Currency overlay The case where a portfolio's currency exposures are managed separately from the management of the portfolio itself.

Currency spot return The percent change in an exchange rate over a specified time period.

Discretion The ability of a firm to implement its intended strategy.

Distinct Business Entity A unit, division, department, or office that is organizationally and functionally segregated from other units, divisions, departments, or offices and that retains discretion over the assets it manages and that should have autonomy over the investment decision-making process.

Domestic currency The currency an investor uses for consumption purposes (e.g., Canadian dollars are the domestic currency for a Canadian investor). Also called *base currency* or *home currency*.

Downside capture ratio A measure of capture when the benchmark return is negative in a given period; downside capture less (greater) than 100% generally suggests out (under) performance relative to the benchmark.

Due diligence Investigation and analysis in support of an investment action, decision, or recommendation.

Economic exposure The risk of loss from a position in an asset class.

Fair value The amount at which an investment could be exchanged in a current arm's length transaction between willing parties in which the parties each act knowledgeably and prudently. The valuation must be determined using the objective, observable, unadjusted quoted market price for an identical investment in an active market on the measurement date. Fair value must include accrued income.

Fee rebate In a short sale, the portion of the income earned on the invested collateral that is returned to the borrower of shares.

Fee Schedule Refers to the firm's current schedule of investment management fees or bundled fees appropriate to prospective clients or prospective investors.

Forward A non-standardized and non-exchange traded contract between two parties to buy or sell an asset at a specified future time at a price agreed upon today.

Forward currency contracts Contracts between two parties for the exchange of a specified amount of currency at a fixed exchange rate at a future date.

GIPS Compliance Notification Form The form that must be filed when the firm initially claims compliance with the GIPS standards and must be updated annually.

GIPS Recommendations Are optional but *should* be followed because they represent best practice in performance presentation.

GIPS Report A presentation for a composite or pooled fund that contains all the information required by the GIPS standards and may also include recommended information or supplemental information.

GIPS Requirements *Must* be followed in order for a firm to claim compliance.

Gross-of-Fees Return The return on investments reduced by any transaction costs.

Hedged return When using currency forward contracts, the return that reflects the foreign asset return in local currency terms and the forward discount or premium.

High-water mark the highest cumulative net asset value attained by the fund, net of fees.

Holdings-based style analysis A bottom-up style analysis that estimates the risk exposures from the actual securities held in the portfolio at a point in time.

Hurdle rate a minimum rate of return below which the fund does not charge an incentive fee.

Independent and identically distributed (IID) When the residuals from a given statistical analysis are independent and identically distributed, the data is said to be IID. Independence means that the data in any one period are not influenced by the data in any other period. If the sample statistics (e.g., mean and standard deviation) from a particular subperiod of the data series being evaluated is the same statistics drawn from another subperiod of the entire data series.

Internal Dispersion Internal dispersion of annual returns of individual portfolios within a composite can be measured in various ways, including but not limited to high/low, interquartile range, and the standard deviation of returns (equal or asset weighted).

Internal rate of return The rate of return based on the cash flows and the terminal value of the company. It takes into account the time value of money and reflects the private equity manager's control over the timing of cash inflows and outflows.

Investment Book of Record (IBOR) It is a set of fund data for trading and portfolio-management purposes.

Investment policy statement A written investment planning document that includes statements of a client's investment objectives and investment constraints.

J-curve The shape of the IRR curve over time. As the private equity fund calls capital early in the fund's life, the IRR dips below zero because fees and expenses erode capital before the manager has had an opportunity to realize returns. As the fund matures and the capital invested starts to create distributions, the IRR turns positive.

Key person risk The risk that results from over-reliance on an individual or individuals whose departure would negatively affect an investment manager.

Limited Distribution Pooled Fund Any pooled fund that is not a broad distribution pooled fund.

Long–short portfolio A portfolio that contains both long positions in assets expected to rise in value and short positions in assets expected to fall in value.

Loss ratio In private equity, the amount of invested capital that is held below cost.

Margin calls A request for the short seller to deposit additional funds to bring their balance up to the initial margin.

Market-neutral strategies Long/short strategies that match long and short risk exposures and are intended to eliminate market exposure.

Modified duration A measure of a bond's price sensitivity to interest rate movements.

Money-Weighted Returns The returns for a period that reflect the change in value and the timing and size of external cash flows.

Moneyness The relationship between the option exercise price and the underlying price.

Multiple of invested capital The current value of the underlying private equity portfolio companies, plus any distributions received, divided by the total invested capital.

Net-of-Fees Return The gross-of-fees return reduced by the investment management fees (including performance-based fees and carried interest).

Notional exposure See *notional market value*.

Notional market value The amount of an underlying security that would cause approximately the same change in value for a given change in the price of the underlying security as the change in the futures and associated cash position. Also called *notional exposure*.

Option delta The change in call option value relative to a change in the value of the underlying.

Overlay Strategy A strategy in which the management of a certain aspect of an investment strategy is carried out separately from the underlying portfolio.

Partially hedged A position in an asset that is not fully hedged.

Performance Examination The process by which an independent verifier conducts testing of a specific composite or pooled fund in accordance with the required performance examination procedures of the GIPS standards.

Plain vanilla bond An option-free bond that makes periodic, fixed coupon payments during the bond's life and a lump-sum payment of principal at maturity. Also called *conventional bond*.

Policy portfolio A conceptual portfolio allocated among asset classes or risk budgets in a manner the investor believes is most appropriate for his or her long-term risk and return objectives.

Pooled Fund A fund whose ownership interests may be held by more than one investor.

Portfolio An individually managed group of investments.

Prospective Client Any person or entity that has expressed interest in one of the firm's composite strategies and qualifies to invest in the composite.

Prospective Investor Any person or entity that has expressed interest in one of the firm's pooled funds and qualifies to invest in the pooled fund.

Public market equivalent The use of cash flow data to replicate the private equity GP's capital calls and distributions to allow comparisons of private equity IRRs with returns of publicly traded equity indexes.

Returns-based style analysis A top-down style analysis that involves estimating the sensitivities of a portfolio to security market indexes.

Risk premium An extra return expected by investors for bearing some specified risk.

Segments Groups of securities within a portfolio, e.g., countries, sectors, or industries.

Segregated Account A portfolio owned by a single client.

Serial correlation When regression errors are correlated across observations; see autocorrelation.

Short extension A portfolio consisting of a long position of 100 plus x percent and a short position of x percent.

Short sale The sale of borrowed securities with the intention to repurchase them later at a lower price and return them to the lender.

Short selling Asset positions designed to profit from negative views on the asset.

Significant Cash Flow The level at which the firm determines that one or more client-directed external cash flows may temporarily prevent the firm from implementing the composite strategy.

Spot curve The yield curve that shows the discount rates for various bond maturities that apply to bonds with a single cash flow.

Spot exchange rate The rate at which one currency can be exchanged for immediate delivery of another currency.

Stop-losses A trading order that sets a selling price below the current market price with a goal of protecting profits or preventing further losses.

Subscription Line of Credit A loan facility that is put in place to facilitate administration when the firm is calling for funds from investors.

Supplemental Information Any performance-related information included as part of a GIPS Report that supplements or enhances the requirements and/or recommendations of the GIPS standards.

Swap An instrument in which the counterparties agree to exchange a series of future cash flows.

Theoretical Performance Performance that is not derived from a portfolio or composite with actual assets invested in the strategy presented.

Time-Weighted Returns A method of calculating period-by-period returns that reflects the change in value and negates the effects of external cash flows.

Total Firm Assets The aggregate fair value of all assets (whether or not discretionary or fee-paying) for which a defined firm has investment management responsibility.

Unrealized performance The performance of underlying companies that are still managed by the private equity manager.

Upside capture ratio A measure of capture when the benchmark return is positive in a given period; upside capture greater (less) than 100% generally suggests out (under) performance relative to the benchmark.

Verification The process by which an independent verifier conducts testing of a firm on a firm-wide basis, in accordance with the required verification procedures of the GIPS standards.

Waterfall The allocation of distributions between the fund's investors and the GP.

Yield to maturity The discount rate that equates the present value of the bond's expected cash flows until maturity with the bond's price.

Made in the USA
Middletown, DE
22 November 2024